CompTIA A+ Complete Study Guid

‖‖ ‖ ‖‖‖‖‖‖‖ ‖ ‖‖‖ ‖ ‖‖‖‖‖‖‖‖‖ ‖‖‖‖‖ ‖‖
W9-AJO-358

A+ Essentials (220-601) Exam Objectives

Sybex®
An Imprint of
🌐WILEY

A+ Depot Technician (220-604) Exam Objectives

Exam objectives are subject to change at any time without prior notice and at CompTIA's sole discretion. Please visit CompTIA's web site (www.comptia.org) for the most current listing of exam objectives.

Sybex®
An Imprint of
WILEY

OBJECTIVE	CHAPTER
7.2 Identify potential hazards and implement proper safety procedures including ESD precautions and procedures, safe work environment and equipment handling	10
7.3 Identify proper disposal procedures for batteries, display devices and chemical solvents and cans	10
Domain 8.0 Professionalism and Communication	
8.1 Use good communication skills including listening and tact / discretion, when communicating with customers and colleagues	11
8.2 Use job-related professional behavior including notation of privacy, confidentiality and respect for the customer and customers' property	11

A+ IT Technician (220-602) Exam Objectives

OBJECTIVE	CHAPTER
Domain 1.0 Personal Computer Components	
1.1 Install, configure, optimize and upgrade personal computer components	12
1.2 Identify tools, diagnostic procedures and troubleshooting techniques for personal computer components	12
1.3 Perform preventative maintenance of personal computer components	12
Domain 2.0 Laptops and Portable Devices	
2.1 Identify fundamental principles of using laptops and portable devices	13
2.2 Install, configure, optimize and upgrade laptops and portable devices	13
2.3 Use tools, diagnostic procedures and troubleshooting techniques for laptops and portable devices	13
Domain 3.0 Operating Systems	
3.1 Identify the fundamental principles of operating systems	14
3.2 Install, configure, optimize and upgrade operating systems	14
3.3 Identify tools, diagnostic procedures and troubleshooting techniques for operating systems	14
3.4 Perform preventative maintenance for operating systems	14
Domain 4.0 Printers and Scanners	
4.1 Identify the fundamental principles of using printers and scanners	15
4.2 Install, configure, optimize and upgrade printers and scanners	15
4.3 Identify tools and diagnostic procedures to troubleshooting printers and scanners	15
4.4 Perform preventative maintenance of printers and scanners	15
Domain 5.0 Networks	
5.1 Identify the fundamental principles or networks	16
5.2 Install, configure, optimize and upgrade networks	16
5.3 Use tools and diagnostic procedures to troubleshoot network problems	16
5.4 Perform preventative maintenance of networks including securing and protecting network cabling	16

NOTE Exam objectives are subject to change at any time without prior notice and at CompTIA's sole discretion. Please visit CompTIA's web site (www.comptia.org) for the most current listing of exam objectives.

Sybex®
An Imprint of
WILEY

A+ Remote Support Technician (220-603) Exam Objectives

Sybex®
An Imprint of
🕸️WILEY

CompTIA A+®
Complete
Study Guide

CompTIA A+®
Complete
Study Guide

Quentin Docter

Emmett Dulaney

Toby Skandier

BICENTENNIAL
1807
WILEY
2007
BICENTENNIAL

Wiley Publishing, Inc.

Acquisitions and Development Editor: Jeff Kellum
Technical Editors: Neil Hester and Mike Harwood
Production Editor: Daria Meoli
Copy Editor: Linda Recktenwald
Production Manager: Tim Tate
Vice President and Executive Group Publisher: Richard Swadley
Vice President and Executive Publisher: Joseph B. Wikert
Vice President and Publisher: Neil Edde
Media Development Specialist: Angela Denny
Book Designer: Judy Fung
Compositor: Craig Woods, Happenstance Type-O-Rama
Proofreader: James Brook, Word One
Indexer: Ted Laux
Anniversary Logo Design: Richard Pacifico
Cover Designer: Margaret Rowlands

ISBN-13: 978-0-470-04830-6

ISBN-10: 0-470-04830-1

The logo of the CompTIA Authorized Quality Curriculum (CAQC) program and the status of this or other training material as "Authorized" under the CompTIA Authorized Quality Curriculum program signifies that, in CompTIA's opinion, such training material covers the content of the CompTIA's related certification exam. CompTIA has not reviewed or approved the accuracy of the contents of this training material and specifically disclaims any warranties of merchantability or fitness for a particular purpose. CompTIA makes no guarantee concerning the success of persons using any such "Authorized" or other training material in order to prepare for any CompTIA certification exam.

The contents of this training material were created for the CompTIA A+ exams covering CompTIA certification objectives that were current as of 2006.

How to become CompTIA certified:

This training material can help you prepare for and pass a related CompTIA certification exam or exams. In order to achieve CompTIA certification, you must register for and pass a CompTIA certification exam or exams.

In order to become CompTIA certified, you must:

1. Select a certification exam provider. For more information please visit http://www.comptia.org/certification/general_information/exam_locations.aspx
2. Register for and schedule a time to take the CompTIA certification exam(s) at a convenient location.
3. Read and sign the Candidate Agreement, which will be presented as the time of the exam(s). The text of the Candidate Agreement can be found at http://www.comptia.org/certification/general_information/candidate_agreement.aspx.
4. Take and pass the CompTIA certification exam(s).

For more information about CompTIA's certifications, such as its industry acceptance, benefits or program news, please visit http://www.comptia.org/certification/.

CompTIA is a not-for-profit trade information technology (IT) trade association. CompTIA's certifications are designed by subject matter experts from across the IT industry. Each CompTIA certification is vendor-neutral, covers multiple technologies and requires demonstration of skills and knowledge widely sought after by the IT industry.

To contact CompTIA with any questions or comments, please call 630-678-8300 or email question@comptia.org.

Sybex®
An Imprint of
WILEY

To Our Valued Readers:

Thank you for looking to Sybex for your CompTIA A+ exam prep needs. We at Sybex are proud of our reputation for providing certification candidates with the practical knowledge and skills needed to succeed in the highly competitive IT marketplace. Certification candidates have come to rely on Sybex for accurate and accessible instruction on today's crucial technologies and business skills.

Just as CompTIA is committed to establishing measurable standards for certifying A+ Technicians, Sybex is committed to providing those individuals with the knowledge needed to meet those standards.

The authors and editors have worked hard to ensure that this edition of the *CompTIA A+ Complete Study Guide* you hold in your hands is comprehensive, in-depth, and pedagogically sound. We're confident that this book will exceed the demanding standards of the certification marketplace and help you, the A+ candidate, succeed in your endeavors.

As always, your feedback is important to us. If you believe you've identified an error in the book, please send a detailed e-mail to `support@wiley.com`. And if you have general comments or suggestions, feel free to drop me a line directly at `nedde@wiley.com`. At Sybex we're continually striving to meet the needs of individuals preparing for certification exams.

Good luck in pursuit of your A+ certification!

Neil Edde
Vice President & Publisher
Sybex, an Imprint of Wiley

Acknowledgments

It continues to amaze me how many people and how much time it takes to create a book of this scope and size. From beginning to end, there are scores of dedicated professionals focused on delivering the best book possible to you the readers.

First, I need to thank my co-authors Emmett Dulaney and Toby Skandier, as they did a tremendous job while being under a serious time crunch. Now on to the rest of the team.

Jeff Kellum kept us on track and moving forward, which was a challenge at times. Daria Meoli kept us organized, which is no small feat during writing. I owe special gratitude to Tech Editor Neil Hester, who kept me on my toes and made excellent suggestions. Copy Editors Linda Recktenwald and Sharon Wilkey provided their usual clairvoyance, and saved me from butchering the English language. Many thanks also go out to the proofreader (James Brook), indexer (Ted Laux), and compositor (Craig Woods). Without their great contributions this book would not have made it to your hands.

—*Quentin Docter*

There are a great many people to thank but three are key; without them this book would not be possible. First and foremost is Jeff Kellum of Sybex, who does his job extremely well and pulls you along with him. Thanks must also go to David Groth for his excellent work on the previous edition. I also thank the Production Editor (Daria Meoli); the Technical Editor (Neil Hester); and the Copy Editor (Linda Recktenwald). Without their hard work, I would have never completed this book.

—*Emmett Dulaney*

I would like to thank my Acquisitions and Development Editor, Jeff Kellum. Jeff has a knack for matching me to the most interesting and challenging projects that enhance my knowledge and proficiency in my area of expertise and then keeping me on track with them.

I'm indebted to my Technical Editor, Neil Hester, for catching some of the most detailed technical issues. This book is vastly more solid for his vigilance. My Production Editor, Daria Meoli, and Copy Editor, Linda Recktenwald, have my deepest gratitude for repairing those things in which I am most certainly not expert.

In addition, I'd like to thank the proofreader (James Brook), indexer (Ted Laux), typesetter (Craig Woods), and CD developers (Angela Denny and Kit Malone).

Thank you to my Embarq Corporation management team and associates for the support and challenges you continue to offer.

Finally, thank you to my incredible kids, Toby, Tiffani, Trey, and Taylor. You guys support and encourage your dad through your own hard work and determination. You're always in my thoughts and plans.

—*Toby Skandier*

Contents at a Glance

Contents

Table of Exercises

Introduction

Welcome to the *CompTIA A+ Complete Study Guide*. This is the fourth edition of our best-selling study guide for the A+ certification sponsored by CompTIA (Computing Technology Industry Association).

This book was written at an intermediate technical level; we assume that you already know how to *use* a personal computer and its basic peripherals, such as modems and printers, but we also recognize that you may be learning how to *service* some of that computer equipment for the first time. The exams cover basic computer service topics as well as some more advanced issues, and they cover some topics that anyone already working as a technician, whether with computers or not, should be familiar with. The exams are designed to test you on these topics in order to certify that you have enough knowledge to fix and upgrade some of the most widely used types of personal desktop computers.

We've included review questions at the end of each chapter to give you a taste of what it's like to take the exams. If you're already working as a technical service or support technician, we recommend you check out these questions first to gauge your level of knowledge. (You can also take the Assessment Test at the end of this Introduction, which is designed to see how much you already know.)

Don't just study the questions and answers—the questions on the actual exams will be different from the practice ones included in this book and on the CD. The exams are designed to test your knowledge of a concept or objective, so use this book to learn the objective *behind* the question.

You can use the book mainly to fill in the gaps in your current computer service knowledge. You may find, as many PC technicians have, that being well versed in all the technical aspects of the equipment is not enough to provide a satisfactory level of support—you must also have customer-relations skills. We include helpful hints to get the customer to help you help them.

What Is A+ Certification?

The A+ certification program was developed by the Computer Technology Industry Association (CompTIA) to provide an industry-wide means of certifying the competency of computer service technicians. The A+ certification is granted to those who have attained the level of knowledge and troubleshooting skills that are needed to provide capable support in the field of personal computers. It is similar to other certifications in the computer industry, such Novell's Certified Novell Engineer (CNE) program and the Microsoft Certified Systems Engineer (MCSE) program. The theory behind these certifications is that if you need to have service performed on any of their products, you would sooner call a technician who has been certified in one of the appropriate certification programs than you would just call the first "expert" in the phone book.

The A+ certification program was created to offer a wide-ranging certification, in the sense that it is intended to certify competence with personal computers from many different makers/vendors. You must pass two tests to become A+ certified:

- The A+ Essentials (220-601) exam, which covers basic computer concepts, hardware troubleshooting, soft skills (such as customer service), and hardware upgrading, security, and safety

- One of three "technician" exams—IT Technician (220-602), Remote Support Technician (220-603), or Depot Technician (220-604)—which cover more of the hands-on aspects of the topics tested on in the Essentials exam.

You don't have to take the Essentials and the technician exams at the same time. The A+ certification is not awarded until you've passed both tests.

 Depending on which technician exam you take, your official A+ certificate will state which exam you took.

Why Become A+ Certified?

There are several good reasons to get your A+ certification. The CompTIA Candidate's Information packet lists five major benefits:

- It demonstrates proof of professional achievement.
- It increases your marketability.
- It provides greater opportunity for advancement in your field.
- It is increasingly a requirement for some types of advanced training.
- It raises customer confidence in you and your company's services.

Provides Proof of Professional Achievement

The A+ certification is quickly becoming a status symbol in the computer service industry. Organizations that include members of the computer service industry are recognizing the benefits of A+ certification and are pushing for their members to become certified. And more people every day are putting the "A+ Certified Technician" emblem on their business cards.

Increases Your Marketability

A+ certification makes individuals more marketable to potential employers. A+ certified employees also may receive a higher base salary because employers won't have to spend as much money on vendor-specific training.

Provides Opportunity for Advancement

Most raises and advancements are based on performance. A+ certified employees work faster and more efficiently, and are thus more productive. The more productive employees are, the more money they make for their company. And, of course, the more money they make for the company, the more valuable they are to the company. So if an employee is A+ certified, their chances of being promoted are greater.

What Is an ASC?

More service companies are becoming CompTIA A+ Authorized Service Centers (ASCs). This means that over 50 percent of the technicians employed by that service center are A+ certified. Customers and vendors alike recognize that ASCs employ the most qualified service technicians. As a result, an ASC gets more business than a nonauthorized service center. And, because more service centers want to reach the AASC level, they will give preference in hiring to a candidate who is A+ certified over one who is not.

Fulfills Training Requirements

A+ certification is recognized by most major computer hardware vendors. Some of these vendors apply A+ certification toward prerequisites in their own respective certification programs, which has the side benefit of reducing training costs for employers.

Raises Customer Confidence

As the A+ Certified Technician moniker becomes more well known among computer owners, more of them will realize that the A+ technician is more qualified to work on their computer equipment than a noncertified technician is.

How to Become A+ Certified

A+ certification is available to anyone who passes the tests. You don't have to work for any particular company. It's not a secret society. It is, however, an elite group. To become A+ certified, you must do two things:

- Pass the A+ Essentials exam
- Pass the one of the three A+ technician exams: IT Technician, Remote Support Technician, Depot Technician exam

If you already have your A+ certification and wish to upgrade, CompTIA is allowing you to only take one of the three technician exams to upgrade you certification.

The exams can be taken at any Thompson Prometric or Pearson VUE testing center. If you pass both exams, you will get a certificate in the mail from CompTIA saying that you have passed, and you will also receive a lapel pin and business card.

To register for the tests, call Thompson Prometric at (800) 77-MICRO (776-4276) or register online at http://www.2test.com. For Pearson VUE, call (877) 551-PLUS (7587) or go to http://www.vue.com. You'll be asked for your name, Social Security Number (an optional number may be assigned if you don't wish to provide your Social Security Number), mailing address, phone number, employer, when and where you want to take the test, and your credit card number (arrangement for payment must be made at the time of registration).

Although you can save money by arranging to take more than one test at the same seating, there are no other discounts. If you have to take a test more than once in order to get a passing grade, you must pay both times.

Who Should Buy This Book?

If you are one of the many people who want to pass the A+ exams, and pass them confidently, then you should buy this book and use it to study for the exams. The A+ Essentials exam is designed to measure essential competencies for an entry-level technician. The technician exams are intended to certify that the exam candidate has the necessary skills to work on microcomputer hardware and typically has at least six months of on-the-job experience.

This book was written with one goal in mind: to prepare you for the challenges of the real IT world, not just to pass the A+ exams. This study guide will do that by describing in detail the concepts on which you'll be tested.

How to Use This Book and CD

We've included several testing features throughout the book and on the CD-ROM. At the beginning of the book (right after this introduction) is an assessment test for each that you can use to check your readiness for the actual exams. Take both of these exams before you begin reading the book. Doing so will help you determine the areas you may need to brush up on. The answers to each assessment test appear on a separate page after the last question of the test. Each answer also includes an explanation and a note telling you the chapter in which this material appears.

To test your knowledge as you progress through the book, there are review questions at the end of each chapter. As you finish each chapter, answer the review questions and then check your answers—the correct answers appear on the page following the last review question. You can go back to reread the section that deals with each question you got wrong to ensure that you answer correctly the next time you are tested on the material. You'll also find flash-card questions. You can use these handy question for on-the-go review. Download them right onto your Palm or handheld device for quick and convenient reviewing.

In addition to the assessment test and the chapter review question, you'll find sample exams for each of the A+ exams. Take these practice exams just as if you were actually taking the A+ exams (without any reference material).

Depending on what edition of the book you have, either the Standard or the Deluxe Edition, you will have either eight exams (two each for the 4 A+ tests) or 12 (three each). In the Deluxe Edition, we've also included a second CD, which contains a series of instructional videos with author Emmett Dulaney. These videos show Emmett performing a number of hands-on tasks and processes you need to be familiar with as a CompTIA A+ technician.

If you are going to travel but still need to study for the A+ exams, and you have a laptop with a CD-ROM drive, you can take this entire book with you just by taking the CD-ROM. This book is in PDF (Adobe Acrobat) format so it can be easily read on any computer.

I'm Studying For _____. Is This Book For Me?

You may have noticed that the exam objectives for the three Technician exams look very similar. In fact, they are word for word. CompTIA did this intentionally. Because the exams are now job-role based, during their Job Task Analysis, they discovered that a number of the tasks that, say, a Remote Tech might perform are the same as what an IT or Depot Tech would perform. However, the percentages are the same.

Because it was not logical to release four versions of the book, or make this book into four parts, each focusing on one of the four A+ exams, we decided to cover all three technician exams in one. However, we have included a very handy tear-out card that maps to each of the exam objectives. In it, you will see which chapters cover which exams, and more specifically, which objectives.

In addition, we have included bonus exams for each of the four A+ tests, using the same percentages they use. For instance, roughly 18 percent of the IT Tech bonus exams deal with operating systems, whereas 45 percent of the questions in the Depot Tech exams are on operating system.

So the answer to your question is yes.

Minimum System Requirements

You should have a minimum of 45MB of disk space, as well as Windows 98 or higher, to use the Sybex Test Engine. You will also need Adobe Acrobat Reader (included).

The Exam Objectives

Behind every computer industry exam you can be sure to find exam objectives—the broad topics in which the exam developers want to ensure your competency.

As mentioned previously, two tests are required to become A+ certified: the Essentials exam and one of three technician exams. In the following sections, we have listed the official CompTIA exam objectives. However, we want to point out that you will notice a lot of overlap between the technician objectives. CompTIA has made an effort to target specific job roles with their A+ certification. A number of the tasks in these job roles are similar, thus the overlap.

Exam objectives are subject to change at any time without prior notice and at CompTIA's sole discretion. Please visit the A+ Certification page of CompTIA's website (http://www.comptia.org/certification/aplus/index.htm) for the most current listing of exam objectives.

The A+ Essentials Exam Objectives

The A+ Essentials exam is designed for candidate with at least 500 hours of hands-on experience. It expects you to understand how to installing, building, upgrading, repairing, configuring, troubleshooting, optimizing, diagnosing, and performing preventative maintenance of basic personal computer hardware and operating systems.

The following are the areas (or *domains*, according to CompTIA) in which you must be proficient in order to pass the A+ Essentials:

Domain 1: Personal Computer Components   21%
Domain 2: Laptop and Portable Devices   11%
Domain 3: Operating Systems   21%
Domain 4: Printers and Scanners   9%
Domain 5: Networks   12%
Domain 6: Security   11%
Domain 7: Safety and Environmental Issues 10%
Domain 8: Communication and Professionalism 5%

Domain 1: Installation, Configuration, and Upgrading

1.1 Identify the fundamental principles of using personal computers

Identify the names, purposes and characteristics of storage devices

- FDD
- HDD
- CD / DVD / RW (e.g. drive speeds, media types)
- Removable storage (e.g. tape drive, solid state such as thumb drive, flash and SD cards, USB, external CD-RW and hard drive)

Identify the names, purposes and characteristics of motherboards

- Form Factor (e.g. ATX / BTX, micro ATX / NLX)
- Components
    - Integrated I/Os (e.g. sound, video, USB, serial, IEEE 1394 / firewire, parallel, NIC, modem)
    - Memory slots (e.g. RIMM, DIMM)
    - Processor sockets

- External cache memory
- Bus architecture
- Bus slots (e.g. PCI, AGP, PCIE, AMR, CNR)
- EIDE / PATA
- SATA
- SCSI Technology
- Chipsets
- BIOS / CMOS / Firmware
- Riser card / daughter board

Identify the names, purposes and characteristics of power supplies, for example: AC adapter, ATX, proprietary, voltage

Identify the names purposes and characteristics of processor / CPUs

- CPU chips (e.g. AMD, Intel)
- CPU technologies
  - Hyperthreading
  - Dual core
  - Throttling
  - Micro code (MMX)
  - Overclocking
  - Cache
  - VRM
  - Speed (real vs. actual)
  - 32 vs. 64 bit

Identify the names, purposes and characteristics of memory

- Types of memory (e.g. DRAM, SRAM, SDRAM, DDR / DDR2, RAMBUS)
- Operational characteristics
  - Memory chips (8, 16, 32)
  - Parity versus non-parity
  - ECC vs. non-ECC
  - Single-sided vs. double-sided

Identify the names, purposes and characteristics of display devices, for example: projectors, CRT and LCD

- Connector types (e.g. VGA, DVI / HDMi, S-Video, Component / RGB)
- Settings (e.g. V-hold, refresh rate, resolution)

Identify the names, purposes and characteristics of input devices for example: mouse, keyboard, bar code reader, multimedia (e.g. web and digital cameras, MIDI, microphones), biometric devices, touch screen.

Identify the names, purposes and characteristics of adapter cards

- Video including PCI / PCI-E and AGP
- Multimedia
- I / O (SCSI, serial, USB, Parallel)
- Communications including network and modem

Identify the names, purposes and characteristics of pots and cables for example: USB 1.1 and 2.0, parallel, serial, IEEE 1394 / firewire, RJ45 and RJ11, PS2 / MINI-DIN, centronics (e.g. mini, 36) multimedia (e.g. 1 / 8 connector, MIDSI COAX, SPDIF)

Identify the names, purposes and characteristics of cooling systems for example heat sinks, CPU and case fans, liquid cooling systems, thermal compound

1.2 Install, configure, optimize and upgrade personal computer components

Add, remove and configure internal and external storage devices

- Drive preparation of internal storage devices including format / file systems and imaging technology

Install display devices

Add, remove and configure basic input and multimedia devices

1.3 Identify tools, diagnostic procedures and troubleshooting techniques for personal computer components

Recognize the basic aspects of troubleshooting theory for example:

- Perform backups before making changes
- Assess a problem systematically and divide large problems into smaller components to be analyzed individually
- Verify even the obvious, determine whether the problem is something simple and make no assumptions
- Research ideas and establish priorities
- Document findings, actions and outcomes

Identify and apply basic diagnostic procedures and troubleshooting techniques for example:

- Identify the problem including questioning user and identifying user changes to computer
- Analyze the problem including potential causes and make an initial determination of software and / or hardware problems

- Test related components including inspection, connections, hardware / software configurations, device manager and consult vendor documentation
- Evaluate results and take additional steps if needed such as consultation, use of alternate resources, manuals
- Document activities and outcomes

Recognize and isolate issues with display, power, basic input devices, storage, memory, thermal, POST errors (e.g. BIOS, hardware)

Apply basic troubleshooting techniques to check for problems (e.g. thermal issues, error codes, power, connections including cables and / or pins, compatibility, functionality, software / drivers) with components for example:

- Motherboards
- Power supply
- Processor / CPUs
- Memory
- Display devices
- Input devices
- Adapter cards

Recognize the names, purposes, characteristics and appropriate application of tools for example: BIOS, self-test, hard drive self-test and software diagnostics test

1.4 Perform preventative maintenance on personal computer components

Identify and apply basic aspects of preventative maintenance theory for example:

- Visual / audio inspection
- Driver / firmware updates
- Scheduling preventative maintenance
- Use of appropriate repair tools and cleaning materials
- Ensuring proper environment

Identify and apply common preventative maintenance techniques for devices such as input devices and batteries

Domain 2: Laptops and Portable Devices

2.1 Identify the fundamental principles of using laptops and portable devices

Identify names, purposes and characteristics of laptop-specific:

- Form factors such as memory and hard drives
- Peripherals (e.g. docking station, port replicator and media / accessory bay)
- Expansion slots (e.g. PCMCIA I, II and III, card and express bus)

- Ports (e.g. mini PCI slot)
- Communication connections (e.g. Bluetooth, infrared, cellular WAN, Ethernet)
- Power and electrical input devices (e.g. auto-switching and fixed-input power supplies, batteries)
- LCD technologies (e.g. active and passive matrix, resolution such as XGA, SXGA+, UXGA, WUXGA, contrast radio, native resolution)
- Input devices (e.g. stylus / digitizer, function (Fn) keys and pointing devices such as touch pad, point stick / track point)

Identify and distinguish between mobile and desktop motherboards and processors including throttling, power management and WiFi

2.2 Install, configure, optimize and upgrade laptops and portable devices

Configure power management

- Identify the features of BIOS-ACPI
- Identify the difference between suspend, hibernate and standby

Demonstrate safe removal of laptop-specific hardware such as peripherals, hot-swappable devices and non-hot-swappable devices

2.3 Identify tools, basic diagnostic procedures and troubleshooting techniques for laptops and portable devices

Use procedures and techniques to diagnose power conditions, video, keyboard, pointer and wireless card issues, for example:

- Verify AC power (e.g. LEDs, swap AC adapter)
- Verify DC power
- Remove unneeded peripherals
- Plug in external monitor
- Toggle Fn keys
- Check LCD cutoff switch
- Verify backlight functionality and pixilation
- Stylus issues (e.g. digitizer problems)
- Unique laptop keypad issues
- Antenna wires

2.4 Perform preventative maintenance on laptops and portable devices

Identify and apply common preventative maintenance techniques for laptops and portable devices, for example: cooling devices, hardware and video cleaning materials, operating environments including temperature and air quality, storage, transportation and shipping.

Domain 3: Operating Systems

3.1 Identify the fundamentals of using operating systems

Identify differences between operating systems (e.g. Mac, Windows, Linux) and describe operating system revision levels including GUI, system requirements, application and hardware compatibility

Identify names, purposes and characteristics of the primary operating system components including registry, virtual memory and file system

Describe features of operating system interfaces, for example:

- Windows Explorer
- My Computer
- Control Panel
- Command Prompt
- My Network Places
- Task bar / systray
- Start Menu

Identify the names, locations, purposes and characteristics of operating system files for example:

- BOOT.INI
- NTLDR
- NTDETECT.COM
- NTBOOTDD.SYS
- Registry data files

Identify concepts and procedures for creating, viewing, managing disks, directories and files in operating systems for example:

- Disks (e.g. active, primary, extended and logical partitions)
- File systems (e.g. FAT 32, NTFS)
- Directory structures (e.g. create folders, navigate directory structures)
- Files (e.g. creation, extensions, attributes, permissions)

3.2 Install, configure, optimize and upgrade operating systems

Identify procedures for installing operating systems including:

- Verification of hardware compatibility and minimum requirements
- Installation methods (e.g. boot media such as CD, floppy or USB, network installation, drive imaging)
- Operating system installation options (e.g. attended / unattended, file system type, network configuration)

- Disk preparation order (e.g. start installation, partition and format drive)
- Device driver configuration (e.g. install and upload device drivers)
- Verification of installation

Identify procedures for upgrading operating systems including:

- Upgrade considerations (e.g. hardware, application and / or network compatibility)
- Implementation (e.g. backup data, install additional Windows components)

Install / add a device including loading, adding device drivers and required software including:

- Determine whether permissions are adequate for performing the task
- Device driver installation (e.g. automated and / or manual search and installation of device drivers)
- Using unsigned drivers (e.g. driver signing)
- Verify installation of the driver (e.g. device manager and functionality)

Identify procedures and utilities used to optimize operating systems for example, virtual memory, hard drives, temporary files, service, startup and applications

3.3 Identify tools, diagnostic procedures and troubleshooting techniques for operating systems

Identify basic boot sequences, methods and utilities for recovering operating systems

- Boot methods (e.g. safe mode, recovery console, boot to restore point)
- Automated System Recovery (ASR) (e.g. Emergency Repair Disk (ERD))

Identify and apply diagnostic procedures and troubleshooting techniques for example:

- Identify the problem by questioning the user and identifying user changes to the computer
- Analyze problem including potential causes and initial determination of software and / or hardware problem
- Test related components including connections, hardware / software configurations, device manager and consulting vendor documentation
- Evaluate results and take additional steps if needed such as consultation, alternate resources and manuals
- Document activities and outcomes

Recognize and resolve common operational issues such as bluescreen, system lock-up, input / output device, application install, start or load and Windows-specific printing problems (e.g. print spool stalled, incorrect / incompatible driver for print)

Explain common error messages and codes for example:

- Boot (e.g. invalid boot disk, inaccessible boot drive, missing NTLDR)
- Startup (e.g. device / service failed to start, device / program in registry not found)

- Event Viewer
- Registry
- Windows reporting

Identify the names, locations, purposes and characteristics of operating system utilities for example:

- Disk management tools (e.g. DEFRAG, NTBACKUP, CHKDSK, Format)
- System management tools (e.g. device and task manager, MSCONFIG.EXE)
- File management tools (e.g. Windows Explorer, ATTRIB.EXE)

3.4 Perform preventative maintenance on operating systems

Describe common utilities for performing preventative maintenance on operating systems for example, software and Windows updates (e.g. service packs), scheduled backups / restore, restore points

Domain 4: Printers and Scanners

4.1 Identify the fundamental principles of using printers and scanners

Identify differences between types of printer and scanner technologies (e.g. laser, inkjet, thermal, solid ink, impact)

Identify names, purposes and characteristics of printer and scanner components (e.g. memory, driver, firmware) and consumables (e.g. toner, ink cartridge, paper)

Identify the names, purposes and characteristics of interfaces used by printers and scanners including port and cable types for example:

- Parallel
- Network (e.g. NIC, print servers)
- USB
- Serial
- IEEE 1394 / firewire
- Wireless (e.g. Bluetooth, 802.11, infrared
- SCSI

4.2 Identify basic concepts of installing, configuring, optimizing and upgrading printers and scanners

Install and configure printers / scanners

- Power and connect the device using local or network port
- Install and update device driver and calibrate the device
- Configure options and default settings
- Print a test page

Optimize printer performance for example, printer settings such as tray switching, print spool settings, device calibration, media types and paper orientation

4.3 Identify tools, basic diagnostic procedures and troubleshooting techniques for printers and scanners

Gather information about printer / scanner problems

- Identify symptom
- Review device error codes, computer error messages and history (e.g. event log, user reports)
- Print or scan test page
- Use appropriate generic or vendor-specific diagnostic tools including web-based utilities

Review and analyze collected data

- Establish probable causes
- Review service documentation
- Review knowledge base and define and isolate the problem (e.g. software vs. hardware, driver, connectivity, printer)

Identify solutions to identified printer / scanner problems

- Define specific cause and apply fix
- Replace consumables as needed
- Verify functionality and get user acceptance of problem fix

Domain 5: Networks

5.1 Identify the fundamental principles of networks

Describe basic networking concepts

- Addressing
- Bandwidth
- Status indicators
- Protocols (e.g. TCP / IP including IP, classful subnet, IPX / SPX including NWLINK, NETBWUI / NETBIOS)
- Full-duplex, half-duplex
- Cabling (e.g. twisted pair, coaxial cable, fiber optic, RS-232)
- Networking models including peer-to-peer and client / server

Identify names, purposes and characteristics of the common network cables

- Plenum / PVC
- UTP (e.g. CAT3, CAT5 / 5e, CAT6)
- STP
- Fiber (e.g. single-mode and multi-mode)

Identify names, purposes and characteristics of network cables (e.g. RJ45 and RJ11, ST / SC / LC, USB, IEEE 1394 / Firewire)

Identify names, purposes and characteristics (e.g. definition, speed and connections) of technologies for establishing connectivity for example:

- LAN / WAN
- ISDN
- Broadband (e.g. DSL, cable, satellite)
- Dial-up
- Wireless (all 802.11)
- Infrared
- Bluetooth
- Cellular
- VoIP

5.2 Install, configure, optimize and upgrade networks

Install and configure network cards (physical address)

Install, identify and obtain wired and wireless connection

5.3 Identify tools, diagnostic procedures and troubleshooting techniques for networks

Explain status indicators, for example speed, connection and activity lights and wireless signal strength

Domain 6: Security

6.1 Identify the fundamental principles of security

Identify names, purposes and characteristics of hardware and software security for example:

- Hardware deconstruction / recycling
- Smart cards / biometrics (e.g. key fobs, cards, chips and scans)
- Authentication technologies (e.g. user name, password, biometrics, smart cards)
- Malicious software protection (e.g. viruses, Trojans, worms, spam, spyware, adware, grayware)
- Software firewalls
- File system security (e.g. FAT32 and NTFS)

Identify names, purposes and characteristics of wireless security for example:

- Wireless encryption (e.g. WEP.x and WPA.x) and client configuration
- Access points (e.g. disable DHCP / use static IP, change SSID from default, disable SSID broadcast, MAC filtering, change default username and password, update firmware, firewall)

Identify names, purposes and characteristics of data and physical security

- Data access (basic local security policy)
- Encryption technologies
- Backups
- Data migration
- Data / remnant removal
- Password management
- Locking workstation (e.g. hardware, operating system)

Describe importance and process of incidence reporting

Recognize and respond appropriately to social engineering situations

6.2 Install, configure, upgrade and optimize security

Install, configure, upgrade and optimize hardware, software and data security for example:

- BIOS
- Smart cards
- Authentication technologies
- Malicious software protection
- Data access (basic local security policy)
- Backup procedures and access to backups
- Data migration
- Data / remnant removal

6.3 Identify tool, diagnostic procedures and troubleshooting techniques for security

Diagnose and troubleshoot hardware, software and data security issues for example:

- BIOS
- Smart cards, biometrics
- Authentication technologies
- Malicious software
- File system (e.g. FAT32, NTFS)
- Data access (e.g. basic local security policy)
- Backup
- Data migration

6.4 Perform preventative maintenance for computer security

Implement software security preventative maintenance techniques such as installing service packs and patches and training users about malicious software prevention technologies

Domain 7: Safety and Environmental Issues

7.1 Describe the aspects and importance of safety and environmental issues

Identify potential safety hazards and take preventative action

Use Material Safety Data Sheets (MSDS) or equivalent documentation and appropriate equipment documentation

Use appropriate repair tools

Describe methods to handle environmental and human (e.g. electrical, chemical, physical) accidents including incident reporting

7.2 Identify potential hazards and implement proper safety procedures including ESD precautions and procedures, safe work environment and equipment handling

7.3 Identify proper disposal procedures for batteries, display devices and chemical solvents and cans

Domain 8: Professionalism and Communication

8.1 Use good communication skills including listening and tact / discretion, when communicating with customers and colleagues

Use clear, concise and direct statements

Allow the customer to complete statements – avoid interrupting

Clarify customer statements – ask pertinent questions

Avoid using jargon, abbreviations and acronyms

Listen to customers

8.2 Use job-related professional behavior including notation of privacy, confidentiality and respect for the customer and customers' property

Behavior

- Maintain a positive attitude and tone of voice
- Avoid arguing with customers and / or becoming defensive
- Do not minimize customers' problems
- Avoid being judgmental and / or insulting or calling the customer names
- Avoid distractions and / or interruptions when talking with customers

Property

- Telephone, laptop, desktop computer, printer, monitor, etc.

The A+ IT Technician (220-602) Exam Objectives

The CompTIA A+ 220-602 exam is targeted at people who work in a remote or corporate technical environment with a high level of face-to-face client interaction. Ideally, they should have passed the CompTIA A+ Essentials exam. Typical job titles include enterprise technician, IT administrator, field service technician and PC technician.

The following are the areas (or *domains*, according to CompTIA) in which you must be proficient in order to pass the A+ IT Technician exam:

Domain 1: Personal Computer Components	18%
Domain 2: Laptop and Portable Devices	9%
Domain 3: Operating Systems	20%
Domain 4: Printers and Scanners	14%
Domain 5: Networks	11%
Domain 6: Security	8%
Domain 7: Safety and Environmental Issues	5%
Domain 8: Communication and Professionalism	15%

Domain 1: Personal Computer Components

1.1 Install, configure, optimize and upgrade personal computer components

Add, remove and configure personal computer components including selection and installation of appropriate components for example:

- Storage devices
- Motherboards
- Power supplies
- Processors / CPUs
- Memory
- Display devices
- Input devices (e.g. basic, specialty and multimedia)
- Adapter cards
- Cooling systems

1.2 Identify tools, diagnostic procedures and troubleshooting techniques for personal computer components

Identify and apply basic diagnostic procedures and troubleshooting techniques

- Isolate and identify the problem using visual and audible inspection of components and minimum configuration

Recognize and isolate issues with peripherals, multimedia, specialty input devices, internal and external storage and CPUs

Identify the steps used to troubleshoot components (e.g. check proper seating, installation, appropriate components, settings and current driver) for example:

- Power supply
- Processor / CPUs and motherboards
- Memory
- Adapter cards
- Display and input devices

Recognize names, purposes, characteristics and appropriate application of tools for example:

Multi-meter

Anti-static pad and wrist strap

Specialty hardware / tools

Loop back plugs

Cleaning products (e.g. vacuum, cleaning pads)

1.3 Perform preventative maintenance of personal computer components

Identify and apply common preventative maintenance techniques for personal computer components for example:

- Display devices (e.g. cleaning, ventilation)
- Power devices (e.g. appropriate source such as power strip, surge protector, ventilation and cooling)
- Input devices (e.g. covers)
- Storage devices (e.g. software tools such as DEFRAG and cleaning of optics and tape heads)
- Thermally sensitive devices such as motherboards, CPU, adapter cards memory (e.g. cleaning, air flow)

Domain 2: Laptops and Portable Devices

2.1 Identify fundamental principles of using laptops and portable devices

Identify appropriate applications for laptop-specific communication connections such as Bluetooth, infrared, cellular WAN and Ethernet

Identify appropriate laptop-specific power and electrical input devices and determine how amperage and voltage can affect performance

Identify the major components of the LCD including inverter, screen and video card

2.2 Install, configure, optimize and upgrade laptops and portable devices

Removal of laptop-specific hardware such as peripherals, hot-swappable and non-hot-swappable devices

Describe how video sharing affects memory upgrades

2.3 Use tools, diagnostic procedures and troubleshooting techniques for laptops and portable devices

Use procedures and techniques to diagnose power conditions, video, keyboard, pointer and wireless card issues for example:

- Verify AC power (e.g. LEDs, swap AC adapter)
- Verify DC power
- Remove unneeded peripherals
- Plug in external monitor

- Toggle Fn keys
- Check LCD cutoff switch
- Verify backlight functionality and pixilation
- Stylus issues (e.g. digitizer problems)
- Unique laptop keypad issues
- Antenna wires

Domain 3: Operating Systems

3.1 Identify the fundamental principles of operating systems

Use command-line functions and utilities to manage operating systems, including proper syntax and switches for example:

- CMD
- HELP
- DIR
- ATTRIB
- EDIT
- COPY
- XCOPY
- FORMAT
- IPCONFIG
- PING
- MD / CD / RD

Identify concepts and procedures for creating, viewing and managing disks, directories and files on operating systems

- Disks (e.g. active, primary, extended and logical partitions and file systems including FAT32 and NTFS)
- Directory structures (e.g. create folders, navigate directory structures)
- Files (e.g. creation, attributes, permissions)

Locate and use operating system utilities and available switches for example:

- Disk management tools (e.g. DEFRAG, NTBACKUP, CHKDSK, Format)
- System management tools
  - Device and Task Manager
  - MSCONFIG.EXE
  - REGEDIT.EXE
  - REGEDT32.EXE

- CMD
- Event Viewer
- System Restore
- Remote Desktop
- File management tools (e.g. Windows EXPLORER, ATTRIB.EXE)

3.2 Install, configure, optimize and upgrade operating systems

Identify procedures and utilities used to optimize operating systems for example:

- Virtual memory
- Hard drives (e.g. disk defragmentation)
- Temporary files
- Services
- Startup
- Application

3.3 Identify tools, diagnostic procedures and troubleshooting techniques for operating systems

Demonstrate the ability to recover operating systems (e.g. boot methods, recovery console, ASR, ERD)

Recognize and resolve common operational problems for example:

- Windows specific printing problems (e.g. print spool stalled, incorrect / incompatible driver form print)
- Auto-restart errors
- Bluescreen error
- System lock-up
- Device drivers failure (input / output devices)
- Application install, start or load failure

Recognize and resolve common error messages and codes for example:

- Boot (e.g. invalid boot disk, inaccessible boot drive, missing NTLDR)
- Startup (e.g. device / service failed to start, device / program in registry not found)
- Event Viewer
- Registry
- Windows reporting

Use diagnostic utilities and tools to resolve operational problems for example:

- Bootable media
- Startup modes (e.g. safe mode, safe mode with command prompt or networking, step-by-step / single step mode)
- Documentation resources (e.g. user / installation manuals, internet / web based, training materials)

- Task and Device Manager
- Event Viewer
- MSCONFIG
- Recover CD / recovery partition
- Remote Desktop Connection and Assistance
- System File Checker (SFC)

3.4 Perform preventative maintenance for operating systems

Demonstrate the ability to perform preventative maintenance on operating systems including software and Windows updates (e.g. service packs), scheduled backups / restore, restore points

Domain 4: Printers and Scanners

4.1 Identify the fundamental principles of using printers and scanners

Describe processes used by printers and scanners including laser, ink dispersion, thermal, solid ink and impact printers and scanners

4.2 Install, configure, optimize and upgrade printers and scanners

Install and configure printers / scanners

- Power and connect the device using local or network port
- Install and update device driver and calibrate the device
- Configure options and default settings
- Install and configure print drivers (e.g. PCL™, Postscript™, GDI)
- Validate compatibility with operating system and applications
- Educate user about basic functionality

Install and configure printer upgrades including memory and firmware

Optimize scanner performance including resolution, file format and default settings

4.3 Identify tools and diagnostic procedures to troubleshooting printers and scanners

Gather information about printer / scanner problems

Review and analyze collected data

Isolate and resolve identified printer / scanner problem including defining the cause, applying the fix and verifying functionality

Identify appropriate tools used for troubleshooting and repairing printer / scanner problems

- Multi-meter
- Screwdrivers
- Cleaning solutions
- Extension magnet
- Test patterns

4.4 Perform preventative maintenance of printers and scanners

Perform scheduled maintenance according to vendor guidelines (e.g. install maintenance kits, reset page counts)

Ensure a suitable environment

Use recommended supplies

Domain 5: Networks

5.1 Identify the fundamental principles or networks

Identify names, purposes and characteristics of basic network protocols and terminologies for example:

- ISP
- TCP / IP (e.g. gateway, subnet mask, DNS, WINS, static and automatic address assignment)
- IPX / SPX (NWLink)
- NETBEUI / NETBIOS
- SMTP
- IMAP
- HTML
- HTTP
- HTTPS
- SSL
- Telnet
- FTP
- DNS

Identify names, purposes and characteristics of technologies for establishing connectivity for example:

- Dial-up networking
- Broadband (e.g. DSL, cable, satellite)
- ISDN networking
- Wireless (all 802.11)
- LAN / WAN
- Infrared
- Bluetooth
- Cellular
- VoIP

5.2 Install, configure, optimize and upgrade networks

Install and configure browsers

- Enable / disable script support
- Configure proxy and security settings

Establish network connectivity

- Install and configure network cards
- Obtain a connection
- Configure client options (e.g. Microsoft, Novell) and network options (e.g. domain, workgroup, tree)
- Configure network options

Demonstrate the ability to share network resources

- Models
- Configure permissions
- Capacities / limitations for sharing for each operating system

5.3 Use tools and diagnostic procedures to troubleshoot network problems

Identify names, purposes and characteristics of tools for example:

- Command line tools (e.g. IPCONFIG.EXE, PING.EXE, TRACERT.EXE, NSLOOKUP.EXE)
- Cable testing device

Diagnose and troubleshoot basic network issue for example:

- Driver / network interface
- Protocol configuration

TCP / IP (e.g. gateway, subnet mask, DNS, WINS, static and automatic address assignment)

IPX / SPX (NWLink)

- Permissions
- Firewall configuration
- Electrical interference

5.4 Perform preventative maintenance of networks including securing and protecting network cabling

Domain 6: Security

6.1 Identify the fundamentals and principles of security

Identify the purposes and characteristics of access control for example:

- Access to operating system (e.g. accounts such as user, admin and guest, Groups, permission actions, types and levels), components, restricted spaces

Identify the purposes and characteristics of auditing and event logging

6.2 Install, configure, upgrade and optimize security

Install and configure software, wireless and data security for example:

- Authentication technologies
- Software firewalls
- Auditing and event logging (enable / disable only)
- Wireless client configuration
- Unused wireless connections
- Data access (e.g. permissions, basic local security policy)
- File systems (converting from FAT32 to NTFS only)

6.3 Identify tool, diagnostic procedures and troubleshooting techniques for security

Diagnose and troubleshoot software and data security issues for example:

- Software firewall issues
- Wireless client configuration issues
- Data access issues (e.g. permissions, security policies)
- Encryption and encryption technology issues

6.4 Perform preventative maintenance for security

Recognize social engineering and address social engineering situations

Domain 7: Safety and Environmental Issues

7.1 Identify potential hazards and proper safety procedures including power supply, display devices and environment (e.g. trip, liquid, situational, atmospheric hazards and high-voltage and moving equipment)

Domain 8: Professionalism and Communication

8.1 Use good communication skills including listening and tact / discretion, when communicating with customers and colleagues

Use clear, concise and direct statements

Allow the customer to complete statements – avoid interrupting

Clarify customer statements – ask pertinent questions

Avoid using jargon, abbreviations and acronyms

Listen to customers

8.2 Use job-related professional behavior including notation of privacy, confidentiality and respect for the customer and customers' property

Behavior

- Maintain a positive attitude and tone of voice
- Avoid arguing with customers and / or becoming defensive

- Do not minimize customers' problems
- Avoid being judgmental and / or insulting or calling the customer names
- Avoid distractions and / or interruptions when talking with customers

Property

- Telephone, laptop, desktop computer, printer, monitor, etc.

The A+ Remote Support Technician (220-603) Exam Objectives

The CompTIA A+ Remote Support Technician exam targets people who work in a remote-based work environment where client interaction, client training, operating system and connectivity issues are emphasized. Typical job titles includes remote support technician, help desk technician, call center technician, specialist, representative. Ideally, they have already passed the CompTIA A+ Essentials.

The following are the areas (or *domains*, according to CompTIA) in which you must be proficient in order to pass the A+ Remote Support Technician exam:

Domain 1: Personal Computer Components	15%
Domain 2: Operating Systems	29%
Domain 3: Printers and Scanners	10%
Domain 4: Networks	11%
Domain 5: Security	15%
Domain 6: Communication and Professionalism	20%

1.0 Personal Computer Components

1.1 Install, configure, optimize, and upgrade personal computer components

Add, remove, and configure display devices, input devices and adapter cards including basic input and multimedia devices.

1.2 Identify tools, diagnostic procedures, and troubleshooting techniques for personal computer components

Identify and apply basic diagnostic procedures and troubleshooting techniques, for example:

- Identify and analyze the problem/potential problem
- Test related components and evaluate results
- Identify additional steps to be taken if/when necessary
- Document activities and outcomes

Recognize and isolate issues with display, peripheral, multimedia, specialty input device and storage.

Apply steps in troubleshooting techniques to identify problems (e.g. physical environment, functionality and software/driver settings) with components including display, input devices and adapter cards

1.3 Perform preventative maintenance on personal computer components

Identify and apply common preventative maintenance techniques for storage devices, for example:

- Software tools (e.g., Defrag, CHKDSK)
- Cleaning (e.g., optics, tape heads)

Domain 2: Operating Systems

2.1 Identify the fundamental principles of using operating systems

Use command-line functions and utilities to manage Windows 2000, XP Professional and XP Home, including proper syntax and switches, for example:

- CMD
- HELP
- DIR
- ATTRIB
- EDIT
- COPY
- XCOPY
- FORMAT
- IPCONFIG
- PING
- MD / CD/ RD

Identify concepts and procedures for creating, viewing, managing disks, directories and files in Windows 2000, XP Professional and XP Home, for example:

- Disks (e.g. active, primary, extended and logical partitions)
- File systems (e.g. FAT 32, NTFS)
- Directory structures (e.g. create folders, navigate directory structures)
- Files (e.g. creation, extensions, attributes, permissions)

Locate and use Windows 2000, XP Professional and XP Home utilities and available switches

- Disk Management Tools (e.g. DEFRAG, NTBACKUP, CHKDSK, Format)
- System Management Tools
    - Device and Task Manager
    - MSCONFIG.EXE
    - REGEDIT.EXE
    - REGEDIT32.EXE
    - CMD

- Event Viewer
- System Restore
- Remote Desktop

File Management Tool (e.g. Windows Explorer, ATTRIB.EXE)

2.2 Install, configure, optimize and upgrade operating systems

Identify procedures and utilities used to optimize the performance of Windows 2000, XP Professional and XP Home, for example:

- Virtual memory
- Hard drives (e.g. disk defragmentation)
- Temporary files
- Services
- Startup
- Applications

2.3 Identify tools, diagnostic procedures and troubleshooting techniques for operating systems.

Recognize and resolve common operational problems, for example:

- Windows-specific printing problems (e.g. print spool stalled, incorrect/incompatible driver form print)
- Auto-restart errors
- Bluescreen error
- System lock-up
- Device drivers failure (input/output devices)
- Application install, start or load failure

Recognize and resolve common error messages and codes, for example:

- Boot (e.g. invalid boot disk, inaccessible boot device, missing NTLDR)
- Startup (e.g. device/service has failed to start, device/program references in registry not found)
- Event viewer
- Registry
- Windows

Use diagnostic utilities and tools to resolve operational problems, for example:

- Bootable media
- Startup Modes (e.g. safe mode, safe mode with command prompt or networking, step-by-step/single step mode)
- Documentation resources (e.g. user/installation manuals, internet/web-based, training materials)

- Task and Device Manager
- Event Viewer
- MSCONFIG
- Recovery CD / Recovery partition
- Remote Desktop Connection and Assistance
- System File Checker (SFC)

2.4 Perform preventative maintenance for operating systems

Perform preventative maintenance on Windows 2000, XP Professional and XP Home including software and Windows updates (e.g. service packs)

Domain 3: Printers and Scanners

3.1 Identify the fundamental principles of using printers and scanners

Describe processes used by printers and scanners including laser, ink dispersion, impact, solid ink and thermal printers.

3.2 Install, configure, optimize and upgrade printers and scanners

Install and configure printers and scanners

- Power and connect the device using network or local port
- Install/update the device driver and calibrate the device
- Configure options and default settings
- Install and configure print drivers (e.g. PCL™, Postscript™ and GDI)
- Validate compatibility with OS and applications
- Educate user about basic functionality

Optimize scanner performance for example: resolution, file format and default settings

3.3 Identify tools, diagnostic procedures and troubleshooting techniques for printers and scanners

Gather information required to troubleshoot printer/scanner problems

Troubleshoot a print failure (e.g. lack of paper, clear queue, restart print spooler, recycle power on printer, inspect for jams, check for visual indicators)

Domain 4: Networks

4.1 Identify the fundamental principles of networks

Identify names, purposes, and characteristics of the basic network protocols and terminologies, for example:

- ISP
- TCP/IP (e.g. Gateway, Subnet mask, DNS, WINS, Static and automatic address assignment)

- IPX/SPX (NWLink)
- NETBEUI/NETBIOS
- SMTP
- IMAP
- HTML
- HTTP
- HTTPS
- o SSL
- Telnet
- FTP
- DNS

Identify names, purposes, and characteristics of technologies for establishing connectivity, for example:

- Dial-up networking
- Broadband (e.g. DSL, cable, satellite)
- ISDN Networking
- Wireless
- LAN/WAN

4.2 Install, configure, optimize and upgrade networks

Establish network connectivity and share network resources

4.3 Identify tools, diagnostic procedures and troubleshooting techniques for networks

Identify the names, purposes, and characteristics of command line tools, for example:

- IPCONFIG.EXE
- PING.EXE
- TRACERT.EXE
- NSLOOKUP.EXE

Diagnose and troubleshoot basic network issues, for example:

- Driver/network interface
- Protocol configuration
    - TCP/IP (e.g. Gatway, Subnet mask, DNS, WINS, static and automatic address assignment)
    - IPX/SPX (NWLink)
- Permissions
- Firewall configuration
- Electrical interference

Domain 5: Security

5.1 Identify the fundamental principles of security

Identify the names, purposes, and characteristics of access control and permissions

- Accounts including user, admin and guest
- Groups
- Permission levels, types (e.g. file systems and shared) and actions (e.g. read, write, change and execute)

5.2 Install, configure, optimizing and upgrade security

Install and configure hardware, software, wireless and data security, for example:

- Smart card readers
- Key fobs
- Biometric devices
- Authentication technologies
- Software firewalls
- Auditing and event logging (enable/disable only)
- Wireless client configuration
- Unused wireless connections
- Data access (e.g. permissions, security policies)
- Encryption and encryption technologies

5.3 Identify tools, diagnostic procedures and troubleshooting techniques for security issues

Diagnose and troubleshoot software and data security issues, for example:

- Software firewall issues
- Wireless client configuration issues
- Data access issues (e.g. permissions, security policies)
- Encryption and encryption technology issues

5.4 Perform preventative maintenance for security

Recognize social engineering and address social engineering situations

Domain 6: Professionalism and Communication

6.1 Use good communication skills, including listening and tact / discretion, when communicating with customers and colleagues

Use clear, concise and direct statements

Allow the customer to complete statements – avoid interrupting

Clarify customer statements – ask pertinent questions

Avoid using jargon, abbreviations and acronyms

Listen to customers

6.2 Use job-related professional behavior including notation of privacy, confidentiality and respect for the customer and customers' property

The A+ Depot Technician (220-604) Exam Objectives

The CompTIA A+ Depot Technician examination is targeted towards people who work in settings with limited customer interaction where hardware related activities are emphasized. Typical job titles include depot technician, bench technician, etc. Ideally, candidates should have passed the CompTIA A+ Essentials exam.

The following are the areas (or *domains*, according to CompTIA) in which you must be proficient in order to pass the A+ Depot Technician exam:

Domain 1: Personal Computer Components	45%
Domain 2: Laptop and Portable Devices	20%
Domain 3: Printers and Scanners	20%
Domain 4: Security	5%
Domain 5: Safety and Environmental Issues	10%

Domain 1: Personal Computer Components

1.1 Install, configure, optimize and upgrade personal computer components

Add, remove and configure internal storage devices, motherboards, power supplies, processor/CPU's, memory and adapter cards, including:

- Drive preparation
- Jumper configuration
- Storage device power and cabling
- Selection and installation of appropriate motherboard
- BIOS set-up and configuration
- Selection and installation of appropriate CPU
- Selection and installation of appropriate memory
- Installation of adapter cards including hardware and software/drivers
- Configuration and optimization of adapter cards including adjusting hardware settings and obtaining network card connection

Add, remove and configure systems

1.2 Identify tools, diagnostic procedures and troubleshooting techniques for personal computer components

Identify and apply diagnostic procedures and troubleshooting techniques, for example:

- Identify and isolate the problem using visual and audible inspection of components and minimum configuration

Identify the steps used to troubleshoot components (e.g. check proper seating, installation, appropriate component, settings, current driver), for example:

- Power supply
- Processor/CPU's and motherboards
- Memory
- Adapter cards

Recognize names, purposes, characteristics and appropriate application of tools, for example:

- Multi-meter
- Anti-static pad and wrist strap
- Specialty hardware/tools
- Loop back plugs
- Cleaning products (e.g. vacuum, cleaning pads)

1.3 Perform preventative maintenance of personal computer components

Identify and apply common preventative maintenance techniques, for example:

- Thermally sensitive devices (e.g. motherboards, CPU's, adapter cards, memory)
    - Cleaning
    - Air flow (e.g. slot covers, cable routing)
- Adapter cards (e.g. driver/firmware updates)

Domain 2: Laptop and Portable Devices

2.1 Identify the fundamental principles of using laptops and portable devices

Identify appropriate applications for laptop-specific communication connections, for example:

- Bluetooth
- Infrared devices
- Cellular WAN
- Ethernet

Identify appropriate laptop-specific power and electrical input devices, for example:

- Output performance requirements for amperage and voltage

Identify the major components of the LCD (e.g. inverter, screen, video card)

2.2 Install, configure, optimize and upgrade laptops and portable devices

Demonstrate the safe removal of laptop-specific hardware including peripherals, hot-swappable and non hot-swappable devices

Identify the affect of video sharing on memory upgrades

2.3 Identify tools, diagnostic procedures and troubleshooting techniques for laptops and portable devices.

Use procedures and techniques to diagnose power conditions, video issues, keyboard and pointer issues and wireless card issues, for example:

- Verify AC power (e.g. LED's, swap AC adapter)
- Verify DC power
- Remove unneeded peripherals
- Plug in external monitor
- Toggle Fn keys
- Check LCD cutoff switch
- Verify backlight functionality and pixilation
- Stylus issues (e.g. digitizer problems)
- Unique laptop keypad issues
- Antenna wires

Domain 3: Printers and Scanners

3.1 Identify the fundamental principles of using printers and scanners

Describe the processes used by printers and scanners including laser, inkjet, thermal, solid ink, and impact printers

3.2 Install, configure, optimize and upgrade printers and scanners

Identify the steps used in the installation and configuration processes for printers and scanners, for example:

- Power and connect the device using network or local port
- Install and update the device driver
- Calibrate the device
- Configure options and default settings
- Print test page

Install and configure printer/scanner upgrades including memory and firmware

3.3 Identify tools, diagnostic methods and troubleshooting procedures for printers and scanners

Gather data about printer/scanner problem

Review and analyze data collected about printer/scanner problems

Implement solutions to solve identified printer/scanner problems

Identify appropriate tools used for troubleshooting and repairing printer/scanner problems

- Multi-meter
- Screw drivers

- Cleaning solutions
- Extension magnet
- Test patterns

3.4 Perform preventative maintenance of printer and scanner problems

Perform scheduled maintenance according to vendor guidelines (e.g. install maintenance kits, reset page counts)

Ensure a suitable environment

Use recommended supplies

Domain 4: Security

4.1 Identify the names, purposes and characteristics of physical security devices and processes

Control access to PC's, servers, laptops and restricted spaces

- Hardware
- Operating systems

4.2 Install hardware security

Smart card readers

Key fobs

Biometric devices

Domain 5: Safety and Environmental Issues

5.1 Identify potential hazards & proper safety procedures including power supply, display devices and environment (e.g. trip, liquid, situational, atmospheric hazards, high-voltage and moving equipment)

Assessment Test

1. What is the common name for where custom BIOS settings are stored?

A. BIOS memory

B. CMOS

C. CPU

D. Hard drive

2. What is the term for a small USB-attached flash memory device?

A. Thumb drive

B. SD

C. CompactFlash

D. Memory Stick

3. Which one of the following is not a video-related technology?

A. DVI

B. S/PDIF

C. HDMI

D. WQUXGA

4. Which of the following offers single-layer storage of 25GB?

A. HD DVD

B. Super-CD

C. DVD+R DL

D. Blu-ray Disc

5. How can you tell a USB 2.0 cable from other USB cables?

A. USB 2.0 connectors are bigger.

B. USB 2.0 connectors are smaller.

C. You can see the metallic shield through the sheath.

D. There is absolutely no difference.

6. Nearly all desktop processors mount using _____ connectors, while a few others use _____ connectors.

A. sleeved, slotted

B. push, pull

C. pin, card edge

D. card edge, pin

7. What is the processor's operational state?

    A. C0

    B. C1

    C. C2

    D. C3

8. Which of the following memory standards are used in laptops? (Choose all that apply.)

    A. DIMM

    B. MicroDIMM

    C. SoDIMM

    D. RIMM

9. Which wireless IEEE standard operates on the 2.4GHz radio frequency and transmits data at speeds up to 54Mbps?

    A. 802.11b

    B. 802.11c

    C. 802.11e

    D. 802.11g

10. In Windows XP, how can you start a search for files and folders?

    A. Click Start ➢ All Programs ➢ Search.

    B. Run SEARCH.EXE at the command prompt.

    C. Left-click a directory and choose Find.

    D. Click Start ➢ Search.

11. Which of the following is not a hive in the Windows Registry?

    A. HKEY_CLASSES_ROOT

    B. HKEY_LOCAL_MACHINE

    C. HKEY_USERS

    D. HKEY_RESOURCES

12. Which of the following upgrade paths is *not* possible?

    A. Windows 95 to Windows XP

    B. Windows NT to Windows 2000

    C. Windows Me to Windows XP

    D. Windows 98 to Windows XP

13. The program that performs an upgrade from Windows NT to Windows XP is called _____.

    A. `INSTALL.BAT`

    B. `SETUP.EXE`

    C. `WINNT.EXE`

    D. `WINNT32.EXE`

14. Which of the following are solutions to hard disk thrashing? (Choose all that apply.)

    A. Formatting the disk

    B. Buying a bigger hard disk

    C. Freeing up disk space

    D. Deleting all files

15. In the Windows 2000 boot sequence, which file loads `NTOSKRNL.EXE`?

    A. `NTDETECT.COM`

    B. `NTLDR`

    C. `BOOT.INI`

    D. `NTBOOTDD.SYS`

16. Which of the following is not a type of printer?

    A. Laser printer

    B. Dot-matrix printer

    C. ScanJet printer

    D. Bubble-jet printer

17. What is the component called that stores the material that ends up printed to the page in a laser printer?

    A. Toner cartridge

    B. Ink cartridge

    C. Laser module

    D. Laser cartridge

18. What form of communication is characterized by two stations transmitting to one another simultaneously?

    A. Simplex

    B. Half-duplex

    C. Full-duplex

    D. Double-duplex

19. Which of the following statements about IP addresses is most accurate?

  A. Class A IP addresses have 8 bits.

  B. Class B IP addresses have 24 bits.

  C. Class C IP addresses have 32 bits.

  D. Class D IP addresses have 0 bits.

20. Which authentication protocol depends on a "secret" known only to the authenticator and that peer?

  A. PAP

  B. SLIP

  C. CHAP

  D. PPP

21. Which wireless protocol is an improvement on WEP?

  A. WAP

  B. WPA

  C. PAW

  D. PWA

22. The electrical contacts on your sound card are oxidizing. Which of the following should you *not* use to clean those contacts? (Choose all that apply.)

  A. Cloth and water

  B. Isopropyl alcohol

  C. A pencil eraser

  D. Your fingers

23. What is the approximate minimum level of static charge that can damage an electronic computer component?

  A. 100 volts

  B. 1,000 volts

  C. 10,000 volts

  D. 100,000 volts

24. The goal of _____ is to prevent or minimize unauthorized access to files and folders and disclosure of data and information.

  A. secrecy

  B. privacy

  C. respect

  D. confidentiality

25. While the laws provide a _____ level of privacy, you should go out of your way to respect the privacy of your users beyond what the law establishes.

    A. minimal

    B. maximum

    C. negligible

    D. unimportant

26. Which of the following is *not* a form of storage device configuration?

    A. Formatting

    B. IDE/SCSI selection

    C. Partitioning

    D. Master/slave selection

27. You currently have an AT-style motherboard. Your power supply has failed. Your new power supply is an ATX format. Which one of the following is true?

    A. You need an adapter to connect to your motherboard.

    B. You need an adapter to connect to your hard drive.

    C. You need an adapter to connect to your floppy drive.

    D. There is no way to use the ATX power supply with the AT motherboard.

28. A Bluetooth network is called what?

    A. Bluenet

    B. Subnet

    C. Micronet

    D. Piconet

29. Which of the following devices provides power so that an LCD monitor is bright enough to be seen?

    A. LCD backlight power adapter

    B. Inverter

    C. Backlight

    D. LCD backlight motherboard circuitry

30. Your computer's sound card is not working. You check your speakers, and they work fine. In Device Manager, what would tell you that the device's driver is not functioning properly?

    A. There is a yellow circle and an exclamation point on the device.

    B. There is a red X on the device.

    C. The device is not listed in Device Manager.

    D. Device Manager does not give information about device drivers.

31. You are at a command prompt. A file called WORD1.DOC has been hidden by another user, and you want to unhide it. Which command should you use to accomplish this?

   A. ATTRIB +H WORD1.DOC

   B. ATTRIB -H WORD1.DOC

   C. ATTRIB -U WORD1.DOC

   D. ATTRIB +U WORD1.DOC

32. In the electrophotographic print process, which step follows the cleaning step?

   A. Writing

   B. Transferring

   C. Fusing

   D. Charging

33. Which of the following are examples of printer communication languages? (Choose all that apply.)

   A. PCL

   B. PS

   C. GDI

   D. OSI

34. Which of following are examples of dispersion printer technologies? (Choose all that apply.)

   A. Dot-matrix

   B. Inkjet

   C. Bubble jet

   D. Solid ink

35. In which of the following printing processes does the ink go from a solid directly to a gas?

   A. Inkjet

   B. Bubble jet

   C. Solid ink

   D. Dye-sublimation

36. While _____ is a database, the easiest way to think of it is as a hierarchical tree with a set number of top-level domains, and then entries beneath each of those.

   A. SMTP

   B. DNS

   C. DHCP

   D. WINS

37. Which NTFS permission, when applied to folders, allows moving through folders to reach other files and folders (even if the users don't have permission for those folders); when applied to files, runs applications and allows all actions permitted by the Read permission?

   A. List

   B. Supervisor

   C. Read&Execute

   D. Modify

38. _____ is intended to ensure that security engineering has been implemented in a product from the early design phases. It's intended for high levels of security assurance.

   A. EAL 1

   B. EAL 2

   C. EAL 3

   D. EAL 5

39. What process involves making an application more difficult for non-authorized individuals to access, exploit, and so on?

   A. Application hardening

   B. Bulletproofing

   C. Pharprotecting

   D. EAL'ing

40. Which character can be used at the beginning of a line in a hosts file to make the line a comment?

   A. @

   B. #

   C. !

   D. (

Answers to Assessment Test

1. B.   The CMOS chip or equivalent stores any changes that are made to the default BIOS settings. BIOS memory is not a valid term. For more information, see Chapter 1.

2. A.   Only thumb drives attach directly to a USB port. The other flash memory devices require card readers to attach to a computer. Generally, they are inserted directly into the device they provide memory for. For more information, see Chapter 1.

3. B.   S/PDIF is a digital audio specification. For more information, see Chapter 1.

4. D.   The *DL* in DVD+R DL stands for double layer. The question referred to a single layer. For DVD+R DL, a single layer holds the same amount of data as regular DVD technologies: 4.7GB. HD DVD maxes out at 15GB. Blu-ray Disc is capable of storing 25GB per layer. For more information, see Chapter 1.

5. C.   A USB 2.0 cable uses the same connectors as any other USB cable. It's shielding is improved over that of older cables. The USB 2.0 cables are made with transparent sheaths that allow you to see the silver metallic shield. For more information, see Chapter 1.

6. C.   Nearly all desktop processors mount using pin connectors, while a few others use card edge connectors. For more information, see Chapter 2.

7. A.   C0 is the operational state; no power is being saved. For more information, see Chapter 2.

8. B, C.   The SoDIMM and MicroDIMM are the common laptop memory standards. DIMMs and RIMMs are both desktop standards. For more information, see Chapter 3.

9. D .   The IEEE standard for 54Mbps wireless transmission over 2.4GHz radio is the 802.11g standard. The 802.11b standard has a maximum transmission speed of 11Mbps. Neither 802.11c nor 802.11e is a commonly implemented standard. For more information, see Chapter 3.

10. D.   In addition to using the Start menu to start a search, you can also right-click a file or folder and choose Search, or you can click the Search button in the Windows Explorer toolbar. For more information, see Chapter 4.

11. D.   There are five basic hives in the Windows registry, and they are `HKEY_CLASSES_ROOT`, `HKEY_CURRENT_USER`, `HKEY_LOCAL_MACHINE`, `HKEY_USERS`, and `HKEY_CURRENT_CONFIG`. `HKEY_RESOURCES` does not exist. For more information, see Chapter 4.

12. A.   Windows 95 cannot be directly upgraded to Windows XP. Instead, you must first upgrade to Windows 98 and then to Windows XP (or just do a fresh install of Windows XP). For more information, see Chapter 5.

13. D.   To upgrade from a 32-bit OS such as Windows NT, you would use `WINNT32.EXE`. The program that performs an upgrade from Windows 9*x* to Windows 2000 is `WINNT.EXE`. For more information, see Chapter 5.

14. B, C.   The solution to thrashing is to free up some disk space. However, it may be easiest to install a bigger hard disk. If that solution isn't practical, you must delete enough unused files that you can make the swap file large enough to be functional. For more information, see Chapter 6.

15. B.   NTLDR loads NTDETECT.COM, NTOSKRNL.EXE, and HAL.DLL. For more information, see Chapter 6.

16. C.   ScanJet is a trade name owned by Hewlett-Packard for their line of scanners. Scanners are not printers. For more information, see Chapter 7.

17. A.   Laser printers use toner, which they melt to the page in the image of the text and graphics being printed. A toner cartridge holds the fine toner dust until it is used in the printing process. For more information, see Chapter 7.

18. C.   The term full-duplex describes simultaneous bidirectional communication. Double-duplex is not a valid term. For more information, see Chapter 8.

19. C.   All IP addresses have 32 bits, regardless of class. While options A and B are accurate in a minimalist sense, option C is most accurate. For more information, see Chapter 8.

20. C.   CHAP depends on a "secret" known only to the authenticator and that peer. Part of configuring CHAP is setting the shared, predefined secret on both the client and server. For more information, see Chapter 9.

21. B.   WPA is an improvement on WEP. For more information, see Chapter 9.

22. A, C, D.   To clean electrical contacts, use denatured isopropyl alcohol and a cotton swab. Water should never touch electrical components. A pencil eraser could leave traces of acids behind, and your fingers have oils on them that will damage the contacts. See Chapter 10 for more information.

23. A.   It takes only about 100 volts to damage an electronic component. Most people can feel an electric shock at about 3,000 volts. See Chapter 10 for more information.

24. D.   The goal of *confidentiality* is to prevent or minimize unauthorized access to files and folders and disclosure of data and information. For more information, see Chapter 11.

25. A.   While the laws provide a minimal level of privacy, you should go out of your way to respect the privacy of your users beyond what the law establishes. For more information, see Chapter 11.

26. B.   You physically configure an IDE (ATA) hard drive by selecting whether it is the master or slave of its controller chain. You then configure it through software by partitioning it as one or more volumes represented by unique drive letters and formatting those drives. You must match your drive to the technology supported by the system—IDE, SCSI, and so on. Doing so is not a matter of configuration but rather product selection. Once you select one type, it cannot be configured as another. For more information, see Chapter 12.

27. A.   Device connectors are the same as they have been since each one was introduced. It's the motherboard power header that changes from time to time. Adapters exist to bridge the discrepancy, which means there is a way to use the ATX power supply with the AT motherboard. For more information, see Chapter 12.

28. D.   A Bluetooth network is called a piconet. Piconets have a limit of eight devices each. For more information, see Chapter 13.

29. B.   The inverter is responsible for powering the LCD backlight. The backlight itself provides the light, but it needs power from the inverter. For more information, see Chapter 13.

30. A.   If the device has been installed, but the driver is not functioning properly, you will see a yellow circle with an exclamation point over the device. A red X means that the device is disabled.

31. B.   The ATTRIB command is used to set file attributes. To add attributes, use the plus sign (+). To remove attributes, use the minus sign (−). The hidden attribute is designated by H.

32. D.   The electrophotographic print process is the one followed by laser printers. The steps in order are cleaning, charging, writing, developing, transferring, and fusing. See Chapter 15 for more information.

33. A, B, C.   Printer Command Language (PCL), PostScript (PS), and Graphical Device Interface (GDI) are all languages that can be used to communicate with a printer. The Open System Interconnect (OSI) model is a networking model, not a printing language. See Chapter 15 for more information.

34. B, C.   Inkjet and bubble jet are the two common types of dispersion printer technologies. See Chapter 15 for more information.

35. D.   In dye-sublimation printers, the solid ink gets transformed into a gaseous state (sublimated) before it gets transferred to the paper. See Chapter 15 for more information.

36. B.   While DNS is a database, the easiest way to think of it is as a hierarchical tree with a set number of top-level domains, and then entries beneath each of those. For more information, see Chapter 16.

37. C.   Read and Execute applied to folders allows moving through folders to reach other files and folders (even if the users don't have permission for those folders). When applied to files, Read and Execute runs applications and allows all actions permitted by the Read permission. For more information, see Chapter 16.

38. D.   EAL 5 is intended to ensure that security engineering has been implemented in a product from the early design phases. It's intended for high levels of security assurance. For more information, see Chapter 17.

39. A.   Application hardening involves making an application more difficult for non-authorized individuals to access, exploit, and so on. For more information, see Chapter 17.

40. B.   The pound sign (#) signifies the line as a comment line to ignore when processing. For more information, see Chapter 17.

Identifying Personal Computer Components

THE FOLLOWING COMPTIA A+ ESSENTIALS EXAM OBJECTIVES ARE COVERED IN THIS CHAPTER:

✓ **1.1 Identify the fundamental principles of using personal computers**

- Identify the names, purposes and characteristics of storage devices
  - FDD
  - HDD
  - CD/DVD/RW (e.g. drive speeds, media types)
  - Removable storage (e.g. tape drive, solid state such as thumb drives, flash and SD cards, USB, external CD-RW and hard drive)
- Identify the names, purposes and characteristics of motherboards
  - Form Factor (e.g. ATX/BTX, micro ATX/NLX)
  - Components
    - Integrated I/Os (e.g. sound, video, USB, serial, IEEE 1394 / firewire, parallel, NIC, modem)
    - Memory slots (e.g. RIMM, DIMM)
    - Processor sockets
    - External cache memory
    - Bus architecture
    - Bus slots (e.g. PCI, AGP, PCIe, AMR, CNR)
    - EIDE/PATA
    - SATA
    - SCSI Technology

- Chipsets
- BIOS / CMOS / Firmware
- Riser card / Daughter board
- Identify the names, purposes and characteristics of power supplies, for example: AC adapter, ATX, proprietary, voltage
- Identify the names, purposes and characteristics of processor / CPUs
  - CPU chips (e.g. AMD, Intel)
  - CPU technologies
    - Hyperthreading
    - Dual core
    - Throttling
    - Micro code (MMX)
    - Overclocking
    - Cache
    - VRM
    - Speed (real vs. actual)
    - 32 vs. 64 bit
- Identify the names, purposes, and characteristics of memory
  - Types of memory (e.g. DRAM, SRAM, SDRAM, DDR / DDR2, RAMBUS)
  - Operational characteristics
    - Memory chips (8, 16, 32)
    - Parity versus non-parity
    - ECC vs. non-ECC
    - Single-sided vs. double-sided
- Identify the names, purposes and characteristics of display devices, for example: projectors, CRT and LCD
  - Connector types (e.g. VGA, DVI / HDMi, S-Video, Component / RGB)
  - Settings (e.g. V-hold, refresh rate, resolution)

- Identify the names, purposes and characteristics of input devices for example: mouse, keyboard, bar code reader, multimedia (e.g. web and digital cameras, MIDI, microphones), biometric devices, touch screen.
- Identify the names, purposes, and characteristics of adapter cards
  - Video including PCI / PCI-E and AGP
  - Multimedia
  - I/O (SCSI, serial, USB, parallel)
  - Communications including network and modem
- Identify the names, purposes and characteristics of ports and cables for example: USB 1.1 and 2.0, parallel, serial, IEEE1394 / firewire, RJ45 and 11, PS2 / MINI-DIN, centronics (e.g. mini, 36) multimedia (e.g. 1 / 8 connector, MIDI COAX, SPDIF)
- Identify the names, purposes and characteristics of cooling systems for example heat sinks, CPU and case fans, liquid cooling systems, thermal compound

A *personal computer (PC)* is a computing device made up of many distinct electronic components that all function together in order to accomplish some useful task (such as adding up the numbers in a spreadsheet or helping you write a letter). By this definition, note that we're describing a computer as having many distinct parts that work together. Most computers today are modular. That is, they have components that can be removed and replaced with a component of similar function in order to improve performance. Each component has a very specific function. In this chapter, you will learn about the components that make up a typical PC, what their function is, and how they work together inside the PC.

Unless specifically mentioned otherwise, throughout this book the terms *PC* and *computer* can be used interchangeably.

In this chapter, you will learn how to identify personal computer components, including the following:

- Motherboards
- Processors
- Memory
- Storage devices
- Power supplies
- Display devices
- Input devices
- Adapter cards
- Ports and cables
- Cooling systems

Identifying Components of Motherboards

The spine of the computer is the *motherboard*, otherwise known as the *system board* (and less commonly referred to as the *planar board*). This is the olive green or brown circuit board that lines the bottom of the computer. It is the most important component in the computer because it connects all the other components of a PC together. Figure 1.1 shows a typical PC system board, as seen from above. All other components are attached on this sheet. On the system board, you will find the central processing unit (CPU), underlying circuitry, expansion slots, video components, random access memory (RAM) slots, and a variety of other chips.

Types of System Boards

There are two major types of system boards: integrated and nonintegrated:

Nonintegrated System Board   Each major assembly is installed in the computer as an expansion card. The major assemblies we're talking about are items like the video circuitry, disk controllers, and accessories. *Nonintegrated system boards* can be easily identified because each expansion slot is usually occupied by one of these components.

It is difficult to find nonintegrated motherboards these days. Many of what would normally be called nonintegrated system boards now incorporate the most commonly used circuitry (such as IDE and floppy controllers, serial controllers, and sound cards) onto the motherboard itself. In the early 1990s, these components had to be installed externally to the motherboard.

FIGURE 1.1   A typical system board

Integrated System Board   Most of the components that would otherwise be installed as expansion cards are integrated into the motherboard circuitry. *Integrated system boards* were designed for simplicity. Of course, there's a drawback to this simplicity: When one component breaks, you can't just replace the component that's broken; the whole motherboard must be replaced. Although these boards are cheaper to produce, they are more expensive to repair.

With integrated system boards, there is a way around having to replace the whole motherboard when a single component breaks. On some motherboards, you can disable the malfunctioning onboard component (for example, the sound circuitry) and simply add an expansion card to replace its functions.

System Board Form Factors

System boards are also classified by their form factor (design): ATX, micro ATX, BTX, or NLX (and variants of these). Exercise care and vigilance when acquiring a motherboard and case separately. Some cases are less flexible than others and might not accommodate the motherboard you choose.

Advanced Technology Extended (ATX)

The *ATX motherboard* has the processor and memory slots at right angles to the expansion cards. This arrangement puts the processor and memory in line with the fan output of the power supply, allowing the processor to run cooler. And because those components are not in line with the expansion cards, you can install full-length expansion cards in an ATX motherboard machine. ATX (and its derivatives) are the primary motherboards sold today.

Micro ATX

One form factor that is designed to work in standard ATX cases, as well as its own smaller cases, is known as micro ATX (also referred to as μATX). Micro ATX follows the same principle of component placement for enhanced cooling over pre-ATX designs but with a smaller footprint. With this smaller form come trade-offs. For the compact use of space, you must give up quantity: quantity of memory modules, quantity of motherboard headers, quantity of expansion slots, quantity of integrated components, even quantity of micro ATX chassis bays, although the same small-scale motherboard can fit into much larger cases, if your original peripherals are still a requirement.

Be aware, however, that micro ATX systems tend to be designed with power supplies of lower wattage, in order to help keep down power consumption and heat production, which is generally acceptable with the standard micro ATX suite of components. As more off-board USB ports are added and larger cases are used with additional in-case peripherals, larger power supplies might be required.

New Low-profile Extended (NLX)

An alternative motherboard form factor, known as *New Low-profile Extended (NLX)*, is used in some low-profile case types. NLX continues the trend of the technology it succeeded, Low Profile Extended (LPX), placing the expansion slots (ISA, PCI, and so on) sideways on a special *riser card* to use the reduced vertical space optimally. Adapter cards, or *daughter boards*, that normally plug into expansion slots vertically in ATX motherboards, for example, plug in parallel to the mother-board, so their most demanding dimension does not affect case height.

LPX, a technology that lacked formal standardization and whose riser card interfaces varied from vendor to vendor, enjoyed great success in the 1990s until the advent of the Pentium II processor and the Accelerated Graphics Port (AGP). These two technologies placed a spotlight on how inadequate LPX was at cooling and accommodating high pin counts. NLX, an official standard from Intel, IBM, and DEC, was designed to fix the variability and other shortcomings of LPX, but NLX never quite caught on the way LPX did. Newer technologies, such as micro ATX, and proprietary solutions have been more successful and have taken even more market share from NLX.

Balanced Technology Extended (BTX)

In 2003, Intel announced its design for a new motherboard, slated to hit the market mid- to late-2004. When that time came, the new BTX motherboard was met with mixed emotions. (Postpone accusations of acronym reverse-engineering until "CTX" is announced as the name of the next generation.) Intel and its consumers realized that the price for faster components that produced more heat would be a retooling of the now-classic (since mid-1990s) ATX design. The motherboard manufacturers saw research and development expense and potential profit loss simply to accommodate the next generation of hotter-running processors, proces-sors manufactured by the same designers of the BTX technology. It was this resistance that caused the BTX form factor to gain very little ground over the next couple of years. Never-theless, with the early support of Gateway, Inc., and later buy-in of Dell, Inc., the BTX design dug in and charted a path for future success.

Marketing aside, the BTX technology is well thought out and serves the purpose for which it was intended. By lining up all heat-producing components between air intake vents and the power supply's exhaust fan, Intel found that the CPU and other components could be cooled properly by passive heat sinks. Fewer fans and a more efficient airflow path create a quieter con-figuration overall. While the BTX design benefits any modern onboard implementation, Intel's recommitment to lower-power CPUs has at once lessened the need to rush to more expensive BTX systems and given the market a bit more time to assimilate this newer technology.

There are other motherboard designs, but these are the most popular and also the ones that are covered on the exam. Some manufacturers (such as Compaq and IBM) design and manufacture their own motherboards, which don't conform to the standards. This style of motherboard is known as a *proprietary design* motherboard.

System Board Components

Now that you understand the basic types of motherboards and their form factors, it's time to look at the components found on the motherboard and their locations relative to each other. Figure 1.2 illustrates many of the following components found on a typical motherboard:

- Chipsets
- Expansion slots
- Memory slots and external cache
- CPU and processor slots or sockets
- Power connectors
- Onboard disk drive connectors
- Keyboard connectors
- Peripheral port and connectors
- BIOS chip
- CMOS battery
- Jumpers and DIP switches
- Firmware

FIGURE 1.2   Components on a motherboard

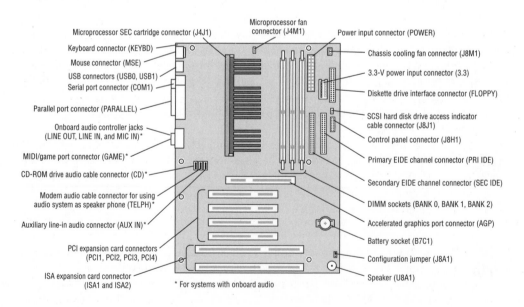

Microprocessor SEC cartridge connector (J4J1)
Microprocessor fan connector (J4M1)
Power input connector (POWER)
Keyboard connector (KEYBD)
Mouse connector (MSE)
USB connectors (USB0, USB1)
Serial port connector (COM1)
Parallel port connector (PARALLEL)
Onboard audio controller jacks (LINE OUT, LINE IN, and MIC IN)*
MIDI/game port connector (GAME)*
CD-ROM drive audio cable connector (CD)*
Modem audio cable connector for using audio system as speaker phone (TELPH)*
Auxiliary line-in audio connector (AUX IN)*
PCI expansion card connectors (PCI1, PCI2, PCI3, PCI4)
ISA expansion card connector (ISA1 and ISA2)
Chassis cooling fan connector (J8M1)
3.3-V power input connector (3.3)
Diskette drive interface connector (FLOPPY)
SCSI hard disk drive access indicator cable connector (J8J1)
Control panel connector (J8H1)
Primary EIDE channel connector (PRI IDE)
Secondary EIDE channel connector (SEC IDE)
DIMM sockets (BANK 0, BANK 1, BANK 2)
Accelerated graphics port connector (AGP)
Battery socket (B7C1)
Configuration jumper (J8A1)
Speaker (U8A1)
* For systems with onboard audio

In this subsection, you will learn about the most-used components of a motherboard, what they do, and where they are located on the motherboard. We'll show what each component looks like so you can identify it on any motherboard you run across. Note, however, that this is just a brief introduction to the insides of a computer. The details of the various devices in the computer and their impact on computer service practices will be covered in later chapters.

Chipsets

A *chipset* is a collection of chips or circuits that perform interface and peripheral functions for the processor. This collection of chips is usually the circuitry that provides interfaces for memory, expansion cards, and onboard peripherals and generally dictates how a motherboard will talk to the installed peripherals.

Chipsets are usually given a name and model number by the original manufacturer. For example, if you see that motherboard has a VIA KT7 chipset, you would know that the circuitry for controlling peripherals was designed by VIA and was given the designation KT7. Typically, that would also mean that you would know that a particular chipset has a certain set of features (for example, onboard video of a certain type/brand, onboard audio of a particular type, and so on).

Chipsets can be made up of one or several integrated circuit chips. Intel-based motherboards typically use two chips, whereas the SiS chipsets typically use one. To know for sure, you must check the manufacturer's documentation.

The functions of chipsets can be divided into two major functional groups, called Northbridge and Southbridge. Let's take a brief look at these groups and the functions they perform.

Northbridge

The *Northbridge* subset of a motherboard's chipset is the set of circuitry or chips that performs one very important function: management of high-speed peripheral communications. The Northbridge subset is responsible primarily for communications with integrated video using AGP and PCIe, for instance, and processor-to-memory communications. Therefore, it can be said that much of the true performance of a PC relies on the performance of the Northbridge chipset and the communications between it and the peripherals it controls.

 When we use the term Northbridge chipset, there isn't actually a Northbridge brand of chipset, but we are referring to the set of chips and circuits that make up a particular subset of a motherboard's chipset.

The communications between the CPU and memory occur over what is known as the *frontside bus (FSB)*, which is just a set of signal pathways between the CPU and main memory. The *backside bus*, on the other hand, is a set of signal pathways between the CPU and Level 2 cache memory (if present).

The Northbridge chipsets also manage the communications between the Southbridge chipset (discussed next) and the rest of the computer. Finally, if a motherboard has onboard video circuitry (especially if it needs direct access to main memory), that circuitry will be found within the Northbridge chipset.

It might help you to remember that the Northbridge plays "traffic cop" with the data within a computer, to ensure that data gets to where it needs to go in a timely fashion.

Southbridge

The *Southbridge* chipset, as mentioned earlier, is responsible for providing support to the myriad onboard peripherals (PS/2, Parallel, IDE, and so on), managing their communications with the rest of the computer and the resources given to them.

Most motherboards today have integrated PS/2, USB, Parallel, and Serial. Some of the optional features handled by the Southbridge include LAN, audio, infrared, and FireWire (IEEE 1394). When first integrated, the quality of onboard audio was marginal at best, but the latest offerings (such as the AC97 audio chipset) rival Creative Labs in sound quality and number of features (even including Dolby Digital Theater Surround technology).

The Southbridge chipset is also responsible for managing communications with the other expansion buses, such as PCI, USB, and legacy buses.

Figure 1.3 shows an example of a typical motherboard chipset (both Northbridge and Southbridge) and the components they interface with. Notice which components interface with which parts of the chipset.

FIGURE 1.3   A typical motherboard chipset

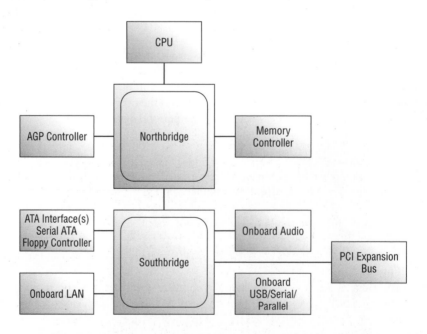

Expansion Slots

The most visible parts of any motherboard are the *expansion slots*. These look like small plastic slots, usually from 3 to 11 inches long and approximately ½ inch wide. As their name suggests, these slots are used to install various devices in the computer to expand its capabilities. Some expansion devices that might be installed in these slots include video, network, sound, and disk interface cards.

If you look at the motherboard in your computer, you will more than likely see one of the main types of expansion slots used in computers today:

- ISA
- PCI
- AGP
- PCIe
- AMR
- CNR

Each type differs in appearance and function. In this section, we will cover how to visually identify the different expansion slots on the motherboard.

ISA Expansion Slots

If you have a computer made before 1997, chances are the motherboard has a few *Industry Standard Architecture (ISA) expansion slots*. They're easily recognizable because they are usually black and have two parts: one shorter and one longer. Computers made after 1997 generally include a few ISA slots for backward compatibility with old expansion cards (although most computers are phasing them out in favor of PCI). Figure 1.4 shows an example of ISA expansion slots.

FIGURE 1.4   ISA expansion slots

PCI Expansion Slots

Most computers made today contain primarily *Peripheral Component Interconnect (PCI)* slots. They are easily recognizable because they are short (around 3 inches long) and usually white. PCI slots can usually be found in any computer that has a Pentium-class processor or higher. Figure 1.5 shows an example of several PCI expansion slots.

AGP Expansion Slots

Accelerated Graphics Port (AGP) slots are very popular for video card use. In the past, if you wanted to use a high-speed, accelerated 3D graphics video card, you had to install the card into an existing PCI or ISA slot. AGP slots were designed to be a direct connection between the video circuitry and the PC's memory. They are also easily recognizable because they are usually brown, are located right next to the PCI slots on the motherboard, and are shorter than the PCI slots. Figure 1.6 shows an example of an AGP slot, along with a PCI slot for comparison. Notice the difference in length between the two.

PCIe Expansion Slots

The newest expansion slot architecture that is being used by motherboards is *PCI Express (PCIe)*. It was designed to be a replacement for AGP and PCI. It has the capability of being faster than AGP while maintaining the flexibility of PCI. And motherboards with PCIe will have regular PCI slots for backward compatibility with PCI.

F I G U R E   1 . 5   PCI expansion slots

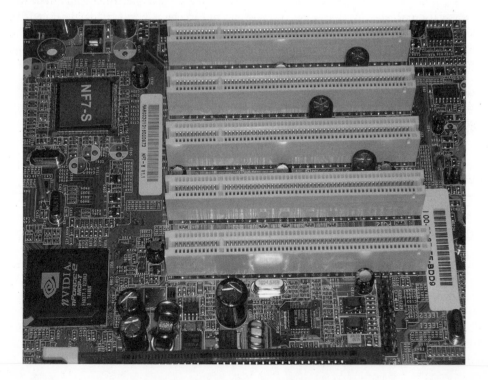

FIGURE 1.6   An AGP slot compared to a PCI slot

There are seven different speed levels for PCIe, and they are designated 1X, 2X, 4X, 8X, 12X, 16X, and 32X. These designations roughly correspond to similarly designated AGP speeds. The slots for PCIe are a bit harder to identify than other expansion slot types because the slot size corresponds to its speed. For example, the 1X slot is extremely short (less than an inch). The slots get longer in proportion to the speed; the longer the slot, the higher the speed. The reason for this stems from the PCIe concept of *lanes*, which are the multiplied units of communication between any two PCIe components and are directly related to physical wiring on the bus. Because all PCIe communications are made up of unidirectional coupling between devices, each PCIe card negotiates for the best mutually supported number of lanes with each communications partner.

 You can, however, use a shorter (lower-speed) card in a longer (higher-speed) slot. For example, you can put an 8X card in a 16X slot. The 8X card won't completely fill the slot, but it will work. The converse, however, is not true.

AMR Expansion Slots

As is always the case, Intel and other manufacturers are constantly looking for ways to improve the production process. One lengthy process that would often slow down the production of motherboards with integrated analog I/O functions was FCC certification. The manufacturers developed a way of separating the analog circuitry, for example, modem and analog audio, onto its own card. This allowed the analog circuitry to be separately certified (it was its own expansion card), thus reducing time for FCC certification.

This slot and riser card technology was known as the *Audio Modem Riser*, or *AMR*. AMR's 46-pin slots were once fairly common on many Intel motherboards, but technologies including CNR and Advanced Communications Riser (ACR) are edging out AMR. In addition and despite FCC concerns, integrated components still appear to be enjoying the most success comparatively. Figure 1.7 shows an example of an AMR slot.

CNR Expansion Slots

The *Communications and Networking Riser (CNR)* slots that can be found on some Intel motherboards are a replacement for Intel's AMR slots. Essentially, these 60-pin slots allow a motherboard manufacturer to implement a motherboard chipset with certain integrated features. Then, if the built-in features of that chipset need to be enhanced (by adding Dolby Digital Surround to a standard sound chipset, for example), a CNR riser card could be added to enhance the onboard capabilities. Additional advantages of CNR over AMR include networking support, Plug and Play compatibility, support for hardware acceleration (as opposed to CPU control only), and no need to lose a competing PCI slot unless the CNR slot is in use. Figure 1.8 shows an example of a CNR slot.

FIGURE 1.7 An AMR slot

FIGURE 1.8 A CNR slot

Memory Slots and External Cache

Memory or random access memory (RAM) slots are the next most prolific slots on a motherboard, and they contain the modules that hold memory chips that make up primary memory, the memory used to store currently used data and instructions for the CPU. Many and varied types of memory are available for PCs today. In this chapter, you will learn the appearance of the slots on the motherboard, so you can identify them.

For the most part, PCs today use memory chips arranged on a small circuit board. Certain of these circuit boards are called *Dual Inline Memory Modules (DIMMs)*. Today's DIMMs differ in the number of conductors, or *pins*, that the particular physical specification uses. Some common examples include 168-, 184-, and 240-pin configurations. In addition, laptop memory comes in smaller form factors known as Small Outline DIMMs (SoDIMMs) and MicroDIMMs. Figure 1.9 shows the form factors for the most popular memory chips. Notice how they basically look the same, but the memory module sizes are different.

Memory slots are easy to identify on a motherboard. DIMM slots are usually black and placed very close together. The number of memory slots varies from motherboard to motherboard, but the appearance of the different slots is similar. Metal pins in the bottom make contact with the soldered tabs on each memory module. Small metal or plastic tabs on each side of the slot keep the memory module securely in its slot.

Sometimes primary memory gets a bit overwhelmed with the requests coming from the processor. To get its bearings, the RAM must obtain the information the CPU wants immediately, but RAM is not as fast the CPU, and the CPU must wait. The result is that the entire system slows down noticeably, on average. One solution for this is to use the hard drive as RAM. This space on the hard drive is known as *virtual RAM (VRAM)*. VRAM is a contiguous, optimized space that can deliver information to RAM faster than if it came from the general storage pool of the drive.

FIGURE 1.9   Different memory module form factors

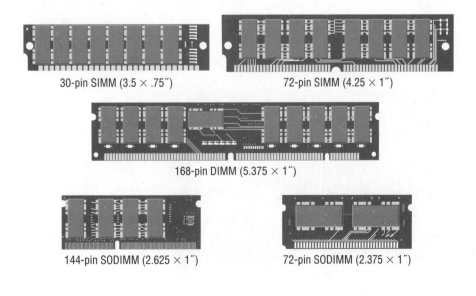

30-pin SIMM (3.5 × .75″)   72-pin SIMM (4.25 × 1″)

168-pin DIMM (5.375 × 1″)

144-pin SODIMM (2.625 × 1″)   72-pin SODIMM (2.375 × 1″)

There is something that can be done on the CPU side of RAM to speed things up a bit as well. That something is adding *cache memory*. Cache memory is a very fast form of memory forged from static RAM, which is discussed in detail in the "Identifying Purposes and Characteristics of Memory" section of this chapter. Cache improves system performance by predicting what the CPU will ask for next and prefetching this information before being asked. This paradigm allows the cache to be smaller in size than the RAM itself. Only the most recently used data and code or that which is expected to be used next is stored in cache. Cache on the motherboard is known as *external cache* because it is external to the processor. Also called *Level 2 (L2) cache*, this is as opposed to the *Level 1 (L1) cache* built into the processor. See the section titled "Identifying Purposes and Characteristics of Processors" later in this chapter for more on L1 cache.

Central Processing Unit (CPU) and Processor Socket or Slot

The "brain" of any computer is the *central processing unit (CPU)*. This component does all the calculations and performs 90 percent of all the functions of a computer. There are many different types of processors for computers—so many, in fact, that you will learn about them later in this chapter in the section "Identifying Purposes and Characteristic of Processors."

Typically, in today's computers, the processor is the easiest component to identify on the motherboard. It is usually the component that has either a fan or a heat sink (usually both) attached to it (as shown in Figure 1.10). These devices are used to draw away the heat a processor generates. This is done because heat is the enemy of microelectronics. Theoretically, a Pentium (or higher) processor generates enough heat that without the heat sink it would self-destruct in a matter of hours.

Sockets and slots on the motherboard are as plentiful and varied as processors. Sockets are basically flat and have several rows of holes arranged in a square, as shown in Figure 1.11. The processor slot is another method of connecting a processor to a motherboard, but one into which an Intel Pentium II or Pentium III–class processor on a special expansion card can be inserted (as shown in Figure 1.12). Newer, more complex processors, such as the Intel Itanium, use a package known as a pin array cartridge (PAC). The socket that receives a PAC works on the very low insertion force (VLIF) principle. To see which socket type is used for which processors, examine Table 1.1.

FIGURE 1.10   Processors with a fan and heat sinks

FIGURE 1.11   An example of a CPU socket

FIGURE 1.12   A Slot 1 connector slot

TABLE 1.1   Socket/Slot Types and the Processors They Support

Socket/Slot	Processors
Socket 4	Pentium 60/66, Pentium 60/66 OverDrive
Socket 5	Pentium 75-133, Pentium 75+ OverDrive, AMD K5
Socket 6*	486DX4, 486 Pentium OverDrive
Socket 7	Pentium 75-200, Pentium 75+ OverDrive, Pentium MMX, AMD K6
Super Socket 7	AMD K6-2, K6-III
Socket 8	Pentium Pro
Slot 1	Pentium II, Pentium III, Celeron, and all SECC and SECC2
Slot 2	Pentium II Xeon, Pentium III Xeon
Slot A	Early AMD Athlon
Socket 370	PPGA processors, including Pentium III and Celeron
Socket 423	Early Pentium 4
Socket A (Socket 462)	AMD Athlon, Athlon XP, Athlon XP-M, Athlon MP, Thunderbird, Duron, Sempron
Socket 478	Pentium 4, Pentium 4 Extreme Edition, Celeron
Socket 479	Pentium M, Celeron M
Socket 486	80486
Socket 563	AMD low-power mobile Athlon XP-M
Socket 603	Intel Xeon
Socket 604	Intel Xeon with Micro FCPGA package
Socket 754	Athlon 64, Sempron, Turion 64
Socket 771	Xeon 50x0 dual-core
Socket T (LGA 775)	Pentium 4, Pentium D dual-core, Celeron D, Pentium Extreme Edition
Socket 939	Athlon 64, Athlon 64 FX, Athlon 64 X2, Opteron 100-series

TABLE 1.1   Socket/Slot Types and the Processors They Support *(continued)*

Socket/Slot	Processors
Socket 940	Athlon 64 FX (FX-51), Opteron
Socket F (Socket 1207)	Replaces Socket 940 when used with Opteron multiprocessor systems
Socket AM2	AMD single-processor systems, replaces Socket 754 and Socket 939
Socket S1	AMD-based mobile platforms, replaces Socket 754 in the mobile sector
PAC418	Itanium
PAC611	Itanium 2

*Socket 6 was a paper standard only and was never implemented in any systems.

Power Connectors

In addition to these sockets and slots on the motherboard, a special connector (shown in Figure 1.13) allows the motherboard to be connected to the power supply to receive power. This connector is where the ATX power connector (mentioned later in this chapter in the section "Identifying Purposes and Characteristics of Power Supplies") plugs in.

FIGURE 1.13   An ATX power connector on a motherboard

Onboard Floppy and Hard Disk Connectors

Almost every computer made today uses some type of disk drive to store data and programs until they are needed. Most drives need a connection to the motherboard so the computer can "talk" to the disk drive. These connections are known as *drive interfaces,* and there are two main types: *floppy drive interfaces* and *hard disk interfaces.* Floppy disk interfaces allow floppy disk drives (FDDs) to be connected to the motherboard and, similarly, hard disk interfaces do the same for hard disks. When you see them on the motherboard, these interfaces are said to be *onboard*, as opposed to being on an expansion card (*off-board*). The interfaces consist of circuitry and a port. Most motherboards produced today include both the floppy disk and hard disk interfaces on the motherboard.

Today, the headers you will find on most motherboards are for Enhanced IDE (EIDE/PATA) or *Serial ATA (SATA).* Advanced Technology Attachment (ATA) is the standard term for what is more commonly referred to as Integrated Drive Electronics (IDE). The AT component of the name was borrowed from the IBM PC/AT, which was the standard of the day. However, because ATA is not the only technology that integrates the drive controller circuitry into the drive assembly (ESDI, for example, was another), IDE is somewhat of a misnomer and not the best term when referring only to ATA drives.

Nevertheless, the original ATA standard was referred to as IDE and had an upper limit of 528MB per logical drive. An enhanced version, Enhanced IDE (EIDE), was developed to circumvent the obstacles to accessing more drive space per volume, increasing the limit to 8GB. Since then, the limit has been increased to 144PB through various enhancements. A petabyte (PB) is the number of bytes represented by 2 raised to the 50th power.

If your motherboard has PATA headers, they will normally be black or some other neutral color if they follow the classic ATA 40-wire standard. If your PATA headers are blue, these represent PATA interfaces that employ the Ultra DMA (UDMA) technology that increases transfer rates by reducing crosstalk in the parallel signal by alternating another 40 wires that act as grounds among the other wires. The connectors and headers are still 40 pins, however. The color coding alerts you to the enhanced performance, which is downward compatible with the 40-wire technology.

The original 40-pin ATA header transfers data between the drive and motherboard multiple bits in parallel, hence the name *Parallel ATA (PATA).* SATA, in comparison, which came out later and prompted the retroactive PATA moniker, transfers data in serial, allowing a higher data throughput because there is no need for more advanced parallel synchronization of data signals. The SATA headers are vastly different from the PATA headers. Figure 1.14 shows an example of the SATA data connector.

Many motherboards, especially higher-end boards like those found in servers, also include the more complex SCSI circuitry built in so that SCSI-attached drives can connect directly to the system board without an external adapter.

FIGURE 1.14   The Serial ATA connector

Keyboard Connectors

The most important input device for a PC is the keyboard. All PC motherboards contain a connector (as shown in Figures 1.15 and 1.16) that allows a keyboard to be connected directly to the motherboard through the case. There are two main types of keyboard connectors. Once, these were the AT and PS/2 connectors. Today, the PS/2-style connector remains popular, but it is quickly being replaced by USB-attached keyboards. The all-but-extinct original AT connector is round, about ½ inch in diameter, in a 5-pin DIN configuration. Figure 1.15 shows an example of the AT-style keyboard connector.

The PS/2 connector (as shown in Figure 1.16) is a smaller 6-pin mini-DIN connector. Most new PCs you can purchase today contain a PS/2 keyboard connector as well as a PS/2 mouse connector right above it on the motherboard. Compare your PC's keyboard connector with Figures 1.15 and 1.16.

Newer motherboards have color coded the PS/2 mouse and keyboard connectors to make connection of keyboards and mice easier. PS/2 mouse connectors are green (to match the standard green connectors on some mice), and the keyboard connectors are purple.

FIGURE 1.15   An AT connector on a motherboard

FIGURE 1.16   A PS/2-style keyboard connector on a motherboard

Peripheral Ports and Connectors

In order for a computer to be useful and have the most functionality, there must be a way to get the data into and out of it. Many different ports are available for this purpose. We will discuss the different types of ports and how they work later in this chapter.

Briefly, the seven most common types of ports you will see on a computer are serial, parallel, Universal Serial Bus (USB), video, Ethernet, sound in/out, and game ports. Figure 1.17 shows some of these and others on a *docking station* or *port replicator* for a laptop. From left to right, the interfaces shown are as follows:

- DC power in

- Analog modem RJ-11

- Ethernet NIC RJ-45
- S-video out
- DVI-D out
- SVGA out
- Parallel (on top)
- Standard serial
- Mouse (on top)
- Keyboard
- S/PDIF (out)
- USB

Figure 1.18 shows an example of a *game port* (also called a *joystick port* because that's the most common device connected to it). As discussed later in this chapter, the game port can be used to connect to *Musical Instrument Digital Interface (MIDI)* devices as well. Game ports connect such peripheral devices to the computer using a DA-15F 15-pin female *D-subminiature (D-sub)* connector.

FIGURE 1.17   Peripheral ports and connectors

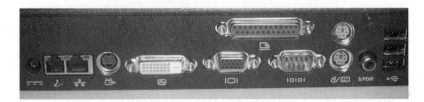

FIGURE 1.18   A game port

Figure 1.19 shows another set of interfaces not shown in Figure 1.17, the sound card jacks. These jacks are known as *1/8-inch* (3.5mm) stereo minijacks, so called for their size and the fact that they make contact with both the left and right audio channels through their tip and ring. Shown in the diagram are an input, the microphone jack on the left, and an output, the speaker jack on the right. Software can use these interfaces to allow you to record and play back audio content in file or CD/DVD form.

Motherboard Attachment

There are two ways of connecting these ports to the motherboard (assuming the circuitry for providing these functions is integrated into the motherboard). The first, called a *header connection*, allows you to mount the ports into the computer's case, usually on the backplane, with a special cable connected to a *header*, or male connector that terminates the motherboard's traces for that function, as shown in Figure 1.20.

FIGURE 1.19 Sound card jacks

FIGURE 1.20 Connecting a port to the header on a motherboard

The second method of connecting a peripheral port is known as the *direct-solder method*. With this method, the individual ports are soldered directly to the motherboard. This method is used mostly in integrated motherboards in non-clone machines. Figure 1.21 shows peripheral ports connected to a motherboard with the direct-solder method. Notice that there is no cable between the port and the motherboard and that the port is part of the motherboard. As discussed earlier, these onboard ports can be disabled in the BIOS setup if necessary.

FIGURE 1.21   Peripheral ports directly soldered to a motherboard

BIOS Chip

Aside from the processor, the most important chip on the motherboard is the Basic Input/Output System (BIOS) chip. This special memory chip contains the BIOS software that tells the processor how to interact with the rest of the hardware in the computer. The BIOS chip is easily identified: If you have a non-clone computer (Compaq, IBM, HP, and so on), this chip has on it the name of the manufacturer and usually the word *BIOS*. For example, the BIOS chip for a Compaq has something like *Compaq BIOS* printed on it. For clones, the chip usually has a sticker or printing on it from one of the major BIOS manufacturers (AMI, Phoenix/Award, Winbond, and so on).

CMOS Battery

Your PC has to keep certain settings when it's turned off and its power cord is unplugged. These settings include the following:

- Date
- Time
- Hard drive configuration
- Memory

Your PC keeps these settings in a special memory chip called the Complimentary Metal Oxide Semi-conductor (CMOS) chip. Actually, CMOS (usually pronounced *see-moss*) is a type of memory chip; it is the parameter memory for the BIOS. But that doesn't translate into an easy-to-say acronym. So because it's the most important CMOS chip in the computer, it has come to be called the CMOS.

To keep its settings, the memory must have power constantly. When you shut off a computer, anything that is left in main memory is lost forever. To prevent CMOS from losing its information (and it's rather important that it doesn't), motherboard manufacturers include a small battery called the *CMOS battery* to power the CMOS memory. The batteries come in different shapes and sizes, but they all perform the same function. Most CMOS batteries look like either large watch batteries or small, cylindrical batteries.

Jumpers and DIP Switches

The last components of the motherboard we will discuss in this section are jumpers and DIP switches. These two devices are used to configure various hardware options on the motherboard. For example, some processors use different voltages (1.5, 3.3, or 5 volts). You must set the motherboard to provide the correct voltage for the processor it is using. You do so by changing a setting on the motherboard with either a jumper or a DIP switch. Figure 1.22 shows both a jumper set and DIP switches. Motherboards often have either several jumpers or one bank of DIP switches. Individual jumpers are often labeled with the moniker JP*x* (where *x* is the number of the jumper).

Many of the motherboard settings that were set using jumpers and DIP switches are now either automatically detected or set manually in the CMOS setup program.

Firmware

Firmware is the name given to any software that is encoded into a read-only memory (ROM) chip and can be run without extra instructions from the operating system. Most computers use firmware in some limited sense. The best example of firmware is a computer's CMOS setup program, which is used to set the options for the computer's BIOS (time/date and boot options, for example). Also, some expansion cards, such as Small Computer System Interface (SCSI) cards, use their own firmware utilities for setting up peripherals.

FIGURE 1.22   Jumpers and DIP switches

Jumper   Rocker-type DIP switch   Slide-type DIP switch

Identifying Purposes and Characteristics of Processors

Now that you've learned the basics of the motherboard, you need to learn about the most important component on the motherboard: the CPU. The role of the CPU, or central processing unit, is to control and direct all the activities of the computer using both external and internal buses. It is a processor chip consisting of an array of *millions* of transistors.

The term *chip* has grown to describe the entire package that a technician might install in a socket. However, the word originally denoted the silicon wafer that is generally hidden within the carrier that you actually see. The external pins you see are structures that can withstand insertion into a socket and that are carefully threaded from the wafer's minuscule contacts. Just imagine how fragile the structures must be that you don't see.

Older CPUs are generally square, with contacts arranged in a Pin Grid Array (PGA). Prior to 1981, chips were found in a rectangle with two rows of 20 pins known as a Dual Inline Package (DIP); see Figure 1.23. There are still integrated circuits that use the DIP form factor. However, the DIP form factor is no longer used for PC CPUs. Most CPUs use either the PGA or the Single Edge Contact Cartridge (SECC) form factor. SECC is essentially a PGA-type socket on a special expansion card.

FIGURE 1.23   DIP and PGA

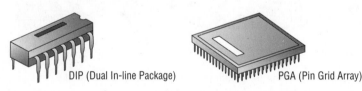

DIP (Dual In-line Package)   PGA (Pin Grid Array)

As processor technology grows and motherboard real estate stays the same, more must be done with the same amount of space. To this end, the *Staggered PGA (SPGA)* layout was developed. An SPGA package arranges the pins in what appears to be a checkerboard pattern, but if you angle the chip diagonally, you'll notice straight rows, closer together than the right-angle rows and columns of a PGA. This feature allows a higher pin count per area.

This discussion only scratches the surface of the topic surrounding chip packaging and carriers. For more information on the various packaging for chips, start with en.wikipedia.org/wiki/Category:Chip_carriers.

You can easily identify which component inside the computer is the CPU because it is a large square lying flat on the motherboard with a very large heat sink and fan (as shown earlier in Figure 1.10). Or if the CPU is installed in a Slot 1 motherboard, it is a large ½-inch-thick expansion card with a large heat sink and fan integrated into the package. It is located away from the expansion cards. Figure 1.24 shows the location of the CPU in relation to the other components on a typical ATX motherboard. Notice how prominent the CPU is.

FIGURE 1.24   The location of a CPU inside a typical computer

Modern processors can feature the following:

Hyperthreading   This term refers to Intel's Hyper-Threading Technology (HTT). HTT is a form of simultaneous multithreading (SMT). SMT takes advantage of a modern CPU's super-scalar architecture. Superscalar processors are able to have multiple instructions operating on separate data in parallel.

HTT-capable processors appear to the operating system to be two processors. As a result, the operating system can schedule two processes at the same time, as in the case of symmetric multiprocessing (SMP), where two or more processors use the same system resources. In fact, the operating system must support SMP in order to take advantage of HTT. If the current process stalls because of missing data caused by, say, cache or branch prediction issues, the execution resources of the processor can be reallocated for a different process that is ready to go, reducing processor downtime.

Multicore   A processor that exhibits a *multicore* architecture has two completely separate processors in the same package. Whether there are multiple dies in the same package or the single

---

Real World Scenario

What's Your CPU?

The surest way to determine which CPU your computer is using is to open the case and view the numbers stamped on the CPU, which today requires removal of the active heat sink. However, you may be able to get an idea without opening the case and removing the heat sink and fan, because many manufacturers indicate the type of processor by placing a very obvious sticker somewhere on the case indicating the processor type. Failing this, you can always go to the manufacturer's website and look up the information on the model of computer you have. If you have a no-name clone, there is always the System Information dialog found by right-clicking My Computer and selecting Properties. The General tab, which is the default, contains such information.

Another way to determine a computer's CPU is to save your work, exit any open programs, and restart the computer. Watch closely as the computer returns to its normal state. You should see a notation that tells you what chip you are using.

---

die contains the equivalent circuitry of multiple processors, the operating system can treat the single processor as if it were two separate processors. As with HTT, the operating system must support SMP. In addition, SMP is not an enhancement if the applications run on the SMP system are not written for parallel processing. *Dual-core* processors are a common specific case for the multi-core technology.

Throttling   CPU *throttling*, or clamping, is the process of controlling how much CPU time is spent on an application. By controlling how individual applications use the CPU, all applications are treated more fairly. The concept of application fairness becomes a particular issue in server environments, where each application could represent the efforts of a different user. Thus, fairness to applications becomes fairness to users, the real customers. Clients of today's terminal servers benefit from CPU throttling.

Microcode   *Microcode* is the set of instructions (known as an *instruction set*) that make up the various microprograms that the processor executes while carrying out its various duties. The Multimedia Extensions (MMX) microcode is a specialized example of a separate microprogram that carries out a particular set of functions. Microcode is at a much lower level than the code that makes up application programs. Each instruction in an application will end up being represented by many microinstructions, on average. The MMX instruction set is incorporated into most modern CPUs from Intel and others. MMX came about as a way to take much of the multimedia processing off the CPU's hands, leaving the processor to other tasks. Think of it as sort of a coprocessor for multimedia, much like the floating-point unit (FPU) is a math coprocessor.

Overclocking   *Overclocking* your CPU offers increased performance, on par with a processor designed to operate at the overclocked speed. However, unlike with the processor designed to run that fast, you must make special arrangements to ensure that an overclocked CPU does not destroy itself from the increased heat levels. An advanced cooling mechanism, such as liquid cooling, might be necessary to avoid losing the processor and other components.

Cache   As mentioned in the "Memory Slots and External Cache" section earlier in this chapter, cache is a very fast chip memory that is used to hold data and instructions that are most likely to be requested next by the CPU. The cache located on the CPU is known as L1 cache and is generally smaller in comparison to L2 cache, which is located on the motherboard. When the CPU requires outside information, it believes it requests that information from RAM. The cache controller, however, intercepts the request and consults its tag RAM to discover if the requested information is already cached, either at L1 or L2. If not, a cache miss is recorded and the information is brought back from the much slower RAM, but this new information sticks to the L1 and L2 cache on its way to the CPU from RAM.

Voltage Regulator Module   The *voltage regulator module (VRM)* is the circuitry that sends a standard voltage level to the portion of the processor that is able to send a signal back to the VRM concerning the voltage level the CPU needs. After receiving the signal, the VRM truly regulates the voltage to steadily provide the requested voltage.

Speed   The speed of the processor is generally described in clock frequency (MHz or GHz). There can be a discrepancy between the advertised frequency and the frequency the CPU uses to latch data and instructions through the pipeline. This disagreement between the numbers comes from the fact that the CPU is capable of splitting the clock signal it receives from the oscillator into multiple regular signals for its own use.

32- and 64-Bit System Bus   The set of data lines between the CPU and the primary memory of the system can be 32 or 64 bits wide, among other widths. The wider the bus, the more data that can be processed per unit of time, and hence the more work that can be performed. Internal registers in the CPU might be only 32 bits wide, but with a 64-bit system bus, two separate pipelines can receive information simultaneously.

Identifying Purposes and Characteristics of Memory

"More memory, more memory, I don't have enough memory!" Today, memory is one of the most popular, easy, and inexpensive ways to upgrade a computer. As the computer's CPU works, it stores information in the computer's memory. The rule of thumb is the more memory a computer has, the faster it will operate.

To identify memory within a computer, look for several thin rows of small circuit boards sitting vertically, packed tightly together near the processor. Figure 1.25 shows where memory is located in a system.

FIGURE 1.25   Location of memory within a system

Parity checking is a rudimentary error-checking scheme that lines up the chips in a column and divides them into an equal number of bits, numbered starting at 0. All the number *n* bits, one from each chip, form a numerical set. If even parity is used, for example, the number of bits in the set is counted up, and if the total comes out even, then the parity bit is set to 0, because the count is already even. If it comes out odd, then the parity bit is set to 1 to even up the count. You can see that this is effective only for determining if there was a blatant error in the set of bits, but there is no indication as to where the error is and how to fix it. This is error checking, not error correction. Finding an error can lock up the entire system and display a memory parity error. Enough of these errors and you need to replace the memory. If that doesn't fix the problem, good luck.

In the early days of personal computing, almost all memory was parity-based. Compaq was one of the first manufacturers to employ non-parity RAM in their mainstream systems. As quality has increased over the years, parity checking in the RAM subsystem has become rarer. If parity checking is not supported, there will generally be fewer chips per module, usually one less per column of RAM.

The next step in the evolution of memory error detection is known as *Error Checking and Correcting (ECC)*. If memory supports ECC, check bits are generated and stored with the data. An algorithm is performed on the data and its check bits whenever the memory is accessed. If the result of the algorithm is all zeros, then the data is deemed valid and processing continues. ECC can detect single- and double-bit errors and actually correct single-bit errors.

In the following sections, we'll outline the four major types of computer memory—DRAM, SRAM, ROM, and CMOS—as well as memory packaging.

DRAM

DRAM is dynamic random access memory. (This is what most people are talking about when they mention RAM.) When you expand the memory in a computer, you are adding DRAM chips. You use DRAM to expand the memory in the computer because it's cheaper than any other type of memory. Dynamic RAM chips are cheaper to manufacture than other types because they are less complex. *Dynamic* refers to the memory chips' need for a constant update signal (also called a *refresh* signal) in order to keep the information that is written there. If this signal is not received every so often, the information will cease to exist. Currently, there are four popular implementations of DRAM: SDRAM, DDR, DDR2, and RAMBUS.

SDRAM

The original form of DRAM had an asynchronous interface, meaning that it derived its clocking from the actual inbound signal, paying attention to the electrical aspects of the waveform, such as pulse width, to set its own clock to synchronize on the fly with the transmitter. *Synchronous DRAM (SDRAM)* shares a common clock signal with the transmitter of the data. The computer's system bus clock provides the common signal that all SDRAM components use for each step to be performed.

This characteristic ties SDRAM to the speed of the FSB and the processor, eliminating the need to configure the CPU to wait for the memory to catch up. Every time the system clock ticks, one bit of data can be transmitted per data pin, limiting the bit rate per pin of SDRAM to the corresponding numerical value of the clock's frequency. With today's processors interfacing with memory using a parallel data-bus width of 8 bytes (hence the term 64-bit processor), a 100MHz clock signal produces 800MBps. That's mega*bytes* per second, not mega*bits*. Such memory is referred to as *PC100*, because throughput is easily computed as eight times the rating.

DDR

Double Data Rate (DDR) SDRAM earns its name by doubling the transfer rate of ordinary SDRAM by double-pumping the data, which means transferring it on both the rising and falling edges of the clock signal. This obtains twice the transfer rate at the same FSB clock frequency. It's the rising clock frequency that generates heating issues with newer components, so keeping the clock the same is an advantage. The same 100MHz clock gives a DDR SDRAM system the impression of a 200MHz clock in comparison to a *single data rate (SDR)* SDRAM system.

You can use this new frequency in your computations or simply remember to double your results for SDR calculations, producing DDR results. For example, with a 100MHz clock, two operations per cycle, and 8 bytes transferred per operation, the data rate is 1600MBps. Now that throughput is becoming a bit tricker to compute, the industry uses this final figure to name the memory modules instead of the frequency, which was used with SDR. This makes the result seem many times better, while it's really only twice as good. In this example, the module is referred to as *PC1600*. The chips that go into making PC1600 modules are named after the perceived double-clock frequency: DDR-200.

DDR2

Think of the *2* in *DDR2* as yet another multiplier of 2 in the SDRAM technology, using a lower peak voltage to keep power consumption down (1.8V vs. the 2.5V of DDR and others). Still double-pumping, DDR2, like DDR, uses both sweeps of the clock signal for data transfer. Internally, DDR2 further splits each clock pulse in two, doubling the number of operations it can perform per FSB clock cycle. Through enhancements in the electrical interface and buffers, as well as through adding off-chip drivers, DDR2 nominally produces four times what SDR is capable of producing.

However, DDR2 suffers from enough additional latency over DDR that identical throughput ratings find DDR2 at a disadvantage. Once frequencies develop for DDR2 that do not exist for DDR, however, DDR2 could become the clear SDRAM leader, although DDR3 is nearing release. Continuing the preceding example and initially ignoring the latency issue, DDR2 using a 100MHz clock transfers data in four operations per cycle and still 8 bytes per operation, for a total of 3200MBps.

Just like DDR, DDR2 names its chips based on the perceived frequency. In this case, you would be using DDR2-400 chips. DDR2 carries on the final-result method for naming modules but cannot simply call them PC3200 modules because those already exist in the DDR world. DDR2 calls these modules *PC2-3200*. The latency consideration, however, means that DDR's PC3200 offering is preferable to DDR2's *PC2-3200*. After reading the "RDRAM" section, consult Table 1.2, which summarizes how each technology in the "DRAM" section would achieve a transfer rate of 3200MBps, even if only theoretically. For example, SDR PC400 doesn't exist.

TABLE 1.2   How Each Memory Type Transfers 3200MBps

Memory Type	Actual/Perceived Clock Frequency (MHz)	Bytes per Transfer
SDR SDRAM PC400*	400/400	8
DDR SDRAM PC3200	200/400	8
DDR2 SDRAM PC2-3200	100/400	8
RDRAM PC800	400/800	4**

* SDR SDRAM PC400 does not exist.
** Running in 32-bit dual-channel mode.

RDRAM

Rambus DRAM, or *Rambus Direct RAM (RDRAM)*, named for the company that designed it, is a proprietary synchronous DRAM technology. RDRAM can be found in fewer new systems today than just a few years ago. This is because Intel once had a contractual agreement with Rambus to create chipsets for the motherboards of Intel and others that would primarily use RDRAM in exchange for special licensing considerations and royalties from Rambus. The contract ran from 1996 until 2002. In 1999, Intel launched the first motherboards with RDRAM support. Until then, Rambus could be found mainly in gaming consoles and home theater components. RDRAM did not impact the market as Intel had hoped, and so motherboard manufacturers got around Intel's obligation by using chipsets from VIA Technologies, leading to the rise of that company.

Although other specifications preceded it, the first motherboard RDRAM model was known as *PC800*. As with non-RDRAM specifications that use this naming convention, PC800 specifies that, using a faster 400MHz clock signal and double-pumping like DDR/DDR2, an effective frequency of 800MHz and a transfer rate of 800Mbps per data pin are created. PC800 uses only a 16-bit (2-byte) bus called a channel, exchanging a 2-byte packet during each read/write cycle, still bringing the overall transfer rate to 1600MBps per channel because of the much higher clock rate. Modern chipsets allow two 16-bit channels to communicate simultaneously for the same read/write request, creating a 32-bit dual-channel. Two PC800 modules in a dual-channel configuration produce transfer rates of 3200MBps.

Today, RDRAM modules are also manufactured for 533MHz and 600MHz bus clock frequencies and 32-bit dual-channel architectures. Termed PC1066 and PC1200, these models produce transfer rates of 2133 and 2400MBps per channel, respectively, making 4266 and 4800MBps per dual-channel. Rambus has road maps to 1333 and 1600MHz models. The section "RIMM" in this chapter details the physical details of the modules.

Despite RDRAM's performance advantages, it has some drawbacks that keep it from taking over the market. Increased latency, heat output, complexity in the manufacturing process, and cost are the primary shortcomings. PC800 RDRAM had a 45ns latency, compared to only 7.5ns for PC133 SDR SDRAM. The additional heat that individual RDRAM chips put out led to the requirement for heat sinks on all modules. High manufacturing costs and high licensing fees led to triple the cost to consumers over SDR, although today there is more parity between the prices.

In 2003, free from its contractual obligations to Rambus, Intel released the i875P chipset. This new chipset provides support for a dual-channel platform using standard PC3200 DDR modules. Now, with 16 bytes (128 bits) transferred per read/write request, making a total transfer rate of 6400MBps, RDRAM no longer holds the performance advantage it once did.

SRAM

The *S* in SRAM stands for *static*. Static random access memory doesn't require a refresh signal like DRAM does. The chips are more complex and are thus more expensive. However, they are faster. DRAM access times come in at 60 nanoseconds (ns) or more; SRAM has access times as fast as 10ns. SRAM is often used for cache memory.

ROM

ROM stands for read-only memory. It is called read-only because the original form of this memory could not be written to. Once information had been written to the ROM, it couldn't be changed. ROM is normally used to store the computer's BIOS, because this information normally does not change very often.

The system ROM in the original IBM PC contained the power-on self-test (POST), Basic Input/Output System (BIOS), and cassette BASIC. Later IBM computers and compatibles include everything but the cassette BASIC. The system ROM enables the computer to "pull itself up by its bootstraps," or *boot* (start the operating system).

Through the years, different forms of ROM were developed that could be altered. The first generation was the programmable ROM (PROM), which could be written to for the first time in the field, but then no more. Following the PROM came erasable PROM (EPROM), which was able to be erased using ultraviolet light and subsequently reprogrammed. These days, our flash memory is a form of electrically erasable PROM (EEPROM), which does not require UV light, but rather a slightly higher than normal electrical pulse, to erase its contents.

CMOS

CMOS is a special kind of memory that holds the BIOS configuration settings. CMOS memory is powered by a small battery, so the settings are retained when the computer is shut off. The BIOS starts with its own default information and then reads information from the CMOS, such as which hard drive types are configured for this computer to use, which drive(s) it should search for boot sectors, and so on. Any conflicting information read from the CMOS overrides the default information from the BIOS. CMOS memory is usually *not* upgradable in terms of its capacity and is very often integrated into the modern BIOS chip.

Memory Packaging

First of all, it should be noted that each motherboard supports memory based on the speed of the frontside bus (FSB) and the memory's form factor. So, for example, if the motherboard's FSB is rated at a maximum speed of 533MHz, and you install memory that is rated at 300Mhz, the memory will operate at only 300MHz, thus making the computer operate slower than what it could. In their specifications, most motherboards list which type(s) of memory they support as well as its maximum speeds.

The memory slots on a motherboard are designed for particular module form factors or styles. In case you run across the older terms, DIP, SIMM, and SIPP are obsolete memory packages. Terms like *double-sided/single-sided memory* and *dual-bank/single-bank memory* are often confused. When speaking of sides, it is correct to refer to the two physical sides of the module and whether they contain chips. However, that says nothing of the number of banks the module satisfies. Satisfying two banks, or channels more often, as in the case of the DDR family, can be accomplished with single-sided memory. The most popular form factors for primary memory modules today are these:

- DIMM
- RIMM
- SoDIMM
- MicroDIMM

DIMM

One type of memory package is known as a DIMM. As mentioned earlier in this chapter, DIMM stands for Dual Inline Memory Module. DIMMs are 64-bit memory modules that are used as a package for the SDRAM family: SDRAM, DDR, and DDR2. The term *dual* refers to the fact that, unlike their SIMM predecessors, DIMMs differentiate the functionality of the pins on one side of the module from the corresponding pins on the other side. With 84 pins per side, this makes 168 independent pins on each standard SDRAM module, as shown with its two keying notches in Figure 1.26.

The DIMM used for DDR memory has a total of 184 pins and a single keying notch, while the DIMM used for DDR2 has a total of 240 pins, one keying notch, and an aluminum cover for both sides, called a *heat spreader*, designed like a heat sink to dissipate heat away from the memory chips and prevent overheating.

RIMM

Not an acronym, RIMM is a trademark of Rambus Inc., perhaps a clever play on the acronym DIMM, a competing form factor. A RIMM is a custom memory module that varies in physical specification based on whether it is a 16-bit or 32-bit module. The 16-bit modules have 184 pins and two keying notches, while 32-bit modules have 232 pins and only one keying notch, reminiscent of the trend in SDRAM-to-DDR evolution. Figure 1.27 shows the two sides of a 16-bit RIMM module, including the aluminum heat spreaders.

The dual-channel architecture can be implemented utilizing two separate 16-bit RIMMs or the newer 32-bit single-module design. Motherboards with the 16-bit single- or dual-channel implementation provide four RIMM slots that must be filled in pairs, while the 32-bit versions provide two RIMM slots that can be filled one at a time. A 32-bit RIMM has two 16-bit modules built in and requires only a single motherboard slot, albeit a physically different slot. So you must be sure of the module your motherboard accepts before upgrading.

FIGURE 1.26   A Dual Inline Memory Module (DIMM)

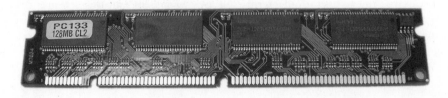

Unique to the use of RIMM modules, a computer must have every RIMM slot occupied. Even one vacant slot will cause the computer not to boot. Any slot not populated with live memory requires an inexpensive (usually less than US$5 for the 16-bit version) blank of sorts called a *continuity RIMM*, or *C-RIMM*, for its role of keeping electrical continuity in the RDRAM channel until the signal can terminate on the motherboard. Think of it like a fusible link in a string of holiday lights. It seems to do nothing, but no light works without it. However, 32-bit modules terminate themselves and do not rely on the motherboard circuitry for termination, so vacant 32-bit slots require a module known as a *continuity and termination RIMM (CT-RIMM)*.

SoDIMM

Notebook computers and other computers that require much smaller components don't use standard RAM packages like the SIMM or the DIMM do. Instead, they can use a much smaller memory form factor called a *Small Outline DIMM (SoDIMM)*. SoDIMMs are available in many physical implementations, including the older 32-bit (72-pin) configuration and newer 64-bit (144-pin EDO, 144-pin SDRAM, and 200-pin DDR/DDR2) configurations. Figure 1.28 shows an example of a 144-pin, 64-bit module.

FIGURE 1.27   A Rambus RIMM module

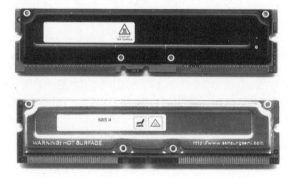

FIGURE 1.28   144-pin SoDIMM

MicroDIMM

The newest, and smallest, RAM form factor is the MicroDIMM. The *MicroDIMM* is an extremely small RAM form factor. In fact, it is over 50 percent smaller than a SoDIMM, only 45.5 millimeters (about 1.75 inches) long and 30 millimeters (about 1.2 inches—a bit bigger than a quarter) wide. It was designed for the ultralight and portable subnotebook style of computer (like those based on the Transmeta Crusoe processor). These modules have 144 pins or 172 pins and are similar to a DIMM in that they use a 64-bit data bus. Often employed in laptop computers, SoDIMMs and MicroDIMMs are mentioned in Chapter 3 as well.

Identifying Purposes and Characteristics of Storage Devices

What good is a computer without a place to put everything? Storage media hold the data being accessed, as well as the files the system needs to operate and data that needs to be saved. The many different types of storage differ in terms of their capacity (how much they can store), access time (how fast the computer can access the information), and the physical type of media used.

Hard Disk Drive Systems

Hard disk drive (HDD) systems (hard disks or hard drives for short) are used for permanent storage and quick access (Figure 1.29). Hard disks typically reside inside the computer (although there are external and removable hard drives) and can hold more information than other forms of storage.

The hard disk drive system contains three critical components:

Controller   Controls the drive. It understands how the drive operates, sends signals to the various motors in the disk, and receives signals from the sensors inside the drive. Most of today's hard disk technologies incorporate the controller and drive into one enclosure.

Hard Disk   The physical storage medium. Hard disk drive systems store information on small disks (between three and five inches in diameter) stacked together and placed in an enclosure.

Host Adapter   The translator, converting signals from the hard drive and controller to signals the computer can understand. Most motherboards today incorporate the host adapter into the motherboard's circuitry, offering headers for drive cable connection.

Floppy Drives

A *floppy disk* is a magnetic storage medium that uses a flexible diskette made of thin plastic enclosed in a protective casing. The floppy disk once enabled information to be transported from one computer to another very easily. Today, floppies are a little too small in capacity to be efficient anymore. They have been replaced by writable CD-ROMs and DVD-ROMs. The original term *floppy disk* referred to the antiquated 8-inch medium used with minicomputers and mainframes. The original PC floppy diskette, which was 5¼ inches square and known as a *minifloppy diskette*, is also obsolete; the *microfloppy diskette* is a diskette that is 3½ inches square. Most computers today use microfloppy diskettes or no floppy at all.

FIGURE 1.29   A hard disk drive system

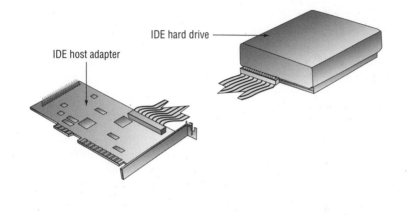

A *floppy drive* (shown in Figure 1.30) is used to read and write information to and from these drives. The advantage of these drives is that they allow portability of data (you can transfer data from one computer to another on a diskette). The downside of a floppy disk drive is its limited storage capacity. Whereas a hard drive can store hundreds of gigabytes of information, most floppy disks were designed to store only about one megabyte. Table 1.3 shows five different floppy diskette drive formats with their corresponding diskette sizes supported in PC systems over the years. The following abbreviations are used: DD means double density; HD means high density; ED means extended density.

TABLE 1.3   Floppy Disk Capacities

Floppy Drive Size	Number of Tracks	Capacity
5¼″ DD	40	360KB
5¼″ HD	80	1.2MB
3½″ DD	80	720KB
3½″ HD	80	1.44MB
3½″ ED	80	2.88MB

Generally speaking, throughout this book we will use the term *floppy drive* to refer to a 3½-inch microfloppy diskette drive.

CD-ROM Drives

Most computers today have a CD-ROM (Compact Disc Read-Only Memory) drive. The compact disks are virtually the same as those used in CD players. The CD-ROM is used for long-term storage of data. CD-ROMs are read-only, meaning that once information is written to a CD, it can't be erased or changed. Also, it takes much longer to access the information on a CD than it does to access data residing on a hard drive. Why, then, are CD-ROMs so popular? Mainly because they make a great software distribution medium. Programs are always getting larger and requiring more disks to install. Instead of installing a program using 100 floppy disks (a real possibility), you can use a single CD, which can hold approximately 650MB. (A second reason they are so popular is that CD-ROMs have been standardized across platforms, with the ISO 9660 standard.) Figure 1.31 shows an example of a typical CD-ROM drive.

FIGURE 1.30   A floppy disk drive

FIGURE 1.31   A typical CD-ROM drive

CD-ROM drives are rated in terms of their data transfer speed. The first CD-ROM drives transferred data at the same speed as home audio CD players, 150KBps. Soon after, CD drives rated as "2X" drives that would transfer data at 300KBps appeared (they just increased the spin speed in order to increase the data transfer rate). This system of ratings continued up until the 8X speed was reached. At that point, the CDs were spinning so fast that there was a danger of the CDs flying apart inside the drive. So, although future CD drives used the same rating (as in 16X, 32X, and so on), their rating was expressed in terms of theoretical maximum transfer rate. The drive isn't necessarily spinning faster or transferring data at 40 or 50 times 150KBps, it is just theoretically possible using the drive's increased buffers and so on.

CD-R and CD-RW Drives

CD-recordable (CD-R) and CD-rewritable (CD-RW) drives (also known as CD *burners*) are essentially CD-ROM drives that allow users to create (or *burn*) their own CD-ROMs. They look very similar to CD-ROM drives, except the front panel of the drive includes a reference to either CD-R or CD-RW.

The difference between these two types of drives is that CD-R drives can write to a CD only once. A CD-RW can erase information from a disc and rewrite to it multiple times. Also, CD-RW drives are rated according to their read, write, and rewrite times. So instead of a single rating like 40X, they have a rating of 32X-16X-4X, which means it reads at 32X, writes at 16X, and rewrites at 4X.

DVD-ROM Drives

A newer type of drive is finding its way into computers: the DVD-ROM drive. DVD (digital video disc) technology is in use in many home theater systems. A DVD-ROM drive is basically the same as the DVD player's drive in a home theater system. As a result, a computer equipped with a DVD-ROM drive and the proper video card can play back DVD movies on the monitor.

However, in a computer, a DVD-ROM drive is much more useful. Because DVD-ROMs use slightly different technology than CD-ROMs, they can store up to 4.3GB of data. This makes them a better choice for distributing large software bundles. Many software packages today are so huge they take multiple CD-ROMs to hold all the installation and reference files. A single DVD-ROM, in a double-sided, double-layered configuration, can hold as much as 17GB (as much as 26 regular CD-ROMs).

A DVD-ROM drive looks very similar to a CD-ROM drive. The only difference is the DVD logo on the front of most drives.

DVD Burners

A DVD burner operates in a similar manner to a CD-R or CD-RW drive: It can store large amounts of data onto a DVD. Today, single-sided, double-layered (DL) discs can be burned right in your home computer, writing 8.5GB of information to a single disc. Common names for the variations of DVD burning technologies include DVD+R, DVD+RW, DVD-R, DVD-RW, DVD-RAM, DVD-R DL, and DVD+R DL. In some cases, the plus variants hold more than their dash counterparts, and drives do not support all types.

Other Storage Media

Many additional types of storage are available for PCs today. Among the other types of storage are tape backup devices, solid-state memory, and advanced optical drives. There are also external hard drives such as the Kangaru drives and new storage media such as the USB memory sticks that can store gigabytes on a single small plastic device that can be carried on a key chain.

Removable Storage

Removable storage once meant something vastly different than what it means today. Sequential tape backup is one of the only remnants of the old forms of removable storage that can be seen in the market today. The more modern solution is random-access, solid-state removable storage. This section presents details of tape backup and the newer removable storage solutions.

Tape Backup Devices

An older form of removable storage is the tape backup. Tape backup devices can be installed internally or externally and use either a digital or analog magnetic tape medium instead of disks for storage. They hold much more data than any other medium but are also much slower. They are primarily used for archival storage.

With hard disks, it's not a matter of "if they fail"; it's "when they fail." So you must back up the information onto some other storage medium. Tape backup devices were once the most common choice in larger enterprises and networks because they were able to hold the most data and were the most reliable over the long term. Today, however, tape backup systems are steadily being phased out by writable and rewritable optical discs, which continue to advance in technology and size.

Flash Memory

Once only for primary memory usage, the same components that sit on your motherboard as RAM can be found in various physical sizes and quantities in today's solid-state storage solutions. These include older removable and nonremovable flash memory mechanisms, Secure Digital (SD) cards and other memory cards, and USB thumb drives. Each of these technologies has the potential to reliably store a staggering amount of information in a minute form factor. Manufacturers are using innovative packaging for some of these products to provide convenient transport options to users, such as key-chain attachments.

For many years, modules and PC Cards known as *flash memory* have offered low- to mid-capacity storage for devices. The name comes from the concept of easily being able to use electricity to instantly alter the contents of the memory. The original flash memory is still used in devices, such as routers and switches, that require a nonvolatile means of storing critical data and code often used in booting the device.

For example, Cisco Systems uses flash memory in various forms to store their Internetwork Operating System (IOS), which is accessed from flash during bootup and, in certain cases, throughout an administrator's configuration sessions. Lesser models store the IOS in compressed form on the flash and then decompress the IOS into RAM, where it is used during configuration. In this case, the flash is not accessed again after the bootup process is complete, unless its contents are being changed, as in an IOS upgrade. Certain devices use externally removable PC Card technology as flash for similar purposes.

The following sections explain a bit more about today's most popular forms of flash memory, memory cards and thumb drives.

SD AND OTHER MEMORY CARDS

Today's smaller devices require some form of removable solid-state memory that can be used for temporary and permanent storage of digital information. Gone are the days of using microfloppies in your digital camera. Even the most popular video-camera medium, mini-DVDs, have solid-state multi-GB models nipping at their heels. These more modern electronics, as well as most contemporary digital still cameras, use some form of removable memory card to store still images permanently or until they can be copied off or printed out. Of these, the *Secure Digital (SD)* format has emerged as the preeminent leader of the pack, which includes the older *MultiMediaCard (MMC)* format on which SD is based. The SD card is slightly thicker than the MMC and has a write-protect notch (and often a switch to open and close the notch), unlike MMC. Figure 1.32 is a photo of an SD card with size reference. Officially, these devices are 32mm by 24mm.

FIGURE 1.32   A typical SD card

Even smaller devices, such as mobile phones, have an SD solution for them. One of these products, known as *miniSD*, is slightly thinner than SD and measures 21.5mm by 20mm. The other, *microSD*, is thinner yet and only 15mm by 11mm. Both of these reduced formats have adapters allowing them to be used in standard SD slots.

Table 1.4 lists additional memory card formats.

TABLE 1.4   Additional Memory Card Formats

Format	Dimensions	Details	Year Introduced
CompactFlash (CF)	36mm by 43mm	Used by IBM for Microdrives; Type I and Type II variants	1994
MiniCard	45mm by 37mm	Defunct; promoted by Intel, AMD, Fujitsu, Sharp	1995

TABLE 1.4   Additional Memory Card Formats *(continued)*

Format	Dimensions	Details	Year Introduced
SmartMedia (SM)	45mm by 37mm	From Toshiba; intended to replace floppies; still sells well	1995
Memory Stick	50mm by 21.5mm	From Sony; standard, pro, duo, and micro formats available	1998

Figure 1.33 shows the memory card slots of an HP PhotoSmart 7550 printer, which is capable of reading these devices and printing them directly or creating a drive letter for access to the contents over its USB connection to the computer. Clockwise from upper left, these slots accommodate CF/Microdrive, SmartMedia, Memory Stick (bottom right), and MMC/SD. Exclusive external card readers and those that can be mounted in a computer's drive bay are common items on the market today. The industry also provides almost any adapter or converter to allow the various formats to work together.

As a final thought on SD cards, SD slots are not for flash memory only. The more general *SDIO* (SD Input/Output) specification, which is based on and compatible with the SD specification, seeks to bring a high-speed, low-power interface to mobile devices, in the same vein as USB for computers. Not that SDIO can't be used with laptops, but it is intended more for PDAs or mobile phones for connectivity to small devices, such as GPS receivers, wireless or wired network adapters, modems, bar-code readers, wireless serial adapters, radio and television tuners, and digital cameras. Even external storage devices, such as hard drives and CD/DVD-ROM drives, could be attached to these smaller handheld devices.

FIGURE 1.33   Card slots in a printer

THUMB DRIVES

Also known as USB flash drives, *thumb drives* are incredibly versatile and convenient devices that allow you to store large quantities of information in a very small form factor. Many such devices are merely extensions of the host's USB connector, extending out from the interface but adding very little to its width, making them very easy to transport, whether in a pocket or laptop bag. Figure 1.34 illustrates an example of one of these components and its relative size.

FIGURE 1.34   A USB thumb drive

Thumb drives capitalize on the versatility of the USB interface, taking advantage of the Plug and Play feature and the physical connector strength. Upon insertion, these devices announce themselves to Windows Explorer as removable drives and show up in the Explorer window with a drive letter. This software interface allows for drag-and-drop copying and most of the other standard Explorer functions performed on standard drives.

USB thumb drives have emerged as the de facto replacement for other removable storage devices, such as floppies, edging out Zip and Jaz offerings from Iomega, as well as other proprietary solutions.

USB-Attached External Disk Drives

Before USB, an external drive used a proprietary adapter and interface/cable combination or the standard RS-232 serial or parallel port generally built into the computer. Since USB, there seems to be no other way to do it. The fact is, there are other ways, but why muddy the water with options when USB covers all the bases and is so ubiquitous in today's systems?

USB-attached external disk drives use the same drives that you might install in a drive bay in your chassis; they simply employ a specialty chassis that houses only the drive and the supporting circuitry that converts the drive interface to USB. Most often, the drive enclosure has a DC power input and a Type-B USB interface, as shown in Figure 1.35. This external chassis has its cover removed, and you can see the internal protective casing with the hard drive mounted in it.

FIGURE 1.35   External drive enclosure

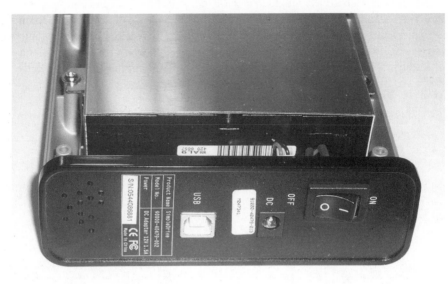

Advanced Digital Storage

There are two technologies on the market today that seek to become the next standard in optical storage; each one offers backward compatibility to the lesser CD and DVD technologies. One of these is known as *High Density (or Definition) DVD (HD DVD)*. The other is known as *Blu-ray Disc (BD)*. Both technologies employ similar blue-violet laser and encoding techniques, as well as disc size, with slightly differing results. The blue laser has a shorter wavelength than the original red laser, which allows more data to be stored in the same space because the laser can be focused more tightly to read data placed more closely.

However, depending on the reception blue-laser technologies receive in the public sector, their times might come and go without much fanfare. Seemingly futuristic technologies, such as perpendicular and holographic recording, might be here before the market realizes it needs blue laser.

HD DVD

HD DVD can hold high-definition video or large quantities of data. HD DVD has a single-layer capacity of 15GB. Dual-layer and triple-layer formats exist that hold two and three times as much data, respectively. Publishers can include both standard DVD and HD DVD formats on a single disc. This coexistence means that consumers, manufacturers, and retailers have options during their transition to HD DVD, because the newer HD DVD discs can play in a standard DVD player. The incentive to upgrade remains, however, due to the higher definition video awaiting owners on the same disc.

If the HD DVD format is applied to standard DVDs that do not use the blue laser, it can result in capacities ranging from 5 to 18GB, offering a lower-cost alternative for those holding off on upgrading to HD DVD. HD DVD uses a single lens in its optical mechanism, unlike Blu-ray technology. Therefore, both red and blue LED lasers can be incorporated into HD DVD drives that are still more compact than those based on Blu-ray.

Blu-ray Disc

Although Blu-ray Disc uses a similar technology to that of HD DVD, it gets the laser closer to the data and is able to store more data per layer, 25GB compared to HD DVD's 15GB. Manufacturers led by Sony make players backward compatible with DVDs and capable of the same high-definition video content. Initially, Blu-ray components were priced a bit higher than those based on HD DVD, but Blu-ray was the first to hit the market with a consumer-recordable version, including drives and media.

Identifying Purposes and Characteristics of Power Supplies

The computer's components would not be able to operate without power. The device in the computer that provides this power is the *power supply* (Figure 1.36). A power supply converts 110 volt or 220 volt AC current into the DC voltages that a computer needs to operate. These are +3.3 volts DC, +5 volts DC, –5 volts DC (ground), +12 volts DC, –12 volts DC (ground), and +5 volts DC standby. The 3.3 volts DC and +5 volts DC standby voltages were first used by ATX motherboards.

You might see *volts DC* abbreviated as *VDC*.

FIGURE 1.36   A power supply

WARNING Power supplies contain transformers and capacitors that can discharge *lethal* amounts of current even when disconnected from the wall outlet. They are not meant to be serviced. *Do not* attempt to open them or do any work on them.

Power supplies are rated in watts. A *watt* is a unit of power. The higher the number, the more power the power supply (and thus your computer) can use. Most computers use power supplies in the 250- to 500-watt range.

Classic power supplies used only three types of connectors to power the various devices within the computer (Figure 1.37): floppy drive power connectors (Berg connectors), AT system connectors (P8 and P9), and standard peripheral power connectors (Molex connectors). Each has a different appearance and way of connecting to the device. In addition, each type is used for a specific purpose. Newer systems have a variety of similar, replacement, and additional connectors.

Floppy Drive Power Connectors

Floppy drive power connectors are most commonly used to power floppy disk drives and other small form factor devices. This type of connector is smaller and flatter (as shown in Figure 1.38) than any of the other types of power connectors. These connectors are also called *Berg connectors*. Notice that there are four wires going into this connector. These wires carry the two voltages used by the motors and logic circuits: +5VDC (carried on the red wire) and +12VDC (carried on the yellow wire); the two black wires are ground wires.

FIGURE 1.37 Standard power supply connectors

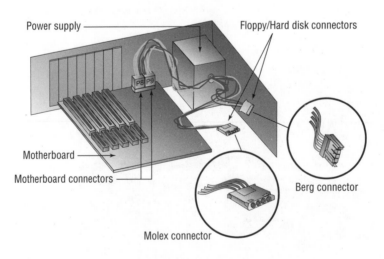

AT System Connectors

The next type of power connector is called the *AT system connector*. There are two 6-wire connectors, labeled P8 and P9 (as shown in Figure 1.39). They connect to an AT-style motherboard and deliver the power that feeds the electronic components on it. These connectors have small tabs on them that interlock with tabs on the motherboard's receptacle. If there are two connectors, you must install them in the correct fashion. To do this (on most systems), place the connectors side by side with their black wires together, and then push the connectors onto the receptacle on the motherboard.

Although it's easy to remove this type of connector from the motherboard, the tabs on the connector make it difficult to reinstall it. Here's a hint: Place the connector at a right angle to the motherboard's connector, interlocking the tabs in their correct positions. Then tilt the connector to the vertical position. The connector will slide into place easily.

FIGURE 1.38   Floppy drive power connector

FIGURE 1.39   AT power supply system board connectors

It is important to note that only computers with AT and baby AT motherboards use this type of power connector.

Most computers today use some form of ATX power connector to provide power to the motherboard.

Standard Peripheral Power Connector

The *standard peripheral power connector* is generally used to power different types of internal disk drives. This type of connector is also called a *Molex connector*. Figure 1.40 shows an example of a standard peripheral power connector. This power connector, though larger than the floppy drive power connector, uses the same wiring color code scheme as the floppy drive connector.

Modern Power Connectors

Modern components have exceeded the capabilities of some of the original power supply connectors. The Molex and Berg peripheral connectors remain, but the P8/P9 motherboard connectors have been consolidated and additional connectors have sprung up.

FIGURE 1.40   A standard peripheral power connector

ATX, ATX12V, and EPS12V Connectors

With ATX motherboards came a new, single connector from the power supply. PCI Express has power requirements that even this connector could not satisfy. Additional 4- and 8-pin connectors supply power to components of the motherboard, such as network interfaces, specialty server components, and the CPU itself, that require a +12V supply in addition to the +12V of the standard ATX connector. These additional connectors follow the *ATX12V* and *EPS12V* standards. The ATX connector was further expanded by an additional four pins in later specifications.

The *ATX system connector* (also known as the *ATX motherboard power connector*) feeds an ATX motherboard. It provides the six voltages required, plus it delivers them all through one connector: a single 20-pin connector. This connector is much easier to work with than the dual connectors of the AT power supply. Figure 1.41 shows an example of an ATX system connector.

When the Pentium 4 processor was introduced, motherboard and power supply manufacturers needed to get more power to the system. The solution was the ATXV12 standard, which added two supplemental connectors. One was a 6-pin auxiliary connector similar to the P8/P9 AT connectors that supplied additional +3.3V and +5V leads and their grounds. The other was a 4-pin square mini version of the ATX connector, referred to as a P4 connector, that supplied two +12V leads and their grounds. EPS12V uses an 8-pin version, called the processor power connector, that doubles the P4's function with four +12V leads and four grounds. Figure 1.42 illustrates the P4 connector. The 8-pin processor power connector is similar but has two rows of four.

FIGURE 1.41 ATX power connector

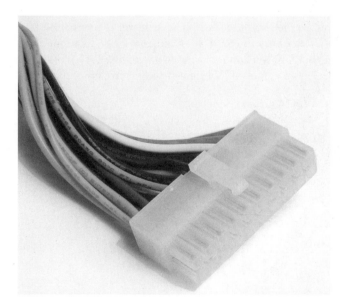

FIGURE 1.42   ATX12V P4 power connector

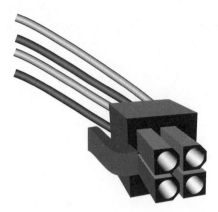

For servers and more advanced ATX motherboards that include PCIe slots, the 20-pin system connector proved inadequate. This led to the *ATX12V 2.0* standard and the even higher-end EPS12V standard for servers. These specifications call for a 24-pin connector that adds additional positive voltage leads directly to the system connector. The 24-pin connector looks like a larger version of the 20-pin connector. There are adapters available if you find yourself with the wrong combination of motherboard and power supply. The 6-pin auxiliary connector disappeared with the ATX12V 2.0 specification and was never part of the EPS12V standard.

SATA Power Connectors

SATA drives arrived on the market with their own power requirements, in addition to their new data interfaces. Refer back to Figure 1.14 and imagine a larger but similar connector for power. You get the SATA power connector, shown in Figure 1.43. This connector is made up of three each of +3.3V, +5V, and +12V leads, as well as five ground leads.

FIGURE 1.43   SATA power connector

Identifying Purposes and Characteristics of Display Devices

The primary method of getting information out of a computer is to use a computer video display unit (VDU). Display systems convert computer signals into text and pictures and display them on a TV-like screen. As a matter of fact, the first personal computers used television screens because it was simple to use an existing display technology rather than to develop a new one. Several types of computer displays are in use today, including the TV. All of them use either the same *cathode ray tube (CRT)* technology found in television sets (many desktop monitors still use this technology) or the *liquid crystal display (LCD)* technology found on all laptop, notebook, and palmtop computers. LCD is steadily gaining in popularity on the desktop, as well.

Display Concepts

Several aspects of display systems make each type of display different. However, most display systems work the same way. First, the computer sends a signal to a device called the *video adapter*—an expansion board installed in an expansion bus slot—telling it to display a particular graphic or character. The adapter then *renders* the character for the display—that is, it converts the single instruction into several instructions that tell the display device how to draw the graphic—and sends the instructions to the display device. The primary differences after that are in the type of video adapter you are using (digital or analog) and the type of display (CRT or LCD).

Video Technologies

Let's first talk about the different types of video technologies. Between digital and analog, there are transistor-transistor logic (TTL) and the technologies that began with video graphics array (VGA). Each video standard differs in two major areas: the highest resolution it supports and the maximum number of colors in its palette.

Resolution depends on how many picture elements (*pixels*) are used to draw the screen. For the same display device, more pixels yield a sharper image. Different CRTs place the physical chemical dots at different intervals, changing the image quality, despite the resolution. The smaller this dot pitch, the better the image, given the same resolution. See the section titled "Monitors" in this chapter for more on dot pitch. The resolution is described in terms of the visible image's dimensions, which indicate how many pixels across and down are used to draw the screen. For example, a resolution of 1,024 × 768 means 1,024 pixels across and 768 pixels down were used to draw the pixel matrix. The video technology in this example would use 786,432 (1,024 × 768 = 786,432) pixels to draw the screen.

In the preceding example, if you were using 24-bit graphics, meaning each pixel requires 24 bits of memory to store that one screen element, 786,432 elements would require 18,874,368 bits or 2,359,296 bytes. Because this boils down to 2.25MB, an early video adapter with only 2MB of RAM would not be capable of such resolution at 24 bits per pixel.

Monochrome

The first video technology for PCs was *monochrome* (from the Latin *mono*, meaning one, and *chroma*, meaning color). This black-and-white video (actually, it was green and white or amber and black) was fine for the main operating system of the day, DOS. DOS didn't have any need for color. Thus, the video adapter was very basic. The first adapter, developed by IBM, was known as the Monochrome Display Adapter (MDA). It could display text but not graphics and used a resolution of 720 × 350 pixels.

The Hercules Graphics Card (HGC), introduced by Hercules Computer Technology, had a resolution of 720 × 350 and could display graphics as well as text. It did this by using two separate modes: a *text mode* that allowed the adapter to optimize its resources for displaying predrawn characters from its onboard library, and a *graphics mode* that optimized the adapter for drawing individual pixels for on-screen graphics. It could switch between these modes on the fly. These modes of operation have been included in all graphics adapters since the introduction of the HGC.

EGA and CGA

The next logical step for displays was to add a splash of color. IBM was the first with color, with the introduction of the Color Graphics Adapter (CGA). CGA could display text, but it displayed graphics with a resolution of only 320 × 200 pixels with four colors. It displayed a better resolution (640 × 200) with two colors—black and one other color. After a time, people wanted more colors and higher resolution, so IBM responded with the Enhanced Graphics Adapter (EGA). EGA could display 16 colors out of a palette of 64 with a resolution of 320 × 200 or 640 × 350 pixels.

These two technologies were the standard for color until the IBM AT was introduced. This PC was to be the standard for performance, so IBM wanted better video technology for it.

VGA

With the PS/2 line of computers, IBM wanted to answer the cry for "more resolution, more colors" by introducing its best video adapter to date: the Video Graphics Array (VGA). This video technology had a whopping 256KB of video memory on board and could display 16 colors at 640 × 480 pixels or 256 colors at 320 × 200 pixels. It became widely used and has since become the standard for color PC video; it's the starting point for today's computers, as far as video is concerned. Your computer should use this video technology at minimum.

One unique feature of VGA is that it's an analog technology, unlike the preceding standards. Thus the 256 colors it uses can be chosen from various shades and hues of a palette of 262,114 colors. VGA sold well mainly because users could choose from almost any color they wanted (or at least one that was close). The reason for moving away from the original digital signal is because for every power of 2 that the number of simultaneously displayed colors increases, you need another pin on the connector to transmit them. Four pins for 16 colors is not a big deal, but 32 pins for over 4 billion colors become a bit unwieldy. The cable has to grow with the connector, as well, affecting transmission quality and cable length.

SuperVGA

Up to this point, IBM set most video standards. IBM made the adapters, everyone bought them, and they became a standard. Some manufacturers didn't like this monopoly and set up the Video Electronics Standards Association (VESA) to try to enhance IBM's video technology and make the enhanced technology a public standard. The result of this work was SuperVGA (SVGA). This new standard was indeed an enhancement, because it could support 16 colors at a resolution of 800×600 (the VESA standard), but it soon expanded to support $1,024 \times 768$ pixels with 256 colors.

Since that time, SVGA has been a term for any resolution and color palette to exceed that of standard VGA. This even includes the resolution presented next, XGA. New names still continue to be introduced, mainly as a marketing tool to tout the new resolution du jour. While display devices must be manufactured to support a certain display resolution, one of the benefits of analog video technology is that modern VGA monitors can advance along with the graphics adapter, in terms of the color palette. The analog signal is what dictates the color palette, and the standard for the signal has not changed since its VGA origin. This makes a discussion of a VGA monitor's color limitations a non-issue. Such a topic makes sense only in reference to graphics adapters.

XGA

IBM introduced a new technology in 1990 known as the Extended Graphics Array (XGA). This technology was available only as a Micro Channel Architecture (MCA) expansion board and not as an ISA or EISA board. (It was rather like IBM saying, "So there. You won't let me be the leader, so I'll lead my own team.") XGA could support 256 colors at $1,024 \times 768$ pixels or 65,536 colors at 800×600 pixels. It was a different design, optimized for GUIs like Windows or OS/2. It was also an *interlaced* technology, meaning that rather than scan every line one at a time to create the image, it scanned every other line on each pass, using the phenomenon known as *persistence of vision* to produce what appears to our eyes as a continuous image.

Later Video Standards

Any standard other than the ones already mentioned are probably extensions of SVGA or XGA. It is becoming easier and easier to predict the approximate resolution of a video specification based on its name. Whenever a known technology is preceded by the letter *W*, you can assume roughly the same vertical resolution but a wider horizontal resolution to accommodate 16:9 or 16:10 wide-screen formats. Preceding the technology with the letter *Q* indicates that the horizontal and vertical resolutions were each doubled, making a final resolution four times (quadruple) the original. To imply four times each, for a final resolution enhancement of 16 times, the letter *H* for hexadecatuple is used.

Therefore, if XGA has a resolution of 1024×768, then QXGA will have a resolution of 2048×1536. If SuperXGA (SXGA) has a resolution of 1280×1024 and an aspect ratio of 5:4, then WSXGA might have a resolution of 1440×900 and a 16:10 aspect ratio. Each of these advanced resolutions has a standard 32-bit color palette, for over four billion different colors per pixel. Table 1.5 details the various video technologies, their resolutions, and the color palettes they support.

TABLE 1.5   Video Display Adapter Comparison

Name	Resolutions	Colors
Monochrome Display Adapter (MDA)	720×350	Mono (text only)
Hercules Graphics Card (HGC)	720×350	Mono (text and graphics)
Color Graphics Adapter (CGA)	320×200	4
	640×200	2
Enhanced Graphics Adapter (EGA)	320×200	16
	640×350	16
Video Graphics Array (VGA)	640×480	16
	320×200	256
SuperVGA (SVGA)	800×600	16
Extended Graphics Array (XGA)	$1,024 \times 768$	256
Super XGA (SXGA)	1280×1024	4,294,967,296
Ultra XGA (UXGA)	1600×1200	4,294,967,296
Widescreen XGA (WXGA), 16:9	1280×720	4,294,967,296
WUXGA, 16:10	1920×1200	4,294,967,296
Quad XGA (QXGA)	2048×1536	4,294,967,296
WQXGA, 16:10	2560×1600	4,294,967,296
WQUXGA, 16:10	3840×2400	4,294,967,296
WHUXGA, 16:10	7680×4800	4,294,967,296

Additional Video Technologies

While the VGA-spawned standards might keep the computing industry satisfied for quite some time to come, there is a sector in the market driving development of non-VGA specifications. These high-resolution, high-performance junkies approach video from the broadcast angle. They are interested in the increased quality of digital transmission. For them, the industry responded with technologies like DVI and HDMI. The computing market benefits from these technologies, as well.

Other consumers desire specialized methods to connect analog display devices by splitting out colors from the component to improve quality. For this group, a few older standards remain viable: component video, S-video, and composite video. The following sections present the details of these five specifications.

DVI

In an effort to return to digital video, which can be transmitted farther and at higher quality than analog, a series of connectors known collectively as the *Digital Visual (or Video) Interface (DVI)* was developed for the technology of the same name. At first glance, the DVI connector might look like a standard D-sub connector, but on closer inspection, it begins to look somewhat different. For one thing, it has quite a few pins, and for another, the pins it has are asymmetrical in their placement on the connector. Figure 1.44 illustrates the five types of connector that the DVI standard specifies.

The three main categories of DVI connector are these:

DVI-A   An analog-only connector

DVI-D   A digital-only connector

DVI-I   A combination analog/digital connector

FIGURE 1.44   Types of DVI connector

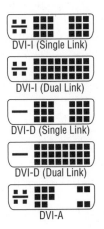

DVI-I (Single Link)

DVI-I (Dual Link)

DVI-D (Single Link)

DVI-D (Dual Link)

DVI-A

The DVI-D and DVI-I connectors come in two varieties: single link and dual link. The dual-link options have more connectors than their single-link counterparts, which accommodate higher speed and signal quality. The additional link can be used to increase resolution from 1920×1080 to 2048×1536 or even from WUXGA to WQUXGA. Of course, all components, as well as the cable, must support the dual-link feature.

DVI-A and DVI-I analog quality is superior to that of VGA, but it's still analog, meaning it is more susceptible to noise. However, the analog signal will travel farther before degrading beyond usability. The analog portion of the connector, if it exists, comprises the four separate pins and the horizontal blade that they surround, which happens to be the analog ground lead.

HDMI

High-Definition Multimedia Interface (HDMI) is an all-digital technology that advances the work of DVI to include higher resolution, higher motion-picture frame rates, and digital audio right on the same connector, as well as a function to share the signals of a remote control throughout the HDMI interconnection. The connector is not the same as the one used for DVI. In June 2006, revision 1.3 of the HDMI specification was released to support the bit rates necessary for HD DVD and Blu-ray Disc. HDMI is compatible with DVI-D through proper adapters, but only single-link is supported and HDMI's audio and remote-control pass-through features are lost. Figure 1.45 shows a DVI-to-HDMI adapter for single-link DVI-D and the Type-A 19-pin HDMI cable. There is also a Type-B connector that has 29 pins and promises higher resolution for the components that use it.

Component Video

When analog technologies outside the VGA realm are used for broadcast video, you are generally able to get better-quality video by splitting the red, green, and blue components in the signal into different streams right at the source. The technology known as *component video* performs a signal-splitting function similar to RGB separation, but it creates a signal called *luminance* (Y) that corresponds to the colorless (call it black and white) portion of the feed. It also creates two color difference signals known as Pb and Pr (or Cb and Cr, in some cases). These *chrominance* signals work together to mathematically approximate the original RGB signal. Figure 1.46 shows the three RCA connectors of a component cable.

FIGURE 1.45   Types of DVI connector

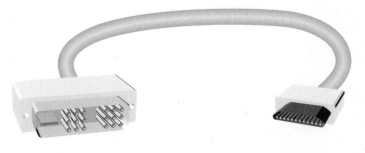

S-video

S-video is a component video technology that combines the two chrominance signals into one, resulting in video quality not quite as high as that of true component video. One example of an S-video connector, shown in Figure 1.47, is a 7-pin mini-DIN, mini-DIN of various pin counts being the most common connector type. The most basic connector is a 4-pin mini-DIN that has, quite simply, one luminance and one chrominance (C) output lead and a ground for each. A 4-pin male connector is compatible with a 7-pin female connector, both in fit and pin functionality. The converse is not also true, however. These are the only two standard S-video connectors.

FIGURE 1.46   A component video cable

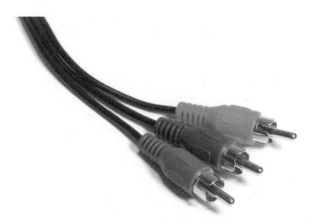

FIGURE 1.47   A 7-pin S-video port

The 6-pin and 7-pin versions are also output only, but they add composite video leads, which are discussed next, as well. ATI uses 8-, 9-, and 10-pin versions of the connector that include such added features as S-video input in addition to output, or even bidirectional pin functionality, and audio input/output.

Composite Video

When the preceding component video technologies are not feasible, the last related standard, *composite video*, combines the luminance and all chrominance leads into one. Composite video is truly the bottom of the analog-video barrel. Very often a single yellow RCA jack, the composite video jack is rather common on computers and home and industrial video components. While still fairly decent in video quality, composite video is more susceptible to undesirable video phenomena and artifacts, such as aliasing, cross coloration, and dot crawl.

Monitors

As already mentioned, an older-style (yet still popular) non-LCD monitor contains a CRT. But how does it work? Basically, a device called an *electron gun* shoots electrons toward the back side of the monitor screen (see Figure 1.48). The back of the screen is coated with special chemicals (called *phosphors*) that glow when electrons strike them. This beam of electrons scans across the monitor from left to right and top to bottom to create the image.

There are two ways to measure a monitor's image quality:

Dot Pitch   The shortest distance between two dots of the same color on the monitor. Usually given in fractions of a millimeter (mm), the dot pitch tells how "sharp" the picture is. The lower the number, the closer together the pixels are, and, thus, the sharper the image. An average dot pitch is 0.28mm. Anything smaller than 0.28mm is considered great.

FIGURE 1.48   How a monitor works

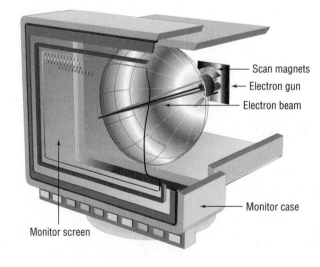

Scan magnets
Electron gun
Electron beam

Monitor case

Monitor screen

Refresh Rate   (Technically called the *vertical scan frequency.*) Specifies how many times in one second the scanning beam of electrons redraws the screen. The phosphors stay bright for only a fraction of a second, so they must constantly be hit with electrons to stay lit. Given in draws per second, or Hertz, the refresh rate specifies how much energy is being put into keeping the screen lit. The refresh rate on smaller monitors, say 14 to 16 inches, does fine in the range 60 to 72Hz. However, the larger a monitor gets, the higher the refresh rate needs to be to reduce eyestrain from perceivable flicker. It is not uncommon to see refresh rates of 85Hz and higher.

One note about monitors that may seem rather obvious: You must use a video card that supports the type of monitor you are using. For example, you can't use a CGA monitor on a VGA adapter.

CRT monitors manufactured today are not susceptible to damage caused by setting the video adapter's refresh rate too high, unlike older monitors. They simply refuse to operate at a rate higher than they are capable of. Refresh rates are set on the video card through the operating system or special utility software. In order to see a proper image, however, the monitor must support the rate you select.

Liquid Crystal Displays (LCDs)

Portable computers were originally designed to be compact versions of their bigger brothers. They crammed all the components of the big desktop computers into a small, suitcase-like box called (laughably) a *portable computer*. No matter what the designers did to reduce the size of the computer, the display remained as large as the desktop version's. That is, until an inventor found that when he passed an electric current through a semicrystalline liquid, the crystals aligned themselves with the current. It was found that by combining transistors with these liquid crystals, patterns could be formed. These patterns could represent numbers or letters. The first application of these *liquid crystal displays* (LCDs) was the LCD watch. It was rather bulky, but it was cool.

As LCD elements got smaller, the detail of the patterns became greater, until one day someone thought to make a computer screen out of several of these elements. This screen was very light compared to computer monitors of the day, and it consumed little power. It could easily be added to a portable computer to reduce the weight by as much as 30 pounds. As the components got smaller, so did the computer, and the laptop computer was born.

LCDs are not just limited to laptops; desktop versions of LCD displays are available as well. They use the same technologies as their laptop counterparts but on a much larger scale. Plus, these LCDs are available in either analog or digital interfaces for the desktop computer. The analog interface is exactly the same as the interface used for most monitors. All digital signals from the computer are converted into analog signals by the video card, which are then sent along the same 15-pin connector as a monitor. Digital LCDs, on the other hand, are directly driven by the video card's internal circuitry. They require the video card to be able to support digital output (through the use of a Digital Visual Interface, or DVI, connector). The advantage is that since the video signal never goes from digital to analog, there is no conversion-related quality loss. Digital displays are generally sharper than their analog counterparts.

Two major types of LCD displays are used today: active-matrix screen and passive-matrix screen. The main differences lie in the quality of the image. However, both types use lighting behind the LCD panel to make the screen easier to view:

Active Matrix   An active-matrix screen works in a similar manner to the LCD watch. The screen is made up of several individual LCD pixels. A transistor behind each pixel, when switched on, activates two electrodes that align the crystals and turn the pixel dark. This type of display is very crisp and easy to look at. The major disadvantage of an active-matrix screen is that it requires large amounts of power to operate all the transistors. Even with the backlight turned off, the screen can still consume battery power at an alarming rate. Most laptops with active-matrix screens can't operate on a battery for more than two hours.

Passive Matrix   Within the passive-matrix screen are two rows of transistors: one at the top, another at the side. When the computer's video circuit wants to turn on a particular pixel (turn it black), it sends a signal to the x- and y-coordinate transistors for that pixel, thus turning them on. This then causes voltage lines from each axis to intersect at the desired coordinates, turning the desired pixel black. Figure 1.49 illustrates this concept.

The main difference between active matrix and passive matrix is image quality. Because the computer takes a millisecond or two to light the coordinates for a pixel in passive-matrix displays, the response of the screen to rapid changes is poor, causing, for example, an effect known as *submarining*: On a computer with a passive-matrix display, if you move the mouse pointer rapidly from one location to another, it will disappear from the first location and reappear in the new location without appearing anywhere in between.

FIGURE 1.49   A passive-matrix display

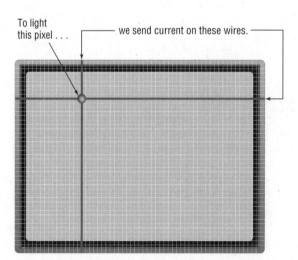

To keep the quality of the image on an LCD the best, the screen must be cleaned often. Liquid crystal displays are typically coated with a clear plastic covering. This covering commonly gets dirtied by fingerprints as well as a generous coating of dust. The best way to clean the LCD lens coating is to wipe it off occasionally with a damp cloth. Doing so will ensure that the images stay crisp and clear.

Identifying Input Devices

An *input device* is one that transfers information outside the computer system to an internal storage location, such as system RAM, video RAM, flash memory, or disk storage. Without input devices, computers would be unable to change state from their originally manufactured personality. This section details six different input devices. It will demonstrate the similarities shared by devices that provide input to computer systems as well as their differences.

Mouse

Although the computer mouse was born in the 1970s at Xerox's Palo Alto Research Center (PARC), it was Apple in 1984 that made the mouse an integral part of the personal computer image with the introduction of the Macintosh. In its most basic form, the mouse is a hand-fitting device that uses some form of motion-detection mechanism to translate its own physical two-dimensional movement into on-screen cursor motion. Many variations of the mouse exist, including trackballs, tablets, touchpads, and pointing sticks. Figure 1.50 illustrates the recognizable form of the mouse.

FIGURE 1.50 A computer mouse

The motion-detection mechanism of the original Apple mouse was a simple ball that protruded from the bottom of the device so that when the bottom was placed against a flat surface that offered a slight amount of friction, the mouse would glide over the surface, but the ball would roll, actuating two rollers that mapped the linear movement to the software interface. This method of motion detection remains popular today.

Later technologies used optical receptors to catch LED light reflected from specially made surfaces purchased with the devices and used like a *mouse pad*. A mouse pad is a special surface to improve mechanical mouse traction while offering very little resistance to the mouse itself. As optical science advanced for the mouse, lasers were used to allow a sharper image to be captured by the mouse and more sensitivity in motion detection. The mouse today can be wired to the computer system or wireless. Wireless versions use batteries to power them, and the optical varieties deplete these batteries more quickly than their mechanical counterparts.

The final topic is one that is relevant for any mouse: buttons. The number of buttons you need for your mouse to have is dependent on the software interfaces you use. For the Macintosh, one button has always been sufficient, but for a Windows-based computer, at least two are recommended, hence the pop-culture term *right-click*. Today, the mouse is commonly found to have a wheel on top to aid in scrolling. The wheel has even developed a click in many models, sort of an additional button underneath the wheel. Buttons on the side of the mouse that can be programmed for whatever the user desires are more common today as well.

Keyboard

More ubiquitous than the mouse, the keyboard is easily the most popular input device, so much so that its popularity is more of a necessity. Very few users would even think of beginning a computing session without a working keyboard. Few would even know how. The U.S. English keyboard places keys in the same orientation as the QWERTY typewriter keyboards, which were first seen in the 1870s.

In addition to the standard QWERTY layout, modern computer keyboards often have separate cursor-movement and numerical keypads. The numerical keys in a row above the alphabet keys send different scan codes to the computer from those sent by the numerical keypad.

Keyboards have also added function keys (not to be confused with the common laptop key labeled Fn), which are often placed in a row across the top of the keyboard above the numerical row. Key functionality can be modified by using one or more combinations of the Ctrl, Alt, Shift, and Fn keys along with the normal QWERTY keys.

Technically speaking, the keys on a keyboard complete individual circuits when each one is pressed. The completion of each circuit leads to a unique scan code that is sent to the keyboard connector on the computer system. The computer uses a keyboard controller chip to interpret the code as the corresponding key sequence. The computer then decides what action to take based on the key sequence and what it means to the computer and the active application.

Bar-code Reader

A *bar-code reader* (or *bar-code scanner*) is a specialized input device commonly used in retail and other industrial sectors that manage inventory. The systems that the reader connects to can be so specialized that they have no other input device. Bar-code readers can use LEDs or lasers as light sources and can scan one- or two-dimensional bar-codes.

Bar-code readers can connect to the host system in a number of ways, but serial connections, such as RS-232 and USB are fairly common. If the system uses proprietary software to receive the reader's input, the connection between the two might be proprietary as well. The simplest software interfaces call for the reader to be plugged into the keyboard's PS/2 connector using a splitter that allows the keyboard to remain connected. The scanner converts all output to keyboard scans so that the system treats the input as if it came from a keyboard. For certain readers, wireless communication with the host is also possible, using IR, RF, Bluetooth, Wi-Fi, and more.

Multimedia Devices

Multimedia input devices vary in functionality based on the type of input being gathered. Two broad categories of input are audio and video. Digital motion and still cameras are incredibly popular as a replacement for similar products that do not transfer information to a computer, simply to make sharing and collaboration so much easier. Microphones and audio recording and playback devices are common components connected to the sound card of many systems so that audio input from these devices can be collected and processed. This includes MIDI devices that provide musical input for further processing.

Biometric Devices

Any device that measures one or more physical or behavioral features of an organism is considered a *biometric device*. When the same device forwards this biometric information to the computer, it becomes an input device. The list includes fingerprint scanners, retinal scanners, voice recognition, and facial recognition, to name a few. A computer can use this input to authenticate the user based on preestablished information regarding this biometric information.

Touch Screens

Touch-screen technology converts stimuli of some sort, which are generated by actually touching the screen, to electrical impulses that travel over serial connections to the computer system. These input signals allow for the replacement of both the keyboard *and* the mouse. However, standard computer systems are not the only application for touch-screen enhancement. This technology can also be seen in PDAs, point-of-sale venues for such things as PIN entry and signature capture, handheld and bar-mounted games, ATMs, remote controls, appliances, and vehicles.

For touch screens there are a handful of solutions for how to convert a touch to a signal. Some less-successful ones rely on warm hands, sound waves, or dust-free screens. The more successful screens have optical or electrical sensors that are quite a bit less fastidious. In any event, the sensory system is added onto a standard monitor at some point in the creation of the monitor.

Identifying Purposes and Characteristics of Adapter Cards

An *adapter card* (also known as an *expansion card*) is simply a circuit board you install into a computer to increase the capabilities of that computer. Adapter cards come in many different kinds, but the important thing to note is that no matter what function a card has, the card being installed must match the bus type of the motherboard you are installing it into (for example, you can install a PCI network card only into a PCI expansion slot).

Five of the most common expansion cards that are installed today are as follows:

- Video card
- Network interface card (NIC)
- Modem
- Sound card
- I/O card

Let's take a quick look at each of these cards, their functions, and what some of them look like.

Video Card

A *video adapter* (more commonly called a *video card*) is the expansion card you put into a computer in order to allow the computer to display information on some kind of monitor or LCD display. A video card also is responsible for converting the data sent to it by the CPU into the pixels, addresses, and other items required for display. Sometimes, video cards can include dedicated chips to perform certain of these functions, thus accelerating the speed of display.

With today's motherboards, most video cards are AGP and, with increasing popularity, PCIe expansion cards that fit in the associated slot on a motherboard. Figure 1.51 shows an example of an AGP-based video card.

Network Interface Card (NIC)

A *network interface card (NIC)* is an expansion card that connects a computer to a network so that it can communicate with other computers on that network. It translates the data from the parallel data stream used inside the computer into the serial data stream of packets used on the network. It has a connector for the type of expansion bus on the motherboard (PCIe, PCI, ISA, and so on) as well as a connector for the type of network (such as RJ-45 for UTP or BNC for coax). In addition to the NIC, you need to install software or drivers on the computer in order for the computer to use the network. Figure 1.52 shows an example of a NIC.

FIGURE 1.51   A video expansion card

FIGURE 1.52   A network interface card (NIC)

Some computers have NIC circuitry integrated into their motherboards. Therefore, a computer with an integrated NIC wouldn't need to have a NIC expansion card installed, unless you were using the second NIC for load balancing, security, or fault-tolerance applications.

Modem

Any computer that connects to the Internet using a dial-up connection needs a modem. A *modem* is a device that converts digital signals from a computer into analog signals that can be transmitted over phone lines and back again. These expansion card devices have one connector for the expansion bus being used (PCIe, PCI, ISA, and so on) and another for connection to the telephone line. Actually, as you can see in Figure 1.53, there are two RJ-11 ports: one for connection to the telephone line and the other for connection to a telephone. This is the case primarily so that putting a computer online still lets someone hook a phone to that wall jack (although he won't be able to use the phone while the computer is connected to the Internet).

FIGURE 1.53   A modem

Sound Card

Just as there are devices to convert computer signals into printouts and video information, there are devices to convert those signals into sound. These devices are known as *sound cards*. Many different manufacturers make sound cards, but the standard has been set by Creative Labs with its SoundBlaster series of cards.

A sound card typically has small, round, 1/8-inch jacks on the back of it for connecting to microphones, headphones, and speakers as well as other sound equipment. Many sound cards also have a DA15 game port (discussed below), which can be used for either joysticks or MIDI connections (it allows a computer to talk to a digital musical instrument, such as a digital keyboard). For MIDI, the DA15 port is bidirectional. MIDI devices use a 5-pin DIN connector like the larger original-style PC keyboard connector. An adapter is required for two of these unidirectional DIN connectors, a MIDI-in and a MIDI-out, to interface with the DA15. Figure 1.54 shows an example of a sound card.

Sound cards today might come with an RCA jack (see the section "Audio/Video Jacks" later in this chapter). This is decidedly not for composite video. Instead, there is a digital audio specification known as the *Sony/Philips Digital Interface (S/PDIF)*. Not only does this format allow you to transmit audio in digital clarity, but in addition to the RCA jack and coaxial copper cabling it specifies optical fiber connectors and cabling for electrically noisy environments, further increasing transmission quality of the digital signal.

FIGURE 1.54   A typical sound card

I/O Card

I/O card is often a catchall phrase for any adapter card that expands the system to interface with devices that offer input to the system, output from the system, or both. Common examples of I/O are the serial and parallel ports of the system, drive interface connections, and so on. A very popular expansion card of the 1980s and early 1990s was known as the Super I/O card. This one adapter had the circuitry for two standard serial ports, one parallel port, two PATA controllers, and one floppy controller. Some versions included more still. For many years, if you wanted to use a SCSI hard drive in your system, you had to install an adapter card that expanded the motherboard's capabilities to allow the use of SCSI hard drives. The drives would them cable to the adapter, and the adapter would perform the requisite conversion of the drive signals to those that the motherboard and the circuits installed on it could use. Today, common I/O adapter cards tend to be USB 2.0 adapters and FireWire adapters.

Identifying Characteristics of Ports and Cables

Now that you've learned the various types of items found in a computer, let's discuss the various types of ports and cables used with computers. A *port* is a generic name for any connector on a computer into which a cable can be plugged. A *cable* is simply a way of connecting a peripheral or other device to a computer using multiple copper or fiber-optic conductors inside a common wrapping or sheath. Typically, cables connect two ports, one on the computer and one on some other device.

Let's take a quick look at some of the different styles of port connector types as well as peripheral port and cable types. We'll begin by looking at peripheral port connector types.

Peripheral Port Connector Types

Computer ports are interfaces that allow other devices to be connected to a computer. Their appearance varies widely, depending on their function. In this section we'll examine the following types of peripheral ports:

- D-subminiature
- RJ-series
- Other types

D-subminiature Connectors

D-sub connectors, for a number of years the most common style of connector found on computers, are typically designated with DXn, where the letter X is replaced by the letters A through E, which refer to the size of the connector, and the letter n is replaced by the number of pins or sockets in the connector. See the discussion on D-sub nomenclature in Chapter 12. D-sub connectors are usually shaped like a trapezoid, as you can see in Figure 1.55. The nice part about these connectors is that only one orientation is possible. If you try to connect them upside down or try to connect a male connector to another male connector, they just won't go together, and the connection can't be made. Table 1.6 lists common D-sub ports and connectors as well as their most common uses.

On the left in Figure 1.55 is a DE15F 15-pin video port, in the center is a DB25F 25-pin female printer port, and on the right is a DE9M 9-pin male serial port.

TABLE 1.6   Common D-sub Connectors

Connector	Gender	Use
DE9	Male	Serial port
DE9	Female	Connector on a serial cable
DB25	Male	Serial port or connector on a parallel cable
DB25	Female	Parallel port, or connector on a serial cable
DA15	Female	Game port or MIDI port
DA15	Male	Connector on a game peripheral cable or MIDI cable
DE15	Female	Video port (has three rows of 5 pins as opposed to two rows)
DE15	Male	Connector on a monitor cable

FIGURE 1.55   D-sub ports and connectors

RJ-Series

Registered jack (RJ) connectors are most often used in telecommunications. Figure 1.56 shows the two most common examples of RJ ports: RJ-11 and RJ-45. RJ-11 connectors are used most often in telephone hookups; your home phone jack is probably an RJ-11 jack. RJ-45 connectors, on the other hand, are most commonly found on Ethernet networks that use twisted-pair cabling. Although RJ-45 is a widely accepted description for the larger connectors, it is not correct. Generically speaking, they are 8-pin modular connectors.

On the left in this picture is an RJ-11 connector and on the right is an RJ-45 connector. Notice the size difference.

As you can see, RJ connectors are typically square with multiple gold contacts on the top (flat) side. A small locking tab on the bottom prevents the connector and cable from falling or being pulled out of the jack accidentally.

FIGURE 1.56   RJ ports

Other Types of Ports

A few other ports are used with computers today. These ports include the following:

- Universal Serial Bus (USB)
- IEEE 1394 (FireWire)
- Infrared
- Audio jacks
- PS/2 (mini-DIN)
- Centronics

Let's look at each one and how it is used.

Universal Serial Bus (USB)

Most computers built after 1997 have one or more flat ports in place of one DE9M serial port. These ports are Universal Serial Bus (USB) ports, and they are used for connecting multiple (up to 127) peripherals to one computer through a single port (and the use of multiport peripheral *hubs*). USB version 1.1 supported data rates as high as 12Mbps (1.5MBps). The newest version, USB 2.0, supports data rates as high as 480Mbps (60MBps). Figure 1.57 shows an example of a set of Type A USB ports. Port types are explained in the "Common Peripheral Interfaces and Cables" section later in this chapter.

The newest version of USB, USB 2.0, uses the same physical connection as the original USB, but it is much higher in transfer rates and requires a cable with more shielding that is less susceptible to noise. You can tell if a computer supports USB 2.0 by looking for the red and blue "High Speed USB" graphic somewhere on the computer (or on the box).

FIGURE 1.57   USB ports

Because of USB's higher transfer rate, flexibility, and ease of use, most devices that in the past used serial interfaces now come with USB interfaces. It's rare to see a newly introduced PC accessory with a standard serial interface cable. For example, PC cameras (such as the Logitech QuickCam) used to come as standard serial-only interfaces. Now you can buy them only with USB interfaces.

IEEE 1394 (FireWire)

Recently, one port has been slowly creeping into the mainstream and is seen more and more often on desktop PCs. That port is the IEEE 1394 port (shown in Figure 1.58), more commonly known as a *FireWire* port. Its popularity is due to its ease of use and very high (400MBps) transmission rates. Originally developed by Apple, it was standardized by IEEE in 1995 as IEEE 1394. It is most often used as a way to get digital video into a PC so it can be edited with digital video editing tools.

FIGURE 1.58   A FireWire port on a PC

Infrared

Increasing numbers of people are getting fed up with being tethered to their computers by cords. As a result, many computers (especially portable computing devices like laptops and PDAs) are now using infrared ports to send and receive data. An *infrared (IR) port* is a small port on the computer that allows data to be sent and received using electromagnetic radiation in the infrared band. The infrared port itself is a small, dark square of plastic (usually a very dark maroon) and can typically be found on the front of a PC or on the side of a laptop or portable. Figure 1.59 shows an example of an infrared port.

FIGURE 1.59   An infrared port

Infrared ports send and receive data at a very slow rate (maximum speed on PC infrared ports is less than 4Mbps). Most infrared ports on PCs that have them support the *Infrared Data Association (IrDA) standard*, which outlines a standard way of transmitting and receiving information by infrared so that devices can communicate with each other.

More information on the IrDA standard can be found at the organization's website: http://www.irda.org.

Note that although infrared is a wireless technology, most infrared communications (especially those that conform to the IrDA standards) are line-of-sight only and take place within a short distance (typically less than four meters). Infrared is typically used for point-to-point communications such as controlling the volume on a device with a handheld remote control.

Audio/Video Jacks

The RCA jack (shown in Figure 1.60) was developed by the RCA Victor Company in the late 1940s for use with its phonographs. You bought a phonograph, connected the RCA plug on the back of your phonograph to the RCA jack on the back of your radio or television, and used the speaker and amplifier in the radio or television to listen to records. It made phonographs cheaper to produce and had the added bonus of making sure everyone had an RCA Victor radio or television (or at the very least, one with the RCA jack on the back). Either way, RCA made money.

FIGURE 1.60   An RCA jack (female) and RCA plug (male)

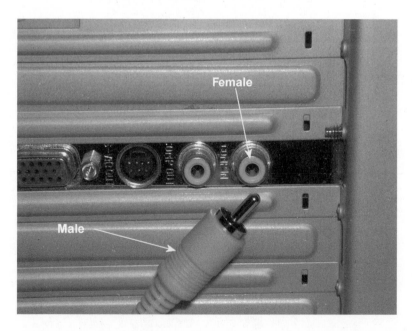

Today, RCA jacks and connectors (or plugs) are used to transmit both audio and video information. Typically, when you see an RCA connector on a PC video card (next to a DE15F connector), it's for composite video output (output to a television or VCR). However, digital audio uses *S/PDIF*, which is an RCA jack. Figure 1.17 showed an S/PDIF jack. Although they aren't used for video, it bears mentioning that the 1/8-inch stereo minijack and mating miniplug are more commonly used on computers these days for analog audio. Your sound card, microphone, and speakers have them.

In the spirit of covering interfaces that support both audio and video, don't forget the HDMI jack, which carries both over the same interface. Only CATV coaxial connections to TV cards can boast that on the PC. An RCA jack and cable carry either audio or video, not both simultaneously.

PS/2 (Keyboard and Mouse)

Another common port, as mentioned earlier, is the PS/2 port. A *PS/2 port* (also known as a *mini-DIN 6* connector) is a mouse and keyboard interface port first found on the IBM PS/2 (hence the name). It is smaller than previous interfaces (the DIN-5 keyboard port and serial mouse connector), and thus its popularity increased quickly. Figure 1.61 shows examples of both PS/2 keyboard and mouse ports. You can tell the difference because usually the keyboard port is purple and the mouse port is green. Also, typically there are small graphics of a keyboard and mouse, respectively, imprinted next to the ports.

FIGURE 1.61   PS/2 keyboard and mouse ports

Centronics

The last type of port connector is the Centronics connector, a micro ribbon connector named for the Wang subsidiary that created it. It has a unique shape, as shown in Figure 1.62. It consists of a central connection bar surrounding by an outer shielding ring. The Centronics connector was primarily used in parallel printer connections and SCSI interfaces. It is most often found on peripherals, not on computers themselves (except in the case of some older SCSI interface cards).

FIGURE 1.62   A Centronics connector

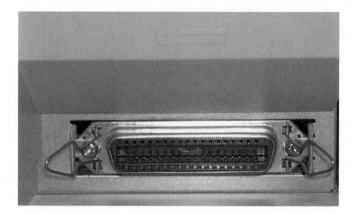

Common Peripheral Interfaces and Cables

An *interface* is a method of connecting two dissimilar items together. A *peripheral interface* is a method of connecting a peripheral or accessory to a computer, including the specification of cabling, connector type, speed, and method of communication used.

The most common interfaces used in PCs today include these:

- Parallel
- Serial
- USB
- IEEE 1394 (FireWire)
- Infrared
- RCA
- PS/2

For each type, let's look at the cabling and connector used as well as the type(s) of peripherals that are connected.

Parallel

For many years, the most popular type of interface available on computers was the parallel interface. Parallel communications take the interstate approach to data communications. Normally, interstate travel is faster than driving on city roads. This is the case mainly because you can fit multiple cars going the same direction on the same highway by using multiple lanes. On the return trip, you take a similar path, but on a completely separate road. The *parallel interface* (an example is shown in Figure 1.55) transfers data eight bits at a time over eight separate transmit wires inside a parallel cable (one bit per wire). Normal parallel interfaces use a DB-25 female connector on the computer to transfer data to peripherals. Parallel was faster than the original serial technology, which was also once used for printers in electrically noisy environments or at greater distances from the computer, but the advent of USB has brought serial, fast serial, back to the limelight.

The most common use of the parallel interface is printer communication. There are three major types: standard, bidirectional, and enhanced parallel ports. Let's look at the differences between the three.

Standard Parallel Ports

The standard parallel port only transmits data *out* of the computer. It cannot receive data (except for a single wire carrying a Ready signal). This parallel port came with the original IBM PC, XT, and AT. It can transmit data at 150KBps and is commonly used to transmit data to printers. This technology also has a maximum transmission distance of 10 feet.

Bidirectional Parallel Ports

As its name suggests, the bidirectional parallel port has one important advantage over a standard parallel port: It can both transmit and receive data. These parallel ports are capable of interfacing with such devices as external CD-ROM drives and external parallel port backup drives (Zip, Jaz, and tape drives). Most computers made since 1994 have a bidirectional parallel port.

In order for bidirectional communication to occur properly, the cable must support bidirectional communication as well.

Enhanced Parallel Ports

As more people began using parallel ports to interface with devices other than printers, they started to notice that the available speed wasn't good enough. Double-speed CD-ROM drives had a transfer rate of 300KBps, but the parallel port could transfer data at only 150KBps, thus limiting the speed at which a computer could retrieve data from an external device. To solve that problem, the Institute of Electrical and Electronics Engineers (IEEE) came up with a standard for enhanced parallel ports called IEEE 1284. The IEEE 1284 standard provides for greater data transfer speeds and the ability to send memory addresses as well as data through a parallel port. This standard allows the parallel port to theoretically act as an extension to the main bus. In addition, these ports are backward compatible with the standard and bidirectional ports.

There are two implementations of IEEE 1284: ECP parallel ports and EPP parallel ports. An *enhanced capabilities port* (ECP port) is designed to transfer data at high speeds to printers. It uses a DMA channel and a buffer to increase printing performance. An *enhanced parallel port* (EPP port) increases bidirectional throughput from 150KBps to anywhere from 600KBps to 1.5MBps.

> The cable must also have full support for IEEE 1284 in order for proper communications to occur in both directions and at rated speeds.

Parallel Interfaces and Cables

Most parallel interfaces use a DB-25 female connector, as shown earlier in this chapter. Most parallel cables use a DB-25 male connector on one end and either a DB-25 male connector or Centronics-36 connector on the other. The original printer cables typically used the DB-25M–to–Centronics-36 configuration. Inside a parallel cable, eight wires are used for transmitting data, so one byte can be transmitted at a time. Figure 1.63 shows an example of a typical parallel cable (in this case, a printer cable).

If a printer today uses a parallel port through which to connect to the computer, the likely interface on the printer is known as a mini-Centronics. Figure 1.64 shows the component end of a mini-Centronics cable. Again, however, nothing is more popular today for printer connectivity than USB.

Serial

If parallel communications are similar to taking the interstate, then serial communications are similar to taking a country road. In serial communications, bits of data are sent one after another (single file, if you will) down one wire, and they return on a different wire in the same cable. Three main types of serial interfaces are available today: standard serial, Universal Serial Bus (USB), and FireWire.

FIGURE 1.63   A typical parallel cable

FIGURE 1.64   The mini-Centronics connector

Standard Serial

Almost every computer made since the original IBM PC has at least one serial port. These computers are easily identified because they have either a DE-9 male or a DB-25 male port (shown in Figure 1.65). Standard serial ports have a maximum data transmission speed of 57Kbps and a maximum cable length of 50 feet.

FIGURE 1.65   Standard DE-9 and DB-25 male serial ports

Serial cables come in two common wiring configurations: *standard serial cable* and *null modem serial cable*. A standard serial cable is used to hook various peripherals such as modems and printers to a computer. A null modem serial cable is used to hook two computers together without a modem. The transmit wires on one end are wired to the receive pins on the other side, so it's as if a modem connection exists between the two computers but without the need for a modem. Figures 1.66 and 1.67 show the wiring differences (the *pinouts*) between a standard serial cable and a null modem cable. In the null modem diagram, notice how the transmit (tx) pins on one end are wired to the receive (rx) pins on the other.

FIGURE 1.66   A standard serial cable wiring diagram

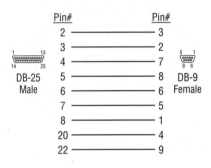
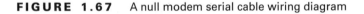

FIGURE 1.67   A null modem serial cable wiring diagram

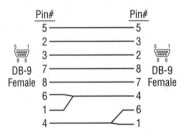

Finally, because of the two different device connectors (DE-9M and DB-25M), serial cables have a few different configurations. Table 1.7 shows the most common serial cable configurations.

TABLE 1.7   Common Serial Cable Configurations

1st Connector	2nd Connector	Description
DE-9 female	DB-25 male	Standard modem cable
DE-9 female	DE-9 male	Standard serial extension cable

TABLE 1.7   Common Serial Cable Configurations *(continued)*

1st Connector	2nd Connector	Description
DE-9 female	DE-9 female	Null modem cable
DB-25 female	DB-25 female	Null modem cable
DB-25 female	DB-25 male	Standard serial cable or standard serial extension cable

Universal Serial Bus (USB)

USB cables are used to connect a wide variety of peripherals to computers, including keyboards, mice, digital cameras, printers, and scanners. The latest version of USB, version 2.0, requires a cable with better shielding than did earlier versions. Not all USB cables work with USB 2.0 ports. The connectors are identical, so look for cables that are transparent with a view to the silver metallic shielding within.

USB's simplicity of use and ease of expansion make it an excellent interface for just about any kind of peripheral. This fact alone makes the USB interface one of the most popular on the modern computer, perhaps behind only the video, input, and network connectors.

The USB interface is fairly straightforward. Essentially, it was designed to be Plug and Play—just plug in the peripheral, and it should work (providing the software is installed to support it). The USB cable varies based on the USB male connector on each end. Because there can be quite a number of daisy-chained USB devices on a single system, it helps to have a scheme to clarify their connectivity. The USB standard specifies two broad types of connector. They are designated Type A and Type B connectors. A standard USB cable has some form of Type A connector on one end and some form of Type B connector on the other end. Figure 1.68 shows four USB cable connectors. From left to right, they are

- Type A
- Standard mini-B
- Type B
- Alternate mini-B

One part of the USB interface specification that makes it so appealing is the fact that if your computer runs out of USB ports, you can simply plug a device known as a *USB hub* into one of your computer's USB ports, which will give you several more USB ports from one USB port. Figure 1.69 shows an example of a USB hub.

From the perspective of the cable's plug, Type A is always oriented toward the system from the component. As a result, you might notice that the USB receptacle on the computer system that a component cables back to is the same as the receptacle on the USB hub that components cable back to. The USB hub is simply an extension of the system and becomes a component that cables back to the system.

FIGURE 1.68   USB cables and connectors

FIGURE 1.69   A USB hub

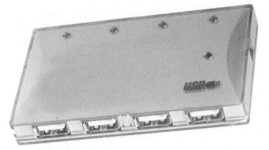

Type B plugs connect in the direction of the component. Therefore, you see a Type B interface on the hub as well as on the end devices to allow them to cable back to the system or another hub. Although they exist, USB cables with both ends of the same type, a sort of extension cable, are in violation of the USB specification. Collectively, these rules make cabling your USB subsystem quite straightforward.

While the system receptacle, the Type A, remains constant, the component receptacle differs, often based on the size of the USB device. For example, a USB-attached printer is large enough for a Type B connector, but a compact digital camera might only be large enough to accommodate a mini-B receptacle of some sort. While the standard calls for one mini-B connector, others have been developed, some common, others a bit rarer. The four connectors shown in Figure 1.68 are the most common. You might also run across mini-A connectors, which are not discussed further in this book.

   USB connectors are keyed and will go into a USB port only one way. If the connector will not go into the port properly, try rotating it.

   For more information on USB, check out http://www.usb.org.

IEEE 1394 (FireWire)

The IEEE 1394 interface is about one thing: speed. Its first iteration, now known as FireWire 400, has a maximum data throughput of 400Mbps. The latest iteration, FireWire 800, has a maximum data throughput of 800Mbps. It carries data at that speed over a maximum cable length of 4.5 meters (FireWire 400) and 100 meters (FireWire 800 over fiber-optic cables).

FireWire (also known as i.Link in Sony's parlance) uses a very special type of cable, as shown in Figure 1.70. Notice the difference in the system end on the left and the component end on the right. It is difficult to mistake this cable for anything but a FireWire cable.

FIGURE 1.70 A FireWire (IEEE 1394) cable

Although most people think of FireWire as a tool for connecting their digital camcorders to their computers, it's much more than that. Because of its high data transfer rate, it is being used more and more as a universal, high-speed data interface for things like hard drives, CD-ROM drives, and digital video editing equipment.

RCA

The RCA cable is simple. There are two connectors, usually male, one on each end of the cable. The male connector connects to the female connector on the equipment. Figure 1.71 shows an example of an RCA cable. An RCA male-to-RCA female connector is also available; it's used to extend the reach of audio or video signals.

FIGURE 1.71 An RCA cable

The RCA male connectors on a connection cable are sometimes plated in gold to increase their corrosion resistance and to improve longevity.

PS/2 (Keyboard and Mouse)

The final interface we'll discuss is the PS/2 interface for mice and keyboards. Essentially, it is the same connector for the cables from both items: a male mini-DIN 6 connector. Most keyboards today still use the PS/2 interface, whereas most mice are gravitating toward the USB interface (especially optical mice). However, mice that have USB cables still may include a special USB-to-PS/2 adapter so they can be used with the PS/2 interface. Figure 1.72 shows an example of a PS/2 keyboard cable.

FIGURE 1.72   A PS/2 keyboard cable

Most often, PS/2 cables have only one connector, because the other end is connected directly to the device being plugged in. The only exception is PS/2 extension cables used to extend the length of a PS/2 device's cable.

Identifying Purposes and Characteristics of Cooling Systems

It's a basic concept of physics: electronic components turn electricity into work and heat. The heat must be dissipated or the excess heat will shorten the life of the components. In some cases (like the CPU), the component will produce so much heat that it can destroy itself in a matter of seconds if there is not some way to remove this extra heat.

Most PCs use air-cooling methods to cool their internal components. With air cooling, the movement of air removes the heat from the component. Sometimes, large blocks of metal called heat sinks are attached to a heat-producing component in order to dissipate the heat more rapidly.

Fans

When you turn on a computer, you will often hear lots of whirring. Contrary to popular opinion, the majority of the noise isn't coming from the hard disk (unless it's about to go bad). Most of this noise is coming from the various fans inside the computer. Fans provide airflow within the computer.

Most PCs have a combination of these six fans:

Front Intake Fan   This fan is used to bring fresh, cool air into the computer for cooling purposes.

Rear Exhaust Fan   This fan is used to take hot air out of the case.

Power Supply Fan   This fan is usually found at the back of the power supply and is used to cool the power supply. In addition, there are fans used to pull hot air from above the CPU into the power supply so that it can be exhausted.

CPU Fan   This fan is used to cool the processor. Typically, this fan is attached to a large heat sink, which is in turn attached directly to the processor.

Chipset Fan   Some motherboard manufacturers replaced the heat sink on their onboard chipset with a heat sink and fan combination. This fan aids in the cooling of the onboard chipset (especially useful when overclocking).

Video Card Chipset Fan   As video cards get more complex and have higher performance, more video cards have cooling fans right on their video cards.

Ideally, the airflow inside a computer should resemble the following:

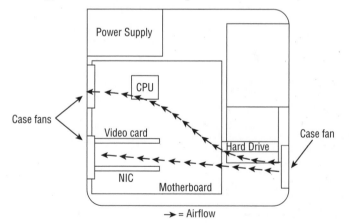

Memory Cooling

If you are going to start overclocking your computer, you will want to do everything in your power to cool all the components in your computer, and that includes the memory.

There are two methods of cooling memory: passive and active. The passive memory cooling method just uses the ambient case airflow to cool the memory through the use of enhanced heat dissipation. For this, you can buy either heat sinks or special "for memory chips only" devices known as heat spreaders. These are special aluminum or copper housings that wrap around memory chips and conduct the heat away from the memory chips.

Active cooling, on the other hand, usually involves forcing some kind of cooling medium (air or water) around the RAM chips themselves or around their heat sinks. Most often, active cooling methods are just high-speed fans directing air right over a set of heat spreaders.

Some memory models allow you to put activity lights on top of your memory coolers.

Hard Drive Cooling

You might be thinking, "Hey, my hard drive is working all the time. Is there anything I can do to cool it off as well?" There are both active and passive cooling devices for hard drives. Most common, however, is the active cooling bay. You install a hard drive in a special device that fits into a 5.25-inch expansion bay. This device contains fans that draw in cool air over the hard drive, thus cooling it. Figure 1.73 shows an example of one of these active hard drive coolers. As you might suspect, you can also get heat sinks for hard drives.

FIGURE 1.73   An active hard disk cooler

Chipset Cooling

Every motherboard has a chip or chipset that controls how the computer operates. As with other chips in the computer, the chipset is normally cooled by the ambient air movement in the case. However, when you overclock a computer, the chipset may need to be cooled more as it is working harder than it normally would be. Therefore, it is often desirable to replace the onboard chipset cooler with a more efficient one.

CPU Cooling

Probably the greatest challenge in cooling is the cooling of the computer's CPU. It is the component that generates the most heat in a computer. As a matter of fact, if it isn't actively cooled all the time, it will generate enough heat to burn itself up in an instant. That's why most motherboards have an internal CPU heat sensor and a CPU_FAN sensor. If no cooling fan is active, these devices will shut down the computer before damage occurs.

There are many different types of CPU cooling methods, but the two most important are air cooling and advanced cooling methods.

Air Cooling

The parts inside most computers are cooled by air moving through the case. The CPU is no exception. However, because of the large amount of heat produced, the CPU must have (proportionately) the largest surface area exposed to the moving air in the case. Therefore, the heat sinks on the CPU are the largest of any inside the computer.

It should be noted that the highest performing CPU coolers use copper plates in direct contact with the CPU. They also use high-speed and high-CFM cooling fans to dissipate the heat produced by the processor. CFM is short for cubic feet per minute, an airflow measurement of the volume of air that passes by a stationary object per minute.

Some CPU heat sinks use heat pipes to transfer heat away from the CPU. With any cooling system, the more surface area exposed to the cooling method, the better the cooling. Plus, the heat pipes can be used to transfer heat to a location away from the heat source before cooling. This is especially useful in small form factor cases where heat is limited.

With advanced heat sinks and CPU cooling methods like this, it is important to improve the thermal transfer efficiency as much as possible. To that end, cooling manufacturers have come up with a compound that helps to bridge the extremely small gaps between the CPU and the heat sink. This compound is known as thermal compound and can be bought in small tubes.

 In addition to using thermal compound, you can enhance the cooling efficiency of a CPU heat sink by lapping (polishing) the heat sink.

If you've ever installed a brand new heat sink onto a CPU, you've most likely used thermal compound or a thermal compound patch. However, some people have designed special thermally conductive compounds such as Arctic Silver, which contain micronized silver in an organic suspension fluid, that are supposed to conduct heat better while filling in the microscopic peaks and valleys in a heat sink's surface.

Advanced CPU Cooling Methods

In addition to standard air-cooling methods, there are other methods of cooling a CPU (and other chips as well). These methods are somewhat unorthodox but usually deliver extreme results. These methods can also result in permanent damage to your computer, so try them at your own risk.

Liquid Cooling

A new trend in PC cooling is *liquid cooling*. Liquid cooling is a technology whereby a special water block is used to conduct heat away from the processor (as well as from chipsets). Water is circulated through this block to a radiator, where it is cooled.

The theory is that you could achieve better cooling performance through the use of liquid cooling. For the most part, this is true. However, with traditional cooling methods (which use air and water), the lowest temperature you can achieve is room temperature. Plus, with liquid cooling, the pump is submerged in the coolant (generally speaking), so as it works, it produces heat, which adds to the overall system temperature.

The main benefit to liquid cooling is silence. There is only one fan needed: the fan on the radiator to cool the water. So a liquid cooled system can run extremely quietly.

Liquid cooling, while more efficient that air cooling and much quieter, has its drawbacks. Most liquid cooling systems start around $100 (although the price is always coming down) and that includes reservoir, pump, water block(s), hose, and radiator. Air-cooling systems are usually cheaper (although if you are really into cooling performance, the prices of all your fans and heat sinks could easily add up to more than $100).

Peltier Cooling Devices

Water- and air-cooling devices are extremely effective by themselves, but they are more effective when used with a device known as a Peltier cooling element. These devices, also known as thermo-electric coolers (TECs), essentially will facilitate the transfer of heat from one side of the element to the other. Thus, they have a hot side and a cold side. The cold side should always be against the CPU die and the hot side against a heat sink or water block so that the heat can be dissipated.

Phase Change Cooling

There is one new type of PC cooling that is just starting to be seen: *phase change cooling*. With this type of cooling, the cooling effect from the change of a liquid to a gas is used to cool the inside of a PC. It is a very expensive method of cooling, but it does work. Most often, external air-conditioner-like pumps, coils, and evaporators cool the coolant, which is sent, ice cold, to the heat sink blocks on the processor and chipset. Think of it as a water-cooling system that chills the water below room temperature. It is possible to get CPU temps in the range of -4°F (-20°C). Normal CPU temperatures hover between 104°F and 122°F (40°C and 50C).

The major drawback to this method is that in higher-humidity conditions, condensation can be a problem. The moisture from the air condenses on the heat sink and can run off onto the processor and motherboard, thus shorting them out. Designers of phase change cooling systems (like the Prometeia Mach II from Chip-Con) ensure this isn't a problem by sealing the processor in insulating foam.

Summary

In this chapter, we took a tour of the components of a PC. You learned about the different components that make up a PC, including the case, motherboard, drives and storage, expansion cards, and display devices. In addition, we discussed common peripheral ports and cables and their appearance. Finally, you learned about the various methods used for cooling a PC. You also learned what each of these items looks like and how they function.

Exam Essentials

Know the types of system boards.   Know the characteristics of and differences between ATX, micro ATX, NTX, and BTX motherboards.

Know the components of a motherboard.   Be able to describe motherboard components, such as chipsets, expansion slots, memory slots and external cache, CPU and processor slots or sockets, power connectors, onboard disk drive connectors, keyboard connectors, peripheral ports and connectors, BIOS chips. CMOS batteries, jumpers and DIP switches, and firmware.

Understand the purposes and characteristics of processors.   Be able to discuss the different processor packaging, old and new, and know the meaning of the terms hyperthreading, multicore, throttling, microcode, overclocking, cache, voltage regulator module, speed, and system bus width (32 or 64 bits).

Understand the purposes and characteristics of memory.   Know about the characteristics that set the various types of memory apart from one another. This includes the actual types of memory, such as DRAM, which includes several varieties, SRAM, ROM, and CMOS, as well as memory packaging, such as DIMMs, RIMMs, SoDIMMS, and MicroDIMMs.

Understand the purposes and characteristics of storage devices.   Be able to compare and contrast the various storage devices, which include hard and floppy drives, CD and DVD drives, and removable storage, such as flash memory and USB-attached drives.

Understand the purposes and characteristics of power supplies.   Know the job the power supply performs, as well as the connectors it uses to connect to the rest of the system to supply power to various components.

Understand the purposes and characteristics of display devices.   Be comfortable with the historical video standards and know the various modern VGA-based standards and their naming convention. Be able to discuss the modern analog and digital video technologies. Know the similarities and differences between CRT and LCD monitors.

Understand the purposes and characteristics of input devices.   Know the various forms of input devices and their categories, such as standard and multimedia. Be able to describe individual devices and their uses.

Understand the purposes and characteristics of adapter cards and their ports and cables. Familiarize yourself with the variety of expansion cards and integrated components in today's computer systems, as well as the ports they use and any cables that connect to external devices.

Understand the purposes and characteristics of cooling systems.   Know the different ways that internal components can be cooled and how overheating can be prevented.

Review Questions

1. Which computer component contains all the circuitry necessary for *all* components or devices to communicate with each other?

    A. Motherboard

    B. Adapter card

    C. Hard drive

    D. Expansion bus

2. Which packaging is used for DDR SDRAM memory?

    A. DIP

    B. SIMM

    C. DIMM

    D. RIMM

3. What technology is used in the original-style monitor?

    A. Video Display Unit

    B. CRT

    C. LCD

    D. Optical Display Unit

4. Which motherboard design style is the most popular?

    A. ATX

    B. AT

    C. Baby AT

    D. NLX

5. Which motherboard socket type is used on the Pentium 4 chip?

    A. Slot 1

    B. Socket A

    C. Socket 370

    D. Socket 478

6. What is the official name for the IDE/EIDE family of drive interfaces?

    A. SCSI

    B. ATA

    C. SATA

    D. TAT

7. Which is another term for the motherboard?

   A. A fiberglass board

   B. A planar board

   C. A bus system

   D. An IBM system board XR125

8. Which of the following is used to store data and programs for repeated use? Information can be added and deleted at will, and it does *not* lose its data when power is removed.

   A. Hard drive

   B. RAM

   C. Internal cache memory

   D. ROM

9. Which motherboard socket type is used with the AMD Athlon XP?

   A. Slot 1

   B. Socket A

   C. Socket 370

   D. Socket 478

10. You want to plug a keyboard into the back of a computer. You know that you need to plug the keyboard cable into a PS/2 port. Which style of port is the PS/2?

   A. RJ-11

   B. DE9

   C. DIN 5

   D. Mini-DIN 6

11. What are the five voltages produced by a common PCs power supply? (Choose all that apply.)

   A. +3.3VDC

   B. −3.3VDC

   C. +5VDC

   D. −5VDC

   E. +12VDC

   F. −12VDC

   G. +110VAC

   H. −110VAC

12. What is the maximum speed of USB 2.0 in Mbps?

  A. 1.5

  B. 12

  C. 60

  D. 480

13. If you wanted to connect a LapLink cable (a parallel data transfer cable) so that you could upload and download files from a computer, which type of parallel port(s) could handle this application? (Choose all that apply.)

  A. Standard

  B. Bidirectional

  C. EPP

  D. ECP

14. What peripheral port type was originally developed by Apple and is currently primarily used for digital video transfers?

  A. DVD

  B. USB

  C. IEEE 1394

  D. IEEE 1284

15. What peripheral port type is expandable using a hub, operates at 1.5MBps, and is used to connect various devices (from printers to cameras) to PCs?

  A. DVD 1.0

  B. USB 1.0

  C. IEEE 1394

  D. IEEE 1284

16. Which peripheral port type was designed to transfer data at high speeds to printers only?

  A. DVD

  B. USB

  C. IEEE 1394

  D. IEEE 1284

17. Which motherboard form factor places expansion slots on a special riser card and is used in low-profile PCs?

  A. AT

  B. Baby AT

  C. ATX

  D. NLX

18. Which Intel processor type(s) use the SEC when installed into a motherboard? (Choose all that apply.)

   A. AMD Athlon

   B. 486

   C. Pentium

   D. Pentium II

19. Which of the following can a DVD-ROM store in addition to movies? (Choose all that apply.)

   A. Audio files

   B. Word documents

   C. Digital photos

   D. All of the above

20. What type of expansion slot is almost always used for high-speed, 3D graphics video cards?

   A. USB

   B. AGP

   C. PCI

   D. ISA

Answers to Review Questions

1. A. The spine of the computer is the system board, otherwise known as the motherboard. On the motherboard you will find the CPU, underlying circuitry, expansion slots, video components, RAM slots, and various other chips.

2. C . DDR SDRAM is manufactured on a DIMM. DIPs are the original chips that memory was delivered in. The SIMM is the predecessor to the DIMM, on which DDR was never deployed. RIMM is the Rambus proprietary competitor for the DIMM that carries RDRAM instead of SDRAM.

3. B . A cathode-ray tube, or CRT, is the technology used in the original televisions and computer monitors.

4. A. Although all the motherboard design styles listed are in use today, the ATX motherboard style (and its derivatives) is the most popular design.

5. D. Most Pentium 4 chips use the Socket 478 motherboard CPU socket.

6. B. Although these drives and their interfaces have become known as IDE and EIDE, the official name for the technology is ATA. Serial ATA is the next generation of this technology and is not the official name for the interface in general. In fact, its interface is different from the PATA interface of IDE and EIDE. SCSI is a competing drive interface, and TAT is not a valid drive-interface technology.

7. B. The spine of the computer is the system board, otherwise known as the motherboard and less commonly referred to as the planar board.

8. A. A hard drive stores data on a magnetic medium, which does not lose its information after the power is removed, and which can be repeatedly written to and erased.

9. B. The Socket A motherboard socket is used primarily with AMD processors, including the Athlon XP.

10. D. A PS/2 port is also known as a mini-DIN 6 connector.

11. A, C, D, E, F. A PC's power supply produces +3.3VDC, +5VDC, −5VDC, +12VDC, and −12VDC from 110VAC.

12. D. The USB 2.0 spec provides for a maximum speed of 480 megabits per second (Mbps—not megabytes per second, or MBps).

13. B, C, D. Bidirectional parallel ports can both transmit and receive data. An ECP was designed to transfer data at high speeds. EPP parallel ports provide for greater transfer speeds and the ability to send memory addresses as well as data through a parallel port. The standard parallel port only transmits data out of the computer. It cannot receive data.

14. C. The 1394 standard provides for greater data transfer speeds and the ability to send memory addresses as well as data through a serial port.

15. B. USBs are used to connect multiple peripherals to one computer through a single port. They support data transfer rates as high as 1.5MBps (for USB 1.0, which is the option listed here).

16. D. IEEE 1284 standard defines the ECP parallel port to use a DMA channel and the buffer to be able to transfer data at high speeds to printers.

17. D. The NLX form factor places expansion slots on a special riser card and is used in low-profile PCs.

18. D. The unique thing about the Pentium II is that it uses a Single Edge Connector (SEC) to attach to the motherboard instead of the standard PGA package.

19. D. The DVD-ROM can store many types of data as well as movies. In the computer world, data can be audio files, Word documents, digital photos, and many other things.

20. B. Although technically PCI and ISA could be used for video adapters, AGP was specifically designed for the use of high-speed, 3D graphic video cards.

Chapter

2

Effectively Working with Personal Computer Components

THE FOLLOWING COMPTIA A+ ESSENTIALS EXAM OBJECTIVES ARE COVERED IN THIS CHAPTER:

✓ **1.2 Install, configure, optimize and upgrade personal computer components**

- Add, remove and configure internal and external storage devices
  - Drive preparation of internal storage devices including format / file systems and imaging technology
- Install display devices
- Add, remove and configure basic input and multimedia devices

✓ **1.3 Identify tools, diagnostic procedures and troubleshooting techniques for personal computer components**

- Recognize the basic aspects of troubleshooting theory for example:
  - Perform backups before making changes
  - Assess a problem systematically and divide large problems into smaller components to be analyzed individually
  - Verify even the obvious, determine whether the problem is something simple and make no assumptions
  - Research ideas and establish priorities
  - Document findings, actions and outcomes
- Identify and apply basic diagnostic procedures and troubleshooting techniques for example:
  - Identify the problem including questioning user and identifying user changes to computer

- Analyze the problem including potential causes and make an initial determination of software and / or hardware problems
- Test related components including inspection, connections, hardware / software configurations, device manager and consult vendor documentation
- Evaluate results and take additional steps if needed such as consultation, use of alternate resources, manuals
- Document activities and outcomes
- Recognize and isolate issues with display, power, basic input devices, storage, memory, thermal, POST errors (e.g. BIOS, hardware)
- Apply basic troubleshooting techniques to check for problems (e.g. thermal issues, error codes, power, connections including cables and / or pins, compatibility, functionality, software / drivers) with components for example:
  - Motherboards
  - Power supply
  - Processor / CPUs
  - Memory
  - Display devices
  - Input devices
  - Adapter cards
- Recognize the names, purposes, characteristics and appropriate application of tools for example: BIOS, self-test, hard drive self-test and software diagnostics test

✓ **1.4 Perform preventative maintenance on personal computer components**

- Identify and apply basic aspects of preventative maintenance theory for example:
  - Visual / audio inspection
  - Driver / firmware updates
  - Scheduling preventative maintenance
  - Use of appropriate repair tools and cleaning materials
  - Ensuring proper environment
- Identify and apply common preventative maintenance techniques for devices such as input devices and batteries

As a PC technician, you need to know quite a bit about hardware. Given the importance and magnitude of this knowledge, the best way to approach it is in sections. The first chapter introduced the topic, and this chapter follows up where it left off.

Installing, Configuring, and Optimizing PC Components

While being able to identify the various components of a personal computer is important, knowing how to install, configure, and optimize them is equally if not more important. The components in question are storage devices (internal and external), display devices, and input/multimedia devices.

The previous chapter introduced you to many of the technologies involved with these components, such as IDE and SCSI. In this chapter, we will focus on the actual implementation of components using these technologies.

There is a great deal of overlap between this chapter and Chapter 12, which deals with these technologies as they relate to the various A+ "technician" exams.

Upgrading Storage Devices

Storage devices come in many shapes and sizes. In addition to IDE and SCSI, two of the old standards, there are now Serial ATA (SATA) and Parallel ATA (PATA), and you can differentiate between internal and external drives. This section looks at storage devices from a number of those different possibilities.

Parallel ATA (PATA) is the name retroactively given to the ATA/IDE standards when SATA became available. PATA uses a normal 40-pin connector, whereas SATA uses a 7-pin connector.

Drive Preparation

Regardless of the type of technology used, some drives need to be formatted prior to use. While many drives come with software for doing this, every operating system includes a utility for this purpose as well. With Windows-based operating systems, you can use the format utility from the command line and the Disk Management graphical utility with XP and newer operating systems.

Subsequent chapters of this book look at the operating systems and contain more information on these and other utilities.

Working with IDE

Traditionally, integrated drive electronics (IDE) drives have been the most common type of hard drive found in computers. Though so often thought of in relation to hard drives, IDE is much more than a hard-drive interface; it's also a popular interface for many other drive types, including CD-ROM, DVD, and Zip.

The design of the IDE is simple: Put the controller right on the drive, and use a relatively short ribbon cable to connect the drive/controller to the IDE interface. This offers the benefits of decreasing signal loss (thus increasing reliability) and making the drive easier to install. The IDE interface can be an expansion board, or it can be built into the motherboard, as is the case on almost all systems today.

IDE generically refers to any drive that has a built-in controller. The IDE we know today is more properly called AT IDE; two previous types of IDE (MCA IDE and XT IDE) are obsolete and incompatible with it.

There have been many revisions of the IDE standard over the years, and each one is designated with a certain AT attachment (ATA) number—ATA-1 through ATA-8. Drives that support ATA-2 and higher are generically referred to as enhanced IDE (EIDE).

With ATA-3, a technology called ATA Packet Interface (ATAPI) was introduced to help deal with IDE devices other than hard disks. ATAPI enables the BIOS to recognize an IDE CD-ROM drive, for example, or a tape backup or Zip drive.

Starting with ATA-4, a new technology was introduced called UltraDMA, supporting transfer modes of up to 33MBps.

ATA-5 supports UltraDMA/66, with transfer modes of up to 66MBps. To achieve this high rate, the drive must have a special 80-wire ribbon cable, and the motherboard or IDE controller card must support ATA-5.

ATA-6 supports UltraDMA/100, with transfer modes of up to 100MBps.

If an ATA-5 or ATA-6 drive is used with a normal 40-wire cable or is used on a system that doesn't support the higher modes, it reverts to the ATA-4 performance level.

ATA-7 supports UltraDMA/133, with transfer modes of up to 150MBps and serial ATA (discussed later).

ATA-8 made only minor revisions to ATA-7 and also supports UltraDMA/133, with transfer modes of up to 150MBps and serial ATA (discussed later).

IDE Pros and Cons

The primary benefit of IDE is that it's nearly universally supported. Almost every motherboard has IDE connectors. In addition, IDE devices are typically the cheapest and most readily available type.

A typical motherboard has two IDE connectors, and each connector can support up to two drives on the same cable. That means you're limited to four IDE devices per system unless you add an expansion board containing another IDE interface. In contrast, with SCSI you can have up to seven drives per interface (or even more on some types of SCSI).

Performance also may suffer when IDE devices share an interface. When you're burning CDs, for example, if the reading and writing CD drives are both on the same cable, errors may occur. SCSI drives are much more efficient with this type of transfer.

IDE Installation and Configuration

To install an IDE drive, do the following:

1. Set the master/slave jumper on the drive.

2. Install the drive in the drive bay.

3. Connect the power-supply cable.

4. Connect the ribbon cable to the drive and to the motherboard or IDE expansion board. There is a colored (usually red) strip down one edge of the ribbon cable that is used to correctly orient the cable both where it connects to the drive and to the motherboard. If there is no marking for pin 1, orient the red stripe toward the power supply.

5. Configure the drive in BIOS Setup if it isn't automatically detected.

6. Partition and format the drive using the operating system.

Each IDE interface can have only one *master* drive on it. If there are two drives on a single cable, one of them must be the *slave* drive. This setting is accomplished via a jumper on the drive. Some drives have a separate setting for Single (that is, master with no slave) and Master (that is, master with a slave); others use the Master setting generically to refer to either case. Figure 2.1 shows a typical master/slave jumper scenario, but different drives may have different jumper positions to represent each state.

Most BIOS Setup programs today support Plug and Play, so they detect the new drive automatically at startup. If this doesn't work, the drive may not be installed correctly, the jumper settings may be wrong, or the BIOS Setup may have the IDE interface set to None rather than Auto. Enter BIOS Setup and find out. Setting the IDE interface to Auto and then allowing the BIOS to detect the drive is usually all that is required.

In BIOS Setup for the drive, you might have the option of selecting a DMA or programmed input/output (PIO) setting for the drive. Both are methods for improving drive performance by allowing the drive to write directly to RAM, bypassing the CPU when possible. For modern drives that support UltraDMA, neither of these settings is necessary or desirable.

FIGURE 2.1   Master/slave jumpers

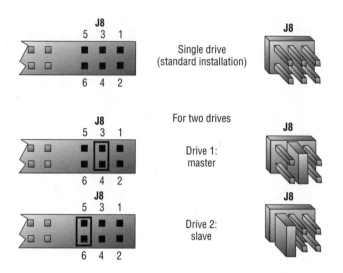

Now that your drive is installed, you can proceed to partition and format it for the operating system you've chosen. Then, finally, you can install your operating system of choice.

For a Windows 2000 or XP system, allow the Windows Setup program to partition and format the drive, or use the Disk Management utility in Windows to perform those tasks. To access Disk Management, from the Control Panel, choose Administrative Tools and then choose Computer Management.

Working with SCSI

Small computer system interface (SCSI) devices can be either internal or external to the computer. Eight-bit SCSI-1 and SCSI-2 internal devices use a SCSI A cable, a 50-pin ribbon cable similar to that of an IDE drive. Sixteen-bit SCSI uses a SCSI P cable, with 68 wires and a DB-style connector. There is also an 80-pin internal connector called SCA used for some high-end SCSI devices. Like IDE and floppy-drive cables, SCSI cables have a colored stripe (usually blue or red) down one side to indicate the orientation of pin 1.

External SCSI connectors depend on the type. SCSI-1 uses a 50-pin Centronics connector, as for a parallel printer. SCSI-2 uses a 25-, 50-, or 68-pin female DB-style connector. SCSI-3 uses a 68- or 80-pin female DB-style connector.

To configure SCSI, you must assign a unique device number (often called a SCSI address, SCSI ID, or SCSI device ID) to each device on the SCSI bus. These numbers are configured through either jumpers or DIP switches. When the computer needs to send data to the device, it sends a signal on the wire addressed to that number. A device called a *terminator* (technically a *terminating resistor pack*) must be installed at both ends of the bus to keep the signals "on the bus." The device then responds with a signal that contains the number of the device that sent the information and the data itself. The terminator can be built into the device and activated/deactivated with a jumper, or it can be a separate block or connector hooked onto the device when termination is required.

Termination can be either active or passive. A *passive terminator* works with resistors driven by the small amount of electricity that travels through the SCSI bus. *Active termination* uses voltage regulators inside the terminator. Active termination is much better, and you should use it whenever you have fast, wide, or Ultra SCSI devices on the chain and/or more than two SCSI devices on the chain. It may not be obvious from looking at a terminator whether it's active or passive.

SCSI Device Installation and Configuration

Installing SCSI devices is more complex than installing an IDE drive. The main issues with installing SCSI devices are cabling, termination, and addressing.

We'll discuss termination and cabling together because they're closely tied. There are two types of cabling:

- Internal cabling uses a 50-wire ribbon cable with several keyed connectors. These connectors are attached to the devices in the computer (the order is unimportant), with one connector connecting to the adapter.

- External cabling uses thick, shielded cables that run from adapter to device to device in a fashion known as *daisy-chaining*. Each device has two ports on it (most of the time). When hooking up external SCSI devices, you run a cable from the adapter to the first device. Then you run a cable from the first device to the second device, from the second to the third, and so on.

Because there are two types of cabling devices, you have three ways to connect them. The methods differ by where the devices are located and whether the adapter has the terminator installed. The guide to remember here is that *both ends* of the bus must be terminated. Let's look briefly at the three connection methods:

Internal Devices Only   When you have only internal SCSI devices, you connect the cable to the adapter and to every SCSI device in the computer. You then install the terminating resistors on the adapter and terminate the last drive in the chain. All other devices are unterminated. This is demonstrated in Figure 2.2.

FIGURE 2.2   Cabling internal SCSI devices only

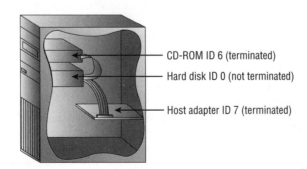

CD-ROM ID 6 (terminated)

Hard disk ID 0 (not terminated)

Host adapter ID 7 (terminated)

Some devices and adapters don't use terminating resistor packs; instead, you use a jumper or DIP switch to activate or deactivate SCSI termination on such devices. Check the documentation to find out what type your device uses.

External Devices Only   In the next situation, you have external devices only, as shown in Figure 2.3. By external devices, we mean that each has its own power supply. You connect the devices in the same manner in which you connected internal devices, but in this method you use several very short (less than 0.5 meters) *stub* cables to run between the devices in a daisy chain (rather than one long cable with several connectors). The effect is the same. The adapter and the last device in the chain (which has only one stub cable attached to it) must be terminated.

Both Internal and External Devices   Finally, there's the hybrid situation in which you have both internal and external devices (Figure 2.4). Most adapters have connectors for both internal and external SCSI devices—if yours doesn't have both, you'll need to see if anybody makes one that will work with your devices. For adapters that do have both types of connectors, you connect your internal devices to the ribbon cable and attach the cable to the adapter. Then you daisy-chain your external devices off the external port. You terminate the last device on each chain, leaving the adapter unterminated.

FIGURE 2.3   Cabling external SCSI devices only

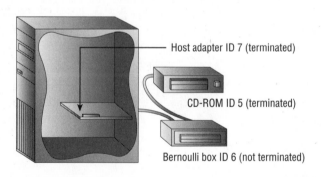

Host adapter ID 7 (terminated)

CD-ROM ID 5 (terminated)

Bernoulli box ID 6 (not terminated)

FIGURE 2.4   Cabling internal and external SCSI devices together

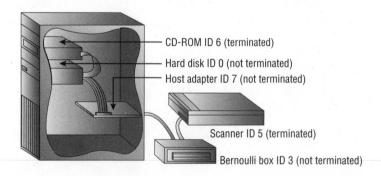

CD-ROM ID 6 (terminated)
Hard disk ID 0 (not terminated)
Host adapter ID 7 (not terminated)

Scanner ID 5 (terminated)

Bernoulli box ID 3 (not terminated)

Even though the third technique described is the technically correct way to install termination for the hybrid situation (in which you have both internal and external devices), some adapter cards still need to have terminators installed. Both ends of a SCSI chain must be terminated.

Each device must also have a unique SCSI ID number. This number can be assigned by the jumper (with internal devices) or with a rotary switch (on external devices). You start by assigning your adapter an address. This can be any number from 0 to 7 on an 8-bit bus, 0 to 15 on a 16-bit bus, and 0 to 31 on a 32-bit bus, as long as no other device is using that ID.

Here are some recommendations that are commonly accepted by the PC community. Remember that these are guidelines, not rules:

- Generally speaking, give slower devices higher priority so they can access the bus whenever they need it. SCSI priorities, from highest to lowest, are established as 1, 2, or 4 groups of 8 descending IDs depending on the width of the address bus, which could be 8, 16, or 32 bits. The tricky part is remembering that with 2 or 4 groups of 8 IDs, each sequence of 8 descending IDs is larger than the last, but lower in priority. Therefore, with a 32-bit bus, the sequence of IDs from highest to lowest priority is 7 through 0, 15 through 8, 23 through 16, and 31 through 24. The ID 7 is always the highest priority, regardless of bus width. This odd priority-sequence came about for the sake of backward compatibility. Originally, the 16-bit bus had to be able to interoperate with the 8-bit bus but had no way of imposing its new IDs on the older technology. So, the new, higher-valued IDs could not trump the older IDs, and yet the descending-group-of-8 convention was maintained. Eventually, the 32-bit bus followed suit for the same reason.

- Set the bootable (or first) hard disk to ID 0.

- Set the CD-ROM to ID 3.

After the devices are cabled and terminated, you have to get the PC to recognize the SCSI adapter and its devices. The SCSI adapter manages all SCSI device resource allocation, so generally all that is required is to make sure the operating system is able to see the SCSI adapter. This involves installing a Windows driver for the adapter in Windows, for example, or a real-mode driver in `CONFIG.SYS` for MS-DOS.

However, if you want to boot from a SCSI drive, the system must be able to read from that drive in order to load the operating system; you must enable the SCSI adapter's own BIOS extension so that the PC can read from it at startup without a driver. Check the documentation for the adapter; sometimes the BIOS Setup program for the SCSI adapter is activated via a function key at startup.

Once the drive is installed and talking to the computer, you can high-level format the media and install the operating system.

If there are problems, double-check the termination and ID numbers. If everything looks correct, try changing the ID numbers one at a time. SCSI addressing is a gray area where many problems arise.

RAID

RAID stands for Redundant Array of Independent Disks. It's a way of combining the storage power of more than one hard disk for a special purpose such as increased performance or fault-tolerance. RAID is more commonly done with SCSI drives, but it can be done with IDE drives.

There are several types of RAID. The following are the most commonly used RAID levels:

RAID 0   Also known as *disk striping*. This is technically not RAID, because it doesn't provide fault tolerance. Data is written across multiple drives, so one drive can be reading or writing while the next drive's read-write head is moving. This makes for faster data access. However, if any one of the drives fails, all content is lost.

RAID 1   Also known as *disk mirroring*. This is a method of producing fault tolerance by writing all data simultaneously to two separate drives. If one drive fails, the other contains all the data and can be switched to. However, disk mirroring doesn't help access speed, and the cost is double that of a single drive.

RAID 5   Combines the benefits of both RAID 0 and RAID 1. It uses a parity block distributed across all the drives in the array, in addition to striping the data across them. That way, if one drive fails, the parity information can be used to recover what was on the failed drive. A minimum of three drives is required.

   RAID works the same with SCSI drives as it does with IDE drives.

External Storage Drives

As prices decrease and capacities increase, the number of external storage drives in use has exponentially climbed. In addition to the SCSI variety discussed above, you can also find drives with USB connections as well as ones that connect directly to the network. USB drives are recognized by the operating system upon connection, and you simply install any additional software you want to use: Dantz Retrospect backup software is commonly included with many drives to allow you to use the external drive for automatic backups.

If the external drive connects directly to the network, simply connect it as outlined in the included instructions and install the optional software on any clients that will be maintaining it. The benefit of connecting directly to the network is that the drive(s) can be easily accessed by all clients.

Upgrading Display Devices

Before connecting or disconnecting a monitor, ensure that the power to both the PC and the monitor is off. Then connect a cable from the monitor to the PC's video card, and connect the monitor's power cord to an AC outlet. This cable may be the traditional VGA (DB-15) or a newer DVI (Digital Visual Interface) cable.

When installing a new display device, the most important component to have is the correct driver. The driver, discussed in more detail in subsequent chapters, is the software interface between the operating system and the hardware monitor. If you do not have the correct driver, it is possible that the display will not match what you should be viewing. The latest drivers can usually be downloaded from the display device manufacturer's website.

Other than the power supply, one of the most dangerous components to try to repair is the monitor, or CRT. We recommend that you *not* try to repair monitors. To avoid the extremely hazardous environment contained inside the monitor—it can retain a high-voltage charge for hours after it's been turned off—take it to a certified monitor technician or television repair shop. The repair shop or certified technician will know and understand the proper procedures to discharge the monitor, which involves attaching a resistor to the flyback transformer's charging capacitor to release the high-voltage electrical charge that builds up during use. The shop will also be able to determine whether the monitor can be repaired or needs to be replaced. Remember, the monitor works in its own extremely protected environment (the monitor case) and may not respond well to your desire to try to open it. The CRT is vacuum-sealed. Be extremely careful when handling it—if you break the glass, the CRT will implode, which can send glass in any direction.

Even though we recommend not repairing monitors, you are expected to know the safety practices to use when you need to do so. If you have to open a monitor, you must first discharge the high-voltage charge on it using a high-voltage probe. This probe has a very large needle, a gauge that indicates volts, and a wire with an alligator clip. Attach the alligator clip to a ground (usually the round pin on the power cord). Slip the probe needle under the high-voltage cup on the monitor. You'll see the gauge spike to around 15,000 volts and slowly reduce to zero. When it reaches zero, you may remove the high-voltage probe and service the high-voltage components of the monitor.

Upgrading Input/Multimedia Devices

The most common upgrades to input devices include transitioning to newer keyboards and mice.

With repeated use, keyboards can begin to wear out over time. The most common problem is a key sticking, or feeling not as responsive as the user would like. You can replace a standard PS/2 101-key keyboard with another by simply unplugging the old one and plugging in the new, and this is a very economical approach. Often today, though, the trend is to replace the older keyboard with a USB keyboard. As long as you are running an operating system that recognizes the keyboard when connected, such as Windows XP, the procedure is the same: Disconnect the old keyboard and connect the new.

Mice tend to age with repeated use as well, and they can be replaced with newer ones. The traditional corded mouse with a PS/2 connection can be replaced with another very inexpensively. You can also replace this mouse with an optical mouse (which gets around the problem of the ball wearing out, collecting dust, and so on) or a wireless mouse (which requires batteries for the signal). While the new mouse may also use PS/2, the more common trend is to utilize USB connections.

Identifying Tools and Diagnostics for PC Components

When you're troubleshooting hardware, there are a few common problems that any experienced technician should know about. These common issues usually have simple solutions. Knowing these problems and their solutions will make you a more efficient troubleshooter.

Most computer technicians spend a great deal of time troubleshooting and repairing systems. You should be familiar with common problems and solutions related to motherboards, hard disks, RAM, cooling, and the other major system components. However, before we talk about troubleshooting, we need to discuss the various tools you'd use.

Gathering Tools

Behind every great technician is an even greater set of tools. Your troubleshooting skills alone can get you only so far in diagnosing a problem; you also need some troubleshooting tools. And once the problem has been identified, you need a different set of tools—to fix the problem.

There are two major types of tools: hardware and software. We'll cover the hardware category first. (Note that there are very few questions on the test about this material; we're including it only for background and reference information.)

Hardware Tools

Hardware tools are those tools that are "hard," meaning you can touch them, as opposed to software tools, which cannot be touched. Several different kinds of hardware tools are used in PC service today. We will discuss the most commonly used tools in this section.

Screwdrivers

The tool that can most often be found in a technician's toolkit is a set of nonmagnetic screwdrivers. Most of the larger components in today's computers are mounted in the case with screws. If these components need to be removed, you must have the correct type of screwdriver available. There are three major types: flat blade, Phillips, and Torx.

Flat-Blade Screwdriver   The first type is often called a *flat-blade* or *flathead screwdriver*, although most people simply refer to it as a *standard screwdriver* (Figure 2.5). The type of screw that this screwdriver removes is not used much anymore (primarily because the screw head can be easily damaged).

We strongly advise against using a flathead screwdriver to *pry* anything open on a computer. Computers are usually put together very well, and if it seems that you need to pry something apart, it's probably because a screw or fastener is still holding it together somewhere.

Phillips Screwdriver   The most commonly used type of screwdriver for computers today is the *Phillips screwdriver* (Figure 2.6). Phillips-head screws are used because they have more surfaces to turn against, reducing the risk of damaging the head of the screw. More than 90 percent of the screws in most computers today are Phillips-head screws.

Phillips screwdrivers come in various sizes, identified by numbers. The most common size is a No. 2 Phillips. It is important to have a few different-sized screwdrivers available. If you use the wrong size (for example, a Phillips driver that is too pointed or too small), it can damage the head of the screw.

FIGURE 2.5   A flat-blade screwdriver and screw

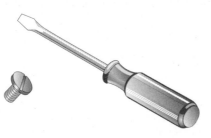

FIGURE 2.6   A Phillips screwdriver and screws

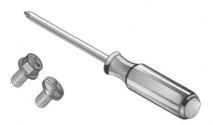

Torx Screwdriver   Finally, there is the type of screwdriver you use when you're working with those maddening little screws found on Compaq and Apple computers (as well as on dashboards of later-model GM cars). Of course, we're referring to the *Torx screwdriver* (Figure 2.7). The Torx type of screw has the most surfaces to turn against and therefore has the greatest resistance to screw-head damage. It is becoming more popular because people like its clean, technical look.

The sizes of Torx drivers are given with the designation T-*xx*, where the *xx* is replaced with a number from 1 through 20. The most common sizes are T-10 and T-15, but for some notebook computers you will need to have much smaller Torx drivers on hand.

Several screwdrivers are available with changeable tips, like bits for a drill. The advantage is that you can easily change these screwdrivers from a flat blade to a Phillips to a Torx just by changing the bits in the driver. The bits are usually stored in the handle of this type of screwdriver.

FIGURE 2.7   A Torx screwdriver and screw

Although it may seem convenient, don't use a multiple-bit driver that is mag-netized. Magnetism and computers don't make good friends. The magnetism can induce currents in conductors and burn out components without your knowledge. It could also erase magnetic disk storage media.

Needle-Nose Pliers

Another great tool to have in your toolkit is a pair or two of needle-nose pliers (Figure 2.8). They are great for grasping connectors or small screws when your hands are large. If a needle-nose is still too large for the job, a standard pair of tweezers will work as well.

FIGURE 2.8   A pair of needle-nose pliers

Flashlight

Another handy tool to have is a small flashlight. You'll know how especially handy it is when you're crawling around under a desk looking for a dropped screw or trying to find a particular component in a dark computer case. Maglite makes a powerful small flashlight that runs on two AA batteries. It also fits well into a toolkit.

Compressed Air

When you work on a computer, typically you'll first remove the case. While the cover is off, it is a good idea to clean the computer and remove the accumulated dust bunnies. These clumps of dust and loose fibers obstruct airflow and cause the computer to run hotter, thus shortening its life. The best way to clean out the dust is with clean, dry, compressed air. If you work for a large company, it will probably have a central air compressor as a source for com-pressed air. If an air compressor is not available, you can use cans of compressed air, but they can be expensive—especially if several are needed. In any case, be sure to take the computer outside before blasting it with compressed air.

Soldering Iron

One tool that is used less and less in the computer service industry is the soldering iron. You might use one occasionally to splice a broken wire; otherwise, you won't have much need for it.

The soldering iron isn't used much anymore because most components have been designed to use quick-disconnect connectors to facilitate easy replacement.

Traditionally, the soldering iron was used to connect electronic components to circuit boards. The most common iron used in electronic applications has a narrow tip rated at 15 to 20 watts. Generally, the component was heated with the iron, and then rosin-core solder (*not* acid-core) was applied to the component. The solder melted and, flowing into the joint, joined the component to the circuit board.

Wire Strippers

When you're soldering, it is a good idea to have a combination wire cutter/stripper available to prepare wires for connection. Stripping a wire simply means to remove the insulation from the portion that will be involved in the connection. The tool shown in Figure 2.9 is a good example of one that does both. However, you must be careful not to cut the wire when stripping it.

Multi-meters

The final hardware device we will discuss is the multi-meter (see Figure 2.10). It gets its name from the fact that it is a combination of several different kinds of testing meters, including an ohmmeter, ammeter, and voltmeter. In trained hands, it can help detect the correct operation or failure of several different types of components.

FIGURE 2.9   A combination wire cutter/stripper

FIGURE 2.10   A common multi-meter

The multi-meter consists of a digital or analog display, two probes, and a function selector switch. This rotary switch not only selects the function being tested, it also selects the range to which the meter is set. If you're measuring a battery using an older meter, you may have to set the range selector manually (to a range close to, but greater than, 1.5 volts). Newer meters, especially digital ones, automatically set their ranges appropriately.

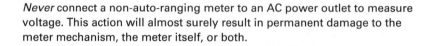

Never connect a non-auto-ranging meter to an AC power outlet to measure voltage. This action will almost surely result in permanent damage to the meter mechanism, the meter itself, or both.

When you're measuring circuits, it is very important to have the meter hooked up correctly so that the readings are accurate. Each type of measurement may require that the meter be connected in a different way. In the following paragraphs, we will detail the most commonly used functions of the multi-meter and how to make measurements correctly with them:

Measuring Resistance with a Multi-meter   *Resistance* is the electrical property most commonly measured in troubleshooting components. Measured in ohms, resistance is most often represented by the Greek symbol omega (Ω). A measurement of infinite resistance indicates that electricity cannot flow from one probe to the other. If you use a multi-meter to measure the resistance in a segment of wire and the result is an infinite reading, there is a very good chance that the wire has a break in it somewhere between the probes.

To measure resistance, you must first set the multi-meter to measure ohms. You do so either through a button on the front or through the selector dial. (Assume for the rest of this chapter that we are using newer auto-ranging multi-meters.) Then you must properly connect the component to be measured between the probes (see the warning and Figure 2.11). The meter will then display the resistance value of the component being measured.

Do not test resistance on components while they are mounted on a circuit board! The multi-meter applies a current to the component being tested. That current may also flow to other components on the board, thus damaging them.

Measuring Voltage with a Multi-meter   You follow a similar procedure when measuring voltage, but with two major differences. First, when measuring voltage, you must be sure you connect the probes to the power source correctly: With DC voltage, the + must connect to the positive side and the – to the negative. (The position doesn't matter with AC voltage.) Second, you must change the selector to VDC (Volts DC) or VAC (Volts AC), whichever is appropriate, to tell the meter what you are measuring (see Figure 2.12). Note that these settings protect the meter from overload. If you plug a meter into a power supply while it's still set to measure resistance, you may blow the meter.

FIGURE 2.11   Connecting a multi-meter to measure resistance

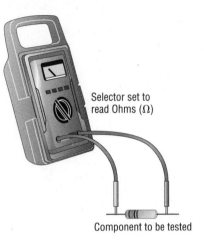

Selector set to
read Ohms (Ω)

Component to be tested

FIGURE 2.12   Connecting a multi-meter to measure voltage

Selector set to
read DC or
AC volts

Red probe (+)   Black probe (−)

Connect directly to terminals of power source

Battery

Measuring Current with a Multi-meter   The final measurement that is commonly made is that of current, in amperes (amps). Again, the procedure is similar to those used for the other measurements. A major difference here is that when you connect an ammeter to measure the current a circuit is drawing, you must connect the ammeter in series with the circuit being measured. Figure 2.13 illustrates the proper connection of a multi-meter to measure current.

FIGURE 2.13 Connecting a multi-meter to measure current

Selector set to
Amps (current)

Connect meter in series
with the circuit being tested

Red
Positive   probe (+)   Black
lead   probe (−)

Power source (unplugged)   Negative   Component being tested
lead

Collecting Software Tools

Hardware tools are used when major failures have occurred. However, a high portion of problems aren't related to a failing component but are due to malfunctioning or incorrectly configured hardware. You can use software diagnostics programs to troubleshoot some hardware problems. There are also programs available (usually from the component manufacturers) for configuring hardware, which relieves some or all of the task of setting jumpers or DIP switches. Finally, there are programs for testing the operation of other programs. In this section, we'll look briefly at two of the most important types of software tools.

Bootable Disks

The very best software diagnostic tool for DOS machines is a *bootable floppy disk*: a disk that has been formatted with a version of DOS and made bootable. It belongs in every technician's bag of essentials. You create a bootable disk by typing **FORMAT A: /S** with a blank floppy in the A: drive. Diagnostic and configuration programs can also be copied onto this disk and run without the possibility of software conflicts.

The advantage to this approach is that when the computer boots from a DOS bootable floppy disk, it doesn't have any drivers loaded that might conflict with your diagnostics. You can thus get real information. Also, if the machine boots successfully with a bootable disk but won't boot normally without it, this tells you that the motherboard, RAM, and major components are probably okay—which means that the problem may be the hard disk, a corrupt operating system (OS), or a device-driver conflict. From this point, you can narrow down the problem.

Software Diagnostics

Several software tools examine the hardware, report its configuration, and identify any errors they find. Programs like CheckIt Pro, QAPlus, and Microsoft's MSD (Microsoft Diagnostics) work in this manner. Other programs serve mainly as reference materials. For example, some manufacturers distribute CD-ROMs that contain all the reference material concerning their brand of computer equipment. (Toshiba, for instance, distributes a set of CD-ROMs to authorized service centers on a quarterly basis, with parts-ordering information, troubleshooting flowcharts, exploded diagrams, and field-replaceable unit (FRU) replacement information. All of the information is searchable—a very handy tool, indeed.)

Basic Aspects of Troubleshooting

Although everyone approaches troubleshooting from a different perspective, a few things should remain constant. Among them is a basic appreciation for data. Any hardware component can be replaced, but data often can't be. For that reason, it's important to always perform backups before making any changes.

It's important to assess every problem systematically and try to isolate the root cause. You always start out with an issue and whittle away at it until you can get down to the point where you can pinpoint the problem—this often means eliminating, or verifying, the obvious.

You must establish priorities—one user being unable to print to the printer of her choice isn't as important as a floor full of accountants unable to run payroll. Prioritize every job and escalate it (or de-escalate it) as you need to.

Last, but perhaps most important, document everything—not just that there was a problem but also the solution you found, the actions you tried, and the outcomes of each.

Basic Diagnostic Procedures

Just as all artists have their own style, all technicians have their own way to troubleshoot. Some people use their instincts; others rely on advice from other people. The most common troubleshooting tips can be condensed into a step-by-step process. You try each step, in order. If the first step doesn't narrow down the problem, you move on to the next step.

In this section, we'll look at each step in the troubleshooting process.

Step 1: Define the Problem

If you can't define the problem, you can't begin to solve it. You can define the problem by asking questions of the user. Here are a few questions to ask the user to aid in determining what the problem is, exactly:

Can you show me the problem?   This question is one of the best. It allows the user to show you exactly where and when he experiences the problem.

How often does this happen?   This question establishes whether this problem is a one-time occurrence that can be solved with a reboot or whether a specific sequence of events causes the problem to happen. The latter usually indicates a more serious problem that may require software installation or hardware replacement.

Has any new hardware been installed recently?   New hardware can mean compatibility problems with existing devices. Some Plug and Play devices install with the same resource settings as an existing device. This can cause both devices to become disabled.

Have any other changes been made to the computer recently?   If the answer is yes, ask if the user can remember approximately when the change was made. Then ask her approximately when the problem started. If the two dates seem related, then there's a good chance that the problem is related to the change. If it's a new hardware component, check to see that the hardware component was installed correctly.

Step 2: Check the Simple Stuff First

This step is the one that most experienced technicians overlook. Often, computer problems are the result of something simple. Technicians overlook these problems because they're so simple that the technicians assume they *couldn't* be the problem. Some examples of simple problems are shown here:

Is it plugged in?   And plugged in at both ends? Cables must be plugged in at *both ends* in order to function correctly. Cables can easily be tripped over and inadvertently pulled from their sockets.

Is it turned on?   This one seems the most obvious, but we've all fallen victim to it at one point or another. Computers and their peripherals must be turned on in order to function. Most have power switches with LEDs that glow when the power is turned on.

Is the system ready?   Computers must be ready before they can be used. *Ready* means the system is ready to accept commands from the user. An indication that a computer is ready is when the operating system screens come up and the computer presents you with a menu or a command prompt. If that computer uses a graphical interface, the computer is ready when the mouse pointer appears. Printers are ready when the Online or Ready light on the front panel is lit.

Do the chips and cables need to be reseated?   You can solve some of the strangest problems (random hang-ups or errors) by opening the case and pressing down on each socketed chip. This remedies the chip-creep problem discussed later in this chapter. In addition, you should reseat any cables to make sure that they're making good contact.

Step 3: Check to See If It's User Error

This error is common but preventable. The indication that a problem is due to user error is when a user says he can't perform some very common computer task, such as printing or saving a file. As soon you hear these words, you should begin asking questions to determine if it's simply a matter of teaching the user the correct procedure. A good question to ask following his statement of the problem is, "Were you *ever* able to perform that task?" If he answers no to this question, it means he's probably doing the procedure wrong. If he answers yes, you must move on to another set of questions.

🌐 Real World Scenario

The Social Side of Troubleshooting

When you're looking for clues as to the nature of a problem, no one can give you more information than the person who was there when it happened. She can tell you what led up to the problem, what software was running, and the exact nature of the problem ("It happened when I tried to print"), and she can help you re-create the problem, if possible.

Use questioning techniques that are neutral in nature. Instead of saying, "What were you doing when it broke?" be more compassionate and say, "What was going on when the computer decided not to work?" It sounds silly, but these types of changes can make your job a lot easier!

Step 4: Restart the Computer

It's amazing how often a simple computer restart can solve a problem. Restarting the computer clears the memory and starts the computer with a clean slate. Whenever we perform phone support, we always ask the customer to restart the computer and try again. If restarting doesn't work, try powering down the system completely and then powering it up again (rebooting). More often than not, that will solve the problem.

Step 5: Determine If the Problem Is Hardware or Software Related

This step is important because it determines on what part of the computer you should focus your troubleshooting skills. Each part requires different skills and different tools.

To determine whether a problem is hardware or software related, you can do a few things to narrow down the issue. For instance, does the problem manifest itself when the user uses a particular piece of hardware (a modem, for example)? If it does, the problem is more than likely hardware related.

This step relies on personal experience more than any of the other steps do. You'll without a doubt run into strange software problems. Each one has a particular solution. Some may even require reinstallation of the software or the entire operating system.

Step 6: If the Problem Is Hardware Related, Determine Which Component Is Failing

Hardware problems are pretty easy to figure out. If the modem doesn't work, and you know it isn't a software problem, the modem is probably the piece of hardware that needs to be replaced.

With some of the newer computers, several components are integrated into the motherboard. If you troubleshoot the computer and find a hardware component to be bad, there's a good chance that the bad component is integrated into the motherboard (for example, the parallel port circuitry) and the whole motherboard must be replaced—an expensive proposition, to be sure.

Step 7: Check Service Information Sources

As you may (or may not) have figured out by now, we're fond of old sayings. Another old saying applies here: "If all else fails, read the instructions." The service manuals are your instructions for troubleshooting and service information. Almost every computer and peripheral made today has service documentation in the form of books, service CD-ROMs, and websites. The latter of the three is growing in popularity as more and more service centers get connections to the Internet.

Step 8: If It Ain't Broke …

When doctors take the Hippocratic oath, they promise to not make their patients any sicker than they already were. Technicians should take a similar oath. It all boils down to "If it ain't broke, don't fix it." When you troubleshoot, make one change at a time. If the change doesn't solve the problem, revert the computer to its previous state before making a different change.

Step 9: Ask for Help

If you don't know the answer, ask one of your fellow technicians. They may have run across the problem you're having and know the solution.

This solution does involve a little humility. You must admit that you don't know the answer. It's said that the beginning of wisdom is "I don't know." If you ask questions, you'll get answers, and you'll learn from the answers. Making mistakes is valuable as well, as long as you learn from them.

Recognizing and Isolating Issues

Your value as a technician increases as you gain experience because of the reduced time it takes you to accomplish common repairs. Your ability to troubleshoot by past experiences and gut feelings will make you more efficient and more valuable, which in turn will allow you to advance and earn a better income. This section will give you some guidelines you can use to evaluate common hardware issues that you're sure to face.

POST Routines

Every computer has a diagnostic program built into its BIOS called the *power-on self-test* (*POST*). When you turn on the computer, it executes this set of diagnostics. Many steps are involved the POST, but they happen very quickly, they're invisible to the user, and they vary among BIOS versions. The steps include checking the CPU, checking the RAM, checking for the presence of a video card, and so on. The main reason to be aware of the POST's existence is that if it encounters a problem, the boot process stops. Being able to determine at what point the problem occurred can help you troubleshoot.

One way to determine the source of a problem is to listen for a *beep code*. This is a series of beeps from the computer's speaker. The number, duration, and pattern of the beeps can sometimes tell you what component is causing the problem. However, the beeps differ depending on the BIOS manufacturer and version, so you must look up the beep code in a chart for your particular BIOS. Different BIOS manufacturers use the beeping differently. AMI BIOS, for example, relies on a raw number of beeps and uses patterns of short and long beeps.

Another way to determine a problem during the POST routine is to use a *POST card*. This is a circuit board that fits into an ISA or PCI expansion slot in the motherboard and reports numeric codes as the boot process progresses. Each of those codes corresponds to a particular component being checked. If the POST card stops at a certain number, you can look up that number in the manual that came with the card to determine the problem.

 BIOS Central is a website containing charts detailing the beep codes and POST error codes for many different BIOS manufacturers: `http://www` `.bioscentral.com/`.

Applying Basic Troubleshooting Techniques

Being able to identify and address basic troubleshooting issues is an important aspect of any PC technician's skill set. In the following sections, we will discuss the basic items to check for common problems.

Identifying Motherboard and CPU Problems

Most motherboard and CPU problems manifest themselves by the system appearing completely dead. However, "completely dead" can be a symptom of a wide variety of problems, not only with the CPU or motherboard but also with the RAM or the power supply. So a POST card (described in the preceding section) may be helpful in narrowing down the exact component that is faulty.

When a motherboard fails, it's usually because it has been damaged. Most technicians can't repair motherboard damage; the motherboard must be replaced. Motherboards can become damaged due to physical trauma, exposure to electrostatic discharge (ESD), or short-circuiting. To minimize the risk of these damages, observe the following rules:

- Handle a motherboard as little as possible, and keep it in an antistatic bag whenever it's removed from the PC case.

- Keep all liquids well away from the motherboard, because water can cause a short circuit.

- Wear an antistatic wrist strap when handling or touching a motherboard.

- When installing a motherboard in a case, make sure you use brass stand-offs with paper washers to prevent any stray solder around the screw holes from causing a short circuit with the metal of the screw.

A CPU may fail because of physical trauma or short-circuiting, but the most common cause for a CPU not to work is failure to install it properly. With a PGA-style CPU, ensure that the CPU is oriented correctly in the socket. With an SECC-style CPU, make sure the CPU is completely inserted into its slot.

Identifying I/O Ports and Cables

I/O ports include legacy parallel and serial, USB, and FireWire ports, all of which are used to connect external peripherals to the motherboard. When a port doesn't appear to be functioning, check the following:

- The cables are snugly connected.

- The port has not been disabled in BIOS Setup.

- The port has not been disabled in Device Manager in Windows.

- No pins are broken or bent on the male end of the port or on the cable being plugged into it.

If you suspect that the cable, rather than the port, may be the problem, swap out the cable with a known good one. If you don't have an extra cable, you can test the existing cable with a multi-meter by setting it to ohms and checking the resistance between one end of the cable and the other.

Use a pin-out diagram, if available, to determine which pin matches up to which at the other end. There is often—but not always—an inverse relationship between the ends. In other words, at one end pin 1 is at the left, and at the other end it's at the right on the same row of pins.

Identifying Cooling Issues

A PC that works for a few minutes and then locks up is probably experiencing overheating because of a heat sink or fan not functioning properly. To troubleshoot overheating, first check all fans inside the PC to ensure they're operating, and make sure any heat sinks are firmly attached to their chips.

In a properly designed, properly assembled PC case, air flows in a specific path from the power supply fan through the vent holes. Cases are designed to cool by making the air flow in a certain way. Therefore, operating a PC with the cover removed can make a PC more susceptible to overheating, even though it's "getting more air."

Similarly, operating a PC with empty expansion slot backplates removed can inhibit a PC's ability to cool itself properly because the extra holes change the airflow pattern from what was intended by its design.

Although CPUs are the most common component to overheat, occasionally chips on other devices, particularly video cards, may also overheat. Extra heat sinks or fans may be installed to cool these chips.

Identifying Case Issues

A PC case holds the drives in its bays, holds the power supply, and has lights and buttons on the front. For the first two of those functions, make sure that the drives and the power supply are tightly fastened in the case with screws.

If one of the lights or buttons on the front of the PC isn't functioning, remove the cover and check the wires that run from the back of that button/light to the motherboard. If the wire has become detached, reattach it. Refer to the motherboard manual or the writing on the motherboard itself to determine what goes where.

Identifying Hard-Disk System Problems

Hard-disk system problems usually stem from one of three causes:

- The adapter (that is, the IDE or SCSI interface) is bad.
- The disk is bad.
- The adapter and disk are connected incorrectly.

The first and last causes are easy to identify, because in either case the symptom will be obvious: The drive won't work. You won't be able to get the computer to communicate with the disk drive.

However, if the problem is a bad disk drive, the symptoms aren't as obvious. As long as the BIOS POST routines can communicate with the disk drive, they're usually satisfied. But the POST routines may not uncover problems related to storing information. Even with healthy POST results, you may find that you're permitted to save information to a bad disk, but when you try to read it back, you get errors. Or the computer may not boot as quickly as it used to, because the disk drive can't read the boot information successfully every time.

In some cases, reformatting the drive can solve the problems described in the preceding paragraph. In other cases, reformatting brings the drive back to life only for a short while. The bottom line is that read and write problems usually indicate that the drive is malfunctioning and should be replaced soon.

WARNING Never low-level format IDE or SCSI drives! They're low-level formatted from the factory, and you may cause problems by using low-level utilities on these types of drives.

Identifying Modem Problems

The most common peripheral problems are those related to modem communications. The symptoms of these problems include the following:

- The modem won't dial.
- The modem keeps hanging up in the middle of the communications session.
- The modem spits out strange characters to the terminal screen.

If the modem won't dial, first check the simple things (for example, that the modem cable is plugged into the correct RJ-11 port on the modem and plugged into a working RJ-11 in the wall). Next, verify that it has been configured correctly in Windows, including its resource assignments. Modem and port settings in Windows XP/2000 can be set through Control Panel ➤ Phone and Modems Options ➤ Modems tab, as shown in Figure 2.14.

Some modems work only under Windows because some of their functions rely on Windows software; these are called *Winmodems* or *software modems*. If such a modem doesn't work immediately upon installation, try running the Setup software that came with the modem.

If the configuration is correct, and Windows recognizes the modem, it should work for dial-up networking connections.

FIGURE 2.14   Configuring a modem in Windows XP

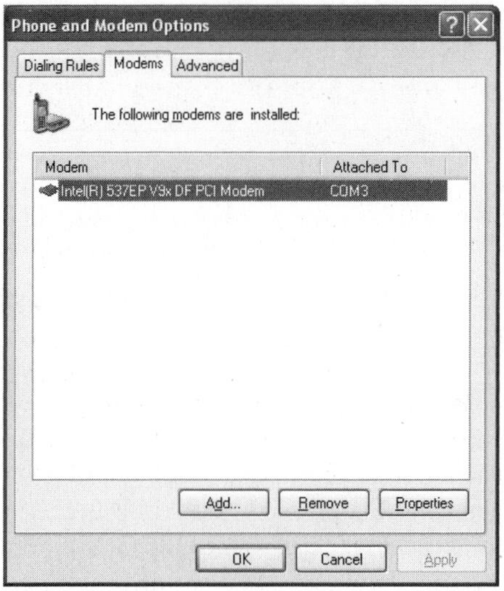

Identifying *AT* Commands

When you're using a terminal application such as HyperTerminal, it's important to use the correct initialization commands. These are the commands sent to the modem by the communications program to initialize it. These commands tell the modem such things as how many rings to wait before answering, how long to wait after the last keystroke was detected for it to disconnect, and at what speed to communicate.

Modem initialization commands are known as the *Hayes command set* or the *AT command set*, because each Hayes modem command starts with the letters AT (presumably calling the modem to ATtention).

Each AT command does something different. The letters AT by themselves ask the modem if it's ready to receive commands. If it returns *OK*, the modem is ready to communicate. If you receive *Error*, there is an internal modem problem that may need to be resolved before communication can take place.

Table 2.1 lists a few of the most common AT commands, their functions, and the problems they can solve. You can send these commands to the modem by opening a terminal program such as Windows Terminal or HyperTerminal and typing them in. All commands should return *OK* if they're successful.

TABLE 2.1   Common AT Commands

Command	Function	Usage
AT	Tells the modem that what follows the letters AT is a command that should be interpreted	Used to precede most commands.

TABLE 2.1 Common AT Commands *(continued)*

Command	Function	Usage
ATDT *nnnnnnn*	Dials the number *nnnnnnn* as a tone-dialed number	Used to dial the number of another modem if the phone line is set up for tone dialing.
ATDP *nnnnnnn*	Dials the number *nnnnnnn* as a pulse-dialed number	Used to dial the number of another modem if the phone line is set up for rotary dialing.
ATA	Answers an incoming call manually	Places the line off-hook and starts to negotiate communication with the modem on the other end.
ATH0 (or +++ and then ATH0)	Tells the modem to hang up immediately	Places the line on-hook and stops communication. (Note: The 0 in this command is a zero, not the letter *O*.)
AT&F	Resets the modem to factory default settings	This setting works as the initialization string when others don't. If you have problems with modems hanging up in the middle of a session or failing to establish connections, use this string by itself to initialize the modem.
ATZ	Resets the modem to power-up defaults	Almost as good as AT&F, but may not work if power-up defaults have been changed with S-registers.
ATS0-*n*	Waits *n* rings before answering a call	Sets the default number of rings that the modem will detect before taking the modem off-hook and negotiating a connection. (Note: The 0 in this command is a zero, not the letter *O*.)
ATS6-*n*	Waits *n* seconds for a dial tone before dialing	If the phone line is slow to give a dial tone, you may have to set this register to a number higher than 2.
,	Pauses briefly	When placed in a string of AT commands, the comma causes a pause to occur. Used to separate the number for an outside line (many businesses use 9 to connect to an outside line) and the real phone number (for example, 9,555-1234).

TABLE 2.1   Common AT Commands *(continued)*

Command	Function	Usage
*70 or 1170	Turns off call waiting	The click you hear when you have call waiting (a feature offered by the phone company) will interrupt modem communication and cause the connection to be lost. To disable call waiting for a modem call, place these commands in the dialing string like so: *70,555-1234. Call waiting will resume after the call is hung up.
CONNECT	Displays when a successful connection has been made	You may have to wait some time before this message is displayed. If this message isn't displayed, the modem couldn't negotiate a connection with the modem on the other end of the line, possibly due to line noise.
BUSY	Displays when the number dialed is busy	If this message is displayed, some programs wait a certain amount of time and try again to dial.
RING	Displays when the modem has detected a ringing line	When someone is calling your modem, the modem displays this message in the communications program. You type **ATA** to answer the call.

If two computers can connect but they both receive garbage on their screens, there's a good chance that the computers don't agree on the communications settings. Settings such as data bits, parity, stop bits, and compression must all agree in order for communication to take place.

Identifying Keyboard and Mouse Problems

Usually, keyboard problems are environmental. Keyboards get dirty, and the keys start to stick.

> **NOTE** If a keyboard is malfunctioning (for example, sending the wrong characters to the display), it's most cost effective to replace it rather than spend hours attempting to fix it, because keyboards are fairly inexpensive.

One way to clean a keyboard is with the keyboard cleaner sold by electronics supply stores. This cleaner foams up quickly and doesn't leave a residue behind. Spray it liberally on the keyboard and keys. Work the cleaner in between the keys with a stiff toothbrush. Blow away the excess with a strong blast of compressed air. Repeat until the keyboard functions properly. If you have to clean a keyboard that's had a soft drink spilled on it, remove the key caps before you perform the cleaning procedure; doing so makes it easier to reach the sticky plungers.

> Remember that most of the dollars spent on systems are for labor. If you spend an hour cleaning a $12.00 keyboard, then you have probably just cost your company $20.00. Knowing how to fix certain things doesn't necessarily mean that you *should* fix them. Always evaluate your workload, the cost of replacement, and the estimated cost of the repair before deciding on a course of action.

Similarly, most mouse problems, such as the pointer failing to move in one direction or the other or the pointer jumping around onscreen, are due to dirt building up inside the mouse. To clean a standard mouse, remove the plate on the bottom of the mouse that holds the ball in place; then remove the ball and clean the inside chamber with an alcohol-dipped cotton swab. Clean the ball itself with mild soap and water. Don't use alcohol on the ball, because it tends to dry out the rubber.

Identifying Display Device Problems

As a general rule, there are two types of video problems: no video and bad video. If there is no video, you should first check the monitor by transferring it to another machine that you know is working and see if it works there. If it does not work, then you should replace it (remember: CompTIA recommends not working on a monitor because of the electrical charge stored within). If the display does work once transferred to another machine, then you should focus on the video card: is it seated? Does it need replaced? etc.

If there is a display, but it is bad, then you should first focus on the settings. Make certain you have the correct driver for the monitor and that you are using settings that are appropriate for that monitor. If the problem persists after you have ruled out those possibilities, then you should focus on the video card and consider replacing it.

Identifying Floppy and Other Removable Disk-Drive Problems

Most floppy-drive problems result from bad media. Your first troubleshooting technique with floppy-drive issues should be to try a new disk.

One of the most common problems that develops with floppy drives is misaligned read-write heads. The symptoms are fairly easy to recognize—you can read and write to a floppy on one machine but not on any others. This is normally caused by the mechanical arm in the floppy drive becoming misaligned. When the disk was formatted, it wasn't properly positioned on the drive, thus preventing other floppy drives from reading it.

Numerous commercial tools are available to realign floppy-drive read-write heads. They use a floppy drive that has been preformatted to reposition the mechanical arm. In most cases, though, this fix is temporary—the arm will move out of place again fairly soon. Given the inexpensive nature of the problem, the best solution is to spend a few dollars and replace the drive.

Another problem you may encounter is a phantom directory listing. For example, suppose you display the contents of a floppy disk, and then you swap to another floppy disk but the listing stays the same. This is almost always a result of a faulty ribbon cable; a particular wire in the ribbon cable signals when a disk swap has taken place, and when that wire breaks, this error occurs.

Identifying Sound Card Problems

Sound cards are traditionally one of the most problem-ridden components in a PC. They demand a lot of PC resources and are notorious for being inflexible in their configuration. The most common problems related to sound cards involve resource conflicts (IRQ, DMA, or I/O address). The problem is much less pronounced on PCI than on ISA cards.

Luckily, most sound-card vendors are aware of the problems and ship very good diagnostic utilities to help resolve them. Use your PC troubleshooting skills to determine the conflict, and then reconfigure until you find an acceptable set of resources that aren't in use.

Some sound cards aren't completely Plug and Play compatible. Windows may detect that new hardware has been installed but be unable to identify the new hardware as a working sound card. To fix this problem, run the Setup software that came with the sound card.

Identifying CD-ROM/DVD Issues

CD-ROM and DVD problems are normally media related. Although compact disc technology is much more reliable than that for floppy disks, it's not perfect. Another factor to consider is the cleanliness of the disc. On many occasions, if a disc is unreadable, cleaning it with an approved cleaner and a lint-free cleaning towel will fix the problem.

If the operating system doesn't see the drive, start troubleshooting by determining whether the drive is receiving power. If the tray will eject, you can assume there is power to it. Next, check BIOS Setup (for IDE drives) to make sure the drive has been detected. If not, check the master/slave jumper on the drive, and make sure the IDE adapter is set to Auto, CD-ROM, or ATAPI in BIOS Setup. Once inside the case, ensure that the ribbon cable is properly aligned with pin 1 and that both the drive and motherboard ends are securely connected.

In order to play movies, a DVD drive must have MPEG decoding capability. This is usually accomplished via an expansion board, but it may be built into the video card or sound card, or it may require a software decoder. If DVD data discs will play but not movies, suspect a problem with the MPEG decoding.

If a CD-RW or DVD drive works normally as a regular CD-ROM drive but doesn't perform its special capability (doesn't read DVD discs or doesn't write to blank CDs), perhaps you need to install software to work with it. For example, with CD-RW drives, unless you're using an operating system such as Windows XP that supports CD writing, you must install CD-writing software in order to write to CDs.

Identifying NIC Issues

In general, network interface cards (NICs) are added to a PC via an expansion slot. The most common issue that prevents network connectivity is a bad or unplugged patch cable.

Cleaning crews and the rollers on the bottoms of chairs are the most common threats to a patch cable. In most cases, wall jacks are placed 4 to 10 feet away from the desktop. The patch cables are normally lying exposed under the user's desk, and from time to time damage is done to the cable, or it's inadvertently snagged and unplugged. When you troubleshoot a network adapter, start with the most rudimentary explanations first. Make sure the patch cable is tightly plugged in, and then look at the card and see if any lights are on. If there are lights on, use the NIC's documentation to help troubleshoot. More often than not, shutting down the machine, unplugging the patch and power cables for a moment, and then reattaching them and rebooting the PC will fix an unresponsive NIC.

 A properly connected NIC should typically have one light illuminated (the link light). If the link light is not illuminated, it indicates a problem with the NIC, the patch cable, or the device the patch cable is connecting to (hub, switch, server, and so on) Other lights that may be illuminated include a speed light, duplex light, and/or activity light.

 Wake On LAN cards have more problems than standard network cards. In our opinion, this is because they're always on. In some cases, you'll be unable to get the card working again unless you unplug the PC's power supply and reset the card.

Identifying BIOS Issues

Computer BIOSs don't go bad; they just become out-of-date. This isn't necessarily a critical issue—they will continue to support the hardware that came with the box. It *does*, however, become an issue when the BIOS doesn't support some component that you would like to install—a larger hard drive, for instance.

Most of today's BIOSs are written to an EEPROM and can be updated through the use of software. Each manufacturer has its own method for accomplishing this. Check out the documentation for complete details.

 If you make a mistake in the upgrade process, the computer can become unbootable. If this happens, your only option may be to ship the box to a manufacturer-approved service center. Be careful!

Identifying Power-Supply Problems

Power-supply problems can manifest themselves as a system that doesn't respond in any way when the power is turned on. When this happens, open the case, remove the power supply, and replace it with a new one. Partial failures, or intermittent power-supply problems, are much less simple. A completely failed power supply gives the same symptoms as a malfunctioning wall socket, UPS or power strip, a power cord that is not securely seated, or some mother-board shorts (such as those caused by an improperly seated expansion card, memory stick, CPU, and the like), and you want to rule out those items before you replace the power supply and find you still have the same problem as when you started. Be aware that different cases have different types of on/off switches. The process of replacing a power supply is a lot easier if you purchase a replacement with the same mechanism.

 Never try to repair or disassemble a power supply. There is a high risk of elec-trocution, and the relatively low cost of a new power supply makes working on them something to avoid.

Identifying Miscellaneous Problems

Some common problems don't fit well into categories. This section lists some common hard-ware issues you'll be faced with.

Dislodged Chips and Cards

The inside of a computer is a harsh environment. The temperature inside the case of some Pentium computers is well over 100° F! When you turn on your computer, it heats up. Turn it off, and it cools down. After several hundred such cycles, some components can't handle the stress and begin to move out of their sockets. This phenomenon is known as *chip creep,* and it can be really frustrating.

Chip creep can affect any socketed device, including ICs, RAM chips, and expansion cards. The solution to chip creep is simple: Open the case, and reseat the devices. It's surprising how often this is the solution to phantom problems of all sorts.

Another important item worth mentioning is an unresponsive but freshly unboxed PC. With the introduction of the Type II– and Type II–style of processors, the number of dead boxes increased dramatically. In fact, at that time I was leading a 2,000-unit migration for a large financial institution. As with any large migration, time and manpower were in short supply. The average dead PC ratio was about 1 out of every 20. When about 10 DOAs had stacked up, I stayed after work one night to assess the problem. After checking the power supply, RAM, and cables on these integrated systems, an examination of the chip provided me with the fix. These large, top-heavy processors can become dislodged during shipment. Shortly after, manufacturers began using a heavier attachment point for the slot style of pro-cessor, which has helped tremendously.

Environmental Problems

Computers are like human beings: They have similar tolerances to heat and cold. In general, anything comfortable to us is comfortable to computers. They need lots of clean, moving air to keep them functioning.

Dirt, grime, paint, smoke, and other airborne particles can become caked on the inside of the components. This is most common in automotive and manufacturing environments. The contaminants create a film that coats the components, causing them to overheat and/or con-duct electricity on their surface. Blowing out these exposed systems with a can of condensed air from time to time can prevent damage to the components. While you're cleaning the components, be sure to clean any cooling fans in the power supply or on the heat sink.

To clean the power supply fan, blow the air from the inside of the case. When you do this, the fan will blow the contaminants out the cooling vents. If you spray from the vents toward the inside of the box, you'll be blowing the dust and grime inside the case or back into the fan motor.

One way to ensure that the environment has the least possible effect on your computer is to always leave the *blanks* in the empty slots on the back of your box. These pieces of metal are designed to keep dirt, dust, and other foreign matter from the inside of the computer. They also maintain proper airflow within the case to ensure that the computer doesn't overheat.

Performing Preventative Maintenance on Personal Computers

This section outlines some preventative maintenance products and procedures. Preventative maintenance is one of the most overlooked ways to reduce the cost of ownership in any environment.

Cleaning a computer system is the most important part of maintaining it. Computer components get dirty. Dirt reduces their operating efficiency and, ultimately, their life. Cleaning them is definitely important. But cleaning them with the right cleaning compounds is equally important. Using the wrong compounds can leave residue behind that is more harmful than the dirt you're trying to remove!

Most computer cases and monitor cases can be cleaned using mild soap and water on a clean, lint-free cloth. Make sure the power is off before you put anything wet near a computer. Dampen (don't soak) a cloth with a mild soap solution, and wipe the dirt and dust from the case. Then wipe the moisture from the case with a dry, lint-free cloth. Anything with a plastic or metal case can be cleaned in this manner.

Don't drip liquid into any vent holes on equipment. CRTs in particular have vent holes in the top.

To clean a monitor screen, use glass cleaner designed specifically for monitors and a soft cloth. Don't use commercial window cleaner, because the chemicals in it can ruin the antiglare coating on some monitors.

To clean a keyboard, use canned air to blow debris out from under keys, and use towelettes designed for use with computers to keep the key tops clean. If you spill anything on a keyboard, you can clean it by soaking it in distilled, *demineralized water*. The minerals and impurities have been removed from this type of water, so it won't leave any traces of residue that might interfere with the proper operation of the keyboard after cleaning. Make sure you let the keyboard dry for at least 48 hours before using it.

The electronic connectors of computer equipment, on the other hand, should never touch water. Instead, use a swab moistened in distilled, *denatured isopropyl alcohol* (also known as electronics cleaner and found in electronics stores) to clean contacts. Doing so will take the oxidation off the copper contacts.

A good way to remove dust and dirt from the inside of the computer is to use compressed air. Blow the dust from inside the computer using a stream of compressed air. However, be sure you do this outdoors, so you don't blow dust all over your work area or yourself. You can also use a vacuum, but it must be designed specifically for electronics—such models don't generate ESD and have a finer filter than normal.

To prevent a computer from becoming dirty in the first place, control its environment. Make sure there is adequate ventilation in the work area and that the dust level isn't excessive. To avoid ESD, you should maintain 50 to 80 percent humidity in the room where the computer is operating.

You should visually inspect the computer for signs of distress within it. Discolored areas on the board are often caused by overheating. The overheating can be caused by power surges or overclocking and is an indication that all is not right.

One unique challenge when cleaning printers is spilled toner. It sticks to everything and should not be inhaled. Use a vacuum designed specifically for electronics. A normal vacuum's filter isn't fine enough to catch all the particles, so the toner may be circulated into the air.

If you get toner on your clothes, use a magnet to get it out (toner is half iron).

Removable media devices such as floppy and CD drives don't usually need to be cleaned during preventative maintenance. Clean one only if you're experiencing problems with it. Cleaning kits sold in computer stores provide the needed supplies. Usually, cleaning a floppy drive involves using a dummy floppy disk made of semi-abrasive material. When you insert the disk in the drive, the drive spins it, and the abrasive action on the read-write head removes any debris.

An uninterruptible power supply (UPS) should be checked periodically as part of the preventative maintenance routine to make sure that its battery is operational. Most UPSs have a Test button you can press to simulate a power outage. You will find that batteries wear out over time, and you should replace the battery in the UPS every couple of years in order to keep the UPS dependable.

The motherboard contains a battery, as well, which is used to maintain internal settings when power is not provided to the unit. Resembling large watch batteries, these entities tend to have a considerable life, on average, but can lose their charge over time. If you boot a system and find that the date and time and other variables have not been maintained, you will want to change the internal battery.

Remember, preventative maintenance is more than just manipulating hardware; it also encompasses running software utilities on a regular basis to keep the file system fit. These utilities can include Disk Defragmenter, ScanDisk, Check Disk, and Disk Cleanup.

Summary

In this chapter, you finished learning about personal computer components, specifically storage devices, display devices, and input and multimedia devices.

In addition, we discussed identifying various problems that can occur, as well as various solutions or approaches to finding a solution. Finally, we walked through troubleshooting theory and techniques and concluded by examining some preventative maintenance recommendations and issues.

Exam Essentials

Know how many pins an IDE/PATA/ATA-5/ATA-6 cable has.   A cable for use with these technologies has 40 pins. You're likely to be asked to choose a cable in a scenario question simply by knowing how many pins the drive requires.

Know how a controller works in a master/slave environment.   When you have a master and a slave, only one of the two controllers controls data transfers. You're likely to be asked a scenario question that relates to this environment.

Know what other devices besides hard drives use IDE interfaces.   With the popularity of IDE technology, manufacturers have introduced tape drives and CD-ROMs that use IDE interfaces.

Know what can be used to clean computer components.   Many types of cleaning solutions can be used to perform these procedures. Be familiar with which option is best for each component. Which ones can be cleaned with water? Which ones require alcohol? Which ones need canned air?

Know why the proper cleaning solutions should be used.   Using the wrong cleaning solution can damage components. Along with choosing the right cleaning solution, understand why the improper solutions are inappropriate for a particular component.

Review Questions

1. Which of the following steps is not necessary when replacing a floppy drive?

   A. Turn off the PC.

   B. Disconnect the power supply from the drive.

   C. Disconnect the ribbon cable from the drive.

   D. Disconnect the audio cable from the drive.

2. When attaching a ribbon cable to a drive, if there is no marking for pin 1, which way should you orient the red stripe?

   A. Closest to the power supply connector

   B. Farthest away from the power supply connector

   C. Facing the top of the drive

   D. Facing the bottom of the drive

3. To fix a bad power supply in a desktop PC, you should _____.

   A. Remove and replace the entire power supply box.

   B. Disassemble the power supply and replace the coils.

   C. Disassemble the power supply and replace the capacitors.

   D. Disassemble the power supply and replace the resistors.

4. How many bits of data does a high-speed serial cable carry simultaneously in a single direction?

   A. 1

   B. 8

   C. 32

   D. Depends on the cable

5. Which of the following could not be connected to an IDE interface on a typical motherboard?

   A. ATA-2

   B. EIDE

   C. ATAPI

   D. All of these could be connected.

6. What do UltraDMA/66 and higher require?

   A. Cable Select configuration

   B. An 80-wire cable

   C. Operating system support

   D. All of the above

7. On the primary IDE channel, if a single hard disk is attached, its jumper should be set to _____.

    A. Slave

    B. Single if available; otherwise Master

    C. Master

    D. Boot

8. Which type of SCSI termination uses voltage regulators inside the terminator?

    A. Active

    B. Passive

    C. High-byte

    D. All of the above

9. You install a new UltraATA/100 hard disk in an old PC, connecting it directly to the primary IDE on the motherboard. You use the 80-wire ribbon cable that came with it. Performance testing indicates that the new drive is not performing up to UltraATA/100 standards. What could you try next?

    A. Reformat the hard disk using NTFS 5.0.

    B. Add an ATA/100-compatible expansion board and connect the drive to it.

    C. Partition the disk into smaller logical drives.

    D. Set up the drive in BIOS Setup to use PIO mode 4.

10. Which AT command resets the modem?

    A. ATH0

    B. ATM0

    C. ATZ

    D. ATDT

11. While inspecting a motherboard, you notice a discolored area. What is usually a cause of this?

    A. Spilled liquid

    B. Improper manufacture

    C. Power surge

    D. Underclocking

12. What does the red stripe on a ribbon cable indicate?

    A. Pin 16

    B. Pin 1

    C. The manufacturer's trademark

    D. Parity

13. Display devices can be connected to a PC using DB-15 connectors or _____.

    A. HDT

    B. DVI

    C. VBA

    D. VBP

14. What utility can be used with Windows XP to format drives?

    A. Disk Design

    B. Disk Plan

    C. Disk Management

    D. Disk Prep

15. Which ATA standard supports UltraDMA/133?

    A. ATA-7

    B. ATA-8

    C. ATA-9

    D. ATA-10

16. What type of female DB-style connector does SCSI-2 use? (Choose all that apply.)

    A. 25-pin

    B. 50-pin

    C. 68-pin

    D. 72-pin

17. Internally, what type of wire ribbon cable does SCSI use?

    A. 25-pin

    B. 50-pin

    C. 68-pin

    D. 72-pin

18. When changing display devices or upgrading to a newer one, what is one of the most crucial components to have?

    A. Manufacturer's resolution recommendations

    B. Antistatic mat

    C. Ribbon cable

    D. Correct driver

19. Every computer has a diagnostic program built into its BIOS called the _____.

    A. CMOS

    B. BIOS

    C. POST

    D. DNS

20. What two devices are commonly used to cool components within a PC? (Choose two.)

    A. Fans

    B. Compressed air

    C. Freon

    D. Heat sinks

Answers to Review Questions

1. D. There is no audio cable associated with a floppy drive; that's only for CD drives. All the other listed actions are necessary when replacing a floppy drive.

2. A. Closest to the power supply connector is a general rule for stripe orientation. Because the cable attaches horizontally to the drive, there is no "facing the top" or "facing the bottom" orientation.

3. A. You should never attempt to disassemble a power supply, because of the risk of electrocution and the relatively low cost of a new power supply.

4. A. By definition, a serial cable carries only one bit of data at a time.

5. D. All of these are types of IDE. ATA-2 and EIDE are the same thing—a rather dated but still useful version of the ATA standard. ATAPI is a non-hard-disk type of IDE device.

6. B. UltraDMA/66 requires a special ribbon cable with extra wires to cut down on crosstalk. It does not require Cable Select to be in use, and it does not require specific operating system support because it operates at a lower level than the OS.

7. B. If there is a Single setting, it should be used. Otherwise use Master. Slave is never appropriate for a single drive. There is no such jumper setting as Boot.

8. A. Active termination uses voltage regulators. Passive termination uses resistors. High-byte termination is a specialty type that terminates only half of the bytes; it's used to transition between a wide and a narrow device on the same chain.

9. B. Because it is an older PC, its IDE interface probably does not support UltraATA/100, so adding an expansion board would be the next step. Repartitioning or reformatting would make no difference. Using a PIO mode in BIOS could actually impede the drive's performance.

10. C. ATZ is a reset command. ATH0 hangs up. ATM0 turns off the speaker. ATDT dials whatever number follows it.

11. C. Discolored areas on the board are often caused by overheating. This can be the result of power surges or overclocking.

12. B. The red stripe on the cable indicates pin 1.

13. B. Digital Visual Interface (DVI) connectors can be used to connect display devices to PCs.

14. C. The Disk Management utility can be used in Windows XP to format drives.

15. A. ATA-7 supports UltraDMA/133.

16. A, B, C. SCSI-2 uses a 25-, 50-, or 68-pin female DB-style connector.

17. B. SCSI internal cabling uses a 50-wire ribbon cable with several keyed connectors.

18. D. The correct driver is needed in order to assure the new display device works as it should.

19. C. Every computer has a diagnostic program built into its BIOS called the power-on self-test (POST).

20. A, D. Heat sinks and fans are commonly used to cool components within a PC.

Understanding Laptops and Portable Devices

THE FOLLOWING COMPTIA A+ ESSENTIALS EXAM OBJECTIVES ARE COVERED IN THIS CHAPTER:

✓ **2.1 Identify the fundamental principles of using laptops and portable devices**

- Identify names, purposes and characteristics of laptop-specific:
    - Form factors such as memory and hard drives
    - Peripherals (e.g. docking station, port replicator and media / accessory bay)
    - Expansion slots (e.g. PCMCIA I, II and III, card and express bus)
    - Ports (e.g. mini PCI slot)
    - Communication connections (e.g. Bluetooth, infrared, cellular WAN, Ethernet)
    - Power and electrical input devices (e.g. auto-switching and fixed-input power supplies, batteries)
    - LCD technologies (e.g. active and passive matrix, resolution such as XGA, SXGA+, UXGA, WUXGA, contrast radio, native resolution)
    - Input devices (e.g. stylus / digitizer, function (Fn) keys and pointing devices such as touch pad, point stick / track point)
- Identify and distinguish between mobile and desktop motherboards and processors including throttling, power management and WiFi

✓ **2.2 Install, configure, optimize and upgrade laptops and portable devices**

- Configure power management
  - Identify the features of BIOS-ACPI
  - Identify the difference between suspend, hibernate and standby
- Demonstrate safe removal of laptop-specific hardware such as peripherals, hot-swappable devices and non-hot-swappable devices

✓ **2.3 Identify tools, basic diagnostic procedures and troubleshooting techniques for laptops and portable devices**

- Use procedures and techniques to diagnose power conditions, video, keyboard, pointer and wireless card issues, for example:
  - Verify AC power (e.g. LEDs, swap AC adapter)
  - Verify DC power
  - Remove unneeded peripherals
  - Plug in external monitor
  - Toggle Fn keys
  - Check LCD cutoff switch
  - Verify backlight functionality and pixilation
  - Stylus issues (e.g. digitizer problems)
  - Unique laptop keypad issues
  - Antenna wires

✓ **2.4 Perform preventative maintenance on laptops and portable devices**

- Identify and apply common preventative maintenance techniques for laptops and portable devices, for example: cooling devices, hardware and video cleaning materials, operating environments including temperature and air quality, storage, transportation and shipping

Just 10 to 15 years ago, portable computers were luxuries that were affordable to only the wealthy or to the select few business-people who traveled extensively. As with all other technologies, though, portable systems have gotten smaller, lighter (more portable), more powerful, and less expensive. Because the technology and price disparity between the two platforms has decreased significantly, more laptops than desktops are now sold every year.

Every indication is that the movement toward mobile computing will continue, so you definitely need to be well versed in portable technologies, which contain both nifty features and frustrating quirks. For this discussion, assume that a *portable computer* is any computer that contains all the functionality of a desktop computer system but is portable. Most people define *portable* in terms of weight and size. So we can discuss things on the same level, let's define *portable* as less than 20 pounds and smaller than an average desktop computer.

Most portable computers fall into one of three categories: luggable, laptop, or PDA.

The original portable computers were hardly portable, hence the unofficial term "luggable." They were the size of a small suitcase and could weigh 50 pounds. Not only were they greatly inferior to desktops in technology, they were also outrageously expensive. It's no wonder few people purchased them. Compaq, Kaypro, and Osborne made some of the first luggable computers.

Laptops were the next type of portable computer. They contain a built-in keyboard, pointing device, and LCD screen in a clamshell design. They are also called *notebook* computers because they resemble large notebooks. Most portable computers in use today are laptop computers.

The final type of portable computer, which has really taken off in the last 10 years, is the palmtop computer, also known as a personal digital assistant (PDA). These computers are designed to keep the information you need close by so you can access it whenever you need it. There are two different approaches to the PDA. Pen-based assistants are basically small digital notepads that use a stylus and handwriting-interpretation software to perform operations. The Palm series of PDAs and HP iPAQ are two examples of this type of PDA.

The other type of PDA is known as a *handheld PC (HPC)*. These are basically shrunken laptops. HPCs run an operating system known as Windows Mobile (the most popular previous mobile version was Windows CE). Windows Mobile is basically Windows XP, shrunk to fit into the limited RAM of the HPC. Instead of using a mouse to point to the icons and menus in Windows Mobile, you use a stylus on the HPC's touch-sensitive screen or a thumbwheel on the side of the device. The RIM BlackBerry is the most common handheld PC.

Many portable computers now also incorporate cell phone features as well. The line between mobile computing and mobile communication has definitely blurred, and we'll likely see a continuation of this technology consolidation for years to come.

In this chapter, you will learn about laptop computer architecture and how it differs from desktops, as well as installing and configuring laptop hardware, troubleshooting laptops, and performing preventative maintenance on laptop computers.

Understanding Laptop Architecture

Laptops are similar to desktop computers in architecture in that they contain many parts that perform similar functions. However, the parts that make up a laptop are completely different from those in desktop computers. The obvious major difference is size; laptops are space-challenged. Another primary concern is heat. Restricted space means less airflow, meaning parts can heat up and overheat faster.

To overcome space limitations, laptop parts are physically much smaller and lighter, and they must fit into the compact space of a laptop's case. (It might not sound like much, but there really is a major difference between a 4.5 pound laptop and a 5.5 pound laptop if you're carrying it around in its case with a shoulder strap all day.) Also, laptop parts are designed to consume less power and to shut themselves off when not being used (although many desktops have components that go into a low-power state when not active, such as video circuitry). Finally, most laptop components, especially the motherboard, are proprietary—the LCD screen from one laptop will not necessarily fit on another.

In this section, you will learn about the various components that make up laptops and how they differ from desktop computer components. If you don't remember exactly what each component does, it may help you to refer back to Chapter 1 occasionally as you read this chapter.

Laptops vs. Desktops

If you've ever shopped for a laptop, you have no doubt noticed that the prices of desktop PCs are often quite a bit lower than for notebook computers, yet they are faster and more powerful. If you've ever wondered what makes a laptop so much different than a PC, here are the primary differences between laptops and desktops:

Portability   This is probably the most obvious difference. Laptops are designed to be portable. They run on batteries, so you aren't tied to one spot at home or at the office. Networking options are available that allow you to connect to a network wirelessly and do work from just about anywhere, including malls, airports, Starbucks, and so on. As anyone who's tried to bring their full-tower PC to a LAN party can tell you, desktops just aren't that portable.

Cost   Laptops cost more—sometimes as much as 60 to 80 percent more—than desktop computers with similar features. The primary reason is that portability requires small components and unique proprietary designs for those components so they fit into the small size necessary. Miniature versions of components cost more money than standard-size (desktop) versions.

Performance   By and large, laptops are always going to lose out somewhere in the performance department. Compromises must often be made between performance and portability, and considering that portability is the major feature of a laptop, performance is what usually suffers. While it is possible to have a laptop with comparable performance to a desktop, the amount of money one would have to spend for a "desktop replacement" laptop is considerable. This is not to say that a laptop can't outperform a desktop, it's just that the "bang for the buck" factor is higher in a desktop.

Expandability Because desktop computers were designed to be modular, their capabilities can be upgraded quite easily. It is next to impossible to upgrade the processor or motherboard on most laptops. Other than memory and hard drives, most laptop upgrades consist of adding an external device though one of the laptop's ports, such as a USB port.

Quality of Construction Considering how much abuse laptops get, it is much more important that the materials used to construct the laptop case and other components be extremely durable. Not that it isn't important in a desktop—but it's more important in a laptop.

🌐 Real World Scenario

Building Your Own

You can't build your own laptop. Because laptop components are designed to fit exacting specifications to fit properly inside the notebook, there generally are no universal motherboards, video boards, and so on for laptops. Memory and hard drives are the exception. You can get different brands of memory and hard drives for laptops, but you can't buy a motherboard from one company and the video circuitry from another. Even things as mundane as floppy drives are designed to work only with a specific model.

Now that we've illustrated the primary differences between laptops and desktops, let's examine the parts of the laptop and what they do.

Laptop Case

A typical laptop case is made up of three main parts: the *display* (usually an LCD display), the *case frame* (the metal reinforcing structure inside the laptop that provides rigidity and strength and that most components mount to), and the laptop's *case* itself (the plastic cover that surrounds the components and provides protection from the elements). The cases are typically made of some type of plastic (usually ABS plastic or ABS composite) to provide for light weight as well as strength.

A few notebooks have cases made of a strong, lightweight metal, such as aluminum or titanium. However, the majority of laptop cases are made of plastic.

Laptop cases are made in what is known as a *clamshell design*. In a clamshell design, the laptop has two halves, hinged together at the back. Usually, the display is the top half and everything else is in the bottom half.

Occasionally, part of the laptop's case will crack and need to be replaced. However, you usually can't just replace the cracked section. Most often, you must remove every component from inside the laptop's case and swap the components over to the new case. This is a labor-intensive process, because the screws in laptops are often very small and hard to reach. Often, repairing a cracked case may cost several hundred dollars in labor alone. Most times, people who have cracked laptop cases wait until something else needs to be repaired before having the case fixed. I have a crack on my laptop that I haven't bothered to fix for this very reason.

Motherboards and Processors

As with desktop computers, the motherboard of a laptop is the backbone structure to which all internal components connect. However, with a laptop, almost all components are integrated onto the motherboard, including onboard circuitry for the serial, parallel, USB, IEEE 1394, video, expansion, and network ports of the laptop.

Laptop Motherboards

The primary differences between a laptop motherboard and a desktop motherboard are the lack of standards and the much smaller form factor. As mentioned earlier, most motherboards are designed along with the laptop case so that all the components will fit inside. Therefore, the motherboard is mostly proprietary. Figure 3.1 shows an example of a laptop motherboard.

FIGURE 3.1   A laptop motherboard

To save space, components of the video circuitry (and possibly other circuits as well) are placed on a thin circuit board that connects directly to the motherboard. This circuit board is often known as a *daughterboard*.

Having components performing different functions (such as video, audio, and networking) integrated on the same board is a mixed bag. On one hand, it saves a lot of space. On the other hand, if one part goes bad, you have to replace the entire board, which is more expensive than just replacing one expansion card.

Laptop Processors

Just like in desktop computers, the processor is the brain of the computer. And just like everything else, compared to desktop hardware laptop hardware means a smaller device that isn't quite as powerful. At the time of this writing, the fastest laptop processor readily available is 2.26 GHz, whereas you can get desktop processors at nearly 4 GHz.

As mentioned earlier (and will be mentioned over and over until you're sick of hearing it), laptops have less space and heat is a major concern. Add to that the fact that processors are the hottest-running component, and you can see where cooling is a major concern. To help combat this heat problem, laptop processors are engineered with the following features:

Laptop processors mount to the motherboard differently than desktop processors.   Nearly all desktop processors mount using pin connectors, while a few others use card edge connectors. Pins and sockets are big and bulky, meaning they're not our friends. Laptop processors are generally either soldered directly to the motherboard or attached using the Micro-FCBGA (Flip Chip Ball Grid Array) standard, which uses balls instead of pins. In most cases, this means that the processor cannot be removed, meaning no processor upgrades are possible.

Laptop processors run at lower voltages and clock speeds than desktop processors.   Two ways to combat heat are to slow the processor down (run it at a lower speed) or give it less juice (run it at a lower voltage). Again, performance will suffer vs. a desktop processor, but lowering heat is the goal here. In addition, most laptops will run in a lower power state when on battery power instead of plugged into an AC outlet, in an effort to extend the life of the battery.

Laptop processors have active sleep and slow-down modes.   This is also known as processor *throttling*. The motherboard works closely with the operating system to determine if the processor really needs to run at full speed. If it doesn't, it's slowed down to save energy and heat. When more processing power is needed, the CPU is throttled back up.

One of the best features of many laptop processors is that they include built-in wireless networking. By far the most common laptop processor is the *Pentium M* chip made by Intel. The Pentium M comprises three separate components:

- The Mobile Intel Express chipset (such as the Mobile Intel 915GM Express or the Mobile Intel 910GML), which is the graphics memory controller hub
- The Intel/PRO Wireless Network Connection, providing an integrated wireless LAN connection
- The Intel Centrino chipset, which is the "brain" of the chipset, designed to run on lower power than the desktop processor

Some portable computers will simply use stripped-down versions of desktop processors such as the Pentium 4. While there's nothing wrong with this, my feeling is that if there's something specifically designed for notebooks, I would rather use that than something that's been retrofitted for notebook use.

Memory

Notebooks don't use standard desktop computer memory chips, because they're too big. In fact, for most of the history of laptops there were no standard types of memory chips. If you wanted to add memory to your laptop, you had to order it from the laptop manufacturer. Of course, because you could get memory from only one supplier, you got the privilege of paying a premium over and above a similar-sized desktop memory chip.

However, there are now two common types of laptop memory package: SoDIMM and the MicroDIMM. To see what kind of memory your laptop uses, check either the manual or the manufacturer's website. You can also check third-party memory producers' websites (such as www.crucial.com).

Interestingly, the Apple iMac desktop uses SoDIMMs.

SoDIMM

The most common memory form factor for laptops is called a *Small Outline DIMM (SoDIMM)*. They're much smaller than standard DIMMs, measuring about 67 millimeters (2.6 inches) long and 32 millimeters (1.25 inches) tall. SoDIMMs are available in a variety of configurations, including 32-bit (72-pin) and 64-bit (144-pin EDO, 144-pin SDRAM, 200-pin DDR, and 200-pin DDR2) options. Figure 3.2 shows an example of the 144-pin variety.

Just like with desktop computers, make sure the SoDIMM you want to put into the laptop is compatible with the motherboard. The same standards that apply to desktop memory compatibility apply to laptops, such as PC2700, PC3200, DDR2, and so forth. Current DDR and DDR2 technologies allow you to get SoDIMMS up to 2GB in size.

FIGURE 3.2   144-pin SoDIMM

MicroDIMM

The newest and smallest RAM form factor is the *MicroDIMM*. The MicroDIMM is an extremely small RAM form factor. In fact, it is over 50 percent smaller than a SoDIMM—only about 45.5 millimeters (about 1.75 inches) long and 30 millimeters (about 1.2 inches, a bit bigger than a quarter) wide. Another major difference is that the MicroDIMM does not have any notches on the bottom. Figure 3.3 shows a 172-pin MicroDIMM.

It was designed for the ultralight and portable subnotebook style of computer. MicroDIMMs have either 144 pins or 172 pins and are similar to DIMMs in that they are 64-bit memory modules. They also have less capacity (currently topping out at 1GB) and cost a bit more than SoDIMMs.

FIGURE 3.3   172-pin MicroDIMM

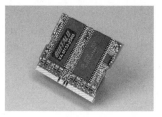

Storage

Nearly all laptops have a hard drive, but not all laptops have both a floppy drive and a CD-ROM drive. Many times there just isn't room for both, and considering floppy drives are practically obsolete, why have one anyway? Often there is a *drive bay* that can be used to hold either drive. If this drive bay exists, users generally keep the CD-ROM drive installed most of the time and leave out the floppy drive. In some cases, the floppy drive is an external device that you connect with a special cable to a proprietary connector. Figure 3.4 shows an example of one of these connectors, and Figure 3.5 shows an example of a laptop floppy drive. Notice how thin the floppy drive is and how compact the electronics are.

FIGURE 3.4   A proprietary floppy connector

FIGURE 3.5   A laptop floppy drive

Laptops don't have the room for the full-size 3¹/₂-inch hard drives that desktop computers use. Instead, they use a small-form-factor hard drive that's only 2¹/₂ inches wide and less than ¹/₂ inch thick! These drives share the same interface technologies (usually ATA and UDMA) as desktop computers; however, they use smaller connectors. Figure 3.6 shows an example of a standard hard drive compared to a laptop hard drive.

FIGURE 3.6   A desktop hard drive compared to a laptop hard drive

Laptop CD-ROM drives come in many different kinds, just like desktop CD-ROM drives. You can get standard CD-ROM, CD-R, CD-RW, DVD, DVD-RAM, and (probably the most popular option) CD-RW/DVD-ROM drives that can both burn CDs and play DVD movies. It is also possible to get CD-ROM drives that manage to cram a floppy drive into the same drive bay along with the CD-ROM.

Often, these drives are very small in form factor (usually less than ¹/₂ inch high). Figure 3.7 shows an example of a desktop CD-ROM drive compared to a laptop CD-ROM drive. Note that the laptop drive is very small, but it has all the functionality of a desktop unit. The drive mechanism and circuits have all been miniaturized to save space. The functionality is basically the same, but the cost is higher. Any time a component's functionality remains the same while its size decreases, you will notice an increase in price over the standard-size item.

FIGURE 3.7   A desktop CD-ROM drive compared to a laptop CD-ROM drive

CD or DVD burners are great to have on laptops as backup devices. Simply copy the contents of the hard drive (or just important files) to the CD or DVD, and store the disc in a safe location.

Displays

Portable computers were originally designed to be compact versions of their bigger brothers. They crammed all the components of the big desktop computers into a small, suitcase-like box called (laughably) a *portable computer*. No matter what the designers did to reduce the size of the computer, the display remained as large as the desktop version's. That is, until an inventor found that when he passed an electric current through a semicrystalline liquid, the crystals aligned themselves with the current. It was found that by combining transistors with these liquid crystals, patterns could be formed. These patterns could represent numbers or letters. The first application of these *liquid crystal displays* (LCDs) was the LCD watch. It was rather bulky, but it was cool.

As LCD elements got smaller, the detail of the patterns became greater, until one day someone thought to make a computer screen out of several of these elements. This screen was very light compared to computer monitors of the day, and it consumed little power. It could easily be added to a portable computer to reduce the weight by as much as 30 pounds. As the components got smaller, so did the computer, and the laptop computer was born.

LCDs are not just limited to laptops; desktop versions of LCD displays are available as well. They use the same technologies as their laptop counterparts but on a much larger scale. Plus, these LCDs are available in either analog or digital interfaces for the desktop computer. The analog interface is exactly the same as the interface used for most monitors. All digital signals from the computer are converted into analog signals by the video card, which are then sent along the same 15-pin connector as a monitor. Digital LCDs, on the other hand, are directly driven by the video card's internal circuitry. They require the video card to be able to support digital output (through the use of a Digital Visual Interface, or DVI, connector). The advantage is that since the video signal never goes from digital to analog, there is no conversion-related quality loss. Digital displays are generally sharper than their analog counterparts.

LCD Technologies

Two major types of LCD displays are used today: active-matrix screen and passive-matrix screen. The main differences lie in the quality of the image. However, both types use lighting behind the LCD panel to make the screen easier to view:

Active matrix   An active-matrix screen works in a similar manner to the LCD watch. The screen is made up of several individual LCD pixels. A transistor behind each pixel, when switched on, activates two electrodes that align the crystals and turn the pixel dark. This type of display is very crisp and easy to look at. The major disadvantage of an active-matrix screen is that it requires large amounts of power to operate all the transistors. Even with the backlight turned off, the screen can still consume battery power at an alarming rate. Most laptops with active-matrix screens can't operate on a battery for more than two hours.

Passive matrix   Within the passive-matrix screen are two rows of transistors: one at the top, another at the side. When the computer's video circuit wants to turn on a particular pixel (turn it black), it sends a signal to the x- and y-coordinate transistors for that pixel, thus turning them on. This then causes voltage lines from each axis to intersect at the desired coordinates, turning the desired pixel black. Figure 3.8 illustrates this concept.

The main difference between active matrix and passive matrix is image quality. Because the computer takes a millisecond or two to light the coordinates for a pixel in passive matrix displays, the response of the screen to rapid changes is poor, causing, for example, an effect known as *submarining*: On a computer with a passive-matrix display, if you move the mouse pointer rapidly from one location to another, it will disappear from the first location and reappear in the new location without appearing anywhere in between.

FIGURE 3.8   A passive-matrix display

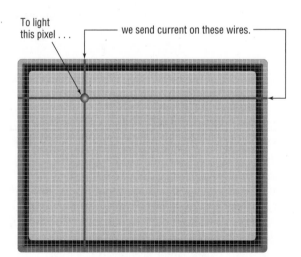

LCD Resolutions

The concept of resolution on an LCD screen is similar to the concept on a standard CRT monitor. Resolution is measured by the number of pixels used to draw the screen. If you use more pixels, you can display a higher the level of detail. Typically, you will see resolution noted like this: 1024 × 768 or 1280 × 1024. At 1024 × 768, the screen will display 768 rows of pixels 1024 columns wide, for a total of 786,432 pixels. At 1280 × 1024, the number of pixels increases to 1,310,720—nearly double the pixels for what doesn't sound like much of a difference! As you might expect, it requires better technology and more video memory to display higher resolutions.

One of the best features about LCD technology is the flexibility to play with the *aspect ratio* of the screen. The aspect ratio gives a proportion of how wide the screen is versus how tall it is (specifically, it's the image width divided by image height). Basically, it's another way of looking at resolution. Standard desktop monitors and televisions have a 4:3 ratio. High-definition televisions (and many new monitors) use 16:9, and widescreen televisions and monitors are often 16:10.

There are over 20 different video standards that various LCD monitors support, including XGA, SXGA+, UXGA, and WUXGA.

XGA

The *Extended Graphics Array (XGA)* was introduced in 1990 by IBM. It's often thought of as a synonym for the 1024 × 768 standard, but it can really support more than just that resolution. XGA was rather limited in that it could support only 65,536 colors in 800 × 600 resolution, and 256 colors in 1024 × 768 resolution. The XGA-2 upgrade provided true color (16 million) options for both resolutions, as well as better refresh rates for monitors.

SXGA+

Common on 14- and 15-inch LCD laptop displays, the *Super eXtended Graphics Array plus (SXGA+)* standard has a resolution of 1400 × 1050 pixels. It's a version of SXGA, which is used in many 17-inch to 19-inch desktop LCD monitors. SXGA+ became popular starting in 2004.

UXGA and WUXGA

Ultra eXtended Graphics Array (UXGA) was the next step in technology after the SXGA standard. It has a resolution of 1600 × 1200. For Dell computers, the standard is called UGA.

If you take a digital video standard and make it widescreen, you need to call it something else. Hence, *Widescreen UXGA (WUXGA)*. It's the same technology as UXGA, with a resolution of 1920 × 1200 and a 16:10 aspect ratio.

Some of the newest standards take digital video to an extremely high level. They include Quad eXtended Graphics Array (QXGA) and its derivatives, which have four times as many pixels as XGA, and Hex eXtended Graphics Array (HXGA) and its derivatives, which has 16 times as many pixels as XGA. One of the newest flavors, Wide Hex Ultra eXtended Graphics Array (WHUXGA), can support resolutions up to 7680 × 4800 pixels (37 million total) at a16:10 aspect ratio.

Table 3.1 highlights the some LCD video standards, their standard resolutions, and their aspect ratio:

TABLE 3.1   LCD Video Standards

Name	Resolution	Ratio
Extended Graphics Array (XGA)	800 × 600	4:3
	1024 × 768	4:3
Super eXtended Graphics Array plus (SXGA+)	1400 × 1050	4.3
Ultra eXtended Graphics Array (UXGA)	1600 × 1200	4.3
Widescreen Ultra eXtended Graphics Array (WUXGA)	1920 × 1200	16:10

Keeping track of all the new developments in digital video can be a tedious and mind-blowing task unless you're immersed in the technology every day. Most of the time, knowing the specifics of the standards does you good only if you're being tested on it. For the "real world" times, just know that there are different standards. Also, be able to find differences if you need to on the Web when you're laptop shopping.

Native Resolution

One of the peculiarities of LCD displays is that they have a single fixed resolution, known as the *native resolution*. As opposed to CRT monitors, which can change resolution to match the frequency emitted by the video signal, LCD monitors are fixed.

What this means in practical terms is that if you have an LCD monitor that isn't totally compatible with your video card, you could see some distortion of the image on the screen. This is because the LCD monitor might be forced to try to scale the image (called interpolation) to fit it on the screen. Depending on how bad the fit is, you might see distortion. This is particularly noticeable when dealing with disparate aspect ratios, like 4:3 (which would be 16:12) versus 16:10. The monitor will try to adjust the picture accordingly, but there isn't a true, even mapping of pixels, and you will probably have distortion.

Normally this isn't much of an issue with laptops, because the displays are usually proprietary to one manufacturer or line of laptops. If you replace one LCD panel with another, it's likely to have the same aspect ratio. It tends to be more of a problem with desktops, where the monitor is easily exchangeable.

Contrast Ratio

The *contrast ratio* is the measure of the ratio between the lightest color and the darkest color the screen is capable of producing. One of the original problems with LCD displays, and a continuing problem with cheaper versions, is that they have low ratios. A display with a low ratio won't show a "true black" very well, and the other colors will look washed out when you have a light source nearby. Try to use the device in full sunshine, and you're not going to see much of anything. Also, lower contrast ratios mean that you'll have a harder time viewing images from the side as opposed to being directly in front of the display.

 A common myth is that too much contrast is a bad thing. Not true. You might pay more for higher contrast ratios, but depending on where you use your laptop, the investment might be worth it.

Ratios for LCD monitors typically start out around 500:1 or 600:1, and 800:1 is common as well. Higher-end displays claim ratios of 1200:1 or higher.

One caveat to contrast ratios is that a manufacturer can boost the ratio simply by increasing how bright the monitor can go. This doesn't do anything to help the display of darker colors, though. All it will do is wash out the lighter colors and make white seem like it's glowing, which is hardly useful to you, the monitor viewer. So while the contrast ratio can be a good thing to consider, don't just take it at face value. Always compare displays to see which one works better for the situation in which you use it.

LCD Maintenance

To keep the quality of the image on an LCD the best, the screen must be cleaned often. Liquid crystal displays are typically coated with a clear plastic covering. This covering commonly gets dirtied by fingerprints as well as a generous coating of dust. The best way to clean the LCD lens coating is to wipe it off occasionally with a damp cloth. Doing so will ensure that the images stay crisp and clear.

A laptop's display takes the most power to run. It is also the device that drains the battery the fastest when the laptop is running on batteries only.

Because the technology behind LCD displays is complex, there are almost no service procedures for the display in a laptop. Most often, when the display is broken, it can be removed by a service technician (usually the display is held in with only a few screws and a plastic bezel) and exchanged with the manufacturer for a new one. This procedure may be under warranty (depending on the length of the manufacturer's warranty).

One particular sore spot with laptop owners and manufacturers is the phenomenon known as *bad pixels*. Most higher-end laptops use active-matrix displays (they have a transistor for each pixel on the screen). With these types of displays, small defects sometimes occur during the manufacturing process, causing a few transistors in the display to not function. The corresponding pixels on the screen are completely black. To put this in perspective, a 15-inch laptop display (at a resolution of 1028×768 pixels) has 789,504 pixels. If one of them is black, you may not notice it (unless it's right in the center of your field of vision).

Manufacturers have warranty stipulations that indicate they will replace the display only if a certain number of pixels go bad. Manufacturers usually consider a display to be fully operational if 99.999 percent of its pixels are operating. On the previously mentioned 1028×768 display, that would mean the manufacturer would replace the screen only if eight of the pixels were bad. This figure is actually pretty good—some manufacturers indicate in their warranties that 99.99 percent is good enough (meaning approximately 79 pixels would have to be bad before they would replace the display).

Many people seem to think that if one pixel is bad, the display should be replaced. However, the pixels are so small that you might hardly notice the problem. Bad pixels are part of the manufacturing process; if you buy a laptop, it's entirely likely that you will have a couple of bad pixels. Be aware of your laptop manufacturer's warranty policy.

Input Devices

Because of laptops' small size, getting data into them presents unique challenges to designers. They must design a keyboard that fits within the case of the laptop. They must also design some sort of pointing device that users can use in graphical interfaces like Windows. The primary challenge in both cases is to design these peripherals so they fit within the design constraints of the laptop (low power and small form factor) while remaining usable.

Keyboards

A standard-size desktop keyboard wasn't designed to be portable. It wouldn't fit well with the portable nature of a laptop. That usually means laptop keys are not normal size; they must be smaller and packed together more tightly. People who learned to type on a typewriter or regular computer often have a difficult time adjusting to a laptop keyboard because the keys are smaller and closer together.

Laptop keyboards are built into the lower portion of the clamshell. Sometimes, they can be removed easily to access peripherals below them (like memory and hard drives, as in the IBM ThinkPad series).

Because of the much smaller space available for keys, some laptop keys (like the number pad, Home, Insert, PgUp, and PgDn keys) are consolidated into special multifunction keys. These keys are accessed through the standard keys by using a special function key (usually labeled Fn in blue lettering). To use a multifunction key, you press the function key (Fn, which is usually located between the Ctrl and Alt keys) and the key that contains the function you want (for example, press Fn + ? for the slash [/] normally found on a numeric keypad on a regular keyboard).

Mice and Pointing Devices

In addition to the keyboard, you must have a method of controlling the on-screen pointer in the Windows interface. There are many methods of doing this, but the most common are as follows:

- Trackball
- Touchpad
- Touchpoint
- Touch screen

Some laptops use multiple pointing devices to appeal to a wider variety of people who have different pointing-device preferences.

Most laptops today include a mouse/keyboard port, a USB port, or both. Either of these ports can be used to add an input device like a mouse or a standard-size keyboard.

Trackball

Many early laptops used trackballs as pointing devices. A *trackball* is essentially the same as a mouse turned upside down. When you move the ball with your thumb or fingers, the on-screen pointer moves in the same direction and at the same speed you move the trackball.

Trackballs were cheap to produce. However, the primary problem with trackballs was that they did not last as long as other types of pointing devices; a trackball picks up dirt and oil from operators' fingers, and those substances clog the rollers on the trackball and prevent it from functioning properly.

Touchpad

To overcome the problems of trackballs, a new technology that has become known as the touchpad was developed. *Touchpad* is actually the trade name of a product. But, like Kleenex, the trade name is now used to describe an entire genre of products that are similar in function.

A *touchpad* is a device that has a pad of touch-sensitive material. The user draws with their finger on the touchpad, and the on-screen pointer follows the finger motions. Included with the touchpad are two buttons for left- or right-clicking (although with some touchpads, you can perform the functions of the left-click by tapping on the touchpad).

Touchpoint

With the introduction of the ThinkPad series of laptops, IBM introduced a new feature known as the *Touchpoint* (also known as a *finger mouse*). The Touchpoint is a pointing device that uses a small rubber-tipped stick. When you push the Touchpoint in a particular direction, the on-screen pointer goes in same direction. The harder you push, the faster the on-screen pointer moves. The Touchpoint allows fingertip control of the on-screen pointer, without the reliability problems associated with trackballs.

Touchpoints have their own problems. Often, the stick does not return to center properly, causing the pointer to drift when not in use.

Touch Screen

The last type of pointing device we'll discuss can be found in use at many department stores: the little informational *kiosks* with screens that respond to your touch and give you information about product specials or bridal registries. Instead of a keyboard and mouse, these computer screens have a film over them that is sensitive to touch. This technology is known as a *touch screen* (see Figure 3.9). With most of the interfaces in use on touch screens, touching a box drawn on the monitor does the same thing as double-clicking that box with a mouse. These screens are most commonly found on monitors; however, with the advent of the *tablet PC* (a laptop designed to be held like a pad of paper), the touch screen is becoming more popular as an input device for a laptop.

FIGURE 3.9   A typical touch screen

Cleaning a touch screen is usually just as easy as cleaning a regular monitor. With optical touch screens, the monitor *is* a regular monitor, so it can be cleaned with glass cleaner. However, if the screen has a capacitive coating, glass cleaner may damage it. Instead, use a cloth dampened with water to clean the dirt, dust, and fingerprints from the screen.

Expansion Bus and Ports

Although laptop computers are less expandable than their desktop counterparts, they can be expanded to some extent. Laptops have expansion ports similar to those found on desktop computers, as well as a couple that are found only on laptops.

PCMCIA (PC Card) Expansion Bus

The tongue-twister *PCMCIA* stands for Personal Computer Memory Card International Association. The PCMCIA was organized to provide a standard way of expanding portable computers. The PCMCIA bus was originally designed to provide a way of expanding the memory in a small, handheld computer. The PCMCIA bus has been renamed *PC Card* to make it easier to pronounce. It uses a small expansion card (about the size of a credit card). Although it is primarily used in portable computers, PC Card bus adapters are available for desktop PCs. The PCMCIA bus now serves as a universal expansion bus that can accommodate any device.

The first release of the PCMCIA standard (PCMCIA 1, the same used in the original handheld computer) defined only the bus to be used for memory expansion. The second release (PCMCIA 2) is the most common; it is used throughout the computer industry and has remained relatively unchanged. PCMCIA 2 was designed to be backward compatible with version 1, so memory cards can be used in the version 2 specification. It was then modified to version 2.1 so card and socket services could be used as a standard driver platform.

Finally, PCMCIA version 3 (PCMCIA 5.0) increased the bus width to 32-bit and the bus speed from 8MHz to a maximum of 33MHz. In addition, the new CardBus adapters used PCI-like access methods, and the throughput speeds increased dramatically (at the time this text was written, speeds up to 132Mbps were possible).

> PCMCIA standards jumped from 2.1 to 5.0 as PCMCIA and JEIDA standards were merged. At the same time, the name officially changed from PCMCIA to CardBus.

Information and Identification

PCMCIA's bus width is either 16-bit or 32-bit, as previously discussed. Also, PC Cards support only one IRQ (a problem if you need to install in a PC Card bus two devices that both need interrupts). PC Cards also do not support bus mastering or Direct Memory Access (DMA). However, because of its flexibility, PCMCIA has quickly become a very popular bus for all types of computers (not just laptops).

Three major types of PC Cards (and slots) are in use today. Each has different uses and physical characteristics (see Figure 3.10). Coincidentally, they are called Type I, Type II, and Type III:

- Type I cards are 3.3mm thick and are most commonly used for memory cards.
- Type II cards are 5mm thick and are mostly used for modems and LAN adapters, but also for sound cards, SCSI controllers, and other devices as well. This is the most common PC Card type found today, and most systems have at least two Type II slots (or one Type III slot).
- The Type III slot is 10.5mm thick. Its most common application is PC Card hard disks.

FIGURE 3.10 PC Card types, by thickness

In addition to the card, the PC Card architecture includes two other components:

- *Socket Services software* is a BIOS-level interface to the PCMCIA bus slot. When loaded, it hides the details of the PC Card hardware from the computer. This software can detect when a card has been inserted and what type of card it is.
- *Card Services software* is the interface between the application and Socket Services. It tells the applications which interrupts and I/O ports the card is using. Applications that need to access the PC Card don't access the hardware directly; instead, they tell Card Services that they need access to a particular feature, and Card Services gets the appropriate feature from the PC Card.

This dual-component architecture allows the PCMCIA architecture to be used in different types of computer systems (that is, not just Intel's). For example, Apple laptop computers currently use PC Cards for modems and LAN interface cards and are based on Motorola processors.

Mini PCI

Mini PCI is an adaptation of the Peripheral Component Interconnect (PCI) standard used in desktop computers. As its name implies, it's just a smaller version (about $1/4$ the size of PCI cards) designed primarily for laptops.

These cards reside internally in the laptop, with their connection ports generally lining up with the edge of the outside of the case.

Mini PCI is functionally identical to the PCI version 2.2, meaning it's a 32-bit, 33MHz bus with a 3.3V-powered connection. It also supports bus mastering and DMA. There are three different Mini PCI form factors: Type I, Type II, and Type III. The size and connector types are listed in Table 3.2.

TABLE 3.2   Mini PCI Form Factors

Type	Connector	Size
IA	100-pin, stacking	7.5 × 70 × 45 millimeters
IB	100-pin, stacking	5.5 × 70 × 45 millimeters
IIA	100-pin, stacking	7.5 × 70 × 45 millimeters
IIB	100-pin, stacking	17.44 × 78 × 45 millimeters
IIIA	124-pin, card edge	2.4 × 59.6 × 50.95 millimeters
IIIB	124-pin, card edge	2.4 × 59.6 44.6 millimeters

The extra 24 pins on Type III connectors allow for routing information back to the system, which is required for audio, phone line, or network connections.

Common Mini PCI devices include sound cards, modems, networking cards, and SCSI, ATA, and SATA controllers. Adapters to convert PCI to Mini PCI and vice versa are widely available.

USB Ports

Just as desktops do, laptops use USB ports for expansion. However, because of the lack of internal expansion in laptops, most peripherals for laptops are found either as PC Cards or USB expansion devices.

For more information about USB ports and their function, refer to Chapter 1.

ExpressBus

ExpressBus was launched as a way to expand USB connectivity for computers. The idea came about in the late 1990s, when USB was really taking off as a standard. While people loved the standard, most computers had limited USB ports, and that was a problem. The solution was the ExpressBus hub. One side of the hub had either four or seven USB ports on it, and the other side plugged into the USB port on the computer via a special USB A/B cable.

The hubs can also be daisy-chained, and the entire chain can support up to 127 devices. Considering most laptops still have only one or two USB ports, ExpressBus hubs can greatly increase expandability.

Mouse/Keyboard Port

Just in case you don't like using your laptop's built-in keyboard or pointing device, most laptops come with a combination *keyboard/mouse port* that allows you to connect either an external keyboard or an external mouse to the laptop. On laptops that don't have USB ports, this port is most often used for a standard PS/2 mouse. On those laptops that do have USB ports, this port is used for an external keypad or keyboard (because the USB port can accommodate an external mouse).

Communications Ports

Laptops are built to make computing mobile. And in this world where it seems like you always need to be in touch with others while you're mobile, it makes sense that laptops have a variety of methods to communicate while you're on the go. There are several wireless communication methods available, and all new laptops have at least one of the following connections: infrared, cellular, Bluetooth, or Ethernet.

Infrared

Laptops were the first computers to use infrared ports regularly. Handheld computers had them before that (including the Palm and HPC platforms). This port is used for many things, although one of the most common uses is to send information to another device (such as a Palm).

An *infrared port* is a small port on the computer that allows data to be sent and received using electromagnetic radiation in the infrared band. The infrared port itself is a small, dark square of plastic (usually a very dark maroon) and can typically be found on the front of a PC or on the side of a laptop or portable. Figure 3.11 shows an example of an infrared port.

FIGURE 3.11 An infrared port

Infrared ports send and receive data at a very slow rate (maximum speed on most PC infrared ports is less than 4Mbps, while Windows XP supports an IrDA port speed of 16Mbps). Most infrared ports on PCs that have them support the *Infrared Data Association (IrDA) standard*, which outlines a standard way of transmitting and receiving information via infrared so that devices can communicate with each other.

 More information on the IrDA standard can be found at the organization's website: http://www.irda.org.

Noted that although infrared is a wireless technology, most infrared communications (especially those that conform to the IrDA standards) are line-of-sight only and take place within a short distance (typically less than 4 meters). Infrared is typically used for point-to-point communications such as controlling the volume on a device with a handheld remote control.

Cellular

Although laptops haven't gotten quite as small as mobile phones yet, the line between the two technologies continues to blur. Phone providers are adding more and more features in an effort to attract subscribers, such as cheaper text messaging (which really is analogous to e-mail) and Internet access. Handheld computers, such as the BlackBerry, offer complete phone, e-mail, and Internet connectivity. At the same time, laptop manufacturers are adding cellular communications to their machines. The antenna is built into the case, and all you have to do is sign up for service just as you would with your cell phone.

Ethernet

Wireless networking and laptops are made for each other like Oreo cookies and milk. The most common wireless networking connection is called *WiFi*, short for wireless fidelity. Specifically, WiFi is a collection of IEEE 802.11*x* standards.

The most common standard for the last several years has been *802.11b*, which provides wireless speeds up to 11Mbps. A newer standard is *802.11g*, which is backward compatible with 802.11b, provides data transmission of up to 54Mbps, and is increasingly popular. Both 802.11b and 802.11g operate in the 2.4GHz band.

Another standard you will occasionally run into is 802.11a. The 802.11a standard operates at a different frequency (the 5GHz band) and uses a different encoding scheme than 802.11b and 802.11g and is not compatible with either of them.

The vast majority of laptops made today come with an internal 802.11 adapter. Often you will see the laptop claim to be 802.11b/g compatible, meaning it can handle either type of network. A few recent adapters are dual-band and support all three standards (802.11a/b/g).

As this text is being written, a new standard (802.11n) is being developed. It is expected to support speeds of over 200Mbps, and the designers of the standard are expected to retain its backward compatibility with 802.11a/b/g devices.

In addition, most laptops have a built-in RJ-45 connector for wired Ethernet networking.

If your laptop does not have a built-in network card, you can purchase USB network adapters from a variety of manufacturers.

Bluetooth

A popular standard for wireless communication is *Bluetooth*. The standard is managed by the Bluetooth Special Interest Group, which includes Microsoft, Intel, Apple, IBM, and Toshiba, along with several cellular phone manufacturers. The technical specification IEEE 802.15.1 describes *Wireless Personal Area Networks (WPANs)* and is based on Bluetooth.

Bluetooth doesn't have the range of cellular communications, nor does it have the bandwidth of current wireless networking standards (WiFi). Bluetooth signals are good only for about 30 feet, and it really helps to have line of sight to make them work. Bluetooth is not designed for wireless networking; it's designed for wireless communication.

The good news is, it's fast and reliable transferring small amounts of data short distances. It also uses little power compared to cellular or WiFi options, making it ideal for laptops as well as handheld computers.

Bluetooth is more popular in cell phones and handheld computers, but it still gets a lot of attention in laptop computers. Common devices are keyboards and mice, printers, cameras, and headsets and microphones.

For complete details of the listed wireless communication methods, see Chapter 8.

Docking Stations

Some laptops are designed to be *desktop replacement laptops*. That is, they will replace a standard desktop computer for day-to-day use and are thus more full-featured than other laptops. These laptops often have a proprietary docking port. A *docking port* (as shown in Figure 3.12) is used to connect the laptop to a special laptop-only peripheral known as a *docking station*. A docking station is basically an extension of the motherboard of a laptop. Because a docking station is designed to stay behind when the laptop is removed, it can contain things like a full-size drive bay and expansion bus slots. Also, the docking station can function as a port replicator.

A *port replicator* reproduces the functions of the ports on the back of a laptop, so that peripherals such as monitors, keyboards, printers, and so on that don't travel with the laptop can remain connected to the dock and don't have to all be physically unplugged each time the laptop is taken away. Finally, there are *accessory bay*s (also called media bays). These external bays allow you to plug your full-size devices into them and take your laptop with you (for example, a full-size hard drive that connects to an external USB or FireWire port). As a point of clarification (or perhaps confusion), media bays and accessory bays are sometimes used to refer to laptop drive bays.

These docking ports and docking stations are *proprietary*. That is, the port works only with docking stations designed by the laptop's manufacturer and vice versa.

FIGURE 3.12   A docking port

Power Systems

Because portable computers have unique characteristics as a result of their portability, they have unique power systems as well. Portable computers can use either of two power sources: batteries or AC power. There are many different sizes and shapes of batteries, but most of them are Nickel-Cadmium (NiCad), Lithium Ion (LiIon), or Nickel Metal Hydride (NiMH). All of these perform equally well, but NiCad batteries can be recharged only a finite number of times. After a time, they develop a memory and must be recharged on a special deep-charging machine. NiMH and LiIon batteries don't usually develop a memory and can be recharged many times, but they're a little more expensive. Some of the much smaller handheld or palmtop computers can use any of these types of battery, but a few vendors such as Hewlett-Packard took a more commonsense approach: They designed their handhelds to use standard AA batteries.

Most notebook computers can also use AC power with a special adapter (called an *AC adapter*) that converts AC power into DC power. The adapter either is integrated into the notebook (as on some Compaq notebooks) or is a separate "brick" with a cord that plugs into the back of the laptop.

Another power accessory that is often used is a *DC adapter*, which allows a user to plug the laptop into the power source (usually a cigarette lighter) inside a car or on an airplane. These adapters allow people who travel frequently to use their laptops while on the road (literally).

Managing Power and Removing Devices

Being free to roam with your laptop wherever you want is a great thing. Unplugging from the wall and running on battery power means you can leap through a field of spring daisies holding your laptop instead of being chained to your gray desk and low cubicle walls. It also presents an opportunity to manage devices and how much power they consume, as batteries don't last forever. Finding a way to manage power efficiently gives batteries longer lives and you more time with your daisies.

In addition, as I mentioned before, laptops were not designed with internal expandability in mind. Most add-on devices are external. Some peripherals can just be plugged in and unplugged, whereas with others you must follow a specific sequence to safely remove the device.

This section focuses on power management as well as the safe removal of hardware devices on laptops.

Understanding Laptop Power Management

As you learned in Chapter 1, the Basic Input/Output System (BIOS) is run when the computer is first powered up. It checks the hardware to make sure there are no major problems, bootstraps the computer, and then hands control over to the operating system. One of the features of most modern BIOS systems is the *Advanced Configuration and Power Interface (ACPI)*, also sometimes referred to as BIOS-ACPI. First released as an open standard in 1996, ACPI defines common interfaces for hardware recognition and configuration and, more important, power management.

ACPI has two important power management features. First, it gives control of power management to the operating system. With older versions of power management, control was BIOS related, and the user had little control through the operating system. Today, the BIOS handles power management communication between the operating system and the device. Second, ACPI allows power management features that were once only found on laptops to be available on desktops as well.

For ACPI to work, the motherboard, CPU, and operating system all need to support the standard. The first Windows operating system to support ACPI was Windows 98.

The ACPI standard defines four power level states, called *global states*. The global states are computer-wide, and there are other device, processor, and performance states as well.

Global States

The normal working state of a computer is called G0 Working. It's assumed that all devices are running at full power. However, while in G0 state, various devices can be put into lower power modes (C and D states, discussed in the next two sections), as the computer sees fit. Most laptops will power down individual devices when they're not being used, to save battery life.

The first power-saving mode is called G1 Sleeping. G1 is divided into four submodes, or sleep modes, called S1–S4. Higher S state numbers indicate more power savings but also longer latency before the device can be powered back up to G0.

- S1 is the most power-hungry sleep mode. The CPU stops executing instructions and the processor cache is flushed, but power is still provided to the CPU and memory. All devices not being used are powered down.

- S2 uses less power than S1 because in this state the processor is powered down. S2 is not typically utilized.

- S3 is also called *Standby* in Windows. When put into S3, the computer maintains power only to the RAM. Because of this, and because all running application information is stored in RAM, when the user brings the computer back from S3, the user can start right where he or she left off. This level is also called Suspend to RAM.

- S4 is called *Hibernation* in Windows. In S4, the information in RAM is written to the hard disk, and the RAM is powered off as well. This means that a user can take the computer from S4 back to G0 and still work from where he or she left off, but it will take longer for the applications to be available. The other good news is, because the information in RAM is written to the hard disk, if a power loss occurs, the user's information will not be lost. If you're in S3 and lose power, all of the information being held in RAM is gone. This level is also called Suspend to disk.

The G2 power state is called *soft off*. You execute a soft off by clicking the Turn Off Computer or Shutdown buttons in Windows or by otherwise letting the operating system shut the computer down, without a physical power outage. To boot back up from G2, the entire boot process must be run.

If a complete power loss occurs (such as by unplugging the cord), the system enters into G3 *mechanical off*. In this state, the computer can be safely disassembled. To bring the computer from G3 to G0, the complete boot process must be run.

Processor States

The processor is one of the most critical components inside a computer, and as such it's often one of the last components to get powered down. There are four processor states:

- C0 is the operational state; no power is being saved.

- C1, or Halt, is a powered-down state, but the processor can return to action nearly instantaneously.

- C2, sometimes called Stop-Clock, uses less power than C1. The processor is still visible to software applications but takes longer to wake up if a request is made.

- C3 is Sleep mode. In this state, the processor cache is flushed, and it will take a few seconds for the processor to be available.

Device States

As with processor states, there are four device states. These apply only to peripheral devices within the computer.

- D0 Fully On is the full operating state.

- D1 and D2 are intermediate power states. Neither uses full power, and each device specifically defines its own D1 and D2 states.

- In D3 Off, the device is completely powered down and not responsive.

Performance States

Think of performance states as sublevels to processor and device states. Processors or devices in normal running modes (C0 or D0 state) can be in a lower power-level using a performance state. Performance states are designated P0-Pn, where n can be 1–16. As with all other states, bigger numbers indicate greater power savings, as well as more latency to become fully operational.

Some manufacturers have tried to brand their performance states. Intel calls its implementation SpeedStep, and AMD labels its version as Cool'n'Quiet.

Managing Power in Windows

As stated in the last section, Windows 98 and newer can handle all aspects of hardware power management. This means you don't need to configure anything in the BIOS other than to ensure that the power management setting (if it has one) is enabled, which it is by default.

To get to the power management features of Windows XP, open Control Panel, and in the Performance and Maintenance category, choose Power Options. Alternatively, you can right-click an empty area on the Desktop, click properties, select the Screen Saver tab, and click the Power button. You will get a screen like the one shown in Figure 3.13.

You can see that there are five different tabs (you can do this on a desktop, too, but desktops don't typically have the Alarms and Power Meter tabs and may add a UPS tab for an uninterruptible power supply). Looking at Figure 3.13, you can see that it's set on the Portable/Laptop scheme, which allows you to define separate settings for when the laptop is plugged in versus running on the battery. Clicking the down arrow for Power Schemes, you have the option to choose from multiple schemes, if they exist. If you want to make your own scheme, configure the settings to your liking, and then click Save As.

The Alarms tab allows you to configure how your system will respond when battery power gets low. The Power Meter tab shows you the current battery life, as shown in Figure3.14.

FIGURE 3.13 Windows power management

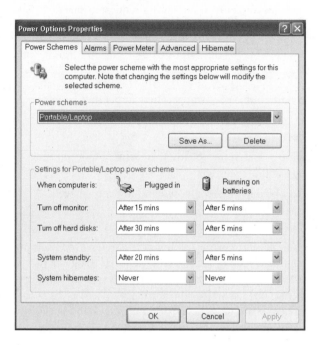

FIGURE 3.14 Power Meter tab

You can also get to the same information by clicking on the battery icon in your system tray, as shown in Figure 3.15. It's good to keep your eye on the battery icon when you're on battery power, so you don't run out.

The Advanced tab, shown in Figure 3.16, lets you configure the function of the power buttons.

Finally, the Hibernate tab allows you to turn off or turn on whether or not your computer can enter hibernation mode.

The default power management settings are pretty relaxed. It's a good idea to be much more conservative, especially if you are on battery power a lot and want to maximize battery life.

FIGURE 3.15   Battery icon

FIGURE 3.16   Advanced options

Power Options Properties

Power Schemes | Alarms | Power Meter | Advanced | Hibernate

Select the power-saving settings you want to use.

Options

☐ Always show icon on the taskbar

☑ Prompt for password when computer resumes from standby

Power buttons

When I close the lid of my portable computer:

Hibernate

When I press the power button on my computer:

Shut down

When I press the sleep button on my computer:

Ask me what to do

OK   Cancel   Apply

Removing Laptop-Specific Hardware

In the grand scheme of things, there are two types of peripherals: internal and external. We've already discussed that laptops weren't exactly made for internal expandability. So when it comes to opportunities to remove internal hardware, you'll find them few and far between. The most likely thing you will do is add or remove memory. To do that, you usually need to remove a screw or two holding a plate on the bottom of the laptop to reveal the memory compartment. Always check with the laptop's manual and your warranty before attempting these types of procedures.

External hardware is much easier to remove from the computer. Just unplug it, right? Well, it's not always quite that simple. If you have USB-type devices plugged in, removing them *is* as easy as disconnecting them, but other peripherals require more work.

 WARNING Although most of the time you can just remove a USB device, make sure it's not in use when you remove it.

The recommended way to remove a device from a laptop is to stop the device first (this is even good policy for USB devices), using the icon in the system tray that looks like a card with a green arrow over it. This is shown in Figure 3.17.

FIGURE 3.17 Safely Remove Hardware icon

Click on the Safely Remove Hardware icon, and you will get a screen similar to the one shown in Figure 3.18.

Highlight the device you want to remove, and click Stop. Windows will then notify you that it's safe to remove the device. If it's a cabled device, just detach it. If it's PCMCIA, then you can press the eject button next to the slot in which the card is located. Other types of hardware in some laptops require you to release a latch. The laptop in Figure 3.19 has modular front-load bays, and the right side has a CD-ROM in it. These modular bays are sometimes referred to as media bays.

Turning the computer over, as in Figure 2.20, you can see the release latch. Slide it to the side, and pull on the grip on the underside of the CD-ROM. Out it comes.

Adding a device to a laptop generally means that the computer will automatically recognize and enable the device for you, unless there's no compatible driver available. In cases like these, Windows will tell you that it detected new hardware and ask you to provide an appropriate driver.

FIGURE 3.18   Removable-hardware list

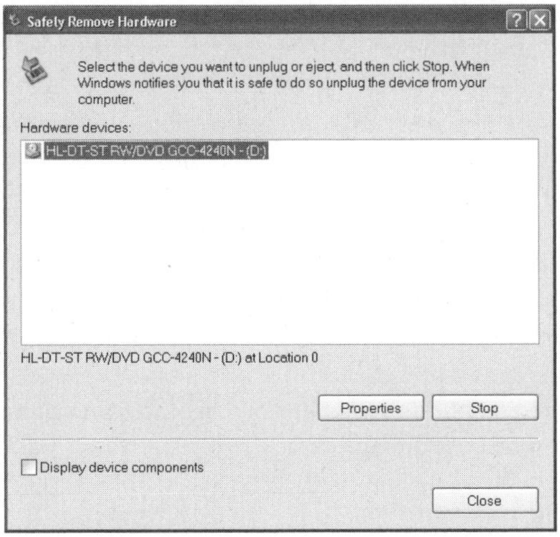

Safely Remove Hardware

Select the device you want to unplug or eject, and then click Stop. When
Windows notifies you that it is safe to do so unplug the device from your
computer.

Hardware devices:

HL-DT-ST RW/DVD GCC-4240N - (D:)

HL-DT-ST RW/DVD GCC-4240N - (D:) at Location 0

Properties   Stop

☐ Display device components

Close

FIGURE 3.19   Modular-bay CD-ROM

FIGURE 3.20   Underside of laptop

Troubleshooting and Performing Preventative Maintenance on Laptops

Laptops use essentially the same types of device as desktops, but troubleshooting the two can feel very different. While the general troubleshooting philosophies never change—steps such as gathering information, isolating the problem, and then testing one fix at a time—the space and configuration limitations can make laptop troubleshooting more frustrating.

Preventative maintenance is critical to the long-term well-being of any computer system. But because laptops are moved around so much, they're often exposed to many environmental hazards that desktops aren't. For example, how many people worry about accidentally sitting on their desktop computer?

This section looks at troubleshooting techniques as well as preventative maintenance measures to keep your laptop running well into its old age.

Diagnosing Laptop Problems

Before getting into specific laptop-type issues, remember that good troubleshooting means acting in a methodical manner. You need to find out if the device or software ever worked, what happened before the problem occurred, and what changes were made (if any), and then you must try to isolate the problem and test one fix at a time.

There are four typical areas where laptops could have different problems than their desktop counterparts: power, video, input, and wireless networking.

Power Concerns

Is it plugged in? Everyone hates getting asked that question if their computer doesn't work. But it's the critical first question to ask. After all, if it's not plugged in, who knows if it will work or not? You can't assume that the battery is working (or is attached) like it's supposed to. Always check power and connections first!

Most laptop power adapters have a light on them indicating they're plugged in. If there's no light, check to make sure the outlet is working, or switch outlets. Also, most laptops have a power-ready indicator light when plugged into a wall outlet as well. Check to see if it's lit. If the outlet is fine, try another power adapter. They do fail on occasion.

If you're working on a DC adapter, the same thing applies. Check for lights, try changing plugs if possible (many newer cars have secondary power sources, such as ones in the console between the seats), or try another adapter if you have one.

Another thing to remember when troubleshooting power problems is to remove all external peripherals. Strip your laptop down to the base computer, so there isn't a short or other power drain coming from an external device.

Video Issues

Video problems are usually caused by the video card (built into the motherboard on most laptops) or the display unit. Of course, since the video section follows the power section, make sure the computer is on before diagnosing it as a video problem!

Here are a few things to try:

- Plug in an external monitor that you know works. On most laptops, you need to press the function key and another key (often F8) to direct the video output to an external monitor.

- Check the LCD cutoff switch. Remember the function+F8 idea? Try toggling it a few times, waiting a few seconds between each press of the toggle key to let the display power up. Most laptops have three display states: LCD only, external only, and both.

- Raise or lower the brightness level. This is usually done with a function key combination as well, such as function+F5 or function+F6. Check your keyboard for function keys that have a sun on them.

- If you have a handheld computer, try turning the backlight feature on or off. For specifics on how to do this, check your manual.

If the display is not working, you can order a new one from the laptop manufacturer. If the computer won't output a display to an external monitor as well, you likely need a new motherboard.

Input Problems

Laptop keyboards aren't as easy to switch out as desktop keyboards. You can, however, very easily attach an external keyboard to your laptop if the keys on your laptop don't appear to work. If you have the wrong type of connector, most electronics stores will have USB-to-PS/2 or PS/2-to-USB converters.

Another unique problem to laptop keyboards is the function key. (It can be your friend or your enemy.) If the function key is "stuck" on, the only keys that will work are those with functions on them. Try toggling it, just as you would a Caps Lock key.

A lot of laptops now have touchpads. While they're usually thought of as very handy (I love mine), some people find that they're annoying. If you are using the Touchpoint, for example, your palm might rest on the touchpad, causing erratic mouse behavior. You can turn the touchpad off through Control Panel. Keeping in mind that you can turn it off on purpose, remember that it can be turned off accidentally as well. Check to make sure it's enabled. Some laptops allow you to disable or change the sensitivity of the Touchpoint as well.

On handhelds or other touch screen devices, the screen input can occasionally fail. This indicates a problem with the digitizer, and it generally means you need a repair or a replacement.

Networking Troubles

Nearly all modern laptops are equipped with wireless networking, built into the computer. In many cases, the wireless antenna is run into the LCD panel. This allows the antenna to stand up higher and pick up a better signal.

If your wireless isn't working, check to make sure that the LEDs on your network card are functioning. If there are no lights, it could indicate a problem with the card itself, or on some cards, that there is no connection or signal. First, make sure that the wireless card is enabled through Windows. You generally do this in Windows XP by right-clicking on My Network Places, selecting Properties, right-clicking the wireless network connection, and selecting Properties in order to look at the network card properties. However, some network cards have their own proprietary configuration software. You can also often check here by clicking the Wireless Networks tab to see if you're getting a signal and the strength of that signal.

 If you have a USB network adapter, try unplugging it and plugging it back in. Make sure that Windows recognizes the card properly.

When wireless fails but the network card appears to be working, plug it in. Most laptops with wireless cards also have wired RJ-45 network ports. Plug the card in and see if you get lights, and see if the network works.

Performing Preventative Maintenance

Many problems people have with their computers can be prevented. By taking good care of your equipment, you can dramatically extend the life of your hardware, and laptops are no exception. Two ways to look at preventative maintenance include being careful of what the computer is exposed to (the environment) and taking steps to proactively protect your computer (tools and techniques).

The Environment

Environmental issues are where laptops usually take a severe beating. Desktops don't have to worry about being constantly moved around, shaken, opened and closed, and occasionally dropped. Laptops live in fear of users who forget to zip their carrying case or those who leave it closed and sitting on the couch.

I'm going to use the term "environment" to refer to all of those external things that can affect a computer. At the top of the list is transportation. Laptops get moved around all the time, and if you're going to carry one around, always put it in a carrying case designed for such a purpose. Too many people just stuff them into a backpack or briefcase and then wonder why things like broken screens happen.

One other interesting issue with laptops is due to their clamshell design. When the laptop is closed, the screen is basically face to face with the keyboard. Any pressure or squeezing together of the sides causes the keys to press into the screen. Over time, the keys will mar the coating of the LCD screen, and you'll be left with permanent marks in your display. One way to prevent this problem is to place a screen-sized piece of foam (they usually come between the keyboard and screen when the laptop is shipped) or heavy cloth between the keyboard and screen when you close your laptop. It will keep the display better for longer.

Computer components get very hot, and that's especially true of laptops because of their confined space. Don't operate your laptop for long periods of time in the sun or in very hot conditions. Laptops have cooling fans, but the fans are small and can only do so much.

Real World Scenario

Potential Wireless and Wired Conflicts

A short time ago, a friend of mine was frustrated because he couldn't get to the network in his office with his laptop plugged into his docking station. He had used the laptop at home the night before and gotten on his wireless network without a problem. But this day, his wired connection would not work. He checked his cables (good first step!) and saw that there were lights (good sign). He had tried to access both the Internet and intranet sites but to no avail.

We opened a command prompt and ran `ipconfig`. He didn't have an IP address, but I noticed that his built-in wireless card was listed and active.

What he needed to do was to disable his built-in wireless card. He had enabled the wireless to work at home, and it was still enabled. Because it was enabled, the wireless card was trying to obtain an IP address, and it refused to let the wired "portion" of the card pick up an address from the company DHCP server (there was no wireless in the building). After disabling his wireless card, his wired connection picked up an IP address, and all was well.

Most laptop network cards have a wired connection in addition to their wireless capabilities. For many of them, the wired connection will not work if the wireless is enabled. It's an attempt to prevent conflicts if both connection types are active.

Speaking of fans, dust and dirt can get into them, rendering them useless for cooling your computer. Make sure the area you're working in doesn't have a lot of dust flying around—a construction site isn't a good place for a laptop, for example.

Tools and Techniques

Heat always has been and probably always will be an enemy of small computers. All those electronic components crammed into a small space just beg for overheating problems. All laptops have fans to keep the processor and memory cool, and laptop components are designed to run cooler than their desktop counterparts, but overheating is still a problem.

You can purchase external cooling devices for your laptop, which promise to keep it cooler and extend the life of your system. The most common version is a cooling pad. It sits on your desk (most are about 1 inch high), and the laptop sits on the cooling pad. Inside the pad are fans that circulate hot air away from the bottom of your laptop, the part that usually gets the hottest. There are dozens of varieties of cooling pads, starting off around $15 and going up to several hundred dollars for exotic cooling fan/docking station combos.

One of the most common "mistakes" people make is when cleaning their laptop display. They figure it's just like cleaning the TV, so they get out the glass cleaner and a paper towel and clean away. Two mistakes there. First, don't use abrasive cloths to clean the screen. The coating on LCD screens will scratch easily, and you'll be left staring at scratch marks until you decide to upgrade. Second, don't use commercial glass cleaners. They often contain chemicals that will damage the LCD screen. To do the job right, there are two ways you can go. One, use a slightly damp (and soft!) cloth. Two, buy a cleaner designed for LCD screens. You can find them at most any office supply store. There are even premoistened towelette versions that are handy to carry with you in your laptop case.

Summary

In this chapter, you learned about the various laptop issues that are on the A+ Essentials exam. We discussed differences between laptops and desktops, including the various components that make up a laptop and how they differ in appearance and function from those on a desktop.

You also learned how to configure power-management in laptops, as well as remove laptop-specific hardware. Finally, we explored troubleshooting procedures and preventative maintenance techniques. Keep in mind that each brand of laptop is different. For a lot of these issues, it is important to refer to the service manual for specific proper procedures.

Exam Essentials

Know the differences between laptop processors and desktop processors.   Laptops have less room in them, so it makes sense that laptop processors are smaller than their desktop brethren. They also operate at lower voltages, have more advanced power-down or sleep modes, and are often soldered directly to the motherboard. Finally, chipsets such as the Intel Pentium M chipset also include built-in video processing and networking capabilities.

Understand the differences between laptop memory standards and desktop memory standards. Continuing a main theme of this chapter, memory in laptops needs to be smaller than in desktops, and so it is. The two main standards for laptop memory are SoDIMM and MicroDIMM.

Know the differences between laptop processors and desktop processors.   Laptops have less room in them, so it makes sense that laptop processors are smaller as well.

Understand key concepts behind LCD technology.   You need to be familiar with active and passive matrix, resolution standards such as XGA and UXGA, and terms such as contrast ratio and native resolution.

Know how laptops handle power management.   Laptops should power down devices much quicker than desktops do, in an effort to save battery life. This is all set up by the Advanced Configuration Power Interface (ACPI) feature of the BIOS and supported by Windows.

Know how to remove laptop-specific hardware.   For most devices, you should use the Safely Remove Hardware icon in the taskbar to stop the device and then physically remove it.

Review Questions

1. You have a floppy drive in your laptop's modular bay, and your laptop is on. What is the recommended first step in removing it so you can put a CD-ROM drive in instead?

    A. Turn off the laptop.

    B. Use the latch on the underside of the laptop to release the drive, and pull gently.

    C. Use the Safely Remove Hardware icon to stop the device.

    D. Use Add/Remove Hardware in Control Panel to remove the device.

2. Which of the following is *not* a benefit of laptop design?

    A. Portability

    B. Increased performance

    C. Desktop replacement

    D. Higher-quality construction

3. Which of the following must be true for BIOS-ACPI to work? (Choose all that apply.)

    A. The BIOS must support ACPI.

    B. You must be running Windows 95 or newer.

    C. The motherboard must support ACPI.

    D. The processor must support ACPI.

4. Which laptop input device was released with the IBM ThinkPad series of laptops?

    A. Touchpad

    B. Touchball

    C. Touchpoint

    D. Touchway

5. Which laptop accessory allows you to power your laptop from a car or airplane?

    A. AC adapter

    B. DC adapter

    C. Battery converter

    D. Automotive Wizard

6. If the video on your laptop is not working, what should you do to troubleshoot it? (Choose all that apply.)

    A. Toggle the video function key.

    B. Try using an external monitor.

    C. Remove the display unit and reattach it.

    D. Power the system off and back on.

7. _____ is the fastest and most modern interface used as an expansion method for external peripherals like mice, web cams, scanners, printers, and so on and is popular on laptops and desktops alike.

   A. Parallel

   B. PS/2

   C. USB

   D. ATA

8. Which kind of laptop was designed to look and function like a paper notebook?

   A. Clamshell PC

   B. Tablet PC

   C. Paper PC

   D. Notebook PC

9. Which of the following power states consumes the least amount of power?

   A. G0

   B. S1

   C. S2

   D. S4

10. Which type of PC Card is used most often for expansion devices like NICs, sound cards, and so on?

   A. Type I

   B. Type II

   C. Type III

   D. Type IV

11. Which wireless IEEE standard operates on the 2.4GHz radio frequency and transmits data at a maximum of 11Mbps?

   A. 802.11b

   B. 802.11c

   C. 802.11e

   D. 802.11g

12. What would be the best thing to use to clean a laptop display?

   A. A dry cloth

   B. Glass cleaner

   C. Abrasive cleaning powder

   D. LCD cleaner

13. PCMCIA expansion cards need which software in order to operate? (Select all that apply.)

　　A. Cardmember Services

　　B. Card Services

　　C. Modem Services

　　D. Socket Services

14. What is the most important function of BIOS-ACPI?

　　A. Bootstrap the operating system

　　B. Detect system hardware

　　C. Manage system power

　　D. Remove unused system components

15. The process by which the processor slows down to conserve power is called _____?

　　A. Dropping

　　B. Cooling

　　C. Disengaging

　　D. Throttling

16. The display on your laptop appears warped and fuzzy. You plug in an external monitor, and the image on it is fine. What is the most likely cause of the problem?

　　A. The video card

　　B. The LCD display

　　C. The motherboard

　　D. The video driver

17. Which of the following types of display has the best performance characteristics?

　　A. Active matrix

　　B. Passive matrix

　　C. Dual matrix

　　D. Quad matrix

18. Which of the following video standards supports 1900×1200 resolution at a 16:10 aspect ratio?

　　A. XGA

　　B. SXGA+

　　C. UXGA

　　D. WUXGA

19. Which laptop input device is a flat surface that you can draw on with your finger to control the mouse pointer?

    A. Touchpad

    B. Touchball

    C. Touchpoint

    D. Touchway

20. Which of the following memory types has the smallest form factor?

    A. RIMM

    B. DIMM

    C. MicroDIMM

    D. SoDIMM

Answers to Review Questions

1. C. Before removing hardware, you should stop the device using the Safely Remove Hardware icon located in your system tray. Turning off the laptop would work, but it's not necessary. After stopping the device, you can use the latch (if your laptop has one) to release the drive.

2. B. By and large, compromises always must be made when comparing laptops to desktops. Although laptops can be used as desktop replacements, their performance is almost always lower than comparably priced desktops.

3. A, C, D. For ACPI power management to work, it first must be a feature of the BIOS. In addition, the motherboard and processor must support the standard. Finally, you need Windows 98 or newer.

4. C. The Touchpoint (aka finger mouse) was released with the IBM ThinkPad series of laptops.

5. B. A DC adapter converts the DC output from a car or airplane accessory power plug into the voltages required by your laptop.

6. A, B. Two helpful things to try are toggling the video output function key (usually Fn+F8) and plugging an external monitor into the laptop. Removing the display is possible but not recommended. Powering the system off and back on isn't likely to correct the problem.

7. C. USB is used most often in laptops as an expansion bus for external peripherals. Although parallel and PS/2 allow for connection of external peripherals, they are not as flexible or widely used for expansion as USB.

8. B. The tablet PC is a notebook with a flip-around screen that allows a user to hold it like a large notebook and write notes directly on the screen with a special stylus.

9. D. The S4 hardware state is also called Hibernation mode, and it consumes very little power. G0 is the fully powered operational state. S1 and S2 consume less power than full power but more than S4.

10. B. A Type II PC Card is the type used most often for expansion devices like NICs, sound cards, SCSI controllers, modems, and so on.

11. A . The IEEE standard for 11Mbps wireless transmission over 2.4GHz radio is the 802.11b standard. The 802.11g standard has a maximum transmission speed of 54Mbps.

12. D. Laptop LCD video displays can scratch easily. To clean them, it's best to use a cleaner designed specifically for LCD screens. They can be found at any office supply store.

13. B, D. The PC Card architecture has two components. The first is the Socket Services software, and the second is the Card Services software.

14. C. BIOS-ACPI is the power management standard introduced in 1996. It's an extension of the system BIOS that is responsible for managing power to devices in your system.

15. D. The processor can adjust how fast it's working, called throttling, to save system power.

16. B. It has to be a problem with the LCD display. If it were the video card, then the display would appear warped and fuzzy on the external monitor as well. While many motherboards contain video circuitry, this answer is not specific enough. If the video driver were corrupt, you would have the same problem on all displays.

17. A. Active-matrix screens have better performance than passive-matrix screens. There are no dual- or quad-matrix display devices.

18. D. The WUXGA standard is the only widescreen standard listed, and it is the only one that supports 1920 × 1200 resolution at a 16:10 aspect ratio.

19. A. The touchpad is a mousing surface built into the laptop. It allows you to use your finger to control the mouse pointer by drawing on the surface.

20. C. The SoDIMM and MicroDIMM are the common laptop memory standards. Of the two, MicroDIMM is smaller.

Chapter

4

Understanding Operating Systems

THE FOLLOWING COMPTIA A+ ESSENTIALS EXAM OBJECTIVES ARE COVERED IN THIS CHAPTER:

✓ **3.1 Identify the fundamentals of using operating systems**

- Identify differences between operating systems (e.g. Mac, Windows, Linux) and describe operating system revision levels including GUI comparison, MAC and Linux system requirements, and application and hardware compatibility comparisons

- Identify names, purposes and characteristics of the primary operating system components including registry, virtual memory and file system

- Describe features of operating system interfaces, for example:
  - Windows Explorer
  - My Computer
  - Control Panel
  - Command Prompt
  - My Network Places
  - Task bar / systray
  - Start Menu

- Identify the names, locations, purposes and characteristics of operating system files for example:
  - BOOT.INI
  - NTLDR
  - NTDETECT.COM
  - NTBOOTDD.SYS
  - Registry data files

- Identify concepts and procedures for creating, viewing, managing disks, directories and files in operating systems for example:
  - Disks (e.g. active, primary, extended and logical partitions)
  - File systems (e.g. FAT 32, NTFS)
  - Directory structures (e.g. create folders, navigate directory structures)
  - Files (e.g. creation, extensions, attributes, permissions)

In the previous three chapters, we looked at the hardware that comprises a personal computer's and laptop's physical components. Hardware is only half the story, though. When poor Thomas Watson, chairman of IBM, said in 1943, "I think there is a world market for maybe five computers," he was looking at a very different machine from the ones we have today. At that time computers were bulky—as in room sized—slow, and difficult to use. As recently as the 1970s, most machines were still using punch cards as a primary data input tool, and anyone wanting to use a computer had to navigate a complex, uninviting interface with only a keyboard to help them. In such an environment, Watson probably was correct to believe that few people would go through the time, effort, and expense to use computers.

As computer technology has evolved toward smaller, more powerful machines, the personal computer has made significant strides toward Microsoft's grandiose stated goal of "a computer in every home." The incredible global computer revolution is not due just to hardware, though. In many ways, the acceleration of computer usage over the last decade has had more to do with the ever-improving operating systems that humans use to interact with these machines. Computers require programmed code (called *software*) to run, and they require an input-output mechanism to allow users to give the machine instructions and to view the results of those commands. The *operating system* (OS) is the primary software used to achieve these ends, and the evolution of more powerful and user-friendly operating systems has made computers less difficult to use and more enjoyable.

In order to understand the emergence of modern personal computer OSs, you should know about the technologies that led to our present systems and about the critical relationship between hardware and software over the course of the PC's development. Graphics, speed, GUI interfaces, and multiple programs running concurrently are all made possible because software designers take full advantage of the hardware for which they are designing their software. As a result, you will see that as computer hardware has improved, software has improved with it. Because the OS is the platform on which all other software builds, it is generally the development of a new OS that drives the development of other software.

This chapter is therefore the story of that very special, and crucial, type of software—the personal computer OS. This chapter looks at several aspects of operating systems: where they've been, where they are, and features of various operating systems. Although there are several commonly used operating systems in the market today, no one operating system family has garnered more market share and attention than Microsoft's Windows operating systems. Therefore, we'll talk briefly about some others, but the focus of this chapter will be on Windows. We'll dive specifically into the two most common end-user operating systems of today's computing world: Windows 2000 and Windows XP.

There are some differences between Windows XP Home and Windows XP Professional. Throughout this chapter and book we'll refer to them collectively as Windows XP (for brevity's sake), unless specific differences exist, in which case we'll point them out.

Understanding Operating Systems

Computers are pretty much useless without software. A piece of hardware makes a good paperweight or doorstop, unless you have an easy way to interface with it. Software is that interface. While there are many types of software, or programs, the most important application you'll ever deal with is the operating system. Operating systems have many different, complex functions, but two of them jump out as being critical: one, interfacing with the hardware, and two, providing a platform on which other applications can run.

Here are three major distinctions of software to be aware of:

Operating System (OS) Provides a consistent environment for other software to execute commands. The OS gives users an interface with the computer so they can send commands (input) and receive feedback or results (output). To do this, the OS must communicate with the computer hardware to perform the following tasks:

- Disk and file management
- Device access
- Memory management
- Output format

Once the OS has organized these basic resources, users can give the computer instructions through input devices (such as a keyboard or a mouse). Some of these commands are built into the OS, whereas others are issued through the use of applications. The OS becomes the center through which the system hardware, other software, and the user communicate; the rest of the components of the system work together through the OS, which coordinates their communication.

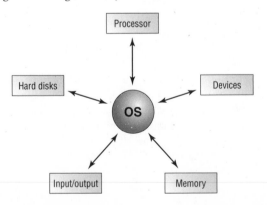

Application   Used to accomplish a particular task, an application is software that is written to supplement the commands available to a particular OS. Each application is specifically compiled (configured) for the OS on which it will run. For this reason, the application relies on the OS to do many of its basic tasks. Examples of applications include complex programs, such as Microsoft Word and Netscape Navigator, as well as simple programs, such as a command-line FTP program. Either way, when accessing devices and memory, the programs can simply request that the OS do it for them. This arrangement saves substantially on programming overhead, because much of the executable code is *shared*—it is written into the operating system and can therefore be used by multiple applications running on that OS.

Driver   Extremely specific software written for the purpose of instructing a particular OS on how to access a piece of hardware. Each modem or printer has unique features and configuration settings, and the driver allows the OS to properly understand how the hardware works and what it is able to do.

In the following sections, we'll look at some terms and concepts central to all operating systems. Then we'll move into specific discussions on Windows and alternative operating systems.

Operating System Terms and Concepts

Before we get too far into our discussion of PC operating systems, it will be useful to define a few key terms. Following are some terms you will come across as you study this chapter and visit with people in the computer industry:

Version   A particular revision of a piece of software, normally described by a number, which tells you how new the product is in relation to other versions of the product. MS-DOS, for instance, is currently in its sixth major version. Major revisions are distinguished from minor ones in this manner: DOS 5.0 to 6.0 was a major revision, whereas 6.0 to 6.2 was a minor revision. This way of marking changes is now relatively standard for other OS and application software. Very minor revisions are indicated with an additional decimal point. Upgrading from DOS version 6.21 to 6.22 involved only a few new files, but it was still an upgrade.

Source   The actual code that defines how a piece of software works. Computer operating systems can be *open source*, meaning the OS can be examined and modified by users, or they can be *closed source*, meaning users cannot modify or examine the code.

Shell   A program that runs on top of the OS and allows the user to issue commands through a set of menus or some other graphical interface. Shells make an OS easier to use by changing the user interface. The two shells we will look at most closely are Microsoft's DOS Shell (a menu-driven system) and Windows (a fully graphical user interface).

Graphical User Interface (GUI)   A method by which a person communicates with a computer. GUIs use a mouse, touchpad, or another mechanism (in addition to the keyboard) to interact with the computer to issue commands.

Network   Any group of computers that have a communication link between them. Networks allow computers to share information and resources quickly and securely.

Cooperative Multitasking   A multitasking method that depends on the application itself to be responsible for using and then freeing access to the processor. This is the way Windows 3.1 managed multiple applications. If any application locked up while using the processor, the application was unable to properly free the processor to do other tasks, and the entire system locked, usually forcing a reboot.

Preemptive Multitasking   A multitasking method in which the OS allots each application a certain amount of processor time and then forcibly takes back control and gives another application or task access to the processor. This means that if an application crashes, the OS takes control of the processor away from the locked application and passes it on to the next application, which should be unaffected. Although unstable programs still lock, only the locked application will stall—not the entire system.

Multithreading   The ability of a single application to have multiple requests in to the processor at one time. This results in faster application performance, because it allows a program to do many things at once. Only 32-bit or higher OSs support multithreading.

Microsoft Windows

Microsoft Windows was born out of the Microsoft Disk Operating System (MS-DOS) world. It was a dark place with no graphical interface. If you wanted something accomplished, you had to know the command and type it in. Although it doesn't sound user friendly, it was pretty advanced for its time.

Any real understanding of the success of DOS after 1987 requires knowledge of Windows. In the early years of its existence, Microsoft's DOS gained great acceptance and became a standard as a PC OS. Even so, as computers became more powerful and programs more complex, the limitations of the DOS command-line interface became apparent.

The solution to the problem was to make the OS easier to navigate, more uniform, and generally friendlier to the user. IBM understood that the average user did not want to receive their computer in pieces but preferred to have it ready to go out of the box. Oddly, the company did not understand that the same user who wanted their hardware to be ready to go also wanted their software to be the same way. They also did not want to edit batch files or hunt through directories using CD or DIR commands. As a result, when Microsoft came to IBM with a graphical user interface (GUI) based on groundbreaking work done by Xerox labs, IBM was not interested, preferring to go onward with the development of OS/2 (a project it had already started with Microsoft).

Regardless of IBM's interest, Microsoft continued on its own with development of the GUI—which it named *Windows* after its rectangular work areas—and released the first version to the market in 1985. Apple filed a lawsuit soon after, claiming that the Microsoft GUI had been built using Apple technology, but the suit was dismissed. Both Apple's Macintosh and Microsoft's DOS-with-Windows combo have continued to evolve, but until a recent deal between Apple and Microsoft, tensions have always been high. Mac and PC *users*, of course, remain adamantly chauvinistic about their respective platforms.

Early Work on Windows

The Xerox Corporation maintains a think tank of computer designers in Palo Alto, California, called the Palo Alto Research Center (PARC). One of the results of its work was the Alto workstation, which is generally thought to be the forerunner of all modern graphical OSs. The Alto had a mouse and a GUI interface, and it communicated with other workstations via Ethernet. Oh, and it was finished in 1974! Although it was never promoted commercially, both Microsoft and Apple viewed the Alto and incorporated its technology into their own systems. The accomplishments of the PARC lab in laying the groundwork for modern graphical computing systems cannot be overstated. Check out `http://www.parc.xerox.com` for more information on PARC past and present.

Oh, the stories that have been told around the glow of a monitor about Gates vs. Jobs. One of the easiest ways to get a bit of the flavor of the struggle is through a movie called *Pirates of Silicon Valley*, in which Anthony Michael Hall of *The Breakfast Club* plays Gates and Noah Wyle of *ER* fame plays Jobs. For more info, visit `http://tnt.turner.com/movies/tntoriginals/pirates`.

The Windows interface to MS-DOS is really just a shell program that allows users to issue DOS commands through a graphical interface—a prettier extension of Microsoft's earlier DOS Shell work. The integration of a mouse for nearly all tasks—a legacy of the Xerox Alto computer on which both the Macintosh and Windows GUIs are based—further freed users from DOS by allowing them to issue common commands without using the keyboard. Word processors, spreadsheets, and especially games were revolutionized as software manufacturers happily took advantage of the ease of use and flexibility that Windows added to DOS.

Windows Versions

After the development of Windows, many of the enhancements made to subsequent versions of DOS were designed to help free up and reallocate resources to better run Windows and Windows-based applications. Similarly, PC hardware continued to evolve far past the limits of DOS's ability to effectively use the power available to it, and later versions of Windows were designed to hide and overcome the limitations of the OS. The combination of MS-DOS and its Windows shell made Microsoft the industry leader and spurred the PC movement to new heights in the early 1990s. Following is a brief examination of the development of the Windows shell and a look at its different versions.

Windows 1

Version 1 of Windows featured the tiling windows, mouse support, and menu systems that still drive next-generation OSs such as Windows 98, Windows CE, and Windows 2000. It also offered *cooperative multitasking*, meaning that more than one Windows application could run concurrently. This was something that MS-DOS, up to this point, could not do.

Windows 1 was far from a finished product. For one thing, it didn't use icons, and it had few of the programs we have come to expect as Windows standards. Windows 1 was basically just an updated, more graphical version of the DOSSHELL.EXE program.

Windows 2

Version 2, released in 1987, added icons and allowed application windows to overlap each other, as well as tile. Support was also added for PIFs (program information files), which allowed the user to configure Windows to run their DOS applications more efficiently.

Windows 3.*x*

Windows 3.0 featured a far more flexible memory model, allowing it to access more memory than the 640KB limit normally imposed by DOS. It also featured the addition of the File Manager and Program Manager, allowed for network support, and could operate in *386 Enhanced mode*. 386 Enhanced mode used parts of the hard drive as *virtual memory* and was therefore able to use disk memory to supplement the RAM in the machine. Windows today is still quite similar to the Windows of version 3.0.

In 1992, a revision of Windows 3, known as Windows 3.1, provided for better graphical display capability and multimedia support. It also improved the Windows error-protection system and let applications work together more easily through the use of object linking and embedding (OLE).

After the introduction of version 3.1, Windows took a marked turn for the better, because Microsoft started making a serious effort to change to a full 32-bit application environment. With version 3.11, also known as Windows for Workgroups, Windows offered support for both 16-bit and 32-bit applications. (Windows 3.1 could support only 16-bit applications.) Significant progress on the 32-bit front was not made until very late in 1995, however, when Microsoft introduced Windows 95. Since that time, the venerable DOS/Windows team has been largely replaced by newer, more advanced systems. You may occasionally still run into a Windows 3.1 machine, but it is not a common occurrence.

With the introduction of Windows for Workgroups, people speaking generically about the two *flavors* of Windows—3.1 and 3.11—started referring to them collectively as Windows 3.*x*, as in the heading of this section.

Windows 95

Although it dominated the market with its DOS operating system and its add-on Windows interface, Microsoft found that the constraints of DOS were rapidly making it difficult to take full advantage of rapidly improving hardware and software developments. The future of computing was clearly a 32-bit, preemptively multitasked system such as IBM's OS/2; but many current users had DOS-based software or older hardware that was specifically designed for DOS and would not operate outside of its cooperatively multitasked Windows 3.1 environment.

Because of this problem, in the fall of 1995 Microsoft released a major upgrade to the DOS/ Windows environment. Called Windows 95, the new product integrated the OS and the shell. Where previous versions of Windows simply provided a graphical interface to the existing DOS OS, the Windows 95 graphical interface *is* part of the OS. Moreover, Windows 95 was designed to be a hybrid of the features of previous DOS versions and newer 32-bit systems. It also supports both 32-bit and 16-bit drivers as well as DOS drivers, although the 32-bit drivers are strongly recommended over the DOS ones because they are far faster and more stable.

Among the most important of the other enhancements debuted by Microsoft with Windows 95 was support for the Plug and Play (PnP) standard. This meant that if a device was designed to be Plug and Play, a technician could install the device into the computer, start the machine, and have the device automatically recognized and configured by Windows 95. This was a major advance; but unfortunately, in order for PnP to work properly, three things had to be true:

- The OS had to be PnP compatible.

- The computer motherboard had to support PnP.

- All devices in the machine had to be PnP compatible.

At the time Windows 95 came out, many manufacturers were creating their hardware for use in DOS/Windows machines, and DOS did not support PnP, so most pre-1995 computer components (sound cards, modems, NICs, and so on) were not PnP compliant. As a result, these components—generally referred to as *legacy* devices—often interfered with the PnP environment. Such devices are not able to dynamically interact with newer systems. They therefore require manual configuration or must be replaced by newer devices, which don't usually need manual configuration. Because of problems managing legacy hardware under Windows 95, many people soured on PnP technology. Worse, they blamed Windows 95 for their problems, not the old hardware. "It worked fine in DOS" was the standard logic! Now, a decade later, nearly all PC components are PnP compliant, and configuring computer systems is far easier than it was under DOS.

The foibles of PnP aside, to say that the new system was a success would be a major understatement. Within just a few years of its release, the Windows 95–style GUI had won over nearly all Windows users, and the more resilient architecture of Windows 95 had won over network administrators and computer technicians. Although it was far from perfect, Windows 95 was a tremendous advance out of the DOS age. Perhaps the only ones not thrilled were the folks at Apple, who continued to make a cottage industry out of starting lawsuits against Microsoft. This time, Apple contended that the Windows 95 interface itself was stolen from the Macintosh. It is undeniable that the Windows 95 interface is nearly a twin of the Mac interface; it turned out that Apple itself got its GUI from PARC Alto! Xerox not only designed the first computer GUI but had created an interface that would not be significantly improved upon in over 20 years of OS development—and both Apple and Microsoft settled on it as the basis for their GUIs. All subsequent versions of Windows (98, NT, 2000, and XP) use an interface essentially identical to the Windows 95 GUI.

Windows 98/Me/NT/2000/XP

After Windows 95, Windows 98 was introduced as its successor, followed by Windows Me (Millennium Edition). Windows 98/Me is still a very common PC OS to find on users' computers, but XP is even more common yet. One of the earlier options that offered more power than Windows 95 is the Windows NT OS. NT (which unofficially stands for New Technology) is an OS that was designed to be far more powerful than any previous Windows version. It uses an architecture based entirely on 32-bit code and is capable of accessing up to 4GB (4,000MB) of RAM.

After Windows 98 and NT, Windows 2000 was released. It used the same interface as Windows 98 (with a few important enhancements). It came in many versions, but the most popular were Windows 2000 Professional (workstation OS) and Windows 2000 Server (server OS).

Then came the introduction of Windows XP. It comes in three versions: XP Home, XP Professional, and Media Center. They are all close to being the same. However, XP Professional contains more corporate and networking features, and Media Center is designed to exploit multimedia connectivity by allowing you to set up your TV through your computer.

We will mostly talk about Windows 2000 and Windows XP in depth throughout the rest of this book, because they are the OSs you need to know for the A+ exam.

Windows Server 2003

The Windows Server 2003 family is the most recent operating system release from Microsoft. (Windows Vista, discussed in the next section, was still in beta testing at the time of this writing.) Server 2003 comes in three varieties: Server 2003 Enterprise Edition and Datacenter Edition, and Small Business Server 2003.

These are operating systems that aren't designed to run on everyday, end-user PCs. They're made to be the backbones of networks small and large. Here are some of the features of Server 2003:

- Support for server-class, 64-bit processors (such as the Itanium 2). Server 2003 Datacenter Edition supports up to 64 processors.

- More memory support: Windows XP is limited to 4GB of RAM. Datacenter can support up to 512GB of RAM.

- Centralized security management.

- Support for network services such as SQL Server, IIS Server, Terminal Server, and Streaming Media.

- Enhanced throughput for network connections and services.

The list of features of Windows Server 2003 is really long and quite impressive. The operating system is designed to compete head-to-head with high-end Unix-based servers produced by companies such as Sun Microsystems and Hewlett-Packard. It's not something you're likely to need to run in a home office any time soon.

Windows Vista

Scheduled to launch in early 2007, Windows Vista (formerly code-named Longhorn) is the newest operating system platform developed by Microsoft. It will be presented in five different versions: Business, Enterprise, Home Premium, Home Basic, and Ultimate.

While Windows XP was offered in several versions as well, those versions were tailored around the hardware that it was installed on. For example, Windows XP Tablet PC Edition is pretty obviously for a Tablet PC. All Windows Vista versions have the same core technology, but the different versions are designed to work around the role your PC (or handheld PC) plays, not the hardware that it uses.

Among the prominent features that will be included with Vista are a new user interface named Windows Aero, Internet Explorer 7, speech and handwriting recognition, and easy-access pop-up sidebars and gadgets.

Neither Windows Server 2003 nor Windows Vista is tested on the A+ exam, but you should be aware of them.

Alternative Operating Systems

Although most people run some version of Windows on their computers, a few OSs out there aren't Microsoft's. And people seem to get by just fine. As a matter of fact, there are software releases for these alternative OSs for major productivity software such as word processing, spreadsheets, and so forth.

Mac OS

The Mac OS isn't a PC OS (although many people are trying hard to get it to be one), in that it runs only on a Macintosh computer. While you should not expect too many (if any) question on the Mac OS, it is a very important part of PC culture. The long-standing holy war between Macintosh users and Windows users is a topic of legend.

One of the long-standing myths about the Mac OS is that it can't be (or has never been) hacked. (Mac users love to point this out every time a new Windows virus makes the headlines.) This simply isn't true. Mac operating systems have vulnerabilities, just as Windows operating systems do. It's just that the install base is much smaller, and so is the shock value impact of writing bugs for it. Why would a hacker want to write a virus that can affect only several thousand computers (and not many businesses) when he or she can write one that can wreak mass destruction and affect millions?

The Mac OS contains a GUI similar to Windows, with icons and a mouse pointer driving much of the action. Older versions of Macintosh operating systems and older versions of Windows (such as Windows for Workgroups 3.11) looked very similar, but the respective lines of operating systems have differentiated their looks over the years.

Mac OS X (Version 10.4) is the most current Macintosh operating system. Here are the system requirements to run it:

- PowerPC, G3, G4, or G5 processor
- 256MB RAM
- 3GB available hard disk space (4GB if you want to install XCode 2 developer tools)

- Apple-supplied video card with compatible or built-in display
- FireWire
- DVD drive (or you can get the OS on CD for an extra charge)

 The PowerPC processor was developed through an Apple-IBM-Motorola alliance. The G3, G4, and G5 processors are made by Motorola. All of the processors are based on Reduced Instruction Set Computer (RISC) technology, as opposed to Intel which bases its processors on the Complex Instruction Set Computer (CISC) standard.

Applications for Macintosh computers need to be written for the Mac. As outlined in the note above, the processor technology is different for the PC and the Mac, making it so software developers need to make a version for each. (Although many models of PowerPC can run both types of software without a problem.) When buying software, ensure that it has a Mac logo on the box (or says it will work with a Mac) if you want to run it on your Mac. A lot of software today is shipped with both Mac and PC versions in the same box.

Linux

Over the past several years, the *open-source* movement has been rallying around Linus Torvalds and his Linux OS. Linux is a Unix-type OS that has been released into the public domain and is being developed as an OS standard, much as TCP/IP is a protocol standard. A number of computer users are uncomfortable with Microsoft's dominance of the crucial OS market, and as a result, Linux has been positioned as an excellent alternative to the Microsoft juggernaut.

Although Linux is making inroads with knowledgeable home users and is even being used as a server in many corporate environments, it has not yet been able to break into the mass home or corporate desktop markets.

The theory behind Linux is to make core OS code available to anyone who wants it, so that the code can then be explored and enhanced by users. Those who choose to can create a full Unix-type OS from the Linux source code, modify it as they see fit, and release it to the world as a Linux *distribution*. Distributions are similar to versions, but where versions are chronological enhancements to a single company's OS, distributions are variations on a single OS theme. For a list of Linux distributions, refer to `http://www.linux.org/dist/english.html`. It's a long list, and because of the nature of Linux, the list is sure to be incomplete. Some of the more popular strains include:

- Red Hat (`http://www.redhat.com`)
- Debian (`http://www.debian.org`)
- Slackware (`http://www.slackware.com`)
- Mandrake (`http://www.linux-mandrake.com`)

Each has different characteristics; it would take a lot of study to understand the details of each version.

Is it free, or is it Free?

Linux the operating system is not owned by anyone, not even Linus Torvalds. It's an open source, free operating system. For a look into the psyche of the Linux community, here's a quote from the `linux.com` website:

"Now, just because it's Free, doesn't necessarily mean it's free. Think 'free' as in 'free speech,' not 'free beer,' as we in the Free Software/Open Source community like to say. In a nutshell, software that is free as in speech, like Linux, is distributed along with its source code so that anyone who receives it is free to make changes and redistribute it. So, not only is it ok to make copies of Linux and give them to your friends, it's also fine to tweak a few lines of the source code while you're at it—as long as you also freely provide your modified source code to everyone else."

As you can see, they're "open" about communication, and have a sense of humor to boot.

The architecture of Linux is based on Unix, the OS used in mainframes and other high-end computers, and it is extremely powerful and stable. Linux is also commonly used as a web server or an e-mail server on the Internet, and it can function as either a network OS or a desktop OS, just as Windows NT can.

Few creatures are more rabid in defense of their cause than Linux fans, and for good reason. The basic philosophy of Linux is that the people who use an OS are the ones who know best what needs to be improved on it and that user feedback should be respected and acted upon. Linux has not always been an OS for the masses, because early distributions were complex to install and had little application support. But a small army of users has sent suggestions, so it has improved markedly.

The Linux vs. Microsoft debate is an interesting one in the computer world, because it is a face-off between idealism and corporate power, open-source and proprietary code. It is a battleground where we will eventually see whether users prefer a system that gives them power (but requires a bit more work) or one that makes everything easy (but gives them fewer choices). Should be fun to watch, if nothing else.

 For detailed information about the world of Linux, two websites are great starting points: http://www.linux.org and http://www.linux.com. Linux.org is probably the better of the two for those interested in simply learning about what Linux is, and it has a great online course called "Getting Started with Linux."

There is really no way to list the minimum hardware requirements for Linux, as each version is different. A generality is that Linux will run on less powerful hardware that Windows-based operating systems, as most versions of Linux have less overhead.

Linux does not specify a graphical user interface. In fact, it's a badge of honor for most Linux users to use the command line as much as possible. However, there are many Linux (and Unix) GUI applications widely available. To run software on a Linux machine, the software must be specifically written for Linux.

Using Operating Systems

In this section, we will look at the Microsoft GUI from the ground up, beginning with a detailed look at its key components and ending with an exploration of basic tasks common across Windows 2000 and XP. The following general topics will be covered:

- Windows GUI components
- My Computer
- My Network Places
- Control Panel
- The command prompt
- The Windows Registry
- Virtual memory
- System files
- Windows Explorer
- File and disk management

The Windows GUI has been incredibly successful since its debut. All Microsoft operating system GUIs share features, but they also have differences.

 For the A+ Essentials exam, you'll need to know various aspects of the GUI interface for the Windows 2000 and XP operating systems.

The Windows Interface

When you look at the monitor of a machine running Windows 98 and then look at the monitor of a machine running Windows Me/NT/2000, it is difficult to tell them apart. If you look closely, you will notice that the names of some of the icons are different, but for the most part they're identical and look very much like the screen in Figure 4.1. If you look at the monitor of a machine running Windows XP, you'll notice that it looks a bit different than the older interfaces. However, don't despair; things still basically work the same way.

FIGURE 4.1   The Windows interface

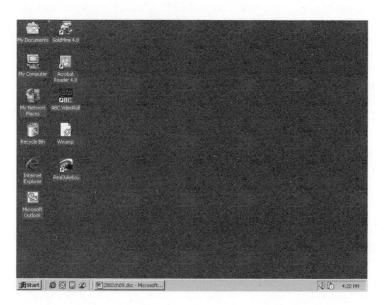

As a technician, you will quickly realize that this overall standardization of Microsoft's graphical interface for all of its OSs is good for you. Most basic tasks are accomplished in almost identical fashion on everything from a Windows 95 workstation computer to a Windows 2000 Advanced Server computer to a Windows XP Professional computer. Also, although the tools that are used often vary between the different OSs, the way you use those tools remains remarkably consistent across *platforms*.

We will begin with an overview of the common elements of the Windows GUI. We will then look at some tasks that are similar across Windows operating systems. If you have a copy of Windows 2000 or XP available, you may want to follow along by exploring each of the elements as they are discussed.

If you are able to follow along, you may notice that there are numerous icons and options we do not mention. Quite honestly, there are too many to cover, and they're out of the scope of this chapter. For now, simply ignore them, or browse through them on your own and then return to the text.

The Desktop

The Desktop is the virtual desk on which all of your other programs and utilities run. By default it contains the *Start menu*, the *Taskbar*, and a number of *icons*. The Desktop can also contain additional elements, such as web page content, through the use of the Active Desktop feature. Because it is the base on which everything else sits, the way the Desktop is configured can have a major effect on how the GUI looks and how convenient it is for users.

You can change the Desktop's background patterns, screensaver, color scheme, and size by right-clicking any area of the Desktop that doesn't contain an icon. The menu that appears allows you to do several things, such as creating new Desktop items, changing how your icons are arranged, or selecting a special command called Properties, similar to the one shown in Figure 4.2. If you're looking at the Desktop of a computer running Windows XP, you'll notice that the Active Desktop option is missing from the menu. This feature is still available, but you access it through Properties ➢ Desktop ➢ Customize Desktop ➢ Web.

FIGURE 4.2   The Desktop context menu

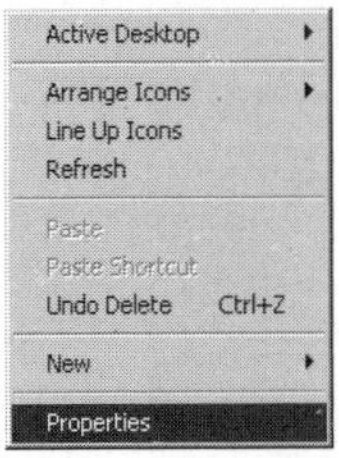

The Three Clicks in Windows

- *Primary mouse click*—A single click used to select an object or place a cursor.

- *Double-click*—Two primary mouse clicks in quick succession. Used to open a program through an icon or for other application-specific functions.

- *Secondary mouse click (or alternate click)*—Most mice have two buttons. Clicking once on the secondary button (usually the one on the right, although that can be modified) is interpreted differently from a left mouse click. Generally in Windows this click displays a context-sensitive menu from which you can perform tasks or view object properties.

When you right-click the Desktop and choose Properties, you will see the Display Properties screen shown in Figure 4.3.

From this screen, you can click the various tabs at the top to move to the different screens of information about the way Windows looks. Tabs are similar to index cards, in that they are staggered across the top so you can see and access large amounts of data within a single small window. Each Properties window has a different set of tabs. Among the tabs in the Display Properties window are the following:

Themes (Windows XP Only)   Used to select a theme that enables you to quickly customize the look and feel of your machine. Selecting a theme sets several items at once, such as a picture to display on the Desktop, the look of icons, sounds to use, and so on. All of these options can also be selected individually through the other Desktop Properties tabs. For example, if you're more comfortable with the look and feel of previous versions of Windows, you can select the Windows Classic theme.

Background (Windows 2000)/Desktop (Windows XP)   The Background tab in Windows 2000 is used to select an HTML document or a picture to display on the Desktop. In addition to letting you perform this same function, the Desktop tab in Windows XP lets you configure other items through the Customize Desktop button. Examples include changing which default icons to display on the Desktop and configuring web content for the Desktop.

Screen Saver   Sets up an automatic screensaver to cover your screen if you have not been active for a certain period of time. Originally used to prevent burned monitors, screensavers are now generally used for entertainment or to password-protect users' Desktops. The Screen Saver tab also gives you access to other power settings.

Appearance   Used to select a color scheme for the Desktop or to change the color or size of other Desktop elements.

Effects (Windows 2000)   Contains numerous assorted visual options. In Windows XP, some of these visual options are available via the Customize Desktop button on the Desktop tab.

Web (Windows 2000)   Lets you configure Active Desktop settings. In Windows XP, you can access this tab via the Customize Desktop button on the Desktop tab.

Settings   Used to set the color depth or screen size. Also contains the Advanced button, which leads to graphics driver and monitor configuration settings.

FIGURE 4.3   The Display Properties screen

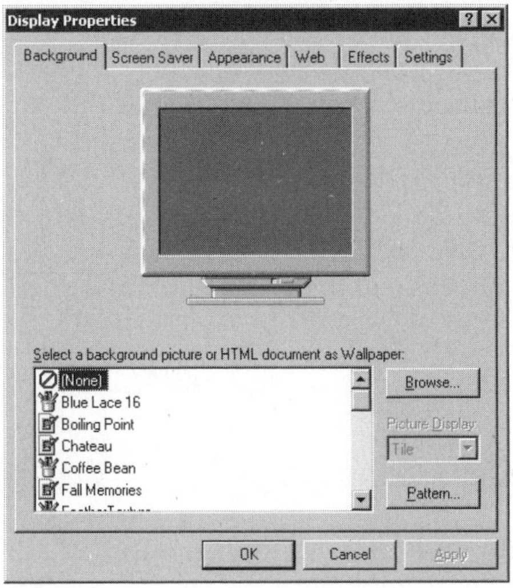

In Windows 2000 you can also access the Display Properties settings by using the Display icon under Start ➢ Settings ➢ Control Panel. In Windows XP, you access the Display icon under Start ➢ Control Panel.

In Exercise 4.1, you will see how to change a screensaver.

EXERCISE 4.1

Changing a Screensaver

To change the screensaver on Windows 2000 or XP, perform the following steps:

1. Right-click the Desktop.

2. Choose Properties from the context menu.

3. Click the Screen Saver tab.

4. Choose 3D Flower Box. Click Preview to see the new screensaver. Move the mouse to cancel the screensaver and return to the Display Properties dialog box.

5. Click the OK button or the Apply button. (OK performs two tasks—Apply and Exit window—whereas Apply leaves the window open.)

The Taskbar

The Taskbar (see Figure 4.4) is another standard component of the Windows interface. Note that although the colors and feel of the Desktop components, including the Taskbar, have changed in Windows XP, the components themselves are the same. The Taskbar contains two major items: the Start menu and the System Tray (systray). The Start menu is on the left side of the Taskbar and is easily identifiable: it is a button that has the word *Start* on it. The *System Tray* is located on the right side of the Taskbar and contains only a clock by default, but other Windows utilities (for example, screensavers or virus-protection utilities) may put their icons here to indicate that they are running and to provide the user with a quick way to access their features.

FIGURE 4.4   The Taskbar

| Start | 2802ch09.doc - Microsoft... | Adobe Photoshop | 4:26 PM |

Windows also uses the middle area of the Taskbar. When you open a new window or program, it gets a button on the Taskbar with an icon that represents the window or program as well as the name of the window or program. To bring that window or program to the front (or to maximize it if it was minimized), click its button on the Taskbar. As the middle area of the Taskbar fills with buttons, the buttons become smaller so they can all be displayed.

You can increase the size of the Taskbar by moving the mouse pointer to the top of the Taskbar and pausing until the pointer turns into a double-headed arrow. Once this happens, click the mouse and move it up to make the Taskbar bigger. Or move it down to make the Taskbar smaller. You can also move the Taskbar to the top or side of the screen by clicking the Taskbar and dragging it to the new location.

> **TIP**
>
> In Windows XP, once you've configured the Taskbar position and layout to your liking, you can configure it so that it can't be changed accidentally. To do so, right-click the Taskbar and select Lock The Taskbar. To unlock the Taskbar and make changes, right-click the Taskbar and select Lock The Taskbar again.

In Exercise 4.2, we will show you how to auto-hide the Taskbar.

EXERCISE 4.2

Auto-Hiding the Taskbar

You can make the Taskbar automatically hide itself when it isn't being used (thus freeing that space for use by the Desktop or other windows):

1. Right-click the Taskbar.

2. Choose Properties, which will bring up the Taskbar And Start Menu Properties screen.

3. In Windows 2000, check the Auto Hide option on the General tab. In Windows XP, check the Auto-Hide The Taskbar option on the Taskbar tab.

4. Click OK.

5. In Windows 2000, move your mouse to the top of the Desktop or click on the Desktop. The Taskbar will retract off the screen. In Windows XP, the Taskbar retracts as soon as you click OK.

6. Move the mouse pointer to the bottom of the screen, and the Taskbar will pop up and be available for normal use.

The Start Menu

Back when Microsoft officially introduced Windows 95, it bought the rights to use the Rolling Stones' song "Start Me Up" in its advertisements and at the introduction party. Microsoft chose that particular song because the Start menu was the central point of focus in the new Windows interface, as it has been in all subsequent versions.

To display the Start menu, click the Start button in the Taskbar. You'll see a Start menu similar to that shown in Figure 4.5. You'll notice that in Windows XP the look of the Start menu has changed quite a bit from earlier versions of Windows. The Windows XP Start menu serves the same function (quick access to important features and programs); however, its layout and options have changed. Note that if you change the Desktop's appearance to the Windows Classic look, this changes only the color scheme and so on—the options and layout of the Windows XP Start menu remain different from those in older versions of Windows. However, the way the Start menu works (the principles it applies) is essentially the same in Windows XP as in older versions.

From the Start menu, you can select any of the various options the menu presents. An arrow pointing to the right indicates that a submenu is available. To select a submenu, move the mouse pointer over the submenu title and pause. The submenu will appear; you don't even have to click. (You have to click to choose an option *on* the submenu, though.) We'll discuss each of the default Start menu's submenu options and how to use them.

One handy feature of the Start menu in pre–Windows XP versions of Windows is that it usually displays the name of the OS type along its side when you activate it. This provides an excellent way to quickly see whether you are on Windows 95, 98, Me, NT, or 2000. In Windows XP you don't see the name of the OS; however, the Start menu looks so different that you'll know you are using Windows XP. (The Windows XP Start menu also displays the name of the currently logged-in user at the top.)

FIGURE 4.5   The Windows XP Start menu

In pre–Windows XP versions of Windows, you can also check which OS you are using by right-clicking the My Computer icon on the Desktop and selecting Properties. The OS type and version are displayed on the first tab. In Windows XP, the My Computer icon may not display on the Desktop by default. You can add the icon to the Desktop by using the Display Properties (click Customize Desktop on the Desktop tab, select My Computer on the General tab, and apply your changes), or you can click Start and then right-click the My Computer option and select Properties.

If you are attached to the look and feel of the pre–Windows XP Start menu, you can configure XP to use the old Start menu layout. To do so, right-click on the Taskbar and select Properties. Click on the Start Menu tab, select Classic Start Menu, and click OK.

Programs (Windows 2000)/All Programs (Windows XP) Submenu

The Programs/All Programs submenu holds the program groups and program icons you can use. When you select this submenu, you will be shown another submenu, with a submenu for each program group. In Windows XP, the look is again a little different, but the functionality is the same. You can navigate through this menu and its submenus and click the program you wish to start.

New in Windows XP, after you install a program, the newly installed program or program group is highlighted on the Start menu so you can find it easily.

The most common way to add programs to this submenu is by using an application's installation program. In Windows 2000 and Windows XP if you're using the Classic Start Menu, you can also add programs to this submenu by using the Taskbar Properties screen (right-click on the Taskbar and choose Properties).

Documents (2000)/My Recent Documents (Windows XP) Submenu

The Documents/My Recent Documents submenu has only one function: to keep track of the last 15 data files you opened. Whenever you open a file, a shortcut to it is automatically made in this menu. To open the document again, click the document in the Documents menu to open it in its associated application. In Windows XP, this feature is not enabled by default. To enable it, in the Taskbar And Start Menu Properties screen, click the Start Menu tab and then click Customize next to Start Menu. Click the Advanced tab, select the List My Most Recently Opened Documents option, and then click OK. An option called My Recent Documents is added to the Start menu; it lists the 15 most recently opened data files.

> To clear the list of documents shown in the Documents/My Recent Documents submenu, go to the Taskbar And Start Menu Properties screen. Then use the Clear button on the Advanced tab. (Remember that you access the Advanced tab in Windows XP via the Customize button on the Start Menu tab.)

Settings Submenu (Windows 2000)

The Settings submenu provides easy access to the configuration of Windows. This menu has numerous submenus, including Control Panel, Printers, and Taskbar & Start Menu. Additional menus are available, depending on which version of Windows you are using. These submenus give you access to the Control Panel, printer driver, and Taskbar configuration areas. You can also access the first two areas from the My Computer icon; they are placed together here to provide a common area to access Windows settings.

In Windows XP, you'll find Control Panel as an option directly off the Start menu (not below a submenu). You can add other options (such as Printers And Faxes) to the Start menu by using the options on the Advanced tab of the Taskbar And Start Menu Properties screen (via the Customize button).

Search (Find) Submenu/Option

The name of this submenu (Windows 2000) or Start menu option (Windows XP) differs between Search and Find in the various versions of Windows, but its purpose doesn't. In all cases, it's used to locate information on your computer or on a network.

In Windows 2000, to find a file or directory, select the Find or Search submenu and then select Files Or Folders (see Figure 4.6). In the Named field in this dialog box, type in the name of the file or directory you are looking for and click Find Now. Windows will search whatever is specified in the Look In parameter for the file or directory. Matches are listed in a window under the Find window. You can use wildcards (* and ?) to look for multiple files and directories. You can also click the Advanced tab to further refine your search.

FIGURE 4.6   Options in the Find submenu

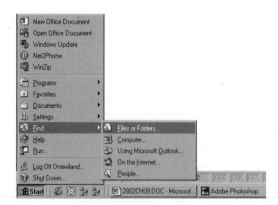

In Windows XP, to find a file or directory, click on the Search option in the Start menu. Doing so opens the Search Results dialog box shown in Figure 4.7. In the left pane, click on All Files And Folders, and then enter the appropriate information in the text fields. Expand the downward-pointing double arrows to access advanced search options. To start the search, click Search. The search results display in the right pane.

Help Command (Windows 2000)/Help And Support Command (Windows XP)

Windows has always included a *very* good Help system. In addition, the Help system was updated with a new interface and new tools in Windows XP. Because of its usefulness and power, it was placed in the Start menu for easy access.

In Windows 2000, when you select the Help command, it brings up the Windows Help window. In Windows XP, when you click Help And Support, the Help And Support Center home page opens. This screen may have been slightly customized by a hardware vendor if Windows XP was preinstalled on your machine. However, all the options and available tools will still be present.

A quick way to access Help is to press the F1 key.

FIGURE 4.7   The Search Results dialog box in Windows XP

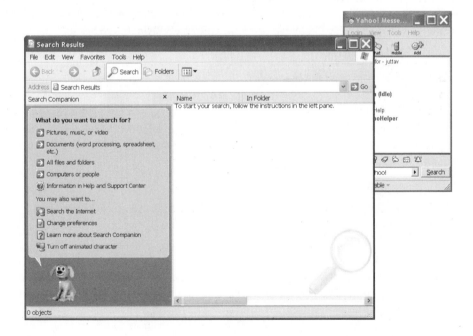

Run Command

You can use the Run command to start programs if they don't have a shortcut on the Desktop or in the Programs submenu. When you choose Run from the Start menu, a screen similar to the one in Figure 4.8 appears. To execute a particular program, type its name in the Open field. If you don't know the exact path, you can browse to find the file by clicking the Browse button. Once you have typed in the executable name, click OK to run the program.

FIGURE 4.8   The Start menu's Run command

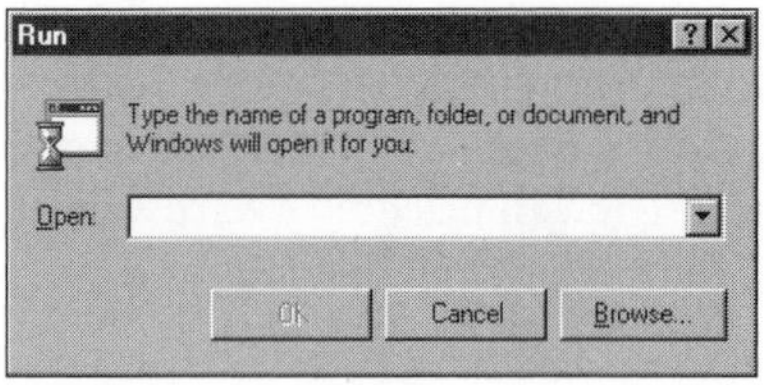

In Exercise 4.3, you will see how to start a program from the Run window.

EXERCISE 4.3

Starting a Program from the Run Window

Applications can easily be started from the Run window; often you will find it faster to open programs this way than search for their icons in the Start menu maze.

1. Click Start ➢ Run.

2. In the Open field, type **notepad**.

3. Click OK. Notepad will open in a new window.

If the program you want to run has been run from the Run window before, you can find it on the Open field's drop-down list. Click the down arrow to display the list, and then select the program you want by clicking its name and clicking OK.

Shut Down Command (Windows 2000)/Turn Off Computer Command (Windows XP)

Windows operating systems are very complex. At any one time, many files are open in memory. If you accidentally hit the power switch and turn off the computer while these files are open, there is a good chance they will be corrupted. For this reason, Microsoft has added the Shut Down (pre–Windows XP) or Turn Off Computer (Windows XP) command under the Start menu. Note that with a configuration called Fast User Switching, Windows XP also displays Shut Down, rather than Turn Off Computer. When you select this option, Windows presents you with several choices. Exactly which options are available depends on the Windows version you are running.

The possible choices are as follows:

Shut Down (Windows 2000)/Turn Off (Windows XP)   This option writes any unsaved data to disk, closes any open applications, and gets the computer ready to be powered off. Depending on the OS, the computer is then powered down automatically, or you'll see a black screen with the message *It's now safe to turn off your computer.* In this case, you can power off the computer or press Ctrl+Alt+Del to reboot the computer.

Restart   This option works the same as the first option, but instead of shutting down completely, it automatically reboots the computer with a warm reboot.

Stand By (Windows XP only)   This option places the computer into a low-power state. The monitor and hard disks are turned off, and the computer uses less power. To resume working, press a key on the keyboard; the computer is returned to its original state. In this state, information in memory is not saved to hard disk, so if a power loss occurs, any data in memory will be lost.

> If you enable Hibernation on a Windows XP machine, you can place the computer into hibernation by holding down the Shift key while clicking Stand By in the Turn Off Computer screen. Using the Hibernation feature, any information in memory is saved to disk before the computer is put into a low power state. Thus, if power is lost while the machine is in hibernation, your data is not lost. However, going into and coming out of hibernation takes more time than going into and coming out of stand-by mode.

Icons

Icons are not nearly as complex in structure, but they are very important nonetheless. Icons are shortcuts that allow a user to open a program or a utility without knowing where that program is located or how it needs to be configured. Icons consist of several major elements:

- Icon label
- Icon graphic
- Program location

The label and graphic simply tell the user the name of the program and give a visual hint about what that program does. The icon for the Solitaire program, for instance, is labeled *Solitaire*, and its icon graphic is a deck of cards. By right-clicking an icon once, you make that icon the active icon, and a drop-down menu appears. One of the selections is Properties. Clicking Properties brings up the icon's attributes (see Figure 4.9) and is the only way to see exactly which program an icon is configured to start and where the program's executable is located. You can also specify whether to run the program in a normal window or maximized or minimized.

FIGURE 4.9   The Properties window of an application with its icon to the left

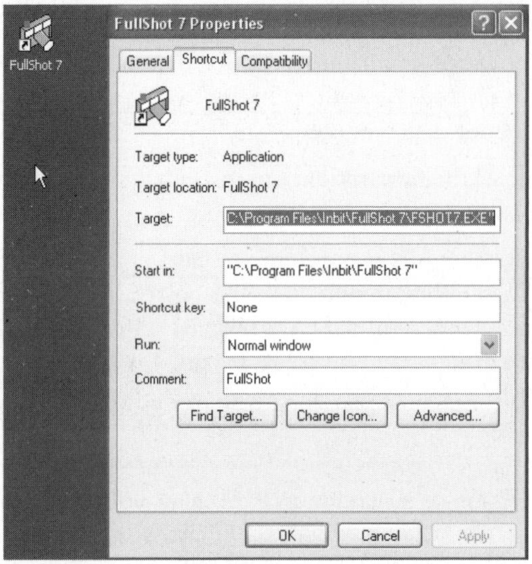

In Windows XP, additional functionality has been added to an icon's Properties to allow for backward compatibility with older versions of Windows. To configure this, click the Compatibility tab and specify the version of Windows for which you want to configure compatibility. Choices include Windows 95, Windows 98/Me, Windows NT 4.0 (Service Pack 5), and Windows 2000. This feature is helpful if you own programs that used to work in older versions of Windows but no longer run under Windows XP. In addition, you can specify different display settings that might be required by older programs.

Standard Desktop Icons

In addition to the options in your Start menu, a number of icons are placed directly on the Desktop. Three of the most important icons are My Computer, Network Neighborhood/My Network Places, and the Recycle Bin. In Windows XP, the My Computer and My Network Places icons no longer display by default on the Desktop; however, you might want to add them. Instructions on how to add My Computer were given earlier in the section "The Start Menu"; you can select My Network Places in the same place you select My Computer to display on the Desktop.

THE MY COMPUTER ICON

If you double-click the My Computer icon, it displays a list of all the disk drives installed in your computer. In pre–Windows XP versions of Windows, it also displays an icon for the Control Panel and Printers folders, which can be used to configure the system.

In Windows XP, My Computer does not by default display an icon for Control Panel (although you can configure it to do so by going to Tools ➢ Folder Options and specifying to show Control Panel in My Computer on the View tab) or for printers; however, in addition to displaying disk drives, it also displays a list of other devices attached to the computer, such as scanners, cameras, mobile devices, and so on. In Windows XP, all the disk devices are sorted into categories such as Hard Disk Drives, Devices With Removable Storage, Scanners And Cameras, and so on. If you double-click a disk drive or device, you will see the contents of that disk drive or device.

You can delve deeper into each disk drive or device by double-clicking it. The contents are displayed in the same window. You can use Tools ➤ Folder to configure each folder to open in a new window. Having multiple windows open makes it easy to copy and move files between drives and between directories using these windows.

In addition to allowing you access to your computer's files, the My Computer icon lets you view your machine's configuration and hardware, also called the System Properties.

In Exercise 4.4, you will see how to view the System Properties.

EXERCISE 4.4

Viewing System Properties

Here is the process to view your System Properties:

1. Right-click the My Computer icon (on the Desktop in pre–Windows XP versions of Windows and in the Start menu in Windows XP).

2. Choose Properties.

3. On the System Properties screen (General screen in Windows XP), look to see what type of processor your computer uses and how much RAM is installed. This screen also tells you what version of Windows is being used. We'll look at the System Properties in much more detail later in this chapter.

MY NETWORK PLACES

Another icon in Windows relates to accessing other computers to which the local computer is connected, and it's called My Network Places (Network Neighborhood pre–Windows 2000).

In Windows XP, the My Network Places icon may not display on the Desktop by default. You can add the icon to the Desktop through the Display Properties (in the same manner you can add the My Computer icon to the Desktop if it isn't there), or you can reach My Network Places by clicking Start ➤ My Network Places.

Opening My Network Places enables you to browse for and access other computers and shared resources to which your computer is connected. This might be another computer in a workgroup, domain, or other network environment (such as a Novell NetWare network). You can also use My Network Places to establish new connections to shared resources.

Through the Properties of My Network Places, you can configure your network connections, including LAN and dial-up connections. You will learn about networking in detail in Chapter 8.

THE RECYCLE BIN

All files, directories, and programs in Windows are represented by icons and are generally referred to as *objects*. When you want to remove an object from Windows, you do so by deleting it. Deleting doesn't just remove the object, though; it also removes the ability of the system to access the information or application the object represents. For this reason, Windows includes a special directory where all deleted files are placed: the Recycle Bin. The Recycle Bin holds the files until it is emptied and allows users the opportunity to recover files that they delete accidentally.

You can retrieve a file you have deleted by opening the Recycle Bin icon and then dragging the file from the Recycle Bin to where you want to restore it to. Alternatively, you can right-click a file and select Restore, and the file will be restored back to the location it was deleted from.

If you have antivirus software installed, option names in the Recycle Bin might change. For example, if you have Norton Antivirus installed and you right-click on a file, you'll see that the Restore option has been renamed to Recover.

To permanently erase files, you need to empty the Recycle Bin, thereby deleting any items in it and freeing the hard-drive space they took up. If you want to delete only specific, but not all, files, you can select those file(s) in the Recycle Bin, right-click, and choose Delete. You can also permanently erase files (bypassing the Recycle Bin) by holding down the Shift key as you delete the file (either by dragging the file and dropping it in the Recycle Bin, pressing the Del key, or clicking Delete on the file's context menu). If the Recycle Bin has files in it, its icon looks like the full trash can shown on the left in Figure 4.10; after it is emptied, its icon reflects this fact, as shown on the right.

FIGURE 4.10   A full (left) and empty (right) Recycle Bin

In Exercise 4.5, you will see how to empty the Recycle Bin.

EXERCISE 4.5

Emptying the Recycle Bin

Did your parents always tell you to take out the trash? Periodically emptying the Recycle Bin helps clean up your hard drive.

1. Right-click the Recycle Bin.

2. Choose Empty Recycle Bin.

3. A window appears asking if you are certain you want to permanently delete the objects. Click Yes.

What's in a Window?

We have now looked at the nature of the Desktop, the Taskbar, the Start menu, and icons. Each of these items was created for the primary purpose of making access to user applications easier, and these applications are in turn used and managed through the use of *windows*, the rectangular application environments for which the Windows family of operating systems is named. We will now examine how windows work and what they are made of.

A program *window* is a rectangular area created on the screen when an application is opened within Windows. This window can have a number of different forms, but most windows include at least a few basic elements.

Elements of a Window

Several basic elements are present in a standard window. Figure 4.11 shows the control box, title bar, Minimize button, Restore button, Close button, and resizable border in a text editor called Notepad (NOTEPAD.EXE) that has all the basic window elements—and little else.

The basic window elements are as follows:

Control Box   In the upper-left corner of the window. Used to control the state of the application. It can be used to maximize, minimize, and close the application. Clicking it once brings into view a selection menu. Double-clicking it closes the window and shuts down the application.

Minimize and Restore Buttons   Used to change the state of the window on the Desktop. They are discussed in the "States of a Window" section later in this chapter.

Close Button   Used to easily end a program and return any resources it was using to the system. It essentially does the same thing as double-clicking the control box, but with one less click.

FIGURE 4.11   The basic elements of a window

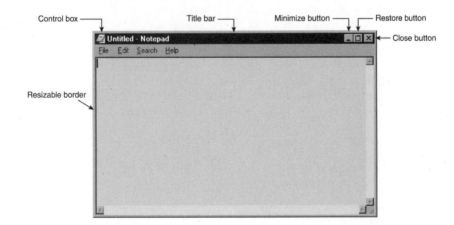

Title Bar   The area between the control box and the Minimize button. It states the name of the program and in some cases gives information about the particular document being accessed by that program. The color of the title bar indicates whether a particular window is the active window.

Menu Bar   Used to present useful commands in an easily accessible format. Clicking one of the menu choices displays a list of related options you may choose from.

Active Window   The window that is currently being used. It has two attributes. First, any keystrokes that are entered are directed there by default. Second, any other windows that overlap the active window are pushed behind it.

Border   A thin line that surrounds the window in its restored state and allows it to be resized.

Not every element is found on every window, because programmers can choose to eliminate or modify them. Still, in most cases they will be constant, with the rest of the window filled in with menus, toolbars, a workspace, or other application-specific elements. For instance, Microsoft Word, the program with which this book was written, adds an additional control box and Minimize and Maximize buttons for each document. It also has a menu bar, a number of optional toolbars, scroll bars at the right and bottom of the window, and a status bar at the very bottom. Application windows can become quite cluttered.

Notepad is a very simple Windows program. It has only a single menu bar and the basic elements seen previously in Figure 4.11. Figure 4.12 shows a Microsoft Word window. Both Word and Notepad are used to create and edit documents, but Word is far more configurable and powerful and therefore has many more optional components available within its window.

FIGURE 4.12   A window with more components

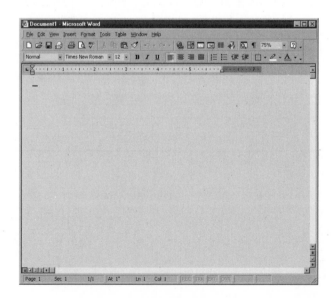

States of a Window

There is more to the Windows interface than the specific parts of a window. Windows also are movable, stackable, and resizable, and they can be hidden behind other windows (often unintentionally!).

When an application window has been launched, it exists in one of three states:

Maximized   A maximized window takes up all available space on the screen. When it is in front of other programs, it is the only thing visible—even the Desktop is hidden. In Figure 4.13, note that Microsoft Word is maximized; it takes up the entire space of the Desktop, and the middle button in the upper-right corner displays two rectangles rather than one. The sides of the window no longer have borders. The window is flush with the edges of the screen. Maximizing a window provides the maximum workspace possible for that window's application, and the window can be accessed actively by the user. In general, maximized mode is the preferred window size for most word-processing, graphics-creation, and other user applications.

Restored   A restored window can be used interactively and is identical in function to a maximized window, with the simple difference that it does not necessarily take up the entire screen. Restored windows can be very small, or they can take up almost as much space as maximized windows. Generally, how large the restored window becomes is the user's choice. Restored windows display a restore box (the middle button in the upper-right corner) with a single rectangle in it; this is used to maximize the window. Restored windows have a border. Figure 4.13 shows an example of Notepad in a restored state.

Minimized   Minimized program windows are represented by nothing but an icon and title on the Taskbar, and they are not usable until they have been either maximized or restored. The only difference between a minimized program and a closed program is that a minimized program is out of the way but is still taking up resources and is therefore ready to use if you need it. It also leaves the content of the window in the same place when you return to it as when you minimized it. In Figure 4.13, Adobe Photoshop is minimized.

When a program is open and you need to open another program (or maybe you need to stop playing a game because your boss has entered the room), you have two choices. First, you can close the program and reopen it later. If you do this, however, your current game will be lost and you will have to start over. Minimizing the game window, on the other hand, removes the open window from the screen and leaves the program open but displays nothing more than an icon and title on the Taskbar, as with the Photoshop icon in Figure 4.13. Later, you can restore the window to its previous size and finish the game in progress.

Keep in mind that applications in the background are still running. Therefore, if you minimize your game, you might return to find that you've been eaten by whatever monster you were running from in the game. Running while minimized can be a good thing, however, if you're running a useful utility such as a long search or a disk defrag.

FIGURE 4.13   Windows in different states

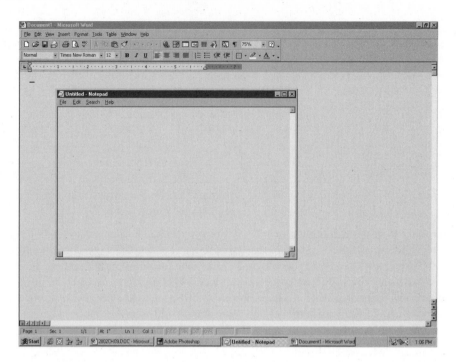

Control Panel

Although for the most part the Windows system is functional from the time it is installed, Microsoft realized that if someone were going to use computers regularly, they would probably want to be able to customize their environment so it would be better suited to their needs—or at least more fun to use. As a result, the Windows environment has a large number of utilities that are intended to give you control over the look and feel of the Desktop.

This is, of course, an excellent idea. It is also a bit more freedom than some less-than-cautious users seem to be capable of handling, and you will undoubtedly serve a number of customers who call you in to restore their configuration after botched attempts at changing one setting or another.

More than likely, you will also have to reinstall Windows yourself a few times because of accidents that occur while you are studying or testing the system's limits. This is actually a good thing, because no competent computer technician can say that they have never had to reinstall because of an error. You can't really know how to fix Windows until you are experienced at breaking it. So it is extremely important to experiment and find out what can be changed in the Windows environment, what results from those changes, and how to undo any unwanted results. To this end, we will examine the most common configuration utility in Windows: Control Panel. The names of some panels are different in various versions of Windows;

different names are indicated in parentheses. And not all panels are available in all versions. You'll see some of the more popular panels described in Table 4.1.

In Windows XP, when you first open Control Panel, it displays in Category view. This view provides you with different categories to choose from, into which Control Panel programs have been organized. Once you choose a category, you can pick a task and the appropriate Control Panel program is opened for you; or you can select one of the Control Panel programs that is part of the category. However, you can change this view to Classic View, which displays all the Control Panel programs in a list, as in older versions of Windows (see Figure 4.14). We suggest that administrators of Windows XP computers change to this view. To do so, click Switch To Classic View in the left pane. Throughout this chapter, when we refer to accessing Control Panel programs, we will assume that you have changed the view to Classic View.

For a quick look at how the Control Panel programs work, the following exercise examines some of the settings in the Date/Time program. The Date/Time program is used to configure the system time, date, and time-zone settings, which can be important for files that require accurate timestamps or to users who don't have a watch. Because it is a simple program, it's a perfect example to use. In pre–Windows XP versions of Windows, the Date/Time program includes only two sets of *tabs* (Date & Time and Time Zone) and one option (whether to use Daylight Savings). Windows XP also has an Internet Time tab, which enables you to synchronize time on the computer with an Internet time server.

FIGURE 4.14   The Control Panel interface in Windows XP

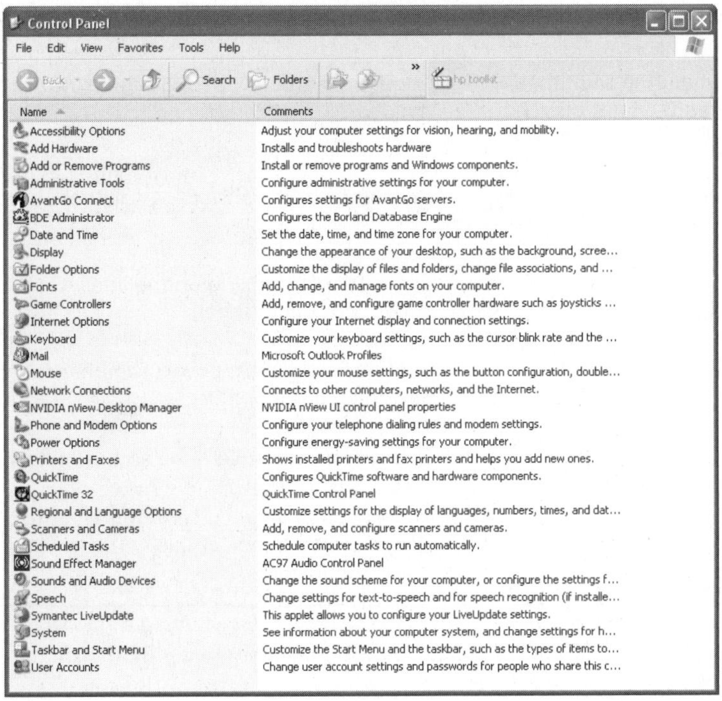

TABLE 4.1   Selected Windows Control Panel Programs (Windows XP Names and Other Variations in Parentheses)

Program Name	Function
Add/Remove Hardware (Add Hardware in Windows XP)	Adds and configures new hardware.
Add/Remove Programs (Add Or Remove Programs)	Changes, adds, or deletes software.
Administrative Tools	Performs administrative tasks on the computer.
Date/Time (Date And Time)	Sets the system time and configures options such as time zone.
Display	Configures screensavers, colors, display options, and monitor drivers.
Folder Options	Configures the look and feel of how folders are displayed in Windows Explorer.
Fonts	Adds and removes fonts.
Internet Options	Sets a number of Internet connectivity options.
Multimedia (Sounds And Multimedia; Sounds And Audio Devices; also Scanners And Cameras)	Configures audio, video, or audio and video options.
Network (Network And Dial-up Connections; Network Connections)	Sets options for connecting to other computers.
Modems (Phone And Modem Options)	Sets options for using phone lines to dial out to a network or the Internet.
Power Options	Configures different power schemes to adjust power consumption.
Printers (Printers And Faxes)	Configures printer settings and print defaults.
System	Allows you to view and configure various system elements. We'll look at this in more detail later in this chapter.

In Exercise 4.6, you will see how to change the time zone.

Changing the Time Zone

Did you recently move from one time zone to the other? Keep up with the time(s)!

1. In pre–Windows XP versions of Windows, click Start ➢ Settings ➢ Control Panel. In Windows XP, click Start ➢ Control Panel.

2. From Control Panel, double-click the Date/Time (Date And Time) icon (by default, the programs are listed alphabetically).

3. Click the Time Zone tab and use the drop-down menu to select (GMT –03:30) Newfoundland, as shown in the graphic.

4. Hop a plane to Newfoundland, secure in the knowledge that you will know what time it is once you get there.

5. If you skipped step 4, change the time zone back to where it should be before closing the window.

The System Control Panel

The System control panel (see Figure 4.15 for the Windows XP System control panel) is one of the most important control panels, and it's nearly all business. From within this one relatively innocuous panel, you can make a large number of configuration changes to a Windows machine. The different versions of Windows have different options available in this panel; as a general rule, the newer the OS, the more options you'll find. The System Properties panel is divided into tabs. They can include some of the following: General, Network Identification, Device Manager,

Hardware, Hardware Profiles, User Profiles, Environment, Startup/Shutdown, Performance, System Restore, Automatic Updates, Remote, Computer Name, and Advanced. The General tab gives you an overview of the system, such as OS version, registration information, basic hardware levels (Processor and RAM), and the Service Pack level that's installed, if any. For the rest of the tabs, we will look a bit more closely at their functionality. For each tab, we identify which versions of Windows contain the tab.

Network Identification (Windows 2000)/Computer Name (Windows XP)

This tab is used to define whether the machine is in a workgroup or a domain environment. We will talk more about networking in Chapter 8, but in general terms, the difference between a workgroup and a domain is this:

Workgroup   Loosely associated computers, each of which is its own security authority.

Domain   A group of computers that is tightly connected. Has a single authority (called a *domain controller*) that manages security for all the computers.

Hardware

This tab includes a number of tools, all of which allow you to change how the hardware on your machine is used:

FIGURE 4.15   The System Properties control panel on a Windows XP computer with the Advanced tab selected

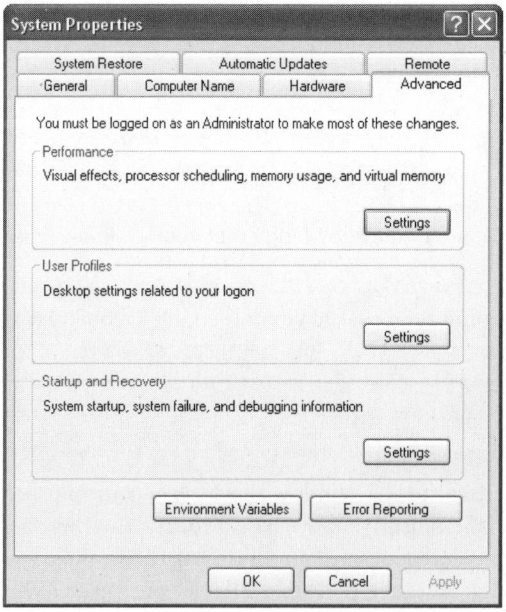

(Add) Hardware Wizard   The Hardware Wizard in Windows 2000 is used, as it says, to "install, uninstall, repair, unplug, eject, and configure" hardware in the system. In Windows XP, you can only install and troubleshoot hardware here. Essentially, this means that if you want to add a new device to the system or uninstall drivers that are already there, this is the place to go. You can also use this tool to temporarily eject *PC Card* devices or other removable components.

WARNING   Even in a Plug and Play system, it is important to properly unplug a device if you wish to remove it while the system is running. If you don't do this, nothing may go wrong, but you can sometimes damage the device or cause the system to become unstable.

Driver Signing   This is an option first introduced in Windows 2000. In order to minimize the risks involved with adding third-party software to your Windows 2000 Professional machine, Microsoft has come up with a technique called *driver signing*. Installing new hardware drivers onto the system is a situation in which both viruses and badly written software can threaten your system's health. To minimize the risks, you can choose to only use drivers that have been *signed*. The signing process is meant to ensure that you are getting drivers that have been checked with Windows 2000/XP and that those drivers have not been modified maliciously.

Device Manager

Although you can make many hardware changes through the Hardware Wizard, it is often easier to use the Device Manager. We'll discuss the Device Manager in more detail later in this chapter.

Hardware Profiles

A hardware profile lets you start the computer with different hardware configurations. This ability is most useful on laptops, which often have docking stations, or at the very least are moved from place to place. You might have one profile that loads a network card driver, and another profile that loads your laptop's modem driver, for example.

User Profiles (Windows 2000; on the Advanced tab in Windows XP)

Unlike Windows 9x, where *user profiles* are an optional setting, in Windows 2000 and XP every user automatically is given a user profile when they log on to the workstation. This profile contains information about the user's settings and preferences. Although it does not happen often, occasionally a user profile becomes corrupt or needs to be destroyed. Alternatively, if a particular profile is set up exceptionally well, you can copy it so that it is available for other users. To do either of these tasks, use the User Profiles tab to select the user profile you want to work with. At that point, you will be given three options:

Delete   Removes the user's profile entirely. When that user logs on again, they will be given a fresh profile taken from the system default. Any settings they have added will be lost, as will any profile-related problems they have caused.

Change Type   Configures a profile as local (the default) or roaming. If a user works at two machines, each machine will use a different profile. Updates to one machine will not be reflected on the other. If you have a network, roaming profiles can be configured to allow a user to have a single profile anywhere on the network. Further discussion of this topic is beyond the scope of this book.

Copy To   Copies a profile from one user to another. Often the source profile is a template set up to provide a standard configuration.

Advanced

The Advanced tab has three subheadings, each of which can be configured separately. They're not identical in Windows 2000/XP, however. (This could also be called the Etc. tab rather than the Advanced tab.) Among its options are the following:

- Performance
- Environment Variables
- User Profiles
- Startup And Recovery

We discussed User Profiles earlier, so we won't cover it again here.

Performance (Windows 2000/XP)   Although it is hidden in the backwaters of Windows 2000/XP's system configuration settings, the Performance option holds some important settings you may need to configure on a 2000/XP Professional system. To access it in Windows 2000, on the Advanced tab, click Performance Options. In Windows XP, on the Advanced tab, click Settings in the Performance area.

Among the settings in the Performance window are the size of your virtual memory (we talk more about virtual memory later in this chapter) and how the system handles the allocation of processor time. In addition, in Windows 2000, this is the place to specify the maximum Registry size (through the Virtual Memory options). In Windows XP, you also use Performance to configure visual effects for the XP GUI.

Letting the Registry fill up is a serious problem. Although the default level is usually fine, if you think this may happen, you should change this option. An extra 10MB today could save a lot of pain tomorrow.

How resources are allocated to the processor is normally not something you will need to modify. It is set by default to optimize the system for foreground applications, making the system most responsive to the user who is running programs. This is generally best, but it means that any applications (databases, network services, and so on) that are run by the system are given less time by the system.

If the Windows machine will be working primarily as a network server, you may want to change this option to Background Services. Otherwise, leave it as is.

Environment Variables   There are two types of *environment variables*, and each can be added through the Environment Variables button:

User Variables   Specify settings that are specific to an individual user and do not affect others who log on to the machine.

System Variables   Set for all users on the machine. System variables are used to provide information needed by the system when running applications or performing system tasks.

System and user variables were extremely important in DOS and Windows 3.1. If you are going to try to run DOS/Win3.1 applications on Windows, you will probably have to add variables in this window to support those applications.

Startup And Recovery   The Windows 2000/XP Startup And Recovery options are relatively straightforward. They involve two areas: what to do during system startup and what to do in case of unexpected system shutdown:

System Startup   The System Startup option defaults to the Windows OS you installed, but you can change this default behavior if you like. Unless you are *dual-booting*, only one option is available; but if you have another OS installed, you can change the Windows boot manager to load that as the default. You can also reduce the time the menu is displayed or remove the menu entirely. In Windows XP, you can also click Edit to edit the BOOT.INI.

If you choose to completely disable the menu on a dual-boot system, you will find that doing so may cause you annoyance in the future when you want to boot into a different OS but no longer have a choice to do so. Thus, you should always let the boot menu appear for at least two to five seconds if you are dual-booting.

System Failure   A number of options are available in the Startup And Recovery screen for use in case of problems. These include writing an event about the problem, sending out an alert to the network, and saving information about the problem to disk. These options come into play only in case of a major system problem, though.

Your options for handling system failures will be covered along with the troubleshooting information later in this chapter.

System Restore (Windows XP)

The System Restore tab lets you disable/enable and configure the new System Restore feature in Windows XP. When it's enabled on one or more drives, Windows XP monitors the changes you make on your drives. From time to time it creates what is called a *restore point*. Then, if you have a system crash, it can restore your data back to the restore point. You can turn on System Restore for all drives on your system or for individual drives. Note that turning off System Restore on the system drive (the drive on which the OS is installed) automatically turns it off on all drives.

Automatic Updates (Windows XP)

The Automatic Updates tab in Windows XP lets you configure how you want to handle updating the OS. You can specify that you want to automatically download updates, notify the user when updates are available (but not automatically install them), or turn off the feature. You can also specify that you want Windows XP to notify you again of updates you declined to download at an earlier point in time.

Remote (Windows XP)

The Remote tab in Windows XP lets you enable or disable Remote Assistance. Remote Assistance allows the local workstation to be used from a remote computer. This can help an administrator or other support person troubleshoot problems with the machine from a remote location.

Remote Assistance is enabled by default. It is handled at two levels. Just having Remote Assistance turned on allows the person connecting only to view the computer's screen. To let that person take over the computer and be able to control the keyboard and mouse, click Advanced and then, in the Remote Control section, click Allow This Computer To Be Controlled Remotely.

The Command Prompt

Although we're talking about the Windows operating system in this book, its ancestor, the Microsoft Disk Operating System (MS-DOS), still plays a role in Windows today. MS-DOS was never meant to be extremely friendly. Its roots are in CP/M, which, in turn, has its roots in Unix. Both of these older OSs are command line–based, and so is MS-DOS. In other words, they all use long strings of commands typed in at the computer keyboard to perform operations. Some people prefer this type of interaction with the computer, including many folks with technical backgrounds (such as yours truly). Although Windows has left the full command-line interface behind, it still contains a bit of DOS, and you get to it through the command prompt.

Although you can't tell from looking at it (see Figure 4.16), the Windows command prompt is actually a 16- or 32-bit Windows program that is intentionally *designed* to have the look and feel of a DOS command line. Because it is, despite its appearance, a Windows program, the command prompt provides all the stability and configurability you expect from Windows.

FIGURE 4.16   The Windows command prompt

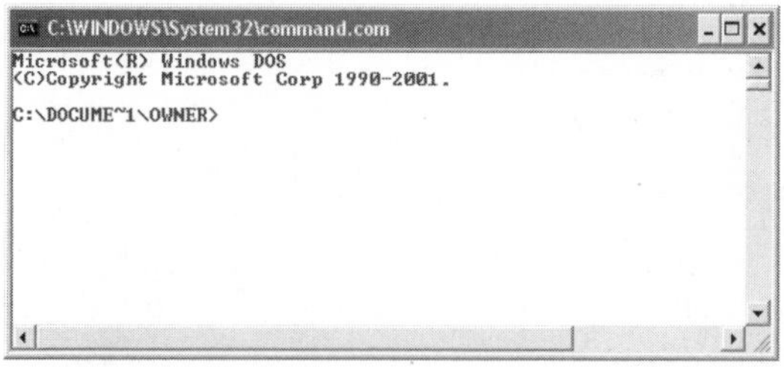

You can access a command prompt by either running the 16-bit COMMAND.COM or the 32-bit CMD.EXE. In Windows 2000 and XP, if you run COMMAND.COM and enter commands at the command prompt, they're actually sent to and handled by CMD.EXE.

There are few actual text-based applications in newer versions of Windows. We'll discuss some specific command-line utilities in Chapter 14.

The Registry

Windows configuration information is stored in a special configuration database known as the *Registry*. This centralized database contains environmental settings for various Windows programs. It also contains *registration* information that details which types of file extensions are associated with which applications. So, when you double-click a file in Windows Explorer, the associated application runs and opens the file you double-clicked.

The Registry was introduced with Windows 95. Most OSs up until Windows 95 were configured through text files, which can be edited with almost any text editor. However, the Registry database is contained in a special binary file that can be edited only with the special Registry Editor provided with Windows.

Windows 2000 and XP have two applications that can be used to edit the Registry, REGEDIT and REGEDT32 (with no *I*). In Windows XP, regedt32 opens regedit. They work similarly, but each has slightly different options for navigation and browsing. In addition, REGEDT32 allows you to configure security-related settings for Registry keys,, such as assigning permissions.

The Registry is broken down into a series of separate areas called *hives*. These keys are divided into two basic sections—user settings and computer settings. In Windows 2000 and XP, a number of files are created corresponding to each of the different hives. Most of these files do not have extensions, and their names are system, software, security, sam, and default. One additional file that does have an extension is NTUSER.DAT.

The basic hives of the Registry are these:

HKEY_CLASSES_ROOT   Includes information about which file extensions map to particular applications.

HKEY_CURRENT_USER   Holds all configuration information specific to a particular user, such as their Desktop settings and history information.

HKEY_LOCAL_MACHINE   Includes nearly all configuration information concerning the actual computer hardware and software.

HKEY_USERS   Includes information about all users who have logged on to the system. The HKEY_CURRENT_USER hive is actually a subkey of this hive.

HKEY_CURRENT_CONFIG   Provides quick access to a number of commonly needed keys that are otherwise buried deep in the HKEY_LOCAL_MACHINE structure.

Modifying a Registry Entry

If you need to modify the Registry, you can modify the values in the database or create new entries or keys. You will find the options for adding a new element to the Registry under the Edit menu. To edit an existing value, double-click the entry and modify it as needed. On Windows 2000 and XP systems, you need administrative-level access to modify the Registry.

Windows uses the Registry extensively to store all kinds of information. Indeed, the Registry holds most, if not all, of the configuration information for Windows. Modifying the Registry in Windows is a potentially dangerous task. Control Panel and other configuration tools are provided so you have graphical tools for modifying system settings. Directly modifying the Registry can have unforeseen—and unpleasant—results. You should only modify the Registry when told to do so by an extremely trustworthy source or if you are absolutely certain you have the knowledge to do so without causing havoc in the Registry.

🌐 Real World Scenario

Beware Editing the Registry

Just in case it hasn't sunk in yet, be careful editing the Registry. There is no Undo button, nor do you have the safety net of choosing not to save your edits before you close. Once you make the change, it's made, for better or for worse.

There have been countless examples throughout my career of where people went in to edit the Registry without really knowing what they were doing. In many cases, making small changes to the Registry, without having a viable backup, means having to reinstall Windows. At the very least, this is inconvenient.

Windows 2000 and Windows XP can help in this regard if you are in a networked environment with Windows-based servers. You can create system policies that prevent users from performing certain tasks, and the one at the top of the importance list is running Registry editors.

Restoring the Registry in Windows 2000 and XP

Windows 2000 and XP store Registry information in files on the hard drive. You can restore this information using the Last Known Good Configuration option, which restores the Registry from a backup of its last functional state. To use this option:

- In Windows 2000/XP, press F8 during startup and then select Last Known Good Configuration from the menu that appears. You can also back up the Registry files to the systemroot\ repair directory by using the Windows 2000/XP Backup program, or you can save them to tape during a normal backup. To repair the Registry from a backup, overwrite the Registry files in `systemroot\system32\config`.

- In Windows 2000, creating an Emergency Repair Disk (ERD) also backs up the Registry files (to floppy disk, in this case). To create an ERD, in Windows 2000, use the Backup utility.

- In Windows XP, the ERD has been replaced with Automatic System Recovery (ASR), which is accessible through the Backup utility.

Note that ERD and ASR are considered last-resort options for system recovery. We'll talk more about ERD and ASR in Chapter 14.

Virtual Memory

Another thing you may need to configure is *virtual memory*. Virtual memory uses what's called a *swap* file, or *paging* file. A swap file is actually hard-drive space into which idle pieces of programs are placed, while other active parts of programs are kept in or swapped into main memory. The programs running in Windows believe that their information is still in RAM, but Windows has moved the data into *near-line* storage on the hard drive. When the application needs the information again, it is swapped back into RAM so that it can be used by the processor.

Because the concept of virtual memory can sometimes be hard to grasp, here is an analogy. When you are working in your office and need a document, you may have to walk to a file cabinet to get it. You then return to your seat and read the document. When you have finished and are ready to go on to another task, you need to put down the current document. If you don't need it again in the near future, you should get up and put it back in the file cabinet. However, if you will need it again, you may just set it on your desk for easier access. When you need the document again, you have to pick it back up (unless you can remember what it said without looking again). Generally, you can think of a computer's disk drive as the file cabinet and virtual memory as the desk.

Random access memory (RAM) is the computer's physical memory. The more RAM you put into the machine, the more items it can remember without looking anything up. And the larger the swap file, the fewer times the machine has to do intensive drive searches. The maximum possible size of your swap file depends on the amount of disk space you have available on the drive where the swap file is placed:

- Windows XP configures the minimum and maximum swap file size automatically, but if you want Windows to handle the size of the swap file dynamically, you have to change the default setting by selecting System Managed Size in the Virtual Memory dialog box. We'll show you how to get there in a moment.

- In Windows 2000, Windows sets the minimum and maximum swap file size for you, and you can adjust these settings. Windows 2000 handles the swap file much the same as Windows XP. In Windows 2000 if you set a minimum and maximum size and the OS dynamically manages the swap file size within those parameters. 2000 automatically creates a virtual-memory swap file during installation that is approximately 1.5 times the size of installed RAM.

In Windows 2000 and XP, the swap file is called PAGEFILE.SYS, and it's located in the root directory of the drive on which you installed the OS files. The swap file is a hidden file, so to see the file in Windows Explorer you must have the folder options configured to show hidden files. Typically, there's no reason to view the swap file in the file system, because you'll use Control Panel to configure it. However, you may want to check its size, and in that case you'd use Windows Explorer.

The moral of the story: As with most things virtual, a swap file is not nearly as good as actual RAM, but it is better than nothing!

To modify the default Virtual Memory settings, follow these steps:

- In Windows 2000, click Start ➤ Settings ➤ Control Panel. Double-click the System icon and select the Advanced tab. Then click Performance Options and, in the Virtual Memory area, click Change.

- In Windows XP, click Start ➤ Control Panel. Double-click the System icon, and select the Advanced tab. In the Performance area, click Settings. Next, click the Advanced tab (yes, another Advanced tab), and then, in the Virtual Memory area, click Change.

Note that in addition to changing the swap file's size and how Windows handles it, you can also specify the drive on which you want to place the file.

You should place the swap file on a drive with plenty of empty space. As a general rule, try to keep 20 percent of your drive space free for the overhead of various elements of the OS, like the swap file.

Do not set the swap file to an extremely small size. Another general rule would be that the swap file should be at least as big as the amount of RAM in the machine. If you make the swap file too small, the system can become unbootable, or at least unstable.

Windows System Files

Among the things you must be familiar with in preparation for the A+ exam are the startup and system files used by Windows 2000 and Windows XP. We will look at each of them individually, but Windows makes nosing around in the startup environment difficult, and so there is a change you need to make first.

To protect Windows system files from accidental deletion, and to get them out of the way of the average user, they are hidden from the user by default. Because of this, many of the files we are about to talk about will not be visible to you.

To make them visible, you need to change the display Properties of Windows Explorer. We will show you how to do this in Exercise 4.7

EXERCISE 4.7

Showing Hidden Files and Folders

Some of the more important files you will need to work on are hidden by default as a security precaution. Let's throw precaution to the wind.

1. Open Windows Explorer.

2. Browse to the root of the C: drive. Look for the IO.SYS system file. It should be hidden and will not appear in the file list.

3. Choose Tools ➤ Folder Options. The Folder Options window opens.

4. Select the View tab, and scroll until you find the Hidden Files option.

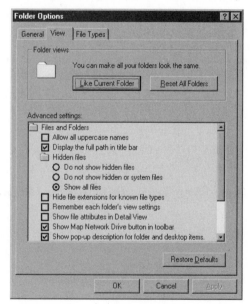

5. Select show all files.

6. Deselect Hide Protected Operating System Files (Recommended).

7. Uncheck Hide File Extensions for Known File Types.

8. Click OK. You will now be able to see the Windows system files discussed in the following sections. For security reasons, you should set these attributes back to the defaults after you've read this chapter.

Windows 2000 and Windows XP are both based on Windows NT, and as such each of their boot processes uses the same key boot files as Windows NT did. In this section, we will discuss these files.

Key Boot Files

Windows 2000 and XP require only a few files, each of which performs specific tasks:

NTLDR   Bootstraps the system. In other words, this file starts the loading of an OS on the computer.

BOOT.INI   Holds information about which OSs are installed on the computer.

BOOTSECT.DOS   In a dual-boot configuration, keeps a copy of the DOS or Windows 9*x* boot sector so that the Windows 9*x* environment can be restored and loaded as needed.

NTDETECT.COM   Parses the system for hardware information each time Windows 2000/XP is loaded. This information is then used to create dynamic hardware information in the Registry.

NTBOOTDD.SYS   On a system with a SCSI boot device, used to recognize and load the SCSI interface. On EIDE systems, this file is not needed and is not even installed.

NTOSKRNL.EXE   The Windows 2000/XP OS kernel.

System Files   In addition to the previously listed files, all of which except NTOSKRNL.EXE are located in the root of the C: partition on the computer, Windows 2000/XP needs a number of files from its system directories (e.g., system and system32), such as the hardware abstraction layer (HAL.DLL).

Numerous other DLL (dynamic link library) files are also required, but usually the lack or corruption of one of them produces a noncritical error, whereas the absence of HAL.DLL causes the system to be nonfunctional.

System Files Configuration Tools in Windows 2000/XP

The MSCONFIG system-configuration tool that was available in Windows 9*x* doesn't exist in Windows 2000. It is, however, included with Windows XP. Some tabs in the Windows XP version of MSCONFIG are the same as those available in the Windows 9*x* version, such as General, System.ini, Win.ini, and Startup. New tabs in the Windows XP version include Boot.ini and Services. The Boot.ini tab lets you modify the BOOT.INI file and also specify other boot options. On the Services tab, you can view the services installed on the system and their current status (running or stopped). You can also enable and disable services as necessary.

 If you want to use the MSCONFIG configuration tool on a Windows NT/2000 computer, you can do so by copying MSCONFIG.EXE from a Windows XP computer to the Windows 2000 computer.

Disk Management

Where there are files, there are disks. That is to say, all the files and programs we've talked about so far reside on *disks*. Disks are physical storage devices, and these disks also need to be managed. There are several aspects to disk management. One is concerned with getting disks ready to be able to store files and programs. Another deals with backing up your data. Yet another involves checking the health of disks and optimizing their performance. We'll look at these aspects in more detail.

Getting Disks Ready to Store Files and Programs

For a hard disk to be able to hold files and programs, it has to be partitioned and formatted. *Partitioning* is the process of creating logical divisions on a hard drive. A hard drive can have one or more partitions. *Formatting* is the process of creating and configuring a file allocation table (FAT) and creating the root directory. Several file system types are supported by the various versions of Windows, such as FAT16, FAT32, and NTFS. Windows *9x*/Me and newer use FAT32, but they recognize and support FAT16. Windows NT/2000/XP also supports a newer, more robust file system type called NTFS (New Technology Filesystem) and recognizes and supports FAT16 and FAT32. The file table for the NTFS is called the Master File Table (MFT).

The following is a list of the major file systems that are used with Windows and the differences among them:

File Allocation Table (FAT)   An acronym for the file on this file system used to keep track of where files are. It's also the name given to this type of file system, introduced in 1981. Many OSs have built their file system on the design of FAT, but without its limitations. A FAT file system uses the *8.3 naming convention* (eight letters for the name, a period, and then a three-letter file identifier). This later became known as *FAT16* (to differentiate it from FAT32) because it used a 16-bit binary number to hold cluster-numbering information. Because of that number, the largest FAT disk partition that could be created was approximately 2GB.

Virtual FAT (VFAT)   An extension of the FAT file system that was introduced with Windows 95. It augmented the 8.3 file-naming convention and allowed filenames with up to 255 characters. It created two names for each file: a *long name* and an 8.3-compatible name so that older programs could still access files. When VFAT was incorporated into Windows 95, it used 32-bit code for improved disk access while keeping the 16-bit naming system for backward compatibility with FAT. It also had the 2GB disk partition limitation.

FAT32   Introduced along with Windows 95 OEM Service Release 2. As disk sizes grew, so did the need to be able to format a partition larger than 2GB. FAT32 was based more on VFAT than on FAT16. It allowed for 32-bit cluster addressing, which in turn provided for a maximum partition size of 2 terabytes (2048GB). It also included smaller cluster sizes to avoid wasted space (discussed later). FAT32 support is included in Windows 98/Me/2000/XP.

Older versions of Windows (Windows 3.*x* and Windows 95 original release) as well as all versions of DOS cannot read FAT32 partitions.

NT File System (NTFS)   Introduced along with Windows NT (and available on 2000/XP). NTFS is a much more advanced file system in almost every way than all versions of the FAT file system. It includes such features as individual file security and compression, RAID support, as well as support for extremely large file and partition sizes and disk transaction monitoring. It is the file system of choice for higher-performance computing.

When you're installing any Windows OS, you will be asked first to format the drive using one of these disk technologies. Choose the disk technology based on what the computer will be doing and which OS you are installing.

To create a FAT16 or FAT32 partition, you can use the FDISK command. To format a partition, you can use the FORMAT command. FDISK.EXE is available only with Windows 9x/Me (not 2000/XP), and you can run it from a command prompt. FORMAT.EXE is available with all versions of Windows. You can run FORMAT from a command prompt or by right-clicking a drive in Windows Explorer and selecting Format. However, when you install Windows it performs the process of partitioning and formatting for you if a partitioned and formatted drive does not already exist.

Be extremely careful with the FORMAT command! When you format a drive, all data on the drive is erased.

In Windows 2000/XP, you can manage your hard drives through the Disk Management component. To access Disk Management, access the Control Panel and double-click Administrative Tools. Then, double-click Computer Management. Finally, double-click Disk Management. The Disk Management screen looks similar to the one shown in Figure 4.17.

The Disk Management screen lets you view a host of information regarding all the drives installed in your system, including CD-ROM and DVD drives. In Figure 4.17, you can see that this computer has three disks (Disk 0, Disk 1, and Disk 2), one DVD (CD-ROM 0), and one CD-ROM (CD-ROM 1) drive installed. In this example, you can see that Disk 0 has four partitions. A different drive letter is assigned to each partition on Disk 0 (C:, D:, G:, and H:). The list of devices in the top portion of the screen shows you additional information for each partition on each drive, such as the file system used, status, free space, and so on. If you right-click a partition in either area, you can perform a variety of functions, such as formatting the partition and changing the name and drive-letter assignment. For additional options and information, you can also access the Properties of a partition by right-clicking it and selecting Properties.

Windows 2000 and XP Professional support both basic and dynamic storage. The partition that the operating system boots from must be designated as *active*. Only one partition on a disk may be marked active. With basic storage, Windows 2000 and XP Professional drives can be partitioned with *primary* or *extended* partitions. The difference is that extended partitions can be divided into one or more logical drives and primary partitions cannot be further subdivided. Each 2000/XP Professional hard disk can be divided into a total of four partitions, either four primary partitions or three primary and one extended partition.

FIGURE 4.17   The Disk Management screen

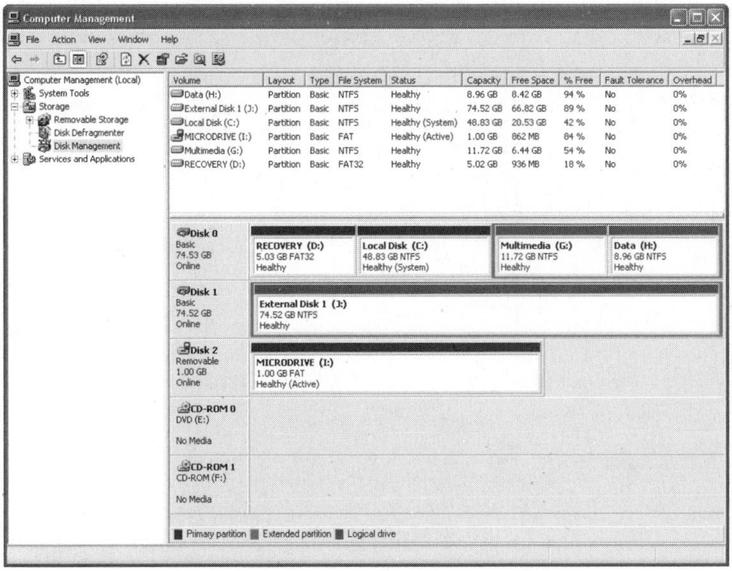

Finally, there is the concept of a *logical partition*. In reality, all partitions are logical in the sense that they don't necessarily correspond to one physical disk. One disk can have several logical divisions (partitions). A logical partition is any partition that has a drive letter.

> Sometimes, you will also hear of a logical partition as one that spans multiple physical disks. For example, a network drive that you know as drive H: might actually be located on several physical disks on a server. To the user, all that is seen is one drive, or H:.

Backing Up the Data on Your Drives

Another very important aspect of disk management is backing up the data on your drives. Sooner or later, you can count on running into a situation where a hard drive fails or data becomes corrupted. Without a backup copy of your data, you're facing a world of trouble trying to re-create the data, if that's even possible or economically feasible. You also shouldn't rely on the Recycle Bin. Although it is a good utility to restore an occasional file or directory that a user has accidentally deleted, it will not help you if your drives and the data on them become unusable.

Toward that end, Windows has a built-in backup feature called, you guessed it, Backup. To access Backup, click Start ➢ Programs (All Programs) ➢ Accessories ➢ System Tools ➢ Backup. This will open the Backup Wizard. To move on to the Backup utility, click Advanced Mode. Figure 4.18 shows the Windows 2000 Backup utility with the Backup tab selected.

FIGURE 4.18   The Windows 2000 Backup utility with the Backup tab selected

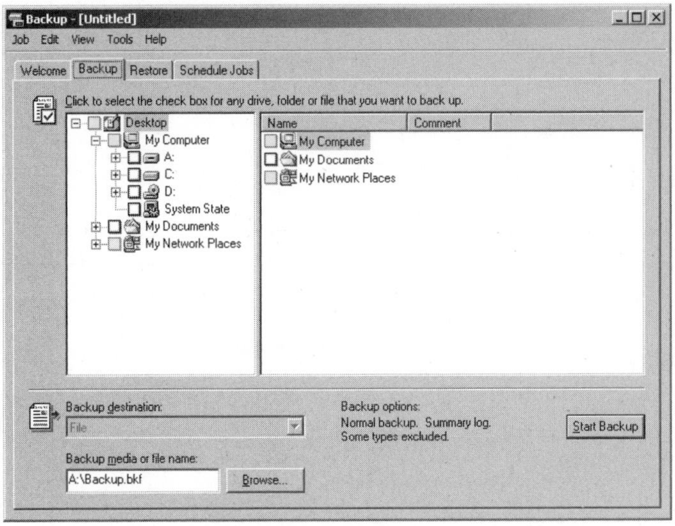

The Backup utility in each of the different versions of Windows has different capabilities, with newer versions having greater capabilities. In general, you can either run a wizard to create a backup job or manually specify the files to back up. You can also run backup jobs or schedule them to run at specific time at a specific interval. Refer to the Windows Help system for in-depth information on how to use Backup.

Checking the Health of Hard Disks and Optimizing Their Performance

As time goes on, it's important to check the health of Windows computers' hard disks and optimize their performance. Windows provides you with several tools to do so, some of which we've already mentioned in this chapter. One important tool is Disk Defragmenter, which exists in all versions of Windows except Windows NT.

When files are written to a hard drive, they're not always written contiguously. As a result, file data is spread out over the disk, and the time it takes to retrieve files from disk increases. Defragmenting a disk involves analyzing the disk and then consolidating fragmented files and folders so they occupy a contiguous space, thus increasing performance during file retrieval.

To access Disk Defragmenter, click Start ➤ Programs (All Programs) ➤ Accessories ➤ System Tools ➤ Disk Defragmenter. In the list of drives, select the drive you want to defragment, and then click Analyze. When the analysis is finished, Disk Defragmenter tells you how much the drive is defragmented and whether defragmentation is recommended. If it is, click Defragment. Be aware that for large disks with a lot of fragmented files, this process can take quite some time to finish.

In Windows 2000/XP, you can also access Disk Defragmenter through the Properties of any partition listed in Disk Management. Click the Tools tab and then click Defragment.

File Management

File management is the process by which a computer stores data and retrieves it from storage. Although some of the file-management interfaces across Windows interfaces may have a different look and feel, the process of managing files is similar across the board.

Files and Folders

For a program to run, it must be able to read information off the disk and write information back to the disk. In order to be able to organize and access information—especially in larger new systems that may have thousands of files—it is necessary to have a structure and an ordering process.

Windows provides this process by allowing you to create *directories*, also known as *folders*, in which to organize files. Windows also regulates the way that files are named and the properties of files. Each file created in Windows has to follow certain rules, and any program that accesses files through Windows also must comply with these rules. Files created on a Windows system must follow these rules:

- Each file has a filename of up to 255 characters.

- Certain characters, such as a period (.) and slash (\ or /), are prohibited in the filename.

- An extension (generally three or four characters) can be added to identify the file's type.

- Filenames are not case sensitive. (You can create files with names that use both upper- and lowercase letters, but to identify the file within the file system, it is not necessary to adhere to the capitalization in the filename.) Thus, you cannot have a file named `working.txt` and another called `WORKING.TXT` in the same directory. To Windows, these filenames are identical, and you can't have two files with the same filename in the same directory. We'll get into more detail on this topic a little later.

- In Windows 3.*x* and DOS, filenames were limited to eight characters and a three-character extension, separated by a period. This is also called the *8.3* file-naming convention. With Windows 95, long filenames were introduced, which allowed the 255-character filename convention.

The Windows file system is arranged like a filing cabinet. In a filing cabinet, paper is placed into folders, which are inside dividers, which are in a drawer of the filing cabinet. In the Windows file system, individual files are placed in subdirectories that are inside directories, which are stored on different disks or different partitions.

Windows also protects against duplicate filenames, so no two files on the system can have exactly the same name and *path*. A path indicates the location of the file on the disk; it is composed of the logical drive letter the file is on and, if the file is located in a directory or subdirectory, the names of those directories. For instance, if a file named AUTOEXEC.BAT is located in the root of the C: drive—meaning it is not within a directory—the path to the file is C:\AUTOEXEC.BAT. If, as another example, a file called FDISK.EXE is located in the Command directory under Windows under the root of C:, then the path to this file is C:\WINDOWS\COMMAND\FDISK.EXE.

> **NOTE** The *root directory* of any drive is the place where the hierarchy of folders for that drive begins. On a C: drive, for instance, C:\ is the root directory of the drive.

Common file extensions you may encounter are .EXE for executable files (applications), .DLL for dynamic linked library (DLL) files, .SYS for system files, .LOG for log files, .DRV for driver files, .TXT for text files, and others. Note that DLL files contain additional functions and commands applications can use and share. In addition, most applications use specific file extensions for the documents created with each application. For example, documents created in Microsoft Word have a .DOC extension. You'll also encounter extensions such as .MPG for video files, .MP3 for music files, .TIF and .JPG for graphics files, .HTM or .HTML for web pages, and so on. Being familiar with different filename extensions is helpful in working with the Windows filesystem.

Capabilities of Windows Explorer

Although it is technically possible to use the command-line utilities provided within the command prompt to manage your files, this generally is not the most efficient way to accomplish most tasks. The ability to use drag-and-drop techniques and other graphical tools to manage the file system makes the process far simpler, and Windows Explorer is a utility that allows you to accomplish a number of important file-related tasks from a single graphical interface, as shown in Figure 4.19.

FIGURE 4.19 The Windows Explorer program

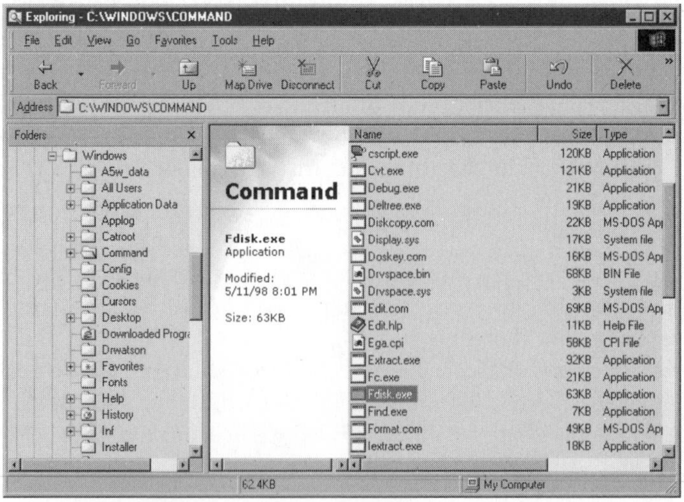

Some of the tasks you can accomplish using Windows Explorer include the following:

- Viewing files and directories
- Opening programs or data files
- Creating directories and files
- Copying objects (files or directories) to other locations
- Moving objects (files or directories) to other locations
- Deleting or renaming objects (files or directories)
- Searching for a particular file or type of file
- Changing file attributes
- Formatting new disks (such as floppy disks)

You can access many of these functions by right-clicking a file or folder and selecting the appropriate option, such as Copy or Delete, from the context menu.

Navigating and Using Windows Explorer

Using Windows Explorer is simple. A few basic instructions are all you need to start working with it. First, Windows Explorer interface has a number of parts, each of which serves a specific purpose. The top area of Windows Explorer is dominated by a set of menus and toolbars that give you easy access to common commands. The main section of the window is divided into two panes: The left pane displays the drives and folders available, and the right pane displays the contents of the currently selected folder. In pre–Windows XP versions, along the bottom of the window, the status bar displays information about the used and free space on the current directory. Some common actions in Explorer include the following:

Expanding a Folder   You can double-click a folder in the left pane to expand the folder (show its subfolders in the left pane) and display the contents of the folder in the right pane. Clicking the plus sign (+) to the left of a folder expands the folder without changing the display in the right pane.

Collapsing a Folder   Clicking the minus sign (–) next to a folder unexpands/collapses it.

Selecting a File   If you click the file in the right pane, Windows highlights the file by marking it with a darker color.

Selecting Multiple Files   The Ctrl and Shift keys allow you to select multiple files at once. Holding down Ctrl while clicking individual files selects each new file while leaving the currently selected file(s) selected as well. Holding down Shift while selecting two files selects both of them and all files in between.

Opening a File   Double-clicking a file in the right pane opens the program if the file is an application; if it is a data file, it will open using whichever file extension is configured for it.

Changing the View Type   Windows 2000 has five different view types: Large Icons, Small Icons, List, Details, and Thumbnail. Then, in Windows XP, the Tiles view was added. In XP, you can still choose to view objects with icons, but you can no longer choose between large and small icons. You can move between these views by clicking the View menu and selecting the view you prefer.

Finding Specific Files   This option is accessed by using the Search button. You can search for files based on their name, file size, file type, and other attributes.

In Exercise 4.8, we will show you how to search for a file type.

EXERCISE 4.8

Searching for a Type of File

Many computers have over 100,000 files. Finding one manually can be like looking for a needle in a haystack.

1. In Windows 2000, click the Search button on the toolbar. In Windows XP, click the Search button on the toolbar and then click All Files And Folders in the left pane.

2. The Search pane appears. You are prompted for the Search information.

3. Type *.TXT in the field that asks for the name of the file(s).

4. In the Look In field, enter C:\, and click Find Now.

5. In Windows 2000, to include subfolders, click Search Options and then select Advanced Options. Once you select Advanced Options, Search Subfolders is automatically selected. In Windows XP, subfolders are searched by default. (To disable this function, click More Advanced Functions and deselect Search Subfolders.)

6. Click Search Now (Windows 2000) or Search (Windows XP).

7. Windows searches the C: drive and eventually displays a Search Results window with all the files it has found.

When you're searching, you can also use wildcards. *Wildcards* are characters that act as placeholders for a character or set of characters, allowing, for instance, a search for all files with a text (.TXT) extension. To perform such a search, you'd type an asterisk (*) as a stand-in for the filename: *.TXT. An asterisk takes the place of any number of characters in a search. A question mark (?) takes the place of a single number or letter. For example, AUTOEX??.BAT would return the file AUTOEXEC.BAT as part of its results.

Creating New Objects   To create a new file, folder, or other object, navigate to the location where you want to create the object, and then right-click in the right pane (without selecting a file or directory). In the menu that appears, select New and then choose the object you want to create, as shown in Figure 4.20.

FIGURE 4.20   Creating a new folder

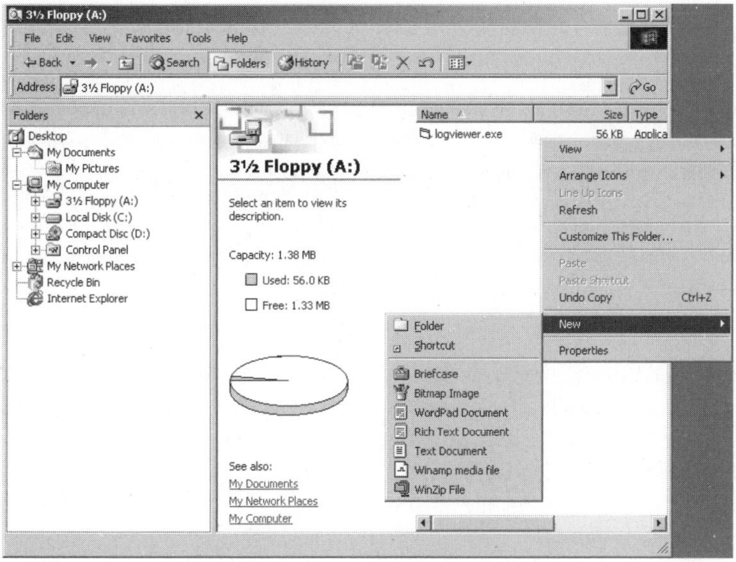

Deleting Objects   Select the object and press the Del key on the keyboard, or right-click the object and select Delete from the menu that appears.

> **WARNING**   The simplicity of deleting in Windows makes it likely that you or one of the people you support will delete or misplace a file or a number of files that are still needed. In such a case, the Recycle Bin (mentioned earlier) is a lifesaver.

In Exercise 4.9, we will show you how to create and delete objects in Windows Explorer.

EXERCISE 4.9

Using Windows Explorer to Create and Delete Objects

The primary file and folder management tool in Windows is Windows Explorer. It's important you be able to navigate through it as well as create and delete objects such as files and folders.

1. Open Windows Explorer. In Windows 2000, click Start ➢ Programs ➢ Accessories ➢ Windows Explorer. In Windows XP, click Start ➢ All Programs ➢ Accessories ➢ Windows Explorer.

2. To see which applications are installed in the Program Files directory, navigate the hierarchy from My Computer to C: to Program Files. You may need to click the + next to one or more of the folders to expand them and see their contents.

3. Navigate back to the root of C: and right-click in the right pane. Select New ➤ Folder and type **TEST** as the name of the folder.

4. Double-click the new TEST folder and examine the right pane after its contents are displayed. The folder was just created, so it is empty. Right-click in the right pane and select New ➤ Text Document. Give the file the name **NEW.TXT**.

5. To delete the file you just created, select it by clicking it once and then right-click it. Choose Delete. You are asked whether you are sure you want to send the file to the Recycle Bin; click Yes.

Besides simplifying most file-management commands as shown here, Windows Explorer also allows you to easily complete a number of disk-management tasks. You can format and label floppy disks and, in some cases, copy the Windows system files to a floppy so that you can use a disk to boot a machine.

Changing File Attributes

File attributes determine what specific users can do to files or directories. For example, if a file or directory is flagged with the Read Only attribute, then users can read the file or directory but not make changes to it or delete it. Attributes include Read Only, Hidden, System, and Archive, as well as Compression, Indexing, and Encryption. Not all attributes are available with all versions of Windows. We'll look at this subject in more detail in a moment.

You can view and change file attributes either with the ATTRIB command-prompt command or through the Properties of a file or directory. To access the Properties of a file or directory in the Windows GUI, right-click the file or directory and select Properties. Figure 4.21 shows the Properties screen of a file in Windows XP. In Windows XP, you can view and configure the Read Only and Hidden file attributes on the General tab. To view and configure additional attributes, click Advanced.

FIGURE 4.21 The General tab of a Windows XP file's Properties screen

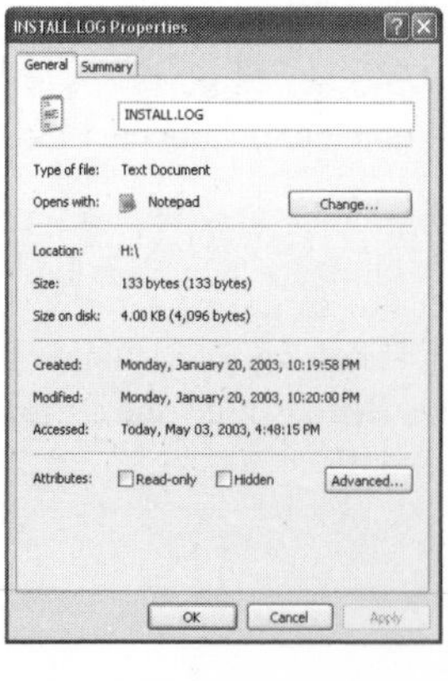

System files are usually flagged with the Hidden attribute, meaning they don't appear when a user displays a directory listing. You should not change this attribute on a system file unless absolutely necessary. System files are required for the OS to function. If they are visible, users might delete them (perhaps thinking they can clear some disk space by deleting files they don't recognize). Needless to say, that would be a bad thing!

File system Advanced Attributes

Windows 2000 and XP use the NT File system (NTFS), which gives you a number of options that are not available on earlier file systems such as FAT or FAT32. A number of these options are implemented through the use of the Advanced Attributes window, shown in Figure 4.22. To reach these options in Windows 2000/XP, right-click the folder or file you wish to modify and select Properties from the menu. On the main Properties page of the folder or file, click the Advanced button in the lower-right corner.

FIGURE 4.22   The Advanced Attributes window in Windows 2000

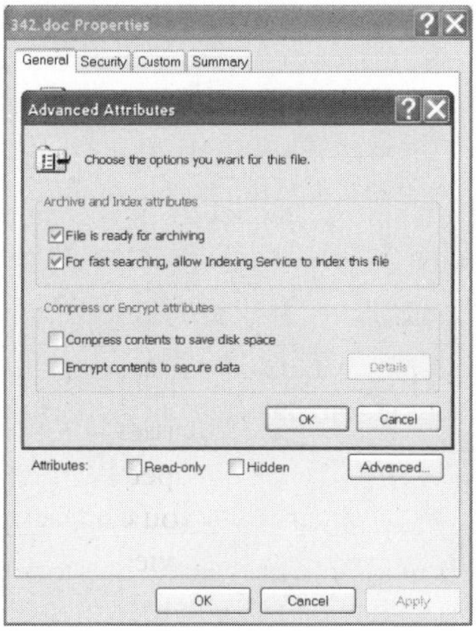

On the Advanced Attributes screen you have access to the following settings:

Archiving   This option tells the system whether the file has changed since the last time it was backed up. Technically it is known as the Archive Needed attribute; if this box is selected, the file should be backed up. If it is not selected, a current version of the file is already backed up.

Indexing   Windows 2000 and XP implement an Index Service to catalog and improve the search capabilities of your drive. Once files are indexed, you can search them more quickly by name, date, or other attributes. Setting the index option on a folder causes a prompt to appear, asking whether you want the existing files in the folder to be indexed as well. If you choose to do this, Windows 2000 and XP automatically reset this attribute on subfolders and files. If not, only new files created in the directory are indexed.

Compression   Windows 2000 and XP support advanced *compression* options, which were first introduced in Windows NT. NTFS files and folders can be dynamically compressed and uncompressed, often saving a great deal of space on the drive. As with Indexing, turning on Compression for a folder results in your being prompted as to whether you want the existing files in the folder to be compressed. If you choose to do this, Windows 2000 and XP automatically compress the subfolders and files. If not, only new files created in the directory are compressed.

>
> Compression works best on such files as word-processing documents and uncompressed images. Word files and MS Paint bitmaps can be compressed up to 80 percent. Files that are already packed well do not compress as effectively; EXE and Zip files generally compress only about 2 percent. Similarly GIF and JPEG images are already compressed (which is why they are used in Internet web pages), so they compress a little or not at all.

Encryption   First introduced in Windows 2000 and also available in Windows XP, *encryption* lets you secure files against anyone else's being able to view them, by encoding the files with a key that only you have access to. This can be useful if you're worried about extremely sensitive information, but in general, encryption is not necessary on the network. NTFS local file security is usually enough to provide users with access to what they need and prevent others from getting to what they shouldn't. If you want to encrypt a file, go through the same process you would for indexing or compression.

> Encryption and Compression are mutually exclusive—you can set one but not both features on a file or folder. Neither feature is available in XP Home edition.

> If a user forgets their password or is unable to access the network to authenticate their account, they will not be able to open encrypted files. By default, if the user's account is lost or deleted, the only other user who can decrypt the file is the Administrator account.

File Permissions

Windows 2000 and XP also support the use of *file permissions*, because these OSs use NTFS, which includes file-level file system security (rather than just share-level security, as is the case with Windows 9x/Me). Permissions serve the purpose of controlling who has access and what type of access to what files or objects. Several permissions are available, such as Read, Write, Execute, Delete, Change Permissions, Take Ownership, Full Control, and so on. The list is quite extensive. For a complete list, consult the Windows Help files. These permissions are called *special permissions*.

Assigning special permissions individually could be a tedious task. To make it easier for administrators to assign multiple permissions at once, Windows incorporates *standard permissions*. Standard permissions are collections of special permissions, including Full Control, Modify, Read & Execute, Read, and Write. As we said, each of these standard permissions automatically assigns multiple special permissions at once. To see which special permissions are assigned by the different standard permissions, enter **File Permissions (List)** into the Help system's index keyword area.

Note that you can assign permissions to individual users or to groups. You assign standard permissions on the Security tab of a file or folder (see Figure 4.23), which you access through the file or folder's Properties.

FIGURE 4.23   The Security tab for a folder on a Windows 2000 Professional computer

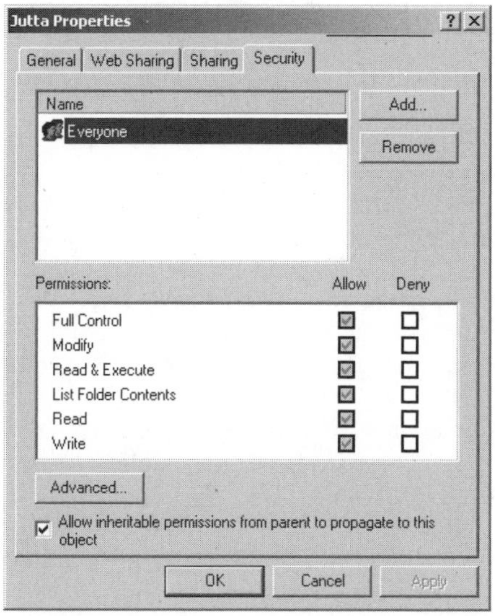

In Exercise 4.10, we will show you how to examine file permissions.

EXERCISE 4.10

Examining File Permissions

Being able to set file permissions is a great reason to use NTFS. Here's how to examine file permissions:

1.   Open Windows Explorer.

2.   Right-click a file or folder and choose Properties.

EXERCISE 4.10 *(continued)*

3. Select and then examine the Security tab. The Security tab will not appear if Simple File Sharing is selected. If this is the case, you can turn off Simple File Sharing by selecting the Tools menu ➢ Folder Options ➢ View tab. Then scroll down in the Advanced Settings area to Use Simple File Sharing and uncheck the box.

4. You'll see the users and/or groups to which permissions have been assigned. Select a user or group in the list and examine the list of standard permissions. (To add a new user or group, click Add and follow the prompts.) Any standard permissions that are checked in the Allow column are applied. If a check box is grayed out, this means the permission was inherited. To revoke a set of standard permissions, click the appropriate check box in the Deny column. If you click the check box in the Deny column for the Full Control permission, all other standard permissions are denied also.

5. Click Advanced to examine advanced options.

6. Click Cancel twice to close the file or folder's Properties.

 WARNING   Be sure you don't accidentally make any changes you're not intending to make. Changing permissions without understanding the ramifications can have negative consequences, such as losing access to files or folders.

Summary

In this chapter, you learned about Windows, where it came from, alternative operating systems, the basics of Windows structure, critical boot files, and window management. Because Windows is a graphical system, the key to success in learning to use it is to click every option and examine every window. By exploring the system to find out what it can do, you will be better prepared to later decipher what a user has done.

First, we covered a brief history of Windows, some alternative operating systems, and operating system concepts. In order to understand why we are where we are today with operating systems, you need to know where they came from and how their features sprang from necessity.

Next, we covered the Windows interface. Among other things, we looked at the layout and components of the Desktop, the Taskbar, and the Start menu, as well as at basic icons present in default Windows installations. Next, we covered what the component that gives Windows its name (the window) actually is and how windows are used.

We then went over how Windows 2000 and Windows XP boot up, including critical files involved in the boot process.

Finally, we covered basic Windows management concepts. Concepts included managing disks, using file systems and managing files, and understanding directory structure.

With the basic knowledge gained in this chapter, you are now ready to learn how to install, upgrade, configure, and optimize two of the most popular operating systems in use today: Windows 2000 and Windows XP, which are covered in the next chapter.

Exam Essentials

Know what operating systems besides Windows are commonly used and how they differ from Windows.   Other than Windows, the most popular operating systems are the Mac OS and Linux. The Mac OS (currently on version 10, or Mac OS X) is used on Apple Macintosh computers. Linux is a derivative of Unix and is popular because it's powerful, easily adaptable (if you can program), and inexpensive.

Understand the fundamental reasons for choosing one operating system over another.   The most important thing when choosing an operating system is to ensure that your hardware and software will be compatible with the operating system. If you have older hardware or mission-critical applications that will not run with Windows XP, for example, then it might make sense to run an older operating system.

Know what the critical Windows interfaces are and how to use them.   This list includes using the Desktop, Taskbar, Start menu, icons, windows, Control Panel, the command prompt, My Computer, My Network Places, the system tray, and the Registry editor.

Know what the Windows 2000 and Windows XP boot files are and the order in which they load.   The order is NTLDR, BOOT.INI, BOOTSECT.DOS (for systems booting into an older operating system, such as Windows 9*x* or DOS), NTDETECT.COM, NTBOOTDD.SYS (for systems using a SCSI boot device), and NTOSKRNL.EXE.

Know what file systems are available in Windows 2000 and Windows XP and what the differences between them are.   The two most commonly used file systems used on Windows 2000 and XP hard drives are FAT32 and NTFS. (FAT16, often referred to as FAT, is also available but is much less efficient than FAT32.) FAT32 is older and perhaps a bit quicker for smaller hard drives. NTFS adds a bunch of important features, including security and auditing.

Understand how to manage files in Windows.   Nearly all file management is accomplished through Windows Explorer, including moving, copying, renaming, and deleting files and changing file attributes, advanced attributes, and permissions.

Review Questions

1. What is the Desktop?

   A. The top of the desk where the computer sits

   B. A tool that keeps track of all the data on disk

   C. Where all of a computer's memory is stored

   D. The virtual desk upon which all of your other programs and utilities run

2. The screensaver can be changed in the _____ dialog box.

   A. Display Properties

   B. Taskbar

   C. Menu Bar

   D. Shortcut Menu

3. Which of the following is a popular open-source operating system?

   A. Mac OS X

   B. Linux

   C. Windows Me

   D. Windows XP

4. The Taskbar can be increased in size by _____.

   A. Right-clicking the mouse and dragging the Taskbar to make it bigger

   B. Left-clicking the mouse and double-clicking the Taskbar

   C. Moving the mouse pointer to the top of the Taskbar, pausing until the pointer turns into a double-headed arrow, and then clicking and dragging

   D. Highlighting the Taskbar and double-clicking in the center

5. Which of the following file attributes are available to files on a FAT32 partition?

   A. Hidden, Read Only, Archive, System

   B. Compression, Hidden, Archive, Encryption, Read Only

   C. Read Only, Hidden, System, Encryption

   D. Indexing, Read Only, Hidden, System, Compression

6. What was the first 32-bit preemptive multitasking system?

   A. Windows 2

   B. Windows 3

   C. Windows 95

   D. Windows 98

7. The Windows Explorer program can be used to do which of the following? (Select all that apply.)

    A. Browse the Internet

    B. Copy and move files

    C. Change file attributes

    D. Create backup jobs

8. Standard permissions are _____.

    A. The same as special permissions

    B. Only the Read, Write, and Execute permissions

    C. Permissions assigned to users but not to groups

    D. Permissions grouped together for easy assignment.

9. Virtual memory is configured through which system tool?

    A. Taskbar

    B. System control panel

    C. Memory Manager

    D. Virtual Configuration

10. If a program doesn't have a shortcut on the Desktop or in the Programs submenu, you can start it by _____.

    A. Using the Shut Down command

    B. Typing **cmd** in the Start Run box

    C. Using the Run command and typing in the name of the program

    D. Typing **cmd** in the Start box followed by the program name

11. What can you do if a program is not responding to any commands and appears to be locked up? (Choose all that apply.)

    A. Open the System control panel and choose Performance to see what process is causing the problem.

    B. Add more memory.

    C. Press Ctrl+Alt+Del to reboot the computer.

    D. Open Task Manager, select the appropriate task, and click End Task.

12. In Windows, a deleted file can be retrieved using which of the following?

    A. My Computer icon

    B. Recycle Bin

    C. Control Panel

    D. Settings panel

13. To turn off a Windows 2000 machine, you should _____.

    A. Run the Shut Down (Turn Off) command at a command prompt.

    B. Turn off the switch and unplug the machine.

    C. Press Ctrl+Alt+Del.

    D. Select Start ➤ Shut Down, choose Shut Down, and turn off the computer.

14. Which type of resource do you configure in Device Manager?

    A. Hardware

    B. Files and folders

    C. Applications

    D. Memory

15. To back up the files on your disks in Windows, which Windows program can you use?

    A. Disk Management

    B. Backup

    C. My Computer

    D. Windows doesn't come with a backup program.

16. Which of the following files bootstraps Windows XP?

    A. NTLDR

    B. BOOT.INI

    C. BOOTSTRAP.EXE

    D. NTBOOTDD.SYS

17. Which of the following partitions is specifically the partition from which the operating system boots?

    A. Primary partition

    B. Extended partition

    C. Active partition

    D. Logical partition

18. Which of the following Registry hives contains information about the computer's hardware?

    A. HKEY_CURRENT_MACHINE

    B. HKEY_LOCAL_MACHINE

    C. HKEY_MACHINE

    D. HKEY_RESOURCES

19. Within Windows 2000, what is the maximum length of a filename?

   A. 8 characters plus a 3-character extension

   B. 64 characters

   C. 255 characters

   D. Unlimited

20. Which of the following utilities will rearrange the files on your hard disk to occupy contiguous chunks of space?

   A. Disk Defragmenter

   B. Windows Explorer

   C. SCANDISK

   D. Windows Backup

Answers to Review Questions

1. D. By default, the Desktop contains the Start menu, the Taskbar, and a number of icons. Because it is the base on which everything else sits, how the Desktop is configured can have a major effect on how the GUI looks and how convenient it is for users.

2. A. The screensaver can be changed in the Display Properties dialog box. To access the Display Properties dialog box, you can either right-click anywhere on the Desktop and choose Properties from the menu that appears or go to the Control Panel and open the Display applet.

3. B. Linux is an open-source operating system. Neither the Mac OS nor any of the Windows operating systems are open source. Linux was born from the world of Unix, which is traditionally an open-source environment.

4. C. You can increase the Taskbar's size by moving the mouse pointer to the top of the Taskbar, pausing until the pointer turns into a double-headed arrow, and then clicking and dragging. Keep in mind that in Windows XP, you have to unlock the Taskbar first by right-clicking on it and deselecting Lock The Taskbar.

5. A. FAT32 does not have as many options as NTFS, such as Encryption and Compression. These attributes are available only on NTFS partitions.

6. C. The first 32-bit preemptive multitasking system was Windows 95. Windows 95 can emulate and support cooperative multitasking for programs that require it. It also supports both 32-bit and 16-bit drivers as well as DOS drivers, although the 32-bit drivers are strongly recommended over the DOS ones because they are far more stable and are faster.

7. B, C. The Windows Explorer program can be used to copy and move files and to change file attributes.

8. D. Standard permissions, unlike special permissions, have been grouped together to make it easier for administrators to assign permissions.

9. B. Virtual memory settings are accessed through the Performance tab or area of the System control panel.

10. C. To run any program, select Start ➢ Run and type the name of the program in the Open field. If you don't know the exact name of the program, you can find the file by clicking the Browse button. Once you have typed in the executable name, click OK to run the program.

11. C, D. If an application is locked up, you can use Ctrl+Alt+Del to reboot. You can also use Task Manager to deal with applications that have stopped responding.

12. B. All deleted files are placed in the Recycle Bin. Deleted files are held there until the Recycle Bin is emptied. Users can easily recover accidentally deleted files from the Recycle Bin.

13. D. To turn off a Windows 2000 machine, select Start ➢ Shut Down, choose Shut Down, and turn off the computer.

14. A. Device Manager is used in Windows to configure all hardware resources that Windows knows about.

15. B. The Backup utility is provided with all versions of Windows, but it has different levels of functionality in the different versions.

16. A. The NTLDR file bootstraps the system (is the initial file that starts the operating system) and in turn loads the BOOT.INI. There is no file called BOOTSTRAP.EXE, and NTBOOTDD.SYS is called only if you're using a SCSI boot device.

17. C. The operating system boots from the active partition. Active partitions must be primary partitions, but a primary partition does not have to be active (as there can be up to four primary partitions per hard drive).

18. B. There are five basic hives in the Windows Registry, and they are HKEY_CLASSES_ROOT, HKEY_CURRENT_USER, HKEY_LOCAL_MACHINE, HKEY_USERS, and HKEY_CURRENT_CONFIG. HKEY_LOCAL_MACHINE stores information about the computer's hardware. HKEY_CURRENT_MACHINE, HKEY_MACHINE, and HKEY_RESOURCES do not exist

19. C. In Windows 2000 (and XP for that matter), filenames can be no longer than 255 characters. Under DOS, files were limited by the 8.3 standard of 8 characters plus a 3-character file extension.

20. A. Windows Disk Defragmenter rearranges files on your hard disk so they occupy contiguous spaces (as much as possible). Windows Explorer lets you view and manage files but not manage their location on the physical hard disk. SCANDISK will check the hard drive for errors, and Windows Backup backs up files but does not manage their physical location.

Understanding Basics of Installing, Configuring, Optimizing, and Upgrading Operating Systems

THE FOLLOWING COMPTIA A+ ESSENTIALS EXAM OBJECTIVES ARE COVERED IN THIS CHAPTER:

✓ **3.2 Install, configure, optimize and upgrade operating systems – references to upgrading from Windows 95 and NT may be made**

- Identify procedures for installing operating systems including:
  - Verification of hardware compatibility and minimum requirements
  - Installation methods (e.g. boot media such as CD, floppy or USB, network installation, drive imaging)
  - Operating system installation options (e.g. attended / unattended, file system type, network configuration)
  - Disk preparation order (e.g. start installation, partition and format drive)
  - Device driver configuration (e.g. install and upload device drivers)
  - Verification of installation

- Identify procedures for upgrading operating systems including:
  - Upgrade considerations (e.g. hardware, application and / or network compatibility)
  - Implementation (e.g. backup data, install additional Windows components)
- Install / add a device including loading, adding device drivers and required software including:
  - Determine whether permissions are adequate for performing the task
  - Device driver installation (e.g. automated and / or manual search and installation of device drivers)
  - Using unsigned drivers (e.g. driver signing)
  - Verify installation of the driver (e.g. device manager and functionality)
- Identify procedures and utilities used to optimize operating systems for example, virtual memory, hard drives, temporary files, service, startup and applications

At some point, an operating system must be installed, reinstalled, or upgraded. Often, this is the case because you have built a new computer and need to install the OS to get the computer up and operating. Or you may have an older OS and want to upgrade it to the newest version. In either case, the ability to install an OS and configure it properly is an important skill to have.

In this chapter, you will learn how to install the Windows 2000 and Windows XP operating systems, as well as upgrade earlier versions of Windows to Windows XP. You will also learn the procedures that must be followed, both pre- and post-installation, to ensure your computer works optimally.

Aside from installing operating systems, technicians are frequently asked to install new hardware devices. Along with installing the physical hardware, you must install the proper software to make the device work. This chapter looks at device driver installation, to help devices work problem-free the first time.

Finally, we'll look at a problem that really doesn't need to be a problem. It's when your perfectly wonderful computer starts showing performance issues and running slower, and slower, and slower. This problem can be often fixed by optimizing your Windows installation, and we'll end the chapter looking at how to do that.

Installing Operating Systems

Usually, you install an OS from scratch—that is, you install it on a computer that currently has no OS. If the computer already has an OS, you will be essentially performing an OS upgrade.

In the following sections, you will learn how to perform an installation of Windows 2000 Professional and Windows XP Professional. You will also learn the prerequisites for installation of each OS.

Installation Prerequisites

Before you can begin to install an OS, there are several items you must consider in order to have a flawless installation. You must perform these tasks before you even put the OS installation CD-ROM into your computer's CD-ROM drive. These items essentially set the stage for the procedure you are about to perform:

- Determining hardware compatibility and minimum requirements
- Determining installation options

- Determining the installation method
- Preparing the computer for installation

Let's begin our discussion by talking about hardware compatibility issues and requirements for installing the various versions of Windows.

Determining Hardware Compatibility and Minimum Requirements

Before you can begin to install any version of Windows, it is important that you determine whether the hardware you will be using is supported by the Windows version you will be running. That is, will the version of Windows have problems running any drivers for the hardware you have?

To answer this question, Microsoft has come up with several versions of its *Hardware Compatibility List (HCL)*. This is a list of all the hardware that works with Windows and which versions of Windows it works with. You can find this list at http://www.microsoft .com/whdc/hcl/search.mspx. With the release of Windows XP, Microsoft expanded the idea of the HCL to include software as well—and a list that includes both hardware and software can hardly be called a Hardware Compatibility List. The new term is the *Windows Catalog*, and eventually the Windows Catalog will completely replace HCLs.

   Another name for the Windows Catalog is the Windows Marketplace, available at http://www.windowsmarketplace.com.

The point is, before you install Windows, you should check all your computer's components against this list and make sure each item is compatible with the version of Windows you plan to install.

In addition to general compatibility, it is important that your computer have enough "oomph" to run the version of Windows you plan to install. For that matter, it is important for your computer to have enough resources to run any software you plan to use. Toward that end, Microsoft (as well as other software publishers) publishes a list of both minimum and recommended hardware specifications that you should follow when installing Windows.

Minimum specifications are the absolute minimum requirements for hardware you should have in your system in order to install and run the OS you have chosen. *Recommended* hardware specifications are what you should have in your system to realize usable performance. Always try to have the recommended hardware (or better) in your system. If you don't, you may have to upgrade your hardware before you upgrade your OS. Table 5.1 lists the minimum and recommended hardware specifications for the versions of Windows tested on in the A+ Essentials exam. Note that in addition to these minimums, the hardware must be compatible with Windows. Also, additional hardware may be required if certain features are installed (for example, a NIC is required for networking support).

TABLE 5.1   Windows 2000 and XP Minimum and Recommended Hardware

Hardware	2000 Professional Requirement	2000 Professional Recommendation	XP Professional Requirement	XP Professional Recommendation
Processor	Pentium 133	Pentium II or higher	233MHz Pentium/Celeron or AMD K6/Athlon/Duron	300 MHz or higher Intel-compatible processor
Memory	64MB	128MB or more	64MB	128MB
Free Hard Disk Space	650MB	2GB, plus what is needed for applications and storage	1.5GB	1.5GB
Floppy Disk	Required only if installing from boot disks	Yes	Not required	Not required
CD-ROM or DVD	Required	Yes	Required	Required
Video	VGA	SVGA	SuperVGA or better	SuperVGA or better
Mouse	Required (but not listed as a requirement)	Required (but not listed as a requirement)	Required	Required
Keyboard	Required	Required	Required	Required

If there is one thing to be learned from Table 5.1, it is that Microsoft is nothing if not optimistic. For your own sanity, though, we *strongly* suggest that you always take the minimum requirements with a grain of salt. They are *minimums*. Even the recommended requirements should be considered minimums. Bottom line: Make sure you have a good margin between your system's performance and the minimum requirements listed. Always run Windows on *more* hardware, rather than less!

Other hardware—sound cards, network cards, modems, video cards, and so on—may or may not work with Windows. If the device is fairly recent, you can be relatively certain that it was built to work with the newest version of Windows. But if it is older, you may need to find out who made the hardware and check their website to see if they have drivers for the version of Windows you are installing.

Determining OS Installation Options

In addition to making sure you have enough and the right kind of hardware, you must determine a few of the Windows installation options. These options control how Windows will be installed, as well as which Windows components will be installed. These options include:

- Installation type
- Network configuration
- File system type
- Dual-boot support

Installation Type

When you install applications, OSs, or any software, you almost always have options as to how that software is installed. Especially with OSs, there are usually many packages that make up the software. You can choose how to install the many different components; these options are usually called something like Typical, Full, Minimal, and Custom:

- A *typical installation* installs the most commonly used components of the software, but not all of the components.

- A *full installation* installs every last component, even those that may not be required or used frequently.

- A *minimal installation* (also known as a *compact installation*) installs only those components needed to get the software functional.

- A *custom installation* usually allows you to choose exactly which components are installed.

> Some Windows Setup programs include a *portable installation* type as well, which installs components needed for portable system installations on laptops. It includes such features as power management and LCD display software.

All Windows versions use these, or derivations of these installation types, and you should decide ahead of time which method you are going to use (which may be dictated by the amount of disk space you have available).

Network Configuration

With many versions of Windows, you can choose whether to install networking options. If you do install networking, you can also choose (with some versions of Windows) which networking components you want installed. With Windows 2000/XP, you also must know which workgroup or domain you are going to install.

File System Type

As Windows has evolved, a number of changes have been made to the basic architecture, as you might expect. One of the architecture items that have changed the most is the disk system structure. There have been multiple changes in the file system since DOS (the first Microsoft OS). The file systems available in Windows are covered in detail in Chapter 4, but your primary choices are the

New Technology File System (NTFS) and File Allocation Table (FAT). For Windows 2000 and Windows XP computers, it's almost always better to go with NTFS, unless you're running an older operating system such as Windows 98 on the same computer as well.

When you're installing any Windows OS, you will be asked first to format the drive using one of the available filesystems. Choose based on what the computer will be doing and which OS you are installing.

Dual-Boot Support

Occasionally, a mission-critical program (one you can't do your business or function without it) doesn't support the OS to which you are upgrading. There may be a newer release in the future, but at the present time it isn't supported. In that case, you may have to install the new OS in a dual-boot configuration.

It is also possible, in some situations, to have a multiboot configuration where you can choose from a list of OSs. However, this setup makes it more difficult to choose compatible disk formats and often requires multiple disks to accomplish properly.

In a *dual-boot configuration*, you install two OSs on the computer (Windows 98 and Windows 2000, for example). At boot time, you have the option of selecting which OS you want to use.

It is possible to multiple-boot to all Microsoft OSs, including DOS and all versions of Windows (95/98/Me/NT/2000/XP). Microsoft recommends that each installation be done to a separate disk (or partition) in order to avoid conflicts with built-in programs like Internet Explorer. In addition, you should install the oldest OS first (usually MS-DOS or Windows 98) and then proceed in chronological order to the newest (Windows XP).

For more information on dual-boot and multiboot configurations, visit the Microsoft support website at http://support.microsoft.com.

Determining the Installation Method

Another item you must determine is which method you are going to use to install Windows. Most versions of Windows come on a CD-ROM (which is bootable for every version after and including Windows 98 Second Edition). It was possible to install older versions of Windows (primarily Windows 95 and, to some degree, Windows 98) using floppy disks. Granted, there were several disks (the first Windows 95 installation used 19 3 1/2-inch floppy diskettes). However, this isn't the most efficient method. CD-ROMs, because of their large storage capacity, are the perfect medium to distribute software.

Windows 2000 and Windows XP each come on a single CD-ROM (not together, of course, but each on its own CD-ROM). It is possible to boot to this CD and begin the installation process. However, your system must have a system BIOS and CD-ROM capable of supporting bootable CDs.

If you don't have a bootable CD, you must first boot the computer using some other bootable media (a floppy disk, for example), which then loads the CD-ROM driver so that you can access the installation program on the CD. With Windows 2000, these bootable disks usually come with the packaged operating system.

There's one more thing to consider when evaluating installation methods. Some methods only work if you're performing a clean installation, and not an upgrade. (For details on performing upgrades, see the "Upgrading the Operating System" section later in this chapter.) Table 5.2 shows you four common unattended installation methods, and when they can be used.

TABLE 5.2   Windows 2000 and XP Unattended Installation Methods

Method	Clean Installation	Upgrade
Unattended Install	Yes	Yes
Bootable Media	Yes	No
Sysprep	Yes	No
Remote Install	Yes	No

 Two common categories of installations are attended and unattended. In an *attended installation*, a user must be present to choose all of the options when the installation program gets to that point. As you can imagine, if you have several hundred computers to install, this isn't exactly efficient. The other option is an *unattended installation*, which does not require human intervention once started and is frequently used when installing over the network.

Let's look at each of these in a bit more detail.

Unattended Installation

Answering the myriad of questions posed by Windows setup doesn't qualify as exciting work for most people. Fortunately, there is a way to answer the questions automatically, and it's through an unattended installation. In this type of installation, an *answer file* is supplied with all of the correct parameters (time zone, regional settings, administrator user name, and so on), so no one needs to be there to tell the computer what to choose or to hit Next 500 times.

Unattended installations are great because they can be used to upgrade operating systems to Windows 2000/XP. The first step is to create an answer file. Generally speaking, you'll want to run a test installation using that answer file first before deploying it on a large scale, because you'll probably need to make some tweaks to it. After you create your answer file, place it on a network share that will be accessible from the target computer. (Most people put it in the same place as the Windows 2000/XP installation files for convenience.)

Boot the computer that you want to install on using a boot disk or CD, and establish the network connection. Once you start the setup process, everything should run automatically.

Sysprep

Another common unattended installation tool is the system preparation tool, or *sysprep*. The sysprep utility works by making an exact image or replica of a computer (called the *master computer*), to be installed on other computers. Sysprep removes the master computer's Security ID, and will generate new IDs for each computer the image is used to install.

 All sysprep does is create the system image. You still need a third-party cloning utility to copy the image to other computers.

Perhaps the biggest caveat to using sysprep is that because you are making an exact image of an installed computer (including drivers and settings), all of the computers that you will be installing the image on need to be identical (or very close) to the configuration of the master computer. Otherwise, you could have to go through and fix driver problems on every installed computer. Sysprep images can be installed across a network or copied to a CD for local installation. Sysprep cannot be used to upgrade a system; plan on all data on the system (if there is any) being lost after a format.

There are several third-party vendors which provide similar services, and you'll often hear it referred to as *disk imaging* or *drive imaging*. The process works the same way as sysprep, except that the third-party utility makes the image as well. Then the image file is transferred to the computer without an OS. You boot the new system with the Ghost (imaging software) floppy and start the image download. The new system's disk drive is made into an exact sector-by-sector copy of the original system.

Imaging has major upsides. The biggest one is speed. In larger networks with multiple new computers, you can configure tens to hundreds of computers by using imaging in just hours, rather than the days it would take to individually install the OS, applications, and drivers.

Bootable Media

For computers not connected to a network, images can be copied to a CD-ROM for local installation. This is a quick way to perform a clean installation of an operating system without consuming all of your network bandwidth. However, keep in mind that most CD-ROMs can only store in the neighborhood of 650MB of data, which can be limiting.

Remote Install

Windows 2000 Server and newer Windows Server operating systems have a feature called Remote Installation Service (RIS), which allows you to perform several network installations at one time. A *network installation* is handy when you have many installs to do and installing by CD is too much work for many computers.

In a network installation, the installation CD is copied to a shared location on the network. Then individual workstations boot and access the network share. The workstations can boot either through a boot disk or through a built-in network boot device known as a *boot ROM*. Boot ROMs essentially download a small file that contains an OS and network drivers and has enough information to boot the computer in a limited fashion. At the very least, it can boot the computer so it can access the network share and begin the installation.

Preparing the Computer for Installation

Once you have verified that the machine on which you are planning to install Windows is capable of running it properly, you're sure all hardware is supported, and you have chosen your installation options, you need to make certain that the system is ready for the install. The primary question is whether you are planning to perform a fresh install of Windows or whether you are going to upgrade an existing system. We'll deal with upgrading later in the chapter; for now, we'll focus on new installations.

Preparing the Hard Drive

If you are installing Windows onto a system that does not already have a functioning OS, you have a bit of work to do before you get to the installation itself. New disk drives need two critical functions performed on them before they can be used:

- *Partitioning* is the process of assigning part or all of the drive for use by the computer.

- *Formatting* is the process of preparing the partition to store data in a particular fashion.

With older operating systems, you dealt with these two procedures by using the `FDISK.EXE` and `FORMAT.COM` commands. Running any sort of command on a machine that has no OS is impossible, though. You need a way to boot the computer: either a floppy disk that is bootable or, more likely, the Windows 2000 or Windows XP CD-ROM.

For Windows 2000/XP the process will always be to boot up (which starts the installation process), partition the drive, and then format the drive.

Partitioning the Hard Drive

Partitioning refers to establishing large allocations of hard-drive space. A partition is a continuous section of sectors that are next to each other. In DOS and Windows, a partition is referred to by a drive letter, such as C: or D:. Partitioning a drive into two or more parts gives it the appearance of being two or more physical hard drives. At the beginning of each hard drive is a special file called the *master boot record* (MBR). The MBR contains the partition information about the beginning and end of each partition.

> The size of a partition determines certain aspects of a file pointer table called the File Allocation Table (FAT). The larger the drive partition, the more space will be wasted on the drive. NTFS partitions are less wasteful of space than FAT partitions are, beecause of limitations in FAT cluster sizes.

Formatting the Hard Drive

The next step in management of a hard drive is formatting, initiated by the `FORMAT` command (or automatically by the installation program). When formatting is performed, the surface of the hard drive platter is briefly scanned to find any possible bad spots, and the areas surrounding a bad spot are marked as bad sectors. Then magnetic tracks are laid down in concentric circles. These tracks are where information is eventually encoded. These tracks, in turn, are split into pieces of 512 bytes called *sectors*. Some space is reserved in between the sectors for error-correction information, referred to as cyclic redundancy check (CRC) information. The OS may use CRC information to re-create data that has been partially lost from a sector. An operating system boot record is created along with the root directory. Finally, the File Allocation Table (FAT) or Master File Table (MFT) is created. This table contains information about the location of files as they are placed onto the hard drive. Windows 2000 Professional Installation

The installation processes for operating systems has arguably gotten easier over time. Being able to boot to a CD and automatically begin the installation is an example. Although modern operating systems have more options for you to choose from, care has also been taken to minimize the stress involved in the process. We will look next at the Windows 2000 installation process and, in doing so, cover the following topics:

- Installation requirements
- Accessing the Setup files
- Running the Setup program
- Partitioning
- Formatting
- Customizing Setup

Installation Prerequisites

Because it is a power workstation, the hardware requirements for Windows 2000 are higher than those for older versions of Windows, and Windows 2000 also is less forgiving of older, less-efficient software. Make sure you have at least the minimum required hardware before you begin—but really, go for at least the recommended level of hardware.

Accessing the Setup Files

Unlike Windows 9*x* Setup, which must run from a functioning OS (an earlier version of DOS or Windows or a boot disk), Windows 2000 is generally a breeze to install on a machine. To start the install process, place the Windows 2000 Professional CD into the CD-ROM drive and restart the computer. After the POST routine for the computer has completed, a message appears that says *Press any key to boot from CD*. Hit a key, any key, and the Windows 2000 Setup program will start.

That is a "perfect world" situation, and sometimes reality intrudes. If the *Press any key* message does not appear, that generally means your PC is not configured to boot from CD-ROM or does not have that capability. In such a case, you need to do one of two things:

- Go into the BIOS to set the machine to boot to its CD drive. Consult your computer's user guide for more information about examining and making changes to the BIOS.
- Create and use Windows 2000 boot disks to start the setup.

Starting a Windows 2000 Installation

The startup options we've listed all eventually lead you to the same point: executing the Setup routine for Windows 2000 Professional. Professional has two different executables used to start Setup, depending on the OS you are using to start the install. These executables are WINNT (used from DOS or Windows 9*x*) and WINNT32 (used from Windows NT/2000). These commands have various options associated with them, as shown in Tables 5.3 and 5.4.

TABLE 5.3   Common WINNT.EXE Options

Option	Function
/s:*sourcepath*	Allows you to specify the location of the Windows 2000 source files.
/t:*tempdrive*	Allows you to specify the drive that Setup uses to store temporary installation files.
/u:*answer file*	Used in an unattended installation to provide responses to questions the user would normally be prompted for.
/udf:*id [,UDB_file]*	If you are installing numerous machines, each must have a unique computer name. This setting lets you specify a file with unique values for these settings.
/e:*command*	Allows you to add a command (such as a batch script) to execute at the end of Setup.
/a	Tells Setup to enable accessibility options.

TABLE 5.4   Common WINNT32.EXE Options

Option	Function
/s:*sourcepath*	Allows you to specify the location of the Windows 2000 source files.
/tempdrive:*drive_letter*	Allows you to specify the drive Setup uses to store temporary installation files.
/unattend	Used to run the install without user intervention.
/unattend[*num]:[answer_file]*	Allows you to specify custom settings for machines during an unattended installation.

TABLE 5.4   Common `WINNT32.EXE` Options *(continued)*

Option	Function
`/cmd:command_line`	Executes a command (such as a batch file at the end of Setup).
`/debug[level]:[filename]`	Used to troubleshoot problems during an upgrade.
`/udf:id[,UDB_file]`	Allows certain values that need to be unique to be set separately for each machine installed.
`/checkupgradeonly`	Performs all the steps of an upgrade, but only as a test. The results are saved to an `UPGRADE.TXT` file that can be examined for potential problems.
`/makelocalsource`	Specifies that the i386 installation directory from the CD should be copied to the hard drive, allowing for easier updates later.

If you start the install from CD-ROM or create the Windows 2000 boot disks, `WINNT.EXE` starts the install by loading a number of files and then presents you with a screen that says, *Welcome to Setup*.

If you use a Windows 9x boot disk, change to the i386 directory and run `WINNT` from that directory.

Partitioning the Drive in Windows 2000

To start Setup, click Enter at the welcome screen, and you will be shown a list of the partitions currently configured on the machine. If one of them is acceptable, select that partition and click Enter. If you wish to create a new partition, you can do so using the Setup program itself, which replaces FDISK as a way to set up the system's hard drive(s).

To delete an existing partition, highlight the partition and press D. You will be asked to confirm your choice and will be reminded that all information on the partition will be lost. If the disk is new or if the old information is no longer needed, this is fine.

If you are not sure what is on the drive, find out before you repartition it!

To create a new partition, highlight some free space and press C. You will be asked how big you want the partition to be. Remember that Windows 2000 Professional wants you to have about 2GB as a minimum, but the partition can be as large as the entire drive.

Formatting the Partition in Windows 2000

Once you have created or decided on a partition to use, you are asked to format that partition. In doing so, you need to choose between NTFS and the FAT filesystem. FAT is the file system of DOS, and its advantages include the following:

- Compatible with DOS and Windows 9x dual-boot configurations

- Excellent speed on small drives

- Accessible and modifiable with many standard DOS disk utilities

NTFS, as you might expect, comes from Windows NT and is a more sophisticated file system that has a number of enhancements that set it apart from FAT:

- Supports larger partition sizes than FAT

- Allows for file-level security to protect system resources

- Supports compression, encryption, disk quotas, and file ownership

 In most cases, you will find that it is better to go with NTFS.

When you choose one of the format options, the machine goes out and formats the installation partition. This generally takes a few minutes, even on a fast PC.

Installing Windows 2000

After the installation partition is formatted, the system checks the new partition for errors and then begins to copy files. While the files are being copied, a progress indicator displays on the screen showing you how far along the process is. Windows installs files into temporary installation folders on the drive and asks you to reboot once the copy is complete. If you do not reboot within 15 seconds of the end of the file copy, the system automatically reboots for you.

 If Setup detects any problems during the partition check, it attempts to fix them and immediately asks you to reboot. At that point the install will need to start over. If problems are found, this often indicates problems with the hard drive, and you may want to run a full SCANDISK before returning to the install.

When Windows 2000 Professional reboots, it automatically brings you into a graphical setup that resembles a massive Windows wizard (as shown in Figure 5.1). This is generally referred to as the graphical phase of Windows 2000 Setup, due to the contrast between this phase and the earlier blue-background-and-text text phase where you configured partitions and copied temporary files.

During this phase, Windows attempts to identify and configure the hardware in the computer, which may take a few minutes. One of the more unsettling parts of Setup occurs during this time, because the screen flickers—and often goes completely black—while monitor detection occurs.

FIGURE 5.1   The Windows 2000 Setup Wizard

Windows 2000 comes packaged with an impressive array of drivers and is able to identify and load most modern hardware. Still, not all devices have compatible drivers on the Windows 2000 CD-ROM. If your hardware is not detected during startup, you can install additional device drivers after Setup completes, as shown later in the chapter.

After hardware detection is completed, the ever-polite Windows 2000 Setup Wizard welcomes you once again. To move through the wizard, click the Next and Back buttons along the bottom of the window. The screens of the setup process are as follows:

Regional Settings   The first screen rarely needs to be modified if you are configuring the machine for use in the U.S., but users in other countries will find that this is where they can change keyboard and language settings.

Personalize Your Software   Enter the name (required) and organization (optional) of the person to whom the software is registered. Both fields are just text boxes. Enter any values that apply.

Personalize Your Software   If you're using a retail version of the OS, you will be prompted for the 25-character product key. You must enter it in to proceed.

Computer Name and Administrator Password   The *computer name* is the name by which a machine will be known if it participates on a network. This name is generally 15 characters or fewer. The administrator password is used to protect access to the powerful Administrator account. Unlike Windows $9x$, where usernames and password security are optional, all users must log on with a username and password to use a Windows 2000 Professional Desktop.

Modem Dialing Information   If a modem has been detected, you are asked for country, area code, and dialing preference information. If you do not have a modem, this screen is skipped.

Date and Time Settings   The Date and Time dialog box also has time zone and daylight savings time information. Any data on this screen can easily be changed later.

Networking Settings/Installing Components   After you enter the date and time, you will wait a minute or two as Windows 2000 installs any networking components it has found and prepares to walk you through the network configuration. As you are waiting, the Status area shows you which components are being installed.

Performing Final Tasks   The Final Tasks page reports on Setup's progress while it does the following:

Installs Start Menu Items   Shortcuts are created to the applications and options installed during Setup.

Registers Components   The Registry is updated with Setup information.

Saves Settings   Configuration information is saved to disk, and other defaults and user selections are applied (such as area code, time zone, and so on).

Removes Any Temporary Files Used   The temporary files saved to the hard drive at the start of Setup and used to install Windows are removed to free drive space.

> This last screen can take quite a long time to complete. In general, the install of Windows 2000 takes about twice as long as an install of Windows 9*x*.

Eventually, the wizard completes, and you are asked to reboot by clicking the Finish button. When the system restarts, Windows 2000 Professional Setup is complete, and the standard Windows 2000 boot process initiates.

Windows XP Installation

As of the writing of this book, Windows XP is the most common end-user operating system in the Microsoft OS family. Installing it is a breeze compared to previous editions of Windows. As a matter of fact, you can install it with a minimum of user interaction. Microsoft has designed Windows XP to be the simplest OS to install yet.

As with other versions of Windows, you will go through various phases of the installation:

- Starting the installation
- Text-based installation phase
- Graphical installation phase

Notice, however, that Windows XP does almost everything for you. It is a very quick OS installation.

> This installation process assumes that there is no OS on the computer already. If there is, check out "Upgrading to Windows XP" later in this chapter.

Starting the Installation

During this phase, you begin the installation of Windows XP, configure the disk system to accept Windows XP, and start the graphical phase of Windows XP Setup.

In order to start a Windows XP installation, as with the other Windows OSs, you must first check your prerequisites (hardware support, available disk space, and so on). Plus, you must ensure that your computer supports booting to a CD-ROM (most do these days, especially those that are able to support Windows XP).

Once you do, to start the installation, power up the computer and quickly insert the Windows XP CD-ROM. If you don't do this quickly enough, you may get an *Operating system not found* message because the CD-ROM wasn't ready as a boot device (it hadn't spun up yet). If this happens, leave the CD in the drive and reboot the computer.

You may have to press a key on some systems. A phrase like *Press any key to boot from CD-ROM* may appear. If it does, press a key to do just that so you can begin the installation.

If the CD is inserted successfully, the screen clears, and the words *Setup is inspecting your computer's configuration* appear. After that, the Windows XP Setup main screen appears, as in Figure 5.2.

If your computer was produced after the release of Windows XP and you need to install a third-party SCSI, IDE, or RAID driver in order to recognize the disk drives, press F6 as soon as the screen turns from black to blue (Setup will prompt you at the bottom of the screen).

FIGURE 5.2   Windows XP main Setup screen

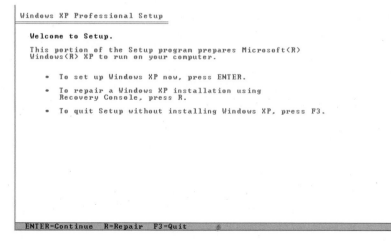

Text-Based Installation Phase

When the Setup screen appears, you can press Enter to begin the installation. The End User License Agreement (EULA) screen appears, which you must accept (otherwise you can't install Windows XP—as with other versions of Windows). Windows Setup then presents you with a series of screens similar to those in previous versions, where you can set up the disk to accept Windows XP with either FAT or NTFS. It is best to choose NTFS for performance reasons.

Windows Setup now formats the partition as you specified and copies the files needed to start the graphical portion of Setup. When it's finished copying and unpacking the files, Setup reboots the computer and starts the graphical portion of Windows XP Setup. If all is successful, you will see a screen similar to that in Figure 5.3.

Graphical Installation Phase

During the graphical installation phase, Windows XP Setup performs almost all of the actions necessary to bring Windows XP to a functional level. The first thing it does is copy files to the hard disk and begin installing devices (as shown in Figure 5.4). This process takes several minutes and should not be interrupted.

Now, follow these steps:

1. Setup asks you for regional and language settings. The defaults are English (United States) for the language, United States for the location, and US Keyboard Layout for the default text-input method. If you are in a different location or prefer a different input method, you can change either item by clicking the button next to that item (Customize for language and location, Details for text-input method). If you accept the displayed options, click Next to continue the installation.

2. Identify yourself to Windows XP Setup by entering your name and company.

3. Windows asks you for the product key. You must enter the product key that comes with your version of Windows XP. This product key can be used only on this computer. To prevent product key theft, Microsoft requires that you go through product activation after the installation is complete.

Windows Activation

New to Windows XP is a process known as *product activation*. To curb software piracy, Microsoft requires that each copy of Windows XP be *activated* (either by phone or Internet) after installation. Without activation, you can run Windows XP, but you can only use it for only 30 days. And during that 30 days, Windows XP will constantly remind you to activate your product.

In addition, the activation records what kind(s) of hardware are in your system, and if three or more pieces change, it requires you to activate again. It's somewhat of a hassle on the part of a system owner if he is constantly upgrading systems. However, some types of Windows XP distributions don't require activation (like those under volume license agreements with Microsoft).

The activation process is simple. After installation is complete, a wizard pops up, asking if you want to activate Windows. You can choose either the Internet or Phone option. If you have a connection to the Internet, the Activation Wizard asks you only which country you live in. No other personal information is required. You can then click Activate, and the Activation Wizard will send a unique identifier built from the different types of hardware in your system across the Internet to Microsoft's activation servers. These servers will send back a code to the Activation Wizard that activates your copy of Windows XP. The phone process is similar, but you must enter the code manually after calling Microsoft and receiving it.

For more information about the process, go to `http://www.microsoft.com/windowsxp/ evaluation/features/activation.mspx`.

FIGURE 5.3   Windows XP Setup

FIGURE 5.4   Installing devices in Windows XP Setup

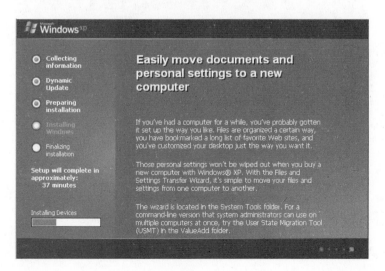

4. Enter a computer name to identify this computer. Use something that will be completely unique on the entire network. Windows XP Setup suggests a name automatically, but you can overwrite it and choose your own. You also must enter a password for the Administrator user account (just as with Windows 2000).

5. Set the time, date, and time zone, as well as whether to adjust for daylight saving time. Click Next.

6. Setup prompts you for the network setup information. You can either have Setup install the network for you or choose the settings yourself. My personal preference is to accept the Typical Settings option and to go back and configure them later if they don't work. The typical settings include TCP/IP set to get its IP address automatically via DHCP (most networks are configured this way).

7. Setup asks you if you want to use a workgroup or a domain, similar to the installation of Windows 2000. Select either choice and continue.

8. Windows finishes the installation by copying all the remaining necessary files, puts items on the Start menu, builds the Registry, and cleans up after itself. This last step should take several minutes to complete. When it's finished, Setup reboots the computer.

Upon reboot, Windows automatically adjusts the screen size for optimum use. You are presented with a screen welcoming you to Windows XP. It walks you through connecting your computer to the Internet and registering and activating your copy of Windows XP, asks you for the names of people who are going to use this computer, and then presents you with the login screen (Figure 5.5). Click on a username you want to log in as, and Windows XP will present you with a Desktop (Figure 5.6).

FIGURE 5.5   A Windows XP login screen

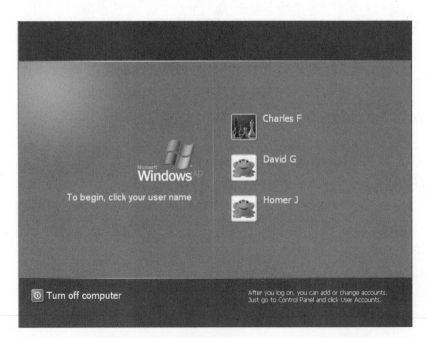

FIGURE 5.6   A Windows XP Desktop

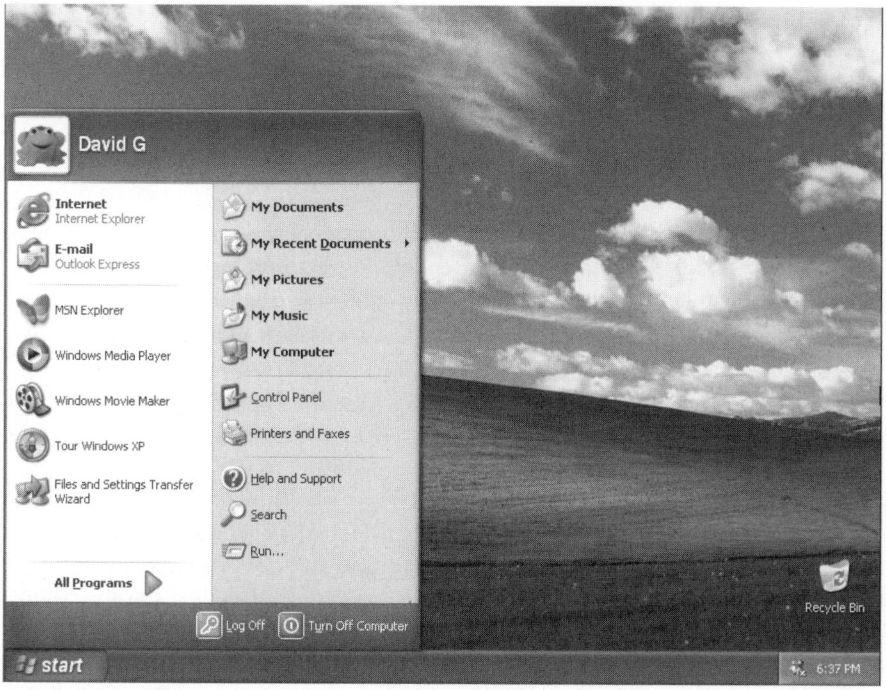

Post-Installation Routines

Even though you have installed your OS, you are not quite finished. There are a few items you must do in order to be truly finished. These items include the following:

- Updating drivers
- Restoring user data files
- Verifying installation

If you don't perform these tasks, you will find using the newly installed OS less than enjoyable.

Updating Drivers

After you have gotten the OS up and running, you may find that a few items aren't configured or working properly. That is somewhat typical. The drivers for some hardware aren't found on the Windows installation CD. Or, more commonly, the drivers on the installation CD are horribly out of date. It's a good idea, then, to go back after an installation and update the drivers for your hardware.

You should check the version of drivers for the following hardware against their manufacturer's website and ensure you have the most current driver for that item:

- Motherboard and chipset
- Video card
- Network card
- Sound card
- Disk controller

To update a driver, download the appropriate driver file package from the hardware manufacturer's website, extract it, and either run the setup utility that is included or use the Add Hardware Wizard that comes with all versions of Windows.

Restoring User Data Files

After you have installed an OS, you will want to use the computer. This involves installing applications and (if applicable) restoring data from either an older computer or this computer if you are reinstalling the OS.

Most often, restoring data files simply involves copying them from a different medium (such as a floppy disk, removable hard disk, magnetic tape, or other removable media). However, it can also involve copying the older data files from another computer. Windows XP includes a utility known as the *Files and Settings Transfer Wizard* that will transfer most of your files and individual application settings from an old computer to a new one. You connect the two computers (either by LAN or by null modem serial cable) and run the wizard on both computers. The files and settings are transferred to the new computer without much trouble.

 NOTE You can find out more about using this utility from Microsoft: http://www .microsoft.com/windowsxp/using/setup/expert/crawford_november12.mspx.

Verifying Installation

The last thing you should do after installing any operating system is to perform a verification. It sounds easy enough, but many people forget to do it, and not doing it can come back to haunt you later. Simply reboot, again (not that the installation didn't reboot a few dozen times already), and log in as a user. Make sure all of the appropriate programs are there and all of the devices (such as the network card and video card) are working properly.

Upgrading the Operating System

In the previous sections, you have learned about installing an operating system from scratch. In this section, you will learn about upgrading an OS to Windows 2000 or Windows XP. Microsoft is constantly releasing new versions of Windows, and upgrading is often the best way to ensure you'll receive the best support. With each version, the hardware requirements go up; however, so does the number of features that are included.

In this section you will learn about the various topics you must understand when upgrading an OS. For the most part, an upgrade is an installation. There are only a few differences, and we will explain them as they apply to the process.

Upgrade Prerequisites

Before you can begin an upgrade, you must plan it so that it goes successfully. An OS upgrade is a major undertaking and shouldn't be taken lightly. You must consider several items, including these:

- Upgrade path
- Hardware compatibility
- Application compatibility
- Service packs and updates
- Backing up data
- Upgrade utility

In this section, you will learn about the various prerequisites that are necessary before beginning an upgrade.

Determine an Upgrade Path

Before you can upgrade your OS, you must determine if it is possible to upgrade directly to the OS you want from your current version. For example, if you have Windows 95 and wish to upgrade to Windows 2000, it is possible to upgrade directly. However, upgrading from Windows 95 to Windows XP requires an intermediate upgrade to Windows 98 first.

Table 5.5 lists the source upgrades and possibilities of upgrading to the various existing versions of Windows. Start with your finger on the version of Windows you currently have on the left side of the table, and then slide it to the right into the column representing the version of Windows you want.

TABLE 5.5   Windows Upgrade Matrix

Your Current Version	Can You Upgrade to Windows 2000?	Can You Upgrade to Windows XP?
Windows 95	Yes	No
Windows 98	Yes	Yes
Windows Me	No	Yes
Windows NT Workstation 4.0	Yes	Yes

TABLE 5.5 Windows Upgrade Matrix *(continued)*

Your Current Version	Can You Upgrade to Windows 2000?	Can You Upgrade to Windows XP?
Windows 2000	N/A	Yes
Windows XP	N/A	N/A

Notice that you can upgrade Windows Me only to Windows XP. That's it! Because Windows Me came out after Windows 2000, it can't be upgraded to that version. Also, this table assumes that the file systems are compatible.

Determine Hardware Compatibility

As mentioned several times during this chapter, when you're doing any kind of installation, you must make sure the hardware onto which you are installing the software is compatible with that OS. Upgrades are no exception. Although the hardware might operate just fine under Windows 98, there's no guarantee it will do so under Windows XP.

To be on the safe side, you should check the Microsoft Hardware Compatibility List (HCL) or Windows Catalog on the Microsoft website given earlier in this chapter for the hardware you have in your computer. Also, you may want to download the drivers that are compatible with the new version of the OS you will have and expand them into a directory on your computer so that they will be available if they are needed during the upgrade.

Determine Application Compatibility

In addition to hardware compatibility, you may have to deal with software application compatibility. Some older software may not work with the newer version of the OS to which you are upgrading. Thankfully, Microsoft has written standards for programmers to use, and if they follow those guidelines correctly, their applications will work on all versions of Windows. However, programmers often need to take shortcuts to make deadlines, and their software may not be 100 percent compatible with certain versions of Windows.

Always make sure you have the most current patch level and version of your critical software before performing an OS upgrade. And make sure all your applications will work properly after the upgrade.

Both Windows 2000 and Windows XP have utilities that will generate hardware and software compatibility reports for you before you upgrade. For upgrades to Windows 2000, you can run the Windows 2000 Readiness Analyzer (called chkupgrd.exe), which is found at http://www.microsoft.com/downloads. If you want to upgrade to XP, you can download the upgrade advisor from http://www.microsoft.com/windowsxp/pro/upgrading/advisor.mspx.

Apply Service Packs and Updates

To ensure that your upgrade will work properly, you may need to update or patch your current OS before doing the upgrade. Most people take the "if it ain't broke, don't fix it" approach to OS patches. However, upgrades can bring out the worst in an OS. So make sure your current OS is up to the most current patch level and that it will be compatible with the upgrade OS.

Backing Up Data

In theory, after the upgrade is complete all of your old data will be there. Usually this is the case. Don't be the victim of the "once-in-a-rarity" times where something goes wrong, and the computer crashes. Back up your data before performing any major system change. An upgrade qualifies as a major system change.

Determine the Correct Upgrade Utility

Finally, you must make sure which utility you need to use when upgrading your OS. For example, you can use the WINNT32.EXE program on the Windows 2000 upgrade disk to upgrade Windows NT to Windows 2000. There are two things to remember about the upgrade utilities:

- WINNT.EXE is for upgrading 16-bit OSs (Windows 9x) to a 32-bit OS (Windows 2000/XP).
- WINNT32.EXE is for upgrading a 32-bit OS to another 32-bit OS.

Upgrading to Windows 2000

If the machine that you want to install Windows 2000 on already has Windows 9x/NT up and running, you may want to upgrade to the advanced security and performance of Windows 2000 without losing your installed programs or system configuration. Windows 2000 allows for this option by providing a sophisticated upgrade mechanism that can check your hardware and software and then update an existing Windows 9x install while preserving the look, feel, and functionality of your current environment.

Windows 2000 cannot upgrade Windows 3.1 or DOS systems to 2000 Professional. Most machines running 3.1 or DOS probably will be running older hardware, but if you do want to upgrade such a system, you must perform a new full install rather than an upgrade. All programs or drivers that were installed on DOS or Windows 3.x will then need to be reinstalled under Windows 2000.

Starting Setup

Compared to the work involved in setting up a new Windows 2000 install, running the 2000 upgrade is almost effortless. The basic requirements are the same for an upgrade as for a new install, and again you have the option of doing either a CD-based install or a network-based install.

Generally, the simplest option is to place the Windows 2000 Professional disk into the CD-ROM drive of the machine to be upgraded. A window (see Figure 5.7) automatically appears, asking if you want to upgrade to Windows 2000.

> When a compact disc is inserted into a drive, it often automatically starts a program, such as an install routine. This is done through the *Autorun* option.

> Upgrading to Windows 2000 Professional from Windows 9*x* and Windows NT Workstation is essentially the same process—just pop the disk in and go. One of the big advantages of the Windows NT upgrade is that because it is a very similar OS to Windows 2000, you should have fewer compatibility issues. Also, Windows NT drivers can be used in Windows 2000, whereas Windows 9*x* drivers cannot, meaning more hardware may be automatically detected and installed.

If you click Yes to accept the offered upgrade, the Windows 2000 Setup Wizard begins. This wizard performs a number of pre-upgrade tasks and then starts the upgrade itself. The screens you may see during the Upgrade Wizard include the following:

Welcome to the Windows 2000 Setup Wizard   The first choice in the wizard is also probably the most important. This screen (shown in Figure 5.8) is where you decide whether to perform an upgrade to your existing system or install a fresh copy of Windows 2000 onto the drive. Both options have their advantages:

Upgrade to Windows 2000 (Recommended)   The upgrade allows you to keep your existing programs, but it also retains any existing *problems*. Because of this, any system configuration glitches or files that are no longer used will continue to plague you in the new install, just as they did in Windows 9*x*.

FIGURE 5.7   The Windows 2000 upgrade auto-run screen

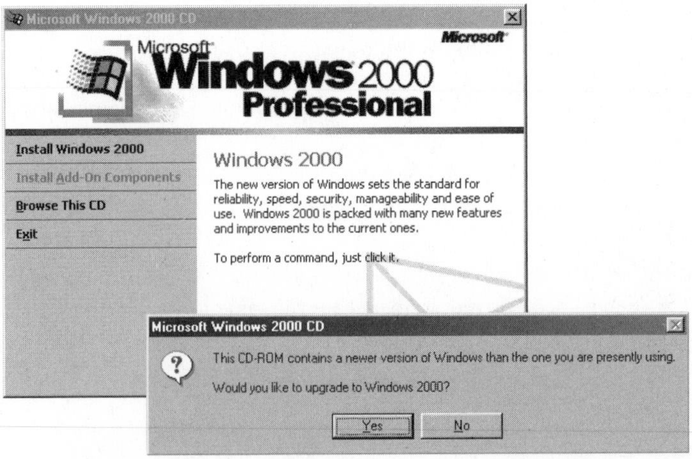

![The Windows 2000 Professional CD auto-run screen. It shows "Microsoft Windows 2000 CD" with a menu of options: Install Windows 2000, Install Add-On Components, Browse This CD, Exit. A dialog box reads: "This CD-ROM contains a newer version of Windows than the one you are presently using. Would you like to upgrade to Windows 2000?" with Yes and No buttons.]

Install a New Copy of Windows 2000 (Clean Install)   A clean install has two major advantages. First, it allows you to start fresh without the baggage of your Windows 9*x* setup. Second, it allows you to dual-boot back to your original Windows 9*x* OS. The disadvantage, of course, is that you have to reinstall all your programs in this scenario.

Windows 2000 and Windows 9*x* can exist on the same computer in a dual-boot scenario. However, because certain drive locations (such as the location of Internet Explorer and Outlook Express) are hard-wired to the same directory for both, software problems would occur if you installed them on the same partition. To install a new copy of Windows 2000 and dual-boot to Windows 9*x*, you need to have a second partition on your disk or a second disk. Windows 9*x* should be installed on the C: partition first, and then Windows 2000 can be installed afterward on the D: partition. The installation of Windows 9*x* *after* Windows 2000 is not supported as a dual-boot scenario.

If you choose to upgrade, you will continue through the wizard. If you choose to install a new copy of the OS, you will be immediately funneled into the process described in the "Windows 2000 Professional Installation" section.

In most cases, I use upgrades as an opportunity to clean up a system. In order to do this, I generally back up any needed data and then reformat the machine's drives and start over from ground zero. It takes a bit more time but is often worth it. Before doing this, though, make sure you still have installation disks for all the applications and other software you will need to reinstall.

FIGURE 5.8   The upgrade and install options

License Agreement and Product Key   Assuming you have continued the upgrade, you're required to complete the next two screens, License Agreement and Product Key. They allow you to accept the Microsoft licensing terms and ask you for a Windows 2000 *product key*. As with the regular install, this key is 25 characters in length and can usually be found on the case of the CD.

Preparing to Upgrade to Windows 2000   With the bookkeeping out of the way, you can now get down to the business of the upgrade itself. Before you start copying files, the Upgrade Wizard examines your existing configuration to see whether there are any problems that will make upgrading difficult (Figure 5.9). The Upgrade Wizard provides a link to Microsoft's Windows Compatibility website for product updates and compatibility information.

During the upgrade, Setup tries to contact Microsoft's website for information and updates, including the upgrade packs it's looking for on the next page of the wizard. If you do not have a connection to the Web as you are upgrading, you will be asked to connect, but you can choose to continue to work offline. If you do work offline, any updates must be applied manually later. If you have an Internet connection, it is recommended that Setup go out to the website and look for updates.

Provide Upgrade Packs   If you choose to work offline, you may need to provide application upgrade packs. Most 32-bit applications will continue to function without any problems. If you have any 16-bit DOS or Windows 3.*x* applications, though, they may not work. Also, any new or odd hardware may not be upgraded properly, as you will see in the next section. If you have been to the Microsoft upgrade site or a vendor site and have obtained updated files for 2000, you can add them now by choosing the Yes, I Have Upgrade Packs option. If not, select the No, I Don't Have Any Upgrade Packs option. In such a case, you can still apply upgrades later if applications do not function after the upgrade.

FIGURE 5.9   Preparing to upgrade to Windows 2000

![Windows 2000 Setup dialog box titled "Preparing to Upgrade to Windows 2000". Text reads "Setup must examine your computer before you upgrade to Windows 2000." Before the upgrade, Setup will: Prompt you to provide software and hardware upgrade files, if you have any. Search for incompatible hardware, software, or settings. Create an upgrade report that you can print or save. Before upgrading, visit the Windows 2000 Web site for the latest information and upgrade files. Click here to connect now. Buttons: Back, Next, Cancel.]

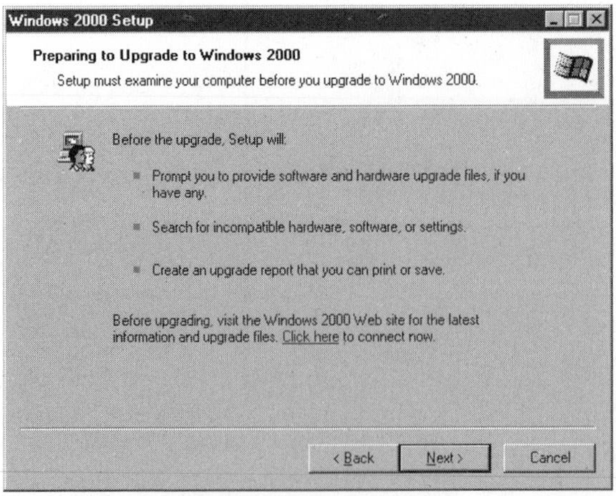

Upgrading to the Windows 2000 NTFS File System   Another upgrade option you are given is to upgrade your drive's file system to Windows 2000's advanced NTFS. The upgrade to NTFS enables increased file security, disk quotas, and disk compression. NTFS also makes better use of large drives by using a more advanced method of saving and retrieving data.

To enable NTFS and sever all ties to Windows 9x, select the Yes, Upgrade My Drive option. To retain your links to the past and allow for dual-boot scenarios, select the No, Do Not Upgrade My Drive option.

Preparing an Upgrade Report   Once you have made your choices, Setup finally goes through and examines your system for compatibility issues. This involves checking to be sure all hardware and software that is currently installed can be found, and it also involves creating a detailed upgrade report. You will be allowed to do two things: provide updated files for any incompatible hardware and view a report of what the compatibility check has found.

Provide Updated Plug and Play Files   In upgrading any system, there is a chance that incompatible hardware may be found. In upgrading certain systems, such as older machines or laptops, the chances are even greater. IBM's ThinkPad series, for example, has hardware support for DVD playback available through an MPEG-2 Decoder Card. This is an optional piece of hardware that is specifically built by IBM for IBM, and as such it is not common enough to be recognized by the Setup process. In order for this device to work, you must obtain updated files from IBM.

If you don't have updated files at present for any unsupported hardware, you can continue with the install, but you will have to update the files before the hardware will function under Windows 2000. If the functioning of the hardware is essential to the operation of the system (network card, video card, and so on), you may want to stop the install and get the new drivers before continuing. For nonessential hardware such as a DVD decoder, you can continue and fix the problem later, but it is a good idea to at least verify that the hardware is compatible with Windows 2000, so you won't be surprised later.

WARNING   As noted earlier, you cannot use the same Windows 9x drivers that are currently installed.

Upgrade Report   The Setup Wizard now provides you with a detailed report (see Figure 5.10) of what it thinks may cause you issues as you upgrade. The following topics are included:

Hardware   Any devices that cannot be confirmed as compatible with Windows 2000 are listed here.

Software   Programs that do not work with Windows 2000 are listed here. In these cases you are directed to uninstall the program before the upgrade, because it will not function and may not uninstall properly after the upgrade.

Program Notes   Some programs need to be reconfigured to work with Windows 2000. The Program Notes area details some of these known issues, such as the fact that Microsoft Outlook 2000 works with Windows 2000 but must be reinstalled after the upgrade.

General Information This section details information best described as "other." Some of the upgrade issues that arose during a recent upgrade concerned hardware profiles, backup files, and the Recycle Bin.

If you want to save the upgrade report information for later use, you have two options: print it or save it to a file. If you feel that the machine has major compatibility issues, you should probably save or print the report and visit http://support.microsoft.com/ph/1131 for information or updates.

Once you have checked out the upgrade report, you have to choose whether to proceed with the upgrade immediately or to exit from the upgrade in order to regroup and obtain needed updates. If you are ready to proceed, click Next to continue with the install. If you would rather wait, click Cancel, and the upgrade will end without affecting your existing Windows installation.

Ready to Install Windows 2000 If you have made it this far, the tough part is over. As the wizard states, *This process is completely automatic, and you will not have to answer any additional questions.*

All you need to do is click the Next button and head off to get some coffee—or preferably some lunch. About one hour and three restarts later, you should find that the process has completed and a Windows 2000 logon screen is waiting for you when you return.

 After the first reboot, the existing Windows install is deleted and Windows 2000 files are copied to the drive. After that, a second graphical setup starts, and your settings from Windows 9*x*/NT are automatically reapplied.

FIGURE 5.10 The completed upgrade report

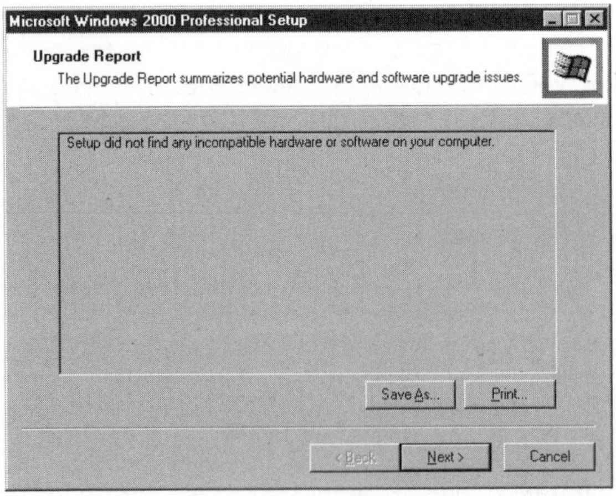

Microsoft Windows 2000 Professional Setup

Upgrade Report
The Upgrade Report summarizes potential hardware and software upgrade issues.

Setup did not find any incompatible hardware or software on your computer.

Save As...   Print...

< Back   Next >   Cancel

Upgrading to Windows XP

Upgrading to XP is probably the simplest OS upgrade of all:

1. Insert the CD and choose Install Windows XP from the menu that appears (Figure 5.11).

FIGURE 5.11   Windows XP installation menu

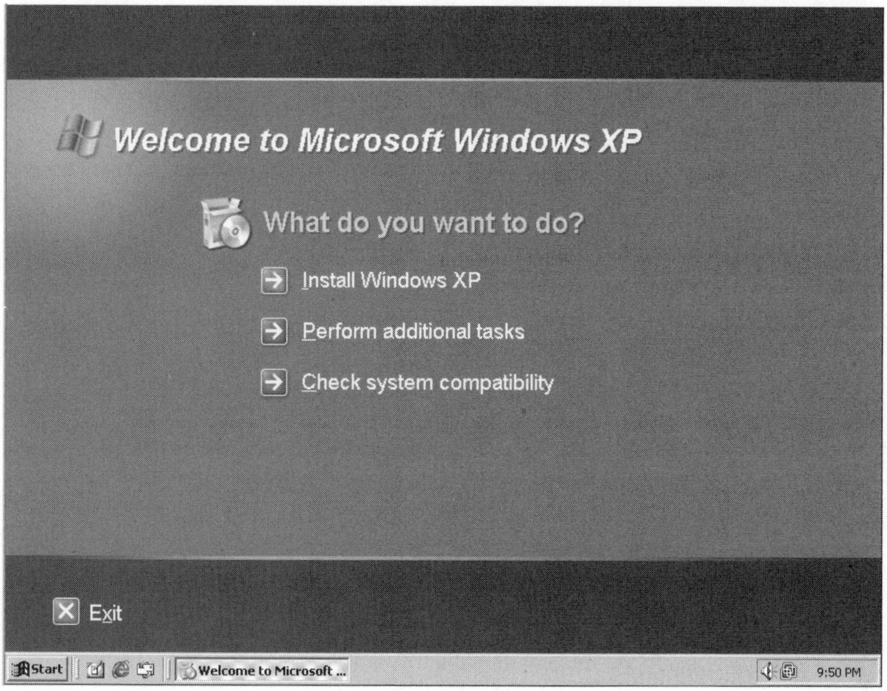

2. The Setup program detects that you already have an OS installed and presents you with a menu that says Upgrade (Recommended), as shown in Figure 5.12. Click Next to begin the upgrade.

3. Setup asks you to agree to the EULA, enter the product key, and download an updated version of the Setup program (if necessary).

4. Setup copies several files over, reboots a couple of times, and continues like a standard Windows XP installation.

Once you have finished the installation, you must activate it (like a standard installation of Windows XP), but that's about it. Windows XP Setup makes most of the decisions about the upgrade for you, so only a minimal amount of interaction is necessary.

FIGURE 5.12   Windows XP upgrade menu

Finalizing Your Upgrade

Now that you've completed your upgrade, you need to think about making this computer functional, like you would have if you had just installed a new operating system. The first step after a reboot should always be to make sure that the newest service patches and updates are applied. Fortunately, both Windows 2000 and Windows XP participate in the automatic *Windows Update* program, which will automatically download new patches if you allow it to. Still, when you've just performed an upgrade (or new installation), it's best to force this action by manually initiating Windows Update in the Start menu.

After your updates and patches are applied, verify that the user's data transferred properly, including checking to ensure that critical programs work. Finally, install any additional services that might be necessary—the computer is ready to go!

Installing Device Drivers

Hardware devices come in all shapes and sizes, adding a variety of capabilities to your computer system. In this section, you will learn the specifics of installing device drivers for many different types of peripherals. You will learn the different methods of connecting a peripheral as well as the steps required to install a driver on Windows 2000 and Windows XP.

As a technician, one task you will constantly be asked to perform is to install a device driver. A *device driver* (or just *driver* for short) is a small piece of software that allows the OS to communicate directly with a specific piece of hardware. Without the driver, the OS wouldn't know the special commands to send to the device to make it do what you want.

Most often, you will be adding a device or component to your computer in order to expand the computer's capabilities. Regardless of function, devices that you can install can be divided into two primary groups:

Plug and Play   *Plug and Play (PnP)* is a standard set of specifications that was developed by Intel to enable a computer to detect a new device automatically and install the appropriate driver. PnP makes a technician's job easier because the system already knows what hardware settings are in use, and it sets the new device's hardware settings (IRQ, I/O address, and so on) to appropriate, nonconflicting settings. Almost every new device introduced since 1995 is a PnP device.

Non–Plug and Play   If you have to configure a device's hardware settings manually in order to install it, the device can be considered a non-PnP device. These devices are nearly obsolete (but you'll still see them out there, hanging on) as manufacturers embrace PnP methods.

The basic process for installing these devices is the same for all versions of Windows. There are simply some minor differences in procedures and the appearance of the dialog boxes.

Rights and Security Issues

Whenever you are installing a new device, Windows 2000 and XP may consider that process a security threat. After all, you might be installing some kind of snooping or monitoring device. Therefore, you must have certain permissions to be able to install a new piece of hardware in Windows.

The primary requirement is that in most cases, in order to install a device, you must be logged in either as an administrator or as a user who is a member of the Administrators group. However, if the device driver has a digital signature, Windows may consider it okay to install without the administrator's permission. A *digitally signed driver* is a driver that has been digitally "signed" by Microsoft with a special value that only Windows can read. This signature tells the Windows installer that the driver being installed has been tested for security and stability on the chosen Windows platform and that the driver is from a reputable source. Using digitally signed drivers increases the stability and reliability of your system.

WARNING   Although more and more companies are signing their drivers, many still do not. Microsoft's official stance on unsigned drivers is "Use them at your own risk!"

Another requirement to installing hardware without the administrator's permission is if the device can be installed without user interaction. That is, a window does not have to be displayed that requires the user to make a choice of some kind.

Basic Procedure for Device Installation

The basic procedure for installing any device into a Windows computer is the same no matter what version of Windows you are using or whether the device is PnP compliant. The process is as follows:

1. Locate drivers for the device.

2. Connect the device to your computer (either internally or externally).

3. Load or install the proper drivers.

4. Configure the device.

The last two steps will not require your intervention if the device you are installing is PnP compliant.

Keep in mind that these are general steps. Whenever possible, it is advisable to follow the manufacturer's exact instructions when installing any piece of hardware. Failure to do so may possibly damage the device and void the device's warranty.

Locating Drivers for the Device

Device drivers are software, and they are distributed much like any other software. Usually, a CD-ROM or floppy disk comes with whatever hardware you are installing. On that CD-ROM is the device driver for the OS version you have. Most driver CD-ROMs contain drivers for all possible compatible OSs (usually the version for each different OS is in its own directory). However, the drivers on these CDs aren't always the most up-to-date ones.

To find more up-to-date drivers, there are many places you can go. Often, if the OS you have installed is newer than the hardware in your computer, a more current driver may be on the OS CD-ROM. The most current driver can often be found on the device manufacturer's support website. Go to that company's main website. Usually, the main page has a link to Support, Product Support, Download Drivers, or something similar.

Once on the support website, you download an archive file that contains all the driver files needed for your device (including any setup program and supporting utilities). Download it to a directory on your computer, and then double-click on the archive to open it and extract all the files (this may also start the installation program).

Connecting the Device

Connecting devices to your computer can be accomplished in many ways. There are many different ports and interfaces to your computer. Each one of them may be used to add a new device to your computer (or upgrade an existing device).

Generally speaking, when you are connecting a device to the inside of your computer (either in an expansion slot or connecting to an existing expansion bus), you should power down the computer, unplug it, and wait at least 30 seconds before attempting to install or remove any device. This is necessary because power in the newer ATX-style motherboards remains supplied to the motherboard for at least that long until the capacitors in the power supply drain completely. Some motherboards have a small LED that indicates whether the board has power (even if the power switch is off). If your motherboard has one of these LEDs, wait until it goes out (usually 20 to 30 seconds) before attempting to add or remove a device.

The procedure for USB devices is contrary to this rule. Generally, you install the driver and software for the USB device first and then plug in the device *while the computer is on.* Doing so allows the computer to recognize the new component and configure it properly.

To connect the device, follow the manufacturer's instructions and insert the card, plug in the cable, or connect the device in whatever method it uses. Make sure it is firmly secured before you attempt to power up the computer.

Loading or Installing the Proper Drivers

There are two main methods of installing device drivers: You can either use the setup program that comes with the hardware driver CD-ROM (or downloaded file) or use the Windows hardware installation wizard. Either method will get the software installed. However, if the driver is for a device that requires a monitoring utility (like a webcam utility for a webcam), you *must* use the setup utility that comes with the driver software. Often, if you try to install hardware that requires such a utility with the Windows Add/Remove Hardware Wizard, the wizard will tell you exactly that and halt the installation.

Often, after installing a device, you must reboot the computer so that Windows will recognize and load the driver properly.

For devices that are not hot swappable (or pluggable), rebooting is a must. However, for many external devices, such as USB devices, rebooting is not necessary. Just plug in the device, let Windows detect it, and use the device.

Configuring the Device

Once the device has been installed, you must configure its various options so that it functions the way you want it to. In the case of a video card, you must ensure that it is set to the right resolution for the monitor you are using, so you get the highest possible performance out of the system.

Often, this step is overlooked. Some people install the driver, and if the device works, that's the key. However, you can often obtain the best performance with only a few more minutes of adjustment.

Usually, in order to configure the device, you must either go to the System control panel in Windows and view the properties of the device you are concerned with, or use the utility that comes with the device. The latter method is more common with many peripherals and complex expansion cards.

Windows Version-Specific Installation Items

For the most part, installing a new device is similar in the different versions of Windows. However, there are a few areas where installation differs. In this section, you will learn the differences between adding hardware on Windows 2000 and Windows XP.

Adding Hardware in Windows 2000

Windows 2000 relies heavily on PnP. Installing a piece of hardware in a Windows 2000 computer basically involves physically installing the device, booting the computer, and letting Windows 2000 automatically install the driver for that device. If it can't find the driver, it will ask you for the location. In addition, the screens have the Windows 2000 look and feel. Finally, you can use the Add/Remove Hardware Wizard to both add new hardware and update drivers for existing hardware.

Follow these steps:

1. Begin the process by double-clicking the Add/Remove Hardware icon (found in Start ➤ Settings ➤ Control Panel). Doing so starts the Add/Remove Hardware Wizard.

2. After clicking Next to move past the first screen, you are asked if you want to add/troubleshoot a device or uninstall/unplug a device. The latter choice allows you to prepare Windows to completely remove a device or temporarily disable a device. To continue adding a hardware device, choose Add/Troubleshoot A Device and click Next.

3. Windows 2000 searches for any uninstalled PnP devices. It also searches for a list of currently installed devices that may or may not need new drivers. The wizard then presents you with a list of devices so you can choose the device for which you want to install a new driver (either a new device or an existing one), as shown in Figure 5.13. If you are installing a new device, choose Add A New Device. If you are updating a driver for an existing device, choose the device whose driver you want to update. When you've made your choice, click Next.

4. At this point, the Add/Remove Hardware Wizard asks you whether you want Windows to search for the hardware or whether you'll select it from a list. The wizard then installs the hardware driver or asks you for the appropriate driver, and the installation finishes.

FIGURE 5.13 Choosing a device for which to install a driver

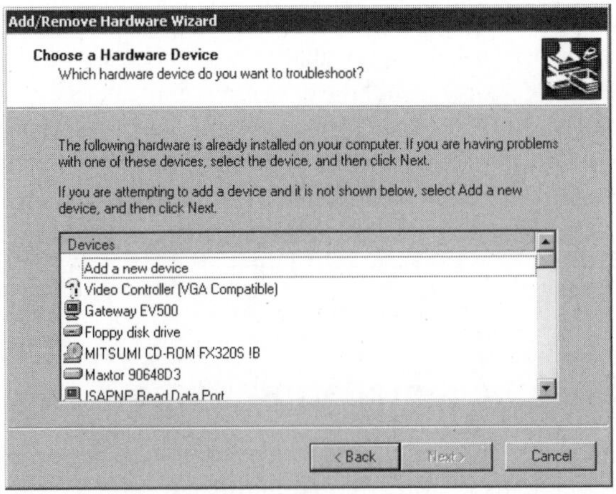

One nice feature of adding hardware is that if the device driver can't be found or won't install correctly, Windows 2000 starts a troubleshooting wizard to help you finish installing the new hardware.

Adding Hardware in Windows XP

You will notice that Microsoft changed the name of the Windows 2000 Add/Remove Hardware Wizard to Add Hardware Wizard under Windows XP. As in previous versions of Windows, to install hardware you can let Windows XP recognize new hardware on boot-up and install drivers then, use the manufacturer's installation program, or manually install hardware using the Add Hardware Wizard.

When you install some hardware under Windows XP, XP will warn you to install software before installing the device. You will notice this requirement mainly on USB devices and some other PnP devices.

To begin installing a driver for a new piece of hardware, follow these steps:

1. Install the hardware (either insert the expansion card or plug in the device).

2. Boot the computer and wait for Windows XP to recognize the new hardware. If XP recognizes the new hardware, it displays a screen similar to the one shown in Figure 5.14, which asks if you want Windows to install the driver automatically for you or if you want to pick the driver from a list. If you go with the default choice of having Windows XP install the driver automatically, XP locates the driver in its database of drivers that come with XP or that have already been installed. It then proceeds to install the driver and activate the new hardware.

You may see a warning telling you that if your hardware came with an installation CD, you should insert it now. That way, XP can find the driver automatically.

FIGURE 5.14   XP detecting new hardware

3. Once XP has found the driver, it determines whether the driver is properly signed (and gives you the chance to stop the installation if it's not).

4. XP tells you that the device has been installed.

Like Windows 2000, if Windows XP can't find the right driver for the device, it will start a troubleshooting wizard to help you along the installation. Clearly, Microsoft has streamlined the hardware-installation process for Windows XP.

 In both Windows 2000 and Windows XP, always check Device Manager to make sure that the device is recognized by the system and the driver is working properly!

Optimizing Windows 2000 and Windows XP

Anyone who's run a Windows computer for any length of time has experienced it: Your computer runs faster than anything when you first get it, but after a while, it seems to slow down. It gets slower and slower until it's almost unusable. This particular problem is partially a result of poor Windows optimization. Windows *optimization* is the process of making Windows run at its best with a given hardware platform.

You can perform several tasks to make your system run better. The most common tasks that will affect performance significantly include these:

- Managing virtual memory
- Defragmenting disks
- Using caches
- Managing temporary files

In this section, you will learn how to use these common tasks to optimize Windows performance.

Managing Virtual Memory

Let's face it. Windows is a resource hog. The more hardware a computer has (memory, hard disk space, and so on), the more resources Windows will use. You can never have enough memory. Toward that end, Microsoft developed for Windows its own virtual memory technology. *Virtual memory* is the general term for a type of computer technology where hard-disk space is used as a kind of backup memory.

Operating systems besides Windows use virtual memory in one form or another. Linux and Macintosh OSs use some kind of virtual memory (although they may call it something different).

The *swap file* is used to provide virtual memory to the Windows system. The swap file is a file (called PAGEFILE.SYS) created on hard-drive space where idle pieces of programs are placed, while active parts of programs are kept in or swapped into main memory. The programs running in Windows believe that their information is still in RAM, but Windows has moved it into near-line storage on the hard drive. When the application needs the information again, the data is swapped back into RAM so it can be used by the processor.

Throughout this section, you will see the terms swap file, page file, and paging file. They are all synonyms.

When you are working in your office and need a document, you may have to walk over to a file cabinet to get it. You then return to your seat and read the document. When you have finished and are ready to go on with another task, you put down the current document. If you don't need it again in the near future, you should get up and put it back in the file cabinet. If you will need it again, though, you may just set it on your desk for easier access. When you need it again, you have to pick it back up (unless you can remember what it said without looking). Generally, you can think of a computer's disk drive as the file cabinet and virtual memory as the desk.

Real memory (RAM) is the computer's memory. The more RAM you put into the machine, the more things it is able to remember without looking anything up. The larger the swap file, the fewer times the computer has to do intensive drive searches.

The moral of the story: As with most things virtual, a swap file is not nearly as good as actual RAM, but it is better than nothing!

🌐 Real World Scenario

Why Do We Have Virtual Memory?

People wonder this all the time: "My computer has two gigs of RAM. Why would I need more?"

Like many other things in the computer industry, virtual memory was born out of necessity. Fairly early on in personal computer evolution, it was decided that a computer would never need more than 640KB (yes, *kilo*bytes) of memory. Oops. For DOS it was fine, mostly, but once graphical operating systems came into the world, the required resources jumped significantly.

Flash back to the late 1980s/early 1990s. If you had 4MB of RAM in your system, you were doing well. Very well, in fact, because RAM cost over $100 *per megabyte*. If you wanted more memory for Windows to use, then you had two choices. One was to mortgage your house, and the other was to use another source: virtual memory.

Hard-disk space was and probably always will be cheaper per megabyte than RAM, simply because of the technology involved. So while hard disks might be slower than RAM, they are bigger and cheaper. Using space on them for virtual memory made a ton of economic sense then and still does today.

Virtual Memory in Windows 2000

The virtual memory settings in Windows 2000 (see Figure 5.15) tell you how much hard-drive space is allocated to the system as a swap file. Windows 2000 recommends a particular virtual memory level, but you can add to or subtract from this value as necessary. Often, certain applications (SQL Server, for instance) need you to raise Windows 2000 Professional's virtual memory limit in order to work properly. Graphics and CAD applications also require you to raise the virtual memory level, but if this is the case, the setup instructions for the application will generally tell you what modifications need to be made.

Adding to the swap-file size is not always helpful and can sometimes slow down the system. Modify this setting only if you have been instructed to or if you are testing to see whether the change speeds up or slows down the computer. Reducing the swap-file size is generally not recommended and can have serious consequences on performance.

To access the virtual memory settings, open the System control panel, click the Advanced tab, and then click the Performance Options button. Doing so will bring up the Performance Options window, where you can view the current virtual memory settings.

To change the size of the paging file, you must be logged on as Administrator. If you're not an administrator, the options will be grayed out. To begin, click Change under the size of the current page file. Type in values for the maximum and minimum sizes of the page file (Microsoft recommends a value at least 1.5 times the amount of RAM as in your system), click Set, and then click OK.

If you reduce the minimum or maximum size of the page file, you will have to reboot your computer. However, in Windows 2000, increases don't require a restart.

If you need to delete a paging file, set both the minimum and maximum sizes to zero.

FIGURE 5.15 The Virtual Memory window in Windows 2000

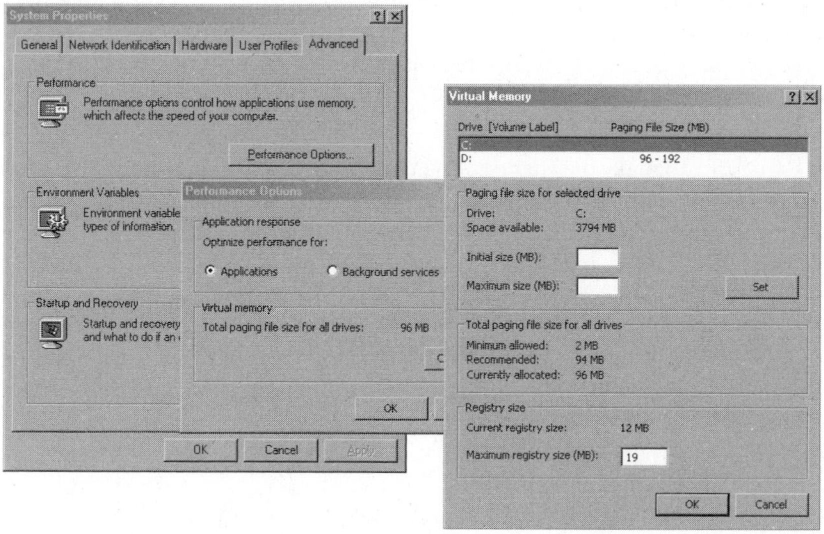

Virtual Memory in Windows XP

Setting the swap-file size and location in Windows XP is almost identical to the process in Windows 2000. The major differences are how you get to the controls and what the screen looks like.

As in Windows 2000, you must be logged on as an administrator. However, the screen that allows you to change your virtual memory settings is buried a bit deeper. To begin, open the System control panel, as shown in Figure 5.16. Click the Advanced tab. On this tab, click the button labeled Settings in the Performance section to access the Performance Options window. Click the Advanced tab.

FIGURE 5.16 Windows XP System control panel

On this tab are various performance-tuning options. At the bottom of the displayed tab are the virtual memory settings (Figure 5.17). This area tells you the total paging-file size for all drives. If you have multiple swap files on multiple drives, the number listed tells the total size for all swap files.

To change the size of your swap files, click the Change button to open the screen in Figure 5.18. In the Drive [Volume Label] section, select the drive that contains the swap file you want to change. Then, in the paging section, change the minimum and maximum numbers as in Windows 2000. Click Set to make the changes, and click OK in each open window. Windows may ask you to reboot to complete the changes, but (as in Windows 2000) only if you've reduced the swap-file size.

To let Windows manage the swap-file size, choose the System Managed Size option on the screen shown in Figure 5.18.

Defragmenting Disks

When Windows is installed on a new disk, all the full clusters are contiguous. That is, they are located one after another rotationally on the disk. However, as files and programs are installed and deleted, the blocks of disk space get less and less contiguous. This can hinder Windows' performance, because it has to constantly go looking for more sections of different files. You've probably seen a symptom of a fragmented disk: the hard-drive light flickers madly, and the system seems slow as a snail when switching programs, starting a new program, or opening a file. This symptom is known as *disk thrashing*.

FIGURE 5.17   Advanced performance settings

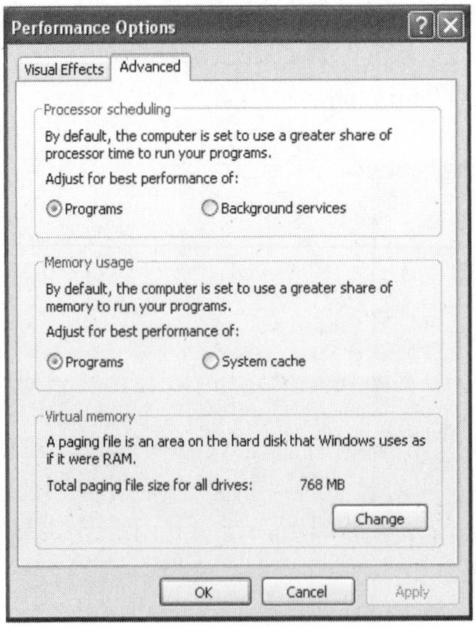

![Performance Options dialog box showing Visual Effects and Advanced tabs with Processor scheduling, Memory usage, and Virtual memory sections. Total paging file size for all drives: 768 MB with a Change button.]

FIGURE 5.18   Changing the Windows XP paging-file size

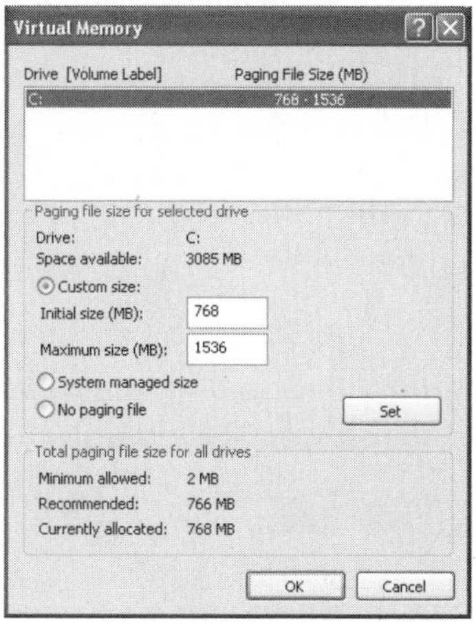

To solve this problem, Microsoft includes a utility with Windows for reorganizing, or *defragmenting*, the hard disk. With earlier versions of Windows, this was a separate utility you ran to defragment your disk; in later versions, it is integrated into the operating system.

> Oddly enough, the Windows NT operating system did not come with a disk defragmentation utility, even though earlier operating systems such as Windows 95 did.

Defragmenting in Windows 2000 Professional

To begin defragmenting, close all programs, and then double-click the My Computer icon. Right-click on the hard disk you want to defragment, and choose Properties to bring up the Local Disk Properties window. In this window, click the Tools tab, and then click the Defragment Now button to start the defragmentation program.

> You can also start the program by going to Start ➤ Programs ➤ Accessories ➤ System Tools ➤ Disk Defragmenter.

Once you have started the Disk Defragmenter, you can do one of two things: analyze a disk to see whether it needs defragmentation (by clicking the Analyze button) or go ahead with the defragmentation (by clicking the Defragment button). If you click the Defragment button to begin the defragmentation, Disk Defragmenter will analyze the disk to get a map of where files are stored and then rearrange them into contiguous disk space. This process will take some time, and it may be best to start it in the evening before you go to bed. Figure 5.19 shows what the defragmentation process looks like while it's proceeding.

Defragmenting in Windows XP Professional

As in other operations that modify key parts of the Windows installation or hardware (especially disk drives), you must be logged in as an administrator in order to perform a defragmentation on Windows XP. However, the process for starting the Disk Defragmenter is exactly the same as in previous versions of Windows. To open the Disk Defragmenter, go to Properties in My Computer on any drive you want to defragment, click the Tools tab, and then click Defragment Now. As with Windows 2000, click Defragment to begin the process. Figure 5.20 shows an example of the defragmentation process in Windows XP.

FIGURE 5.19   Defragmenting a disk using the Windows 2000 Disk Defragmenter

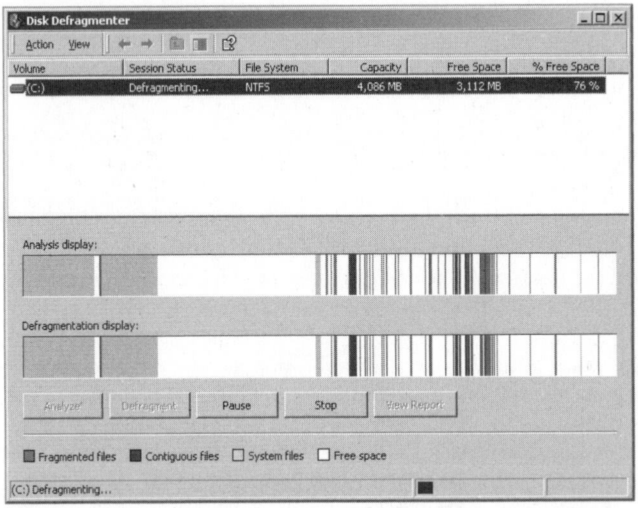

FIGURE 5.20   Defragmenting a disk using the Windows XP Disk Defragmenter

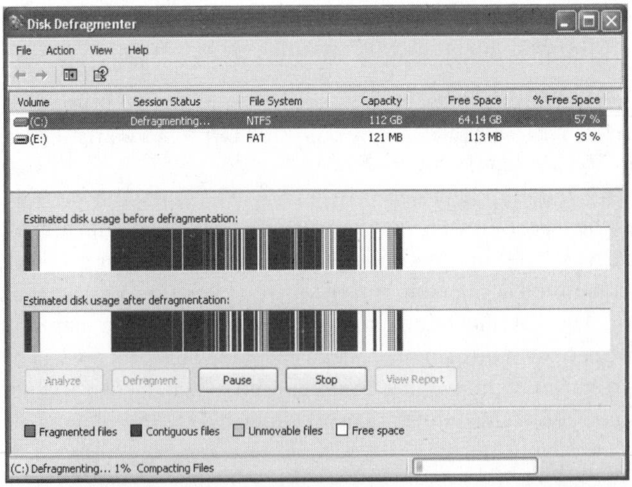

In all versions of Windows, you an also begin a disk defragmentation by using the command-line DEFRAG.EXE.

Using Disk Caches

A *disk cache* is a small amount of memory that is used to hold data that is frequently accessed from the hard disk. Various utilities and software handle disk caching for the different versions of Windows. If you use disk caching and it is configured properly, you can greatly increase the performance of Windows and, thus, your system.

Disk Caching in Windows 2000 and Windows XP

Windows 2000 and XP take care of most of their own disk caching. However, you can modify one disk-cache setting by changing the Large System Cache entry in the Registry. This option, when enabled, takes all memory not being used by applications, the system, or data, and uses it for disk caching. Otherwise, only 4MB of memory is used for disk caching. This option is off by default in Windows 2000 Professional and Windows XP.

You should normally enable this setting only if you have at least 96MB of RAM or more in your computer. Otherwise, you may hamper performance.

You can enable this feature by changing one key:

1. Launch either REGEDIT.EXE or REGDT32.EXE.

2. Navigate to the Registry key HKey_Local_Machine \System\CurrentControlSet\ Control\Session Manager\Memory Management.

3. Double-click on the item labeled LargeSystemCache.

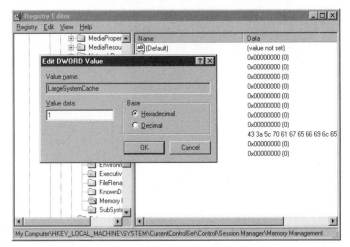

4.   The Value Data field should have a 0 in it. Change it to a 1 and click OK.

5.   Close Registry Editor and reboot the computer to enable the settings.

Cached Internet Explorer Files

The other type of disk caching you can tweak to increase your system's performance is the cache of often-visited web pages in Internet Explorer. IE copies to your hard disk any images or HTML files from websites you visit frequently. That way, the next time you visit the website, you don't need to redownload the images for that web page; IE instead gets them from its local disk cache. IE's local disk cache is also known as the *Temporary Internet Files* directory, which is a special directory set up for storing these images and pages.

However, this disk cache can become too large or contain outdated information. Therefore, you can modify some settings to change how this feature works from within IE.

This procedure is for IE 5.*x* and 6.*x* for Windows. Other versions have this feature, but it looks slightly different.

To configure IE's disk cache settings, do the following from within IE:

1.   Select Tools ➢ Internet Options to open the Internet Options control panel. (You can also open it by choosing Start ➢ Settings ➢ Control Panel and double-clicking Internet Options. Opening it this way, the window will say Internet Properties at top, as opposed to Internet Options if you do it through IE. However, they're both the same.)

2. Click the Settings button in the Temporary Internet Files section. The settings on the window that appears allow you to modify how IE's disk cache works.

By default, IE uses automatic settings. Each time a page is requested, the local page is compared to the page from the web server to determine if a new download is necessary. If the pages are the same, IE uses the local version. For the most part, this provides the best performance. However, if you are constantly getting older pages, you may want to modify the settings.

3. You can change the size of the disk cache by either moving the slider or modifying the numbers next to the slider. Increasing these numbers or moving the slider to the right increases the amount of disk space used for caching Internet pages.

4. You can also put this disk cache on a different disk, thus reducing the burden on your boot hard disk. Click the Move Folder button, navigate to the drive and directory where you would like the cache to be, and click OK. IE will move the cache to the new location and use it from there.

If you ever need to clear the disk cache (for example, if you always get the same outdated page and you know there is a new version), you can delete all the temporary files. To do so, open the Internet Options control panel and click Delete Files.

Managing Temporary Files

A *temporary file (temp file)* is just that—temporary. It is designed to store information for a short period of time and then be deleted. Almost every program of any size today uses temp files. There is one problem, however: Often, the temp files remain permanently. Eventually, they begin taking up considerable disk space.

One thing you can do to improve system performance is to delete any temporary files that exist on your system. Temp files can be found in a variety of locations, including:

```
C:\TEMP
C:\TMP
C:\WINDOWS\TEMP
C:\WINDOWS\TMP
```

The way to know for sure where they're located is to determine what values the TEMP and TMP environment variables are set to. An *environment variable* is a setting that stays permanent throughout a Windows or DOS session. It is set by an entry in an INI file, the Registry, or one of the MS-DOS configuration files (CONFIG.SYS or AUTOEXEC.BAT).

To find out where the temporary files are stored in your machine, start a command-line session (choose Start ➢ Run and type in either **CMD** or **COMMAND**). At the command prompt, type **SET**. This command returns all the environment variables for your system. Look for TEMP= or TMP= (or both). These variables point to directories on your hard disk; in these locations, you will find the temporary files.

In Windows XP, you can find where your temp files are going by opening the System control panel, clicking the Advanced tab, and then clicking the Environment Variables button. The temp location will be shown in the User Variables box at the top as well as the System Variables at the bottom.

Once you have found the temporary files, use Windows Explorer to delete them. You may need to reboot, and then try to delete the temp files. Otherwise, some of them may be in use, and you won't be able to delete them.

Summary

In this chapter, you learned the different methods of installing and upgrading Windows 2000 and Windows XP. For each type of OS installation, you learned the installation prerequisites and how to install that OS.

You also learned the methods used to upgrade from one OS to Windows XP, as well as which OSs can be upgraded directly to XP. We looked at the steps necessary to upgrade as well as how an upgrade differs from a standard installation.

Next, you learned how to install and configure peripherals. A peripheral is any device that is not part of the computer itself. Examples of peripherals include modems, printers, scanners, and so on.

Finally, you learned about the methods used to optimize system performance on the various Windows platforms. We explained some little tricks you can use to bump up speed and efficiency. These include managing virtual memory and swap files on the Windows platforms, defragmenting hard drives, and managing disk caches and temporary files.

For the most part, Windows manages virtual memory on its own, but sometimes you can tweak performance by increasing the size of the page file. Windows disks frequently become fragmented, thus causing disk thrashing to occur. We described how to solve this problem using the built-in Disk Defragmenter program. We explained how to manage the disk caches not only in Windows but in Internet Explorer as well. You also learned how to locate the temporary files that Windows uses and how to delete them when they begin causing problems.

In the next chapter, we'll look at specific methods to diagnose Windows problems and how to fix those problems. In addition, we'll look at ways to help reduce the chance of those problems from happening in the first place through preventative maintenance.

Exam Essentials

Know how to check to ensure that your hardware and applications are compatible with Windows 2000 or Windows XP.   Always check the Windows Catalog (formerly known as the Hardware Compatibility List) to ensure that your hardware and software will work with whatever operating system you choose to install.

Understand the differences between minimum hardware requirements and recommended hardware levels.   Not only do you need to know what the minimums and recommended levels are for Windows 2000 and Windows XP, but you must understand that the minimums are just that—the very lowest you can possibly go and still have hope that the operating system will run. If you want any sort of reasonable performance, you should go with at least the recommended levels.

Know how to begin the Windows 2000 and Windows XP installation processes.   With both Windows 2000 and Windows XP, you can insert a bootable installation CD, turn on the computer (provided that your system can boot to the CD-ROM), and the installation will begin. Also, with Windows 2000 you have the option of booting to floppy disks to begin the installation.

Know what it means to have a dual-boot installation.   Dual-booting means you have more than one operating system, usually an older one such as Windows 95/98 and a newer one such as Windows XP. There's no limit to the number of operating systems you can have on one machine, but common sense says to limit it to no more than two or three.

Know the requirements for creating a dual-boot system.   If you are going to dual-boot with an operating system older than Windows 2000, your first partition needs to be the active partition and needs to be formatted FAT. If not, operating systems such as Windows 9x/Me will not be able to boot, as they cannot translate NTFS. Secondary partitions can be NTFS, but from within Windows 9x/Me, you won't be able to access files on those partitions.

Know the commands to perform an upgrade to Windows 2000 or Windows XP.   If you have a 16-bit operating system such as Windows 9x, you should run the WINNT.EXE command. If you have a true 32-bit OS such as Windows NT, you need to run WINNT32.EXE. Also, be familiar with various switches, especially those used for network installations.

Understand how to add hardware in Windows 2000 and Windows XP.   Both operating systems are Plug and Play OSs, meaning that once you install new hardware, it should automatically be detected, and Windows will attempt to install a driver for it. If it can't find one (and many times even if it does), you will want to install a newer driver from the disk or CD that came with the device or from the manufacturer's website. You can also add hardware through the Add/Remove Hardware (Windows 2000) or Add Hardware (Windows XP) Control Panel wizards.

Understand how and when to manage virtual memory.   Virtual memory is managed through the System control panel. For the most part, Windows can manage virtual memory pretty well on its own. But if you are seeing performance issues, one way to help the system out is to give it additional virtual memory.

Know how to defragment hard drives.   The longer you use a computer, the more fragmented the files on a hard disk become. This will slow down performance. Use the Disk Defragmenter utility to give better structure to the files on your hard drive.

Understand why disk caches and temporary files are used.   Disk caches and temporary files are both used to speed up the operation of the computer. However, if the number of files in a cache or temporary area becomes unwieldy, it can slow down the performance of your machine. It's good to go in and periodically clean out these temporary areas to ensure the best performance.

Review Questions

1. Which of the following is *not* a possible upgrade?

    A. Windows 98 to Windows XP

    B. Windows Me to Window 2000

    C. Windows 2000 to Windows XP

    D. Windows NT to Windows 2000

2. Which of the following is *not* a requirement to install Windows XP?

    A. 233MHz Pentium processor or equivalent

    B. 64MB memory

    C. 1GB free hard-disk space

    D. CD-ROM

3. What is the first step when installing Windows onto a system that doesn't already have a functioning operating system?

    A. Formatting

    B. Partitioning

    C. Redirecting

    D. Installing the OS

4. Which of the following is/are performed by formatting the hard drive? (Choose all that apply.)

    A. Formatting scans the surface of the hard-drive platter to find bad spots and marks the areas surrounding a bad spot as bad sectors.

    B. Formatting lays down magnetic tracks in concentric circles.

    C. The tracks are split into pieces of 512 bytes called sectors.

    D. Formatting creates a File Allocation Table that contains information about the location of files.

5. The program that performs an upgrade from Windows *9x* to Windows 2000 is called _____.

    A. INSTALL.BAT

    B. SETUP.EXE

    C. WINNT.EXE

    D. WINNT32.EXE

6. Where is the best place to find Windows hardware compatibility information?

    A. Windows manuals

    B. Hardware manuals

    C. Microsoft website

    D. Manufacturer's website

7. You've successfully completed an upgrade to Windows 2000 Professional. Several days later, you add your old printer, using the driver that originally came with it. Now the printer, which has never had a problem, won't print. What do you need to do to fix the problem?

    A. Older printers are often not compatible with Windows 2000. You may need to replace the printer.

    B. Your printer driver is out of date. Contact the vendor or visit its website for an updated driver.

    C. Uninstall, and then reinstall the printer using the original driver.

    D. None of the above.

8. Which of the following methods correctly adds new hardware to a Windows 2000 system if Plug and Play does not work? (Select all that apply.)

    A. Exit to a command prompt and use the software that came with the device to run the installation.

    B. Choose Start ➢ Settings ➢ Control Panel and then double-click the Add/Remove Hardware icon.

    C. If Plug and Play does not work, there is no way to get the hardware working in the Windows 2000 environment.

    D. On the Desktop, double-click the My Computer icon, double-click the Control Panel icon, and then double-click the Add/Remove Hardware icon.

9. Plug and Play includes a troubleshooting wizard on which operating system?

    A. Windows 95

    B. Windows 98

    C. Windows NT

    D. Windows 2000

10. Which version of Windows does *not* come with a disk-defragmentation utility?

    A. 9*x*

    B. NT

    C. 2000

    D. XP

11. The _____ is hard-drive space in which idle pieces of programs are placed, while other active parts of programs are kept in or swapped into main memory.

    A. Swap file

    B. Location file

    C. Temporary file

    D. Program file

12. Where do Windows 2000 and Windows XP keep the disk cache setting?

    A. `WIN.INI`

    B. `SYSTEM.INI`

    C. Registry

    D. `REGEDIT.EXE`

13. Which utility that comes with Windows 2000 Professional is used to create an image of an existing computer for network installation?

    A. Ghost

    B. Sysprep

    C. Sysimage

    D. RIS

14. How do you start the Disk Defragmenter program in Windows 2000?

    A. Start ➤ Settings ➤ Control Panel ➤ Disk Defragmenter

    B. Start ➤ Programs ➤ Accessories ➤ Disk Defragmenter

    C. Start ➤ Programs ➤ Accessories ➤ System Tools ➤ Disk Defragmenter

    D. None of the above

15. The name of the swap file is _____ in Windows 2000/XP.

    A. `SWAPFILE.SYS`

    B. `PAGEFILE.SYS`

    C. `SWAPPINGFILE.SYS`

    D. `PAGINGFILE.SYS`

16. If you have 256MB of RAM in a Windows 2000 machine, what is the minimum recommended size for the swap file?

    A. 128MB

    B. 256MB

    C. 384MB

    D. 512MB

17. Which of the following is *not* a common location for Windows temporary files?

    A. C:\TEMP

    B. C:\WINDOWS\TEMP

    C. C:\TMP

    D. None of the above

18. Which of the following operations requires a system reboot? (Select all that apply.)

    A. Increasing the swap-file size in Windows 2000.

    B. Decreasing the swap-file size in Windows 2000.

    C. Increasing the swap-file size in Windows XP.

    D. Decreasing the swap-file size in Windows XP.

19. In Windows XP, where can you check to see the location of where your temporary files are being stored?

    A. System control panel, Advanced tab, Environment Variables button

    B. System control panel, Advanced tab, Temporary Files button

    C. System control panel, Advanced tab, Windows XP Temp Files button

    D. Your temp files are always in the same directory in Windows XP.

20. You have a computer running Windows 98 that you want to upgrade to a more current operating system. It is a Pentium 166 with 128MB of RAM and has 2GB of free hard disk space. Which of the following can you upgrade to?

    A. Windows 2000 only

    B. Windows XP only

    C. Both Windows 2000 and Windows XP

    D. You cannot upgrade to Windows 2000 or Windows XP

Answers to Review Questions

1. B. Because Windows Me was released *after* Windows 2000, the Setup program doesn't know about the particulars of Windows Me and therefore can't upgrade.

2. C. To install Windows XP, you need at least 1.5GB of free hard-disk space.

3. B. New disk drives or PCs with no OS need to have two critical functions performed on them before they can be used: partitioning and formatting. These two functions are performed by two commands, `FDISK.EXE` and `FORMAT.COM`, or by the Windows 2000/XP installation program itself.

4. A, B, C, D. Formatting does all of the listed processes.

5. C. The program that performs an upgrade from Windows 9*x* to Windows 2000 is `WINNT.EXE`. To upgrade from a 32-bit OS such as Windows NT, you would use `WINNT32.EXE`.

6. C. Although D might seem like a good answer (and you might find the information), the best (and most current) place to find hardware compatibility information for Windows is the Microsoft Hardware Compatibility List on the Microsoft website.

7. B. When installing a printer, or any hardware device for that matter, you must always be sure to have an updated driver. Many device problems originate with out-of-date hardware drivers.

8. B, D. Plug and Play will automatically detect new hardware and install the proper software. If it is not successful, you can use the Add/Remove Hardware Wizard.

9. D. When Plug and Play does not work, Windows 2000/XP has a troubleshooting wizard to assist the user. The Add New Hardware Wizard in Windows 2000/XP can also be used to add new hardware and update drivers for existing hardware.

10. B. Windows NT does not come with a version of either `DEFRAG` or Disk Defragmenter. All other versions of Windows include some kind of disk-defragmentation utility.

11. A. A swap file is a file used for virtual memory. It is where the information that was swapped from main memory resides on the hard disk. It's also referred to as a page file or paging file.

12. C. The settings for `LargeSystemCache` are located in the Windows Registry.

13. B. The sysprep utility comes with Windows 2000 Professional (and Windows XP), and is used to make an image of a computer. Ghost is a third-party utility made by Norton. Sysimage is not a known Windows utility, and RIS only comes with Server operating systems.

14. C. The proper sequence for Windows 2000 is Start ➢ Programs ➢ Accessories ➢ System Tools ➢ Disk Defragmenter.

15. B . The name of the virtual memory swap file is `PAGEFILE.SYS`.

16. C. The minimum recommended swap-file size under Windows 2000 is 1.5 times the amount of physical RAM. 1.5 × 256MB = 384MB.

17. D. All of the listed options are common places where Windows temporary files are located.

18. B, D. Windows 2000 and XP require a reboot only when you decrease the size of the swap file.

19. A. In Windows XP, you can find where your temp files are going by opening the System control panel, clicking the Advanced tab, and then clicking the Environment Variables button. The temp location will be shown in the User Variables box at the top as well as the System Variables at the bottom.

20. A. With the hardware in your system, you can upgrade only to Windows 2000. Windows XP requires at least a 233MHz processor.

Chapter

6

Identifying Operating System Troubleshooting and Diagnostic Procedures

THE FOLLOWING COMPTIA A+ ESSENTIALS EXAM OBJECTIVES ARE COVERED IN THIS CHAPTER:

- ✓ **3.3 Identify tools, diagnostic procedures and troubleshooting techniques for operating systems**
    - Identify basic boot sequences, methods and utilities for recovering operating systems
        - Boot methods (e.g. safe mode, recovery console, boot to restore point)
        - Automated System Recovery (ASR) (e.g. Emergency Repair Disk (ERD))
    - Identify and apply diagnostic procedures and troubleshooting techniques for example:
        - Identify the problem by questioning the user and identifying user changes to the computer
        - Analyze problem including potential causes and initial determination of software and / or hardware problem
        - Test related components including connections, hardware / software configurations, device manager and consulting vendor documentation
        - Evaluate results and take additional steps if needed such as consultation, alternate resources and manuals
        - Document activities and outcomes

- Recognize and resolve common operational issues such as bluescreen, system lock-up, input / output device, application install, start or load and Windows-specific printing problems (e.g. print spool stalled, incorrect / incompatible driver for print)
- Explain common error messages and codes for example:
  - Boot (e.g. invalid boot disk, inaccessible boot drive, missing NTLDR)
  - Startup (e.g. device / service failed to start, device / program in registry not found)
  - Event Viewer
  - Registry
  - Windows reporting
- Identify the names, locations, purposes and characteristics of operating system utilities for example:
  - Disk management tools (e.g. DEFRAG, NTBACKUP, CHKDSK, Format)
  - System management tools (e.g. device and task manager, MSCONFIG.EXE)
  - File management tools (e.g. Windows Explorer, ATTRIB.EXE)

✓ **3.4 Perform preventative maintenance on operating systems**

- Describe common utilities for performing preventative maintenance on operating systems for example, software and Windows updates (e.g. service packs), scheduled backups / restore, restore points

Troubleshooting involves asking a lot of questions of yourself and of other people. Beginners (and yes, we were all beginners once upon a time) like the trial-and-error method of fixing things, but in the long run, a methodological approach works better. The reason beginners often choose trial and error is that they don't yet have a good enough background to analyze problems.

Analysis is the act of breaking down a structure or system into its component parts and their relationships.

More than occasionally, a technician will unwittingly create new problems in an attempt to fix a real problem. For example, if a program will not run and displays an *Out of Memory* error, it might seem logical to add more memory.

But certain types of memory currently on the market will not work in older computers—what happens if the memory the technician installs is the wrong type for the computer? Now there are two problems.

And what if the computer with the mismatched memory actually starts up but eventually locks up because of the memory problem? The lockups could create an interruption in writing information to the hard drive, and a program could become corrupted. That would make three problems total.

Once the technician has sorted out all the problems, it's time to repair whatever went wrong. In this example, it is quite likely that the source of the original *Out of Memory* error was corrupted program code. Many times, a Windows program with damage to one or more components will cause that error to be displayed.

The first pillar of good troubleshooting is an understanding of how things are *supposed* to work. If you're not sure of that, how are you supposed to make it work right? To that end, you need to build your fundamental knowledge of how Windows works, which you can do through the previous two chapters. This chapter will continue to build upon your Windows knowledge, point out specific areas where troubles are likely to happen, and give you advice on how to approach solving those problems. You'll learn the steps to methodically go about troubleshooting Windows and other applications.

In addition, you can often prevent problems from happening in the first place by performing preventative maintenance. The old adage that an ounce of prevention is worth a pound of cure definitely holds true. After we look at troubleshooting, we'll examine steps you can take to stave off as many problems as possible.

Troubleshooting Steps

In a computer system, you need to consider at least four main parts, each of which is in turn made up of many pieces:

1. A *collection of hardware pieces* integrated into a working system. As you know, the hardware can be quite complex, what with motherboards, hard drives, video cards, and so on. Software can be equally perplexing.

2. An *operating system*, which in turn is dependent on the hardware.

3. An *application* or software program that is supposed to do something. Programs such as Microsoft Word and Excel are bundled with a great many features.

4. A *computer user*, ready to take the computer system to its limits (and beyond). A technician can often forget that the user is a very complex and important part of the puzzle.

Effective troubleshooting requires some experience just for the background required to analyze the problem at hand, but you also need to remember some other logical steps. Ask yourself, "Is there a problem?" Perhaps it is as simple as a customer expecting too much from the computer. If there is a problem, is it just one problem or multiple issues? To help during the troubleshooting process, follow these steps.

Many of these steps also require you to have good communication and soft skills, which CompTIA is emphasizing more. These are addressed in Chapter 11.

Step 1: Talk to the Customer

One of the keys to working with customers is to ensure, much like a medical professional, that you have good bedside manner. Most people are not as technically hip as you, and when something goes wrong they become confused or even fearful that they'll take the blame. Assure them that you're just trying to fix the problem, but that they can probably help because they know what went on before you got there. It's important to instill trust with your customer. Believe what they are saying, but also believe that they might not tell you everything right away. It's not that they're necessarily lying, they just might not know what's important to tell.

It's a classic IT story that almost sounds like a joke, but it's happened. A customer calls technical support because his computer won't turn on. After 20 minutes of troubleshooting, the technician is becoming frustrated ... maybe it's a bad power supply? The technician asks the user to read some numbers off of the back of his computer, and the user tells him, "Hold on, I need to get a flashlight. It's dark in here with the power out."

Help clarify things by having the customer show you what the problem is. The best method I've seen of doing this is to say to him, "Show me what 'not working' looks like." That way, you see the conditions and methods under which the problem occurs. The problem may be a simple matter of an improper method. The user may be performing an operation incorrectly or performing the operation in the wrong order. During this step, you have the opportunity to observe how the problem occurs, so pay attention.

Step 2: Gather Information

Something happened between the time when the computer worked and when it didn't. Your job as the detective with the screwdriver is to find out what that "something" is. Ask the user what has changed recently. Was hardware or software added? Did the computer get moved? Has someone who normally doesn't use the computer used it? Was there a storm recently? Pick at things from the environment that might have caused the problem.

Probing further, find out when the last time the computer worked. Did anything happen right then? Can you make the problem happen again? (If a problem can't be replicated, then it's not a problem you can fix.) The key is, find out everything you can that might be related to the problem. If the power is out in the house, like in the story I related earlier, then there's no sense in trying the power plug in another outlet.

Step 3: Eliminate Possibilities

Now that you know what the problem is, it's time to form your hypothesis as to what's causing it. If you haven't identified the problem yet, then you have a lot more work to do. Start eliminating possibilities. For example, if the hard drive won't read, then there are likely one of three culprits: the drive itself, the cable it's on, or the connector on the motherboard. Try plugging the drive into the other connector or using a different cable. Narrow down the options.

A common troubleshooting technique is to strip the system down to the bare bones. In a hardware situation, this could mean removing all interface cards except those absolutely required for the system to operate. In a software situation, this usually means booting up in safe mode so most of the drivers do not load.

Once you have eliminated all options and isolated the problem, slowly rebuild the system to see if the problem comes back (or goes away). This helps you identify what is really causing the problem, and if there are other factors affecting the situation. For example, I have seen memory problems that are fixed by switching the slot that the memory chips are in.

Before starting to eliminate possibilities, check the vendor's website for any information that might help you. For example, typing in a specific error message on a vendor's website might get you directly to specific steps to fix the problem.

Step 4: Evaluate Your Results

If your fix worked, then you're done and you can move on to step 5. If not, then you need to re-evaluate and look for the next option. So you tried the hard drive with a new (verified) cable and it still doesn't work. Now what? Your sound card won't play and you've just deleted and reinstalled the driver. Next steps? Move on and try the next logical thing in line.

When evaluating your results and looking for that golden "next step," don't forget other resources you might have available. Use the Internet to look at the manufacturer's website. Read the manual. Talk to your friend who knows everything about obscure hardware (or arcane versions of Windows). When fixing problems, two heads can be better than one.

Step 5: Document Your Work

Lots of people can fix problems. But the key is whether you can remember what you did when you fixed a problem a month ago. Maybe. Can one of your co-workers remember something you did to fix the same problem on that machine a month ago? Unlikely. Always document your work so that you or someone else can learn from that experience. Good documentation of past troubleshooting can save hours of stress in the future.

Understanding Boot Sequences

When working with any operating system, it's imperative that you know the important files, know the files involved in the boot process, understand the boot process itself, and know how to prepare for a situation in which you have to perform an emergency boot. In this section, we will first look at the system files required to boot the Windows 2000 and Windows XP operating systems. We will then acquaint you with the various boot processes and sequences each OS goes through during bootup if there are problems. Finally, we'll show how you can create emergency boot disks you can use to boot the OS to help you recover in the event of a system failure.

Listing the Important Files

Among the things you must be familiar with in preparation for the A+ Essentials exam are the startup and system files used by Windows 2000 and Windows XP. We will look at each of them individually, but Windows makes nosing around in the startup environment difficult, and so there is a change you need to make first.

To protect Windows system files from accidental deletion, and to get them out of the way of the average user, they are hidden from the user by default. Because of this, many of the files we are about to talk about will not be visible to you. To make them visible, you need to change the display properties of Windows Explorer. Exercise 6.1 shows how to make files visible in Windows 2000/XP.

Real World Scenario

Document Everything!

One thing I always recommend to new technicians is to purchase a notebook and carry it around with them everywhere. The kind of notebook doesn't matter really, but I prefer the spiral-bound ones (to keep the papers secure) with lots of pages (because I'll be using it a lot).

Whenever you come across a term that you're not familiar with, write it down. You can look it up later when you have more access to resources. If you're trying to fix a problem, write down exact error messages. Document exactly each step you take in fixing a problem. Cause and effect: What did you change and what happened when you changed it? Sometimes the answer of "nothing changed" helps you eliminate potential causes of the problem.

When you first start out, this notebook will be invaluable. It's not likely to have a lot of organization, and many of the things you write down might be tricky to decipher later. But those notes will help you out in a big way when you need them because no one can remember everything. Especially when you're new at something.

Eventually you might become less and less reliant upon the notebook, but it's still good practice to keep one handy. Organize it in a way that suits your needs, and it can be the best troubleshooting tool you'll ever find.

EXERCISE 6.1

Making Files Visible in Windows 2000 and Windows XP

To make files visible, follow these steps:

1. Open Windows Explorer.

2. Choose Tools ➢ Folder Options. The Folder Options window opens.

3. Select the View tab, and scroll until you find the Hidden files and folders option.

4. Select Show hidden files and folders.

5. Deselect Hide protected operating system files (Recommended).

6. Uncheck Hide extensions for known file types.

7. Click OK. You will now be able to see the Windows system files discussed in the following sections. For security reasons, you should set these attributes back after you've read this chapter.

Identifying Important Files in Windows 2000/XP

Windows 2000 and XP use different startup procedures and different startup files than older versions of Windows. Windows 2000/XP are both based on Windows NT, and so they use the same key boot files as Windows NT. In this section, we will discuss these files.

Key Boot Files

Windows 2000 and Windows XP require only a few files, each of which performs specific tasks:

NTLDR   *Bootstraps* the system. In other words, this file starts the loading of an OS on the computer.

BOOT.INI   Holds information about what OSs are installed on the computer.

BOOTSECT.DOS   In a dual-boot configuration, keeps a copy of the DOS or Windows *9x* boot sector so that the Windows *9x* environment can be restored and loaded as needed.

NTDETECT.COM   Parses the system for hardware information each time Windows 2000/XP is loaded. This information is then used to create dynamic hardware information in the Registry.

NTBOOTDD.SYS   On a system with a SCSI boot device, used to recognize and load the SCSI interface. On EIDE systems, this file is not needed and is not even installed.

NTOSKRNL.EXE   The Windows 2000/XP OS kernel.

System Files   In addition to the previously listed files, all of which except NTOSKRNL.EXE are located in the root of the C: partition on the computer, Windows 2000/XP also needs a number of files from its system directories, such as the Hardware Abstraction Layer (HAL.DLL).

Numerous other dynamic link library (DLL) files are also required, but usually the lack or corruption of one of them produces a noncritical error, whereas the absence of HAL.DLL causes the system to be nonfunctional.

System Configuration Tools in Windows 2000 and Windows XP

The SYSEDIT configuration tool used a lot in Windows *9x* also exists in Windows 2000/XP. Its usefulness is limited, however, because it opens the WIN.INI, SYSTEM.INI, AUTOEXEC.BAT, and CONFIG.SYS files for you to edit. WIN.INI and SYSTEM.INI contain information for application backward-compatibility reasons. AUTOEXEC.BAT and CONFIG.SYS are empty and should stay that way.

The MSCONFIG system configuration tool, which was also used frequently in Windows *9x*, doesn't exist in Windows 2000. It is, however, included with Windows XP.

 MSCONFIG was discussed in detail in Chapter 4.

Understanding the Windows 2000/XP Boot Process

We'll now look at the Windows 2000/XP boot process. It's a pretty long and complicated process, but keep in mind that these are complex operating systems, providing you with a lot more functionality than older versions of Windows could offer:

1. System self-checks and enumerates hardware resources. Each machine has a different startup routine, called the POST (power-on self-test), which is executed by the commands written to the motherboard of the computer. Newer PnP boards not only check memory and processors, they also poll the systems for other devices and peripherals.

2. MBR loads and finds the boot sector. Once the system has finished with its housekeeping, the Master Boot Record is located on the first hard drive and loaded into memory. The MBR finds the bootable partition and searches it for the boot sector of that partition.

3. MBR determines the file system and loads NTLDR. Information in the boot sector allows the system to locate the system partition and to find and load into memory the NTLDR.EXE file located there.

4. NTLDR switches the system from real mode to protected mode and enables paging. Protected mode enables the system to address all of the available physical memory. It's also referred to as *32-bit flat mode*. At this point, the file system is also started.

5. NTLDR processes BOOT.INI. BOOT.INI is a text file that resides in the root directory. It specifies what OSs are installed on the computer. During this step of the boot process, you may be presented with a list of the installed OSs (depending on how your startup options are configured and whether you have multiple OSs installed). If you're presented with the list, you can choose an OS, or, if you don't take any action, the default selection is chosen automatically. If you have multiple OSs installed and you choose a DOS-based OS from the list (such as Windows *9x*), NTLDR processes BOOTSECT.DOS and does a warm boot. The MBR code contained in BOOTSECT.DOS is run after the computer goes through the POST, and IO.SYS is loaded, starting the DOS-based OS's boot process. We will, however, continue with the 2000/XP boot process.

6. NTLDR loads and runs NTDETECT.COM. NTDETECT.COM checks the system for installed devices and device configurations and initializes the devices it finds. It passes the information to NTLDR, which collects this information and passes it to NTOSKRNL.EXE after that file is loaded.

7. NTLDR loads NTOSKRNL.EXE and HAL.DLL. NTOSKRNL.EXE holds the OS kernel and also what's known as the *Executive subsystems*. Executive subsystems are software components that parse Registry control set configuration information and start services and drivers. HAL.DLL enables communication between the OS and the installed hardware.

8. NTLDR loads the HKEY_LOCAL_MACHINE\SYSTEM Registry hive and loads device drivers. The drivers that load at this time serve as boot drivers, using an initial value called a *Start value*.

9. NTLDR transfers control to NTOSKRNL.EXE. NTOSKRNL.EXE initializes loaded drivers and completes the boot process.

10. Winlogon loads. At this point, you are presented with the Logon screen. After you enter a username and password, you're taken to the Windows Desktop.

Advanced Startup Options

In addition to performing a regular boot into the OS of your choice, you can make additional selections for advanced startup options. In Windows 2000/XP, you access the options by pressing the F8 key when you're presented with the list of OSs installed on the computer. If you don't have the system configured to display the list of OSs (for example, if you have only one OS installed), press F8 when a message on the screen tells you that you can do so.

In most cases you will be able to just boot into your OS without worrying about the advanced options. Occasionally, though, problems may arise. If you have a problem that makes it difficult to get Windows up and running, the advanced options offer a number of useful tools. The options are not identical on the various versions of Windows. Here are the advanced startup options available in Windows 2000 and Windows XP:

Safe Mode   Starts Windows 2000/XP using only basic files and drivers (mouse, except serial mice; monitor; keyboard; mass storage; base video; default system services; and no network connections). Once in safe mode, you can restore files that are missing or fix a configuration error.

Safe Mode with Networking   Same as safe mode but tries to load networking components as well.

Safe Mode with Command Prompt   Similar to safe mode but doesn't load the Windows GUI. Presents the user with a Windows 2000/XP command-prompt interface.

Enable Boot Logging   Logs all boot information to a file called NTBTLOG.TXT. This file can be found in the \WINNT directory. You can then check the log for assistance in diagnosing system startup problems.

Enable VGA Mode   Starts Windows 2000/XP using the basic VGA driver but loads the rest of the system as normal. If you happen to install an incorrect video driver or a video driver corrupts, this allows you to get into the system to fix the problem.

Last Known Good Configuration   Useful if you have changed a configuration setting in the Registry, which then causes the system to have serious problems, and you're not able to log in. Use Last Known Good Configuration to restore the system to a prior, functional state, which will allow you to log in again. It will not save you from a corrupt file or a deleted file error.

Directory Services Restore Mode   Used only with domain controllers. If chosen, boots into a mode that doesn't load directory services. This enables you to restore directory services, such as Active Directory, to the machine. (You can't restore directory services if directory services are running.)

Debugging Mode   A sort of advanced boot logging. Requires that another machine be hooked up to the computer through a serial port. The debug information is then passed to that machine during the boot process. This option is rarely used and should not be bothered with in most cases. If it comes to this, reinstalling is far faster!

Boot Normally (Start Windows Normally)   Continues the boot normally. It's equivalent to the Normal option in Windows 9*x*.

Reboot (Windows XP Only)   As the name implies, reboots the computer (warm boot).

Return to OS Choices Menu (Windows XP Only)   Self-explanatory; returns you to the choice of installed OSs.

Using the Recovery Console

The Recovery Console is another option you can use if Windows is not booting properly and Safe Mode and other startup options don't work. The Recovery Console is a command-line utility you can use to format drives, read data from and write data to local hard drives, stop and start services, and perform several other administrative tasks.

You can run the Recovery Console as an advanced boot option if you install it on the hard drive first. Otherwise, you need to run it from the Windows installation CD. Here's how to install the Recovery Console:

1. Put the Windows installation CD in the CD-ROM drive.
2. Click Start and then Run.
3. In the Run box, type **D:\i386\winnt32.exe /cmdcons** (where D:\ is your CD-ROM drive letter).
4. Follow the instructions on screen.

To run the Recovery Console, you must be an administrator or have administrative privileges. Once you log in to the Recovery Console, you can perform activities such as changing directories or viewing files, as well as administrative duties such as trying to repair the boot sector of the hard drive. The Recovery Console is a command-line interface; much as in a Windows command prompt, you can type **help** at the Recovery Console prompt to get a list of available commands. Table 6.1 lists the available Recovery Console commands and a brief description of their functions.

TABLE 6.1 Recovery Console commands

Command	Function
ATTRIB	Changes the attributes of a file or folder.
BATCH	Runs the commands specified in a text file so that you can perform many tasks in one step.
CD or CHDIR	Changes directories.
CHKDSK	Runs the hard disk checker.
CLS	Clears the screen of previous output.
COPY	Copies files from removable media to the system folders. (Note: With the console, you cannot use wildcards!)
DEL or DELETE	Deletes files.
DIR	Lists the contents of a directory.
DISABLE	Disables a specified service or driver.
DISKPART	Creates or deletes disk partitions.
ENABLE	Enables a specified service or driver.
EXTRACT	Extracts compressed installation files (ones with .CAB extensions) to the system partition. This command only works if you run the console from the installation CD.
FIXBOOT	Writes a new boot sector on the system partition.
FIXMBR	Writes a new Master Boot Record for the partition boot sector.
FORMAT	Formats the selected disk.
HELP	Displays a list of available Recovery Console commands.
LISTSVC	Lists all services and drivers running in Windows.
LOGON	Logs on to Windows.
MAP	Displays the drive letter mappings currently recognized. Can be helpful to use before DISKPART.
MD or MKDIR	Creates a directory.

TABLE 6.1   Recovery Console commands *(continued)*

Command	Function
MORE or TYPE	Displays the contents of a specified file.
RD or RMDIR	Deletes a directory.
REN or RENAME	Renames a file.
SYSTEMROOT	Makes the current directory the system root of the drive you are logged in to.

While the console can do many things, it's important to note the things that the console *can't* do. Most notably, it can't be used to back up files. Files can be copied from media to the local hard drive (specifically, to the system partition), but not the other way around. In addition, although you can change to partitions other than the system partition, you can't read files on them. So the console is handy but it's not a save-all; don't think of it as a duplicate of the command prompt.

 The key functions of the Recovery Console are to be able to repair your system partition or make minor tweaks to Windows to get the operating system functional.

Creating Boot Disks or an Emergency Repair Disk

Most of the time, you won't bump into serious problems running any of the Windows versions we have been discussing. However, someday you might find yourself in a situation where the system won't boot up anymore or where you are experiencing some other type of critical error. It is extremely important to be prepared for these types of scenarios. One thing you can do when the system is running smoothly is to create startup disks or emergency repair disks (depending on your OS). (You might also find these disks referred to as boot disks.) These disks typically enable you to at least boot the machine and access drives (and thus data) and also to troubleshoot the problem. In this section, we'll look at the different types of disks you can create in Windows.

Boot Disks and ERD in Windows 2000

To prepare for a Windows 2000 emergency, you need four OS boot disks, as well as an *Emergency Repair Disk (ERD)*. To create the set of four boot disks, you need the Windows 2000 Operating System CD. To create an ERD, you need to use the Emergency Repair Disk utility in the Windows Backup utility (see Figure 6.1). Let's look at this process in more detail.

FIGURE 6.1 The Emergency Repair Disk utility in Windows 2000

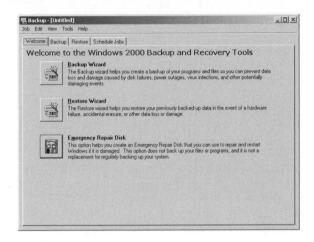

To create the four Windows 2000 boot disks, insert the Windows 2000 Operating System CD into the CD-ROM drive. On the CD, browse to the Bootdisk directory and run MAKEBOOT.EXE. The program walks you through the process of creating the boot disks. Make sure you have four blank floppy disks ready. Once you have created the boot disks, you need to create an ERD.

Make sure you store these disks in a safe place. If you have an emergency, you can use the boot disks to start the Windows 2000 Setup program. At some point, you'll be asked if you want to install or repair Windows 2000. Choose Repair. Windows 2000 Setup will continue and at a later point ask you for the ERD.

Automated System Recovery in Windows XP

In Windows XP, things are different. Windows XP introduces *Automated System Recovery (ASR)*. As in Windows 2000, this feature is integrated into the Backup utility. It first creates a backup of your system partition and then creates a recovery disk. Using these two components, you can recover from a system crash and restore the system back to a functional state. Exercise 6.2 demonstrates how to use ASR to restore the system in Windows XP.

EXERCISE 6.2

Using ASR in Windows XP

To restore the system using ASR in Windows XP, follow these steps:

1. Click Start ➢ All Programs ➢ Accessories ➢ System Tools ➢ Backup. If Backup starts in Wizard mode, deselect Always Start In Wizard Mode and click Cancel. Then start Backup again. You're taken directly to the Backup interface.

2.   Click the Automated System Recovery Wizard button. In the Welcome dialog box, click Next.

3.   You're prompted for the Backup Destination. By default, this is A:\BACKUP.BKF. You need to change this location, because a backup of your system partition won't fit onto a floppy disk. Use a drive other than the C: drive, because this drive will be formatted as part of the recovery process. Click Next, and then click Finish.

4.   The backup procedure starts. When it's finished, you're prompted to insert a floppy disk. Do so and click OK.

5.   When the disk-creation process has completed, click OK. Keep the ASR disk in a safe place.

To use ASR to recover from a system failure, run Setup from the Windows XP CD. During the text portion of the Setup program, you'll see a message to press F2; do so, and you'll be prompted to insert the ASR disk. The system then guides you through the rest of the process.

To obtain setup boot disks for Windows XP, you have to go to Microsoft's download website at www.microsoft.com/downloads and download them. These disks can be used to install XP if you can't boot from CD-ROM. You'll need six floppy disks during the download; they should be formatted and blank.

Identifying Windows File-Related Problems

The first set of specific Windows problems we'll discuss are those that can be traced to missing, corrupt, or misconfigured files. These issues can cause consternation to no end because they can be troublesome to fix. Thankfully, the error message usually gives an indication of which file is the problem.

In this section, you will learn about some of the various file-related problems that can occur in Windows, as well as their solutions. These problems can be categorized into four main areas:

- System files not found

- Configuration file issues

- Swap file issues

- Boot issues

Because the most easily fixed problems are related to missing system files, that's the next topic we'll cover.

System Files Not Found

Every operating system or operating environment has certain key system files that must be present in order for it to function. If these files are missing or corrupt, the OS will cease to function properly. Files can be deleted by accident rather easily, so it's important to know what these system files are, where they are located, and how to replace them.

When you boot, the presence of the system files is checked, and each file is loaded. If you remember, the computer's BIOS first checks the PC's hardware and then looks for a boot sector on one of the disks and loads the OS found in that boot sector. However, if the computer can't find a boot sector with an OS installed on any of the disks, it displays an error similar to the following:

```
No operating system found
```

This error means the computer's BIOS checked all the drives it knew about and couldn't find any disk with a bootable sector. This could be due to any number of reasons, including these:

- An operating system wasn't installed.
- The boot sector has been corrupted.
- The boot files have been corrupted.

Thankfully, there are a couple of solutions to these problems. First, if the file or files are missing, copy them from the original setup diskettes or CD-ROM, or copy them from a backup (assuming you have one). The same holds true if you have a corrupt file, except you must delete the corrupt file first and then replace it with a new copy.

These same concepts hold true for another system file–related problem:

```
Missing NTLDR
```

This error means that the NTLDR file is either missing or corrupt. Just replace it with a fresh copy. The error should go away, and the computer will function properly. In the worst-case scenario, an OS reinstall should take care of these issues.

Configuration File Issues

In older versions of Windows, this was a common problem because users could easily edit their configuration files. Now, the Windows Registry stores nearly every configuration parameter available, but on many computers it's not secured: People can edit it. And worse yet, its structure is incredibly complex and there's no "undo" feature or Save button. Once you delete something, it's immediately gone. In addition, most software installation programs modify the Registry when a new program is installed. An error you might see is this:

```
A device referenced in the Registry can not be found
```

If you just added hardware, then it might make sense that the particular piece of hardware or its driver might be causing the problem. If not, then you would have to use the Registry Editor (REGEDIT.EXE or REGEDT32.EXE) to search for corrupt or invalid entries.

Swap File Issues

Windows uses swap files (also called page files or paging files) to increase the amount of usable memory by using hard-disk space as memory. However, sometimes problems can occur when a computer doesn't have enough disk space to make a proper swap file. Because Windows relies on swap files for proper operation, if a swap file isn't big enough, Windows will slow down and start running out of usable memory. All sorts of memory-related problems can stem from swap files that are incorrect or too small. Symptoms of swap-file problems include an extremely slow system and a disk that is constantly being accessed. This condition, known as hard disk *thrashing*, occurs because Windows doesn't have enough memory to contain all the programs that are running, and there isn't enough disk space for a swap file to contain them all. This situation causes Windows to swap between memory and the hard disk.

The solution to this problem is to first free up some disk space. With hard drives big and cheap these days, the easiest thing to do is install a bigger hard disk. If that solution isn't practical, you must delete enough unused files that the swap file can be made large enough to be functional.

Windows Boot Issues

Troubleshooting Windows boot issues is another type of Windows troubleshooting that is commonly performed. To understand Windows boot issues, you must first understand the Windows boot process, which was described a few sections ago.

Let's take a brief look at some common Windows 2000/XP boot errors, what might be causing them, and how to solve them:

Invalid Boot Disk   You get the *Invalid Boot Disk* error when the BIOS finds a partition that could be bootable but is missing the essential system files. You can correct this problem by reinstalling the OS.

Operating System Not Found   This error means exactly what it says. Essentially, the system could not find an OS, or even a valid boot partition, on any of the boot devices (floppy, hard disk, or CD-ROM). You will get this error on a brand-new computer that you have just built, until you install the OS.

Inaccessible Boot Device   If, on bootup, you receive an error that states *STOP: 0x0000007B Inaccessible Boot Device*, you may have one of several problems. The most common is that Windows could not load the driver for the disk controller on the boot device. This could be because it is the wrong driver or because the disk controller is conflicting with some other hardware in the system.

This issue could also be caused by a unique installation procedure. If you are trying to run Windows 2000/XP Setup from a SCSI CD-ROM, Setup will not allow you to install a third-party SCSI driver when you boot from the SCSI CD-ROM. You will have to try using the boot disks to install 2000/XP.

Missing NTLDR As you've learned, NTLDR is relied on heavily during the boot process. If it is missing or corrupted, Windows NT will not be able to boot, and you'll get an error similar to *Can't find NTLDR*.

On the other hand, if you get an error such as *NTOSKRNL.EXE missing or corrupt* on bootup, it may be an error in the BOOT.INI file. This is a common occurrence if you have improperly used the multi(0)disk(0)rdisk(0)partition(1)\WINDOWS="Microsoft Windows XP Professional" syntax for partition entries or had the partition table modified in a multidisk setup. If these entries are correct, the NTOSKRNL.EXE file may be corrupt or missing. Boot from a startup disk and replace the file from the setup disks or CD-ROM.

Troubleshooting Other Common Problems

Some common Windows problems don't fall into any category other than "common Windows problems." They include the following:

General Protection Faults (GPFs) A *general protection fault (GPF)* happens in Windows when a program accesses memory that another program is using or when a program accesses a memory address that doesn't exist. Generally, GPFs are the result of sloppy programming. To fix this type of problem, a simple reboot will usually clear memory. If GPFs keep occurring, check to see which software is causing the error. Then find out if the manufacturer of the software has a patch to prevent it from GPFing.

Illegal Operation Occasionally a program will quit, apparently for no reason, and present you with a window that says *This program has performed an illegal operation and will be shut down. If the problem persists, contact the program vendor.* An *illegal operation error* usually means that a program was forced to quit because it did something Windows didn't like. Windows then displays this error window. The name of the program that quit appears at the top of the window, along with three buttons: OK, Cancel, and Details. The OK and Cancel buttons do the same thing: dismiss the window. The Details button opens the window a little farther and shows the details of the error, including which module experienced the problem, the memory location being accessed at the time, and the registers and flags of the processor at the time of the error.

System Lock-Up It is obvious when a system lockup occurs. The system simply stops responding to commands and stops processing completely. System lockups can occur when a computer is asked to process too many instructions at once with too little memory. Usually, the cure for a system lockup is to reboot. If the lockups are persistent, it may be a hardware-related problem instead of a software problem.

Dr. Watson Windows 2000 and Windows XP include a special utility known as Dr. Watson. This utility intercepts all error conditions and, instead of presenting the user with a cryptic Windows error, displays a slew of information that can be used to troubleshoot the problem.

Failure to Start GUI Occasionally, the Windows GUI won't appear. The system will hang just before the GUI appears. Or, sometimes, the *Blue Screen of Death (BSOD)*—not a technical term, by the way—appears. The BSOD is another way of describing the blue-screen error condition that occurs when Windows 2000/XP fails to boot properly or quits unexpectedly. Because it is at this stage that the device drivers for the various pieces of hardware are installed, if your Windows GUI fails to start properly, more than likely the problem is related to a mis-configured driver or misconfigured hardware. Try booting Windows in safe mode to bypass this problem.

If you happen to get a BSOD with a *Fatal Exception error 0D* message, chances are that the culprit is a problem relating to the video card.

Option (Sound Card, Modem, SCSI Card, or Input Device) Will Not Function   When you are using Windows, you are constantly interacting with pieces of hardware. Each piece of hardware has a Windows driver that must be loaded in order for Windows to be able to use it. In addition, the hardware must be installed and functioning properly. If the device driver is not installed properly or the hardware is misconfigured, the device won't function properly.

Cannot Log On to the Network (Option—NIC Not Functioning)   If your computer is hooked up to a network (and more and more computers today are), you need to know when your computer is not functioning on the network properly and what to do about it. In most cases, the problem can be attributed to either a malfunctioning network interface card (NIC) or improperly installed network software. The biggest indicator in Windows that some com-ponent of the network software is nonfunctional is that you can't log on to the network or access any network service. To fix this problem, you must first fix the underlying hardware problem (if one exists) and then properly install or configure the network software.

Networking software is covered in Chapter 8

Application Will Not Install   We've all experienced this frustration. You are trying to install the coolest new program, and, for whatever reason, it just won't install properly. It may give you one of the previously mentioned errors or a cryptic installation error. If a software program won't install and it gives you any of the errors we've mentioned (such as a GPF or illegal oper-ation), use the solutions for those errors first. If the error that occurs during install is unique to the application being installed, check the application manufacturer's website for an explanation or update. These errors generally occur when you're trying to install over an application that already exists or when you're trying to replace a file that already exists but that another appli-cation has in use. When you're installing an application, it is extremely important that you first quit all running programs so the installer can replace any files it needs to.

Application Will Not Start   Once you have an application successfully installed, you may run into a problem getting it to start properly. This problem can come from any number of sources, including an improper installation, a software conflict, or system instability. If your application was installed incorrectly, the files required to properly run the program may not be present, and the program can't function without them. If a shared file that's used by other programs is installed, it could be a different version than should be installed that causes conflicts with other already-installed programs. Finally, if one program GPFs, it can cause memory problems that can destabilize the system and cause other programs to crash. The solution to these problems is to uninstall and reinstall the offending application, first making sure that all programs are closed.

Invalid Working Directory   Some Windows programs are extremely processor intensive. These programs require an area on the hard disk to store their temporary files while they work. This area is commonly known as a *working directory*, and its location is usually specified during that program's installation. However, if that directory changes after installation and the program still thinks its working directory is in the same location, the program will issue an error that says something such as *Invalid working directory*. The solution is to reinstall the program with the correct parameters for the working directory.

For this reason, many programs use the Windows TEMP directory as their working directory. You will see this error only if the programmer chose to use a user-settable working directory.

Remember that there are two universal solutions to Windows problems: rebooting and obtaining an update from the software manufacturer.

🌐 Real World Scenario

Did You Reboot Your Computer?

Quick quiz: You just got an error in Windows, and it appears that you are on the verge of a crash (of your application or the whole system). What do you do?

The first thing is to write down any error messages that appear. Then, save your work (if possible) and reboot your computer.

Anyone who has called tech support, or been a tech support person, knows how demeaning this phrase can seem. When you ask someone, "Did you restart your computer?" it's almost as if you're insulting their intelligence. Most people respond with an indignant, "Of course!" when the reality is they might or might not have actually done it.

Whenever there's a software problem, always, always reboot the computer before trying to troubleshoot. The vast majority of the time, the problem will disappear and you'll have just saved yourself half an hour of frustration. If the same problem continues, then you know you have work to do.

> Why does rebooting help? When an application is running, it creates one or more tempo-
> rary files that it uses to store information, and it also stores information in memory (RAM).
> If a temporary file or information in RAM becomes corrupt (such as by application A
> writing its information into application B's memory space), the application can have
> problems. Rebooting will clear the memory registers and most often remove problematic
> temporary files, eliminating the issue.
>
> It might sound trite, but the first axiom in troubleshooting software really is to reboot. Even
> if the user says she did it, do it again. (Tell her you want to see the opening screen for any pos-
> sible error messages, or make up another good excuse.) If the problem doesn't come back, it's
> not a problem. If it does, then you can use your software skills to fix it.

Understanding Windows Reporting

One of the new features of Windows XP Professional is Windows error reporting. If a program
error occurs (such as Internet Explorer crashing, but non-Microsoft programs will also do it),
a window will pop up asking if you want to report the problem to Microsoft. It only works
if you have an active Internet connection. If you choose to report the problem, then technical
information about the problem is gathered and sent to Microsoft. If others have reported the
same problem, then additional technical information will be available to you, to help you solve
the problem.

According to Microsoft, the information gathered is only used by programming groups to
help solve technical problems. Your individual information is not stored or tracked in any way.

To configure (or disable) Windows reporting, open your System properties by right-
clicking on My Computer and selecting Properties. On the Advanced tab, click on the Error
Reporting button at the bottom of the screen to open a window similar to the one shown in
Figure 6.2.

FIGURE 6.2   Windows Error Reporting options

Your two major choices are to disable or enable error reporting. If you choose to disable it, you can still be notified when errors occur. After choosing to enable error reporting, you can make the selection of reporting Windows operating system and/or program errors. By clicking on the Programs button, you can configure which programs you want to report errors on. By default, all program errors from all programs get reported, but you can configure the reporting of errors on an app-by-app basis.

Identifying Windows-Based Troubleshooting Utilities

In addition to learning about the many common problems and troubleshooting techniques for Windows, you should know about the different tools that Microsoft provides with Windows to troubleshoot Windows. These resources are the best to use if you have no other trouble-shooting tools available. They can also be used as a starting point for troubleshooting a computer. The built-in Windows tools that you should be aware of include the following:

- Disk management tools including Format, CHKDSK, DEFRAG, and NTBACKUP
- System management tools such as Device Manager, Computer Management, Task Manager, MSCONFIG, REGEDIT, REGEDT32, CMD, Event Viewer, and System Restore
- File management tools including Windows Explorer and ATTRIB

Disk Management Tools

Preserving information on hard drives has never been more important than today. Not only do you want to keep your own information, you have the legal obligation to manage company records if you work for a publicly held firm. Here are some disk management utilities to be familiar with.

FORMAT.EXE

If you want to wipe out all information on a disk or prepare a disk for an operating system, you can use the FORMAT command. FORMAT.EXE is a DOS program that allows you to wipe partitions clean. Before installing a new operating system, always format the hard drive.

CHKDSK

You can use the Windows CHKDSK utility to create and display status reports for the hard disk. CHKDSK can also correct file system problems (such as cross-linked files) and scan for and attempt to repair disk errors. You can manually start CHKDSK by right-clicking the problem disk and selecting Properties. This will bring up the Properties dialog box for that disk, which shows the current status of the selected disk drive.

By clicking the Tools tab at the top of the dialog box, and then clicking the Check Now button in the Error-checking section, you can start CHKDSK. Exercise 6.3 walks you through starting CHKDSK in Windows XP.

EXERCISE 6.3

Running *CHKDSK* in Windows XP

In this exercise, you will check your hard disk for errors.

1.   Open Windows Explorer by holding down the Windows key and pressing E.

2.   Right-click C: and choose Properties.

3.   Click the Tools tab and then click the Check Now button.

4.   Choose your options: You can automatically fix filesystem errors and/or scan for and attempt recovery of bad sectors.

5.   After you have selected your options, click Start.

DEFRAG.EXE

Defragmenting a disk involves analyzing the disk and then consolidating fragmented files and folders so they occupy a contiguous space, thus increasing performance during file retrieval. The command-line DEFRAG utility allows you to run a defrag from a command prompt. You can also run a defrag in Windows through the Disk Defragmenter in the Computer Management utility or by right-clicking on a hard drive in Windows Explorer, choosing Properties, then the Tools tab, and clicking the Defragment Now button.

NTBACKUP.EXE

If you want to back up your system, you can run the NTBACKUP.EXE utility located in the \WINDOWS\system32 directory. You can also run it by clicking Start ➢ All Programs ➢ Accessories ➢ System Tools ➢ Backup.

   Back up your files early and often.

System Management Tools

Windows 2000 and Windows XP are very complicated operating systems, and it's fortunate that there are plenty of system management tools to help us in our daily computer management activities.

Device Manager

From Windows 9x forward, Microsoft has provided the Device Manager, a tool that analyzes hardware-related problems. The Device Manager displays all of the devices installed in a computer (as shown in Figure 6.3). If a device is malfunctioning, a yellow circle with an exclamation point inside it is displayed (as with the Iomega Parallel Port Interface in Figure 6.3).

With this utility, you can view the devices installed in a system and any of those devices that are failing, and you can also double-click on a device and view and set its properties (as shown in Figure 6.4). On the General tab, you will see the status of the device (whether it's working), as well as find the Troubleshoot button, which can help you solve problems. The other tabs are used to configure the individual devices, add or update drivers, and verify the version of drivers installed.

FIGURE 6.3   The Windows 9x Device Manager

FIGURE 6.4   Properties of a network card

In Windows 2000 and XP, you can access the Device Manager by right-clicking the My Computer icon, choosing Properties, and then clicking the Hardware tab. On the Hardware tab are many buttons, but to access the Device Manager, click the Device Manager button.

Computer Management

Windows 2000/XP includes a new piece of software to manage computer settings: the Computer Management Console. Because Windows 2000/XP is more advanced as a platform, the Computer Management Console can manage more than just the installed hardware devices. In addition to containing a Device Manager that functions almost identically to the one in Windows 9x, the Computer Management Console can also manage all the services running on that computer. It contains an Event Viewer to show any system errors and events, as well as methods to configure the software components of all the computer's hardware. Figure 6.5 shows an example of the Computer Management Console running on Windows 2000.

FIGURE 6.5   Windows 2000 Computer Management Console

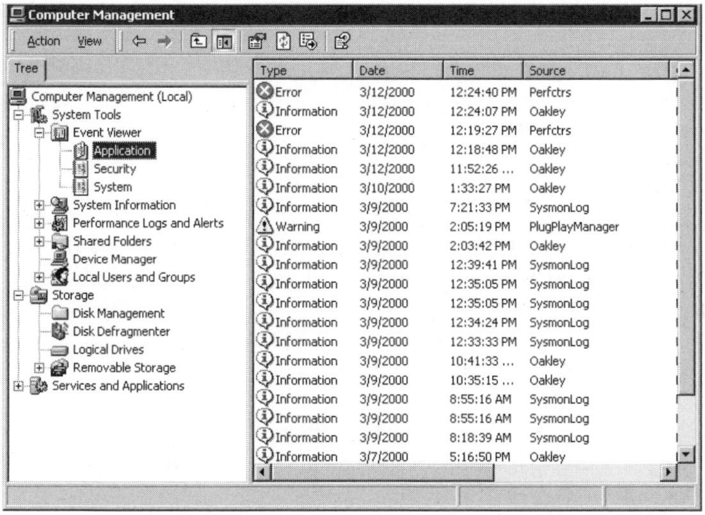

To access the Computer Management Console, go to Start ➢ Settings ➢ Control Panel ➢ Administrative Tools ➢ Computer Management. Alternatively, you can right-click My Computer and choose Manage. You will see all of the computer management tools, including the Device Manager. You can then use the Computer Management Console to manage hardware devices and software services.

Task Manager

Another tool you can use to check on and control your Windows 2000/XP environment is the Task Manager. Any time you run a program, it displays as a button on the Taskbar. Sometimes, however, you may run into problems with running tasks. For example, a task (program) may hang. You'll know this has happened because you won't be able to use any of the program's functions—the program will be unresponsive. To deal with this situation, as well as for other reasons, you can use the Task Manager (see Figure 6.6).

FIGURE 6.6   The Task Manager in Windows XP

To access the Task Manager, press Ctrl+Alt+Del. In Windows 2000, you then have to click Task Manager on the Windows Security screen. By default, Windows XP does not display the Windows Security screen if you press Ctrl+Alt+Del; instead, Task Manager opens right away. You can change this by opening User Accounts in Control Panel and clicking Change the way users log on or off.

To get to the Task Manager directly in any of the Windows versions that include it, you can press Ctrl+Shift+Esc.

In Windows 2000, the Task Manager has three tabs: Applications, Processes, and Performance. In Windows XP, the Task Manager can have two additional tabs: Networking and Users. Let's look at these tabs in more detail:

Applications   The Applications tab lets you see what tasks are open on the machine. You also see the status of each task, which can be either Running or Not Responding. If a task or application has stopped responding (that is, it's hung), you can select the task in the list and click End Task. Doing so closes the program, and you can try to open it again. Often, although certainly not always, if an application hangs, you'll have to reboot the computer to prevent the same thing from happening again shortly after you restart the application. You can also use the Applications tab to switch to a different task or create new tasks.

Processes   The Processes tab lets you see the names of all the processes running on the machine. You also see the user account that's running the process, as well as how much CPU and RAM resources each process is using. To end a process, select the process in the list and click End Process.

Performance   The Performance tab contains a variety of information, including overall CPU Usage percentage, a graphical display of CPU usage history, page-file usage in MB, and a graphical display of page-file usage. This tab also provides you with additional memory-related information such as physical and kernel memory usage, as well as the total number of handles, threads, and processes. Total, limit, and peak commit-charge information also displays. Some of the items are beyond the scope of this book, but it's good to know that you can use the Performance tab to keep track of system performance. Note that the number of processes, CPU usage percentage, and commit charge always display at the bottom of the Task Manager window, regardless of which tab you have currently selected.

Networking (Windows XP Only)   This tab only appears if you are connected to a network. The Networking tab provides you with a graphical display of the performance of your network connection. It also tells you the network adapter name, link speed, and state. If you have more than one network adapter installed in the machine, you can select the appropriate adapter to see graphical usage data for that adapter.

Users (Windows XP Only)   The Users tab, which is available if you have more than one user account on your computer, provides you with information about the users connected to the local machine. You'll see the username, ID, status, client name, and session type. You can right-click on any connected user to perform a variety of functions, including sending the user a message, disconnecting the user, logging off the user, and initiating a remote control session to the user's machine.

MSCONFIG.EXE (Windows XP Only)

A new utility was introduced with Windows 98: MSCONFIG.EXE (aka the System Configuration Utility). Windows 2000 does not include it, but it's back in Windows XP. It allows a user to manage his computer system's configuration. MSCONFIG.EXE allows a user to boot Windows in diagnostic mode, in which he can select which drivers to load interactively. If you suspect a certain driver is causing problems during boot, you can use MSCONFIG.EXE to prevent that driver from loading. In addition, each of the major configuration files (CONFIG.SYS, AUTOEXEC.BAT, WIN.INI, SYSTEM.INI) and the programs loaded at startup can be reconfigured and reordered using a graphical interface.

REGEDIT.EXE and REGEDT32.EXE

The most dangerous utility in the Windows troubleshooting arsenal is the Registry Editor, also known by its executable names REGEDIT.EXE and REGEDT32.EXE. The Registry stores all Windows configuration information. If you edit the Registry, you are essentially changing the configuration of Windows. (This is why it's dangerous. There's no Save button and any changes made happen immediately, for better or for worse. To undo changes, you must do so manually.) The Registry Editor is used to manually change settings that are usually changed by other means (such as through Setup programs and other Windows utilities).

In addition to changing Windows settings, you can use REGEDIT to back up and restore the Registry. To back up the Registry, choose the Export Registry File command under the Registry menu (or File ➤ Export in later versions). This command allows you to save the Registry file to a backup medium. You can restore it later by choosing the Import Registry File command (or File ➤ Import) under the Registry menu.

CMD

If you ever need to type in a command, for example, you want to view your environment variables the old-fashioned way or you want to test network connectivity, go to the Start button. From Start, choose Run, type CMD, and press Enter. That will open a command prompt, where you can enter your commands.

Event Viewer

Windows 2000/XP employs comprehensive error and informational logging routines. Every program and process theoretically could have its own logging utility, but Microsoft has come up with a rather slick utility, Event Viewer, which, through log files, tracks all events on a particular Windows 2000/XP computer. Normally, though, you must be an administrator or a member of the Administrators group to have access to Event Viewer.

To start Event Viewer, log in as an administrator (or equivalent) and go to Start ➤ Programs ➤ Administrative Tools ➤ Event Viewer. From here, you can view the System, Application, and Security log files:

- The System log file displays alerts that pertain to the general operation of Windows.

- The Application log file logs server application errors.

- The Security log file logs security events such as login successes and failures.

These log files can give a general indication of a Windows computer's health.

One situation that does occur with the Event Viewer is that the Event Viewer log files get full. Although this isn't really a problem, it can make viewing log files confusing because there are many entries. Even though each event is time- and date-stamped, you should clear the Event Viewer every so often. To do this, open the Event Viewer and choose Clear All Events from the Log menu. Doing so erases all events in the current log file, allowing you to see new events more easily when they occur.

ConfigSafe

One utility that has become popular for keeping the stability of Windows in check is ConfigSafe. ConfigSafe, by ImagineLan, is a utility that technicians and IT professionals use when they are installing new, untested software or to keep their systems stable.

ConfigSafe works by taking a snapshot of the current system configuration, including file lists, Registry settings, icons, and so on, and storing that information in a file. Then, if you install a new piece of software or a driver or make other configuration changes, and that change causes your system to stop functioning, you can roll back to the last good configuration.

File Management Tools

Windows comes with several utilities to manage files on your hard drives. Some simply allow you to see what's out there and move files around, whereas others offer you the ability to make modifications to the contents or properties of those files.

Windows Explorer

Windows Explorer is a utility that allows you to accomplish a number of important file-related tasks from a single graphical interface. Among the tasks you can accomplish with Windows Explorer are viewing files and directories, opening programs or files, creating files and directories, copying or moving objects, deleting files and directories, changing file attributes, and formatting floppy disks.

Windows Explorer was discussed in detail in Chapter 4. It's highly recommended that you become very familiar with how to use Windows Explorer, as it will be one of the most common interfaces you use in Windows.

ATTRIB.EXE

Every OS since DOS provides four attributes that can be set for files to modify their interaction with the system. These attributes are as follows:

Read-only   Prevents a file from being modified, deleted, or overwritten.

Archive   Used by backup programs to determine whether the file has changed since the last backup and needs to be backed up.

System   Used to tell the OS that this file is needed by the system and should not be deleted.

Hidden   Used to keep files from being seen in a normal directory search. This attribute is useful to prevent system files and other important files from being accidentally moved or deleted.

While you can use Windows Explorer to set these attributes, you can also set attributes for files using the external DOS command ATTRIB.EXE, which uses the following syntax:

```
ATTRIB <filename> [+ or -][attribute]
```

To set the Read-only attribute on the file TESTFILE.DOC, use the following series of commands:

```
ATTRIB TESTFILE.DOC +r
```

Proper attribute management is important to the well-being of Windows. Many critical system files are marked with the System attribute, which is important to be aware of. The Archive attribute is important as well, so you can tell if the file has been backed up or not. The Hidden attribute is really there for everyone's own protection. After all, if a user doesn't know a file exists, how can he accidentally delete it?

If a file is set to read-only, you won't be able to make changes to it. Some users won't understand why they can't change a file (because they don't know about attributes), but if they for some reason can't save a file, this is one of the first things to check.

EXTRACT.EXE

Many versions of Windows have setup files that come compressed in cabinet (CAB) files. These files are extracted during the Windows Setup process by the EXTRACT.EXE utility. You can also use this utility to extract one or multiple files from a CAB file to replace a corrupt file. If you have one Windows file that is corrupt, you can extract a replacement from the Windows setup CAB files. If you don't know which CAB file contains a particular Windows system file, you can look it up in the CABS.TXT file.

For example, to extract the UNIDRV.DLL file from the WIN95_10.CAB file on a CD-ROM in drive D: to the C:\WINDOWS\SYSTEM directory, use the following command syntax:

```
EXTRACT D:\WIN95_10.CAB UNIDRV.DLL /L C:\WINDOWS\SYSTEM
```

The new file will be extracted to the new location and replace the old corrupt version in that location.

EDIT.COM

Occasionally, you need to quickly edit a configuration file or other text file. For this purpose, a simple editor named EDIT.COM has been included with all Microsoft OSs since DOS version 6. To edit a file, start a command-line session and type in the following:

```
EDIT <filename>
```

Replace <filename> with the name of the file you wish to edit. Once EDIT comes up, it works like any other word processor or text editor. When you have finished editing the file, save it, and it will be saved as a standard ASCII text file.

If you're in Windows, you can also use the Windows NOTEPAD.EXE editor for the same function.

Identifying Diagnostic Resources

In addition to the many diagnostic tools you have available, there are some diagnostic resources you should use to make troubleshooting easier. Although most people don't necessarily think of these resources as tools, they aid in the troubleshooting process. These resources include the following:

- Manuals
- Internet resources
- Training materials

User/Installation Manuals

Technicians are the guiltiest of not using this readily available resource when troubleshooting a system. In fact, most often, a technician will rely on his own experience and try to install a new component without reading the manual. Then, when the installation doesn't work, he might go back and look at the manual after spending time looking for the solution to a problem that might have been avoided in the first place.

Typically, in addition to the steps needed to install software or a device, a manual includes a section on the most common problems and the solutions to those problems. This area of the manual would be especially useful for the technician we just described.

Internet/Web Resources

Possibly the most useful resource to the technician is the Internet. As mentioned throughout this book, a manufacturer's website is the best place to get the most current drivers, fixes, and technical information. Often, you can search a hardware or software vendor's website for a problem you might be having with that hardware or software, and find the fix for it. In addition, Microsoft's website contains a wide variety of known problems and issues with Windows and its interaction with other software. Sometimes a solution that can't be found at the software vendor's website can be found by viewing the Microsoft support website because Microsoft has a larger staff and has been able to document a larger variety of problems. If you can't find an answer at the manufacturer's or Microsoft's website, you might try entering your problem into one of the many search engines, such as Yahoo (`http://www.yahoo.com`) or Google (`http://www.google.com`).

There are websites dedicated to communities of technical individuals (such as yourself) that can be a great source of information. Chances are, if you're having a computer or technical problem, someone else, somewhere in the world, has the solution—and the Internet can bring you together. You can post your problem to any number of website bulletin boards and newsgroups and receive a response, possibly within minutes.

Training Materials

The final resource is one that most people overlook. Individuals do not acquire knowledge magically—they either learn it by themselves with self-study materials or are taught by an experienced instructor. In either case, books and other training materials (like the one you are reading right now) are excellent sources of information. Although training materials don't often contain patches or updates, they can and do teach concepts you can apply to help you with troubleshooting. After all, if you had not read this book, you might not have gotten the information you needed to pass the A+ exam.

Now ask yourself: Did I learn anything? Will the information I learned be able to help me troubleshoot a computer problem?

Performing Preventative Maintenance on Operating Systems

For the most part, modern Windows operating systems are pretty resilient. There are a mind-boggling number of ways that systems could crash, but crashes don't happen often under normal circumstances. However, you do play an important role in the stability of the operating system on your computer. If you neglect to maintain it, you could be in for significant problem that would impact your productivity or someone else's.

In this section we'll take a look at some preventative steps you can take to help keep Windows 2000 and Windows XP running smoothly. They include the following:

- Using hardware that's in the Windows Catalog
- Obtaining the right drivers for your hardware (that's in the Windows Catalog)
- Installing Windows properly
- Shutting down properly
- Updating Windows regularly
- Scheduling backups
- Creating restore points
- Guarding against viruses and their kin

Let's dive in.

Using Recommended Hardware

Back in Chapter 5, when we looked at installing Windows, we talked about ensuring that your hardware was in the Windows Catalog (formerly the Hardware Compatibility List). A surefire way to make sure Windows *doesn't* work right is to install hardware that Windows won't play nice with. Realistically, the vast majority of hardware on the market will work fine with Windows, considering how ubiquitous the operating system family is. However, don't just assume that the hardware will work. Always check it against the Windows Catalog to ensure that you won't have problems after it's installed.

You can find the Windows Catalog at `http://www.windowsmarketplace.com/`.

Obtaining Current Drivers

This topic goes right along with making sure that your hardware will work with Windows. When you purchase a hardware device, odds are it's been in that box for a while. By the time it gets made, packaged, stored, delivered to the store, stored again at the retailer, and then purchased by you, it's entirely likely that the company that made the device has updated the driver—even possibly a few times if there have been a lot of reported problems.

When you install a device, always go to the manufacturer's website to see if a newer driver is available. The old driver might work fine, but the newest driver is the one most likely to be bug-free and have all of the most current bells and whistles for your device.

Installing Windows Properly

Chapter 5 went into a great amount of detail about how to install Windows 2000 and Windows XP. You'll probably remember that there were a lot of steps you needed to take before the installation, as planning is crucial. In addition, there are quite a few choices you can make during the installation. Making the wrong choice isn't usually fatal, but it could have long-lasting consequences. If you think your installation is bad, reinstall. Just make sure to choose the right options the second time to avoid needing to install a third time. Whenever you reinstall because you think there are problems, make sure to completely wipe out any possibility of an old problem lingering by formatting the hard drive.

We also talked quite a bit about upgrading from earlier versions of Windows in Chapter 5. Most of the time, upgrades work well and you won't have any problems. However, there is a bigger chance of having a problem with your operating system if you upgrade as opposed to performing a clean installation on a freshly formatted hard drive. If there seem to be problems as a result of an upgrade, back up everything that's critical, reformat the hard drive, and perform a fresh installation.

Shutting Down Properly

Not shutting down properly can result in lost data from open applications or corrupted operating system files. Neither option is good.

You would think that people are pretty aware of how to shut down, but sadly it's not always true. When it comes to your own computers, always shut down properly by clicking

Start ➤ Turn Off Computer in Windows XP or Start ➤ Shut Down in Windows 2000. If you are a technician at a company, it's your responsibility to train all users on how to properly shut down as well.

Updating Windows

Windows 2000 and Windows XP include *Windows Update*, a feature designed to keep Windows current by automatically downloading updates such as patches and security fixes and installing these fixes automatically.

By default, Windows Update will run automatically when any administrator user is logged in. However, if you want to run it manually, you can do so by clicking Start ➤ All Programs ➤ Windows Update in Windows XP, or by clicking Start Windows Update (Windows XP), or by clicking Start ➤ Programs ➤ Windows Update in Windows 2000. You can also go to http:// windowsupdate.microsoft.com to start the process.

Often, major updates to Windows are called *service packs*.

Here is an overview of how Windows Update works:

1. Windows Update starts (either by itself or manually).
2. Windows Update goes online to check to see what updates are available. It compares the update list to the updates that have already been applied to the computer or have been refused by the administrator.
3. If updates are available, they are downloaded automatically in the background.
4. Once the updates are downloaded, Windows Update notifies you that the download is complete and asks you if you want to install them.

If you choose not to install the updates right away, Windows will do so for you when you shut off the computer. Instead of shutting off right away, Windows Update will install the updates first and then perform a proper shutdown.

By default, Windows Update is enabled. But there might be times you want to configure it. Exercise 6.4 steps through the process of configuring Windows Update in Windows XP.

EXERCISE 6.4

Configuring Windows Update in Windows XP

To configure Windows Update in Windows XP, follow these steps:

1. Open the System Properties box (right-click My Computer and choose Properties, or double-click the System icon in Control Panel).

EXERCISE 6.4 *(continued)*

2. Click on the Automatic Updates tab.

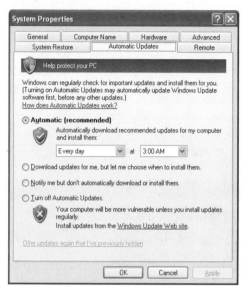

3. Choose the option that best suits your needs. You have four choices:

Automatically download recommended updates for my computer and install them.

Download updates for me, but let me choose when to install them.

Notify me but don't automatically download or install them.

Turn off Automatic Updates.

It's not a problem if you want to choose to have control over which updates get installed and when. However, it really is in your best interest to have Windows Update enabled to ensure that you have the most current patches available.

Scheduling Backups

This is one of the areas where most users, and even most companies, fail to manage properly. At the same time, it's one of the most important. Backups serve several key purposes, such as protecting against hard drive failure, protecting against accidental deletion, protecting against malicious deletion or attacks, and making an archive of important files for later use. Any time you make major changes to your system, including installing new software, you should perform a backup of important files before making those changes.

Both Windows 2000 and Windows XP allow you to schedule backups, which is a great feature that not all versions of Windows have had.

Now that you know you can schedule backups to make your life easy, and of course you want to make backups because it's the right thing to do, the question becomes: How often do you need to back up your files?

The answer really depends on what the computer does and what you do on the computer. How often does your data change? Every day? Every week or every month? How important are your files? Can you afford to lose them? How much time or money will it cost to replace lost files? Can they be replaced? By answering these questions, you can get an idea of how often you want to run scheduled backups. As a rule of thumb, the more important the data is and the more often it changes, the more often you want to back up. If you don't care about losing the data, then there's no need for backups—but most of us do care about losing our stuff. Exercise 6.5 demonstrates how to schedule backups in Windows XP.

EXERCISE 6.5

Scheduling Backups in Windows XP

To schedule a backup in Windows XP, follow these steps:

1. Open Windows Backup by going to Start ≻ All Programs ≻ Accessories ≻ System Tools ≻ Backup. This will open the Backup or Restore Wizard. The wizard will walk you through all of the options you can use, or you can click the Advanced Mode link to set up things manually.

2. On the Backup or Restore Wizard screen, click Next to continue.

3. Choose Back Up Files And Settings, and click Next.

4. Choose what you want to back up (as shown in the graphic), and click Next.

EXERCISE 6.5 *(continued)*

5. Confirm the backup type and the destination, and give the backup file a name (it will have a .BKF extension). For the destination, you can click the Browse button to select the right location, which might be a floppy drive, a CD or DVD burner, or a network drive. Click Next.

6. Specify the type of backup. If you're not sure, choose Normal. Click Next.

7. Choose your backup options: Verify Data, Hardware Compression, and Disable Volume Shadow Copy. It's a good idea to verify data, but it does take extra time. Click Next.

8. Choose to replace the current backup file (if one exists) or append the data to the end of the backup. Click Next.

9. Here is where you can schedule the backup. Choose Later, and then click the Set Schedule button. (If you don't want to schedule but want to back up the files now, click Now.)

10. In the Schedule Job window, choose how often and at what time you would like to run backups, and click OK. Then click Next.

11. You will be prompted for a username and password to run the backup. This is because only certain user accounts (such as the Administrator account) have the ability to run backups. When the process starts, Windows will log itself in as the user account you specify to perform the backup. Click Next.

12. Review the information on the confirmation page, and click Finish.

One key thing to remember is that for the backups to run properly as scheduled, the computer needs to be on when the scheduled backup is supposed to take place.

Real World Scenario

Learning Lessons about Backups

People don't back up data enough, plain and simple. Scheduling regular backups is a good protective measure, but just because you are backing up your data doesn't mean you're completely saved if something goes wrong.

Several years ago, one of my former students related a story to me about a server crash at his company. A server had mysteriously died over the weekend, and the technicians were greeted with the problem first thing Monday morning. Not to worry, they thought, because they made regular backups.

After several attempts to restore the backup tape, a second, more serious problem was readily apparent. The backup didn't work. They couldn't read the data from the tape, and it was the only backup tape they had. It wasn't going to be a very good Monday. Ultimately, they ended up losing extensive data from the server because their backup didn't work.

How do you prevent tragedies like this from happening? Test your backups. After you make a backup, ensure that you can read from it. If you've just backed up a small amount of data, restore it to an alternate location and make sure you can read it. If you are backing up entire computers, a good idea is to run a test restore on a separate computer. No matter what your method, test your backup, especially when it's the first one you've made after setting up backups or you have made backup configuration changes. It isn't necessary to fully test each single backup after that, but it is a good idea to spot-check backups on occasion.

Here are two more ideas that will help too. One, rotate backup tapes (or CDs). Alternate tapes every other backup period, or use a separate tape for each day of the week. This lessens the risk of having a bad tape bring you down. Two, store your backups offsite. If your backup is sitting on top of the server, and you have a fire that destroys the building, then your backup didn't do you any good. There are data archiving firms that will, for a small fee, come and pick up your backup tapes and store them in their secure location.

Be religious about backing up your data, and in the event of a failure, you'll be back up and running in short order.

Creating Restore Points

There are times when bad things happen to good computers. No matter how hard you've tried to keep a system running flawlessly, karma is against you, and your computer crashes. There are several ways to get your computer back up and running, but many of them (such as reinstalling the operating system) take a lot of time. A new feature of Windows XP, System Restore, allows you to create restore points to make recovery of the operating system easier.

A *restore point* is a copy of your system configuration at a given point in time. Restore points are created one of three ways. One, Windows creates them automatically by default. Two, you can manually create them yourself. Three, during the installation of some programs, a restore point is created before the installation (that way, if the install fails, you can "roll back" the system to a preinstallation configuration). Restore points are useful for when Windows fails to boot but the computer appears to be fine otherwise, or if Windows doesn't seem to be acting right and you think it was because of a recent configuration change.

To open System Restore, click on Start ➢ All Programs ➢ Accessories ➢ System Tools ➢ System Restore. It will open a screen like the one in Figure 6.7.

Notice in Figure 6.7 that you have two options. The first is to restore your computer to an earlier time (if you feel Windows is misbehaving), and the second is to manually create a restore point.

> If you need to use a restore point and Windows won't boot, you can reboot into safe mode. After safe mode loads, you will have the option to work in safe mode or use System Restore. Choose System Restore and you'll be presented with restore points (if any) you can use.

FIGURE 6.7   System Restore

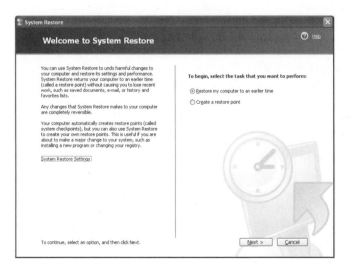

One other option in Figure 6.7 is a link on the left side, which takes you to System Restore settings. You can also get to the same place by opening the System control panel (right-clicking on My Computer and choosing Properties) and selecting the System Restore tab, as shown in Figure 6.8.

First, notice that you can turn off System Restore. Don't, unless you really don't care if your computer crashes and you can't recover it without a reinstall. The other option is to select how much disk space is available for System Restore. The less disk space you make available, the fewer restore points you will be able to have. If you have multiple hard drives, you can allocate a different amount of space per hard drive.

Creating a restore point manually is also done through the System Restore utility. In Exercise 6.6, we'll walk through the process of creating a restore point in Windows XP.

EXERCISE 6.6

Creating a Restore Point in Windows XP

To create a restore point, follow these steps:

1.   Open System Restore by clicking on Start ➢ All Programs ➢ Accessories ➢ System Tools ➢ System Restore.

2.   Choose Create A Restore point, and click Next.

3.   Provide a restore point description. Click Create.

4.   Within a minute, you will be presented with a confirmation screen with the time, date, and name of your restore point.

FIGURE 6.8   System Restore options

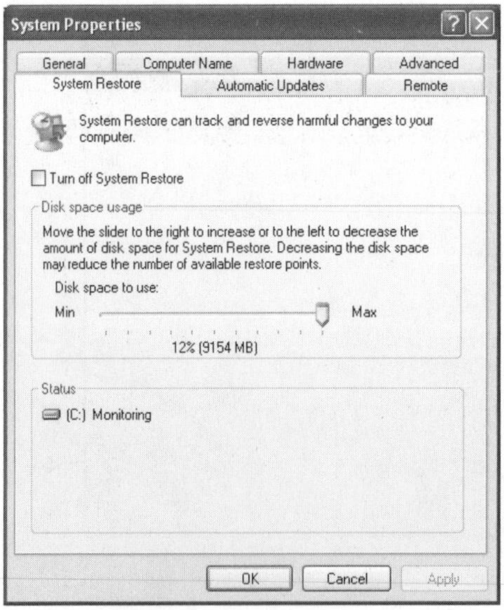

Now that you have created a restore point, it's time to look at how to perform a system restoration. To restore your system to a previous state, choose the Restore My Computer To An Earlier Time radio button, as shown in Figure 6.6. Click Next. On the next screen, you will be shown a calendar and available restore points, as shown in Figure 6.9.

On days when restore points were created, the calendar date will be bolded. You can choose any restore point you want, and click Next. The next screen confirms the restore point you have chosen, as shown in Figure 6.10.

FIGURE 6.9   Available restore points

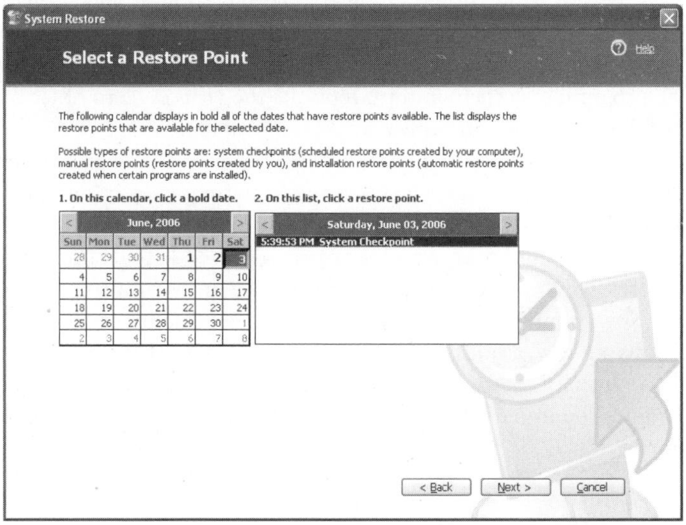

FIGURE 6.10   Confirming restore point selection

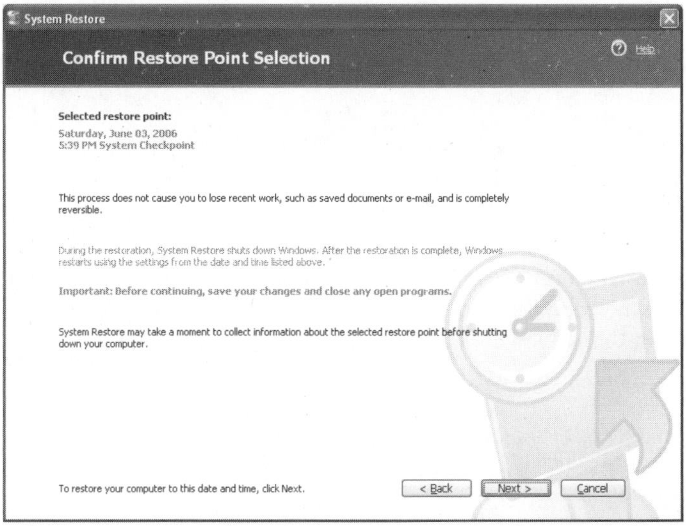

Note that at the bottom of the screen, you are told to click Next and the system will be restored to the point you selected. And, as the screen tells you, restoring the system restores only the configuration and does not cause you to lose recently saved files or documents.

Guarding against Viruses

This type of preventative maintenance is absolutely critical these days if you have a connection to the Internet. A computer *virus* is a small, deviously ingenious program that replicates itself to other computers, generally causing those computers to behave abnormally. Generally speaking, a virus's main function is to reproduce. A virus attaches itself to files on a hard disk and modifies those files. When the files are accessed by a program, the virus can infect the program with its own code. The program may then, in turn, replicate the virus code to other files and other programs. In this manner, a virus may infect an entire computer.

When an infected file is transferred to another computer (via disk or modem download), the process begins on the other computer. Because of the frequency of downloads from the Internet, viruses can run rampant if left unchecked. For this reason, antivirus programs were developed. They check files and programs for any program code that shouldn't be there and either eradicate it or prevent the virus from replicating. An antivirus program is generally run in the background on a computer, and it examines all the file activity on that computer. When it detects a suspicious activity, it notifies the user of a potential problem and asks the user what to do about it. Some antivirus programs can also make intelligent decisions about what to do. The process of running an antivirus program on a computer is known as *inoculating* the computer against a virus.

For a listing of most of the viruses that are currently out there, refer to Symantec's Anti-Virus Research Center (SARC) at http://www.symantec .com/avcenter/index.html.

Real World Scenario

But Where Do I Stick the Needle?

You may notice that a lot of the language surrounding computer viruses sounds like language we use to discuss human illness. The moniker *virus* was given to these programs because a computer virus functions much like a human virus, and the term helped to anthropomorphize the computer a bit. Somehow, if people can think of a computer as getting sick, it breaks down the computer phobia that many people have.

There are two categories of viruses: benign and malicious. Benign viruses don't do much besides replicate themselves and exist. They may cause the occasional problem, but it is usually an unintentional side effect. Malicious viruses, on the other hand, are designed to destroy things. Once a malicious virus (for example, the Michelangelo virus) infects your machine, you can usually kiss the contents of your hard drive good-bye.

To prevent virus-related problems, you can install one of any number of antivirus programs (Norton AntiVirus or McAfee Anti-Virus, for example). These programs will periodically scan your computer for viruses, monitor regular use of the computer, and note any suspicious activity that might indicate a virus. In addition, these programs have a database of known viruses and the symptoms each one causes.

These databases should be updated frequently (about once a week, although more often is better) to keep your antivirus program up-to-date with all the possible virus definitions. Most antivirus programs will automatically update themselves (if configured properly) just like Windows Update will update Windows. It's a good idea to let them automatically update, just in case you forget to do it yourself.

Summary

In this chapter, we gave you some tips for troubleshooting the Windows environment. Just as with troubleshooting hardware, it is important that you know how to troubleshoot software problems. However, troubleshooting software is actually more difficult because the problems can appear to be more phantom-like.

In the first section, you learned the basic steps to troubleshooting software problems. You also learned how to apply these troubleshooting steps to problems. These steps are as follows:

1. Talk to the customer.
2. Gather information.
3. Eliminate possibilities.
4. Test your results.
5. Document the solution.

In the next section, you learned how to troubleshoot boot problems. Booting the OS is a complex process that involves many different phases. Without a successful boot, the OS won't be usable. If that's ever the case, it's important to know how to recover and regain access.

To that end, we first covered the boot process and boot files for the Windows 2000/XP operating systems. We also showed you how to use system configuration tools to troubleshoot and configure booting-related options and how to use advanced boot options. We then showed you how to create boot emergency repair disks in Windows 2000 and use Windows XP's Automated System Recovery feature.

Next, you learned how to troubleshoot file-related problems. We described some of the more common file-related problems and their solutions. Some of the problems you learned about are missing or corrupt system files, configuration file problems, Windows 2000/XP boot problems, and swap-file issues.

You learned in the next section how to troubleshoot Windows problems that don't fall into any particular category. Some of these issues include general protection faults, invalid page faults, and applications that won't install. We explained how to recognize the symptoms of each of these problems and how to solve them when they occur.

Next, you learned how to use the various built-in Windows troubleshooting utilities. You learned what each utility is for and how to use it. We also discussed when to apply a particular utility to a problem.

We then considered some resources for troubleshooting that are often overlooked but are potentially very helpful: user guides, web resources, and training materials (like the book you are holding now!).

Finally, we ended this chapter by moving from troubleshooting into important ideas that will hopefully keep you from needing to troubleshoot too much: preventative maintenance. Keeping your computer healthy will save you a lot of stress if things don't break. Examples we discussed included using approved hardware and making sure you have the right driver, installing and shutting down Windows properly, updating Windows, performing backups, creating restore points, and protecting against viruses.

Exam Essentials

Know the five steps of proper troubleshooting.   To troubleshoot effectively, you need to follow a regimented procedure. Talk to the consumer first. Then, continue to gather information, eliminate possibilities, and test your results. Finally, document your work.

Understand the Windows 2000/XP boot process, in order.   The NTLDR utility bootstraps Windows and calls the BOOT.INI file. Then, NTLDR loads NTDETECT.COM, NTOSKRNL.EXE, and HAL.DLL. After the Registry loading begins, control is handed over to NTOSKRNL.EXE, and the Winlogon process starts.

Know what the advanced boot options are.   Advanced boot options available in Windows 2000 and Windows XP include Safe Mode, Enable Boot Logging, VGA Mode, Last Known Good Configuration, Directory Services Restore Mode, and Debugging Mode.

Know how to create an Emergency Repair Disk (ERD) or enable Automated System Recovery (ASR).   Both the ERD (Windows 2000) and ASR (Windows XP) can help you recover a system that has crashed because of Windows problems. However, before either option is available, you must first go to Windows Backup and create the appropriate disk.

Understand how to fix software-related problems.   Most software problems boil down to a missing or corrupted file. If this is the case, then reinstalling that file (or the application) can often fix the problem. Try rebooting first, and if the problem doesn't go away, you might need to reinstall.

Know a variety of Windows troubleshooting tools available to you.   Windows has several built-in utilities that can help you fix problems. They include disk management tools such as DEFRAG, NTBACKUP, CHKDSK and SCANDISK, and Format. System management tools include Device Manager, Task Manager, MSCONFIG, REGEDIT and REGEDT32, Event Viewer, and System Restore.

Understand how to update Windows.   Windows 2000 and Windows XP are automatically updated (by default) through the Windows Update utility.

Know how to schedule backups.   Backups are scheduled through the Windows Backup utility.

Know how to create restore points.   Restore points can be created in Windows XP through the System Restore utility.

Review Questions

1. What do you use in Windows XP to create a recovery disk?

   A. Automated System Recovery (ASR)

   B. RDISK.EXE

   C. Enhanced Startup Disk (ESD)

   D. Emergency Recovery System (ERS)

2. What is the first file used in the boot-up of Windows 2000?

   A. NTOSKRNL.EXE

   B. CONFIG.SYS

   C. AUTOEXEC.BAT

   D. NTLDR

   E. NTBOOTDD.SYS

3. What does safe mode allow you to do?

   A. Run Windows without processing AUTOEXEC.BAT and CONFIG.SYS.

   B. Boot the system without scanning drives.

   C. Start Windows using only basic files and drivers.

   D. Skip loading the Registry.

4. All of the following are Windows-based troubleshooting or modification utilities except _____.

   A. SYSEDIT

   B. PSCRIPT

   C. MSCONFIG

   D. DEFRAG

5. In order to delete and/or replace system files, which command do you use to remove the Hidden, System, and Read-only attributes on the file before you replace the file?

   A. UNDELETE

   B. ERASE

   C. ATTRIB

   D. DELETE

6. All of the following are common problems faced in troubleshooting Windows and applications except _____.

   A. General protection faults

   B. Valid working directory

   C. System lockup

   D. Application will not start or load

7. What is the first step in the troubleshooting process?

   A. Talk to the customer.

   B. Gather information.

   C. Eliminate possibilities.

   D. Document your work.

8. All of the following are Windows file-related problems except _____.

   A. System files not found

   B. Configuration file issues

   C. AUTOEXEC.BAT issues

   D. Swap-file issues

   E. Boot file issues

9. Symptoms of swap-file problems include extremely slow system speed and a disk that is constantly being accessed, which is referred to as _____.

   A. Clocking

   B. Thrashing

   C. Booting

   D. Filtering

10. What is the quickest solution to fixing a corrupt NTOSKRNL.EXE file?

   A. Reinstall Windows.

   B. Replace the corrupt file with a new one.

   C. Modify the BOOT.INI file to point to the backup NTOSKRNL.EXE file.

   D. Boot from a startup disk and replace the file from the setup disks or CD-ROM.

11. Which of the following is the most common error in Windows, and it happens when a program accesses memory another program is using or when a program accesses a memory address that doesn't exist?

   A. General protection fault

   B. Windows protection error

   C. Illegal operation

   D. System lockup

12. Which Windows error message is displayed when a program is forced to quit because it did something Windows didn't like?

   A. General protection fault

   B. Windows protection error

   C. Illegal operation

   D. System lockup

13. In Windows 2000, NTDETECT.COM _____.

    A. Parses the system for hardware information each time Windows 2000 is loaded

    B. Detects information about what OSs are installed on the computer

    C. Bootstraps the system

    D. Recognizes and loads the SCSI interface

14. In Windows XP, how do you access advanced startup options?

    A. By pressing the spacebar when prompted to do so

    B. By holding down Ctrl+Alt+Del after the Windows logo displays for the first time

    C. By pressing Esc after the OS menu displays

    D. By pressing F8 during the first phase of the boot process

15. Which advanced startup option in Windows 2000 would you use to be able to return to a previously functioning environment?

    A. Command Prompt Only

    B. Safe Mode

    C. Step-By-Step Configuration

    D. Debugging Mode

    E. Last Known Good Configuration

16. In Windows 2000, which utility do you use to create an ERD?

    A. Disk Management

    B. Backup

    C. SYSEDIT

    D. Windows 2000 doesn't support making an ERD.

17. In Windows XP, which of the following utilities is responsible for finding, downloading, and installing Windows service packs?

    A. Update Manager

    B. Service Pack Manager

    C. Windows Update

    D. Download Manager

18. Windows XP includes a feature called a _____, which is a copy of your system configuration that can be used to roll back the system to a previous state if a configuration error occurs.

    A. Restore point

    B. Repair point

    C. Roll back point

    D. Registry

19. In Windows 2000 and Windows XP, which of the following files is specifically responsible for enabling communication between the system hardware and the operating system?

   A. NTDETECT.COM

   B. NTOSKRNL.EXE

   C. NTBOOTDD.SYS

   D. HAL.DLL

   E. NTLDR

20. You have an application open in Windows 2000 that is not responding. Which of the following utilities can you use to forcibly close the nonresponsive application?

   A. Application Manager

   B. Task Manager

   C. Windows Explorer

   D. Device Manager

Answers to Review Questions

1. A. Windows XP introduced a new feature for system recovery, Automated System Recovery (ASR). It makes a backup of your system partition and creates a recovery disk.

2. D. The first file used in the Windows 2000/XP boot process is NTLDR. Both the NTOSKRNL.EXE and NTBOOTDD.SYS files are used in the boot process, but neither is the first file run. Neither AUTOEXEC.BAT nor CONFIG.SYS is involved in the Windows XP/2000 boot process.

3. C. Safe mode is a good option to choose to restore files that are missing or to fix a configuration error. With only basic files and drivers loaded, you can more easily identify the source of the problem.

4. B. PSCRIPT is not a Windows-based utility. SYSEDIT, MSCONFIG, and DEFRAG are all utilities used to troubleshoot or modify Windows.

5. C. In order to delete and/or replace system files, you must use the ATTRIB command to remove the Hidden, System, and Read-only attributes on the file.

6. B. A valid working directory is not a common problem faced in troubleshooting Windows and applications.

7. A. The first step in the troubleshooting process is to talk to the customer. It is best to obtain as much information as possible from the user so you have an idea of where to begin your troubleshooting.

8. C. Windows file-related problems do not include AUTOEXEC.BAT issues. AUTOEXEC.BAT is a DOS batch file that is automatically executed during bootup if the file is present.

9. B. Thrashing means an extremely slow system speed and a disk that is constantly being accessed. This condition occurs because Windows doesn't have enough memory to contain all the programs that are running.

10. D. The solution to a corrupt NTOSKRNL.EXE file is to boot from a startup disk and replace the file from the setup disks or CD-ROM. Replacing the corrupt NTOSKRNL.EXE file might also be the solution, but the quickest fix (provided it's the problem) is to look at the BOOT.INI file.

11. A. A general protection fault is the most common error in Windows. It happens when a program accesses memory that another program is using or when a program accesses a memory address that doesn't exist. Generally, GPFs are the result of sloppy programming; they can often be fixed by clearing the memory with a reboot.

12. C. *Illegal operation* is the Windows error message displayed when a program is forced to quit because it did something Windows didn't like. The error's details include which module experienced the problem, the memory location being accessed at the time, and the registers and flags of the processor at the time of the error.

13. A. The information detected by NTDETECT.COM is used to create dynamic hardware information in the Registry.

14. D. Pressing F8 during the first phase of the boot process brings up the Advanced Startup Options menu in Windows 2000/XP.

15. E. Last Known Good Configuration enables you to restore the system to a prior, functional state if a change was made to the Registry that turned out to be problematic.

16. B. The Backup utility lets you create an ERD in Windows 2000.

17. C. Windows Update is responsible for finding updates, patches, and service packs, downloading them, and installing them on your computer.

18. A. Windows XP automatically creates restore points, which are copies of your system configuration. You can also create them manually through the System Restore utility.

19. D. HAL, or the Hardware Abstraction Layer, is the translator between the hardware and the operating system.

20. B. Task Manager will show you a list of running processes and applications and allow you to close applications that are not responsive (or even ones that are running normally). The easiest way to open Task Manager is to press Ctrl+Alt+Del in Windows.

Understanding the Basics of Printers and Scanners

THE FOLLOWING COMPTIA A+ ESSENTIALS EXAM OBJECTIVES ARE COVERED IN THIS CHAPTER:

✓ **4.1 Identify the fundamental principles of using printers and scanners**

- Identify differences between types of printer and scanner technologies (e.g. laser, inkjet, thermal, solid ink, impact)

- Identify names, purposes and characteristics of printer and scanner components (e.g. memory, driver, firmware) and consumables (e.g. toner, ink cartridge, paper)

- Identify the names, purposes and characteristics of interfaces used by printers and scanners including port and cable types for example:

  - Parallel
  - Network (e.g. NIC, print servers)
  - USB
  - Serial
  - IEEE 1394 / firewire
  - Wireless (e.g. Bluetooth, 802.11, infrared)
  - SCSI

✓ **4.2 Identify basic concepts of installing, configuring, optimizing and upgrading printers and scanners**

- Install and configure printers / scanners

  - Power and connect the device using local or network port

  - Install and update device driver and calibrate the device

- Configure options and default settings
- Print a test page

- Optimize printer performance for example, printer settings such as tray switching, print spool settings, device calibration, media types and paper orientation

✓ **4.3 Identify tools, basic diagnostic procedures and troubleshooting techniques for printers and scanners**

- Gather information about printer / scanner problems
  - Identify symptom
  - Review device error codes, computer error messages and history (e.g. event log, user reports)
  - Print or scan test page
  - Use appropriate generic or vendor-specific diagnostic tools including web-based utilities

- Review and analyze collected data
  - Establish probable causes
  - Review service documentation
  - Review knowledge base and define and isolate the problem (e.g. software vs. hardware, driver, connectivity, printer)

- Identify solutions to identified printer / scanner problems
  - Define specific cause and apply fix
  - Replace consumables as needed
  - Verify functionality and get user acceptance of problem fix

Let's face it. Our society is dependent on paper. When we conduct business, we use different types of paper documents. Contracts, letters, and, of course, money are all used to conduct business. As more and more of those documents are created on computers, printers will become increasingly important.

Printers are electromechanical output devices that are used to put information from the computer onto paper. They have been around since the introduction of the computer. Other than the display monitor, the printer is the most popular peripheral purchased for a computer, because most people need to have paper copies of the documents they create.

Scanners are electromechanical devices used to convert text and illustrations on paper into electronic form. Any form of paper, like documents, photographs, receipts, and so on can be scanned into a computer and converted into electronic form. Think of it like this: a printer takes data from the computer and turns it into paper form. A scanner takes paper and turns it into data.

In this chapter, we will discuss the details of each major type of printer, including impact printers, ink printers, and laser (page) printers, as well as the different types of scanners (including flatbed, sheet-fed, and handheld). We'll also talk about printer and scanner interfaces and the supplies used for printers. Finally, we'll go over some of the problems that arise during printer use and how to troubleshoot them.

Take special note of the section on laser and page printers. The A+ exams test these subjects in detail, so we'll cover them in just as much depth.

Understanding Printer and Scanner Fundamentals

There are several different types of printers and scanners available on the market today. In this section, you will learn about the different types of printers and scanners that you will see as a technician, their basic components, and how they function. In this section you will learn about

- Impact printers
- Bubble-jet printers
- Laser printers (page printers)
- Other printers

- Printer interfaces and supplies
- Scanners and their components
- Flatbed scanners
- Sheet-fed scanners
- Handheld scanners
- Scanner interfaces

Impact Printers

The most basic type of printer is the category known as *impact printers*. Impact printers, as their name suggests, use some form of impact and an inked ribbon to make an imprint on the paper. In a manner of speaking, typewriters are like impact printers. Both use an inked ribbon and an impact head to make letters on the paper. The major difference is that the printer can accept input from a computer.

There are two major types of impact printers: daisy wheel and dot matrix. Each type has its own service and maintenance issues.

Daisy-Wheel Printers

Although they aren't really covered on the A+ exam, the first type of impact printer we're going to discuss is the *daisy-wheel printer*. These printers contain a wheel (called the *daisy wheel* because it looks like a daisy) with raised letters and symbols on each "petal" (see Figure 7.1). When the printer needs to print a character, it sends a signal to the mechanism that contains the wheel. This mechanism is called the *printhead*. The printhead rotates the daisy wheel until the required character is in place. An electromechanical hammer (called a *solenoid*) then strikes the back of the petal containing the character. The character pushes up against an inked ribbon that ultimately strikes the paper, making the impression of the requested character.

FIGURE 7.1   A daisy-wheel printer mechanism

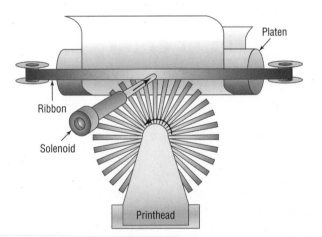

Daisy-wheel printers were one of the first types of impact printer developed. Their speed is rated by the number of *characters per second (cps)* they can print. The early printers could only print between two and four characters per second. Aside from their poor speed, the main disadvantage to this type of printer is that it makes a lot of noise when printing—so much, in fact, that special enclosures were developed to contain the noise.

The daisy-wheel printer has a few advantages, of course. First, because it is an impact printer, you can print on multipart forms (like carbonless receipts), assuming they can be fed into the printer properly. Second, it is relatively inexpensive compared to the price of a laser printer of the same vintage. Finally, the print quality is comparable to that of a typewriter because it uses a very similar technology. This typewriter level of quality was given a name: *letter quality (LQ)*.

Dot-Matrix Printers

The other type of impact printer we'll discuss is the *dot-matrix printer*. These printers work in a manner similar to daisy-wheel printers, but instead of a spinning, character-imprinted wheel, the printhead contains a row of *pins* (short, sturdy stalks of hard wire). These pins are triggered in patterns that form letters and numbers as the printhead moves across the paper (see Figure 7.2).

FIGURE 7.2   Formation of images in a dot-matrix printer

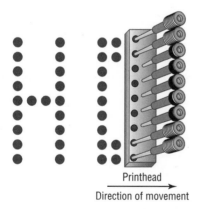

Printhead

Direction of movement

The pins in the printhead are wrapped with coils of wire to create a solenoid and are held in the rest position by a combination of a small magnet and a spring. To trigger a particular pin, the printer controller sends a signal to the printhead, which energizes the wires around the appropriate print wire. This turns the print wire into an electromagnet, which repels the print pin, forcing it against the ink ribbon and making a dot on the paper. The arrangement of the dots in columns and rows creates the letters and numbers you see on the page. Figure 7.2 shows this process.

The main disadvantage of dot-matrix printers is their image quality, which can be quite poor compared to the quality produced with a daisy wheel. Dot-matrix printers use patterns of dots to make letters and images, and the early dot-matrix printers used only nine pins to make those patterns. The output quality of such printers is referred to as *draft quality*—good mainly for providing your initial text to a correspondent or reviser. Each letter looked fuzzy because the dots were spaced as far as they could be and still be perceived as a letter or image. As more pins were crammed into the printhead (17-pin and 24-pin models were eventually developed), the quality increased because the dots were closer together. Dot-matrix technology ultimately improved to the point that a letter printed on a dot-matrix printer was *almost* indistinguishable from typewriter output. This level of quality is known as *near letter quality (NLQ)*.

Dot-matrix printers are noisy, but the print wires and printhead are covered by a plastic dust cover, making them quieter than daisy-wheel printers. They also use a more efficient printing technology, so the print speed is faster (typically in the range of 36 to 72cps). Some dot-matrix printers (like the Epson DFX series) can print at close to a page per second! Finally, because dot-matrix printers are also impact printers, they can use multipart forms. Because of these advantages, dot-matrix printers quickly made daisy-wheel printers obsolete.

Bubble-Jet Printers

The next category of printer technology is one of the most popular in use today. This category is actually an advanced form of an older technology known as *inkjet printers*. Both types of printers spray ink on the page, but inkjet printers used a reservoir of ink, a pump, and an ink nozzle to accomplish this. They were messy, noisy, and inefficient. Bubble-jet printers work much more efficiently and are much cheaper.

In a *bubble-jet printer,* bubbles of ink are sprayed onto a page and form patterns that resemble the items being printed. In this section, you will learn the parts of a bubble-jet printer, as well as how bubble-jet printers work.

Parts of a Typical Bubble-Jet Printer

Bubble-jet printers are simple devices. They contain very few parts (even fewer than dot-matrix printers) and, as such, are inexpensive to manufacture. It's common today to have a $99 bubble-jet printer with print quality that rivals that of basic laser printers.

In this section, you will learn the parts of a typical bubble-jet printer and what they do. The printer parts can be divided into the following categories:

- Printhead/ink cartridge
- Head carriage, belt, and stepper motor
- Paper-feed mechanism
- Control, interface, and power circuitry

Printhead/Ink Cartridge

The first part of a bubble-jet printer is the one people see the most: the *printhead*. This part of a printer contains many small nozzles (usually 100–200) that spray the ink in small dots onto the page. Many times the printhead is part of the *ink cartridge*, which contains a reservoir of ink and the printhead in a removable package. Color bubble-jet printers include multiple printheads, one for each of the *CMYK* print inks (cyan, magenta, yellow, and black).

Every bubble-jet printer works in a similar fashion. As we just mentioned, each bubble-jet printer contains a special part called an ink cartridge (see Figure 7.3) that contains the printhead and ink supply (although some printers separate them so they can be replaced separately). The print cartridge must be replaced as the ink supply runs out.

FIGURE 7.3   A typical ink cartridge (size: approximately 3 inches by ½ inches)

Inside the ink cartridge are several small chambers. At the top of each chamber are a metal plate and a tube leading to the ink supply. At the bottom of each chamber is a small pinhole. These pinholes are used to spray ink on the page to form characters and images as patterns of dots (similar to the way a dot-matrix printer works but with much higher resolution).

There are two methods of spraying the ink out of the cartridge. The first was developed by Hewlett-Packard (HP): When a particular chamber needs to spray ink, an electric signal is sent to the heating element, energizing it. The elements heat up quickly, causing the ink to vaporize. Because of the expanding ink vapor, the ink is pushed out the pinhole and forms a bubble. As the vapor expands, the bubble eventually gets large enough to break off into a droplet. The rest of the ink is pulled back into the chamber by the surface tension of the ink. When another drop needs to be sprayed, the process begins again. The second method, developed by Epson, uses a piezoelectric element that flexes when energized. The outward flex pushes the ink from the nozzle; on the return, it sucks more ink from the reservoir.

When the printer is done printing, the printhead moves back to its maintenance station. The *maintenance station* contains a small suction pump and ink-absorbing pad. To keep the ink flowing freely, before each print cycle the maintenance station pulls ink through the ink nozzles using vacuum suction. This expelled ink is absorbed by the pad. The station serves two functions: to provide a place for the printhead to rest when the printer isn't printing and to keep the printhead in working order.

Head Carriage, Belt, and Stepper Motor

Another major component of the bubble-jet printer is the head carriage and the associated parts that make it move. The *printhead carriage* is the component of a bubble-jet printer that moves back and forth during printing. It contains the physical as well as electronic connections for the printhead and (in some cases) the ink reservoir. Figure 7.4 shows an example of a head carriage. Note the clips that keep the ink cartridge in place and the electronic connections for the ink cartridge. These connections cause the nozzles to fire, and if they aren't kept clean, you may have printing problems.

The stepper motor and belt make the printhead carriage move. A *stepper motor* is a precisely made electric motor that can move in the same very small increments each time it is activated. That way, it can move to the same position(s) time after time. The motor that makes the printhead carriage move is most often called the *carriage motor* or *carriage stepper motor*. Figure 7.5 shows an example of a stepper motor.

FIGURE 7.4 A printhead carriage in a bubble-jet printer

FIGURE 7.5 A carriage stepper motor

In addition to the motor, a belt is placed around two small wheels or pulleys and attached to the printhead carriage. This belt, called the *carriage belt*, is driven by the carriage motor and moves the printhead back and forth across the page while it prints. To keep the printhead carriage aligned and stable while it traverses the page, the carriage rests on a small metal *stabilizer bar*. Figure 7.6 shows the stabilizer bar, carriage belt, and pulleys.

Paper-Feed Mechanism

In addition to getting the ink onto the paper, the printer must have a way to get the paper into the printer. That's where the paper-feed mechanism comes in. The *paper-feed mechanism* picks up paper from the paper drawer and feeds it into the printer. This assembly consists of several smaller assemblies. First are the *pickup rollers* (Figure 7.7), which are several rubber rollers with a slightly flat spot; they rub against the paper as they rotate, and feed the paper into the printer. They work against small cork or rubber patches known as *separator pads* (Figure 7.8), which help keep the rest of the paper in place (so only one sheet goes into the printer). The pickup rollers are turned on a shaft by the *pickup stepper motor*.

Sometimes the paper that is fed into a bubble-jet printer is placed into a *paper tray*, which is simply a small plastic tray in the front of the printer that holds the paper until it is fed into the printer by the paper-feed mechanism. On smaller printers, the paper is placed vertically into a *paper feeder* at the back of the printer; it uses gravity, in combination with feed rollers and separator pads, to get the paper into the printer. No real rhyme or reason dictates which manufacturers use these different parts; some models use them, and some don't. Generally, more expensive printers use paper trays, because they hold more paper. Figure 7.9 shows an example of a paper tray on a bubble-jet printer.

FIGURE 7.6 Stabilizer bar, carriage belt, and pulleys in a bubble-jet printer

FIGURE 7.7   Bubble-jet pickup rollers

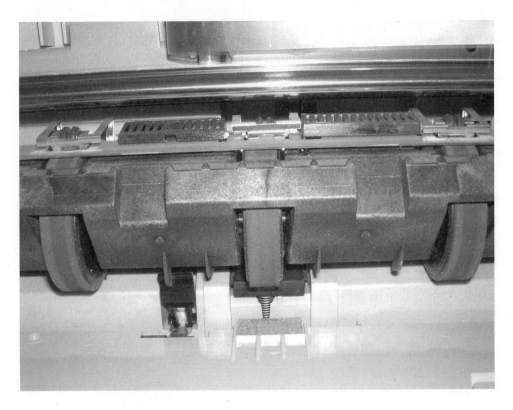

FIGURE 7.8   Bubble-jet separator pads

The final part of the paper-feed mechanism is the *paper-feed sensors*. These components tell the printer when it is out of paper, as well as when a paper jam has occurred during the paper-feed process. Figure 7.10 shows an example of a paper-feed sensor.

FIGURE 7.9   A paper tray on a bubble-jet printer

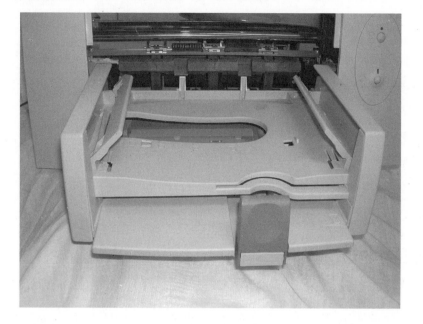

FIGURE 7.10   A paper-feed sensor on a bubble-jet printer

Identifying the Parts of a Bubble-jet Printer

Being able to identify the parts of a bubble-jet printer is an important skill for an A+ candidate. For this exercise, you'll need a bubble-jet printer.

1.   Unplug the bubble-jet printer from power and the computer.

2.   Open the top cover to expose the inner print mechanism.

3.   Locate and identify the paper tray.

4.   Locate and identify the paper-feed sensor.

5.   Locate and identify the pickup roller(s).

6.   Locate and identify the separator pad(s).

7.   Locate and identify the printhead and carriage assembly.

Control, Interface, and Power Circuitry

The final component group is the electronic circuitry for printer control, printer interfaces, and printer power. The *printer control circuits* are usually on a small circuit board that contains all the circuitry to run the stepper motors the way the printer needs them to work (back and forth, load paper and then stop, and so on). These circuits are also responsible for monitoring the health of the printer and reporting that information back to the PC.

Next, the interface circuitry (commonly called a *port*) not only makes the physical connection to whatever signal is coming from the computer (parallel, serial, SCSI, network, infrared, and so on) but also connects the interface to the control circuitry. The interface circuitry converts the signals from the interface into the datastream that the printer uses.

The last set of circuits the printer uses is the *power circuits*. Essentially, these conductive pathways convert 110V or 220V house current into the voltages the bubble-jet printer uses (usually 12V and 5V) and distribute those voltages to the other printer circuits and devices that need it. This is accomplished through the use of a transformer. A transformer, in this case, takes the 110V AC current and changes it to 12V DC (among others). This transformer can be either internal (incorporated into the body of the printer) or external. Today's bubble-jets can use either design, although the integrated design is preferred because it is simpler and doesn't show the bulky transformer.

The Bubble-Jet Printing Process

Just as with other types of printing, the bubble-jet printing process consists of a set of steps the printer must follow in order to put the data onto the page being printed. The following steps happen whenever you click the Print button in your favorite software (like Microsoft Word or Internet Explorer):

1. You click the Print button (or similar) that initiates the printing process.

2. The software you are printing from sends the data to be printed to the printer driver you have selected.

The function and use of the printer driver are discussed later in this chapter.

3. The printer driver uses a page-description language to convert the data being printed into the proper format that the printer can understand. The driver also ensures that the printer is ready to print.

4. The printer driver sends the information to the printer via whatever connection method is being used (parallel, USB, network, and so on).

5. The printer stores the received data in its onboard *print buffer* memory. A print buffer is a small amount of memory (typically 512KB to 16MB) used to store print jobs as they are received from the printing computer. This buffer allows several jobs to be printed at once and helps printing to be completed quickly.

6. If the printer has not printed in a while, the printer's control circuits activate a cleaning cycle. A *cleaning cycle* is a set of steps the bubble-jet printer goes through in order to purge the printheads of any dried ink. It uses a special suction cup and sucking action to pull ink through the printhead, dislodging any dried ink or clearing stuck passageways.

7. Once the printer is ready to print, the control circuitry activates the paper-feed motor. This causes a sheet of paper to be fed into the printer until the paper activates the paper-feed sensor, which stops the feed until the printhead is in the right position and the leading edge of the paper is under the printhead. If the paper doesn't reach the paper-feed sensor in a specified amount of time after the stepper motor has been activated, the Out of Paper light is turned on and a message is sent to the computer.

8. Once the paper is positioned properly, the printhead stepper motor uses the printhead belt and carriage to move the printhead across the page, little by little. The motor is moved one small step, and the printhead sprays the dots of ink on the paper in the pattern dictated by the control circuitry. Typically, this is either a pattern of black dots or a pattern of *cyan, magenta, yellow, and black (CMYK)* inks that are mixed to make colors. Then the stepper motor moves the printhead another small step; the process repeats all the way across the page. This process is so quick, however, that the entire motion of starts and stops across the page looks like one smooth motion.

9. At the end of a pass across the page, the paper-feed stepper motor advances the page a small amount. Then the printhead repeats step 8. Depending on the model, the printhead either returns to the beginning of the line and prints again in the same direction only, or it moves backward across the page so that printing occurs in both directions. This process continues until the page is finished.

10. Once the page is finished, the feed-stepper motor is actuated and ejects the page from the printer into the output tray. If more pages need to print, printing the next page begins again at step 7.

11. Once printing is complete and the final page has been ejected from the printer, the print-head is *parked* (locked into rest position) and the print process is finished.

Laser Printers

Laser printers and inkjet printers are referred to as *page printers* because they receive their print job instructions one page at a time (rather than receiving instructions one line at a time). There are two major types of page printers: those that use the electrophotographic (EP) print process and those that use the light-emitting diode (LED) print process. Each works in basically the same way, with slight differences.

Electrophotographic (EP) Laser Printers

Xerox, Hewlett-Packard, and Canon were pioneers in developing the laser printer technology we use today. Scientists at Xerox developed the electrophotographic (EP) process in 1971. The first successful desktop laser printer was introduced by HP in 1984 using Canon hardware that used the EP process. This technology uses a combination of static electric charges, laser light, and a black powdery substance called *toner*. Printers that use this technology are called EP process laser printers, or just *laser printers*. Every laser printer technology has its foundations in the EP printer process.

Let's discuss the basic components of the EP laser printer and how they operate so you can understand the way an EP laser printer works.

Basic Components

Most printers that use the EP process contain eight standard assemblies: the toner cartridge, laser scanner, high-voltage power supply, DC power supply, paper transport assembly (including paper-pickup rollers and paper-registration rollers), transfer corona, fusing assembly, printer controller circuitry, and ozone filter. Let's discuss each of the components individually before we examine how they all work together to make the printer function.

THE TONER CARTRIDGE

The EP toner cartridge (Figure 7.11), as its name suggests, holds the toner. Toner is a black carbon substance mixed with polyester resins (to make it flow better) and iron oxide particles (to make the toner sensitive to electrical charges). These two components make the toner capable of being attracted to the photosensitive drum and of melting into the paper. In addition to these components, toner contains a medium called the *developer* (also called the *carrier*), which carries the toner until it is used by the EP process. The toner cartridge also contains the EP print drum. This drum is coated with a photosensitive material that can hold a static charge when not exposed to light (but *cannot* hold a charge when it *is* exposed to light—a curious phenomenon and one that EP printers exploit for the purpose of making images). Finally, the drum contains a cleaning blade that continuously scrapes the used toner off the photosensitive drum to keep it clean.

FIGURE 7.11   An EP toner cartridge

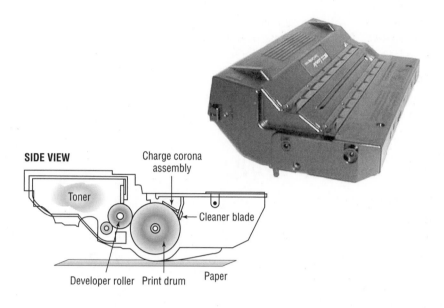

SIDE VIEW   Charge corona
                        assembly

Toner

— Cleaner blade

Developer roller   Print drum   Paper

 In most laser printers, *toner cartridge* means an EP toner cartridge that contains toner and a photosensitive drum in one plastic case. In some laser printers, however, the toner and photosensitive drum can be replaced separately instead of as a single unit. If you ask for a toner cartridge for one of these printers, all you will receive is a cylinder full of toner. Consult the printer's manual to find out which kind of toner cartridge your laser printer uses.

THE LASER SCANNING ASSEMBLY

As we mentioned earlier, the EP photosensitive drum can hold a charge if it's not exposed to light. It is dark inside an EP printer, except when the laser scanning assembly shines on particular areas of the photosensitive drum. When it does that, the drum discharges, but only in that area. As the drum rotates, the laser scanning assembly scans the laser across the photosensitive drum. Figure 7.12 shows the laser scanning assembly.

Laser light is damaging to human eyes. Therefore, the laser is kept in an enclosure and will operate only when the laser printer's cover is closed.

HIGH-VOLTAGE POWER SUPPLY (HVPS)

The EP process requires high-voltage electricity. The high-voltage power supply (HVPS) provides the high voltages used during the EP process. This component converts house AC current (120V, and 60Hz) into higher voltages that the printer can use. This high voltage is used to energize both the charging corona and the transfer corona.

FIGURE 7.12 The EP laser scanning assembly (side view and simplified top view)

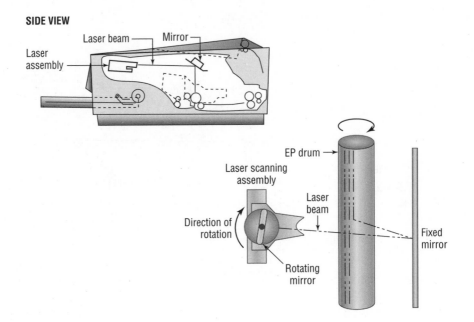

DC POWER SUPPLY (DCPS)

The high voltages used in the EP process can't power the other components in the printer (the logic circuitry and motors). These components require low voltages, between +5 and +24VDC. The DC power supply (DCPS) converts house current into three voltages: +5VDC and −5VDC for the logic circuitry and +24VDC for the paper-transport motors. This component also runs the fan that cools the internal components of the printer.

PAPER-TRANSPORT ASSEMBLY

The paper-transport assembly is responsible for moving the paper through the printer. It consists of a motor and several rubberized rollers that each performs a different function.

The first type of roller found in most laser printers is the *feed roller*, or *paper-pickup roller* (Figure 7.13). This D-shaped roller, when activated, rotates against the paper and pushes one sheet into the printer. This roller works in conjunction with a special rubber separator pad to prevent more than one sheet from being fed into the printer at a time.

Another type of roller that is used in the printer is the *registration roller* (also shown in Figure 7.13). There are actually two registration rollers, which work together. These rollers synchronize the paper movement with the image-formation process in the EP cartridge. The rollers don't feed the paper past the EP cartridge until the cartridge is ready for it.

Both of these rollers are operated with a special electric motor known as an *electronic stepper motor*. This type of motor can accurately move in very small increments. It powers all the paper-transport rollers as well as the fuser rollers.

FIGURE 7.13   Paper-transport rollers

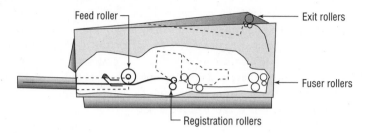

THE TRANSFER CORONA ASSEMBLY

When the laser writes the images on the photosensitive drum, the toner then sticks to the exposed areas; we'll cover this in the next section, "Electrophotographic (EP) Print Process." How does the toner get from the photosensitive drum onto the paper? The *transfer corona assembly* (Figure 7.14) is given a high-voltage charge, which is transferred to the paper which pulls the toner from the photosensitive drum.

Included in the transfer corona assembly is a *static-charge eliminator strip* that drains away the charge imparted to the paper by the corona. If you didn't drain away the charge, the paper would stick to the EP cartridge and jam the printer.

There are two types of transfer corona assemblies: those that contain a transfer *corona wire* and those that contain a transfer *corona roller*. The transfer corona wire is a small-diameter wire that is charged by the HVPS. The wire is located in a special notch in the floor of the laser printer (under the EP print cartridge). The transfer corona roller performs the same function as the transfer corona wire, but it's a roller rather than a wire. Because the transfer corona roller is directly in contact with the paper, it supports higher speeds. For this reason, the transfer corona wire is no longer used much in laser printers.

FIGURE 7.14   The transfer corona assembly

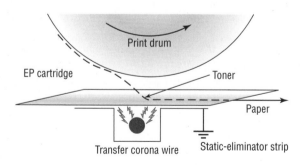

FUSING ASSEMBLY

The toner in the EP toner cartridge will stick to just about anything, including paper. This is true because the toner has a negative static charge and most objects have a net positive charge. However, these toner particles can be removed by brushing any object across the page. This could be a problem if you want the images and letters to stay on the paper permanently!

To solve this problem, EP laser printers incorporate a device known as a *fuser* (Figure 7.15), which uses two rollers that apply pressure and heat to fuse the plastic toner particles to the paper. You may have noticed that pages from either a laser printer or a copier (which uses a similar device) come out warm. This is because of the fuser.

FIGURE 7.15   The fuser

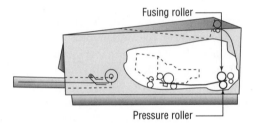

The fuser is made up of three main parts: a halogen heating lamp, a Teflon-coated aluminum fusing roller, and a rubberized pressure roller. The fuser uses the halogen lamp to heat the fusing roller to between 329° F (165° C) and 356° F (180° C). As the paper passes between the two rollers, the pressure roller pushes the paper against the fusing roller, which melts the toner into the paper.

PRINTER CONTROLLER CIRCUITRY

The final component in the laser printer we need to discuss is the *printer controller assembly*. This large circuit board converts signals from the computer into signals for the various assemblies in the laser printer, using a process known as *rasterizing*. This circuit board is usually mounted under the printer. The board has connectors for each type of interface and cables to each assembly.

When a computer prints to a laser printer, it sends a signal through a cable to the printer controller assembly. The controller assembly formats the information into a page's worth of line-by-line commands for the laser scanner. The controller sends commands to each of the components, telling them to wake up and begin the EP print process.

OZONE FILTER

Your laser printer uses various high-voltage biases inside the case. As anyone who has been outside during a lightning storm can tell you, high voltages create ozone. Ozone is a chemically reactive gas that is created by the high-voltage coronas (charging and transfer) inside the printer. Because ozone is chemically reactive and can severely reduce the life of laser printer components, most laser printers contain a filter to remove ozone gas from inside the printer as it is produced. This filter must be removed and cleaned with compressed air periodically (cleaning it whenever the toner cartridge is replaced is usually sufficient). Many newer laser printers don't have ozone filters. This is because these printers don't use transfer corona wires but instead use transfer corona rollers, which dramatically reduce ozone emissions.

Electrophotographic (EP) Print Process

The *EP print process* is the process by which an EP laser printer forms images on paper. It consists of six major steps, each for a specific goal. Although many different manufacturers call these steps different things or place them in a different order, the basic process is still the same. Here are the steps in the order you will see them on the exam:

1. Cleaning
2. Charging
3. Writing
4. Developing
5. Transferring
6. Fusing

 To help you remember the steps of the EP print process in order, learn the first letter of each step: CCWDTF. The most often used mnemonic sentence for this combination of letters is "Charlie Can Walk, Dance, and Talk French."

Before any of these steps can begin, however, the controller must sense that the printer is ready to start printing (toner cartridge installed, fuser warmed to temperature, and all covers in place). Printing cannot take place until the printer is in its ready state, usually indicated by an illuminated Ready LED light or a display that says something like 00 READY (on HP printers).

STEP 1: CLEANING

In the first part of the laser print process, a rubber blade inside the EP cartridge scrapes any toner left on the drum into a used toner receptacle inside the EP cartridge, and a fluorescent lamp discharges any remaining charge on the photosensitive drum (remember that the drum, being photosensitive, loses its charge when exposed to light). This step is called the *cleaning step* (Figure 7.16).

FIGURE 7.16 The cleaning step of the EP process

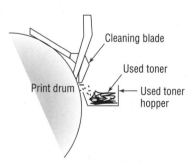

The EP cartridge is constantly cleaning the drum. It may take more than one rotation of the photosensitive drum to make an image on the paper. The cleaning step keeps the drum fresh for each use. If you didn't clean the drum, you would see ghosts of previous pages printed along with your image.

 The amount of toner removed in the cleaning process is quite small. The cartridge will run out of toner before the used toner receptacle fills up.

STEP 2: CHARGING

The next step in the EP process is the *charging step* (Figure 7.17). In this step, a special wire or roller (called a *charging corona*) within the EP toner cartridge (above the photosensitive drum) gets a high voltage from the HVPS. It uses this high voltage to apply a strong, uniform negative charge (around −600VDC) to the surface of the photosensitive drum.

STEP 3: WRITING

Next is the *writing step*. In this step, the laser is turned on and scans the drum from side to side, flashing on and off according to the bits of information the printer controller sends it as it communicates the individual bits of the image. Wherever the laser beam touches, the photosensitive drum's charge is severely reduced from −600VDC to a slight negative charge (around −100VDC). As the drum rotates, a pattern of exposed areas is formed, representing the image to be printed. Figure 7.18 shows this process.

At this point, the controller sends a signal to the pickup roller to feed a piece of paper into the printer, where it stops at the registration rollers.

STEP 4: DEVELOPING

Now that the surface of the drum holds an electrical representation of the image being printed, its discrete electrical charges need to be converted into something that can be transferred to a piece of paper. The EP process step that accomplishes this is the *developing step* (Figure 7.19). In this step, toner is transferred to the areas that were exposed in the writing step.

FIGURE 7.17   The charging step of the EP process

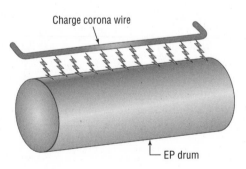

Charge corona wire

EP drum

FIGURE 7.18   The writing step of the EP process

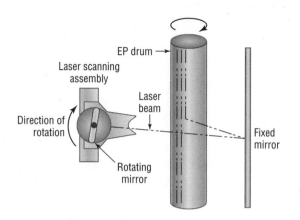

FIGURE 7.19   The developing step of the EP process

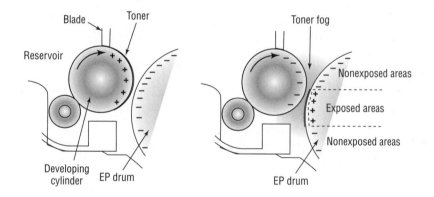

A metallic roller called the *developing roller* inside an EP cartridge acquires a –600VDC charge (called a *bias voltage*) from the HVPS. The toner sticks to this roller because there is a magnet located inside the roller and because of the electrostatic charges between the toner and the developing roller. While the developing roller rotates toward the photosensitive drum, the toner acquires the charge of the roller (–600VDC). When the toner comes between the developing roller and the photosensitive drum, the toner is attracted to the areas that have been exposed by the laser (because these areas have a lesser charge, of –100VDC). The toner also is repelled from the unexposed areas (because they are at the same –600VDC charge, and like charges repel). This toner transfer creates a fog of toner between the EP drum and the developing roller.

The photosensitive drum now has toner stuck to it where the laser has written. The photosensitive drum continues to rotate until the developed image is ready to be transferred to paper in the next step.

STEP 5: TRANSFERRING

At this point in the EP process, the developed image is rotating into position. The controller notifies the registration rollers that the paper should be fed through. The registration rollers move the paper underneath the photosensitive drum, and the process of transferring the image can begin, with the *transferring step*.

The controller sends a signal to the charging corona wire or roller (depending on which one the printer has) and tells it to turn on. The corona wire/roller then acquires a strong *positive* charge (+600VDC) and applies that charge to the paper. The paper, thus charged, pulls the toner from the photosensitive drum at the line of contact between the roller and the paper, because the paper and toner have opposite charges. Once the registration rollers move the paper past the corona wire, the static-eliminator strip removes all charge from that line of the paper. Figure 7.20 details this step. If the strip didn't bleed this charge away, the paper would attract itself to the toner cartridge and cause a paper jam.

The toner is now held in place by weak electrostatic charges and gravity. It will not stay there, however, unless it is made permanent, which is the reason for the fusing step.

STEP 6: FUSING

In the final step, the *fusing step*, the toner image is made permanent. The registration rollers push the paper toward the fuser rollers. Once the fuser grabs the paper, the registration rollers push for only a short time more. The fuser is now in control of moving the paper.

As the paper passes through the fuser, the 350° F fuser roller melts the polyester resin of the toner, and the rubberized pressure roller presses it permanently into the paper (Figure 7.21). The paper continues on through the fuser and eventually exits the printer.

FIGURE 7.20   The transferring step of the EP process

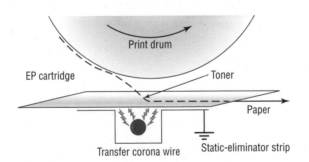

FIGURE 7.21   The fusing step of the EP process

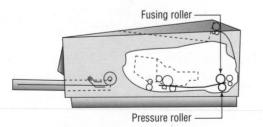

Once the paper completely exits the fuser, it trips a sensor that tells the printer to finish the EP process with the cleaning step. At this point, the printer can print another page, and the EP process can begin again.

SUMMARY OF THE EP PRINT PROCESS

Figure 7.22 summarizes all the EP process printing steps. First, the printer uses a rubber scraper to clean the photosensitive drum. Then the printer places a uniform –600VDC charge on the photosensitive drum by means of a charging corona. The laser "paints" an image onto the photosensitive drum, discharging the image areas to a much lower voltage (–100VDC). The developing roller in the toner cartridge has charged (–600VDC) toner stuck to it. As it rolls the toner toward the photosensitive drum, the toner is attracted to (and sticks to) the areas of the photosensitive drum that the laser has discharged. The image is then transferred from the drum to the paper at its line of contact by means of the transfer corona wire (or corona roller) with a +600VDC charge. The static-eliminator strip removes the high, positive charge from the paper, and the paper, now holding the image, moves on. The paper then enters the fuser, where a fuser roller and the pressure roller make the image permanent. The paper exits the printer, and the printer begins printing the next page or returns to its ready state.

FIGURE 7.22   The EP print process

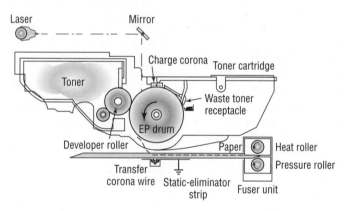

LED Page Printers

Now we'll discuss another laser printer: the light-emitting diode (LED) page printer. This technology is primarily developed and used by Okidata and Panasonic. Because the A+ exam does not currently cover LED page printers, we will discuss only the differences between them and laser printers.

The two main differences between a LED page printer and a laser printer are the toner cartridges and the print process.

LED Page Printer Toner Cartridges

One problem with laser printers is that the toner usually runs out before the photosensitive drum needs to be replaced. But because they're usually both housed in the same replaceable unit, every time you replace the toner, you're also replacing the drum, whether it needs replacing or not. So the designers of LED page printers made the photosensitive drum and toner separate, replaceable items.

 The main parts of the LED page printer toner assembly are integrated into the printer. The charging corona (or roller) and erasing lamps are also integrated into the printer. The average user cannot replace these items; an authorized service technician must replace them.

When replacing the photosensitive drum, you swing the photosensitive drum/toner cartridge out of the printer first. Then you remove the drum from its carrier and install the new one (this also replaces the waste toner receptacle).

Filling the toner hopper is fairly easy. On most LED page printers, you place the new toner cartridge over the toner hopper and lock it in place. Between the new toner cartridge and the toner hopper are a lever and door. When you slide the lever over, it opens the door and allows the toner to fall through the opening. Once all the toner is out of the cartridge and hopper, you slide the lever back, closing the door. You can then remove the cartridge and throw it away.

The LED Page Printer Process

The LED page printer uses the same process as a laser printer, with one major exception. It uses a row of small light-emitting diodes held very close to the photosensitive drum to expose it. Each LED is about the same size as the diameter of the laser beam used in laser printers. These printers are basically the same as EP process printers, except that in the writing step, they use LEDs instead of a laser.

LED page printers offer several benefits over laser printers. First, because they use LEDs instead of lasers, LED page printers are much cheaper than similar laser printers—they're about half the cost. Also, because the LEDs are close to the drum, the whole printer is smaller—about two-thirds the size of a comparable laser printer. Finally, LEDs aren't as dangerous to the eye as lasers (you could probably damage your eyes if you stared at one long enough, but it's unlikely you'd do such a thing).

If they have so many advantages, why isn't everyone using them? Mainly because LED technology isn't as advanced as laser technology. The resolutions of LED page printers have yet to break the 800 dots-per-inch (dpi) mark. Another reason is that the toner system in an LED printer, although more efficient, is also messier. Because of its slight static charge, toner isn't easy to remove from surfaces.

 Never ship a printer anywhere with a toner cartridge installed! If the printer is a laser printer, remove the toner cartridge first. If it's an LED page printer, there is a method to remove the photosensitive drum and toner hopper (check your manual for details).

Other Types of Printers

The types of printers you have learned about so far in this chapter account for 90 percent of all printers used with home or office computers and that you will see as a repair technician. The other 10 percent consist of other types of printers that primarily differ by the method they use to put colored material on the paper to represent what is being printed.

The three other major types of printers in use today are as follows:

- Solid ink
- Thermal
- Dye sublimation

Keep in mind throughout this section that for the most part, these printers operate like other printers in many ways: They all have a paper-feed mechanism (sheet-fed or roll); they all require consumables; they all use the same interfaces, for the most part, as other types of printers; and they are usually about the same size.

Solid-Ink Printers

Solid-ink printers work much like bubble-jet printers: However, in a solid-ink printer, the ink is in a waxy solid form rather than in liquid form, which allows it to stay fresh and not cause problems like spillage. In addition, solid-ink printers usually print an entire line at one time, which makes them faster than bubble-jet printers. Because of the type of ink used, solid-ink printers are better for graphics companies that need true color at a price lower than a color laser printer.

Thermal Printers

You almost surely have seen a direct thermal printer. They can be found in many older fax machines (most newer ones use either inkjet or laser printing). They print on a kind of special, waxy paper that comes on a roll; the paper turns black when heat passes over it. *Thermal printers* work by using a printhead the width of the paper. When it needs to print, the printhead heats and cools spots on the printhead. The paper below the heated printhead turns black in those spots. As the paper moves through the printer, the pattern of blackened spots forms an image on the page of what is being printed. Another type of thermal printer uses a heat-sensitive ribbon instead of heat-sensitive paper. A thermal printhead melts wax-based ink from the ribbon onto the paper. These are called thermal transfer or thermal wax-transfer printers.

Thermal direct printers typically have long lives because they have few moving parts. However, the paper is somewhat expensive, doesn't last long (especially if it is left in a very warm place, like a closed car in summer), and produces poorer-quality images than most of the other printing technologies.

Dye-Sublimation Printers

The last type of printer you will learn about in this chapter is the *dye-sublimation printer*. These printers use sheets of solid ink that *sublimate*, or go from the solid phase directly to gas. During printing, a printhead passes over these sheets (one each of cyan, magenta, yellow, and gray for tonal change) inside the printer. As it passes over the page, spots on the printhead heat up, causing the ink under those spots to sublimate into gas. This gas then passes through the paper being printed, where the ink turns back into a solid, embedded into the paper. The print-head in most printers makes four passes, one for each color.

Dye-sublimation printers are used most often in the graphics or printing industries, because they really do only one thing well: photo-quality images. They take time to produce their images, but those images are of extremely high quality. It would expensive and impractical to use a dye-sublimation printer for word processing.

Printer Interfaces and Supplies

Besides understanding the printer's operation, for the A+ exam you need to understand how the printer talks to a computer and all the items involved in that process. You must also under-stand how the different types of print media affect the print process.

Interface Components

A printer's *interface* is the collection of hardware and software that allows the printer to com-municate with a computer. The hardware interface is commonly called a port. Each printer has at least one interface, but some printers have several, in order to make them more flexible in a multiplatform environment. If a printer has several interfaces, it can usually switch between them on the fly so that several computers can print at the same time.

An interface incorporates several components, including its communication type as well as the *interface software*. Each aspect must be matched on both the printer and the computer. For example, an HP LaserJet 4L has only a parallel port. Therefore, you must use a parallel cable as well as the correct software for the platform being used (for example, a Macintosh HP LaserJet 4L driver if you connect it to a Macintosh computer).

Communication Types

When we say *communication types*, we're talking about the ports used in getting the printed information from the computer to the printer. There are eight major types: serial, parallel, Uni-versal Serial Bus (USB), network, infrared, SCSI, IEEE 1394, and wireless. You've learned about these connections in earlier chapters, but now you will learn how they apply to printers

SERIAL

When computers send data serially, they send it one bit at a time, one after another. The bits stand in line like people at a movie theater, waiting to get in. Just as with modems, you must set the communication parameters (baud, parity, start and stop bits) on both entities—in this case, the computer and its printer(s)—before communication can take place.

PARALLEL

When a printer uses parallel communication, it is receiving data eight bits at a time over eight separate wires (one for each bit). Parallel communication was the most popular way of commu-nicating from computer to printer for many years, mainly because it's faster than serial.

A parallel cable consists of a male DB-25 connector that connects to the computer and a male 36-pin Centronics connector that connects to the printer. Most of the cables are less than 10 feet long. Parallel cables should be IEEE 1284-compliant.

WARNING
Keep printer cable lengths to less than 10 feet. Some people try to run printer cables more than 50 feet. If the length is greater than 10 feet, communications can become unreliable due to cross talk (described in Chapter 1).

UNIVERSAL SERIAL BUS (USB)

The most popular type of printer interface as this book is being written is the Universal Serial Bus (USB). In fact, it is the most popular interface for just about every peripheral. The convenience for printers is that it has a higher transfer rate than either serial or parallel and it automatically recognizes new devices.

NETWORK

Some of the newer printers (primarily laser and LED printers) have a special interface that allows them to be hooked directly to a network. These printers have a *network interface card (NIC)* and ROM-based software that allow them to communicate with networks, servers, and workstations.

The type of network interface used on the printer depends on the type of network to which the printer is being attached. For example, if you're using a Token Ring network, the printer should have a Token Ring interface.

INFRARED

With the explosion of personal digital assistants (PDAs), the need grew for printing under the constraints they provide. The biggest hurdle faced by PDA owners who need to print is the lack of any kind of universal interface. Most interfaces are too big and bulky to be used on handheld computers such as PDAs. The solution was to incorporate the standardized technology used on some remote controls: infrared transmissions. *Infrared transmissions* are simply wireless transmissions that use radiation in the infrared range of the electromagnetic spectrum. Many laser printers (and some computers) come with infrared transmitter/receivers (transceivers) so that they can communicate with the infrared ports on many handhelds. This allows the user of a PDA, handheld, or laptop to print to that printer by pointing the device at the printer and initiating the print process.

As far as configuring the interface is concerned, very little needs to be done. The infrared interfaces are enabled by default on most computers, handhelds, and printers equipped with them. The only additional item that must be configured is the print driver on the PDA, handheld, or computer. The driver must be the correct one for the printer to which you are printing.

SCSI

Only a few types of printers use SCSI interfaces to the PC, and most of them are laser printers, dye-sublimation printers, or typesetters. When these printers were introduced, they all came with an option for a SCSI interface. The benefits in these situations were as follows:

- There could be more than one device on a single SCSI connection through daisy chaining.
- It was fairly simple to implement.
- It had relatively large throughput compared to other interfaces of the time.

Because of the advent of higher-speed peripheral connection methods, like IEEE 1394/ FireWire and USB 2.0, SCSI interfaces for printers are rapidly becoming obsolete.

IEEE 1394 FIREWIRE

The IEEE 1394 interface (also known as *FireWire*—an Apple trademark) has had an explosion of popularity recently. As discussed in Chapter 1, this interface currently supports devices with a maximum throughput of 800MBps and is capable of speeds up to 3.2Gbps, so more and more devices that need to send a lot of data in a short period of time will use this interface. Printers used for tasks such as graphics and typesetting that need to receive hundreds of megabytes of camera-ready art and graphics have IEEE 1394 ports. Not many home printers use IEEE 1394, however, because it is an extra feature most people wouldn't use (and thus don't want to pay for). In addition, not every computer has an IEEE 1394 port (except for most Macintosh computers sold today).

WIRELESS

The latest boom in printer interface technology is wireless (of many different kinds). With the advent of IEEE 802.11 wireless networking, it is possible for people to roam around an office and still remain connected to one another and to their corporate network. So someone had the idea that it would be nice if printers could be that mobile as well (after all, many are on carts with wheels). Some printers either have built-in 802.11 interfaces or are hooked to 802.11 bridges with their built-in network cards.

Another wireless technology that has been gaining acceptance rapidly, especially among peripheral manufacturers, is *Bluetooth*. Bluetooth is a wireless technology that is used to replace the myriad of interface cables that run between your computer and all its peripherals. It's not meant to work over long distances (its absolute maximum range is 100 meters, and most devices are specified to work within 10 meters). Printers such as the HP 955c have Bluetooth capability.

When printing with a Bluetooth-enabled device (like a PDA or cell phone) and a Bluetooth-enabled printer, all you need to do is get within range of the device (that is, move closer), select the print driver from the device, and choose Print. The information is transmitted wirelessly through the air using radio waves and is received by the device.

For more information about the Bluetooth specification and its details, visit www.bluetooth.org.

Interface Software

Computers and printers can't talk to each other by themselves. They need interface software to translate software commands into commands the printer can understand.

There are two factors to consider with interface software: the page-description language and the driver software. The page-description language determines how efficient the printer is at converting the information to be printed into signals the printer can understand. The driver software understands and controls the printer. It is very important that you use the correct interface software for your printer. If you use either the wrong page-description language or the wrong driver software, the printer will print garbage—or possibly nothing at all.

PAGE-DESCRIPTION LANGUAGES

A *page-description language* works just as its name says it does. It describes the whole page being printed by sending commands that describe the text as well as the margins and other settings. The controller in the printer interprets these commands and turns them into laser pulses (or pin strikes).

Real World Scenario

Life without a Page-Description Language

The most basic page-description language is no page-description language. The computer sends all the instructions the printer needs in a serial stream, like so: Position 1, print nothing; Position 2, strike pins 1 and 3; Position 3, print nothing. This type of description language works great for dot-matrix printers, but it can be very inefficient for laser printers. For example, if you wanted to print a page using a standard page-description language and there was only one character on the page, there would be a lot of wasted signal for the "print nothing" commands.

With graphics, the commands to draw a shape on the page are relatively complex. For example, to draw a square, the computer (or printer) has to calculate the size of the square and convert that into lots of "strike pin *x*" (or "turn on laser") and "print nothing" commands. This is where the other types of page-description languages come into the picture.

The first page-description language was PostScript. Developed by Adobe, it was first used in the Apple LaserWriter printer. It made printing graphics fast and simple. Here's how PostScript works: The PostScript printer driver describes the page in terms of "draw" and "position" commands. The page is divided into a very fine grid (as fine as the resolution of the printer). When you want to print a square, a communication like the following takes place:

```
POSITION 1,42%DRAW 10%POSITION 1,64%DRAW10D%  . . .
```

These commands tell the printer to draw a line on the page from line 42 to line 64 (vertically). In other words, a page-description language tells the printer to draw a line on the page, gives it the starting and ending points, and that's that. Rather than send the printer the location of each and every dot in the line and an instruction at each and every location to print that location's individual dot, PostScript can get the line drawn with fewer than five instructions. As you can see, PostScript uses commands that are more or less in English. The commands are interpreted by the processor on the printer's controller and converted into the print-control signals.

Another page-description language is the Printer Control Language (PCL). Currently in revision 6 (PCL 6), it was developed by Hewlett-Packard for its LaserJet series of printers as a competitor to PostScript. PCL works in much the same manner as PostScript, but it's found mainly in HP printers (including the DeskJet bubble-jet printers). Other manufacturers use PCL, however. In fact, some printers support both page-description languages and will automatically switch between them.

The main advantage of page-description languages is that they move some of the processing from the computer to the printer. With text-only documents, they offer little benefit. However, with documents that have large amounts of graphics or that use numerous fonts, page-description languages make the processing of those print jobs happen much faster. This makes them an ideal choice for laser printers. However, other printers can use them as well (the aforementioned Desk-Jets, as well as some dot-matrix printers).

DRIVER SOFTWARE

The *driver software* controls how the printer processes the print job. When you install a printer driver for the printer you are using, it allows the computer to print to that printer correctly (assuming you have the correct interface configured between the computer and printer).

 Installation and configuration of printer drivers will be covered in Chapter 15.

When you need to print, you select the printer driver for your printer from a preconfigured list. The driver you select has been configured for the type, brand, and model of printer as well as the computer port to which it is connected. You can also select which paper tray the printer should use, as well as any other features the printer has (if applicable). Also, each printer driver is configured to use a particular page-description language.

 If the wrong printer driver is selected, the computer will send commands in the wrong language. If that occurs, the printer will print several pages full of garbage (even if only one page of information was sent). This "garbage" isn't garbage at all but the printer page-description language commands printed literally as text instead of being interpreted as control commands.

Printer Supplies

Just as it is important to use the correct printer interface and printer software, you must use the correct printer supplies. These supplies include the print media (what you print on) and the consumables (what you print with). The quality of the final print job has a great deal to do with the print supplies.

Print Media

The *print media* is what you put through the printer to print on. There are two major types of print media: paper and transparencies. Of the two types, paper is by far the most commonly used.

PAPER

Most people don't give much thought to the kind of paper they use in their printers. It's a factor that can have tremendous effect on the quality of the hard-copy printout, however, and the topic is more complex than people think. For example, if the wrong paper is used, it can cause the paper to jam frequently and possibly even damage components.

Several aspects of paper can be measured; each gives an indication as to the paper's quality. The first factor is *composition*. Paper is made from a variety of substances. Paper used to be made from cotton and was called *rag stock*. It can also be made from wood pulp, which is cheaper. Most paper today is made from the latter or a combination of the two.

Another aspect of paper is the property known as *basis weight* (or simply *weight* for short). The weight of a particular type of paper is the actual weight, in pounds (lb.), of 500 sheets of the standard (basic) size of that paper made of that material. For regular bond paper, that size is 17×22. The most common paper used in printers is 20 lb. bond paper. Manufacturers divide the standard size into four sheets, resulting in the 8.5×11 size we are all familiar with. So a ream of 500 sheets of 20 lb. bond paper weighs 5 pounds.

The final paper property we'll discuss is the *caliper* (or thickness) of an individual sheet of paper. If the paper is too thick, it may jam in feed mechanisms that have several curves in the paper path. (On the other hand, a paper that's too thin may not feed at all.)

These are just three of the categories we use to judge the quality of paper. Because there are so many different types and brands of printers as well as paper, it would be impossible to give the specifications for the "perfect" paper. However, the documentation for any printer will give specifications for the paper that should be used in that printer.

For best results with any printer, buy the paper that has been designated specifically for that printer by the manufacturer. It will be more expensive, but you'll have fewer problems related to having the wrong type of paper for the printer. The print quality will also be the best it can possibly be.

TRANSPARENCIES

Transparencies are still used for presentations made with overhead projectors, even with the explosion of programs like PowerPoint (from Microsoft) and peripherals like LCD computer displays, both of which let you show a whole roomful of people exactly what's on your computer screen. PowerPoint has an option to print slides, and you can also use any program to print to a transparent sheet of plastic or vinyl for use with an overhead projector. The problem is these "papers" are *exceedingly* difficult for printers to work with. That's why special transparencies were developed for use with laser and bubble-jet printers.

Each type of transparency was designed for a particular brand and model of printer. Again, check the printer's documentation to find out which type of transparency works in that printer. Don't use any other type of transparency!

Never run transparencies through a laser printer without first checking to see if it's the type recommended by the printer manufacturer. The heat from the fuser will melt most other transparencies, and they will wrap themselves around it. It is impossible to clean a fuser after this has happened. The fuser will have to be replaced. *Use only the transparencies that are recommended by the printer manufacturer.*

Print Consumables

Besides print media, other things in the printer run out and need to be replenished. These items are the *print consumables*. Most consumables are used to form the images on the print media. There are two main types of consumables in printers today: ink and toner. Toner is used primarily in laser printers; most other printers use ink.

INK

Ink is a liquid that is used to stain the paper. Printers use several different colors of ink, but the majority use some shade of black or blue. Both dot-matrix printers and bubble-jet printers use ink, but with different methods.

Dot-matrix printers use a cloth or polyester ribbon soaked in ink and coiled up inside a plastic case. This assembly is called a *printer ribbon* (or *ribbon cartridge*). It's very similar to a typewriter ribbon, but instead of being coiled into the two rolls you'd see on a typewriter, the ribbon is continuously coiled inside the plastic case. Once the ribbon has run out of ink, it must be discarded and replaced. Ribbon cartridges are developed closely with their respective printers. For this reason, ribbons should be purchased from the same manufacturer as the printer. The wrong ribbon could jam in the printer as well as cause quality problems.

It is possible to re-ink a ribbon. Some vendors sell a bottle of ink solution that can be poured into the plastic casing, where the cloth ribbon will soak up the solution.

Bubble-jet cartridges have a liquid ink reservoir. The ink in these cartridges is sealed inside. Once the ink runs out, the cartridge must be removed and discarded. A new, full one is installed in its place. Because the ink cartridge contains the printing mechanism as well as ink, it's like getting a new printer every time you replace the ink cartridge.

In some bubble-jet printers, the ink cartridge and the printhead are in separate assemblies. This way, the ink can be replaced when it runs out, and the printhead can be used several times. This works fine if the printer is designed to work this way. However, some people think they can do this on their integrated cartridge/printhead system, using special ink cartridge refill kits. These kits consist of a syringe filled with ink and a long needle. The needle is used to puncture the top of an empty ink cartridge, and the syringe is then used to refill the reservoir. Don't use these kits! See the warning about using them for more information.

Do not use ink cartridge refill kits! These kits (the ones you see advertised with a syringe and a needle) have several problems. First, the kits don't use the same kind of ink that was originally in the ink cartridges. The new ink may be thinner, causing the ink to run out or not print properly. Also, the printhead is supposed to be *replaced* around this same time. Refilling the cartridge doesn't replace the printhead, so you'll have print-quality problems. Finally, the hole the syringe leaves cannot be plugged and may allow ink to leak out. The bottom line: *Buy new ink cartridges from the printer manufacturer.* Yes, they are a bit more expensive, but you will actually save money because you won't have any of the problems described here.

TONER

The final type of consumable is toner. Each model of laser printer uses a specific toner cartridge. We covered the types of toner cartridges in the discussions of the different types of printers. You should check the printer's manual to see which toner cartridge it needs.

⊕ Real World Scenario

Think Before You Refill

Just as with ink cartridges, you should always buy the exact model recommended by the manufacturer. The toner cartridges have been designed specifically for a particular model. Additionally, *never* refill toner cartridges, for most of the same reasons we don't recommend refilling ink cartridges. The printout quality will be poor, and the fact that you're just refilling the toner means you're *not* replacing the photosensitive drum (which is usually inside the cartridge), and the drum might *need* to be replaced. Simply replacing refilled toner cartridges with proper, name-brand toner cartridges has solved most laser printer quality problems we have run across. We keep recommending the right ones, but clients keep coming back with the refilled ones. The result is that we take our clients' money to solve their print-quality problems when all it involves is a toner cartridge, our (usually repeat) advice to buy the proper cartridge next time, and the obligatory minimum charge for a half hour of labor (even though the job of replacing the cartridge takes all of five minutes!).

Options/Upgrades

Most printers (especially laser printers) can be upgraded with different capabilities. This is done to add functions or to increase the printing capacity of a printer. As the complexity of laser printers increases, they are often becoming what are known as *mopiers* (short for multiple original copiers). Rather than your having to print one copy of a document and then copy it with double-sided and stapling or hole-punch options, the laser printer manufacturer has included those functions in the printer, so each printed "copy" is essentially an original.

Each manufacturer, with the documentation for each printer, includes a list of all the accessories, options, and upgrades available for that printer. These options include the following:

- Memory
- Hard drives
- NICs
- Trays and feeders
- Finishers
- Scanners, fax modems, and copiers

MEMORY

One of the most common options for a printer is to add memory to it to increase its buffer size. The larger the buffer, the larger a print job it can handle. So, by adding memory, you can increase the performance of a printer.

For the most part, printer memory is specific to the make and model of printer being upgraded. You can check with the manufacturer of your printer to see what kind of memory it takes and how best to upgrade it. The procedures are slightly different for each make and model of printer.

HARD DRIVES

In order to print properly, the type style or *font* being printed must be downloaded to the printer along with the job being printed. Desktop-publishing and graphic-design businesses that print color pages on slower color printers are always looking for ways to speed up their print jobs. So they install multiple fonts into the onboard memory of the printer to make them *printer-resident fonts*.

But there's a problem: Most printers have a limited amount of storage space for these fonts. To solve this problem, printer manufacturers made it possible for hard drives to be added to many printers. These hard drives can be used to store many fonts used during the print process and are also used to store the large document file while it is being processed for printing.

NICS

Networks are everywhere. Almost every business has one, as do some homes. They are used to share information and resources between computers. In the past, you could share your printer with your neighbor over the network through software installed on your computer. But doing so had two drawbacks: It was slow, because your computer does other things in addition to sharing the printer, and it was cumbersome, because your computer had to be on in order for someone to print to your printer. Thus, the network interface card (NIC) option for a printer became popular as more and more people needed their printers to be on the network without the need for a host computer.

The NIC in a printer is similar to the NIC in a computer, with a couple of important differences. First, the NIC in a printer has a small processor on it to perform the management of the NIC interface (functions that the software on a host computer would do). Second, the NIC in a printer is proprietary, for the most part. It is made by the same manufacturer as the printer.

When a person on the network prints to a printer with a NIC, they are printing right to the printer and not going through any third-party device (although in some situations, that is desirable and possible with NICs). Because of its dedicated nature, the NIC option installed in a printer makes printing to that printer faster and more efficient—that NIC is dedicated to receiving print jobs and sending printer status to clients.

Some printer NICs have small web servers installed that allow clients to check their print jobs' status as well as toner levels from any computer on the network.

TRAYS AND FEEDERS

One option that is popular in office environments is the addition of paper trays. Most laser and bubble-jet printers come with at least one paper tray (usually 250 sheets or less). The addition of a paper tray allows a printer to print more sheets between paper refills, thus reducing its operating cost. In addition, some printers can accommodate multiple paper trays, which can be loaded with different types of paper, stationery, and envelopes. The benefit is that you can print a letter and an envelope from the same printer without having to leave your desk or change the paper in the printer.

Related to trays is the option of *feeders*. Some types of paper products need to be watched as they are printed, to make sure the printing happens properly. One example is envelopes: You usually can't put a stack of envelopes in a printer, because they won't line up straight or may get jammed. An accessory that you might add for this purpose is the *envelope feeder*. An envelope feeder typically attaches to the front of a laser printer and feeds in envelopes, one at a time. It can hold usually between 100 and 200 envelopes.

 If you're curious about the procedure for installing an envelope feeder, go to www.hp.com and search on "Envelope Feeder Install."

FINISHERS

A printer's *finisher* does just what it says: It finishes the document being printed. It does this by folding, stapling, hole punching, sorting, or collating the sets of documents being printed into their final form. So rather than your printing out a bunch of paper sheets and then having to collate and staple them, the finisher can do the same thing for you.

This particular option, while not cheap, is becoming more popular on laser printers in order to turn them into the aforementioned mopiers. As a matter of fact, many copiers are now digital and can do all the same things a laser printer can, but much faster and for a much cheaper cost per page.

SCANNERS, FAX MODEMS, AND COPIERS

The last few options are a bit of a stretch for laser printers, but they do somewhat fit. First, it is possible to add a scanner to a laser printer. A *scanner* is an accessory that takes a document and puts it into digital form. From there it can be edited or printed. If you use the scanner and print directly from the scanned-in image, you have just made a copy and turned the laser printer into a digital version of a copier. You can also add a device known as a fax modem to a printer configured with a scanner to turn the printer into a fax machine. A *fax modem* is a device you install into a computer or other device that takes the signals from that device and turns them into signals a fax machine can understand over a phone line.

By adding these two accessories, you can turn your simple printer into a home office copier capable of sending faxes as well. In this age of home offices, such devices are becoming commonplace. Several printer companies manufacture *multifunction printers*. These peripherals are essentially a printer, copier, scanner, and fax machine all in one. They're perfect for the home office without a lot of desk space.

Scanners and Their Components

As discussed earlier, a scanner converts paper into data that the computer can use. But how exactly does it do that? The various components work together to change the light reflected off the item being scanned (known as the *original*) into a stream of data that the computer can use. The reason a scanner is so named is because the data is converted one line at a time or *scanned* down the page as the scanning head (discussed later) moves down the page.

The following components (in various forms) are used inside most scanners:

- Glass plate and cover
- Scanning head
- Stepper motor
- Interface

Let's take a quick look at each component and how it works. Figure 7.23 illustrates a typical scanner and the location of each component. We will also look at the various types of scanners, including

- Flatbed scanners
- Sheet-fed scanners
- Handheld scanners

Finally, we will look at various scanner interfaces.

Glass Plate and Cover

The glass plate and cover are the majority of what users see when they use a scanner. The *glass plate* is the transparent plate that the original is placed on so that the scanner can scan it. Although originally made of glass, there are scanners with cheaper, clear acrylic plates. The cover comes down over the original (in the case of flatbed scanners) and keeps out stray light that can affect the accuracy of the scan. Most often, the side of the cover that sits on top of the original is white so that any part of the glass plate that the original doesn't cover is shown as white in the document as it is scanned.

 Flatbed scanners (discussed later) are the only types of scanner that use a glass plate and cover.

Scanning Head

The scanning head is the most important part of a scanner. It is the component that does the actual scanning. It moves down the page underneath the glass plate, controlled by the computer and moved by the stepper motor (discussed next). It contains several components, including these:

- Light source and mirrors
- Stabilizer bar
- Charge coupled device (CCD) array or contact image sensor (CIS)

FIGURE 7.23   A typical scanner and its components

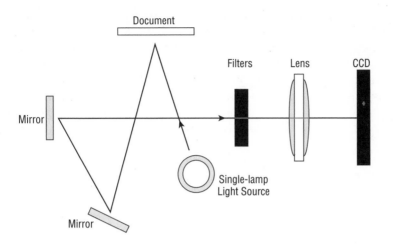

Light Source and Mirrors

The light source in a scanner is the bright white light that is used to illuminate the original as it is being scanned. The light from this light source bounces off the original and is reflected off several mirrors and into the CCD or off the original and into the CIS (both discussed in the next section).

Depending on the type of scanner, the light source can be either a fluorescent bulb, a cold cathode fluorescent lamp (CCFL), or a xenon lamp. The differences between them are cost, trueness of color reproduction, and bulb life.

 If you are using a scanner with a CIS (discussed later), they most often use multicolor LEDs as their light source.

Stabilizer Bar

The stabilizer bar is what the scanning head rides on inside a flatbed scanner. It is a long stainless steel rod, usually about ½ inch in diameter that is securely fastened to the case of the scanner. It provides a smooth ride as the scanner scans down the page. If the scanning head were to wobble or stutter as it makes its pass, the image would look funny and the scan would be of no use. Thus, the smooth ride produces a smooth image.

Charge Coupled Device (CCD) Array or Contact Image Sensor (CIS)

All scanners in use today use one of these two devices to convert the light energy into a data stream. A *charge coupled device (CCD) array* is a device inside a scanner that converts photons (particles of light) into electricity. The more light that falls on one of the *photosites* (single cell within the CCD array), the more electricity that site produces and thus the brighter the representation of the image on the computer. Any scanner that uses a CCD uses a lens to focus the light coming from the mirrors within the scanning head.

On the other hand, some cheaper scanners use a technology known as the *contact image sensor (CIS)*. This technology replaces the mirrors and CCD array with a sensor as long as the glass plate is wide. The light source is a set of LEDs that runs the length of the glass plate as well.

Either of these two devices (depending on the type used) will determine the overall *resolution* of a scanner. The resolution is the definition of how many pixels a scanner can use to make up a square inch of an image. For example, a scanner's resolution is given as a number such as 300×300 dpi. That means that the scanner uses $300 \times 300 = 90,000$ dots to represent one square inch. The higher the number, the higher the quality of the scan (but the higher the file size when transferred to the computer).

Stepper Motor

As with many types of printers, scanners use a stepper motor to make movements within the device. The stepper motor in a scanner moves the scan head down the page during the scan cycle. Often, the stepper motor is located either on the scan head itself or attached to a belt to drive the scanner head.

Interface

Like printers, scanners use various types of cables to connect to their host computers. You will learn about the different types of interfaces later in this chapter.

FIGURE 7.24 A flatbed scanner

Flatbed Scanners

If there is a mainstay of the scanner family, it is the flatbed scanner. A *flatbed scanner* is a scanner wherein the paper is put on a flat glass plate and the scanner head moves up and down the page inside the body of the scanner. It is the most common type of scanner. Figure 7.24 shows a typical flatbed scanner.

Flatbed scanners are the most popular because they are inexpensive and produce the best results for scanning single photographs or documents (which is 80 percent of what scanners are used for).

Sheet-Fed Scanners

Essentially, a *sheet-fed scanner* is similar to a flatbed scanner, but instead of a moving scan head, the scan head remains stationary and the paper is fed past it. As a matter of fact, there are sheet-feeder attachments for some flatbed scanners that will turn them into sheet-fed scanners. Figure 7.25 shows an example of a sheet-fed scanner.

The main advantage of a sheet-fed scanner over a flatbed scanner is speed. Sheet-fed scanners are designed to scan large numbers of documents in a short amount of time at the sacrifice of quality. Many sheet-fed scanners can scan 50–150 pages per minute, but the image resolution isn't as good because the CCD can't read the image that quickly at a high resolution. Thus, fewer pixels are scanned per inch to be able to move the paper that quickly.

Handheld Scanners

One type of scanner you may run into as a technician is the handheld scanner. Basically, a *handheld scanner* is the scanning head from a flatbed scanner that you hold in your hand. You then move the scanning head down the page yourself as you hold the page on a table or other flat surface. They aren't seen much anymore because the price of flatbed scanners has come down so much (they are now available for less than $30) and the image quality isn't as great. No human hand, no matter how steady, can be as precise as a stepper motor.

FIGURE 7.25   A sheet-fed scanner

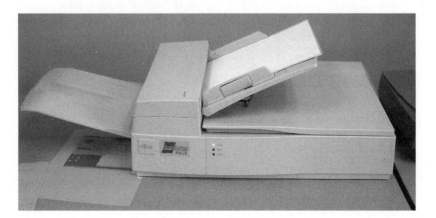

Scanner Interfaces

Scanners often use some of the same interfaces as printers. However, there are limitations. Most scanners today use one of the following interfaces:

- USB
- Parallel
- SCSI
- IEEE 1394/FireWire

You can refer the section earlier in this chapter regarding printer interfaces for explanations of how they work and how they connect. It is important to note that scanners don't currently use wireless. The main reason is that since scanners produce a steady stream of data, any interruption in the data stream will produce an unacceptable image from the scanner.

Installing, Configuring, and Upgrading Printers and Scanners

At some point during the ownership of their computer, any owner will want to add capability to it. Two of the most popular peripherals are printers and scanners. The A+ Essentials exam tests your knowledge of the procedures to install printers and scanners. In this section, you will learn the proper procedures for installing, configuring, and upgrading printers and scanners. You will not only learn how to install and configure printers and scanners but how to optimize their performance as well.

Printer and Scanner Installation Procedures

Although every device is different, there are certain accepted methods used for installing any device. Printers and scanners are just two sides of the same coin. Both devices use similar hookups, but one is an input device, and the other is an output device. The following procedure works for installing both kinds of devices:

- Attach the device to a local or network port and connect power.
- Install and update the device driver and calibrate the device.
- Configure options and default settings.
- Print/scan a test page.

Before doing any of this, read your device's installation instructions. There are exceptions to every rule.

Step 1: Attach the Device Using a Local or Network Port and Connect Power

When installing a printer or scanner, you must first take the device out of its packaging and set it up on a flat, stable surface. Then connect the device to either the host computer with its power off (if it is a stand-alone device) or to the network (if it is a network device). However, USB devices usually require that you install the software first and then connect the device.

Once you have connected the device, connect power to it using whatever supplied power adapter comes with it. Some devices have their own built-in power supply and just need an AC power cord connecting the device to the wall outlet, while others rely on an external transformer and power supply. Finally, turn on the device.

Some USB scanners are very low power and run off the power supplied by the USB cable.

Step 2: Install and Update the Device Driver and Calibrate the Device

Once you have connected and powered up the device, boot up the computer and wait for Windows to recognize the device. It will pop up a screen similar to the one shown in Figure 7.26. This wizard will allow you to configure the driver for the printer or scanner (depending on the device). You can insert the driver CD-ROM that comes with the device, and the wizard will guide you through the device driver installation. If Windows fails to recognize the device, you can use the Add Hardware Wizard to troubleshoot the installation and to install the device drivers.

FIGURE 7.26 The Windows Add Hardware Wizard

Once the driver is installed, the device will function. But some devices, such as inkjet printers and scanners, require that you calibrate the device. *Calibration* is the process by which a device is brought within functional specifications. For example, inkjet printers need their printheads aligned so they print evenly and don't print funny-looking letters and unevenly spaced lines. The process is part of the installation of all inkjet printers.

Each manufacturer's process is different, but a typical alignment/calibration works like so:

1. During software installation, the installation wizard asks you if you would like to calibrate now, to which you respond Yes or OK.

2. The printer prints out a sheet with multiple sets of numbered lines. Each set of lines represents an alignment instance.

3. The software will ask you which set(s) looks the best. Enter the number and click OK or Continue.

4. Some alignment routines end at this point. Others will reprint the alignment page and see if the alignment "took." If not, you can reenter the number of which one looks the best.

5. Click Finish to end the alignment routine.

Scanners, on the other hand, may need to be color calibrated with the monitor so that what scans in is accurate to what's on screen. Many include a test pattern that can be scanned in and the color on the screen corrected for variations in color. This pattern is commonly known as an *IT8 scanner target*.

 When working with print media, it is especially important to calibrate all your hardware to ensure color matching, including your monitor, scanner, printer, and digital camera.

Step 3: Configure Options and Default Settings

Once you have installed the software and calibrated the device, you can configure any options for either the scanner or printer. Scanners may require setting options such as configuring sheet feeders within the driver software. These settings and how to change them can be found in your hardware's manual.

Step 4: Print/Scan a Test Page

Once you have done all of these steps, you are finished and can print a test page to test the output of the printer. Windows has a built-in function for doing just that. Right-click on the printer you installed from within the printer control panel and click Properties. In the window that appears (Figure 7.27), there will be a Print Test Page button. If you click that button, Windows will send a test page to the printer. If the page prints, congratulations! Your printer is working.

For scanners, run the scanning software that came with the scanner. Place a single page on the scanner. Press the Scan button on the scanner (or in the software) to initiate a test scan. If the scan comes through on the screen, congratulations! Everything was done correctly.

FIGURE 7.27   Printer Properties window

hp officejet 4200 series Properties

General | Sharing | Ports | Advanced | Color Management | About

hp officejet 4200 series

Location:

Comment:

Model: hp officejet 4200 series

Features

Color: Yes   Paper available:

Double-sided: Yes

Staple: No

Speed: Unknown

Maximum resolution: Unknown

Printing Preferences...   Print Test Page

OK   Cancel   Apply

If your test scan or print doesn't work, proceed to the "Scanner Troubleshooting" section.

EXERCISE 7.2

Installing a USB printer

In this exercise, you will install a printer. You will need the following:

- A USB printer
- A USB printer cable
- The software driver CD or disk that came with the printer
- A computer with a free USB port and a CD-ROM

1. Turn on the computer.
2. Plug in the printer and turn it on.

3. Insert the CD into the computer's CD-ROM drive. The driver CD's auto-run should automatically start the installation program. If not, click on Start ➢ Run and type in **D:\setup** or **D:\install** (if your CD-ROM drive letter is different than *D* substitute that letter for *D*).

4. Follow the prompts in the installation program to install the driver.

5. Once the software has been installed, plug one end of the USB cable into the printer and the other end into the free USB port. Some installation programs will prompt you for this step.

6. Windows will automatically detect the new printer, install the driver, and configure it automatically. Windows will display a balloon in the lower-right-hand corner of the screen saying "Your hardware is now installed and is ready to use."

7. Print a test page to see if the printer can communicate and print properly.

Optimizing Printer and Scanner Performance

As a general rule, printers and scanners either work or they don't. There is very little you can do to optimize their performance from the hardware side. However, the software that comes with them often has many settings that will affect the quality of the job. For example, you can set inkjet printers to use less ink, but the quality of the print job goes down as well.

Troubleshooting Printers and Scanners

As we mentioned, other than the monitor, the most popular peripheral purchased for computers today is the printer. Printers are also the most complex peripheral, as far as troubleshooting is concerned. In this section, we will cover the most common types of printer problems you will run into. We will break the section into four areas: three areas for the three major types of printers and one area for scanner troubleshooting.

Dot-Matrix Printer Problems

Dot-matrix printers are relatively simple devices. Therefore, only a few problems usually arise. We will cover the most common problems and their solutions here.

Low Print Quality

Problems with print quality are easy to identify. When the printed page comes out of the printer, the characters may be too light or have dots missing from them. Table 7.1 details some of the most common print quality problems, their causes, and their solutions.

TABLE 7.1   Common Dot-Matrix Print Quality Problems

Characteristics	Cause	Solution
Consistently faded or light characters	Worn-out printer ribbon	Replace the ribbon with a new, vendor-recommended ribbon.
Print lines that go from dark to light as the printhead moves across the page	Printer ribbon-advance gear slipping	Replace the ribbon-advance gear or mechanism.
A small, blank line running through a line of print (consistently)	Printhead pin stuck inside the printhead	Replace the printhead.
A small, blank line running through a line of print (intermittently)	A broken, loose, or shorting printhead cable	Secure or replace the printhead cable.
A small, dark line running through a line of print	Printhead pin stuck in the out position	Replace the printhead. (Pushing the pin in may damage the printhead.)
Printer makes a printing noise, but no print appears on the page	Worn, missing, or improperly installed ribbon cartridge	Replace the ribbon cartridge correctly.
Printer prints garbage	Cable partially unhooked, wrong driver selected, or bad printer control board (PCB)	Hook up the cable correctly, select the correct driver, or replace the PCB (respectively).

Printout Jams inside the Printer (aka "The Printer Crinkled My Paper")

Printer jams are very frustrating because they always seem to happen more than halfway through your 50-page print job, requiring you to take time to remove the jam before the rest of your pages can print. A paper jam happens when something prevents the paper from advancing through the printer evenly. Print jobs jam for two major reasons: an obstructed paper path and stripped drive gears.

Obstructed paper paths are often difficult to find. Usually it means disassembling the printer to find the bit of crumpled-up paper or other foreign substance that's blocking the paper path. A common obstruction is a piece of the *perf*—the perforated sides of tractor-feed paper—that has torn off and gotten crumpled up and then lodged in the paper path. It may be necessary to remove the platen roller and feed mechanism to get at the obstruction.

Use extra caution when printing peel-off labels in dot-matrix printers. If a label or even a whole sheet of labels becomes misaligned or jammed, *do not* roll the roller backward to realign the sheet. The small plastic paper guide that most dot-matrix printers use to control the forward movement of the paper through the printer will peel the label right off its backing if you reverse the direction of the paper. Once the label is free, it can easily get stuck under the platen, causing paper jams. A label stuck under the platen is almost impossible to remove without disassembling the paper-feed assembly. If a label is misaligned, try realigning the whole sheet of labels *slowly* using the *feed roller,* with the power off, moving it in very small increments.

Stepper Motor Problems

Printers use stepper motors to move the printhead back and forth as well as to advance the paper (these are called the *carriage motor* and *main motor*, respectively). These motors get damaged when they are forced in any direction while the power is on. This includes moving the printhead over to install a printer ribbon as well as moving the paper-feed roller to align paper. These motors are very sensitive to stray voltages. If you are rotating one of these motors by hand, you are essentially turning it into a small generator and thus damaging it.

A damaged stepper motor is easy to detect. Damage to the stepper motor will cause it to lose precision and move farther with each step. Lines of print will be unevenly spaced if the main motor is damaged (which is more likely). Characters will be scrunched together if the printhead motor goes bad. If the motor is bad enough, it won't move at all in any direction; it may even make high-pitched squealing noises. If any of these symptoms appear, it's time to replace one of these motors.

Stepper motors are usually expensive to replace—about half the cost of a new printer! Damage to them is easy to avoid, using common sense.

Real World Scenario

Which Printer Would You Take to a Desert Island and Why?

If I had a wish for the service department I worked in, it would be that all the dot-matrix printers ever bought would be made by Okidata. An Okidata dot-matrix printer (such as the Microline 390) is a technician's dream machine. With nothing but a flat-bladed screwdriver and your hands, you can completely disassemble an Okidata dot-matrix printer in less than 10 minutes. Replacing parts on them is just as easy. All parts snap into place, including the covers. They also have an excellent reputation. If a customer asks you for a recommendation when buying a dot-matrix printer, you can't go wrong recommending an Okidata.

Bubble-Jet Printer Problems

Bubble-jet printers are the most commonly sold printers for home use. For this reason, you need to understand the most common problems with these printers so your company can service them effectively. Let's take a look at some of the most common problems with bubble-jet printers and their solutions.

Print Quality

The majority of bubble-jet printer problems are quality problems. Ninety-nine percent of these can be traced to a faulty ink cartridge. With most bubble-jet printers, the ink cartridge contains the printhead and the ink. The major problem with this assembly can be described by "If you don't use it, you lose it." The ink will dry out in the small nozzles and block them if they are not used at least once a week.

An example of a quality problem is when you have thin, blank lines present in every line of text on the page. This is caused by a plugged hole in at least one of the small, pinhole ink nozzles in the print cartridge. Replacing the ink cartridge solves this problem easily.

WARNING As we warned earlier, some people try to save a buck by refilling their ink cartridge when they need to replace it. If you are one of them, *stop it!* Don't refill your ink cartridges! Almost all ink cartridges are designed *not* to be refilled. They are designed to be used once and thrown away! By refilling them, you make a hole in them—ink can leak out, and the printer will need to be cleaned. The ink will probably also be of the wrong type, and print quality can suffer. Finally, using a refilled cartridge may void the printer's warranty.

If an ink cartridge becomes damaged or develops a hole, it can put too much ink on the page and the letters will smear. Again, the solution is to replace the ink cartridge. (You should be aware, however, that a very small amount of smearing is normal if the pages are laid on top of each other immediately after printing.)

One final print quality problem that does not directly involve the ink cartridge occurs when the print quickly goes from dark to light and then prints nothing. As we already mentioned, ink cartridges dry out if not used. That's why the manufacturers include a small suction pump inside the printer that primes the ink cartridge before each print cycle. If this priming pump is broken or malfunctioning, this problem will manifest itself and the pump will need to be replaced.

TIP If the problem of the ink quickly going from dark to light and then disappearing ever happens to you, and you really need to print a couple of pages, try this trick I learned from a fellow technician: Take the ink cartridge out of the printer. Squirt some window cleaner on a paper towel and gently tap the printhead against the wet paper towel. The force of the tap plus the solvents in the window cleaner should dislodge any dried ink, and the ink will flow freely again.

If you need to install a new cartridge, the printheads in that cartridge must be aligned. *Printhead alignment* is the process by which the printhead is calibrated for use. A special utility that comes with the printer software is used to do this. You run the alignment utility, and the printer prints several vertical and horizontal lines with numbers next to them. It then shows you a screen and asks you to choose the horizontal and vertical lines that are the most "in line." Once you enter the numbers, the software understands whether the printhead(s) are out of alignment, which direction, and by how much. The software then makes slight modifications to the print driver software to tell it how much to offset when printing. Sometimes alignment must be done several times to get the images to align properly.

Paper Jams

Bubble-jet printers usually have simple paper paths. Therefore, paper jams due to obstructions are less likely. They are still possible, however, so an obstruction shouldn't be overlooked as a possible cause of jamming.

Paper jams in bubble-jet printers are usually due to one of two things:

- A worn pickup roller
- The wrong type of paper

The pickup roller usually has one or two D-shaped rollers mounted on a rotating shaft. When the shaft rotates, one edge of the D rubs against the paper, pushing it into the printer. When the roller gets worn, it gets smooth and doesn't exert enough friction against the paper to push it into the printer.

If the paper used in the printer is too smooth, it causes the same problem. Pickup rollers use friction, and smooth paper doesn't offer much friction. If the paper is too rough, on the other hand, it acts like sandpaper on the rollers, wearing them smooth. Here's a rule of thumb for paper smoothness: Paper slightly smoother than a new dollar bill will work fine.

Laser and Page Printer Problems

I have good news and bad news. The bad news is that laser printer problems are the most complex, because the printer is the most complex. The good news is that most problems are easily identifiable and have specific fixes. Most of the problems can be diagnosed with knowledge of the inner workings of the printer and a little common sense. Let's discuss the most common laser and page printer problems and their solutions.

Paper Jams

Laser printers today run at copier speeds. Because of this, their most common problem is paper jams. Paper can get jammed in a printer for several reasons. First, feed jams happen when the paper-feed rollers get worn (similar to feed jams in bubble-jet printers). The solution to this problem is easy: Replace the worn rollers.

Another cause of feed jams is related to the drive gear of the pickup roller. The drive gear (or clutch) may be broken or have teeth missing. Again, the solution is to replace it. To determine if the problem is a broken gear or worn rollers, print a test page, but leave the paper tray out. Look into the paper-feed opening with a flashlight and see if the paper pickup roller(s) are turning evenly and don't skip. If they turn evenly, the problem is probably worn rollers.

If your paper-feed jams are caused by worn pickup rollers, there is something you can do to get your printer working while you're waiting for the replacement pickup rollers. Scuff the feed roller(s) with a Scotch-Brite pot-scrubber pad (or something similar) to roughen up the feed rollers. This trick works only once. After that, the rollers aren't thick enough to touch the paper.

Worn exit rollers can also cause paper jams. These rollers guide the paper out of the printer into the paper-receiving tray. If they are worn or damaged, the paper may catch on its way out of the printer. These types of jams are characterized by a paper jam that occurs just as the paper is getting to the exit rollers. If the paper jams, open the rear door and see where the paper is. If the paper is very close to the exit roller, the exit rollers are probably the problem.

The solution is to replace all the exit rollers. You must replace all of them at the same time because even one worn exit roller can cause the paper to jam. Besides, they're inexpensive. Don't be cheap and skimp on these parts if you need to have them replaced.

⊕ Real World Scenario

Printer Triage

I was in our local hospital ER a while ago having my hand looked at (I had cut it pretty badly on some glass). The receptionist who examined me asked me a few questions and filled out a report in the medical database on her computer. When she had finished asking me questions, she got up to get the printout from her laser printer.

I was shocked to see what she did next. When the paper starting coming out of the laser printer, she grabbed it and "ripped" it from the printer as you might do if the paper were in an old type-writer! The printer's exit rollers complained bitterly and made a noise that made me cringe. I don't know what hurt worse, my hand or my ears. She did this for every sheet of paper she printed. I didn't say anything, because my health was of primary concern at the time.

The following week, I noticed a familiar laser printer come in for service from that same hospital. As the technician started to work on it, I sauntered over and said, "I bet you 20 dollars it's the exit rollers." He said, "You're on!" Needless to say, I had a really good steak dinner that night with my wife.

I had a word with the person in charge of computer repair at that hospital the next day. They were surprised at what I told them but glad that I pointed it out. I saved them from many future repairs, and they were grateful. As far as I know, the ER receptionist doesn't rip the pages from the printer anymore, because we haven't seen that printer back in for service in a while.

Paper jams can also be the fault of the paper. If your printer consistently tries to feed multiple pages into the printer, the paper isn't dry enough. If you live in an area with high humidity, this could be a problem. I've heard some solutions that are pretty far out but that work (like keeping the paper in a Tupperware-type airtight container or microwaving it to remove moisture). The best all-around solution, however, is humidity control and keeping the paper wrapped until it's needed. Keep the humidity around 50 percent or lower (but above 25 percent if you can, in order to avoid problems with electrostatic discharge).

Finally, a grounded metal strip called the static-eliminator strip inside the printer drains the transfer corona charge away from the paper after it has been used to transfer toner from the EP cartridge. If that strip is missing, broken, or damaged, the charge will remain on the paper and may cause it to stick to the EP cartridge, causing a jam. If the paper jams after reaching the transfer corona assembly, this may be the cause.

Blank Pages

There's nothing more annoying than printing a 10-page contract and receiving 10 pages of blank paper from the printer. Blank pages are a somewhat common occurrence in laser and page printers. Somehow, the toner isn't being put on the paper. There are three major causes of blank pages:

- The toner cartridge
- The transfer corona assembly
- The high-voltage power supply (HVPS)

Toner Cartridge

As we have already discussed, the toner cartridge is the source of most quality problems because it contains most of the image-formation pieces for laser and page printers. Let's start with the obvious. A blank page will come out of the printer if there is no toner in the toner cartridge. I know it sounds simple, but some people think these things last forever. It's easy to check: Just open the printer, remove the toner cartridge, and shake it. You will be able to hear if there's toner inside the cartridge. If it's empty, replace it with a known, good, manufacturer-recommended toner cartridge.

Another issue that crops up rather often is the problem of using refilled or reconditioned toner cartridges. During their recycling process, these cartridges may be filled with the wrong kind of toner (for example, one with an incorrect charge). This can cause toner to be repelled from the EP drum instead of attracted to it. Thus, there's no toner on the page because there was no toner on the EP drum to begin with. The solution once again is to replace the toner cartridge with the type recommended by the manufacturer.

A third problem related to toner cartridges happens when someone installs a new toner cartridge and forgets to remove the sealing tape that is present to keep the toner in the cartridge during shipping. The solution to this problem is as easy as it is obvious: Remove the toner cartridge from the printer, remove the sealing tape, and reinstall the cartridge.

Transfer Corona Assembly

The second cause of the blank-page problem is a damaged or missing transfer corona wire or damaged transfer corona roller. If a wire is lost or damaged, the developed image won't transfer from the EP drum to the paper. Thus, no image appears on the printout. To determine if this is causing your problem, do the first half of the self-test (described later in this chapter). If there is an image on the drum but not on the paper, you know that the transfer corona assembly isn't doing its job.

To check if the transfer corona assembly is causing the problem, open the cover and examine the wire (or roller, if your printer uses one). The corona wire is hard to see, so you may need a flashlight. You will know if it's broken or missing just by looking (it will either be in pieces or just not there). If it's not broken or missing, the problem may be related to the HVPS.

The transfer corona wire (or roller) is a relatively inexpensive part and can be easily replaced with the removal of two screws and some patience.

High-Voltage Power Supply (HVPS)

The HVPS supplies high-voltage, low-current power to both the charging and transfer corona assemblies in laser and page printers. If it's broken, neither corona will work properly. If the self-test shows an image on the drum but none on the paper, and the transfer corona assembly is present and not damaged, then the HVPS is at fault.

All-Black Pages

Only slightly more annoying than 10 blank pages are 10 black pages. This happens when the charging unit (the charging corona wire or charging corona roller) in the toner cartridge malfunctions and fails to place a charge on the EP drum. Because the drum is grounded, it has no charge. Anything with a charge (like toner) will stick to it. As the drum rotates, all the toner is transferred to the page and a black page is formed.

This problem wastes quite a bit of toner but can be fixed easily. The solution (again) is to replace the toner cartridge with a known, good, manufacturer-recommended one. If that doesn't solve the problem, then the HVPS is at fault (it's not providing the high voltage that the charging corona needs to function).

Repetitive Small Marks or Defects

Repetitive marks occur frequently in heavily used (as well as older) laser printers. The problem may be caused by toner spilled inside the printer. It can also be caused by a crack or chip in the EP drum (this mainly happens with recycled cartridges), which can accumulate toner. In both cases, some of the toner gets stuck onto one of the rollers. Once this happens, every time the roller rotates and touches a piece of paper, it leaves toner smudges spaced a roller circumference apart.

The solution is relatively simple: Clean or replace the offending roller. To help you figure out which roller is causing the problem, the service manuals contain a chart like the one in Figure 7.28. To use the chart, place the printed page next to it. Align the first occurrence of the smudge with the top arrow. The next smudge will line up with one of the other arrows. The arrow it lines up with tells you which roller is causing the problem.

Remember that the chart in Figure 7.28 is only an example. Your printer may have different-sized rollers (and thus need a different chart). Check your printer's service documentation for a chart like this. It is valuable in determining which roller is causing a smudge.

FIGURE 7.28 Laser printer roller circumference chart

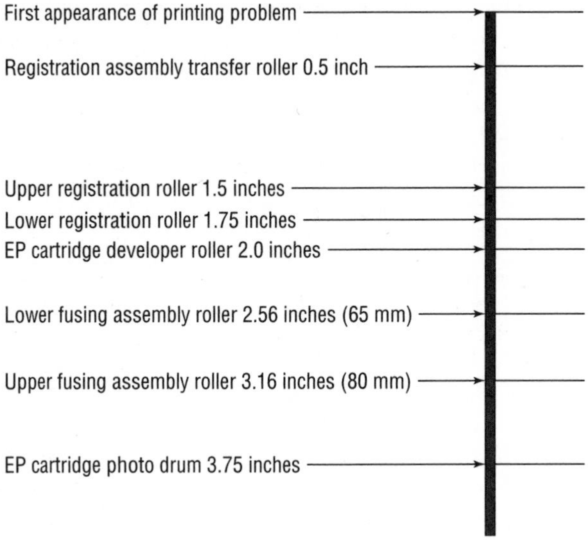

First appearance of printing problem ⟶

Registration assembly transfer roller 0.5 inch ⟶

Upper registration roller 1.5 inches ⟶
Lower registration roller 1.75 inches ⟶
EP cartridge developer roller 2.0 inches ⟶

Lower fusing assembly roller 2.56 inches (65 mm) ⟶

Upper fusing assembly roller 3.16 inches (80 mm) ⟶

EP cartridge photo drum 3.75 inches ⟶

Vertical Black Lines on the Page

A groove or scratch in the EP drum can cause the problem of vertical black lines running down all or part of the page. Because a scratch is lower than the surface, it doesn't receive as much (if any) of a charge as the other areas. The result is that toner sticks to it as though it were discharged. The groove may go around the circumference of the drum, so the line may go all the way down the page.

Another possible cause of vertical black lines is a dirty charging corona wire. A dirty charging corona wire prevents a sufficient charge from being placed on the EP drum. Because the charge on the EP drum is almost zero, toner sticks to the areas that correspond to the dirty areas on the charging corona.

The solution to the first problem is, as always, to replace the toner cartridge (or EP drum, if your printer uses a separate EP drum and toner). You can also solve the second problem with a new toner cartridge, but in this case that would be an extreme solution. It's easier to clean the charging corona with the brush supplied with the cartridge.

Vertical White Lines on the Page

Vertical white lines running down all or part of the page are a relatively common problem on older printers, especially ones that don't see much maintenance. They are caused by foreign matter (more than likely toner) caught on the transfer corona wire. The dirty spots keep the toner from being transmitted to the paper (at those locations, that is), with the result that streaks form as the paper progresses past the transfer corona wire.

The solution is to clean the corona wires. LaserJet Series II printers contain a small corona wire brush to help in this procedure. It's usually a small, green-handled brush located near the transfer corona wire. To use it, remove the toner cartridge and run the brush in the charging corona groove on top of the toner cartridge. Replace the cartridge and use the brush to remove any foreign deposits on the transfer corona. Be sure to put it back in its holder when you're finished.

Image Smudging

If you can pick up a sheet from a laser printer, run your thumb across it, and have the image come off on your thumb, you have a fuser problem. The fuser isn't heating the toner and fusing it into the paper. This could be caused by a number of things—but all of them can be taken care of with a fuser replacement. For example, if the halogen light inside the heating roller has burned out, that would cause the problem. The solution is to replace the fuser. The fuser can be replaced with a rebuilt unit, if you prefer. Rebuilt fusers are almost as good as new ones, and some even come with guarantees. Plus, they cost less.

> The whole fuser may not need to be replaced. Fuser components can be ordered from parts suppliers and can be rebuilt by you. For example, if the fuser has a bad lamp, you can order a lamp and replace it in the fuser.

A similar problem occurs when small areas of smudging repeat themselves down the page. Dents or cold spots in the fuser heat roller cause this problem. The only solution is to replace either the fuser assembly or the heat roller.

Ghosting

Ghosting is what you have when you can see light images of previously printed pages on the current page. This is caused by one of two things: bad erasure lamps or a broken cleaning blade. If the erasure lamps are bad, the previous electrostatic discharges aren't completely wiped away. When the EP drum rotates toward the developing roller, some toner sticks to the slightly discharged areas. A broken cleaning blade, on the other hand, causes old toner to build up on the EP drum and consequently present itself in the next printed image.

Replacing the toner cartridge solves the second problem. Solving the first problem involves replacing the erasure lamps in the printer. Because the toner cartridge is the least expensive cure, you should try that first. Usually, replacing the toner cartridge will solve the problem. If it doesn't, you will have to replace the erasure lamps.

Printer Prints Pages of Garbage

This has happened to everyone at least once. You print a one-page letter, and 10 pages of what looks like garbage come out of the printer. This problem comes from one of two different sources: the print driver software or the formatter board.

Printer Driver

The correct printer driver needs to be installed for the printer you have. For example, if you have an HP LaserJet III, then that is the driver you need to install. Once the driver has been installed, it must be configured for the correct page-description language: PCL or PostScript. Most HP LaserJet printers use PCL (but can be configured for PostScript). Determine what page-description language your printer has been configured for and set the printer driver to the same setting. If this is not done, you will get garbage out of the printer.

> Most printers that have LCD displays will indicate that they are in PostScript mode with a *PS* or *PostScript* somewhere in the display.

If the problem is the wrong driver setting, the garbage the printer prints will look like English. That is, the words will be readable, but they won't make any sense.

Formatter Board

The other cause of several pages of garbage being printed is a bad formatter board. This circuit board takes the information the printer receives from the computer and turns it into commands for the various components in the printer. Usually, problems with the formatter board produce wavy lines of print or random patterns of dots on the page.

It's relatively easy to replace the formatter board in a laser printer. Usually this board is installed under the printer and can be removed by loosening two screws and pulling out the board. Typically, replacing the formatter board also replaces the printer interface, which is another possible source of garbage printouts.

Example Printer Testing: HP LaserJet

Now that we've defined some of the possible sources of problems with laser printers, let's discuss a few of the testing procedures you use with them. We'll discuss HP LaserJet laser printers because they are the most popular type of laser printer, but the topics covered here apply to other types of laser printers as well.

When you troubleshoot laser printers, you can perform three tests to narrow down which assembly is causing the problem: the engine self-test, the engine half self-test, and the secret self-test. (These tests are internal diagnostics for the printers and are included with most laser printers.). In addition to these tests, laser printers with LCD displays can display error codes that help in the diagnosing of laser printer problems.

Self-Tests

As we mentioned, there are three significant printer self-tests—tests the printer runs on its own (albeit when directed by the user). These are the engine self-test, the print engine half self-test, and the secret self-test:

Engine Self-Test   The engine self-test tests the print engine of the LaserJet, bypassing the formatter board. This test causes the printer to print a single page with vertical lines running its length. If an engine self-test can be performed, you know the laser print engine can print successfully. To perform an engine self-test, you must press the printer's self-test button, which is hidden behind a small cover on the side of the printer (see Figure 7.29). The location of the button varies from printer to printer, so you may have to refer to the printer manual. Using a pencil or probe, press the button, and the print engine will start printing the test page.

Half Self-Test   A print engine half self-test is performed the same way as the self-test, but you interrupt it halfway through the print cycle by opening the cover. This test is useful in determining which part of the print process is causing the printer to malfunction. If you stop the print process and part of a developed image is on the EP drum and part has been transferred to the paper, you know that the pickup rollers, registration rollers, laser scanner, charging roller, EP drum, and transfer roller are all working correctly. You can stop the half self-test at various points in the print process to determine the source of a malfunction.

Secret Self-Test   To activate this test, you must first put the printer into service mode. To accomplish this, turn on the printer while simultaneously holding down the On Line, Continue, and Enter buttons (that's the first secret part, because nobody knows it unless somebody tells them). When the screen comes up blank, release the keys and press, in order, Continue and then Enter. The printer will perform an internal self-test and then display 00 READY. At this point you are ready to initiate the rest of the secret self-test: Take the printer offline, press the Test button on the front panel, and hold the button until you see the 04 Self Test message. Then release the Test button. This will cause the printer to print one self-test page. (If you want a continuous printout, instead of releasing the Test button at the 04 Self Test message, keep holding the Test button until the message 04 Self Test is displayed. The printer will print continuous self-test pages until you power off the printer or press On Line, or until the printer runs out of paper.)

FIGURE 7.29   Print engine self-test button location (the location may vary on different printers)

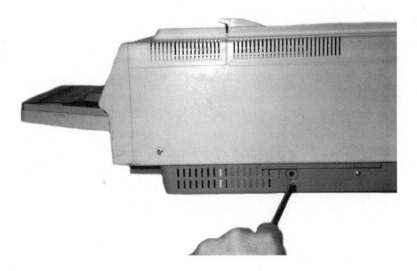

Error Codes

In addition to the self-tests, you have another tool for troubleshooting HP laser printers. Error codes are a way for the LaserJet to tell the user (and a service technician) what's wrong. Table 7.2 details some of the most common codes displayed on an HP LaserJet.

TABLE 7.2 HP LaserJet Error Messages

Message	Description
00 Ready	The printer is in standby mode and ready to print.
02 Warming Up	The fuser is being warmed up before the 00 Ready state.
05 Self-Test	A full self-test has been initiated from the front panel.
11 Paper Out	The paper tray sensor is reporting that there is no paper in the paper tray. The printer will not print as long as this error exists.
13 Paper Jam	A piece of paper is caught in the paper path. To fix this problem, open the cover and clear the jam (including all pieces of the jam). Close the cover to resume printing. The printer will not print as long as this error exists.
14 No EP Cart	There is no EP cartridge (toner cartridge) installed in the printer. The printer will not print as long as this error exists.
15 Engine Test	An engine self-test is in progress.
16 Toner Low	The toner cartridge is almost out of toner. Replacement will be necessary soon.
50 Service	A fuser error has occurred. This problem is most commonly caused by fuser lamp failure. Power off the printer and replace the fuser to solve the problem. The printer will not print as long as this error exists.
51 Error	There is a laser-scanning assembly problem. Test and replace, if necessary. The printer will not print as long as this error exists.
52 Error	The scanner motor in the laser-scanning assembly is malfunctioning. Test and replace as per the service manual. The printer will not print as long as this error exists.
55 Error	There is a communication problem between the formatter and the DC controller. Test and replace as per the service manual. The printer will not print as long as this error exists.

Troubleshooting Tips for HP LaserJet Printers

Printer technicians usually use a set of troubleshooting steps to help them solve HP LaserJet printing problems. Let's detail each of them to bring our discussion of laser printer troubleshooting to a close:

1. **Is the exhaust fan operational?** This is the first component to receive power when the printer is turned on. If you can feel air coming out of the exhaust fan, this confirms that AC voltage is present and power is turned on, that +5VDC and +24VDC are being generated by the AC power supply (ACPS), and that the DC controller is functional. If there is no power to the printer (no lights, fan not operating), the ACPS is at fault. Replacement involves removing all printer covers and removing four screws. You can purchase a new ACPS module, but it is usually cheaper to replace it with a rebuilt unit.

If you are into electronics, you can probably rebuild the ACPS yourself simply and cheaply. The main rectifier is usually the part that fails in these units; it can easily be replaced if you know what you're doing.

2. **Do the control panel LEDs work?** If so, the formatter board can communicate with the control panel. If the LEDs do not light, it could mean the formatter board is bad, the control panel is bad, or the wires connecting the two are broken or shorting out.

3. **Does the main motor rotate at power up?** Turn off the power. Remove the covers from the sides of the printer. Turn the printer back on and carefully watch and listen for main motor rotation. If you see and hear the main motor rotating, this indicates that a toner cartridge is installed, all photosensors are functional, all motors are functional, and the printer can move paper (assuming there are no obstructions).

4. **Does the fuser heat lamp light after the main motor finishes its rotation?** You will need to remove the covers to see this. The heat lamp should light after the main motor rotation and stay lit until the control panel says 00 Ready.

5. **Can the printer perform an engine test print?** A sheet of vertical lines indicates that the print engine works. This test print bypasses the formatter board and indicates whether the print problem resides in the engine. If the test print is successful, you can rule out the engine as a source of the problem. If the test print fails, you will have to further troubleshoot the printer to determine which engine component is causing the problem.

6. **Can the printer perform a control panel self-test?** This is the final test to ensure printer operation. If you can press the Test Page control panel button and receive a test printout, this means the entire printer is working properly. The only possibilities for problems are outside the printer (interfaces, cables, and software problems).

Scanner Troubleshooting

There are several problems unique to scanners that you should know about for the A+ Essentials exam. These problems include the following:

- Scanner won't turn on
- Strange noises from scanner
- Scanner won't scan

Scanner Won't Turn On

Many times when you go to power up the scanner it won't turn on. The simplest explanation is that the power cord has become unplugged. Check that both ends of the power cord for the scanner are plugged in correctly.

Strange Noises from Scanner

Actually, many people mistake noises coming from the scanner as a problem when in reality it is just the normal operation of the scanner. The scanner will make noise when first turned on as it performs its own internal calibration. The stepper motor will run, and the light source will turn on and off.

Scanner Won't Scan

Sometimes, for whatever reason, a scanner won't scan. You click the Scan button in the software but nothing happens. The first thing to do is to try again. Many people give up when they first notice an error. However, strange things can and do happen with computers, so if at first you don't succeed, try, try again.

If that doesn't solve the problem, try shutting down and rebooting the computer. Software isn't always written with the greatest care, and bugs can and do happen. Something that doesn't work after multiple tries may work after a reboot.

Once you've exhausted those possibilities, examine the simple things. For example, many scanners contain a scanning head lock to keep the scanning head from moving during shipping. There is always a possibility that this lock could have been switched back to the lock position by accident or by small, probing fingers (spoken by someone with two small children and many damaged peripherals).

Summary

In this chapter, we discussed how the different types of printers and scanners work as well as the most common methods of connecting them to computers. You learned how computers use page-description languages to format data before they send it to printers. You also learned about the various types of consumable supplies and how they relate to each type of printer.

The most basic category of printer currently in use is the impact printer. Impact printers form images by striking something against a ribbon, which in turn makes a mark on the paper. You learned how these printers work and the service concepts associated with them.

One of the most popular types of printer today is the bubble-jet printer, so named because of the mechanism used to put ink on the paper.

The most complex type of printer is the laser printer. The A+ Essentials exam covers this type of printer more than any other. You learned about the steps in the electrophotographic (EP) process, the process that explains how laser printers print. We also explained the various components that make up this printer and how they work together.

You then learned about the interfaces used to connect printers to PCs and the consumable supplies printers use. We discussed various interfaces and how they are used and how printer supplies can affect print output quality.

Finally, you learned about the various methods used to troubleshoot printing and print quality for both bubble-jet and laser printers. We also explained what causes failures and the best way to fix them.

Exam Essentials

Know the differences between types of printer and scanner technologies (e.g., laser, inkjet, thermal, solid ink, impact).   Laser printers use a laser and toner to create the page. Inkjet printers spray ink onto the page. Thermal printers use heat to form the characters on the page. Solid ink printers use ink in solid form that is then melted, or sublimed, and passed onto the page. Impact printers use a mechanical device to strike a ribbon, thus forming an image on the page.

Know the names, purposes, and characteristics of printer and scanner components (e.g., memory, driver, firmware) and consumables (e.g., toner, ink cartridge, paper).   Each printer contains different components that allow the printer to do its job. The components work together to form the image on the page. Each printer has a print mechanism, power supply, and interface. But each printer differs in how those components work.

Know the names, purposes, and characteristics of interfaces used by printers and scanners, including port and cable types.   Most printers today use the same interfaces, no matter what their type. Printers use parallel, USB, serial, IEEE 1394 (FireWire), wireless, Bluetooth, or network interfaces to connect to their host computers.

Know how to install and configure printers/scanners.   The basic procedure is as follows:

- Power and connect the device using a local or network port.
- Install and update the device driver and calibrate the device.
- Configure options and default settings.
- Print/scan a test page.

Know how to optimize printer performance.   Printers will perform their intended functions out of the box without too much trouble, but to truly get the most out of their performance, you may have to modify settings such as tray switching, print spool settings, device calibration, media types, and paper orientation in their driver or host software.

Know how to identify printer/scanner problems. The basic procedure during troubleshooting is to identify the problem first. To do this, you must first identify the symptom, review any error codes or device history, and then print or scan a test page (noting when and how the symptom manifests itself).

Know how to use appropriate generic or vendor-specific diagnostic tools including web-based utilities to troubleshoot problems. In order to troubleshoot a problem, you must follow this procedure:

- Review and analyze collected data.
- Establish probable causes.
- Review the service documentation.
- Review the knowledge base and define and isolate the problem (e.g., software vs. hardware, driver, connectivity, printer).
- Identify solutions to identified printer/scanner problems.
- Define the specific cause and apply a fix.
- Replace consumables as needed.
- Verify functionality and get user acceptance of the problem fix.

Review Questions

1. Which step in the EP print process uses a laser to discharge selected areas of the photosensitive drum, thus forming an image on the drum?

   A. Writing

   B. Transferring

   C. Developing

   D. Cleaning

2. What is the correct order of the steps in the EP print process?

   A. Developing, writing, transferring, fusing, charging, cleaning

   B. Charging, writing, developing, transferring, fusing, cleaning

   C. Transferring, writing, developing, charging, cleaning, fusing

   D. Cleaning, charging, writing, developing, transferring, fusing

3. What is the most basic printer type?

   A. Impact printer

   B. Bubble-jet printer

   C. Laser printer

   D. Interfaces and print media

4. Which voltage is applied to the paper to transfer the toner to the paper in an EP process laser printer?

   A. +600VDC

   B. –600VDC

   C. +6000VDC

   D. –6000VDC

5. What is the result of an absent or broken static-eliminator strip in either an EP process or HP LaserJet printer?

   A. Nothing. Both printers will continue to function normally.

   B. Nothing will happen in EP process printers, but HP LaserJet printers will flash a "–671 error" message.

   C. Paper jams may occur in both types of printers because the paper may curl around the photosensitive drum.

   D. Nothing will happen in HP LaserJet printers, but EP process printers will flash a "-671 error" message.

6. Which types of printers are referred to as page printers, because they receive their print job instructions one page at a time? (Select all that apply.)

    A. Daisy wheel

    B. Dot matrix

    C. Bubble jet

    D. Laser

7. Which of the following are possible interfaces for printers? (Select all that apply.)

    A. Parallel

    B. Mouse port

    C. Serial

    D. Network

8. Which laser printer component formats the print job for the type of printer being used?

    A. Corona assembly

    B. DC power supply

    C. Printer controller assembly

    D. Formatter software

9. Which of the following are page-description languages? (Select all that apply.)

    A. Page Description Language (PDL)

    B. PostScript

    C. PageScript

    D. Printer Control Language (PCL)

10. The basis weight is the weight in pounds of 500 sheets of bond paper for what size of paper?

    A. $8\frac{1}{2} \times 11$ inch

    B. 11×17 inch

    C. 17×22 inch

    D. $8\frac{1}{2} \times 17$ inch

11. Any printer that uses the electrophotographic process contains how many standard assemblies?

    A. Five

    B. Six

    C. Four

    D. Eight

12. Which type of printers can be used with multipart forms?

    A. Bubble-jet printers

    B. EP process laser printers

    C. HP process laser printers

    D. Dot-matrix printers

13. LED page printers differ from EP process laser printers in which step?

  A. Writing

  B. Charging

  C. Fusing

  D. Cleaning

  E. Developing

  F. Transferring

14. What part of both EP process and HP LaserJet process printers supplies the voltages for the charging and transfer corona assemblies?

  A. High-voltage power supply (HVPS)

  B. DC power supply (DCPS)

  C. Controller circuitry

  D. Transfer corona

15. With EP process laser printers, the laser discharges the charged photosensitive drum to _____ VDC.

  A. +600

  B. 0

  C. –100

  D. –600

16. Which impact printer has a printhead that contains a row of pins that are triggered in patterns that form letters and numbers as the printhead moves across the paper?

  A. Laser printer

  B. Daisy-wheel printer

  C. Dot-matrix printer

  D. Bubble-jet printer

17. Which printer contains a wheel that looks like a flower with raised letters and symbols on each petal?

  A. Bubble-jet printers

  B. Daisy-wheel printer

  C. Dot-matrix printer

  D. Laser printer

18. Which of the following is *not* an advantage of the daisy-wheel printer?

  A. Can print multipart forms

  B. Relatively inexpensive

  C. Print quality is comparable to a typewriter

  D. Speed

19. Which printer part gets the toner from the photosensitive drum onto the paper?

    A. Laser -scannering assembly

    B. Fusing assembly

    C. Corona assembly

    D. Drum

20. Which of the following is *not* an advantage of a Universal Serial Bus (USB) printer interface?

    A. It has a higher transfer rate than a serial connection.

    B. It has a higher transfer rate than a parallel connection.

    C. It automatically recognizes new devices.

    D. It allows the printer to communicate with networks, servers, and workstations.

Answers to Review Questions

1. A. The writing step uses a laser to discharge selected areas of the photosensitive drum, thus forming an image on the drum.

2. D. The correct sequence in the EP print process is cleaning, charging, writing, developing, transferring, and fusing.

3. A. Of the types listed here, the impact printer is the most basic.

4. A. Because the toner on the drum has a slight negative charge (−100VDC), it requires a positive charge to transfer it to the paper; +600VDC is the voltage used in an EP process laser printer.

5. C. If the static-eliminator strip is absent (or broken) in either an EP process or HP LaserJet printer, the paper will maintain its positive charge. Should this occur, paper jams may result due to the paper curling around the photosensitive drum.

6. C, D. A page printer is a type of computer printer that prints a page at a time. Common types of page printers are the laser printer and the inkjet printer.

7. A, C, D. Printers can communicate via parallel, serial, USB, infrared, SCSI, 1394, wireless, and network connections.

8. C. The printer controller assembly is responsible for formatting the print job for the type of printer being used. It formats the information into a page's worth of line-by-line commands for the laser scanner.

9. B, D. Of those listed, only PostScript and PCL are page-description languages.

10. C. The basis weight is the weight in pounds of 500 sheets of bond 17×22–inch paper.

11. D. There are eight standard assemblies in an electrophotographic process printer. Early laser printers using the electrographic process contained eight standard assemblies. Newer laser printers do not require an ozone filter and contain only seven standard assemblies.

12. D. Of the choices listed, only dot-matrix printers are impact printers and therefore can be used with multipart forms.

13. A. LED page printers differ from EP process laser printers in the writing step. They use a different process to write the image on the EP drum.

14. A. The high-voltage power supply is the part of both EP process and HP LaserJet process printers that supplies the voltages for the charging and transfer corona assemblies.

15. C. With EP process laser printers, the laser discharges the charged photosensitive drum to −100VDC.

16. C. The dot-matrix impact printer's printhead contains a row of pins that are triggered in patterns that form letters and numbers as the printhead moves across the paper.

17. B. The daisy-wheel printer gets its name because it contains a wheel with raised letters and symbols on each "petal."

18. D. The daisy-wheel printer is much slower when compared to the dot-matrix printer, and therefore speed is a *disadvantage*.

19. C. The transfer corona assembly gets the toner from the photosensitive drum onto the paper. For some printers, this is a transfer corona wire, and for others, it is a transfer corona roller.

20. D. The rate of transfer and the ability to automatically recognize new devices are two of the major advantages that make USB the current most popular type of printer interface. However, it is the network printer interface that allows the printer to communicate with networks, servers, and workstations.

Chapter 8

Networking Fundamentals

THE FOLLOWING COMPTIA A+ ESSENTIALS EXAM OBJECTIVES ARE COVERED IN THIS CHAPTER:

✓ **5.1 Identify the fundamental principles of networks**

- Describe basic networking concepts
  - Addressing
  - Bandwidth
  - Status indicators
  - Protocols (e.g. TCP / IP including IP, classful subnet, IPX / SPX including NWLINK, NETBWUI / NETBIOS)
  - Full-duplex, half-duplex
  - Cabling (e.g. twisted pair, coaxial cable, fiber optic, RS-232)
  - Networking models including peer-to-peer and client / server
- Identify names, purposes and characteristics of the common network cables
  - Plenum / PVC
  - UTP (e.g. CAT3, CAT5 / 5e, CAT6)
  - STP
  - Fiber (e.g. single-mode and multi-mode)
- Identify names, purposes and characteristics of network cables (e.g. RJ45 and RJ11, ST / SC / LC, USB, IEEE 1394 / Firewire)
- Identify names, purposes and characteristics (e.g. definition, speed and connections) of technologies for establishing connectivity for example:
  - LAN / WAN
  - ISDN

- Broadband (e.g. DSL, cable, satellite)
- Dial-up
- Wireless (all 802.11)
- VoIP

✓ **5.2 Install, configure, optimize and upgrade networks**

- Install and configure network cards (physical address)
- Install, identify and obtain wired and wireless connection

✓ **5.3 Identify tools, diagnostic procedures and troubleshooting techniques for networks**

- Explain status indicators, for example speed, connection and activity lights and wireless signal strength

Imagine working in an office 20 years ago with little or no computer equipment. It's hard to envision now, isn't it? We take for granted a lot of what we have gained in technology the past few decades. Now, imagine having to send a memo to everyone in the company. Back then we used interoffice mail; today we use e-mail. This is an example of one form of communication that only became available due to the introduction and growth of networks.

This chapter focuses on the basic concepts surrounding how a network works, including the way it sends information and what tools it uses to send information. This information is covered only to a minor degree by the A+ Essentials exam. However, if you're interested in becoming a service technician, this information will prove to be very useful, because you will in all likelihood be asked to troubleshoot both hardware and software problems on existing networks. Included in this chapter is information on the following topics:

- Understanding fundamental networking principles
- Installing, configuring, and troubleshooting networks

If the material in this chapter interests you, you might consider studying for, and eventually taking, CompTIA's Network+ exam. It is a generic networking certification (similar to A+, but for network-related topics). You can study for it using Sybex's *CompTIA Network+ Study Guide* materials, available at www.sybex.com.

Understanding Networking Principles

Stand-alone personal computers, first introduced in the late 1970s, gave users the ability to create documents, spreadsheets, and other types of data and save them for future use. For the small-business user or home-computer enthusiast, this was great. For larger companies, however, it was not enough. The larger the company, the greater the need to share information between offices and sometimes over great distances. Stand-alone computers were insufficient for the following reasons:

- Their small hard-drive capacities were insufficient.
- To print, each computer required a printer attached locally.

- Sharing documents was cumbersome. People grew tired of having to save to a diskette and then take that diskette to the recipient. (This procedure was called *sneakernet*.)

- There was no e-mail. Instead, there was interoffice mail, which was not reliable and frequently was not delivered in a timely manner.

To address these problems, *networks* were born. A network links two or more computers together to communicate and share resources. Their success was a revelation to the computer industry as well as businesses. Now, departments could be linked internally to offer better performance and increase efficiency.

You have heard the term *networking* in the business context, where people come together and exchange names for future contact and to give them access to more resources. The same is true with a computer network. A computer network allows computers to link to each other's resources. For example, in a network, every computer does not need a printer connected locally in order to print. Instead, one computer has a printer connected to it and allows the other computers to access this resource. Because they allow users to share resources, networks offer an increase in performance as well as a decrease in the outlay for new hardware and software.

In the following sections, we will discuss the fundamentals of networking, as well as the specifics of networking media and components.

Understanding Networking Fundamentals

Before you can understand networking and the procedures involved in installing a network, you must first understand the fundamentals. The fundamentals include the following:

- LANs vs. WANs
- Primary network components
- Network operating systems (NOSs)
- Network topologies
- Network communications
- Network communication protocols
- Protocol addressing
- Network architectures

LANs vs. WANs

Local area networks (LANs) were introduced to connect computers in a single office. *Wide area networks (WANs)* expanded the LANs to include networks outside the local environment and also to distribute resources across distances. Today, LANs exist in many businesses, from small to large. WANs are becoming more widely accepted as businesses become more mobile and as more of them span greater distances. It is important to understand LANs and WANs as a service professional, because when you're repairing computers you are likely to come in contact with problems that are associated with the computer's connection to a network.

Local Area Networks (LANs)

The 1970s brought us the minicomputer, which was a smaller version of the mainframe. Whereas the mainframe used *centralized processing* (all programs ran on the same computer), the minicomputer used *distributed processing* to access programs across other computers. As depicted in Figure 8.1, distributed processing allows a user at one computer to use a program on another computer as a *back end* to process and store the information. The user's computer is the *front end*, where the data entry is performed. This arrangement allowed programs to be distributed across computers rather than centralized. This was also the first time computers used cable to connect rather than phone lines.

FIGURE 8.1   Distributed processing

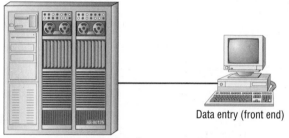

Data entry (front end)

Data processing and storage (back end)

By the 1980s, offices were beginning to buy PCs in large numbers. Portables were also introduced, allowing computing to become mobile. Neither PCs nor portables, however, were efficient in sharing information. As timeliness and security became more important, diskettes were just not cutting it. Offices needed to find a way to implement a better means to share and access resources. This led to the introduction of the first type of PC LAN: ShareNet by Novell. LANs are simply the linking of computers to share resources within a closed environment. The first simple LANs were constructed a lot like Figure 8.2.

FIGURE 8.2   A simple LAN

After the introduction of ShareNet, more LANs sprouted. The earliest LANs could not cover a great distance. Most of them could only stretch across a single floor of the office and could support no more than 30 users. Further, they were still simple, and only a few software programs supported them. The first software programs that ran on a LAN were not capable of permitting more than one user at a time to use a program (this constraint was known as *file locking*). Nowadays, we can see multiple users accessing a program at one time, limited only by restrictions at the record level.

Wide Area Networks (WANs)

By the late 1980s, networks were expanding to cover ranges considered geographical in size and were supporting thousands of users. WANs, first implemented with mainframes at massive government expense, started attracting PC users as networks went to this new level. Businesses with offices across the country communicated as if they were only desks apart. Soon the whole world saw a change in its way of doing business, across not only a few miles but across countries. Whereas LANs are limited to single buildings, WANs can span buildings, states, countries, and even continental boundaries. Figure 8.3 gives an example of a simple WAN.

FIGURE 8.3 A simple WAN

Networks of today and tomorrow are no longer limited by the inability of LANs to cover distance and handle mobility. WANs play an important role in the future development of corporate networks worldwide. Although the primary focus of this chapter is LANs, we will feature a section on WAN connectivity. This section will briefly explain the current technologies and what you should expect to see in the future. If you are interested in more information about LANs or WANs, or if you plan to become a networking technician, check your local library resources or the Internet.

Primary Network Components

Putting together a network is not as simple as it was with the first PC network. You can no longer consider two computers cabled together a fully functional network. Today, networks consist of three primary components:

- Servers
- Clients or workstations
- Resources

> Every network requires two more items to tie these three components together: a network operating system (NOS) and some kind of shared medium. These components are covered later in their own sections.

No network would be complete without these three components working together.

Servers

Servers come in many shapes and sizes. They are a core component of the network, providing a link to the resources necessary to perform any task. The link the server provides could be to a resource existing on the server itself or a resource on a client computer. The server is the "leader of the pack," offering directions to the client computers regarding where to go to get what they need.

Servers offer networks the capability of centralizing the control of resources and can thus reduce administrative difficulties. They can be used to distribute processes for balancing the load on computers and can thus increase speed and performance. They can also compartmentalize files for improved reliability. That way, if one server goes down, not all of the files are lost.

Servers perform several tasks. For example, servers that provide files to the users on the network are called *file servers*. Likewise, servers that host printing services for users are called *print servers*. (There are other tasks, as well, such as remote-access services, administration, mail, and so on.) Servers can be *multipurpose* or *single-purpose*. If they are multipurpose, they can be, for example, both a file server and a print server at the same time. If the server is a single-purpose server, it is a file server only or a print server only. Another distinction we use in categorizing servers is whether they are *dedicated* or *nondedicated*:

Dedicated Servers   Assigned to provide specific applications or services for the network and nothing else. Because a *dedicated server* specializes in only a few tasks, it requires fewer resources from the computer that is hosting it than a nondedicated server might require. This savings in overhead may translate to a certain efficiency and can thus be considered as having a beneficial impact on network performance. A web server is an example of a dedicated server: It is dedicated to the task of serving up web pages.

Nondedicated Servers   Assigned to provide one or more network services *and* local access. A *nondedicated server* is expected to be slightly more flexible in its day-to-day use than a dedicated server. Nondedicated servers can be used not only to direct network traffic and perform administrative actions but also often to serve as a front end for the administrator to work with other applications or services or perform services for more than one network. For example, a nondedicated web server might serve out more than one website, where a dedicated web server serves out just one website. The nondedicated server is not really what some would consider a true server, because it can act as a workstation as well as a server. The workgroup server at your office is an example of a nondedicated server. It might be a combination file, print, and e-mail server. Plus, because of its nature, a nondedicated server could also function well in a peer-to-peer environment. It could be used as a workstation, in addition to being a file, print, and e-mail server.

Many networks use both dedicated and nondedicated servers in order to incorporate the best of both worlds, offering improved network performance with the dedicated servers and flexibility with the nondedicated servers.

Workstations

Workstations are the computers on which the network users do their work, performing activities such as word processing, database design, graphic design, e-mail, and other office or personal tasks. Workstations are basically everyday computers, except for the fact that they are connected to a network that offers additional resources. Workstations can range from diskless computer systems to desktop systems. In network terms, workstations are also known as *client computers*. As clients, they are allowed to communicate with the servers in the network in order to use the network's resources.

It takes several items to make a workstation into a client. You must install a *network interface card (NIC)*, a special expansion card that allows the PC to talk on a network. You must connect it to a cabling system that connects to another computer (or several other computers). And you must install special software, called *client software*, which allows the computer to talk to the servers and request resources from them. Once all this has been accomplished, the computer is "on the network."

To the client, the server may be nothing more than just another drive letter. However, because it is in a network environment, the client can use the server as a doorway to more storage or more applications, or through which it may communicate with other computers or other networks. To users, being on a network changes a few things:

- They can store more information, because they can store data on other computers on the network.

- They can share and receive information from other users, perhaps even collaborating on the same document.

- They can use programs that would be too large or complex for their computer to use by itself.

Network Resources

We now have the server to share the resources and the workstation to use them, but what about the resources themselves? A *resource* (as far as the network is concerned) is any item that can be used on a network. Resources can include a broad range of items, but the most important ones include the following:

- Printers and other peripherals

- Files

- Applications

- Disk storage

When an office can purchase paper, ribbons, toner, or other consumables for only one, two, or maybe three printers for the entire office, the costs are dramatically lower than the costs for supplying printers at every workstation. Networks also give more storage space to files. Client computers can't always handle the overhead involved in storing large files (for example, database files) because they are already heavily involved in users' day-to-day work activities. Because servers in a network can be dedicated to only certain functions, a server can be allocated to store all the larger files that are worked with every day, freeing up disk space on client computers. Similarly, applications (programs) no longer need to be on every computer in the office. If the server is capable of handling the overhead an application requires, the application can reside on the server and be used by workstations through a network connection.

The sharing of applications over a network requires a special arrangement with the application vendor, which may wish to set the price of the application according to the number of users who will be using it. The arrangement allowing multiple users to use a single installation of an application is called a *site license*.

🌐 Real World Scenario

Being on a Network Brings Responsibilities

You are part of a community when you are on a network, which means you need to take responsibility for your actions. First, a network is only as secure as the users who use it. You cannot randomly delete files or move documents from server to server. You do not own your e-mail, so anyone in your company's management can choose to read it. In addition, printing does not mean that if you send something to print it will print immediately—your document may not be the first in line to be printed at the shared printer. Plus, if your workstation has also been set up as a nondedicated server, you cannot turn it off.

Network Operating Systems (NOSs)

PCs use a disk operating system that controls the file system and how the applications communicate with the hard disk. Networks use a network operating system (NOS) to control the communication with resources and the flow of data across the network. The NOS runs on the server. Many companies offer software to start a network. Some of the more popular NOSs at this time include Unix, Novell's NetWare, Linux, and Microsoft's Windows NT Server, Windows 2000 Server, and Windows Server 2003. Although several other NOSs exist, these are the most popular.

Back in the early days of mainframes, it took a full staff of people working around the clock to keep the machines going. With today's NOSs, servers are able to monitor memory, CPU time, disk space, and peripherals, without a babysitter. Each of these operating systems allows processes to respond in a certain way with the processor.

With the new functionality of LANs and WANs, you can be sitting in your office in Milwaukee and carry on a real-time electronic chat with a coworker in France, or maybe print an invoice at the home office in California, or manage someone else's computer from your own while they are on vacation. Gone are the days of disk passing, phone messages left but not received, or having to wait a month to receive a letter from someone in Hong Kong. NOSs provide this functionality on a network.

Network Resource Access

Now that we have discussed the makeup of a typical network, let's examine the way resources are accessed on a network. There are generally two resource-access models: peer-to-peer and client-server. It is important to choose the appropriate model. How do you decide what type of resource model is needed? You must first think about the following questions:

- What is the size of the organization?
- How much security does the company require?
- What software or hardware does the resource require?
- How much administration does it need?
- How much will it cost?
- Will this resource meet the needs of the organization today and in the future?
- Will additional training be needed?

Networks cannot just be put together at the drop of a hat. A lot of planning is required before implementation of a network to ensure that whatever design is chosen will be effective and efficient, and not just for today but for the future as well. The forethought of the designer will lead to the best network with the least amount of administrative overhead. In each network, it is important that a plan be developed to answer the previous questions. The answers will help the designer choose the type of resource model to use.

Peer-to-Peer Networks

In a peer-to-peer network, the computers act as both service providers and service requestors. An example of a peer-to-peer resource model is shown in Figure 8.4.

Peer-to-peer networks are great for small, simple, inexpensive networks. This model can be set up almost immediately, with little extra hardware required. Windows 3.11, Windows 9x, Windows NT, Windows 2000, Windows XP, Linux, and Mac OS are popular operating system environments that support a peer-to-peer resource model.

Generally speaking, there is no centralized administration or control in the peer-to-peer resource model. Every station has unique control over the resources the computer owns, and each station must be administrated separately. However, this very lack of centralized control can make it difficult to administer the network; for the same reason, the network isn't very secure. Moreover, because each computer is acting as both a workstation and server, it may not be easy to locate resources. The person who is in charge of a file may have moved it without anyone's knowledge. Also, the users who work under this arrangement need more training, because they are not only users but also administrators.

FIGURE 8.4 The peer-to-peer resource model

Will this type of network meet the needs of the organization today and in the future? Peer-to-peer resource models are generally considered the right choice for small companies that don't expect future growth. For example, the business might be small, possibly an independent subsidiary of a specialty company, and has no plans to increase its market size or number of employees. Small companies that expect growth, on the other hand, should not choose this type of model. Although it could very well meet the company's needs today, the growth of the company will necessitate making major changes over time. Choosing to set up a peer-to-peer resource model simply because it is cheap and easy to install could be a costly mistake. A company's management may find that it costs them more in the long run than if they had chosen a server-based resource model.

Client-Server Resource Model

The client-server (also known as server-based) model is better than the peer-to-peer model for large networks (say, more than 10 computers) that need a more secure environment and centralized control. Server-based networks use a dedicated, centralized server. All administrative functions and resource sharing are performed from this point. This makes it easier to share resources, perform backups, and support an almost unlimited number of users. This model also offers better security. However, the server needs more hardware than a typical workstation/server computer in a peer-to-peer resource model. In addition, it requires specialized software (the NOS) to manage the server's role in the environment. With the addition of a server and the NOS, server-based networks can easily cost more than peer-to-peer resource models. However, for large networks, it's the only choice. An example of a client-server resource model is shown in Figure 8.5.

FIGURE 8.5   The client-server resource model

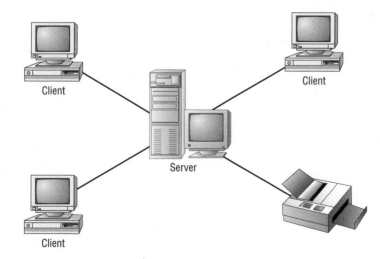

Will this type of network meet the needs of the organization today and in the future? Client-server resource models are the desired models for companies that are continually growing or that need to initially support a large environment. Server-based networks offer the flexibility to add more resources and clients almost indefinitely into the future. Hardware costs may be more, but, with the centralized administration, managing resources becomes less time consuming. Also, only a few administrators need to be trained, and users are responsible for only their own work environment.

> If you are looking for an inexpensive, simple network with little setup required, and there is no need for the company to grow in the future, then the peer-to-peer network is the way to go. If you are looking for a network to support many users (more than 10 computers), strong security, and centralized administration, consider the server-based network your only choice.

Whatever you decide, be sure to take the time to plan. A network is not something you can just throw together. You don't want to find out a few months down the road that the type of network you chose does not meet the needs of the company—this could be a time-consuming and costly mistake.

Network Topologies

A *topology* is a way of laying out the network. Topologies can be either physical or logical. *Physical topologies* describe how the cables are run. *Logical topologies* describe how the network messages travel. Deciding which type of topology to use is the next step when designing your network.

You must choose the appropriate topology in which to arrange your network. Each type differs by its cost, ease of installation, fault tolerance (how the topology handles problems such as cable breaks), and ease of reconfiguration (like adding a new workstation to the existing network).

There are five primary topologies (some of which can be both logical and physical):

- Bus (can be both logical and physical)
- Star (physical only)
- Ring (can be both logical and physical)
- Mesh (can be both logical and physical)
- Hybrid (usually physical)

Each topology has advantages and disadvantages. At the end of this section, check out Table 8.1, which summarizes the advantages and disadvantages of each topology.

Bus Topology

A bus is the simplest physical topology. It consists of a single cable that runs to every workstation, as shown in Figure 8.6. This topology uses the least amount of cabling. Each computer shares the same data and address path. With a logical bus topology, messages pass through the trunk, and each workstation checks to see if the message is addressed to itself. If the address of the message matches the workstation's address, the network adapter copies the message to the card's onboard memory.

FIGURE 8.6   The bus topology

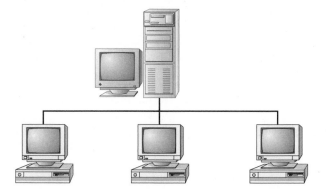

Cable systems that use the bus topology are easy to install. You run a cable from the first computer to the last computer. All the remaining computers attach to the cable somewhere in between. Because of the simplicity of installation, and because of the low cost of the cable, bus topology cabling systems (such as Ethernet) are the cheapest to install.

Although the bus topology uses the least amount of cabling, it is difficult to add a workstation. If you want to add another workstation, you have to completely reroute the cable and possibly run two additional lengths of it. Also, if any one of the cables breaks, the entire network is disrupted. Therefore, such a system is very expensive to maintain.

Star Topology

A physical star topology branches each network device off a central device called a *hub*, making it very easy to add a new workstation. Also, if any workstation goes down, it does not affect the entire network. (But, as you might expect, if the central device goes down, the entire network goes down.) Some types of Ethernet, ARCNet, and Token Ring use a physical star topology. Figure 8.7 gives an example of the organization of the star network.

FIGURE 8.7   The star topology

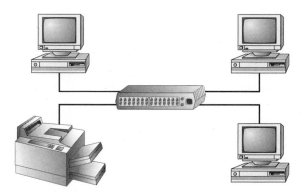

Star topologies are easy to install. A cable is run from each workstation to the hub. The hub is placed in a central location in the office (for example, a utility closet). Star topologies are more expensive to install than bus networks, because several more cables need to be installed, plus the hubs. But the ease of reconfiguration and fault tolerance (one cable failing does not bring down the entire network) far outweigh the drawbacks.

Although the hub is the central portion of a star topology, many networks use a device known as a switch *instead* of a hub. The primary difference between them is that the switch makes a virtual connection between sender and receiver instead of simply sending each message to every port. Thus, a switch provides better performance over a hub for only a small price increase.

Ring Topology

A physical ring topology is a unique topology. Each computer connects to two other computers, joining them in a circle and creating a unidirectional path where messages move from workstation to workstation. Each entity participating in the ring reads a message and then regenerates it and hands it to its neighbor on a different network cable. See Figure 8.8 for an example of a ring topology.

FIGURE 8.8   The ring topology

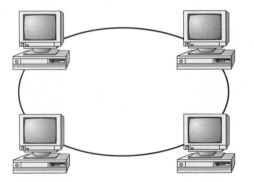

The ring makes it difficult to add new computers. Unlike a star topology network, the ring topology network will go down if one entity is removed from the ring. Physical ring topology systems rarely exist anymore, mainly because the hardware involved was fairly expensive and the fault tolerance was very low. However, one type of logical ring still exists: IBM's Token Ring technology. We'll discuss this technology later in the "Network Architectures" section.

Token Ring does *not* use a physical ring. It actually uses a physical star topology. Remember that physical topologies describe how the cables are connected, and logical topologies describe information flow.

Mesh Topology

The *mesh topology* is the simplest logical topology in terms of data flow, but it is the most complex in terms of physical design. In this physical topology, each device is connected to every other device (Figure 8.9). This topology is rarely found in LANs, mainly because of the complexity of the cabling. If there are x computers, there will be $(x \times (x-1)) \div 2$ cables in the network. For example, if you have five computers in a mesh network, it will use $5 \times (5-1) \div 2 = 10$ cables. This complexity is compounded when you add another workstation. For example, your 5-computer, 10-cable network will jump to 15 cables if you add just one more computer. Imagine how the person doing the cabling would feel if you told them they had to cable 50 computers in a mesh network—they'd have to come up with $50 \times (50-1) \div 2 = 1225$ cables!

FIGURE 8.9   The mesh topology

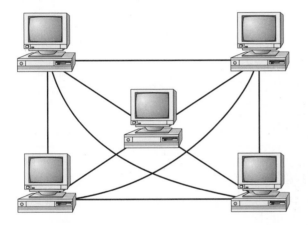

Because of its design, the physical mesh topology is very expensive to install and maintain. Cables must be run from each device to every other device. The advantage you gain is high fault tolerance. With a logical mesh topology, there will always be a way to get the data from source to destination. The data may not be able to take the direct route, but it can take an alternate, indirect route. For this reason, the mesh topology is found in WANs to connect multiple sites across WAN links. It uses devices called *routers* to search multiple routes through the mesh and determine the best path. However, the mesh topology does become inefficient with five or more entities because of the number of connections that need to be maintained.

Hybrid Topology

The hybrid topology is simply a mix of the other topologies. It would be impossible to illustrate it, because there are many combinations. In fact, *most* networks today are not only hybrid but heterogeneous (they include a mix of components of different types and brands). The hybrid network may be more expensive than some types of network topologies, but it takes the best features of all the other topologies and exploits them.

Summary of Topologies

Table 8.1 summarizes the advantages and disadvantages of each type of network topology.

TABLE 8.1   Topologies—Advantages and Disadvantages

Topology	Advantages	Disadvantages
Bus	Cheap. Easy to install.	Difficult to reconfigure. Break in the bus disables the entire network.
Star	Cheap. Easy to install. Easy to reconfigure. Fault tolerant.	More expensive than bus.
Ring	Efficient. Easy to install.	Reconfiguration is difficult. Very expensive.
Mesh	Simplest for data flow. Most fault tolerant.	Reconfiguration is extremely difficult. Extremely expensive. Very complex.
Hybrid	Gives a combination of the best features of each topology used.	Complex (less so than mesh, however).

Network Communications

You have chosen the type of network and arrangement (topology). Now the computers need to understand how to communicate. Network communications use protocols. A *protocol* is a set of rules that govern communications. Protocols detail what "language" the computers are speaking when they talk over a network. If two computers are going to communicate, they both must be using the same protocol.

Different methods are used to describe the different protocols. We will discuss two of the most common: the OSI model and the IEEE 802 standards.

OSI Model

The International Organization for Standardization (ISO) introduced the *Open Systems Interconnection (OSI)* model to provide a common way of describing network protocols. The ISO put together a seven-layer model providing a relationship between the stages of communication, with each layer adding to the layer above or below it.

 This OSI model is just that: a model. It can't be implemented. You will never find a network that is running the "OSI protocol."

The theory behind the OSI model is that as transmission takes place the higher layers pass data through the lower layers. As the data passes through a layer, the layer tacks its information (also called a *header*) onto the beginning of the information being transmitted until it reaches the bottom layer. A layer may also add a trailer to the end of the data. At this point, the bottom layer sends the information out on the wire.

At the receiving end, the bottom layer receives the information, reads its information from its header, removes its header and any associated trailer from the information, and then passes the remainder to the next highest layer. This procedure continues until the topmost layer receives the data that the sending computer sent.

The OSI model layers from top to bottom are listed here. We'll *describe* each of these layers from bottom to top, however. After the descriptions, we'll summarize the entire model:

- Application layer
- Presentation layer
- Session layer
- Transport layer
- Network layer
- Data Link layer
- Physical layer

Physical Layer   Describes how the data gets transmitted over a physical medium. This layer defines how long each piece of data is and the translation of each into the electrical pulses that are sent over the wires. It decides whether data travels unidirectionally or bidirectionally across the hardware. It also relates electrical, optical, mechanical, and functional interfaces to the cable.

Data Link Layer   Arranges data into chunks called *frames*. Included in these chunks is control information indicating the beginning and end of the data stream. This layer is very important because it makes transmission easier and more manageable and allows for error checking within the data frames. The Data Link layer also describes the unique physical address (also known as the *MAC address*) for each NIC.

Network Layer   Addresses messages and translates logical addresses and names into physical addresses. At this layer, the data is organized into chunks called *packets*. The Network layer is something like the traffic cop. It is able to judge the best network path for the data based on network conditions, priority, and other variables. This layer manages traffic through packet switching, routing, and controlling congestion of data.

Transport Layer   Signals "all clear" by making sure the data segments are error-free. This layer also controls the data flow and troubleshoots any problems with transmitting or receiving datagrams. This layer's most important job is to provide error checking and reliable, end-to-end communications. It can also take several smaller messages and combine them into a single, larger message.

Session Layer   Allows applications on different computers to establish, use, and end a session. A session is one virtual conversation. For example, all the procedures needed to transfer a single file make up one session. Once the session is over, a new process begins. This layer enables network procedures such as identifying passwords, logons, and network monitoring. It can also handle recovery from a network failure.

Presentation Layer   Determines the "look," or format, of the data, network security, and file transfers. This layer performs protocol conversion and manages data compression, data translation, and encryption. The character set information also is determined at this level. (The character set determines which numbers represent which alphanumeric characters.)

Application Layer   Allows access to network services. This is the layer at which file services and print services operate. It also is the layer that workstations interact with, and it controls data flow and, if there are errors, recovery.

Figure 8.10 shows the complete OSI model. Note the relation of each layer to the others and the function of each layer.

FIGURE 8.10   OSI model and characteristics

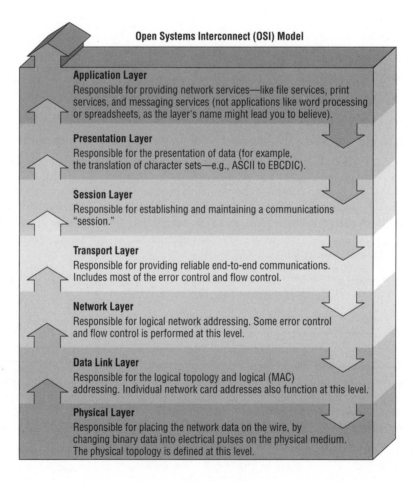

Open Systems Interconnect (OSI) Model

Application Layer
Responsible for providing network services—like file services, print services, and messaging services (not applications like word processing or spreadsheets, as the layer's name might lead you to believe).

Presentation Layer
Responsible for the presentation of data (for example, the translation of character sets—e.g., ASCII to EBCDIC).

Session Layer
Responsible for establishing and maintaining a communications "session."

Transport Layer
Responsible for providing reliable end-to-end communications. Includes most of the error control and flow control.

Network Layer
Responsible for logical network addressing. Some error control and flow control is performed at this level.

Data Link Layer
Responsible for the logical topology and logical (MAC) addressing. Individual network card addresses also function at this level.

Physical Layer
Responsible for placing the network data on the wire, by changing binary data into electrical pulses on the physical medium. The physical topology is defined at this level.

IEEE 802 Project Models

The Institute of Electrical and Electronics Engineers (IEEE) formed a subcommittee to create the 802 standards for networks. These standards specify certain types of networks, although not every network protocol is covered by the IEEE 802 committee specifications. This model breaks down into several categories, but the following are the most popularly referenced:

- 802.1 Internetworking
- 802.2 Logic Link Control
- 802.3 CSMA/CD LAN
- 802.4 Token Bus LAN
- 802.5 Token Ring LAN
- 802.6 Metropolitan Area Network
- 802.7 Broadband Technical Advisory Group
- 802.8 Fiber Optic Technical Advisory Group
- 802.9 Integrated Voice/Data Networks
- 802.10 Network Security
- 802.11 Wireless Networks
- 802.12 Demand Priority Access LAN

The IEEE 802 standards were designed primarily for enhancements to the bottom three layers of the OSI model. The IEEE 802 model breaks the Data Link layer into two sublayers: a Logical Link Control (LLC) sublayer and a Media Access Control (MAC) sublayer. In the Logical Link Control sublayer, data link communications are managed. The Media Access Control sublayer watches out for data collisions, as well as assigning physical addresses.

We will focus on the two predominant 802 models on which existing network architectures have been based: 802.3 CSMA/CD and 802.5 Token Ring.

IEEE 802.3 CSMA/CD

The original *802.3 CSMA/CD* model defines a bus topology network that uses a 50-ohm coaxial baseband cable and carries transmissions at 10Mbps. This standard groups data bits into frames and uses the Carrier Sense Multiple Access with Collision Detection (CSMA/CD) cable access method to put data on the cable. Currently, the 802.3 standard has been amended to include speeds up to 10Gbps.

CSMA/CD specifies that every computer can transmit at any time. When two machines transmit at the same time, a *collision* takes place, and no data can be transmitted for either machine. The machines then back off for a random period of time and try to transmit again. This process repeats until transmission takes place successfully. The CSMA/CD technology is also called *contention*.

The only major downside to 802.3 is that with large networks (more than 100 computers on the same cable), the number of collisions increases to the point where more collisions than transmissions are taking place.

Ethernet is an example of a protocol based on the IEEE 802.3 CSMA/CD standard.

CSMA/CD and Ethernet are discussed in more detail later in this chapter.

IEEE 802.5 TOKEN RING

The IEEE *802.5* standard specifies a physical star, logical ring topology that uses a token-passing technology to put the data on the cable. IBM developed this technology for its mainframe and minicomputer networks. IBM's name for it was Token Ring. The name stuck, and any network using this type of technology is called a Token Ring network.

In *token passing*, a special chunk of data called a *token* circulates through the ring from computer to computer. Any computer that has data to transmit must wait for the token. A transmitting computer that has data to transmit waits for a free token and takes it off the ring. Once it has the token, this computer modifies it in a way that tells the computers which one has the token. The transmitting computer then places the token (along with the data it needs to transmit) on the ring, and the token travels around the ring until it gets to the destination computer. The destination computer takes the token and data off the wire, modifies the token (indicating it has received the data), and places the token back on the wire. When the original sender receives the token back and sees that the destination computer has received the data, the sender modifies the token to set it free. It then sends the token back on the ring and waits until it has more data to transmit.

The main advantage of the token-passing access method over contention (the 802.3 model) is that it eliminates collisions. Only workstations that have the token can transmit. It would seem that this technology has a lot of overhead and would be slow. But remember that this whole procedure takes place in a few milliseconds.

This technology scales very well. It is not uncommon for Token Ring networks based on the IEEE 802.5 standard to reach hundreds of workstations on a single ring.

IEEE 802.5

The story of the IEEE 802.5 standard is rather interesting. It's a story of the tail wagging the dog. With all the other IEEE 802 standards, the committee either saw a need for a new protocol on its own or got a request for one. They would then sit down and hammer out the new standard. A standard created by this process is known as a *de jure* ("by law") standard. With the IEEE 802.5, however, everyone was already using this technology, so the IEEE 802 committee got involved and simply declared it a standard. This type of standard is known as a *de facto* ("from the fact") standard—a standard that was being followed without having been formally recognized.

Network Communication Protocols

As already discussed, a communication protocol is a standard set of rules governing communications. Protocols cover everything from the order of transmission to how to address the stations on a network. Without network protocols, no communication could take place on a network.

Four major protocols are in use today:

- TCP/IP
- IPX/SPX
- NetBEUI/NetBIOS
- AppleTalk

TCP/IP

The *Transmission Control Protocol/Internet Protocol (TCP/IP) suite* is called a suite because it's a collection of protocols. The two most important protocols are used to name the suite (TCP and IP). Although the name represents a collection of multiple protocols, the suite is usually referred to as simply TCP/IP.

TCP/IP is the only protocol suite used on the Internet. In order for any workstation or server to communicate with the Internet, it must have TCP/IP installed. TCP/IP was designed to get information delivered to its destination even in the event of a failure of part of the network. It uses various routing protocols to discover the network it is traveling on and to keep apprised of network changes.

The TCP/IP suite includes many protocols. A few of the more important are these:

Internet Protocol (IP)   Handles the movement of data between computers as well as network node addressing

Transmission Control Protocol (TCP)   Handles the reliable delivery of data

Internet Control Message Protocol (ICMP)   Transmits error messages and network statistics

User Datagram Protocol (UDP)   Performs a similar function to TCP, with less overhead and more speed, but with lower reliability

IPX/SPX

The *Internetwork Packet Exchange/Sequenced Packet Exchange (IPX/SPX)* is the default communication protocol for versions of the Novell NetWare operating system before Net-Ware 5. It is often used with Windows networks as well, but in Windows networks, the implementation of the IPX/SPX protocol is known as *NWLINK*.

IPX/SPX is a communication protocol similar to TCP/IP, but it's used primarily in LANs. It has features for use in WAN environments as well; before the mid-1990s, most corporate networks ran IPX/SPX because it was easy to configure and could be routed across WANs.

The two main protocols in IPX/SPX are IPX and SPX. IPX provides similar functions to TCP, and SPX provides functions similar to the TCP/IP suite protocols IP and UDP.

For information about IPX/SPX, search Novell's knowledgebase by using the Search link at support.novell.com.

NetBEUI/NetBIOS

NetBIOS (pronounced "net-bye-os") is an acronym formed from *network basic input/output system*. It's a Session-layer network protocol originally developed by IBM and Sytek to manage data exchange and network access. NetBIOS provides an interface with a consistent set of commands for requesting lower-level network services to transmit information from node to node, thus separating the applications from the underlying NOS. Many vendors provide either their own version of NetBIOS or an emulation of its communications services in their products.

NetBEUI (pronounced "net-boo-ee") is an acronym formed from *NetBIOS Extended User Interface*. It's an implementation and extension of IBM's NetBIOS transport protocol from Microsoft. NetBEUI communicates with the network through Microsoft's Network Driver Interface Specification (NDIS). NetBEUI is shipped with all versions of Microsoft's operating systems today and is generally considered to have a lot of overhead. NetBEUI also has no networking layer and therefore no routing capability, which means it is suitable only for small networks; you cannot build internetworks with NetBEUI, so it is often replaced with TCP/IP. Microsoft has added extensions to NetBEUI in Windows NT to remove the limitation of 254 sessions per node; this extended version of NetBEUI is called the NetBIOS Frame (NBF).

Together, these protocols make up a very fast protocol suite that most people call NetBEUI/NetBIOS. It is a very good protocol for LANs because it's simple and requires little or no setup (apart from giving each workstation a name). It allows users to find and use the network services they need easily, by simply browsing for them. However, because it contains no Network-layer protocol, it cannot be routed and thus cannot be used on a WAN. It also would make a poor choice for a WAN protocol because of the protocol overhead involved.

NetBIOS can be used over other protocols in addition to NetBEUI. Many Windows computers use NetBIOS over TCP/IP. This allows them to have NetBIOS functionality over a routed network.

AppleTalk

AppleTalk is not just a protocol; it is a proprietary network architecture for Macintosh computers. It uses a bus and typically either shielded or unshielded cable.

AppleTalk uses a Carrier Sense Multiple Access with Collision Avoidance (CSMA/CA) technology to put data on the cable. Unlike Ethernet, which uses a CSMA/CD method (where the CD stands for *Collision Detection*), this technology uses smart interface cards to detect traffic *before* it tries to send data. A CSMA/CA card listens to the wire. If there is no traffic, it sends a small amount of data. If no collisions occur, it follows that amount of data with the data it wants to transmit. In either case, if a collision happens, it backs off for a random amount of time and tries to transmit again.

A common analogy is used to describe the difference between CSMA/CD and CSMA/CA. Sending data is like walking across the street. With CSMA/CD, you just cross the street. If you get run over, you go back and try again. With CSMA/CA, you look both ways and send your little brother across the street. If he makes it, you can follow him. If either of you get run over, you both go back and try again.

Another interesting point about AppleTalk is that it's fairly simple. Most Macintosh computers already include AppleTalk, so it is relatively inexpensive. It assigns itself an address. In its first revision (Phase I), it allowed a maximum of 32 devices on a network. With its second revision (Phase II), it supports faster speeds and multiple networks with EtherTalk and Token-Talk. EtherTalk allows AppleTalk network protocols to run on Ethernet coaxial cable (used for Mac II and above). TokenTalk allows the AppleTalk protocol to run on a Token Ring network, and FDDITalk allows the AppleTalk protocol to run on a Fiber Distributed Data Interface (FDDI) network.

Protocol Addressing

Every network address in either TCP/IP or IPX has both a network portion and a node portion. The network portion is the number that is assigned to the network segment to which the station is connected. The node portion is the unique number that identifies that station on the segment. Together, the network portion and the node portion of an address ensure that a network address is unique across the entire network.

IPX addresses use an eight-digit hexadecimal number for the network portion. This number, called the *IPX network address*, can be assigned randomly by the installation program or manually by the network administrator. The node portion is the 12-digit hexadecimal MAC address assigned to the card by the manufacturer. A colon separates the two portions. The first six digits identify the hardware manufacturer and are assigned to the manufacturer by the IEEE. The last six digits are a unique number given to that card by the manufacturer.

MAC addresses, if necessary, can be changed in the properties of the NIC driver under Windows 9x and later.

Here is a sample IPX address:

Network Address   Node Address

00004567:006A7C11FB56

TCP/IP addresses, on the other hand, use a dotted decimal notation in the format xxx.xxx.xxx.xxx, as shown here:

199.217.67.34 IP Address

255.255.255.0 Subnet Mask

The address consists of four collections of eight-digit binary numbers (or up to three decimal digits) called *octets*, separated by periods. Each decimal number in an IP address is typically a number in the range 0 through 255. Which portion is the network and which portion is the node depend on the class of the address and the *subnet mask* assigned with the address. A subnet mask is also a dotted-decimal number with numbers in the range 0 through 255. If a subnet mask contains 255 in a position (corresponding to a binary number of all ones), the corresponding part of the IP address is the network address. For example, if you have the mask 255.255.255.0, the first three octets are the network portion, and the last portion is the node.

TCP/IP Address Classifications

In a TCP/IP address, the default number of bits used to identify the network and the host varies according to the network class of the address. While other methods, such as Classless Inter-Domain Routing, are currently more popular for specifying address space boundaries for entities of various sizes, the following classes of IP addresses originally offered a default set of boundaries for varying sizes of address space and still provide a fallback mechanism for end and intermediate devices in the absence of ample subnetting information:

- Class A was designed for very large networks only. The default network portion for Class A networks is the first 8 bits, leaving 24 bits for host identification. The high-order bit is always binary 0, which leaves 7 bits available for IANA to define 127 networks. The remaining 24 bits of the address allow each Class A network to hold as many as 16,777,214 hosts. Examples of Class A networks include General Electric, IBM, Hewlett-Packard, Apple, Xerox, Compaq, Columbia University, MIT, and the private network 10.0.0.0. All possible Class A networks are in use; no more are available.

- Class B was designed for medium-sized networks. The default network portion for Class B networks is the first 16 bits, leaving 16 bits for host identification. The 2 high-order bits are always binary 10, and the remaining 14 bits are used for IANA to define 16,384 networks, each with as many as 65,534 hosts attached. Examples of Class B networks include Microsoft, Exxon, and the 16 private networks ranging from 172.16.0.0 to 172.31.0.0, inclusive. Class B networks are generally regarded as unavailable, but address-conservation techniques have made some of these addresses available from time to time over the years.

- Class C was designed for smaller networks. The default network portion for Class C networks is the first 24 bits, leaving 8 bits for host identification. The 3 high-order bits are always binary 110, and the remaining 21 bits are used by IANA to define 2,097,152 networks, but each network can have a maximum of only 254 hosts. Examples of Class C networks are the 256 private networks ranging from 192.168.0.0 to 192.168.255.0. Class C networks are still available.

- Class D is the multicast address range and cannot be used for networks. There is no network/host structure to these addresses. They are taken as a complete address and used as destination addresses only, just like broadcast addresses. The 4 high-order bits are always 1110, and the remaining 28 bits allow access to more than 268 million possible addresses.

- Class E is reserved for experimental purposes. The first 4 bits in the address are always 1111.

One trick that works well, when faced with determining the class of an IP address written entirely in binary, is to assign the letters *A* through *D* to the first 4 bits, in alphabetical order. Wherever the first 0 falls signifies the class of address with which you are dealing. If none of the first 4 bits are set to 0, then you have a Class E address.

Figure 8.11 illustrates the relationships among these classes and shows how the bits are allocated by the Internet Network Information Center (InterNIC), an Internet Corporation for Assigned Names and Numbers (ICANN) licensed service mark.

FIGURE 8.11   The IP address structure

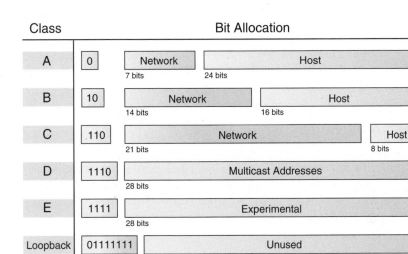

Because the bits used to identify the class are combined with the bits that define the network address, we can draw the following conclusions from the size of the first octet, or byte, of the address:

- A value of 126 or less indicates a Class A address. The first octet is the network number; the next three, the host ID.

- A value of exactly 127, while technically in the Class A range, is reserved as a software loopback test address. If you send an echo request to 127.0.0.1, the ping doesn't actually generate any network traffic. It does, however, test that TCP/IP is installed correctly. Using this number as a special test address has the unfortunate effect of wasting almost 17 million possible IP addresses, a case of early-seventies shortsightedness, much like the theory that 64KB of RAM should be enough for PCs.

- A value of 128 through 191 is a Class B address. The first two octets are the network number, and the last two are the host address.

- A value of 192 through 223 is a Class C address. The first three octets are the network address, and the last octet is the host address.

- A value of 224 through 239 is a Class D multicast address. Again, there are no network or host portions to multicast addresses.

- A value greater than 239 indicates a reserved Class E address.

> **TIP**
>
> The private address spaces listed with each class description are specified in RFC 1918 as being available to anyone who wants to use IP addressing on a private network but does not want to connect these networks directly to the Internet. Private addresses are those addresses that are not permitted to be routed by Internet routers. In fact, ISPs can be fined for passing traffic with these addresses as source or destination. Conversely, public addresses are those IP addresses that are allowed to be passed by Internet routers. You can use the private address space without the risk of compromising someone else's registered network address space. If you use a private address and decide to interconnect your intranet with the Internet, you may use Network Address Translation (NAT) to do so.

Network Architectures

Network architectures define the structure of the network, including hardware, software, and layout. We differentiate each architecture by the hardware and software required to maintain optimum performance levels. A network architecture's performance is usually discussed in terms of *bandwidth*, or how much data a particular network technology can handle in a period of time. The major architectures in use today are Ethernet, Token Ring, and ARCNet.

Ethernet

The original definition of the 802.3 model included a bus topology using a baseband coaxial cable. From this model came the first Ethernet architecture. *Ethernet* was originally codeveloped by Digital, Intel, and Xerox and was known as *DIX Ethernet*.

Ethernet has several specifications, each one specifying the speed, communication method, and cable. The original Ethernet was given a designation of 10Base5. The *10* in Ethernet 10Base5 stands for the 10Mbps transmission rate, *Base* stands for the baseband communications used, and *5* stands for the maximum distance of 500 meters to carry transmissions. This method of identification soon caught on, and as vendors changed the specifications of the Ethernet architecture, they followed the same pattern in the way they identified these specifications.

After 10Base5 came 10Base2 and 10BaseT. These quickly became standards in Ethernet technology. Many other standards (including 100BaseF, 10BaseF, and 100BaseT) developed since then, but those three are the most popular.

Ethernet 10Base2 uses thin coaxial cables and bus topology, and it transmits at 10Mbps with a maximum distance of 185 meters. Ethernet 10BaseT uses twisted-pair cabling, transmitting at 10Mbps with a maximum distance of 100 meters, and a physical star topology with a logical bus topology.

Token Ring

Token Ring networks are exactly like the IEEE 802.5 specification because the specification is based on IBM's Token Ring technology. Token Ring uses a physical star, logical ring topology. All workstations are cabled to a central device called a *multistation access unit (MAU)*. The ring is created within the MAU by connecting every port together with special circuitry in the MAU. Token Ring can use shielded or unshielded cable and can transmit data at either 4Mbps or 16Mbps.

ARCNet (Attached Resource Computing Network)

A special type of network architecture that deserves mention is the *Attached Resource Computer Network (ARCNet)*. Developed in 1977, it was not based on any existing IEEE 802 model. However, ARCNet is important to mention because of its ties to IBM mainframe networks and also because of its popularity. Its popularity came from its flexibility and price. It was flexible because its cabling used large trunks and physical star configurations, so if a cable came loose or was disconnected, the network did not fail. In addition, because it used cheap coaxial cable, networks could be installed fairly cheaply.

Even though ARCNet enjoyed an initial success, it died out as other network architectures became more popular. The main reason was its slow transfer rate of only 2.5Mbps. Thomas-Conrad (a major developer of ARCNet products) developed a version of ARCNet that runs at 100Mbps, but most people have abandoned ARCNet for other architectures. ARCNet is also not based on any standard, which makes it difficult to find compatible hardware from multiple vendors.

Identifying Common Network Media

We have looked at the types of networks, network architectures, and the way a network communicates. To bring networks together, we use several types of media. A *medium* is the material on which data is transferred from one point to another. There are two parts to the medium: the NIC and the cabling. The type of NIC you use depends on the type of cable you are using, so let's discuss cabling first.

Cabling

When the data is passing through the OSI model and reaches the Physical layer, it must find its way onto the medium that is used to physically transfer data from computer to computer. This medium is *cable* (or in the case of wireless networks, the air). It is the NIC's role to prepare the data for transmission, but it is the cable's role to properly move the data to its intended destination. It is not as simple as just plugging it into the computer. The cabling you choose must support both the network architecture and topology. There are five main types of cabling methods: coaxial cable, twisted-pair cable, fiber-optic cable, RS-232 Serial, and wireless. We'll summarize all four cabling methods after the brief descriptions that follow.

Coaxial

Coaxial cable (or coax) contains a center conductor made of copper, surrounded by a plastic jacket, with a braided shield over the jacket (as shown in Figure 8.12). Either Teflon or a plastic such as PVC covers this metal shield. The Teflon-type covering is frequently referred to as a *plenum-rated* coating. That simply means that the coating does not produce toxic gas when burned (as PVC does) and is rated for use in ventilation plenums that carry breathable air. This type of cable is more expensive but may be mandated by electrical code whenever cable is hidden in walls or ceilings. Plenum rating applies to all types of cabling.

NOTE   Other types of cabling (namely, twisted pair) can be rated for plenum use.

FIGURE 8.12   Coaxial cable

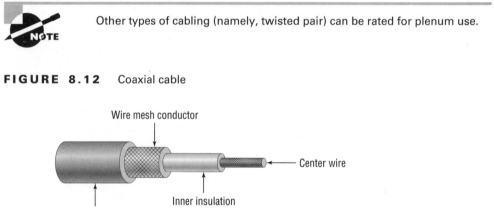

Coaxial cable is available in different specifications that are rated according to the *RG* Type system. Different cables have different specifications and, therefore, different RG grading designations (according to the U.S. military specification MIL-C-17). Distance and cost are considerations when selecting coax cable. The thicker the copper, the farther a signal can travel—and with that comes a higher cost and a less-flexible cable.

Coaxial cable comes in many thicknesses and types. The most common use for this type of cable is Ethernet 10Base2 cabling. It is known as Thinnet or Cheapernet. Table 8.2 shows the different types of RG cabling and their uses.

TABLE 8.2   Coax RG Types

RG #	Popular Name	Ethernet Implementation	Type of Cable
RG-6	Satellite/cable TV cable	N/A	Solid copper
RG-8	Thicknet	10Base5	Solid copper
RG-58 U	N/A	None	Solid copper

TABLE 8.2 Coax RG Types *(continued)*

RG #	Popular Name	Ethernet Implementation	Type of Cable
RG-58 AU	Thinnet	10Base2	Stranded copper
RG-62	ARCNet	N/A	Solid/stranded copper

COAX CONNECTOR TYPES

With coax cable used in networking, generally you use *BNC* connectors (see Figure 8.13) to attach stations to a Thinnet network. It is beyond our province to settle the long-standing argument over the meaning of the abbreviation BNC. We have heard BayoNet Connector, Bayonet Nut Connector, and British Naval Connector. What is relevant is that the BNC connector locks securely with a quarter-twist motion.

With Thick Ethernet, a station attaches to the main cable via a vampire tap, which clamps onto the cable. A *vampire tap* is so named because a metal tooth sinks into the cable, thus making the connection with the inner conductor. The tap is connected to an external transceiver that in turn has a 15-pin AUI connector (also called *DIX* or DB-15 connector) to which you attach a cable that connects to the station (shown in Figure 8.14). DIX got its name from the companies that worked on this format—Digital, Intel, and Xerox.

Twisted-Pair

Twisted-pair is one of the most popular methods of cabling because of its flexibility and low cost. It consists of several pairs of wire twisted around each other within an insulated jacket, as shown in Figure 8.15. Twisted-pair is most often found in 10BaseT Ethernet networks, although other systems can use it.

FIGURE 8.13 Male and female BNC connectors

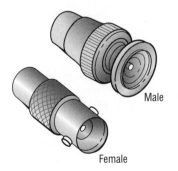

Male

Female

FIGURE 8.14 Thicknet and vampire taps

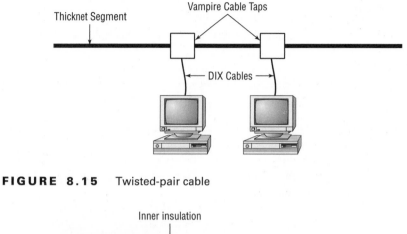

FIGURE 8.15 Twisted-pair cable

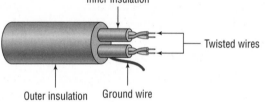

Twisted-pair cabling is usually classified in two types: unshielded twisted-pair (UTP) and shielded twisted-pair (STP). UTP is simply twisted-pair cabling that is unshielded. STP is the same as UTP, but it has a braided foil shield around the twisted wires (to decrease electrical interference).

UTP comes in seven grades to offer different levels of protection against electrical interference:

- Category 1 is for voice-only transmissions and is in most phone systems today. It contains two twisted pairs.

- Category 2 is able to transmit data at speeds up to 4Mbps. It contains four twisted pairs of wires.

- Category 3 is able to transmit data at speeds up to 10Mbps. It contains four twisted pairs of wires with three twists per foot.

- Category 4 is able to transmit data at speeds up to 16Mbps. It contains four twisted pairs of wires.

- Category 5 is able to transmit data at speeds up to 100Mbps. It contains four twisted pairs of copper wire to give the most protection.

- Category 5e is able to transmit data at speeds up to 1Gbps. It also contains four twisted pairs of copper wire, but they are physically separated and contain more twists per foot than Category 5 to provide maximum interference protection.

- Category 6 is able to transmit data at speeds up to 1Gbps and beyond. It also contains four twisted pairs of copper wire, and they are oriented differently than in Category 5 or 5e.

Each of these levels has a maximum transmission distance of 100 meters.

> CompTIA (and many others) usually shorten the word *category* to "Cat" and use the form Cat-5 to refer to Category 5, for example. This is a common way to refer to these categories, and you can feel free to use these terms interchangeably.

TWISTED-PAIR CONNECTOR TYPES

Clearly, a BNC connector won't fit easily on UTP cable, so you need to use an *RJ (registered jack)* connector. You are probably familiar with RJ connectors. Most telephones connect with an RJ-11 connector. The connector used with UTP cable is called RJ-45. The RJ-11 has four wires, or two pairs, and the network connector RJ-45 has four pairs, or eight wires.

In almost every case, UTP uses RJ connectors. Even the now-extinct ARCNet used RJ connectors. You use a crimper to attach an RJ connector to a cable, just as you use a crimper with the BNC connector. The only difference is that the die that holds the connector is a different shape. Higher-quality crimping tools have interchangeable dies for both types of cables.

In addition to the RJ series used on UTP, STP (when used with Token Ring) often uses a special connector known as the *IBM data connector (IDC)*, *universal data connector (UDC)*, or *hermaphroditic data connector*. An example of this type of connector is shown in Figure 8.16. The IDC is unique in many ways. First, it isn't as universal as the other types of network connectors. Second, there aren't male and female versions, as with the others—the IDC is both male and female, so any two data connectors can connect. This connector is most commonly used with IBM's Token Ring technology and Type 1 or 2 STP cable.

FIGURE 8.16   An IDC/UDC

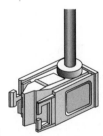

Four-position data
connectors used
for IBM Type 1
cabling system

The IDC also uses a tab to hold the connectors together, but this tab is a little more rigid than the tab on the RJ series connectors and doesn't move as much. Therefore, breakage is not much of an issue.

Fiber-Optic

Fiber-optic cabling has been called one of the best advances in cabling. It consists of a thin, flexible glass or plastic fiber surrounded by a rubberized outer coating (see Figure 8.17). It provides transmission speeds from 100Mbps to 10Gbps and a maximum distance of several miles. Because it uses pulses of light instead of electric voltages to transmit data, it is immune to electrical interference and to wiretapping.

FIGURE 8.17   Fiber-optic cable

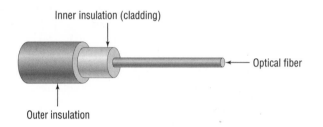

Fiber-optic cable has not been widely adopted for local area networks, however, because of its high cost of installation. Networks that need extremely fast transmission rates, transmissions over long distances, or have had problems with electrical interference in the past often use fiber-optic cabling.

Fiber-optic cable is referred to as either single-mode or multimode fiber. The term *mode* refers to the bundles of light that enter the fiber-optic cable. Single-mode fiber-optic cable uses only a single mode of light to propagate through the fiber cable, whereas multimode fiber allows multiple modes of light to propagate. In multimode fiber-optic cable, the light bounces off the cable walls as it travels through the cable, which causes the signal to weaken more quickly.

Multimode fiber-optic is most often used as horizontal cable. It permits multiple modes of light to propagate through the cable and this lowers cable distances and has a lower available bandwidth. Devices that use multimode fiber-optic cable typically use light-emitting diodes (LEDs) to generate the light that travels through the cable; however, higher bandwidth network devices such as Gigabit Ethernet are now using lasers with multimode fiber-optic cable. ANSI/TIA/EIA-568-B recognizes two-fiber (duplex) 62.5/125-micron multimode fiber; ANSI/TIA/EIA-568-B also recognizes 50/125-micron multimode fiber-optic cable.

Single-mode optical fiber cable is commonly used as backbone cabling; it is also usually the cable type used in phone systems. Light travels through single-mode fiber-optic cable using only a single mode, meaning it travels straight down the fiber and does not bounce off the cable walls. Because only a single mode of light travels through the cable, single-mode fiber-optic cable supports higher bandwidth and longer distances than multimode fiber-optic cable. Devices that use single-mode fiber-optic cable typically use lasers to generate the light that travels through the cable.

ANSI/TIA/EIA-568-B recognizes 62.5/125-micron, 50/125-micron, and 8.3/125-micron single-mode optical fiber cables. ANSI/TIA/EIA-568-B states that the maximum backbone distance using single-mode fiber-optic cable is 3,000 meters (9,840 feet), and the maximum backbone distance using multimode fiber is 2,000 meters (6,560 feet).

FIBER-OPTIC CONNECTOR TYPES

The *subscriber connector* (SC; also sometimes known as a *square connector*) is a type of fiber-optic connector, as shown in Figure 8.18. As you can see, SCs are latched connectors. This makes it impossible for you to pull out the connector without releasing the connector's latch, usually by pressing a button or release.

FIGURE 8.18   A sample SC

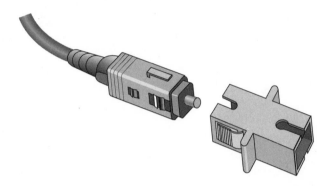

SCs work with either single- or multimode optical fibers and last for around 1,000 matings. They are currently seeing increased use, but they still aren't as popular as ST connectors for LAN connections.

The *straight tip (ST)* fiber-optic connector, developed by AT&T, is probably the most widely used fiber-optic connector. It uses a BNC attachment mechanism, similar to the Thinnet Ethernet connection mechanism, which makes connections and disconnections fairly easy. The ease of use of the ST is one of the attributes that makes this connector so popular. Figure 8.19 shows some examples of ST connectors. Notice the BNC attachment mechanism.

Because it is so widely available, adapters to other fiber connector types are available for this connector type. The ST connector type also has a maximum mating cycle of around 1,000 matings.

RS-232 (Serial Cables)

Occasionally, networks use *RS-232 cables* (also known as *serial cables*) to carry data. The classic example is in older mainframe and minicomputer terminal connections. Connections from the individual terminals go to a device known as a *multiplexer* that combines the serial connections into one connection and connects all the terminals to the host computer. This cabling system is seen less and less as a viable LAN cabling method, however, because LAN connections such as twisted-pair Ethernet are faster, more reliable, and easier to maintain.

FIGURE 8.19   Examples of ST connectors

Wireless Networks

One of the most fascinating cabling technologies today—actually, it doesn't really *use* cable—is wireless. Wireless networks offer the ability to extend a LAN without the use of traditional cabling methods. Wireless transmissions are made through the air by infrared light, laser light, narrow-band radio, microwave, or spread-spectrum radio.

Wireless LANs are becoming increasingly popular as businesses become more mobile and less centralized. You can see them most often in environments where standard cabling methods are not possible or wanted. However, they are still not as fast or efficient as standard cabling methods. They are also more susceptible to eavesdropping and interference than standard cabling methods.

Summary of Cabling Types

Each type of cabling has its own benefits and drawbacks. Table 8.3 details the most common types of cabling in use today. As you look at this table, pay particular attention to the cost, length, and maximum transmission rates of each cabling type.

TABLE 8.3   Cable Types

Characteristics	Twisted-Pair	Coaxial	Fiber-Optic	Wireless
Cost	Least expensive	More than twisted-pair	Expensive	N/A
Maximum length	100 meters (328 feet)	185 meters (607 feet) to 500 meters (1640 feet)	>10 miles	Up to 2 miles
Transmission rate	10Mbps to 100Mbps	10Mbps	100Mbps or more	2Mbps to 54Mbps
Flexibility	Most flexible	Fair	Fair	Limited
Ease of installation	Very easy	Easy	Difficult	Depends on the implementation
Interference	Susceptible	Better than UTP; more susceptible than STP	Not susceptible	Susceptible
Special features	Often prein-stalled; similar to the wiring used in tele-phone systems	Easiest installation	Supports voice, data, and video at the highest transmission speeds	Very flexible
Preferred uses	Networks	Medium-size networks with high security needs	Networks of any size requiring high speed and data security	WANs and radio/TV communications
Connector	RJ-45	BNC-T and AUI	Special (SC, ST, and others)	Dish, transceiver, or access point
Physical topology	Star	Bus	Star (typically)	Bus or star

Network Interface Cards (NICs)

The *network interface card (NIC)* provides the physical interface between computer and cabling. It prepares data, sends data, and controls the flow of data. It can also receive and translate data into bytes for the CPU to understand. It communicates at the Physical layer of the OSI model and comes in many shapes and sizes.

Different NICs are distinguished by the PC bus type and the network for which they are used. This section describes the role of the NIC and how to choose the appropriate one. The following factors should be taken into consideration when choosing a NIC:

- Preparing data
- Sending and controlling data
- Configuration
- Drivers
- Compatibility
- Performance

Preparing Data

In the computer, data moves along buses in parallel, as on a four-lane interstate highway. But on a network cable, data travels in a single stream, as on a one-lane highway. This difference can cause problems when you're transmitting and receiving data, because the paths traveled are not the same. It is the NIC's job to translate the data from the computer into signals that can flow easily along the cable. It does this by translating digital signals into electrical signals (and in the case of fiber-optic NICs, to optical signals).

Sending and Controlling Data

For two computers to send and receive data, the cards must agree on several things. These include the following:

- The maximum size of the data frames
- The amount of data sent before giving confirmation
- The time needed between transmissions
- The amount of time to wait before sending confirmation
- The amount of data a card can hold
- The speed at which data transmits

If the cards can agree, then the sending of the data is successful. If the cards cannot agree, the sending of data does not occur.

In order to successfully send data on the network, you need to make sure the NICs are the same type (such as all Ethernet, all Token Ring, all ARCNet, and so on) and they are connected to the same piece of cable. If you use cards of different types (for example, one Ethernet and one Token Ring), neither of them will be able to communicate with the other (unless you use a gateway device, such as a router).

In addition, NICs can send data using either full-duplex or half-duplex mode. *Half-duplex communication* means that between the sender and receiver, only one of them can transmit at any one time. In *full-duplex communication*, a computer can send and receive data simultaneously. The main advantage of full-duplex over half-duplex communication is performance. NICs (specifically Fast Ethernet NICs) can operate twice as fast (200Mbps) in full-duplex mode as they do normally in half-duplex mode (100Mbps).

NIC Configuration

The NIC's configuration includes such things as a manufacturer's hardware address, IRQ address, base I/O port address, and base memory address. Some may also use Direct Memory Access (DMA) channels to offer better performance.

Each card must have a unique hardware address. If two cards on the same network have the same hardware address, neither one will be able to communicate. For this reason, the IEEE committee has established a standard for hardware addresses and assigns blocks of these addresses to NIC manufacturers, which then hard-wire the addresses into the cards.

Configuring a NIC is similar to configuring any other type of expansion card. The NIC usually needs a unique IRQ channel and I/O address and possibly a DMA channel. Token Ring cards often have two memory addresses that must be excluded in reserved memory to work properly.

NIC Drivers

For the computer to use the NIC, it is very important to install the proper device drivers. These drivers communicate directly with the network redirector and adapter. They operate in the Media Access Control sublayer of the Data Link layer of the OSI model.

PC Bus Type

When you're choosing a NIC, use one that fits the bus type of your PC. If you have more than one type of bus in your PC (for example, a combination PCI/PCI Express), use a NIC that fits into the fastest type (the PCI Express, in this case). This is especially important in servers, because the NIC can quickly become a bottleneck if this guideline isn't followed.

Refer back to Chapter 1 to refresh your memory about the bus architectures mentioned in this discussion.

Network Interface Card Performance

The most important goal of the network adapter card is to optimize network performance and minimize the amount of time needed to transfer data packets across the network. There are several ways of doing this, including assigning a DMA channel, using a shared memory adapter, and deciding to allow bus mastering.

If the NIC can use DMA channels, then data can move directly from the card's buffer to the computer's memory, bypassing the CPU. A shared memory adapter is a NIC that has its own RAM. This feature allows transfers to and from the computer to happen much more quickly, increasing the performance of the NIC. Shared system memory allows the NIC to use a section of the computer's RAM to process data. Bus mastering lets the card take temporary control of the computer's bus to bypass the CPU and move directly to RAM. This process is more expensive, but it can improve performance by 20 to 70 percent. However, the PCI bus supports bus mastering.

Each of these features can enhance the performance of a NIC. Most cards today have at least one, if not several, of these features.

Media Access Methods

You have put the network together in a topology. You have told the network how to communicate and send the data, and you have told it how to send the data to another computer. You also have the communications medium in place. The next problem you need to solve is how to put the data on the cable. What you need now are the *cable access methods*, which define a set of rules for how computers put data on and retrieve it from a network cable. We've mentioned a few of these earlier in this chapter, but now let's take a closer look at four methods of data access:

Carrier Sense Multiple Access with Collision Detection (CSMA/CD)   As we've already discussed, NICs that use CSMA/CD listen to or "sense" the cable to check for traffic. They compete for a chance to transmit. Usually, if access to the network is slow, too many computers are trying to transmit, causing traffic jams.

Carrier Sense Multiple Access with Collision Avoidance (CSMA/CA)   Instead of monitoring traffic and moving in when there is a break, CSMA/CA allows the computer to send a signal that it is ready to transmit data. If the ready signal transmits without a problem, the computer then transmits its data. If the ready signal is not transmitted successfully, the computer waits and tries again. This method is slower and less popular than CSMA/CD.

Token Passing   As previously discussed, token passing is a way of giving every NIC equal access to the cable. A special packet of data is passed from computer to computer. Any computer that wants to transmit has to wait until it has the token. It can then transmit its data.

Polling   Polling is an old method of media access that is still in use. Not many topologies support polling anymore, mainly because it has special hardware requirements. This method requires a central, intelligent device (meaning the device contains either hardware or software intelligence to enable it to make decisions) that asks each workstation in turn if it has any data to transmit. If the workstation answers "yes," the controller allows the workstation to transmit its data.

The polling process doesn't scale well. That is, you can't take this method and simply apply it to any number of workstations. Also, the high cost of the intelligent controllers and cards has made the polling method all but obsolete.

Understanding Networking Components

The cabling links computer to computer. Most cabling allows networks to be hundreds of feet long. But what if your network needs to be bigger than that? What if you need to connect your LANs to other LANs to make a WAN? What if the architecture you've picked for your network is limiting the growth of your network along with the growth of your company? The answer to these questions is found in a special class of networking devices known as *connectivity devices*. These devices allow communications to break the boundaries of local networks and let your computers talk to other computers in the next building, the next city, or the next country.

There are several categories of connectivity devices, but we are going to discuss the six most important and frequently used:

- Repeaters
- Hubs/switches
- Bridges
- Routers
- Brouters
- Gateways

These connectivity devices have made it possible to lengthen networks to almost unlimited distances.

Repeaters

Repeaters are simple devices. They allow a cabling system to extend beyond its maximum allowed length by amplifying the network voltages so they travel farther. Repeaters are nothing more than amplifiers and, as such, are very inexpensive.

Repeaters operate at the Physical layer of the OSI model. Because of this, repeaters can only be used to regenerate signals between similar network segments. For example, you can extend an Ethernet 10Base2 network to 400 meters with a repeater. But you can't connect an Ethernet network and a Token Ring network together with one.

The main disadvantage of repeaters is that they just amplify signals. These signals include not only the network signals but any noise on the wire as well. Eventually, if you use enough repeaters, you could possibly drown out the signal with the amplified noise. For this reason, repeaters are used only as a temporary fix.

Hubs/Switches

Hubs are devices used to link several computers together. They are most often used in 10BaseT Ethernet networks. They are also simple devices. In fact, they are just multiport repeaters: They repeat any signal that comes in on one port and copy it to the other ports (a process that is also called *broadcasting*).

There are two types of hubs: active and passive. *Passive hubs* connect all ports together electrically and are usually not powered. *Active hubs* use electronics to amplify and clean up the signal before it is broadcast to the other ports. In the category of active hubs, there is also a class called *intelligent* hubs, which are hubs that can be remotely managed on the network.

Switches operate very similarly to hubs because they connect several computers (usually twisted-pair Ethernet networks). However, switches don't repeat everything they receive on one port to every other port as hubs do. Rather, switches examine the header of the incoming packet and forward it properly to the right port and only that port. This greatly reduces overhead and thus performance as there is essentially a virtual connection between sender and receiver.

If it helps you to remember their functions, a hub is essentially a multiport repeater, whereas a switch functions like a multiport bridge (and in some cases, a multiport router).

Bridges

Bridges operate in the Data Link layer of the OSI model. They join similar topologies and are used to divide network segments. Bridges keep traffic on one side from crossing to the other. For this reason, they are often used to increase performance on a high-traffic segment.

For example, with 200 people on one Ethernet segment, performance will be mediocre, because of the design of Ethernet and the number of workstations that are fighting to transmit. If you divide the segment into two segments of 100 workstations each, the traffic will be much lower on either side and performance will increase.

Bridges are not able to distinguish one protocol from another, because higher levels of the OSI model are not available to them. If a bridge is aware of the destination address, it can forward packets; otherwise, it forwards the packets to all segments.

Bridges are more intelligent than repeaters but are unable to move data across multiple networks simultaneously. Unlike repeaters, bridges *can* filter out noise.

The main disadvantage of bridges is that they can't connect dissimilar network types or perform intelligent path selection. For that function, you need a router.

Routers

Routers are highly intelligent devices that connect multiple network types and determine the best path for sending data. They can route packets across multiple networks and use routing tables to store network addresses to determine the best destination. Routers operate at the Network layer of the OSI model.

The advantage of using a router over a bridge is that routers can determine the best path for data to take to get to its destination. Like bridges, they can segment large networks and can filter out noise. However, they are slower than bridges because they are more intelligent devices; as such, they analyze every packet, causing packet-forwarding delays. Because of this intelligence, they are also more expensive.

Routers are normally used to connect one LAN to another. Typically, when a WAN is set up, at least two routers are used.

Brouters

Brouters are truly an ingenious idea, because they combine the best of both worlds—bridges and routers. They are used to connect dissimilar network segments and also to route only one specific protocol. The other protocols are bridged instead of being dropped. Brouters are used when only one protocol needs to be routed or where a router is not cost-effective (as in a branch office).

Gateways

Gateways connect dissimilar network environments and architectures. Some gateways can use all levels of the OSI model, but frequently they are found in the Application layer. There, gateways convert data and repackage it to meet the requirements of the destination address. This makes gateways slower than other connectivity devices and more costly. An example of a gateway is the NT Gateway Service for NetWare, which, when running on a Windows NT Server, can connect a Microsoft Windows NT network with a Novell NetWare network.

Installing, Configuring, and Troubleshooting Networks

Now that you have learned about the fundamentals of networking, you should learn the basics behind installing and configuring networks. Because networks are so complex, this chapter will provide you with only a sliver of knowledge of how to install and configure networks. However, as an A+ technician, you will, from time to time, be asked to install, configure, and troubleshoot those components of a network that are part of a PC—namely, the NICs.

 If you are interested in networking, please consider taking the CompTIA Network+ exam as well. It goes into much more detail about networking, and you will open yourself up to a much larger world of computing.

In this section, you will learn how to do the following:

- Install and configure a network interface card
- Obtain wired and wireless Internet connections
- Troubleshoot network interface cards

Installing and Configuring Network Interface Cards

In the old days (1980s) of personal computers, NICs were a pain to install. Not only did you have to configure the hardware manually, but you had to configure the network protocol stack manually. This usually involved a configuration program of some kind and was very cumbersome. With Windows, it's much simpler.

 The CompTIA A+ exam tests your ability to install a NIC. For the exam, you must understand how to both install and configure a NIC.

Before you can begin configuring your network, you must have a NIC installed in the machine. Installing a NIC is a fairly simple task if you have installed any expansion card before; a NIC is just a special type of expansion card. In Exercise 8.1, you will learn how to install a NIC.

 Sometimes older NICs conflict with newer Plug and Play (PnP) hardware. In addition, some newer NICs with PnP capability don't like some kinds of networking software. To resolve a PnP conflict of the latter type, disable PnP on the NIC either with a jumper or with the software setup program. In this chapter, we will assume that your NIC is installed and the drivers are loaded.

EXERCISE 8.1

Installing a NIC

Follow these steps to install a NIC.

1. Power off the PC, remove the case and the metal or plastic blank covering the expansion slot opening, and insert the expansion card into an open slot.

2. Secure the expansion card with the screw provided.

Note: These first two steps may not be necessary if you have an onboard NIC.

3. Put the case back on the computer and power it up (you can run software configuration at this step, if necessary). If there are conflicts, change any parameters so that the NIC doesn't conflict with any existing hardware.

4. Install a driver for the NIC for the type of operating system that you have. Windows should auto-detect the NIC and install the driver automatically. It may also ask you to provide a copy of the necessary driver if it does not recognize the type of NIC you have installed. If the card is not detected at all, run the Add New Hardware Wizard by double-clicking Add New Hardware in the Control Panel.

5. After installing a NIC, you must hook the card to the network using the cable supplied by your network administrator. Attach this patch cable to the connector on the NIC and to a port in the wall, thus connecting your PC to the rest of the network.

Obtaining Wired and Wireless Internet Connections

One of the procedures performed most often by today's technicians is setting up a computer to connect to the Internet. The Internet is no longer just a buzzword, it's a reality. The majority of homes in America have computers and the majority of those computers are connected to the Internet.

Before we can discuss connecting Windows to the Internet, we need to discuss the Internet itself. There are some common terms and concepts every technician must understand about the Internet. First, the Internet is really just a bunch of private networks connected using public telephone lines. These private networks are the access points to the Internet and are run by companies called *Internet service providers (ISPs)*. They sell you a connection to the Internet for a monthly service charge (kind of like your cable bill or phone bill). Your computer talks to the ISP using public phone lines, or even using technologies such as cable or wireless.

Types of Connections

Your computer might use several designations and types of Internet connections to talk to an ISP, ranging in speeds from 56Kbps to several megabits per second (Mbps). Remember that these same types of phone lines connect the ISPs to one another to form the Internet.

Dial-Up/POTS

The most common of Internet access still seen in most parts of the United States is dial-up. In a *dial-up* Internet connection, the computer connecting to the Internet uses a modem to connect to the ISP over a standard telephone line. The telephone company technicians usually call the phone line that goes into your house a *POTS line* (short for *plain old telephone service*). However, the proper, more formal acronym is *public switched telephone network (PSTN)*.

Dial-up Internet connections are relatively slow when compared to the other methods listed here. At the most, dial-up connections are theoretically limited to 56Kbps and practically limited to 53Kbps by FCC rules. In reality, the 53Kbps speed is for downloads only (from the Internet to your computer) and only under ideal conditions. In the real world, you are most likely to get speeds around 40Kbps. The maximum upload speed (from your computer to the Internet) for this connection is around 33.6Kbps.

To make a connection with POTS, you must have a modem installed in your computer. You also must connect your home phone line to the line port on your modem. Then you must configure some software on your computer known as a *dialer*. A *dialer* is a special program that initiates the connection with the ISP, takes the phone off the hook, dials the ISP's access number, and establishes the connection. Most versions of Windows have a built-in dialer known as dial-up networking.

Other ISPs may have their own dialer program that they give you on disk or CD-ROM when you sign up for their service. ISPs such as AOL and AT&T WorldCom have their own dialer software (AOL has its own program, which encompasses dialer, browser, and other functions in one software package but can also function as an Internet dialer).

Dial-up networking is basic Internet access. Most people use the Internet so much that they are moving on to higher-speed methods of Internet access. These higher-speed methods are generally lumped together and called *broadband Internet access*.

Digital Subscriber Line (DSL)

One of the first methods of broadband Internet access to become popular was a technology called *digital subscriber line (DSL)*. DSL uses the existing phone line from your home to the phone company to carry digital signals at higher speeds. Essentially, DSL piggybacks a digital signal on the line used for analog communication (your voice). So, with DSL it is possible to have high-speed Internet access and use your phone at the same time.

However, DSL has some drawbacks. It's more expensive than dial-up; in some areas, DSL can run at least $30 per month more than dial-up connections. Plus, there are distance limitations. You must be within a certain distance of the phone company's central office (usually less than one mile, but it varies on the type of DSL being used). Also, because the phone line is carrying digital signals, many phone lines in older homes and neighborhoods may not be up to par.

When connecting to DSL, you need a special device, most often called a DSL modem. This is actually a misnomer, because modems change digital to analog and back again. Because DSL is digital, the signals are never changed into analog. The proper term for the device used to access DSL is a *DSL endpoint*. Endpoints often have the functions of network bridges or routers.

Endpoints can be either internal or external. Internal endpoints go inside a computer as an expansion card, but that means only that computer can access the Internet directly. External endpoints can be hooked to a hub, switch, or router, which can share the Internet connection with multiple computers.

To see if DSL is available in your area, go to www.dslreports.com. You can also talk to your local telephone provider.

Cable

One of the most popular broadband Internet access methods these days is *cable Internet*. Cable Internet provides broadband Internet access via the television cable that runs to your home via a specification known as *Data Over Cable Service Internet Specification (DOCSIS)*. It is relatively cheap and provides fast Internet download speeds (typically up to 3Mbps of shared bandwidth). It is theoretically available to anyone with a cable TV connection and a cable provider that provides the service.

Although cable sounds great, it has a few drawbacks. If you have a cable Internet connection, because of the way it is designed, essentially you are on a LAN with all the neighbors in your cable segment. Thus, if you (or your cable company) don't protect your connection, theoretically you could see your neighbors' computers and they could see yours. So security might be a problem.

Also, in some markets, the cable itself may not be in the best condition to provide the higher-speed data services. It may need to be replaced (at cost to the cable provider), so cable may not be available in some markets.

For detailed information about cable Internet availability and performance, check out www.cablemodemhelp.com.

INTEGRATED SERVICES DIGITAL NETWORK (ISDN)

Integrated Services Digital Network (ISDN) is a digital, point-to-point network capable of maximum transmission speeds of about 2Mbps, although speeds of 128Kbps are more common. ISDN uses the same UTP wiring as POTS, but it can transmit data at much higher speeds. That's where the similarity ends. What makes ISDN different from a regular POTS line is how it uses the copper wiring. Instead of carrying an analog (voice) signal, it carries digital signals.

A computer connects to an ISDN line via an *ISDN terminal adapter* (often incorrectly referred to as an ISDN modem). An ISDN terminal adapter is not a modem because it does not convert a digital signal to an analog signal; ISDN signals are digital.

An ISDN line has two types of channels. The data is carried on special *Bearer, or B, channels*, each of which can carry 64Kbps of data. A typical *basic rate interface (BRI)* ISDN line has two B channels. One channel can be used for a voice call while the other is being used for data transmissions, and this occurs on one pair of copper wires. The second type of channel is used for call setup and link management and is known as the *signal, or D, channel* (also referred to as the *Delta channel)*. This channel has only 16Kbps of bandwidth. BRI ISDN is also known as 2B+D because of the number and type of channels used.

You can also obtain a *Primary Rate Interface (PRI)* known as 23B+D, which means it has 23 B channels and one D channel. The total bandwidth of a 23B+D ISDN line is 1536Kbps (23 B channels × 64Kbps per channel+64Kbps for the D channel).

In many cases, to maximize throughput, the two Bearer channels are combined into one data connection for a total bandwidth of 128Kbps. This is known as *bonding* or *inverse multiplexing*. This still leaves the Delta channel free for signaling purposes. In rare cases, you may see user data, such as e-mail, on the D line. This was introduced as an additional feature of ISDN, but it hasn't caught on.

The main advantages of ISDN are these:

- Fast connection

- Higher bandwidth than POTS; bonding yields 128Kb bandwidth

- No conversion from digital to analog

However, ISDN does have a few disadvantages:

- It's more expensive than POTS.

- Specialized equipment is required at the phone company and at the remote computer.

- Not all ISDN equipment can connect to every other type of equipment.

- ISDN is a type of dial-up connection and therefore the connection must be initiated.

Satellite

One type of Internet connection that does not get much fanfare is satellite Internet. *Satellite Internet* is not much like any other type of broadband connection. Instead of a cabled connection, it uses a satellite dish to received data from a satellite and relay station that is connected to the Internet.

There are two types of satellite connection: *unidirectional* and *bidirectional*. In unidirectional satellite Internet, the satellite connection is used for only one part of the connection: the download of information from the Internet. The request for information is made via some other transmission method (usually a phone line). The request goes to a relay station, where it is made on behalf of the user. The response is then transmitted back to the user via the satellite. The benefit is that downloads happen at a much higher speed (currently up to 1Mbps), and you use your Internet connection for much more downloading than uploading. The downside is you still need to use a phone line for part of the connection.

In bidirectional satellite Internet, the satellite is used for both uploads and downloads. However, uploads are still slower than downloads. This type relieves you of needing a phone line for part of the Internet connection, but you still need a satellite dish.

The need for a satellite dish and the reliance upon its technology is one of the major drawbacks to satellite Internet. People who own satellite dishes will tell you that there are occasional problems due to weather and satellite alignment. You must keep the satellite dish aimed precisely at the satellite, or your signal strength (and thus your connection reliability and speed) will suffer. Plus, cloudy or stormy days can cause interference with the signal, especially if there are high winds that could blow the satellite dish out of alignment.

Another drawback to satellite technology is the *delay* (also called *propagation delay*). The delay occurs because of the length of time required to transmit the data and receive a response via the satellite. This delay (between 250 and 350 milliseconds) comes from the time it takes to transmit data the approximately 35,000 kilometers into space and return. To compare it with other types of broadband signals, cable and DSL have a delay between customer and ISP of 10 to 30 milliseconds. With standard web and e-mail traffic, this delay, while slightly annoying, is acceptable. However, with technologies like Voice over IP and live Internet gaming, this delay is intolerable.

 Online gamers are especially sensitive to propagation delay. They often refer to it as *ping time*. The higher the ping time (in milliseconds), the worse the response time in the game is. It sometimes means the difference between winning and losing an online game.

Satellite Internet is best used in remote rural areas where other types of Internet may not be practical or available and speeds higher than dial-up are required. In most other cases, land-based Internet is preferable.

Wireless

The final type of Internet access technology you will learn about is wireless. There are many different types of wireless access technology, but all of them have one thing in common: no physical cable between the computer and the ISP. *Wireless Internet* is an Internet access technology that uses radio frequency signals to communicate between ISP and user. It allows the user to roam about a particular area while remaining connected to the Internet. Speeds typically range from 128Kbps to 1.544Mbps (and in some cases, higher).

Wireless Internet comes in two forms: local and wide area. Local wireless is usually available within a particular room or building only. Once you leave that area, it is no longer available. Local wireless has an operating range of around 100 meters outdoors and about 30 meters indoors. It usually conforms to either the 802.11b or 802.11g standard and has speeds of 1Mbps, 11Mbps, and 54Mbps maximum, with 802.11n promising speeds in excess of 500Mbps. However, note that this is not an Internet access technology in itself unless the wireless host device (known as an *access point [AP]*) is connected in some way to the Internet (usually via a cabled connection).

 Intel's Centrino technology integrates local area wireless access cards into laptops.

Wide-area wireless, on the other hand, is typically used to cover an entire metropolitan area from a few, strategically placed towers. Speeds range from 64Kbps to 784Kbps (higher for point-to-point connections between two towers).

The biggest advantage of wireless is that you can be anywhere in the vicinity of the wireless devices and get Internet access. You don't need to be near an outlet or jack. This technology is catching on quickly with PDA and laptop users because they can get their e-mail and browse the Web from just about anywhere (as long as there is an AP within range).

There are a few downsides to wireless Internet as well. The first is cost. Typically, wireless Internet costs more than an equivalent cabled service. This will change as wireless becomes more widespread (and it is rapidly becoming so). Another limitation is availability. At the time of this writing, wireless Internet is still not available everywhere; it doesn't have the availability of wired technologies, such as cable or DSL.

Finally, most wide-area wireless Internet technologies that allow you to be anywhere don't have the same speed as wired broadband technologies, although as the standards mature, that too is changing.

Voice over IP

Voice over IP, or VoIP, is a technology that is rapidly gaining acceptance. VoIP breaks up telephone conversations into data packets that are then sent over a TCP/IP network (such as the Internet). This means that the average person can make free long-distance phone calls via the Internet. A great example of this technology is the service known as Vonage. It works by connecting a telephone to a special black box that is, in turn, connected to the Internet through your home's broadband Internet connection. The box samples the voice coming in from the telephone and converts the samples into the packets that travel over the Internet to the VoIP service provider, where they are then routed to either the traditional telephone network or to another subscriber.

Summary of Connection Types

Table 8.4 details a few of the more common connection types and speeds.

TABLE 8.4   Common Connection Types and Speeds

Designation	Download Speed Range	Description
POTS	2400bps to 53Kbps	Plain old telephone service. A regular analog phone line.
ISDN	64Kbps to 1.544Mbps	Integrated Services Digital Network. Once popular for home office Internet connections.
DSL	256Kbps to 10Mbps	Digital subscriber line. Shares existing phone wires with voice service.
Cable	128Kbps to 3Mbps	Inexpensive broadband Internet access method with wide availability.
Satellite	128Kbps to 1Mbps	Great for rural areas without cabled broadband methods.
Wireless (local)	1Mbps to 54Mbps	Allows a user to roam around a small area such as an office or building while remaining connected to the access point and the Internet.

TABLE 8.4 Common Connection Types and Speeds *(continued)*

Designation	Download Speed Range	Description
Wireless (wide area)	64Kbps to 784Kbps	Allows a user to roam around a metropolitan area while remaining connected to a broadband-level Internet service.

> **NOTE** It should be noted that these speed ranges will most likely be out of date as of the time of publication of this book because speeds are increasing rapidly.

Connection Protocols

Whichever connection type you use, there must be a plan for how to transmit data across a network's lines. Network connection types use different protocols to communicate, just as computers do, so we also need to mention these connection protocols. For instance, TCP/IP Internet traffic runs over two different analog connection protocols: Serial Line Internet Protocol (SLIP) and Point-to-Point Protocol (PPP). Both work to get you on the Internet, but PPP is more commonly used because it is more easily configured; it's also more stable because it includes enhanced error-checking capabilities. Other common connection protocols include X.25, Frame Relay, and ATM (the name is used for both the network and the connection protocol controlling traffic across it).

Installing a Wireless Home Network for Internet Access

A wireless network connection consists of a wireless NIC installed into a computer, a wireless access point, and the Internet connection (for example, cable modem or DSL). Figure 8.20 shows an example of wireless network connected to the Internet.

As you can see, there are two main parts to any wireless network: the wireless access point and the wireless NIC. The access point is the gateway between the wired network and the wireless network. It is usually just a small box with one or more antennae. In your home, you might connect an access point to your broadband Internet connection (cable, DSL, or something similar).

The *wireless card*, on the other hand, is simply a NIC that can transmit and receive information from a wireless network. It is installed like any other NIC.

FIGURE 8.20   A wireless network

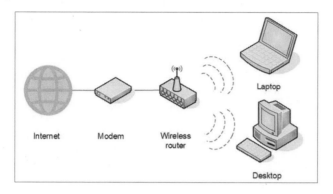

There are two main steps to connecting your computer wirelessly to any network (including one that is connected to the Internet):

1. Install and configure the access point.

2. Install and configure the wireless card.

Let's discuss each of these procedures.

Installing and Configuring the Access Point

Access points are pretty simple devices, and they require little configuration. The configuration that you must do involves setting certain parameters. Although each access point manufacturer is different, you can usually configure these parameters with the built-in, web-based configuration utility included with most wireless access points. The items that require configuration depend on the choices you make about your wireless network. The parameter that most needs attention is the *service-set identifier (SSID)*.

SSID is the unique name given to the wireless network. All hardware that is to participate on the network must be configured to use the same SSID. Essentially, the SSID is the network name. When you are using Windows to connect to a wireless network, all available wireless networks will be listed by their SSID when you select View Available Wireless Networks.

CONFIGURING A LINKSYS WAP11 WIRELESS ACCESS POINT

In order to demonstrate the simplicity of installing a wireless access point, in this section we will show you how to install one of the most popular wireless access points: the WAP11 by Linksys.

This installation procedure makes two assumptions: that you have a wired network using Cat 5 Ethernet connections already set up and functioning, and that it uses the IP addressing scheme similar to that of the default configuration of the WAP11 (192.168.1.x node addresses).

After unwrapping the WAP11 from its packaging (and reading the instructions, of course), you must choose a place for the unit. If it is supplying wireless access to your home network and the Internet, locate it where you can receive access in the most places. Keep in mind that the more walls the signal has to travel through, the lower the signal strength.

Place the WAP11 in the center of your home, close to a network connection. Or if you have only one computer, place it close to the broadband Internet connection you are using (i.e., the cable modem or DSL line).

Once you have chosen the location, plug the unit into a wall outlet and connect the two antennae that come with the unit. They will screw onto two bungs on the back of the unit. Once the unit is plugged in, you need to connect it to your home network. Plug the included Cat5 cable into an unused network port, and make sure that you get a link light on that connection.

At this point, the access point is configured for a home network, with a few basic caveats. First, the default SSID, Linksys, will be used, along with the default administrative password and the default IP addressing scheme. Also, there will be no encryption on the connection, but if you have nothing to protect, except for the Internet connection, you can leave that off. This is known as an *open access point*. Linksys has made the WAP11 so easy to configure that for most networks it is Plug and Play.

If you have personal data on your home network and more than one computer, you should never keep the default settings. Anyone could snoop your access point from the road in front of or behind your house and possibly get on your home network. It's too easy for identity theft!

From a computer on the home network, insert the WAP11 setup CD-ROM into the computer's CD-ROM drive. It will automatically start and present you with a wizard that will walk you through setting the name of the SSID of this new access point, as well as changing the default setup password, setting any security keys (encryption keys, or WEP keys) for this connection, and generally configuring the unit for your network's specific configuration.

That's it! You're finished. Your WAP11 is configured for use with your home network.

Installing and Configuring the Wireless Card

Installing and configuring wireless cards need not be complicated, if you break it into the two component steps:

1. Install the wireless card.

2. Configure the wireless card and connection.

WIRELESS CARD INSTALLATION

Installing a wireless NIC is just like installing a normal, wired NIC. The only difference is in the configuration of the NIC. You must configure the NIC to connect to your preferred wireless network (by its SSID) and configure any security settings (such as wireless encryption keys).

To configure a wireless card under Windows XP, first you must install the wireless card. For a desktop, this means powering off the computer, removing the case cover, and inserting the card into an open slot (assuming the wireless card expansion card type and bus slot type match). Then you can power the computer back up, and the computer should recognize that a new card was installed and prompt you install the driver.

On a laptop, simply insert the wireless PC Card into any open PC Card slot with the laptop powered up. Once you have done this, Windows will recognize the card and ask you to install the driver. With the Intel Centrino, no external adapter needs to be added, but you might need to use a key combination to enable the antenna. USB-attached NICs are an option for modern computers of all types.

For both a desktop and a laptop, once Windows recognizes the card, it will prompt you to search for the card's driver, as it does with the installation of other hardware, or it will use a distribution driver for the card. This is common for devices that Microsoft knew about before publishing the operating system. You can then proceed as with other expansion cards that have more complex installation methods. If prompted, insert the driver CD-ROM and let Windows finish installing the driver.

Once the driver is installed, you may have to reboot (but only in very unique cases). Then the wireless card should be ready to use.

Bear in mind that these are general steps. Always consult the documentation that comes with the hardware to ensure that there isn't a special step that is unique to that card.

WIRELESS CONNECTION CONFIGURATION

Now that your card is installed in your computer, you can configure the connection so you can use it. Windows XP is beautiful for wireless use because it has utilities for connecting to wireless networks built into the operating system. Windows uses the Wireless Zero Configuration Service to automatically connect to wireless access points using IEEE 802.11 protocols (WiFi).

To configure a wireless connection, you can simply bring a Windows XP laptop or computer within range of a wireless access point, and Windows XP will detect the presence of an access point and alert you to its presence. Alternatively, if you would like control over the connection, you can open the network control panel (Start ➢ Control Panel ➢ Network Connections in Windows XP), right-click on the wireless card, and choose View Available Wireless Connections. This will bring up the figure shown in Figure 8.21.

From this screen you can view the SSIDs of the available wireless networks, including the one to which you are connected (the one that says "Connected" next to it). The bars in the far-right column indicate the relative signal strength of each connection. The more green bars showing, the stronger the signal, and the better (and faster) the connection.

If the connection shows a lock icon underneath it, it is a secured wireless network and you will need to enter some sort of password to gain access to that network.

To connect to any network, double-click on it, and Windows will try to connect to that network. You'll see a window similar to the one in Figure 8.22 that shows you the connection is in process. Once you are connected, Windows will display "Connected" next to that connection.

The weaker the signal, the longer the connection will take.

FIGURE 8.21 Available wireless connections

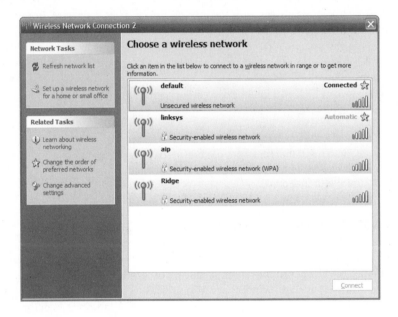

FIGURE 8.22 · Connecting to a wireless network

Troubleshooting Network Interface Cards

NICs are like any other expansion card in that they use resources of the computer. Troubleshooting them should be handled like troubleshooting any other expansion card. However, networks cards have two troubleshooting aids: the link and collision lights. These *status indicators* allow a more casual form of troubleshooting. Without status indicators, all troubleshooting would be more in depth and with so many NICs in the network, every suspicion of failure would result in potentially wasted time.

The *link light* is a small light-emitting diode (LED) found on both the NIC and the hub. It is typically green and is labeled "link" (or some abbreviation). A link light indicates that the NIC and hub (in the case of 10BaseT) are making a logical (Data Link layer) connection. You can usually assume that the workstation and hub are communicating if the link lights are lit on both the workstation's NIC and the hub port to which the workstation is connected.

 The link lights on some NICs aren't activated until the driver is loaded. So if the link light isn't on when the system is first turned on, you may have to wait until the operating system loads the NIC driver.

The *collision light* is also a small LED, typically amber in color. It usually can be found on both Ethernet NICs and hubs. When lit, it indicates that an Ethernet collision has occurred. It is important to know that this light will blink occasionally because collisions are somewhat common on busy Ethernet networks. However, if this light stays on continuously, too many collisions are happening for legitimate network traffic to get through. The problem could be a malfunctioning NIC or another malfunctioning network device.

Be careful not to confuse the collision light with the network activity or network traffic light (usually green). The network activity light indicates that a device is transmitting. This particular light should be blinking on and off continually as the device transmits and receives data on the network.

Summary

In this chapter, you learned about the various network hardware topics on which you will be tested in the A+ exam. A few years ago, you wouldn't have seen many computers with NICs come in for service; networks were found only in offices and large companies. Now, networks can be found in many homes. For this reason, the A+ exam requires that you have at least a basic understanding of network hardware.

In the first section, you learned exactly what a network is. You also learned what components make up a network, what the network resource models are, and what a network topology is. We discussed the OSI model and the IEEE 802 committee and their impact on networks. Finally, we examined the various network architectures in use today.

In the next section, you learned about the different kinds of network media used to connect computers to a network. These media include copper cable, fiber-optic cable, and wireless media. You also learned about the different kinds of NICs used to connect computers to the network media. Then we discussed the methods of network access (contention, token passing, and so on) each major network technology uses to gain access to the network media.

Next, you learned to differentiate between the types of devices that connect to networks. These network connectivity devices are very important to facilitating communications on a network. We explained how each device (including hubs, routers, bridges, brouters, and so forth) works and how it relates to network communications.

Then, you learned about the different methods of connecting to the Internet: POTS, ISDN, DSL, cable, satellite, and wireless Internet connections. We discussed how each of these methods differs in terms of speed and method of connection.

Finally, you learned about installing, configuring, and troubleshooting networks and NICs.

Exam Essentials

Be able to describe basic networking concepts.   You should know the basics of network addressing, bandwidth, status indicators, protocols, full-duplex, half-duplex, cabling, and networking models.

Be able to Identify the differences between the various types of cabling.   You should know the differences between plenum/PVC, UTP/STP, and fiber-optic cable (single mode vs. multimode).

Be able describe the different network connectors.   You should know the appearance and specifications of RJ-11, RJ-45, ST, SC, LC, USB, and IEEE1394 connectors.

Be able to describe the major network technologies.   You should know the definitions and descriptions of LANs, WANs, ISDN networks, broadband connections, dial-up connections, wireless connections, infrared, cellular, and VoIP.

Be able to install a network interface card.   To install a NIC in a desktop PC, with the power off remove the case cover, locate an unused slot that matches the NIC's expansion slot type, insert the NIC into the available slot, and secure it with a screw or other retainer. Finally, reinstall the case cover, power up the computer, and install the driver software.

Be able to set up a wireless connection.   Windows uses the Wireless Zero Configuration Service to automatically connect to wireless access points using IEEE 802.11 protocols (WiFi). Simply locate the wireless access point you wish to connect to and double-click on it. Windows will connect you automatically.

Know how to use link lights as status indicators.   When a link light is illuminated on a NIC, there is a basic level of communication between the NIC and the network.

Review Questions

1. Which device is most efficient at moving packets between similar network topologies?

   A. Gateway

   B. Router

   C. Brouter

   D. Bridge

2. Which IEEE 802 standard uses a bus topology and coaxial baseband cable and is able to transmit at 10Mbps?

   A. 802.4

   B. 802.3

   C. 802.2

   D. 802.1

3. _____ is immune to electromagnetic or radio-frequency interference.

   A. Broadband coaxial cabling

   B. Fiber-optic cabling

   C. Twisted-pair cabling

   D. CSMA/CD

4. Printers, files, and e-mail can all be categorized as _____.

   A. Office equipment

   B. Peer-to-peer networking

   C. Resources

   D. Protocols

5. Which OSI layer signals "all clear" by making sure the data segments are error-free?

   A. Application layer

   B. Session layer

   C. Transport layer

   D. Network layer

6. Which topology is the easiest to modify?

   A. Star

   B. Bus

   C. Ring

   D. Token Ring

7. The _____ protocol within TCP/IP is responsible for network addressing.
   A. IPX
   B. UDP
   C. IP
   D. TCP

8. Which layer of the OSI model has the important role of providing error checking?
   A. Session layer
   B. Presentation layer
   C. Application layer
   D. Transport layer

9. Which type of cabling is easiest to install?
   A. Twisted-pair
   B. Coaxial
   C. Fiber-optic
   D. Wireless

10. _____ is the type of media access method used by NICs that listen to or sense the cable to check for traffic and send only when they hear that no one else is transmitting.
    A. Token passing
    B. CSMA/CD
    C. CSMA/CA
    D. Demand priority

11. A physical star topology consists of several workstations that branch off a central device called a _____.
    A. Repeater
    B. Brouter
    C. Router
    D. Hub

12. A _____ links two or more computers together to communicate and share resources.
    A. Table
    B. Resource
    C. Network
    D. Client

13. Which access method uses smart interface cards to detect traffic *before* it tries to send data?

    A. CSMA/CD

    B. CSMA/CA

    C. Token passing

    D. Demand priority

14. _____ offers the longest possible segment length.

    A. Unshielded twisted-pair cabling

    B. Coaxial cable

    C. Fiber-optic cabling

    D. Shielded twisted-pair cabling

15. _____ uses a thin baseband coaxial cable and bus topology, transmits at 10Mbps, with a distance up to 185 meters.

    A. Token Ring

    B. Ethernet 10BaseT

    C. Ethernet 10Base5

    D. Ethernet 10Base2

16. Which topology uses the least amount of cabling?

    A. Bus

    B. Star

    C. Mesh

    D. Hybrid

17. Which layer describes how the data is transmitted over a physical medium?

    A. Session layer

    B. Data Link layer

    C. Physical layer

    D. Application layer

18. What is another name for IEEE 802.3?

    A. Logic link control

    B. Token passing

    C. CSMA/CD LAN

    D. Token Ring LAN

19. What type of cabling is the cable used to connect traditional cable television?

    A. Twisted-pair

    B. Coaxial

    C. Fiber-optic

    D. Wireless

20. What devices transfer packets across multiple networks and use tables to store network addresses to determine the best destination?

    A. Brouters

    B. Routers

    C. Gateways

    D. Bridges

Answers to Review Questions

1. D. Bridges keep traffic on one side from crossing to the other. For this reason they are often used to increase performance on a high-traffic segment.

2. B. The IEEE 802.3 standard specifies the use of a bus topology, typically using coaxial baseband cable, and can transmit data up to 10Mbps.

3. B. Companies that want to ensure the safety and integrity of their data should use fiber-optic cable, because it cannot be affected by electromagnetic or radio-frequency interference. Even though some copper cables have shielding, they are not immune to EMI or RFI.

4. C. Resources are any items that can be used on a network by multiple people. Therefore, printers, files, and e-mail are all considered resources when they are available on a network.

5. C. It is the responsibility of the Transport layer to signal an "all clear" by making sure the data segments are error-free. It also controls the data flow and troubleshoots any problems with transmitting or receiving data frames.

6. A. The star topology is the easiest to modify. A physical star topology branches each network device off a central device called a hub, making it easy to add a new workstation.

7. C. The Internet Protocol is responsible for network addressing as part of TCP/IP.

8. D. The most important role of the Transport layer is to provide error checking. The Transport layer also provides functions such as reliable end-to-end communications, segmentation and reassembly of larger messages, and combination of smaller messages into a single larger message.

9. A. Of the choices listed here, twisted-pair cabling is generally considered the easiest to install. It is lighter than coaxial and doesn't require a lot of special tools or knowledge like fiber-optic cable.

10. B. CSMA/CD (Carrier Sense Multiple Access with Collision Detection) specifies that the NIC pause before transmitting a packet to ensure that the line is not being used. If no activity is detected, then it transmits the packet. If activity is detected, it waits until it is clear. In the case of two NICs transmitting at the same time (a collision), both NICs pause to detect and then retransmit the data.

11. D. The hub provides the central connecting device in a star topology. All workstations must therefore connect to the hub in order to gain access to each other or any other resources present on the network. The one disadvantage is that the hub becomes a single point of failure. If the hub stops working, no one connected to the hub has network connectivity.

12. C. The purpose of a network is to link computers together so that they can communicate and share available resources such as printers, data, and applications.

13. B. CSMA/CA (Carrier Sense Multiple Access with Collision Avoidance) is slightly more sophisticated than CSMA/CD. It transmits a very small packet on the network. If it is successful, then the NIC transmits the actual data. This initial transmission can be viewed as an "Is it okay for me to send?" message. Therefore, it is said to avoid causing collisions.

14. C. Fiber-optic cable can span distances of several kilometers, because it has much lower crosstalk and interference in comparison to copper cables.

15. D. The name of each option tells you exactly what it is. In the case of Ethernet 10Base2, the *Ethernet* part states that it uses Ethernet architecture, *10* means it can transmit up to 10Mbps, *Base* signifies baseband transmission, and *2* is the distance (in this case, it equates to the 185-meter limitation of coaxial Thinnet cable).

16. A. Because of its design, which includes a central trunk that runs the distance between the two most distant computers (as long as it does not exceed the maximum distance allowed for the cabling), a bus topology requires the least amount of cable.

17. C. The Physical layer is responsible for formatting the final packet of data for transmission over a physical medium.

18. C. The IEEE 802.3 specification states that CSMA/CD is the standard access method for Ethernet networks.

19. B. Television cable is actually a form of coaxial cable.

20. B. Routers are designed to route (transfer) packets across networks. They are able to do this routing, and determine the best path to take, based on internal routing tables they maintain.

Chapter

9

Understanding Network Security Fundamentals

THE FOLLOWING COMPTIA A+ ESSENTIALS EXAM OBJECTIVES ARE COVERED IN THIS CHAPTER:

✓ **6.1 Identify the fundamental principles of security**

- ▪ Identify names, purposes and characteristics of hardware and software security for example:
  - ▪ Hardware deconstruction / recycling
  - ▪ Smart cards / biometrics (e.g. key fobs, cards, chips and scans)
  - ▪ Authentication technologies (e.g. user name, password, biometrics, smart cards)
  - ▪ Malicious software protection (e.g. viruses, Trojans, worms, spam, spyware, adware, grayware)
  - ▪ Software firewalls
  - ▪ File system security (e.g. FAT32 and NTFS)
- ▪ Identify names, purposes and characteristics of wireless security for example:
  - ▪ Wireless encryption (e.g. WEP.x and WPA.x) and client configuration
  - ▪ Access points (e.g. disable DHCP / use static IP, change SSID from default, disable SSID broadcast, MAC filtering, change default username and password, update firmware, firewall)
- ▪ Identify names, purposes and characteristics of data and physical security
  - ▪ Data access (basic local security policy)
  - ▪ Encryption technologies
  - ▪ Backups

- Data migration
- Data / remnant removal
- Password management
- Locking workstation (e.g. hardware, operating system)
- Describe importance and process of incidence reporting
- Recognize and respond appropriately to social engineering situations

✓ **6.2 Install, configure, upgrade and optimize security**

- Install, configure, upgrade and optimize hardware, software and data security for example:
  - BIOS
  - Smart cards
  - Authentication technologies
  - Malicious software protection
  - Data access (basic local security policy)
  - Backup procedures and access to backups
  - Data migration
  - Data / remnant removal

✓ **6.3 Identify tool, diagnostic procedures and troubleshooting techniques for security**

- Diagnose and troubleshoot hardware, software and data security issues for example:
  - BIOS
  - Smart cards, biometrics
  - Authentication technologies
  - Malicious software
  - File system (e.g. FAT32, NTFS)
  - Data access (e.g. basic local security policy)
  - Backup
  - Data migration

✓ **6.4 Perform preventative maintenance for computer security.**

- Implement software security preventative maintenance techniques such as installing service packs and patches and training users about malicious software prevention technologies

It is next to impossible to pick up a trade paper or magazine these days and not find a leading story about security. As our world—and our networks—has become more connected, the need to secure data and keep it out of the eyes of those who can do harm has exponentially increased.

CompTIA has added the security domain to the current A+ exams because it is a topic that every administrator and technician must be aware of and care about. In the world of production, quality may be job one, but in the IT world, it is security.

This chapter looks at security primarily from the standpoint of the network. All of the topics relevant to the Essentials exam are covered, and a thorough overview of the topic is given.

Understanding Security

Security is unlike any other topic in computing. The word *security* is so encompassing that it's impossible to know exactly what you mean when you say it. When you talk about security, do you mean physical security of servers and workstations from those who might try to steal them or damage that may occur if the side of the building collapses? Or do you mean the security of data from viruses and worms and the means by which you keep those threats from entering the network? Or do you mean security of data from hackers and miscreants who have targeted you and have no other purpose in life than to keep you up at night? Or is security the comfort that comes from knowing you can restore files if a user accidentally deletes them?

The first problem with security is that it's next to impossible to have everyone agree on what it means, because it can include all these items. The next problem is that we don't *really* want things to be completely secured. For example, if you wanted your customer-list file to be truly secure, you wouldn't put it on the server and make it available. It's on the server because you need to access it, and so do 30 other people. In this sense, security means that only 30 select people can get to the data.

The next problem is that although everyone wants security, no one wants to be inconvenienced by it. To use an analogy, few travelers don't feel safer by watching airport personnel pat down everyone who heads to the terminal—they just don't want it to happen to them. This is true in computing, as well; we all want to make sure data is accessed only by those who truly should be working with it, but we don't want to have to enter 12-digit passwords and submit to retinal scans.

As a computer professional, you have to understand all these concerns. You have to know that a great deal is expected of you, but few people want to be hassled or inconvenienced by the measures you must put in place. You have a primary responsibility to protect and safeguard the information your organization uses. Many times, that means educating your users and making certain they understand the "why" behind what is being implemented. When discussing computer security, you must be able to identify the names, purposes, and characteristics of three key areas: hardware/software security, wireless security, and physical/data security. These topic areas are discussed following an overview of authentication technologies.

Authentication Technologies

Authentication proves that a user or system is actually who they say they are. This is one of the most critical parts of a security system. It's part of a process that is also referred to as *identification and authentication (I&A)*. The identification process starts when a user ID or logon name is typed into a sign-on screen. Authentication is accomplished by challenging the claim about who is accessing the resource. Without authentication, anybody can claim to be anybody.

Authentication systems or methods are based on one or more of these three factors:

- Something you know, such as a password or PIN
- Something you have, such as a smart card or an identification device
- Something physically unique to you, such as your fingerprints or retinal pattern

Systems authenticate each other using similar methods. Frequently, systems pass private information between each other to establish identity. Once authentication has occurred, the two systems can communicate in the manner specified in the design.

Several common methods are used for authentication. Each has advantages and disadvantages that must be considered when you're evaluating authentication schemes.

Username/Password

A username and password are unique identifiers for a logon process. When users sit down in front of a computer system, the first thing a security system requires is that they establish who they are. Identification is typically confirmed through a logon process. Most operating systems use a user ID and password to accomplish this. These values can be sent across the connection as plain text or can be encrypted.

The logon process identifies to the operating system, and possibly the network, that you are who you say you are. Figure 9.1 illustrates this logon and password process. Notice that the operating system compares this information to the stored information from the security processor and either accepts or denies the logon attempt. The operating system may establish privileges or permissions based on stored data about that particular ID.

Password Authentication Protocol (PAP)

Password Authentication Protocol (PAP) offers no true security, but it's one of the simplest forms of authentication. The username and password values are both sent to the server as clear text and checked for a match. If they match, the user is granted access; if they don't match, the user is denied access. In most modern implementations, PAP is shunned in favor of other, more secure, authentication methods.

FIGURE 9.1   A logon process occurring on a workstation

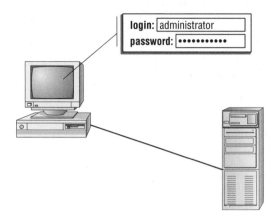

Logon or Security Server

Challenge Handshake Authentication Protocol (CHAP)

Challenge Handshake Authentication Protocol (CHAP) challenges a system to verify identity. CHAP doesn't use a user ID/password mechanism. Instead, the initiator sends a logon request from the client to the server. The server sends a challenge back to the client. The challenge is encrypted and then sent back to the server. The server compares the value from the client and, if the information matches, grants authorization. If the response fails, the session fails, and the request phase starts over. Figure 9.2 illustrates the CHAP procedure. This handshake method involves a number of steps and is usually automatic between systems after it's configured.

 CHAP depends on a "secret" known only to the authenticator and that peer. Part of configuring CHAP is setting the shared, predefined secret on both the client and server. For more information, see the *Network+ Study Guide, 4th Edition.*

Certificates

Certificates are another common form of authentication. A server or *certificate authority (CA)* can issue a certificate that will be accepted by the challenging system. Certificates can be stored on physical access devices such as smart cards or stored on the user's computer as a digital signature used as part of the logon process. A *Certificate Practice Statement (CPS)* outlines the rules used for issuing and managing certificates. A *Certificate Revocation List (CRL)* lists the revocations that must be addressed (often due to expiration) in order to stay current.

A simple way to think of certificates is like hall passes at school. Figure 9.3 illustrates a certificate being handed from the server to the client once authentication has been established. If you have a hall pass, you can wander the halls of your school. If your pass is invalid, the hallway monitor can send you to the principal's office. Similarly, if you have a certificate, then you can prove to the system that you are who you say you are and are authenticated to work with the resources.

Security Tokens

Security tokens are similar to certificates. They contain the rights and access privileges of the token bearer as part of the token. Think of a token as a small piece of data that holds a sliver of information about the user.

FIGURE 9.2 CHAP authentication

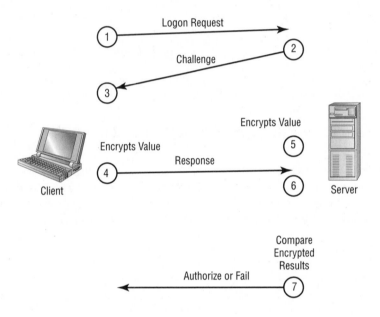

FIGURE 9.3 A certificate being issued once identification has been verified

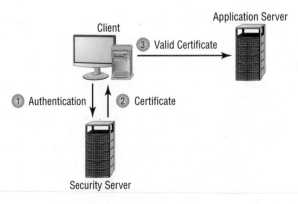

Many operating systems generate a token that is applied to every action taken on the computer system. If your token doesn't grant you access to certain information, then either that information won't be displayed or your access will be denied. The authentication system creates a token every time a user connects or a session begins. At the completion of a session, the token is destroyed. Figure 9.4 shows the security token process.

Kerberos

Kerberos is an authentication protocol named after the mythical three-headed dog that stood at the gates of Hades. Originally designed by MIT, Kerberos is becoming very popular as an authentication method. It allows for a single sign-on to a distributed network.

Kerberos authentication uses a *key distribution center (KDC)* to orchestrate the process. The KDC authenticates the *principal* (which can be a user, a program, or a system) and provides it with a ticket. Once this ticket is issued, it can be used to authenticate against other principals. This occurs automatically when a request or service is performed by another principal.

Kerberos is quickly becoming a common standard in network environments. Its only significant weakness is that the KDC can be a single point of failure. If the KDC goes down, the authentication process will stop. Figure 9.5 shows the Kerberos authentication process and the ticket being presented to systems that are authorized by the KDC.

Multifactor Authentication

When two or more access methods are included as part of the authentication process, you're implementing a *multifactor* system. A system that uses smart cards and passwords is referred to as a *two-factor authentication* system. Two-factor authentication is shown in Figure 9.6. This example requires both a smart card and a logon password process.

FIGURE 9.4   Security token authentication

FIGURE 9.5 Kerberos authentication process

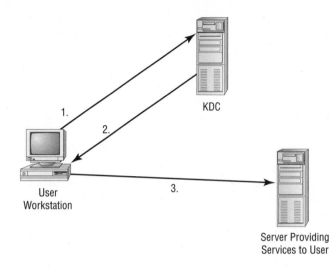

1. User requests access to service running on a different server.
2. KDC authenticates user and sends a ticket to be used between the user and the service on the server.
3. User's workstation sends a ticket to the service.

FIGURE 9.6 Two-factor authentication

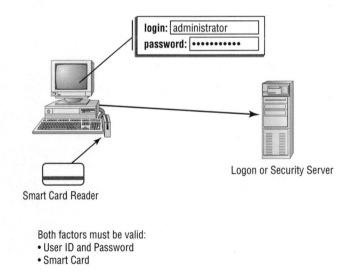

Working with Hardware and Software Security

When it comes to hardware, it's important to understand that although the user interacts with software, the hardware actually stores the data. The hardware in question can be a hard disk, a backup tape, or some other storage device. This overly simplistic concept is important when it comes to choosing how to dispose of hardware.

If it's possible to verify beyond a reasonable doubt that a piece of hardware that's no longer being used doesn't contain any data of a sensitive or proprietary nature, then that hardware can be recycled (sold to employees, sold to a third party, donated to a school, and so on). That level of assurance can come from wiping a hard drive, reformatting it, or using specialized utilities. When computer systems are retired, the disk drives should be zeroed out, and all magnetic media should be degaussed. Degaussing involves applying a strong magnetic field to initialize the media (this is also referred to as *disk wiping*). Erasing files on a computer system doesn't guarantee that the information isn't still on the disk; a low-level format can be performed on the system, or a utility can be used to completely wipe the disk clean. This process helps ensure that information doesn't fall into the wrong hands.

Degaussing hard drives is difficult and may render the drive unusable. Degaussing works better for floppy drives while utilities are often used for hard drives.

If you can't be assured that the hardware in question doesn't contain important data, then the hardware should be destroyed. You cannot, and should not, take a risk that the data your company depends on could fall into the wrong hands.

In the following sections, we'll discuss a number of the elements you need to know as you study for the exam.

Smart Cards

A *smart card* is a type of badge or card that gives you access to resources including buildings, parking lots, and computers. It contains information about your identity and access privileges. Each area or computer has a card scanner or a reader in which you insert your card.

The reader is connected to the workstation and validates against the security system. This increases the security of the authentication process, because you must be in physical possession of the smart card to use the resources. Of course, if the card is lost or stolen, the person who finds the card can access the resources it allows. Smart cards are difficult to counterfeit, but they're easy to steal. Once a thief has a smart card, she has all the access the card allows. To prevent this, many organizations don't put any identifying marks on their smart cards, making it harder for someone to utilize them.

Most smart cards also require the use of a PIN, just in case the card is lost or stolen.

Many European countries are beginning to use smart cards instead of magnetic-strip credit cards because they offer additional security and can contain more information.

Biometrics

Biometric devices use physical characteristics to identify the user. Such devices are becoming more common in the business environment. Biometric systems include hand scanners, retinal scanners, and soon, possibly, DNA scanners. To gain access to resources, you must pass a physical screening process. In the case of a hand scanner, this may include identifying fingerprints, scars, and markings on your hand. Retinal scanners compare your eye's retinal pattern to a stored retinal pattern to verify your identity. DNA scanners will examine a unique portion of your DNA structure in order to verify that you are who you say you are.

Key Fobs

Key fobs are named after the chains that used to be used to hold pocket watches to clothes. They are security devices that you carry with you that display a randomly generated code that you can then use for authentication. This code usually changes very quickly (every 60 seconds is probably the average), and you combine this code with your PIN for authentication.

The term key fob is used to describe a great many things. While something dangling from your key chain that can be used for keyless entry can constitute a key fob as well, when it comes to computer security, there usually needs to be some challenge/authentication process involved for it to be of any great value.

Authentication Issues to Consider

You can set up many different parameters and standards to force the people in your organization to conform. In establishing these parameters, it's important that you consider the capabilities of the people who will be working with these policies. If you're working in an environment where people aren't computer savvy, you may spend a lot of time helping them remember and recover passwords. Many organizations have had to reevaluate their security guidelines after they've invested great time and expense to implement high-security systems.

Setting authentication security, especially in supporting users, can become a high-maintenance activity for network administrators. On one hand, you want people to be able to authenticate themselves easily; on the other hand, you want to establish security that protects your company's resources.

Understanding Software Exploitation

The term *software exploitation* refers to attacks launched against applications and higher-level services. They include gaining access to data using weaknesses in the data-access objects of a database or a flaw in a service. This section briefly outlines some common exploitations that have been successful in the past. The following exploitations can be introduced using viruses, as in the case of the Klez32 virus, or by using access attacks described later in this chapter:

Real World Scenario

Check the Movie Listings

Be wary of popular names or current trends that make certain passwords predictable. For example, during the first release of Star Wars, two of the most popular passwords used on college campuses were C3PO and R2D2. This created a security problem for campus computer centers.

A few years back, characters from the Matrix trilogy became popular passwords as those working in offices tried to live out their lives in fantasy. While you may truly like a movie or character that is popular at the moment, you need to understand that those names will be tried as password possibilities very quickly.

Viruses can be stored/transported through any media. They can enter your system on thumb drives, CDs, e-mail, or just about any way imaginable.

Database Exploitation Many database products allow sophisticated access queries to be made in the client-server environment. If a client session can be hijacked or spoofed, the attacker can formulate queries against the database that disclose unauthorized information. For this attack to be successful, the attacker must first gain access to the environment through one of the attacks outlined later.

Application Exploitation The macro virus is another example of software exploitation. A macro virus is a set of programming instructions in a language such as VBScript that commands an application to perform illicit instructions. Users want more powerful tools, and manufacturers want to sell users what they want. The macro virus takes advantage of the power offered by word processors, spreadsheets, or other applications. This exploitation is inherent in the product, and all users are susceptible to it unless they disable all macros.

E-mail Exploitation Hardly a day goes by without another e-mail virus being reported. This is a result of a weakness in many common e-mail clients. Modern e-mail clients offer many shortcuts, lists, and other capabilities to meet user demands. A popular exploitation of e-mail clients involves accessing the client address book and propagating viruses. There is virtually nothing a client user can do about these exploitations, although antivirus software that integrates with your e-mail client does offer some protection. To be truly successful, the software manufacturer must fix the weaknesses—an example is Outlook's option to protect against access to the address book. This type of weakness isn't a bug, in many cases, but a feature that users wanted.

Some viruses won't damage a system in an attempt to spread into all the other systems in a network. These viruses use that system as the carrier of the virus.

One of the most important measures you can take to proactively combat software attacks is to know common file extensions and the applications they're associated with. For example, .SCR files are screensavers, and viruses are often distributed through the use of these files. No legitimate user should be sending screensavers via e-mail to your users, and all .SCR attachments should be banned from entering the network.

Table 9.1, although not comprehensive, contains the most common file extensions that should or should not, as a general rule, be allowed into the network as e-mail attachments. This chart simply lists file extensions that would (or would not) commonly be expected as e-mail attachments. It does not mean that viruses and other malware won't be propagated using the allowed file extensions.

As a general rule, never open an attachment in e-mail from any unknown sender or from a sender you are not expecting an attachment from.

TABLE 9.1 Common File Extensions for E-mail Attachments

Should Be Allowed	Should *Not* Be Allowed
.DOC	.BAT
.PDF	.COM
.TXT	.EXE
.XLS	.HLP
.ZIP	.PIF
	.SCR

Spyware   *Spyware* differs from other malware in that it works—often actively—on behalf of a third party. Rather than self-replicating, like viruses and worms, spyware is spread to machines by users who inadvertently ask for it. The users often don't know they have asked for it but have done so by downloading other programs, visiting infected sites, and so on.

The spyware program monitors the user's activity and responds by offering unsolicited pop-up advertisements (sometimes known as *adware*), gathers information about the user to pass on to marketers, or intercepts personal data such as credit-card numbers. One thing separating spyware from most other malware is that it almost always exists to provide commercial gain. The operating systems from Microsoft are the ones most affected by spyware, and Microsoft has released Windows Defender to combat the problem.

All OSs are susceptible to these problems, and Microsoft gets the most attention because of its wide use. As we state in Chapter 3, "Although there are several commonly used operating systems in the market today, no one operating system family has garnered more market share and attention than Microsoft's Windows operating systems."

Rootkits   Recently, *rootkits* have become the software exploitation program du jour. Rootkits are software programs that have the ability to hide certain things from the operating system. With a rootkit, there may be a number of processes running on a system that don't show up in Task Manager, or connections may be established/available that don't appear in a netstat display—the rootkit masks the presence of these items. The rootkit does this by manipulating function calls to the operating system and filtering out information that would normally appear.

Unfortunately, many rootkits are written to get around antivirus and antispyware programs that aren't kept up-to-date. The best defense you have is to monitor what your system is doing and catch the rootkit in the process of installation.

Viruses   A *virus* is a piece of software designed to infect a computer system. The virus may do nothing more than reside on the computer. A virus may also damage the data on your hard disk, destroy your operating system, and possibly spread to other systems. Viruses get into your computer in one of three ways: on a contaminated floppy, DVD, memory card, or CD-ROM, through e-mail, or as part of another program.

Important distinguishing elements of viruses are that they attach themselves to a program or file (a host) and that they cannot spread without human interaction (such as running an infected program).

Viruses can be classified as several types: polymorphic, stealth, retroviruses, multipartite, armored, companion, phage, and macro viruses. Each type of virus has a different attack strategy and different consequences.

A symptom of many viruses is unusual activity on the system disk.

Trojan Horses   *Trojan horses* are programs that enter a system or network under the guise of another program. A Trojan horse may be included as an attachment or as part of an installation program. The Trojan horse can create a back door or replace a valid program during installation. It then accomplishes its mission under the guise of another program. Trojan horses can be used to compromise the security of your system, and they can exist on a system for years before they're detected.

The best preventative measure for Trojan horses is to not allow them entry into your system. Immediately before and after you install a new software program or operating system, back it up! If you suspect a Trojan horse, you can reinstall the original programs, which should delete the Trojan horse. A port scan may also reveal a Trojan horse on your system. If an application opens a TCP or IP port that isn't supported in your network, you can track it down and determine which port is being used.

Worms   A *worm* is different from a virus in that it can reproduce itself, it is self-contained, and it doesn't need a host application to be transported. Many of the so-called viruses that have made the papers and media were actually worms. However, it's possible for a worm to contain or deliver a virus to a target system.

By their nature and origin, worms are supposed to propagate, and they use whatever services they're capable of to do that. Early worms filled up memory and bred inside the RAM of the target computer. Worms can use TCP/IP, e-mail, Internet services, or any number of possibilities to reach their target.

Spam   *Spam* is defined as any unwanted, unsolicited e-mail. Not only can the sheer volume of it be irritating, but it can often provide the door to larger problems. Some of the sites advertised in spam may be infected with viruses, worms, and other unwanted programs. If users begin to respond to spam by visiting those sites, then your problems will only multiply.

Just as you can, and must, install good antivirus software programs, you should also consider similar measures for spam. Filtering messages and preventing them from ever entering the network is the most effective method of dealing with the problem.

Grayware   *Grayware* is a term used to describe any application that is annoying or negatively affecting the performance of your computer. If an application doesn't fall into the virus or Trojan category, it can get lumped under grayware. Spyware and adware are often considered types of grayware, as are programs that log user keystrokes and certain hacking programs.

Firewalls

Firewalls are one of the first lines of defense in a network. There are different types of firewalls, and they can be either stand-alone systems or included in other devices such as routers or servers. You can find firewall solutions that are marketed as hardware-only and others that are software-only. Many firewalls, however, consist of add-in software that is available for servers or workstations.

 Although solutions are sold as hardware-only, the hardware still runs some sort of software. It may be hardened and in ROM to prevent tampering, and it may be customized—but software is present, nonetheless.

The basic purpose of a firewall is to isolate one network from another. Firewalls are becoming available as appliances, meaning they're installed into the network between two networks. *Appliances* are freestanding devices that operate in a largely self-contained manner, requiring less maintenance and support than a server-based product.

Firewalls function as one or more of the following:

- Packet filter
- Proxy firewall
- Stateful inspection

A firewall operating as a *packet filter* passes or blocks traffic to specific addresses based on the IP address, protocol, type of application being addressed (identified by a port number) or many other attributes. The packet filter doesn't analyze the contents of a packet; it decides whether to pass it based on the packet's addressing information. For instance, a packet filter may allow web traffic on port 80 and block Telnet traffic on port 23. This type of filtering is included in many routers. If a received packet request asks for a port that isn't authorized, the filter may reject the request or ignore it. Many packet filters can also specify which IP addresses can request which ports and allow or deny them based on the security settings of the firewall.

Telnet shouldn't be used if possible. Telnet sends user ID and password information to the Telnet server unencrypted. This creates a potential security problem in an Internet environment.

You can think of a *proxy firewall* as an intermediary between your network and any other network. Proxy firewalls are used to process requests from an outside network; the proxy firewall examines the data and makes rules-based decisions about whether the request should be forwarded or refused. The proxy intercepts all the packages and reprocesses them for use internally. This process includes hiding IP addresses.

Stateful inspection is also referred to as *stateful packet filtering*. Most of the devices used in networks don't keep track of how information is routed or used. Once a packet is passed, the packet and path are forgotten. In stateful inspection (or stateful packet filtering), records are kept using a state table that tracks every communications channel. Stateful inspections occur at all levels of the network and provide additional security.

Filesystem Security

Microsoft's earliest filesystem was referred to as File Allocation Table (FAT). FAT was designed for relatively small disk drives. It was upgraded first to FAT16 and finally to FAT32. FAT32 (also written as FAT-32) allows large disk systems to be used on Windows systems.

FAT allows only two types of protection: share-level and user-level access privileges. Share-level security is security that applies to the file as it is shared, while user-level security bases access on the login of the user. If a user has write or change access to a drive or directory, he has access to any file in that directory. This is very unsecure in an Internet environment.

The New Technology Filesystem (NTFS) was introduced with Windows NT to address security problems. Before Windows NT was released, it had become apparent to Microsoft that a new filesystem was needed to handle growing disk sizes, security concerns, and the need for more stability. NTFS was created to address those issues.

With NTFS, files, directories, and volumes can each have their own security. NTFS's security is flexible and built in. Not only does NTFS track security in Access Control Lists (ACLs), which can hold permissions for local users and groups, but each entry in the ACL can also specify what type of access is given—such as Read-Only, Change, or Full Control—none of which is possible with FAT. This allows a great deal of flexibility in setting up a network. In addition, special file-encryption programs were developed to encrypt data while it was stored on the hard disk.

Microsoft strongly recommends that all network shares be established using NTFS.

Understanding Wireless Security

Wireless systems are those that don't use wires to send information but rather transmit data through the air. The growth of wireless systems creates several opportunities for attackers. These systems are relatively new, they use well-established communications mechanisms, and they're easily intercepted. Wireless controllers use *service-set identifiers* (SSIDs) that must be configured in the network cards to allow communications with a specific access point. However, using SSID configurations doesn't necessarily prevent wireless networks from being monitored.

This section discusses the various types of wireless systems that you'll encounter, and it mentions some of the security issues associated with this technology. Specifically, this section deals with Wireless Transport Layer Security (WTLS), the IEEE 802 wireless standards, Wired Equivalent Privacy (WEP)/Wireless Applications Protocol (WAP) applications, and the vulnerabilities that each presents.

Wireless Transport Layer Security

Wireless Transport Layer Security (WTLS) is the security layer of WAP, discussed in the section "WEP/WAP." WTLS provides authentication, encryption, and data integrity for wireless devices. It's designed to utilize the relatively narrow bandwidth of these types of devices, and it's moderately secure. WTLS provides reasonable security for mobile devices, and it's being widely implemented.

WTLS is part of the WAP environment: WAP provides the functional equivalent of TCP/IP for wireless devices. Many devices, including newer cell phones and PDAs, include support for WTLS as part of their networking protocol capabilities.

IEEE 802.11*x* Wireless Protocols

The IEEE 802.11*x* family of protocols provides for wireless communications using radio frequency transmissions. The frequencies in use for 802.11 standards are the 2.4GHz and the 5GHz frequency spectrum. Several standards and bandwidths have been defined for use in wireless environments, and they aren't extremely compatible with each other:

802.11 The *802.11* standard defines wireless LANs transmitting at 1Mbps or 2Mbps bandwidths using the 2.4GHz frequency spectrum and using either frequency-hopping spread spectrum (FHSS) or direct-sequence spread spectrum (DSSS) for data encoding.

802.11a   The *802.11a* standard provides wireless LAN bandwidth of up to 54Mbps in the 5GHz frequency spectrum. The 802.11a standard also uses orthogonal frequency division multiplexing (OFDM) for encoding rather than FHSS or DSSS.

802.11b   The *802.11b* standard provides for bandwidths of up to 11Mbps (with fallback rates of 5.5, 2, and 1Mbps) in the 2.4GHz frequency spectrum. This standard is also called *WiFi* or *802.11 high rate*. The 802.11b standard uses only DSSS for data encoding.

802.11g   The *802.11g* standard provides for bandwidths of 54Mbps+ in the 2.4GHz frequency spectrum.

We have mentioned three signal modulation techniques used in the 802.11 standards:

Direct-Sequence Spread Spectrum (DSSS)   DSSS accomplishes communication by adding the data that is to be transmitted to a higher-speed transmission. The higher-speed transmission contains redundant information to ensure data accuracy. Each packet can then be reconstructed in the event of a disruption.

Frequency-Hopping Spread Spectrum (FHSS)   FHSS accomplishes communication by hopping the transmission over a range of predefined frequencies. The changing or hopping is synchronized between both ends and appears to be a single transmission channel to both ends.

Orthogonal Frequency Division Multiplexing (OFDM)   OFDM accomplishes communication by breaking the data into subsignals and transmitting them simultaneously. These transmissions occur on different frequencies or subbands.

The mathematics and theories of these transmission technologies are beyond the scope of this book and far beyond the scope of this exam.

WEP/WAP/WPA

Wireless systems frequently use WAP for network communications. WEP is intended to provide the equivalent security of a wired network protocol. WPA is an improvement on WEP. This section briefly discusses these two terms and provides you with an understanding of their relative capabilities.

WAP

The *Wireless Access Protocol (WAP)* is the technology designed for use with wireless devices. WAP has become a standard adopted by many manufacturers including Motorola, Nokia, and others. WAP functions are equivalent to TCP/IP functions in that they're trying to serve the same purpose for wireless devices. WAP uses a smaller version of HTML called *Wireless Markup Language (WML)*, which is used for Internet displays. WAP-enabled devices can also respond to scripts using an environment called *WMLScript*. This scripting language is similar to JavaScript, which is a programming language.

The ability to accept web pages and scripts produces the opportunity for malicious code and viruses to be transported to WAP-enabled devices. No doubt this will create a new set of problems, and antivirus software will be needed to deal with them.

WAP systems communicate using a WAP gateway system. The gateway converts information back and forth between HTTP and WAP, and it also encodes and decodes the security protocols. This structure provides a reasonable assurance that WAP-enabled devices can be secured. If the interconnection between the WAP server and the Internet isn't encrypted, packets between the devices may be intercepted, creating a potential vulnerability. This vulnerability is called a *gap in the WAP*.

WEP

Wired Equivalent Privacy (WEP) is a security standard for wireless devices. WEP encrypts data to provide data security. The protocol has always been under scrutiny for not being as secure as initially intended.

 The CompTIA objectives use the notation WEP.x, which refers to the key size. 64-bit, 128-bit, and 256-bit keys are commonly supported (WEP 64, WEP 128, and WEP 256).

WEP is vulnerable due to weaknesses in the encryption algorithms. These weaknesses allow the algorithm to potentially be cracked in less than five hours using available PC software. This makes WEP one of the more vulnerable protocols available for security.

 MAC filtering can be used on a wireless network to prevent certain clients from accessing the Internet. You can choose to deny service to a set list of MAC addresses (and allow all others) or allow service only to a set of MAC addresses (and deny all others).

WPA

WiFi Protected Access (WPA) is an improvement on WEP that implements some of the 802.11i standards. An improvement over WPA is WPA2, which implements the full 802.11i standard.

Wireless Vulnerabilities to Know

Wireless systems are vulnerable to all the different attacks that wired networks are vulnerable to. However, because these protocols use radio frequency signals, they have an additional weakness: All radio frequency signals can be easily intercepted. To intercept 802.11*x* traffic, all you need is a PC with an appropriate 802.11*x* card installed. Simple software on the PC can capture the link traffic in the WAP and then process this data in order to decrypt account and password information.

An additional aspect of wireless systems is the *site survey*. Site surveys involve listening in on an existing wireless network using commercially available technologies. Doing so allows intelligence, and possibly data capture, to be performed on systems in your wireless network.

The term *site survey* initially meant determining whether a proposed location was free from interference. When used by an attacker, a site survey can determine what types of systems are in use, the protocols used, and other critical information about your network. It's the primary method used to gather data about wireless networks. Virtually all wireless networks are vulnerable to site surveys.

In reality, wardriving is probably a more current threat that emphasizes the need for paying attention to wireless security. Make sure your limiting your network to those who need access to it and not those sitting in the parking lot.

Understanding Data and Physical Security

Physical security, as the name implies, involves protecting your assets and information from physical access by unauthorized personnel. In other words, you're trying to protect those items that can be seen, touched, and stolen. These threats often present themselves as service technicians, janitors, customers, vendors, or even employees. They can steal your equipment, damage it, or take documents from offices, garbage cans, or filing cabinets. Their motivation may be retribution for some perceived misgiving, a desire to steal your trade secrets to sell to a competitor as an act of vengeance, or just greed. They might steal $1,000 worth of hardware that they can sell to a friend for a fraction of that and have no concept of the value of the data stored on the hardware.

Physical security is relatively easy to accomplish. You can secure facilities by controlling access to the office, shredding unneeded documents, installing security systems, and limiting access to sensitive areas of the business. Most office buildings provide perimeter and corridor security during unoccupied hours, and it isn't difficult to implement commonsense measures during occupied hours as well. Sometimes just having a person present—even a guard who spends much of the time sleeping—can be all the deterrent needed to prevent petty thefts.

The first layer of access control is always perimeter security. Perimeter security is intended to delay or deter entrance into a facility.

Many office complexes also offer roving security patrols, multiple-lock access control methods, and electronic or password access. Typically, the facility managers handle these arrangements. They won't generally deal with internal security as it relates to your records, computer systems, and papers; that is your responsibility in most situations.

The first component of physical security involves making a physical location less tempting as a target. If the office or building you're in is open all the time, gaining entry into a business in the building is easy. You must prevent people from seeing your organization as a tempting target. Locking doors and installing surveillance or alarm systems can make a physical location a less-desirable target. You can also add controls to elevators requiring keys or badges in order to reach upper floors. Plenty of wide-open targets are available, involving less risk on the part of the people involved. Try to make your office not worth the trouble.

The second component of physical security involves detecting a *penetration* or theft. You want to know what was broken into, what is missing, and how the loss occurred. Passive videotape systems are one good way to obtain this information. Most retail environments routinely tape key areas of the business to identify how thefts occur and who was involved. These tapes are admissible as evidence in most courts. Law enforcement should be involved as soon as a penetration or theft occurs. More important from a deterrent standpoint, you should make it well known that you'll prosecute anyone caught in the act of theft to the fullest extent of the law. Making the video cameras as conspicuous as possible will deter many would-be criminals.

The third component of physical security involves recovering from a theft or loss of critical information or systems. How will the organization recover from the loss and get on with normal business? If a vandal destroyed your server room with a fire or flood, how long would it take your organization to get back into operation and return to full productivity?

Recovery involves a great deal of planning, thought, and testing. What would happen if the files containing all your bank accounts, purchase orders, and customer information became a pile of ashes in the middle of the smoldering ruins that used to be your office? Ideally, critical copies of records and inventories should be stored off site in a secure facility.

Encryption Technologies

Cryptographic algorithms are used to encode a message from its unencrypted or clear-text state into an encrypted message. The three primary methods are hashing, symmetric, and asymmetric.

Hashing is the process of converting a message, or data, into a numeric value. The numeric value that a hashing process creates is referred to as a *hash total* or *value*. Hashing functions are considered either one-way or two-way. A one-way hash doesn't allow a message to be decoded back to the original value. A two-way hash allows a message to be reconstructed from the hash. Most hashing functions are one-way hashing. Two primary standards exist that use the hashing process for encryption:

Secure Hash Algorithm (SHA)   The *Secure Hash Algorithm (SHA)* was designed to ensure the integrity of a message. The SHA is a one-way hash that provides a hash value that can be used with an encryption protocol. This algorithm produces a 160-bit hash value. SHA has been updated; four new standards, collectively called SHA-2, have been developed.

Message Digest Algorithm (MDA)   The *Message Digest Algorithm (MDA)* also creates a hash value and uses a one-way hash. The hash value is used to help maintain integrity. There are several versions of MD; the most common are MD5, MD4, and MD2.

Symmetric algorithms require both ends of an encrypted message to have the same key and processing algorithms. Symmetric algorithms generate a secret key that must be protected. A secret key—sometimes referred to as a *private key*—is a key that isn't disclosed to people who aren't authorized to use the encryption system. The disclosure of a private key breaches the security of the encryption system. If a key is lost or stolen, the entire process is breached. These types of systems are common, and examples include AES and IDEA.

Asymmetric algorithms use two keys to encrypt and decrypt data. These keys are referred to as the *public key* and the *private key*. The public key can be used by the sender to encrypt a message, and the private key can be used by the receiver to decrypt the message. Symmetrical systems require the key to be private between the two parties, but with asymmetric systems, each circuit has one key. Examples include Diffie-Hellman and RSA.

The public key may be truly public or it may be a secret between the two parties. The private key is kept private and is known only by the owner (receiver). If someone wants to send you an encrypted message, he can use your public key to encrypt the message and then send you the message. You can use your private key to decrypt the message. One of the keys is always kept private. If both keys become available to a third party, the encryption system won't protect the privacy of the message.

Perhaps the best way to think about this system is that it's similar to a safe-deposit box. Two keys are needed: The box owner keeps the public key, and the bank retains the second or private key. In order to open the box, both keys must be used simultaneously.

Backups

Backups are duplicate copies of key information, ideally stored in a location other than the one where the information is currently stored. Backups include both paper and computer records. Computer records are usually backed up using a backup program, backup systems, and backup procedures.

The primary starting point for disaster recovery involves keeping current backup copies of key data files, databases, applications, and paper records available for use. Your organization must develop a solid set of procedures to manage this process and ensure that all key information is protected. A security professional can do several things in conjunction with system administrators and business managers to protect this information. It's important to think of this problem as an issue that is larger than a single department.

The information you back up also must be immediately available for use when needed. If a user loses a critical file, she won't want to wait several days while data files are sent from a remote storage facility. Several different types of storage mechanisms are available for data storage:

Working Copies   *Working copy* backups—sometimes referred to as *shadow copies*—are partial or full backups that are kept at the computer center for immediate recovery purposes. Working copies are frequently the most recent backups that have been made.

Typically, working copies are intended for immediate use. These copies are usually updated on a frequent basis.

Many filesystems used on servers include *journaling*. Journaled (or journaling) filesystems (JFS) include a log file of all changes and transactions that have occurred within a set period of time (the last few hours, and so on). If a crash occurs, the operating system can look at the log files to see which transactions have been committed and which ones haven't. This technology works well and allows unsaved data to be written after the recovery and the system usually to be successfully restored to its precrash condition.

Onsite Storage   *Onsite storage* usually refers to a location on the site of the computer center that is used to store information locally. Onsite storage containers are available that allow computer cartridges, tapes, and other backup media to be stored in a reasonably protected environment in the building.

Onsite storage containers are designed and rated for fire, moisture, and pressure resistance. These containers aren't *fireproof* in most situations, but they're *fire-rated*: A fireproof container should be guaranteed to withstand damage regardless of the type of fire or temperatures, whereas fire ratings specify that a container can protect the contents for a specific amount of time in a given situation.

If you choose to depend entirely on onsite storage, make sure the containers you acquire can withstand the worst-case environmental catastrophes that could happen at your location. Make sure, as well, that those containers are in locations where you can easily find them after the disaster and access them (near exterior walls, and so on).

Offsite Storage   *Offsite storage* refers to a location away from the computer center where paper copies and backup media are kept. Offsite storage can involve something as simple as keeping a copy of backup media at a remote office, or it can be as complicated as a nuclear-hardened high-security storage facility. The storage facility should be bonded, insured, and inspected on a regular basis to ensure that all storage procedures are being followed.

Determining which storage mechanism to use should be based on the needs of the organization, the availability of storage facilities, and the budget available. Most offsite storage facilities charge based on the amount of space you require and the frequency of access you need to the stored information.

Three methods exist to back up information on most systems:

Full Backup   A *full backup* is a complete, comprehensive backup of all designated files on a disk or server. The full backup is current only at the time it's performed. Once a full backup is made, you have a complete archive of the system or designated files at that point in time. A system shouldn't be in use while it undergoes a full backup because some files may not get backed up. Once the system goes back into operation, the backup is no longer current. A full backup can be a time-consuming process on a large system.

Incremental Backup   An *incremental backup* is a partial backup that stores only the information that has been changed since the last full or the last incremental backup. If a full backup were performed on a Sunday night, an incremental backup done on Monday night would contain only the information that changed since Sunday night. Such a backup is typically considerably smaller than a full backup. This backup system requires that each incremental backup be retained until a full backup can be performed. Incremental backups are usually the fastest backups to perform on most systems, and each incremental tape is relatively small.

> **NOTE**   Restoring data using incremental backups takes longer, however, since the restoration must use the last full backup and every incremental backup made since the last full backup (in order).

Differential Backup   A differential backup is similar in function to an incremental backup, but it backs up any files that have been altered since the last full backup; it makes duplicate copies of files that haven't changed since the last differential backup. If a full backup were performed on Sunday night, a differential backup performed on Monday night would capture the information that was changed on Monday. A differential backup completed on Tuesday night would record the changes in any files from Monday and any changes in files on Tuesday. As you can see, during the week each differential backup would become larger; by Friday or Saturday night, it might be nearly as large as a full backup. This means the backups in the earliest part of the weekly cycle will be very fast, and each successive one will be slower.

> Restoring data using differential backups can be faster than the incremental method, however, since you only need to restore the last full backup and the most recent differential backup.

When these backup methods are used in conjunction with each other, the risk of loss can be greatly reduced. However, you should never combine an incremental backup with a differential backup. One of the major factors in determining which combination of these three methods to used is time—ideally, a full backup would be performed everyday. Several commercial backup programs support these three backup methods. You must evaluate your organizational needs when choosing which tools to use to accomplish backups.

Almost every stable operating system contains a utility for creating a copy of configuration settings necessary to reach the present state after a disaster. As an administrator, you must know how to do backups and be familiar with all the options available to you.

In Exercise 9.1, you'll learn how to use the Backup Utility in Windows XP to create an ASR.

EXERCISE 9.1

Automated System Recovery in Windows XP

In this exercise, you'll use the Backup Utility included with Windows XP to create an ASR backup:

1. Start the Backup Utility by choosing Start ➢ All Programs ➢ Accessories ➢ System Tools ➢ Backup.

2. Choose the Automated System Recovery Wizard.

3. Walk through the wizard and answer the questions appropriately. When you finish, you'll create the backup set first and then a floppy. The floppy contains files necessary to restore system settings after a disaster.

Incidence Reporting

Incident Response policies define how an organization will respond to an incident. These policies may involve third parties, and they need to be comprehensive. The term *incident* is somewhat nebulous in scope; for our purposes, an incident is any attempt to violate a security policy, a successful penetration, a compromise of a system, or any unauthorized access to information. This term includes system failures and disruption of services in the organization.

It's important that an Incident Response policy minimally establish the following items:

- Outside agencies that should be contacted or notified in case of an incident
- Resources used to deal with an incident
- Procedures to gather and secure evidence
- List of information that should be collected about the incident
- Outside experts who can be used to address issues if needed
- Policies and guidelines regarding how to handle the incident

According to the Computer Emergency Response Team (more commonly known as CERT), a Computer Security Incident Response Team (CSIRT) can be a formalized team or ad hoc. You can toss a team together to respond to an incident after it arises; but investing time in the development process can make an incident more manageable, because many decisions about dealing with an incident will have been considered earlier. Incidents are high-stress situations; therefore, it's better to simplify the process by considering important aspects in advance. If civil or criminal actions are part of the process, evidence must be gathered and safeguarded properly.

Assume you've discovered a situation where a fraud has been perpetrated internally using a corporate computer. You're part of the investigating team. Your Incident Response policy lists the specialists you need to contact for an investigation. Ideally, you've already met the investigator or investigating firm, you've developed an understanding of how to protect the scene, and you know how to properly deal with the media (if they become involved).

While a response policy is important to have, don't let it stop there. You must make certain the policy is followed when an incident occurs. The importance of responding to, and acting upon an incident—including correctly reporting it—is imperative.

Social Engineering

Social engineering is a process in which an attacker attempts to acquire information about your network and system by social means, such as talking to people in the organization. A social-engineering attack may occur over the phone, by e-mail, or by a visit. The intent is to acquire access information, such as user IDs and passwords.

These types of attacks are relatively low-tech and are more akin to con jobs. Take the following example. Your help desk gets a call at 4:00 a.m. from someone purporting to be the vice president of your company. She tells the help desk personnel that she is out of town to attend a meeting, her computer just failed, and she is sitting in a Kinko's trying to get a file from her desktop computer back at the office. She can't seem to remember her password and user ID. She tells the help desk representative that she needs access to the information right away or the company could lose millions of dollars. Your help desk rep knows how important this meeting is and gives the vice president her user ID and password over the phone.

Another common approach is initiated by a phone call or e-mail from your software vendor, telling you that they have a critical fix that must be installed on your computer system.

If this patch isn't installed right away, your system will crash and you'll lose all your data. For some reason, you've changed your maintenance account password and they can't log on. Your systems operator gives the password to the person. You've been hit again.

In Exercise 9.2, you'll test your users to determine the likelihood of a social-engineering attack.

EXERCISE 9.2

Testing Social Engineering

The following are suggestions for tests; you may need to modify them slightly to be appropriate at your workplace. Before doing any of them, make certain your manager knows that you're conducting such an exam and approves of it:

1. Call the receptionist from an outside line when the sales manager is at lunch. Tell her that you're a new salesman, that you didn't write down the username and password the sales manager gave you last week, and that you need to get a file from the e-mail system for a presentation tomorrow. Does she direct you to the appropriate person?

2. Call the human resources department from an outside line. Don't give your real name, but instead say that you're a vendor who has been working with this company for years. You'd like a copy of the employee phone list to be e-mailed to you, if possible. Do they agree to send you the list, which would contain information that could be used to try to guess usernames and passwords?

3. Pick a user at random. Call them and identify yourself as someone who does work with the company. Tell them that you're supposed to have some new software ready for them by next week and that you need to know their password in order to finish configuring it. Do they do the right thing?

The best defense against any social-engineering attack is education. Make certain the employees of your company would know how to react to the requests presented here.

Security Solutions

There are a number of security solutions that can be implemented to help make your systems and networks more secure—remember that the network is only as secure as the weakest host connected to it.

BIOS Security

The system Basic Input/Output System (BIOS) is used to power up the system and can also allow you to assign a password. Once enabled/activated, that password is stored in CMOS and must be given before the system will fully boot.

This provides a simple security solution for a workstation/laptop. The casual hacker's most common way of working around the password requirement is to remove the battery (thus erasing the CMOS). You should be aware, however, that many BIOS manufacturers include a backdoor password that can be given to bypass the one set by the user. Many of these values can be found on the Internet and are known by more professional hackers.

 Another method for getting around the password is to change the jumper for resetting CMOS settings to defaults.

Malicious Software Protection

Computer *viruses*—applications that carry out malicious actions—are one of the most annoying trends happening today: they are but one form of threat. Malicious software—also called malware—also includes worms, Trojan horses, spyware, and adware. It seems that almost every day someone invents a new virus. Some of these viruses do nothing more than give you a big "gotcha"; others destroy systems, contaminate networks, and wreak havoc on computer systems. A virus may act on your data or your operating system, but it's intent on doing harm and doing so without your consent. Viruses often include replication as a primary objective and try to infect as many machines as they can, as quickly as possible.

The business of providing software to computer users to protect them from viruses has become a huge industry. Several very good and well-established suppliers of antivirus software exist, and new virus-protection methods come on the scene almost as fast as new viruses. Antivirus software scans the computer's memory, disk files, and incoming and outgoing e-mail. The software typically uses a virus-definition file that is updated regularly by the manufacturer. If these files are kept up-to-date, the computer system will be relatively secure. Unfortunately, most people don't keep their virus definitions up-to-date. Users will exclaim that a new virus has come out, because they just got it. Upon examination, you'll often discover that their virus-definition file is months out-of-date. As you can see, the software part of the system will break down if the definition files aren't updated on a regular basis.

Data Access

Access control defines the methods used to ensure that users of your network can access only what they're authorized to access. The process of access control should be spelled out in the organization's security policies and standards. Several models exist to accomplish this. This section will briefly explain the following models:

- Bell La-Padula
- Biba
- Clark-Wilson
- Information Flow model
- Noninterference model

Bell La-Padula Model

The *Bell La-Padula model* was designed for the military to address the storage and protection of classified information. The model is specifically designed to prevent unauthorized access to classified information. The model prevents the user from accessing information that has a higher security rating than she is authorized to access. The model also prevents information from being written to a lower level of security.

For example, if you're authorized to access Secret information, you aren't allowed to access Top Secret information, nor are you allowed to write to the system at a level lower than the Secret level. This creates upper and lower bounds for information storage. This process is illustrated in Figure 9.7. Notice in the illustration that you can't *read up* or *write down*. This means that a user can't read information at a higher level than she's authorized to access. A person writing a file can't *write down* to a lower level than the security level she's authorized to access.

The process of preventing a *write down* keeps a user from accidentally breaching security by writing Secret information to the next lower level, Confidential. In our example, you can read Confidential information, but because you're approved at the Secret level, you can't write to the Confidential level. This model doesn't deal with integrity, only confidentiality. A user of Secret information can potentially modify other documents at the same level she possesses.

To see how this model works, think about corporate financial information. The chief financial officer (CFO) may have financial information about the company that he needs to protect. The Bell La-Padula model keeps him from inadvertently posting information at an access level lower than his access level (writing down), thus preventing unauthorized or accidental disclosure of sensitive information. Lower-level employees can't access this information because they can't read up to the level of the CFO.

The Biba Model

The *Biba model* was designed after the Bell La-Padula model. It's similar in concept to the Bell La-Padula model, but it's more concerned with information integrity, an area that the Bell La-Padula model doesn't address. In this model, there is no *write up* or *read down*. In short, if you're assigned access to Top Secret information, you can't read Secret information or write to any level higher than the level to which you're authorized. This keeps higher-level information pure by preventing less-reliable information from being intermixed with it. Figure 9.8 illustrates this concept in more detail. The Biba model was developed primarily for industrial uses, where confidentiality is usually less important than integrity.

FIGURE 9.7   The Bell La-Padula model

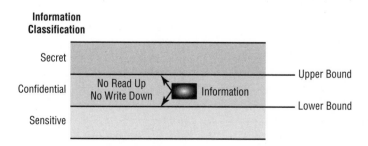

FIGURE 9.8   The Biba model

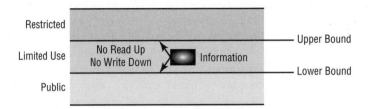

Think about the data that is generated by a researcher for a scientific project. The researcher is responsible for managing the results of research from a lower-level project and incorporating it into her research data. If bad data were to get into her research, the whole research project would be ruined. With the Biba model, this accident can't happen. The researcher doesn't have access to the information from lower levels: That information must be promoted to the level of the researcher. This system keeps the researcher's data intact and prevents accidental contamination.

The Clark-Wilson Model

The *Clark-Wilson model* was developed after the Biba model. The approach is a little different from either the Biba or the Bell La-Padula method. In this model, data can't be accessed directly: It must be accessed through applications that have predefined capabilities. This process prevents unauthorized modification, errors, and fraud from occurring. If a user needs access to information at a certain level of security, a specific program is used. This program may allow only read access to the information. If a user needs to modify data, another application must be used. This allows a separation of duties in that individuals are granted access only to the tools they need. All transactions have associated audit files and mechanisms to report modifications. Figure 9.9 illustrates this process. Access to information is gained by using a program that specializes in access management; this can be either a single program that controls all access or a set of programs that controls access. Many software-management programs work using this method of security.

Let's say you're working on a software product as part of a team. You may need to access certain code to include in your programs. You aren't authorized to modify this code; you're merely authorized to use it. You use a checkout program to get the code from the source library. Any attempt to put modified code back is prevented. The developers of the code in the source library are authorized to make changes. This process ensures that only people authorized to change the code can accomplish the task.

FIGURE 9.9   The Clark-Wilson model

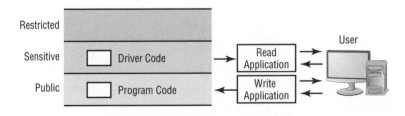

Information Flow Model

The *Information Flow model* is concerned with the properties of information flow, not only the direction of the flow. Both the Bell La-Padula and Biba models are concerned with information flow in predefined manners; they're considered information-flow models. However, this particular Information Flow model is concerned with all information flow, not just up or down. This model requires that each piece of information have unique properties, including operation capabilities. If an attempt is made to write lower-level information to a higher level, the model evaluates the properties of the information and determines whether the operation is legal. If the operation is illegal, the model prevents it from occurring. Figure 9.10 illustrates this concept.

Let's use the previous software project as an example. A developer may be working with a version of the software to improve functionality. When the programmer makes improvements to the code, he wants to put that code back into the library. If the attempt to write the code is successful, the code replaces the existing code. If a subsequent bug is found in the new code, the old code has been changed. The solution is to create a new version of the code that incorporates both the new code and the old code. Each subsequent change to the code requires a new version to be created. This process may consume more disk space, but it prevents things from getting lost, and it provides a mechanism to use or evaluate an older version of the code.

Noninterference Model

The *Noninterference model* is intended to ensure that higher-level security functions don't interfere with lower-level functions. In essence, if a higher-level user changes information, the lower-level user doesn't know about and isn't affected by the changes. This approach prevents the lower-level user from being able to deduce what changes are being made to the system. Figure 9.11 illustrates this concept. Notice that the lower-level user isn't aware that any changes have occurred above him.

Let's take one last look at the software project with which we've been working. If a systems developer is making changes to the library that's being used by a lower-level programmer, changes may be made to the library without the lower-level programmer being aware of them. This lets the higher-level developer work on prototypes without affecting the development effort of the lower-level programmer. When the developer finishes the code, she publishes it to lower-level programmers. At this point, all users have access to the changes, and they can use them in their programs.

FIGURE 9.10   The Information Flow model

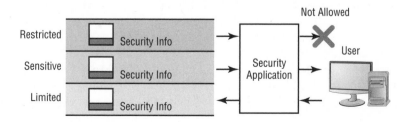

FIGURE 9.11   The Noninterference model

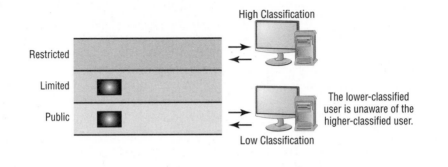

> **NOTE**   This topic is revisited again in Chapter 17 with a focus on OS-specific authentication, authorization, and audit (e.g., rights, permissions, sharing files and folders).

Backup Procedures

An organization's *backup policy* dictates what information should be backed up and how it should be backed up. Ideally, a backup plan is written in conjunction with the Business Continuity Plan.

Backup policies also need to set guidelines for information archiving. Many managers and users don't understand the difference between a backup and an archive. A *backup* is a restorable copy of any set of data that is needed on the system; an *archive* is any collection of data that is removed from the system because it's no longer needed on a regular basis.

The CompTIA objectives also include a mention of the access to backups. If data is valuable enough to spend the resources required to back it up, it is clearly important enough to protect carefully. As a backup, all of your company's data is in an easily transported form and should be protected from access by those who should not see it.

Data Migration

When migrating data from one operating system to another, one platform to another, or even one system to another, it's imperative that you focus on availability and reparability. Depending on the migration being undertaken, it's possible that the system you're migrating to (if changing operating systems) doesn't use the same ACLs, granularity, or defaults that exist on the system you're coming from. This can result in users who are unable to access data they should be able to use and/or result in inappropriate access to data for users.

To identify and plan for this scenario, it's important to always do a test of the migration in a controlled environment (lab, pilot, and so on) before instigating it on production systems.

It's also crucial that you do a full backup of all data before the migration. That backup can't be considered complete until you verify that you can restore it. The last thing you want is to need to restore data, only to find out that the media was improperly formatted and you're unable to do so.

Data Remnant Removal

Data remnant removal is typically the name given to removing all usable data from media (typically hard drives, but any media can be included). Earlier in this chapter, the topic of wiping a hard drive, reformatting it, or using specialized utilities was covered. Remember that when computer systems are retired, the disk drives should be zeroed out, and all magnetic media should be degaussed.

On a related topic, when data ages, it must often be archived and removed from live systems—it must often be archived and able to be retrieved at a later point in time if needed. Policies should be in place to dictate who has access to the archives, how and where the archives are stored, and how they're cataloged. The latter is of key importance because you want to be able to find data as expeditiously as possible, even when it has been removed from the system.

Password Management

One of the strongest ways to keep a system safe is to employ strong passwords and educate your users. To be strong, passwords should include upper- and lowercase letters, numbers, and other characters as allowed (which characters are allowed may differ based upon the operating system).

Users should be educated to understand how valuable data is and why it is important to keep their password strong, secret, and regularly changed.

Locking Workstations

Just as you would not park your car in a public garage and leave its doors wide open with the key in the ignition, you should educate users to not leave a workstation that they are logged in to when they attend meetings, go to lunch, etc. They should log out of the workstation, or lock it. Locking the workstation should require a password (usually the same as their user password) in order to resume working at the workstation.

Identifying Security Problem Areas

The landscape of security is changing at a very fast pace. You, as a security professional, are primarily responsible for keeping current on the threats and changes that are occurring. You're also responsible for ensuring that systems are kept up-to-date. The following list briefly summarizes the areas you must be concerned about:

Operating System Updates   Make sure all scheduled maintenance is performed and updates and service packs are installed on all the systems in your environment. Many manufacturers are releasing security updates on their products to deal with newly discovered vulnerabilities. For example, Novell, Microsoft, and Linux manufacturers offer updates on their websites. In some cases, you can have the OS automatically notify you when an update becomes available; this notification helps busy administrators remember to keep their systems current.

As a security administrator, you understand the importance of applying all patches and updates to keep systems current and to close found weaknesses.

Application Updates   Make sure all applications are kept to the most current levels. Older software may contain vulnerabilities that weren't detected until after the software was released. New software may have recently discovered vulnerabilities as well as yet-to-be-discovered ones. Apply updates to your application software when they're released to help minimize the impact of attacks on your systems.

One of the biggest exploitations that occur today involves application programs such as e-mail clients and word-processing software. The manufacturers of these products regularly release updates to attempt to make them more secure. Like operating system updates, these should be checked regularly and applied.

Network Device Updates   Most newer network devices can provide high levels of security, or they can be configured to block certain types of traffic and IP addresses. Make sure logs are reviewed and, where necessary, ACLs (Access Control Lists) updated to prevent attackers from disrupting your systems. These network devices are also frequently updated to counter new vulnerabilities and threats. Network devices should have their BIOS updated when the updates become available; doing so allows for an ever-increasing level of security in your environment.

ACL, like many other acronyms in computing, can stand for more than one thing. Access Control Lists are used with both permissions for files/folders and network access.

Cisco, 3Com, and other network manufacturers regularly offer network updates. These can frequently be applied online or by web-enabled systems. These devices are your front line of defense: You want to make sure they're kept up-to-date.

Policies and Procedures   A policy that is out-of-date may be worse than no policy. Be aware of any changes in your organization and in the industry that make existing policies out-of-date. Many organizations set a review date as part of their policy-creation procedures. Periodically review your documentation to verify that your policies are effective and current.

In addition to focusing on these areas, you must also stay current on security trends, threats, and tools available to help you provide security. The volume of threats is increasing, as are the measures, methods, and procedures used to counter them.

You must keep abreast of what is happening in the field, as well as the current best practices of the systems and applications you support. You're basically going to be functioning as a clearinghouse and data repository for your company's security. Make it a point to become a walking encyclopedia on security issues: Doing so will improve your credibility and demonstrate your expertise. Both of these aspects enhance your career opportunities and equip you to be a leader in the field.

You should also make it a priority to train and educate users about malicious software. The more they know about the threats that are present—and the harm they can inflict—the more likely they are to act accordingly when they encounter a possible threat.

Table 9.2 summarizes the items where problems may occur and ways to identify that a problem exists.

TABLE 9.2 Identifying Problem Issues

Area	Identifying Symptoms
BIOS	Problems/compromises involving the BIOS typically prevent the system from starting properly. You may be asked to enter a password you don't know, or control of the system is never handed to the OS after POST.
Smart cards	Problems with smart cards become apparent when users are unable to access data or logs show that they accessed data they never truly did.
Biometrics	If there is a problem with biometrics, the user is unable to authenticate and unable to access resources.
Malicious software	Malicious software should be first detected by an antivirus program or other routine operation. If not, it will begin to show itself in the actions taking place on the system (deletion of executables, mass mailing, and so on).
Filesystem	Filesystem problems can fall into the category of users not being able to access data as they need to or everyone being granted access to data that they should not see.
Data access	Data-access problems, as with filesystem issues, are usually those where users legitimately needing access to data can't access it, or too much permission is granted to users who don't need such access. Chapter 14 deals with specific OS approaches to data access.
Backup	Issues with backups are their inability to successfully complete and include all files, or media failure when a restore needs to be done. Always verify that the backup completed successfully, and routinely verify that you can restore.
Data migration	Data-migration problems, as they pertain to security, usually result from the source and target not having the same one-to-one permission sets. Work closely with test data ahead of time to resolve any issues that may arise before doing a migration of production data.

Summary

In this chapter, you learned about the various issues related to security that appear on the A+ Essentials exam. We discussed various principles of security and solutions.

You also learned of security problem areas and issues that can be easily identified.

Exam Essentials

Know the names, purpose, and characteristics of hardware and software security. Many types of hardware and software are used to provide security to an organization. These can range from firewalls (which can be software or hardware based) to smart cards. It's important to also know the different types of authentication technologies available and the various types of malicious software that exist.

Know the names, purpose, and characteristics of wireless security. Wireless networks can be encrypted through WEP and WPA technologies. Wireless controllers use SSIDs that must be configured in the network cards to allow communication with a specific access point. However, using SSIDs doesn't necessarily prevent wireless networks from being monitored, and there are vulnerabilities specific to wireless devices.

Know the names, purpose, and characteristics of data and physical security. Know the different types of backups that can be done as well as the basics of encryption. You should also be aware of social-engineering concerns and the need for a useful Incident Response policy.

Implement software security preventative maintenance techniques. Know the importance of keeping the systems current, applying patches as they're released/needed, and keeping your knowledge/skills up-to-date.

Install, configure, upgrade, and optimize hardware, software, and data security. For this objective, you're expected to know the basics of the following items: BIOS, smart cards, authentication technologies, malicious software protection, data access, backup procedures and access to backups, data migration, and data remnant removal.

Diagnose and troubleshoot procedures and troubleshooting techniques for security. It's important to know the symptoms that may arise in the problem areas and to be able to quickly identify them. This allows you to then hone in on the source of the problem and begin troubleshooting in earnest.

Review Questions

1. Which component of physical security addresses outer-level access control?

   A. Perimeter security

   B. Mantraps

   C. Security zones

   D. Locked doors

2. Which technology uses a physical characteristic to establish identity?

   A. Biometrics

   B. Surveillance

   C. Smart card

   D. CHAP authenticator

3. As part of your training program, you're trying to educate users on the importance of security. You explain to them that not every attack depends on implementing advanced technological methods. Some attacks, you explain, take advantage of human shortcoming to gain access that should otherwise be denied. What term do you use to describe attacks of this type?

   A. Social engineering

   B. IDS system

   C. Perimeter security

   D. Biometrics

4. You've recently been hired by ACME to do a security audit. The managers of this company feel that their current security measures are inadequate. Which information-access control prevents users from writing information down to a lower level of security and prevents users from reading above their level of security?

   A. Bell La-Padula model

   B. Biba model

   C. Clark-Wilson model

   D. Noninterference model

5. Although you're talking to her on the phone, the sound of the administrative assistant's screams of despair can be heard down the hallway. She has inadvertently deleted a file that the boss desperately needs. Which type of backup is used for the immediate recovery of a lost file?

   A. Onsite storage

   B. Working copies

   C. Incremental backup

   D. Differential backup

6. You're trying to rearrange your backup procedures to reduce the amount of time they take each evening. You want the backups to finish as quickly as possible during the week. Which backup system backs up only the files that have changed since the last backup?

   A. Full backup

   B. Incremental backup

   C. Differential backup

   D. Backup server

7. Which backup system backs up all the files that have changed since the last full backup?

   A. Full backup

   B. Incremental backup

   C. Differential backup

   D. Archival backup

8. You've been assigned to mentor a junior administrator and bring him up to speed quickly. The topic you're currently explaining is authentication. Which method uses a KDC to accomplish authentication for users, programs, or systems?

   A. CHAP

   B. Kerberos

   C. Biometrics

   D. Smart cards

9. Which authentication method sends a challenge to the client that is encrypted and then sent back to the server?

   A. Kerberos

   B. PAP

   C. DAC

   D. CHAP

10. After a careful risk analysis, the value of your company's data has been increased. Accordingly, you're expected to implement authentication solutions that reflect the increased value of the data. Which of the following authentication methods uses more than one authentication process for a logon?

   A. Multifactor

   B. Biometrics

   C. Smart card

   D. Kerberos

11. Which of the following services or protocols should be avoided in a network if possible in order to increase security?

    A. E-mail

    B. Telnet

    C. WWW

    D. ICMP

12. Of the following services, which one would be most likely to utilize a retinal scan?

    A. Auditing

    B. Authentication

    C. Access control

    D. Data confidentiality

13. One of the vice presidents of the company calls a meeting with information technology after a recent trip to competitors' sites. She reports that many of the companies she visited granted access to their buildings only after fingerprint scans, and she wants similar technology employed at this company. Of the following, which technology relies on a physical attribute of the user for authentication?

    A. Smart card

    B. Biometrics

    C. Mutual authentication

    D. Tokens

14. Your company provides medical data to doctors from a worldwide database. Because of the sensitive nature of the data you work with, it's imperative that authentication be established on each session and be valid only for that session. Which of the following authentication methods provides credentials that are valid only during a single session?

    A. Tokens

    B. Certificate

    C. Smart card

    D. Kerberos

15. Your help desk has informed you that they received an urgent call from the vice president last night requesting his logon ID and password. What type of attack is this?

    A. Spoofing

    B. Replay attack

    C. Social engineering

    D. Trojan horse

16. Internal users are reporting repeated attempts to infect their systems as reported to them by pop-up messages from their virus-scanning software. According to the pop-up messages, the virus seems to be the same in every case. What is the most likely culprit?

A. A server is acting as a carrier for a virus.

B. You have a caterpillar virus.

C. Your antivirus software has malfunctioned.

D. A DoS attack is underway.

17. You're working late one night, and you notice that the hard disk on your new computer is very active even though you aren't doing anything on the computer and it isn't connected to the Internet. What is the most likely suspect?

A. A disk failure is imminent.

B. A virus is spreading in your system.

C. Your system is under a DoS attack.

D. TCP/IP hijacking is being attempted.

18. You're the administrator for a large bottling company. At the end of each month, you routinely view all logs and look for discrepancies. This month, your e-mail system error log reports a large number of unsuccessful attempts to log on. It's apparent that the e-mail server is being targeted. Which type of attack is most likely occurring?

A. Software exploitation attack

B. Backdoor attack

C. Worm

D. TCP/IP hijacking

19. Upper management has decreed that a firewall must be put in place immediately, before your site suffers an attack similar to one that struck a sister company. Responding to this order, your boss instructs you to implement a packet filter by the end of the week. A packet filter performs which function?

A. Prevents unauthorized packets from entering the network

B. Allows all packets to leave the network

C. Allows all packets to enter the network

D. Eliminates collisions in the network

20. Which media is susceptible to viruses?

A. Tape

B. Memory stick

C. CD-R

D. All of the above

Answers to Review Questions

1. A . The first layer of access control is perimeter security. Perimeter security is intended to delay or deter entrance into a facility.

2. A. Biometrics is a technology that uses personal characteristics, such as a retinal pattern or fingerprint, to establish identity.

3. A. Social engineering uses the inherent trust in the human species, as opposed to technology, to gain access to your environment.

4. A. The Bell La-Padula model is intended to protect confidentiality of information. This is accomplished by prohibiting users from reading above their security level and preventing them from writing below their security level.

5. B. Working copies are backups that are usually kept in the computer room for immediate use in recovering a system or lost file. While onsite storage may be kept in the computer room, it is not a backup type.

6. B. An incremental backup backs up files that have changed since the last full or incremental backup.

7. C. A differential backup backs up all the files that have changed since the last full backup.

8. B. Kerberos uses a key distribution center to authenticate a principle. The KDC provides a credential that can be used by all Kerberos-enabled servers and applications.

9. D. Challenge Handshake Authentication Protocol (CHAP) sends a challenge to the originating client. This challenge is sent back to the server, and the encryption results are compared. If the challenge is successful, the client is logged on.

10. A. A multifactor-authentication process uses two or more processes for logon. A two-factor method might use smart cards and biometrics for logon.

11. B. Telnet shouldn't be used if possible. Telnet sends user ID and password information to the Telnet server unencrypted. This creates a potential security problem in an Internet environment.

12. B. Authentication is a service that requests the principal user to provide proof of his identity. A retinal scan is a very secure form of evidence used in high-security companies and government agencies.

13. B. Biometric technologies rely on a physical characteristic of the user to verify identity. Biometric devices typically use either a hand pattern or a retinal scan to accomplish this.

14. A. Tokens are created when a user or system successfully authenticates. The token is destroyed when the session is over.

15. C. Someone trying to con your organization into revealing account and password information is launching a social-engineering attack.

16. A . Some viruses won't damage a system in an attempt to spread into all the other systems in a network. These viruses use that system as the carrier of the virus.

17. B. A symptom of many viruses is unusual activity on the system disk. This is caused by the virus spreading to other files on your system.

18. A. A software exploitation attack attempts to exploit weaknesses in software. A common attack attempts to communicate with an established port to gain unauthorized access.

19. A. Packet filters prevent unauthorized packets from entering or leaving a network. Packet filters are a type of firewall that block specified traffic based on IP address, protocol, and many other attributes.

20. D. All of these devices can store and pass viruses to uninfected systems. Make sure that all files are scanned for viruses before they're copied to these media.

Chapter

10

Identifying Safety and Environmental Issues

THE FOLLOWING COMPTIA A+ ESSENTIALS EXAM OBJECTIVES ARE COVERED IN THIS CHAPTER:

✓ **7.1 Describe the aspects and importance of safety and environmental issues**

- Identify potential safety hazards and take preventative action

- Use Material Safety Data Sheets (MSDSs) or equivalent documentation and appropriate equipment documentation

- Use appropriate repair tools

- Describe methods to handle environmental and human (for example, electrical, chemical, physical) accidents including incident reporting

✓ **7.2 Identify potential hazards and implement proper safety procedures including ESD precautions and procedures, safe work environment, and equipment handling**

✓ **7.3 Identify proper disposal procedures for batteries, display devices, and chemical solvents and cans**

THE FOLLOWING COMPTIA A+ IT TECHNICIAN EXAM OBJECTIVES ARE COVERED IN THIS CHAPTER:

✓ **7.1 Identify potential hazards and proper safety procedures including power supply, display devices, and environment (for example, trip, liquid, situational, atmospheric hazards, and high-voltage and moving equipment)**

THE FOLLOWING COMPTIA A+ DEPOT TECHNICIAN EXAM OBJECTIVES ARE COVERED IN THIS CHAPTER:

✓ **5.1 Identify potential hazards and proper safety procedures including power supply, display devices, and environment (for example, trip, liquid, situational, atmospheric hazards, and high-voltage and moving equipment)**

There's little doubt that computers have revolutionized the way we live and work. Computers allow us to be more productive, stay in touch with friends and family, and learn about any topic under the sun with just a few clicks of the mouse.

The proliferation of computers in today's society has created jobs for countless technicians. Presumably that's why you're reading this book: You want to get your CompTIA A+ certification. Many others who don't fix computers professionally do like tinkering with them as a hobby. Regardless of your reason, if you're going to be inside a computer, you always need to be aware of safety issues. There's no sense in getting yourself hurt or killed—literally.

Another consequence of modern technology is the potential harm to the environment. Few would consider computer components to be biodegradable, and sure enough they aren't. Many people, though, aren't aware of how to handle computer components or properly dispose of them to help prevent damage to our external environment.

This chapter looks at two issues: safety and the environment. Observing proper safety procedures can help prevent injury or death, which obviously we want to avoid. The environment is a two-sided discussion. The environment affects computers (via things like dust, sunlight, and water), but computers can also affect the environment. We'll consider both sides as we move through this chapter.

Because of the similarity of the A+ Essentials exam and the technician exams, we are covering the Safety and Environmental Issues domain for both of the exams in this chapter.

Understanding Safety and Environmental Issues

As a provider of a hands-on service (repairing, maintaining, or upgrading someone's computer), you need to be aware of some general safety tips, because if you are not careful, you could harm yourself or the equipment. You also need to be aware of the environment, considering that it plays a role in how the computer can perform and for how long. In the following sections, we'll talk about identifying hazards and environmental concerns, understanding safety documentation, using the right tools for the job, and accident handling.

Identifying Potential Safety Hazards

Anything can be a potential safety hazard, right? Okay, maybe that statement is a bit too paranoid, but there *are* many things, both human-created and environmental, that can cause safety problems when working with and around computers.

Perhaps the most important aspect of computers that you should be aware of is that they not only *use* electricity, they *store* electrical charge after they're turned off. This makes the power supply and the monitor pretty much off-limits to anyone but a repair person trained specifically for those devices. In addition, the computer's processor and various parts of the printer run at extremely high temperatures, and you can get burned if you try to handle them immediately after they've been in operation.

Those are just two general safety measures that should concern you. There are plenty more. When discussing safety issues with regard to PCs, let's break them down into three general areas:

- Computer components
- Natural elements
- Work environment

Computer Components

As mentioned earlier, computers use electricity. And as you're probably aware, electricity can hurt or kill you. The first rule when working inside a computer is to always make sure it's powered off. So if you have to open the computer to inspect or replace parts (as you will with most repairs), be sure to turn off the machine before you begin. Leaving it plugged in is fine in most cases (we'll talk about that more in the section titled "Preventing Electrostatic Discharge [ESD]," later in this chapter).

There's one exception to the power-off rule: You don't have to power off the computer when working with hot-swappable parts, which are designed to be unplugged and plugged back in when the computer is on. Most of these components have an externally accessible interface (such as USB devices or hot-swappable hard drives), so you don't need to crack the computer case.

🌐 Real World Scenario

Don't Forget the Case

One aspect people frequently overlook is the case. Cases are generally made of metal, and some computer cases have very sharp edges inside, so be careful when handling them. You can, for example, cut yourself by jamming your fingers between the case and the frame when you try to force the case back on. Also of particular interest are drive bays. Countless technicians have scraped or cut their hands on drive bays when trying in vain to plug a drive cable into the motherboard. Particularly sharp edges can be covered with duct tape—just make sure you're covering only metal, and nothing with electrical components on it.

The Power Supply

Do not take the issue of safety and electricity lightly. Removing the power supply from its case can be dangerous. The current flowing through the power supply normally follows a complete circuit; when your body breaks the circuit, your body becomes part of that circuit.

The two biggest dangers with power supplies are burning yourself and electrocuting yourself. These risks usually go hand in hand. If you touch a bare wire that is carrying current, you could get electrocuted. A large-enough current passing through the wire (and you) can cause severe burns. (It can also cause your heart to stop, your muscles to seize, and your brain to stop functioning. In short, it can kill you.) Electricity always finds the best path to ground. And because people are basically bags of salt water (an excellent conductor of electricity), electricity will use us as a conductor if we are grounded.

Real World Scenario

Fire Safety

Repairing a computer isn't often the cause of an electrical fire. However, you should know how to extinguish such a fire properly. Four major classes of fire extinguishers are available, one for each type of flammable substance: A for wood and paper fires, B for flammable liquids, C for electrical fires, and D (metal powder or NaCl [salt]) for flammable metals such as phosphorus and sodium.

The most popular type of fire extinguisher today is the multipurpose, or ABC-rated, extinguisher. It contains a dry chemical powder (e.g., sodium bicarbonate, monoammonium phosphate) that smothers the fire and cools it at the same time. For electrical fires (which may be related to a shorted-out wire in a power supply), make sure the fire extinguisher will work for class C fires. If you don't have an extinguisher that is specifically rated for electrical fires (type C), you can use an ABC-rated extinguisher.

Although it is possible to open a power supply to work on it, doing so is *not* recommended. Power supplies contain several capacitors that can hold *lethal* charges *long after they have been unplugged!* It is extremely dangerous to open the case of a power supply. Besides, power supplies are pretty cheap. It would probably cost less to replace one than to try to fix it, and this approach would be much safer.

In the late 1990s, a few mass computer manufacturers experimented with putting open power supplies in their computers to save money. I don't know if any deaths occurred because of such incompetence, but it was definitely a very bad idea.

Unless you have been specifically trained to do so, *never* open a power supply.

Current vs. Voltage—Which Is More Dangerous?

When talking about power and safety, you will almost always hear the saying, "It's not the volts that kill you, it's the amps." That's mostly true. However, an explanation is in order.

The number of volts in a power source represents its potential to do work. But volts don't do anything by themselves. Current (amperage, or amps) is the force behind the work done by electricity. Here's an analogy to help explain this concept. Say you have two boulders; one weighs 10lbs, the other 100lbs, and each is 100 feet off the ground. If you drop them, which one will do more work? The obvious answer is the 100lb boulder. They both have the same potential to do work (100 feet of travel), but the 100lb boulder has more mass and thus more force. Voltage is analogous to the distance the boulder is from the ground, and amperage is analogous to the mass of the boulder.

This is why you can produce static electricity on the order of 50,000 volts and not electrocute yourself. Even though this electricity has a great *potential* for work, it does very little work because the amperage is so low. This also explains why you can weld metal with 110 volts. Welders use only 110 (sometimes 220) volts, but they also use anywhere from 50 to 200 amps!

If you ever have to work on a power supply, for safety's sake you should discharge all capacitors within it. To do this, connect a resistor across the leads of the capacitor with a rating of 3 watts or more and a resistance of 100 ohms (Ω) per volt. For example, to discharge a 225-volt capacitor, you would use a 22.5kΩ resistor (225 volts times 100Ω = 22,500Ω or 22.5 kΩ).

The Printer

If you've ever attempted to repair a printer, have you sometimes thought there was a little monster in there hiding all the screws from you? Besides missing screws, here are some things to watch out for when repairing printers:

- When handling a toner cartridge from a laser printer or page printer, do not turn it upside down. You will find yourself spending more time cleaning the printer and the surrounding area than fixing the printer.

- Do not put any objects into the feeding system (in an attempt to clear the path) when the printer is running.

- Laser printers generate a laser that is hazardous to your eyes. Do not look directly into the source of the laser.

- If it's an inkjet printer, do not try to blow in the ink cartridge to clear a clogged opening—that is, unless you like the taste of ink.

- Some parts of a laser printer (such as the EP cartridge) will be damaged if you touch them. Your skin produces oils and has a small surface layer of dead skin cells. These substances can collect on the delicate surface of the EP cartridge and cause malfunctions. Bottom line: Keep your fingers out of where they don't belong!

- Laser printers can get extremely hot. Don't burn yourself on internal components.

When working with printers, I follow some pretty simple guidelines. If there's a messed-up setting, paper jam, or ink or toner problem, I will fix it. If it's something other than that, I call a certified printer repair person. The inner workings of printers can get pretty complex, and it's best to call someone trained to make those types of repairs.

The Monitor

Other than the power supply, the most dangerous component to try to repair is the monitor, or cathode-ray tube (CRT). In fact, we recommend that you *do not* try to repair monitors of any kind.

To avoid the extremely hazardous environment contained inside the monitor—it can retain a high-voltage charge for hours after it's been turned off—take it to a certified monitor technician or television repair shop. The repair shop or certified technician will know and understand the proper procedures to discharge the monitor, which involve attaching a resistor to the flyback transformer's charging capacitor to release the high-voltage electrical charge that builds up during use. They will also be able to determine whether the monitor can be repaired or needs to be replaced. Remember, the monitor works in its own extremely protected environment (the monitor case) and may not respond well to your desire to try to open it.

WARNING   The CRT is vacuum sealed. Be extremely careful when handling the CRT. If you break the glass, it will implode, which can send glass in any direction.

Even though we recommend not repairing monitors, the A+ exam tests your knowledge of the safety practices to use when you need to do so. If you have to open a monitor, you must first discharge the high-voltage charge on it by using a *high-voltage probe*. This probe has a very large needle, a gauge that indicates volts, and a wire with an alligator clip. Attach the alligator clip to a ground (usually the round pin on the power cord). Slip the probe needle underneath the high-voltage cup on the monitor. You will see the gauge spike to around 15,000 volts and slowly reduce to zero. When it reaches zero, you may remove the high-voltage probe and service the high-voltage components of the monitor.

WARNING   Do *not* use an ESD strap when discharging the monitor; doing so can lead to a fatal electric shock.

The Keyboard and Mouse

Okay, we know you're thinking, "What danger could a keyboard or mouse cause?" We admit that not much danger is associated with these components, but there are a couple of safety concerns you should always keep in mind.

First, the mouse usually has a cord, and you can trip over it, so make sure it's safely out of the way. Second, you could short-circuit your keyboard if you accidentally spill liquid on it. Keyboards don't function well with half a can of cola in their innards!

⊕ **Real World Scenario**

Play It Safe with Common Sense

When you're repairing a PC, do not leave it unattended. Someone could walk into the room and inadvertently bump the machine, causing failure. Worse, they could step on pieces that may be lying around and get hurt. It is also not a good idea to work on the PC alone. If you're injured, someone should be around to help if you need it. Finally, if you're fatigued, you may find it difficult to concentrate and focus on what you are doing. There are real safety measures related to repairing PCs, so the most important thing to remember is to pay close attention to what you are doing.

Natural Elements

Computers should always be operated in cool environments away from direct sunlight and water sources. This is also true when you're working on computers. We know that heat is an enemy of electrical components. Dirt and dust act as great insulators, trapping heat inside components. When components run hotter than they should, they have a greater chance of breaking down faster.

It pretty much should go without saying, but I'll say it anyway: Water and electricity don't mix. Keep liquids away from computers. If you need your morning coffee while fixing a PC, make sure the coffee has a tight and secure lid.

Water and Servers Don't Mix

This situation happened at one of the companies one of the authors used to work for. The building needed some roof repairs. Repairs went on for several days, and then the week-end came. It just so happened that the area they were working on was over the server room. That weekend was a particularly rainy one, and of course over the weekend no one was in the office.

Monday morning came, and the IT staff arrived to find that the server room was partially flooded. Rain had come in through weaknesses in the roof, caused by the maintenance, and had flooded through the drop ceiling and into the server room. Nearly half a million dollars of equipment was ruined.

Although this isn't too common, the main point is this: Always be aware of the environment you're working in, and be alert to potential sources of problems for your computer equipment.

Work Environment

We've already talked about some work environment issues to be aware of. For example, don't put a computer next to the break room sink, and keep computers out of direct sunlight (even if the desk location is great).

A couple of other things to watch out for include trip hazards, atmospheric conditions, and high-voltage areas.

Cables are a common cause of tripping. If at all possible, run cables through drop ceilings or through conduits to keep them out of the way. If you need to lay a cable through a trafficked area, use a cable floor guard to keep the cables in place and safe from crushing. Floor guards come in a variety of lengths and sizes (for just a few cables or for a lot of cables). Figure 10.1 shows a cable guard.

FIGURE 10.1   Floor cable guard

 In a pinch, and without a floor cable guard, you can use tape such as duct tape to secure your cables to the floor. This is recommended only as a temporary fix for two reasons. First, it's not much less of a trip hazard than just having the cables run across the floor. Second, duct tape doesn't protect the cables from being crushed if people step on them or heavy objects are moved over them.

Atmospheric conditions that you need to be aware of include areas with high static electricity or inordinate humidity.

 We'll talk more about atmospheric conditions in the section "Preventing Electrostatic Discharge (ESD)," later in this chapter.

Finally, be aware of high-voltage areas. Computers do need electricity to run but only in measured amounts. Running or fixing computers in high-voltage areas can cause problems for the electrical components and can cause problems for you if something should go wrong.

Identifying Environmental Concerns

It is estimated that more than 25 percent of all the lead (a poisonous substance) in landfills today is a result of consumer electronics components. Because consumer electronics (televisions, VCRs, stereos) contain hazardous substances, many states require that they be disposed of as hazardous waste. Computers are no exception. Monitors contain several carcinogens and phosphors, as well as mercury and lead. The computer itself may contain several lubricants and chemicals as well as lead. Printers contain plastics and chemicals such as toners and inks that are also hazardous. All of these items should be disposed of properly.

Remember all those 386 and 486 computers that came out in the late 1980s and are now considered antiques? Where did they all go? Is there an Old Computers Home somewhere that is using these computer systems for good purposes, or are they lying in a junkyard somewhere? Or could it be that some folks just cannot let go, and have a stash of old computer systems and computer parts in the dark depths of their basements?

Although it is relatively easy to put old machines away, thinking you might be able to put them to good use again someday, doing so is not realistic. Most computers are obsolete as soon as you buy them. And if you have not used them recently, your old computer components will more than likely never be used again.

We recycle cans, plastic, and newspaper, so why not recycle computer equipment? The problem, as we mentioned, is that most computers contain small amounts of hazardous substances. Some countries are exploring the option of recycling electrical machines, but most have still not enacted appropriate measures to enforce their proper disposal. However, we can do a few things as consumers and caretakers of our environment to promote the proper disposal of computer equipment:

- Check with the manufacturer. Some manufacturers will take back outdated equipment for parts (and may even pay you for them).

- Properly dispose of solvents or cleaners used with computers, as well as their containers, at a local hazardous waste disposal facility.

- Disassemble the machine and reuse the parts that are good.

- Check out businesses that can melt down the components for the lead or gold plating.

- Contact the Environmental Protection Agency (EPA) for a list of local or regional waste disposal sites that accept used computer equipment. The EPA's web address is http://www.epa.gov.

- Check with local nonprofit or education organizations interested in using the equipment.

- Check out the Internet for possible waste disposal sites. Table 10.1 lists a few websites we came across that deal with disposal of used computer equipment.

- Check with the EPA to see if what you are disposing of has a Material Safety Data Sheet (MSDS). These sheets contain information about the toxicity of a product and whether it can be disposed of in the trash. They also contain lethal-dose information.

TABLE 10.1   Computer Recycling Websites

Site Name	Web Address
Computer Recycle Center	http://www.recycles.com
Computer Recycling Center	http://www.crc.org
RE-PC	http://www.repc.com

In addition to hardware recycling, there are businesses that offer to recycle consumables, such as ink cartridges or printer ribbons. However, although these businesses are doing us a favor in our quest to recycle, it might not be the best way to keep up with the recycling agenda. Why? Well, we don't recommend the use of recycled ink cartridges; they may clog, the ink quality is not as good, and the small circuit board on the cartridge may be damaged. Similarly, recycled printer ribbons will lose their ability to hold ink after a while and don't last as long as new ribbons. And recycled toner cartridges don't operate properly after refilling. However, when you are through with the old cartridges, give them to organizations that do recycle so they can have some fresh cores. That way, you can safely dispose of your cartridge and benefit the environment at the same time.

Remember that recycling is a way to keep our environment clean and our landfills empty. If we can take one step to recycle or redistribute outdated computer equipment, we are one step closer to having a healthier environment. However, we should not have to sacrifice quality in the process.

In particular, you should make a special effort to recycle batteries. Batteries contain several chemicals that are harmful to the environment and won't degrade safely. Batteries should not be thrown away; they should be recycled according to your local laws. Check with your local authorities to find out how batteries should be recycled.

Cleaning Systems

The cleanliness of a computer is extremely important. Buildup of dust, dirt, and oils can prevent various mechanical parts of a computer from operating. Because this topic is important, the A+ exam will test your knowledge of the proper way to use various cleaning products on computer systems.

Computer components get dirty. Dirt reduces their operating efficiency and, ultimately, their life. Cleaning them is definitely important. But cleaning them with the right cleaning compounds is equally important. Using the wrong compounds can leave residue behind that is more harmful than the dirt you are trying to remove.

Most computer cases and monitor cases can be cleaned by using mild soapy water on a clean, lint-free cloth. Do *not* use any kind of solvent-based cleaner on either monitor or LCD screens, because doing so can cause discoloration and damage to the screen surface. Most often, a simple dusting with a damp cloth (moistened with water) will suffice. Make sure the power is off before you put anything wet near a computer. Dampen (don't soak) a cloth in mild soap solution and wipe the dirt and dust from the case. Then wipe the moisture from the case with a dry, lint-free cloth. Anything with a plastic or metal case can be cleaned in this manner.

Additionally, if you spill anything on a keyboard, you can clean it by soaking it in distilled, demineralized water and drying it off. The extra minerals and impurities have been removed from this type of water, so it will not leave any traces of residue that might interfere with the proper operation of the keyboard after cleaning. The same holds true for the keyboard's cable and its connector.

The electronic connectors of computer equipment, on the other hand, should never touch water. Instead, use a swab moistened in distilled, denatured isopropyl alcohol (also known as electronics or contact cleaner and found in electronics stores) to clean contacts. Doing so will take oxidation off of the copper contacts.

Some technicians say you can use a pencil eraser to clean the oxidation from contacts. You should *never* do this, because erasers contain trace amounts of acids from their manufacturing process that can damage the contacts after cleaning.

Finally, the best way to remove dust and dirt from the inside of the computer is to use compressed air instead of vacuuming. Compressed air can be more easily directed and doesn't easily produce electrostatic discharge (ESD) damage (as vacuuming could). Simply blow the dust from inside the computer by using a stream of compressed air. However, make sure to do this outside, so you don't blow dust all over your work area or yourself. Nonstatic vacuum cleaners are available that are specially made for cleaning computer components (such as keyboards and case fans). Their nozzles are grounded to prevent ESD from damaging the components of the computer. However, compressed air is usually a better method, as long as it's done outside.

One unique challenge when cleaning printers is spilled toner. It sticks to everything. There are two methods to deal with this. First, blow all the loose toner out of the printer by using compressed air, being careful not to blow the toner into any of the printing mechanisms. Then, using a cool, damp cloth, wipe any remaining particles out of the printer.

Environmental Problems

Computers in manufacturing plants are particularly susceptible to environmental hazards. One technician reported a situation with a computer that had been used on the manufacturing floor of a large equipment manufacturer. The computer and keyboard were covered with a black substance that would not come off. (It was later revealed to be a combination of paint mist and molybdenum grease.) There was so much diesel fume residue in the power supply fan that it would barely turn. The insides and components were covered with a thin, greasy layer of muck. To top it all off, the computer *smelled terrible*!

Despite all this, the computer still functioned. However, it was prone to reboot itself every now and again. The solution was (as you may have guessed) to clean every component thoroughly and replace the power supply. The muck on the components was able to conduct a small current. Sometimes that current would go where it wasn't wanted, and zap!—a reboot. In addition, the power supply fan is supposed to partially cool the inside of the computer. In this computer, the fan was detrimental to the computer because it got its cooling air from the shop floor, which contained diesel fumes, paint fumes, and other chemical fumes. Needless to say, those fumes aren't good for computer components.

Computers are like human beings. They have similar tolerances to heat and cold (although computers like the cold better than we do). In general, anything comfortable to us is comfortable to a computer. Computers need lots of clean, moving air to keep them functioning. They don't, however, require food or drink (except maybe a few RAM chips now and again)—keep those away from the computer.

 WARNING It's bad practice to eat, drink, or smoke around your computer. Smoke particles contain tar that can get inside the computer and cause problems similar to those described earlier.

One way to ensure that the environment has the least possible effect on your computer is to always leave the blanks in the empty slots on the back of your box. These pieces of metal are designed to keep dirt, dust, and other foreign matter out of the inside of the computer. They also maintain proper airflow within the case to ensure that the computer does not overheat.

Using Safety Documentation

Each piece of computer equipment you purchase comes with a manual. Inside the manual are detailed instructions on the proper handling and use of that component. In addition, many manuals give information on how to open the device for maintenance, or on whether you should even open the device at all.

Don't throw manuals away. Keep a drawer of a file cabinet (and keep it organized!) specifically for hardware manuals. You can always look up information on the Internet as well, but having paper manuals on hand is useful for two reasons. One, you may need to fix something when Internet access isn't readily available (router problems, anyone?). Two, some companies are required to keep hardware documentation in case of an audit (such as for ISO 9000–compliant organizations).

Another place to find safety information is in *Material Safety Data Sheets (MSDSs)*. MSDSs include information such as physical product data (boiling point, melting point, flash point, and so forth), potential health risks, storage and disposal recommendations, and spill/leak procedures. With this information, technicians and emergency personnel know how to handle the product as well as respond in the event of an emergency.

MSDSs are typically associated with hazardous chemicals. Indeed, chemicals do not ship without them. MSDSs are not intended for consumer use; rather, they're made for employees or emergency workers who are consistently exposed to the risks of the particular product.

The United States *Occupational Safety and Health Administration (OSHA)* mandates MSDSs only for products that

- Meet OSHA's definition of *hazardous* (it poses a physcial or health hazard)

  and

- Are "known to be present in the workplace in such a manner that employees may be exposed under normal conditions of use or in a foreseeable emergency"

We will look at OSHA more closely in the section "Working in a Safe Environment" later in this chapter.

One of the interesting things about MSDSs is that OSHA does not require companies to distribute them to consumers. Most companies will be happy to distribute one for their products, but again, they are under no obligation to do so.

If employees are working with materials that have MSDSs, those employees are required by OSHA to have "ready access" to MSDS sheets. This means that employees need to be able to get to the sheets without having to fetch a key, contact a supervisor, or submit a procedure request. Remember the file cabinet drawer you have for the hardware manuals? MSDSs should also be kept readily accessible.

At this point, you might stop to think for a second. Do computers really come with hazardous chemicals? Do I really need an MSDS? Consider this as an example: oxygen. Hardly a dangerous chemical, considering we need to breathe it to live, right? In the atmosphere, oxygen is at 21 percent concentration. At 100 percent concentration, oxygen is highly flammable and can even spontaneously ignite some organic materials. In that sense, and in the eyes of OSHA, nearly everything can be a dangerous chemical.

If you are interested in searching for free MSDSs, two free websites are http://www.msds.com and http://www.msdssearch.com. Many manufacturers of components will also provide MSDSs on their websites.

Here is a sample MSDS for ammonium hydrogen sulfate:

```
**** MATERIAL SAFETY DATA SHEET ****

Ammonium Hydrogen Sulfate
90009

       **** SECTION 1-CHEMICAL PRODUCT AND COMPANY IDENTIFICATION ****

MSDS Name: Ammonium Hydrogen Sulfate
Catalog Numbers:
```

A/5400

Synonyms:

Sulfuric acid, monoammonium salt; Acid ammonium sulfate; Ammonium acid sulfate.

Company Identification:

For information, call:

For emergencies, call:

**** SECTION 2—COMPOSITION, INFORMATION ON INGREDIENTS ****

CAS#	Chemical Name	%	EINECS#
7803-63-6	Ammonium hydrogen sulfate	100 %	232-265-5
	Hazard Symbols: C		
	Risk Phrases: 34		

**** SECTION 3—HAZARDS IDENTIFICATION ****

EMERGENCY OVERVIEW

Causes burns. Corrosive. Hygroscopic (absorbs moisture from the air).

Potential Health Effects

Eye:

Causes eye burns.

Skin:

Causes skin burns.

Ingestion:

May cause severe gastrointestinal tract irritation with nausea, vomiting, and possible burns.

Inhalation:

Causes severe irritation of upper respiratory tract with coughing, burns, breathing difficulty, and possible coma.

Chronic:

No information found.

**** SECTION 4—FIRST-AID MEASURES ****

Eyes:

Immediately flush eyes with plenty of water for at least 15 minutes, occasionally lifting the upper and lower eyelids. Get medical aid immediately.

Skin:

Get medical aid immediately. Immediately flush skin with plenty of water for at least 15 minutes while removing contaminated clothing and shoes.

Ingestion:

Do not induce vomiting. If victim is conscious and alert, give 2-4 cupfuls of milk or water. Never give anything by mouth to an unconscious person. Get medical aid immediately.

Inhalation:

Get medical aid immediately. Remove from exposure and move to fresh air immediately. If not breathing, give artificial respiration. If breathing is difficult, give oxygen.

Notes to Physician:

**** SECTION 5—FIREFIGHTING MEASURES ****

General Information:

As in any fire, wear a self-contained breathing apparatus in pressure-demand, MSHA/NIOSH (approved or equivalent), and full protective gear. During a fire, irritating and highly toxic gases may be generated by thermal decomposition or combustion.

Extinguishing Media:

Substance is noncombustible; use agent most appropriate to extinguish surrounding fire.

**** SECTION 6—ACCIDENTAL RELEASE MEASURES ****

General Information: Use proper personal protective equipment as indicated in Section 8.

Spills/Leaks:

Vacuum or sweep up material and place into a suitable disposal container. Reduce airborne dust and prevent scattering by moistening with water. Clean up spills immediately, observing precautions in the Protective Equipment section.

**** SECTION 7—HANDLING and STORAGE ****

Handling:

Wash thoroughly after handling. Wash hands before eating. Use only in a well-ventilated area. Do not get in eyes, on skin, or on   clothing. Do not ingest or inhale.

Storage:

Store in a cool, dry place. Keep container closed when not in use.

**** SECTION 8—EXPOSURE CONTROLS, PERSONAL PROTECTION ****

Engineering Controls:

Use adequate general or local exhaust ventilation to keep airborne concentrations below the permissible exposure limits.

Personal Protective Equipment

Eyes:

Not available.

Skin:

Wear appropriate protective gloves to prevent skin exposure.

Clothing:

Wear appropriate protective clothing to prevent skin exposure.

Respirators:

Follow the OSHA respirator regulations found in 29 CFR 1910.134 or European Standard EN 149. Always use a NIOSH or European Standard EN 149 approved respirator when necessary.

**** SECTION 9—PHYSICAL AND CHEMICAL PROPERTIES ****

Physical State:	Solid
Color:	White
Odor:	Not available
pH:	Not available
Vapor Pressure:	Not available
Viscosity:	Not available
Boiling Point:	Not available
Freezing/Melting Point:	147 deg C
Autoignition Temperature:	Not applicable
Flash Point:	Not applicable
Explosion Limits, lower:	Not available
Explosion Limits, upper:	Not available
Decomposition Temperature:	Not available
Solubility in Water:	Soluble in water
Specific Gravity/Density:	Not available
Molecular Formula:	NH_4HSO_4
Molecular Weight:	115.0993

**** SECTION 10—STABILITY AND REACTIVITY ****

Chemical Stability:

Stable under normal temperatures and pressures.
Conditions to Avoid:
Incompatible materials, dust generation, exposure to moist air or water.
Incompatibilities with Other Materials:
Strong oxidizing agents and moist air.
Hazardous Decomposition Products:
Oxides of nitrogen, oxides of sulfur.
Hazardous Polymerization: Has not been reported.

**** SECTION 11–TOXICOLOGICAL INFORMATION ****

RTECS#:
CAS# 7803-63-6: BS4400500
LD50/LC50:
Not available.
Carcinogenicity:
Ammonium hydrogen sulfate -
Not listed by ACGIH, IARC, NIOSH, NTP, or OSHA.
See actual entry in RTECS for complete information.

**** SECTION 12–ECOLOGICAL INFORMATION ****

**** SECTION 13–DISPOSAL CONSIDERATIONS ****

Products which are considered hazardous for supply are classified as Special
Waste, and the disposal of such chemicals is covered by regulations which may
vary according to location. Contact a specialist disposal company or the local
waste regulator for advice. Empty containers must be decontaminated before
returning for recycling.

**** SECTION 14–TRANSPORT INFORMATION ****

IATA
Shipping Name: AMMONIUM HYDROGEN SULPHATE
Hazard Class: 8
UN Number: 2506
Packing Group: II
IMO
Shipping Name: AMMONIUM HYDROGEN SULPHATE

              Hazard Class: 8
                 UN Number: 2506
            Packing Group: II
      RID/ADR
            Shipping Name: AMMONIUM HYDROGEN SULPHATE
            Hazard Class: 8
                 UN Number: 2506
            Packing group: II

                **** SECTION 15-REGULATORY INFORMATION ****

European/International Regulations
      European Labeling in Accordance with EC Directives
            Hazard Symbols: C
            Risk Phrases:
                        R 34 Causes burns.
            Safety Phrases:
      S 26 In case of contact with eyes, rinse immediately with plenty of water
and seek medical advice.
                        S 28 After contact with skin, wash immediately
                        with...
  WGK (Water Danger/Protection)
            CAS# 7803-63-6: 1
United Kingdom Occupational Exposure Limits

United Kingdom Maximum Exposure Limits

   Canada
            CAS# 7803-63-6 is listed on Canada's DSL List.
            CAS# 7803-63-6 is not listed on Canada's Ingredient Disclosure List.
      Exposure Limits
 US FEDERAL
      TSCA
            CAS# 7803-63-6 is listed on the TSCA inventory.

                **** SECTION 16-ADDITIONAL INFORMATION ****

   MSDS Creation Date: 6/23/2004 Revision #0 Date: Original.

The information above is believed to be accurate and represents the best
information currently available to us. However, we make no warranty of

merchantability or any other warranty, express or implied, with respect to such information, and we assume no liability resulting from its use. Users should make their own investigations to determine the suitability of the information for their particular purposes. In no way shall the company be liable for any claims, losses, or damages of any third party or for lost

profits or any special, indirect, incidental, consequential or   exemplary damages, howsoever arising, even if the company has been advised of the possibility of such damages.

Using Appropriate Repair Tools

Whether building a shed, fixing a car, or troubleshooting a computer, you need the right tools for the job at hand. Most of the time, computers can be opened and devices removed with nothing more than a simple screwdriver. But if you do a lot of work on PCs, you'll definitely want to have additional tools on hand.

Computer toolkits are readily available on the Internet or at any electronics store. They come in versions from inexpensive (under $10) kits that have around 10 pieces, to several-hundred-dollar kits that have more tools than you will probably ever need. Figure 10.2 shows an example of a basic 11-piece PC toolkit. All of these tools come in a handy zippered case so it's harder to lose them.

FIGURE 10.2   PC toolkit

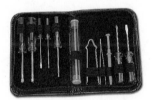

Looking at Figure 10.2, from left to right you have two nut drivers (1/4″ and 3/16″), a 1/8″ flat screwdriver, a #0 Phillips screwdriver, a T-15 Torx driver, a screw tube, an integrated circuit (IC) extractor, tweezers, a three-claw retriever, a #1 Phillips screwdriver, and a 3/16″ flat screwdriver. Most of these tools are incredibly useful, but the IC extractor probably won't be. In today's environment, it's rare to find an IC that you can extract, much less find a reason to extract one.

This section looks at some of the tools of the PC troubleshooting trade.

Screwdrivers

Every PC technician worth his or her weight in pocket protectors needs to have a screwdriver. At least one. There are three major categories of screwdrivers: flat-blade, Phillips, and Torx. In addition, there are devices that look like screwdrivers, except they have a hex-shaped indented head on them. They're called hex drivers and belong in the screwdriver family.

Whenever picking a screwdriver, always keep in mind that you want to match the size of the screwdriver head to the size of the screw. Using a screwdriver that's too small will cause it to spin inside the head of the screw, stripping the screw and making it useless. And if the screwdriver is too large, you won't be able to get the head in far enough to generate any torque to loosen the screw. Of course, if the screwdriver is way too big, it won't even fit inside the screw head at all. Common sizes for Phillips-head screws are 000, 00, 0, 1, 2, and 3. When dealing with Torx screws, the two most common sizes are T-10 and T-15.

When tightening screws, you don't need to make them so tight that they could survive the vibrations of an atmospheric reentry. Snug is fine. Making them too tight can cause problems loosening them, which could cause you (or someone else not so strong) to strip the head.

Using an electric screwdriver is fine if you have one. The only problem with them is that they tend to be larger than manual screwdrivers and can be difficult to get inside a case.

Using magnetic-tipped screwdrivers is not recommended. Many computer disks contain magnetically coded information, and the magnetic tip of a screwdriver could cause a problem. Keep a retrieving tool handy, instead, just in case you drop a screw.

Anti-static Wrist Straps

Essential to any PC technician's arsenal is an anti-static wrist stap. These don't typically come with smaller PC toolkits, but you should always have one or two handy.

We'll talk more about these straps in the "Preventing Electrostatic Discharge (ESD)" section later in this chapter.

Other Useful Tools

Some other things that PC techs commonly carry include the following:

Pliers   Pliers are useful for a variety of tasks, especially gripping something. Long-nose or needle-nose pliers extend your reach.

Wire Cutters   Wire cutters come in a variety of forms but are primarily used for cutting cables. It's not likely you'll need any sort of heavy-duty metal cutters.

Strippers   If you are making your own network cables or fixing them, having a cable stripper (and crimper) is essential.

Mirrors   Mirrors are handy inside tight spaces. Many techs like to use a dentist-style mirror because of its compact size and good reach.

Flashlight   Never underestimate the utility of a good flashlight. You never know what your lighting situation will be like when you're at a repair site. Smaller flashlights with good output are great to have, because they can fit into tight spaces and light up your life.

Compressed Air   For as much as computers and dust don't get along, it sure seems like they are attracted to each other. In all seriousness, computer components are powered by electricity, which causes the components to have a slight electrical charge. Dust is also electrically charged, so it's attracted to computer components. Compressed air can help you clean off components, especially in hard-to-reach places.

> Be judicious about your use of compressed air. Oftentimes, you will find yourself just blowing the dust from one part of a computer to another.

Multimeter   If you're having power issues, a multimeter can be an invaluable tool. (You'll also hear of voltmeters, and while the two have somewhat different functions, both of them can be used to troubleshoot power problems.) Using a voltmeter you can see if a computer power supply is producing the right amount of current for the devices that depend upon it.

> Some of these tools were also discussed in Chapter 2.

Handling Accidents

Accidents happen. Hopefully, they don't happen too often, but we know that they do. So what do you do when one happens? First, handle the situation. Second, report the incident. Two major classifications of accidents are environmental and human.

Environmental Accidents

When related to computers, environmental accidents typically come in one of two forms: electricity or water. Too much electricity is bad for computer components. If lightning is striking in your area, you run a major risk of frying computer parts. Even if you have a surge protector, you could still be at risk.

The best bet in a lightning storm is to power off your equipment and unplug it from outlets. Make the lightning have to come inside a window and hit your computer directly in order to fry it.

> Those cheap $10 surge suppresors will fry right along with your computer. And don't be fooled, most power strips do *not* protect against power surges.

> Modems are particularly susceptible to surges in electricity. If you're having a storm, be sure to unplug your modem from the wall outlet, just as you would a power cord.

Water is obviously also bad for computer components. If there is water in the area, and you believe it will contact your computers, it's best to get the machines powered off as quickly as possible. If components are not powered on but get wet, they may still work after thoroughly drying out. But if they're on when they get wet, they're likely cooked. Water + electronic components = bad. Water + electronic components + electricity = *really* bad.

Many server rooms have raised floors. Although this serves several purposes, one is that equipment stored on the floor is less suceptible to water damage if flooding occurs.

Human Accidents

Human nature dictates that we are not infallible, so of course we're going to make mistakes and have accidents. The key is to minimize the damage caused when an accident happens.

If a chemical spill occurs, make sure that the area gets cordoned off as soon as possible. Then clean up the spill. The specific procedure on how to do that depends on the chemical, and that information can be found on an MSDS. Depending on the severity of the spill or the chemical released, you may also need to contact the local authorities. Again, the MSDS should have related information.

Physical accidents are more worrisome. People can trip and fall on wires, cut or burn themselves repairing computers, and incur a variety of other injuries as well. Computer components can be replaced, but that's not always true of human parts (or lives). The first thing to keep in mind is to always be careful and use common sense. If you're trying to work inside a computer case and you see sharp metal edges inside the case, see whether the metal (or component you are working on) can be moved to another location until you finish. Before you stick your hand into an area, make sure nothing is hot or is going to grab and cut you.

When an accident does happen (or almost happens), be sure to report it. Many companies pay for workers' compensation insurance. If you're injured on the job, you're required to report the incident, and you might also get temporary payments if you are unable to work because of the accident. Also, if the accident was anything but minor, seek medical attention. Just as victims in auto accidents might not feel pain for a day or two, victims in other physical accidents might be in the same position. If you never reported the accident, the insurance companies may find it less plausible that your suffering was work related.

Applying Proper Safety and Disposal Procedures

Safety is usually something that's talked about only during company-mandated training or after someone has an accident. Instead of just talking about safety after a problem, proper safety procedures should be ingrained into the culture of an organization. It will take a while to change some people's behaviors, but constantly reinforcing the benefits of safe operations will eventually become second nature.

One of the ways to implement safety in the IT workplace is to educate technicians and users on the dangers of electrostaic discharge. Relatively simple steps can keep your equipment running longer by avoiding this dangerous phenomenon. In addition, management and all employees must work together to promote a safe work environment, which includes handling and moving equipment the right way. Finally, we owe it to ourselves and others to minimize the possible damage to our environment by disposing of used parts and chemicals in the right way.

This section specifically looks at preventing ESD, promoting a safe work environment, properly handling equipment, and following recommended disposal procedures.

Preventing Electrostatic Discharge (ESD)

ESD can cause problems such as making a computer hang or reboot. Electrostatic discharge (ESD) happens when two objects of dissimilar charge come in contact with one another. The two objects exchange electrons in order to standardize the electrostatic charge between them. This charge can, and often does, damage electronic components.

CPU chips and memory chips are particularly sensitive to ESD. Be extremely cautious when handling these chips.

When you shuffle your feet across the floor and shock your best friend on the ear, you are discharging static electricity into the ear of your friend. The lowest static voltage transfer you can feel is around 3,000 volts (it doesn't electrocute you because there is extremely little current). A static transfer that you can *see* is at least 10,000 volts! Just by sitting in a chair, you can generate around 100 volts of static electricity. Walking around wearing synthetic materials can generate around 1,000 volts. You can easily generate around 20,000 volts simply by dragging your smooth-soled shoes across a shag carpet in the winter. (Actually, it doesn't have to be winter to run this danger. This voltage can occur in any room with very low humidity—like a heated room in wintertime.)

Relative humidity has a significant impact on the electricity you generate. Walking around and generating 1,500 volts at 65–90 percent relative humidity produces 35,000 volts if the relative humidity is in the 10–25 percent range.

It makes sense that these thousands of volts can damage computer components. However, a component can be damaged with under 100 volts! That means if a small charge is built up in your body, you could damage a component without realizing it.

Symptoms of ESD damage may be subtle, but they can be detected. One of the authors relates this experience:

"When I think of ESD, I always think of the same instance. A few years ago, I was working on an Apple Macintosh. This computer seemed to have a mind of its own. I would troubleshoot it, find the defective component, and replace it. The problem was that as soon as I replaced the component, it failed. I thought maybe the power supply was frying the boards, so I replaced both at the same time, but to no avail.

"I was about to send the computer off to Apple when I realized that it was winter. Normally this would not be a factor, but winters where I live are extremely dry. Dry air promotes static electricity. At first I thought my problem couldn't be that simple, but I was at the end of my rope. So, when I received my next set of new parts, I grounded myself with an anti-static strap for the time it took to install the components, and prayed while I turned on the power. Success! The components worked as they should, and a new advocate of ESD prevention was born."

Do you have long hair or (gasp!) have to wear a tie when fixing computers? Tie it back. Long hair or dangling cloth inside an open computer case is asking for trouble, as both are notorious for carrying and conducting static electricity.

The good news is that there are measures you can implement to help contain the effects of ESD. The first and easiest item to implement is the anti-static wrist strap, also referred to as an ESD strap. We will look at the anti-static wrist strap, as well as other ESD prevention tools in the following sections.

Anti-static Wrist Straps

To use the ESD strap, you attach one end to an earth ground (typically, the ground pin on an extension cord) and wrap the other end around your wrist. This strap grounds your body and keeps it at a zero charge. Figure 10.3 shows the proper way to attach an anti-static strap. There are several varieties of wrist straps available. The one in Figure 10.3 uses a banana clip, while others use alligator clips and are attached to the computer case itself.

An ESD strap is a specially designed device to bleed electrical charges away *safely*. It uses a 1-megohm resistor to bleed the charge away slowly. A simple wire wrapped around your wrist will not work correctly and could electrocute you!

FIGURE 10.3   Proper ESD strap connection

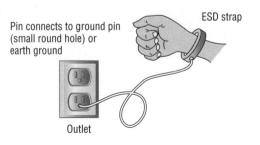

Pin connects to ground pin (small round hole) or earth ground

ESD strap

Outlet

WARNING Never wear an ESD strap if you're working inside a monitor or inside a power supply. If you wear one while working on the inside of these components, you increase the chance of getting a lethal shock.

Anti-static Bags for Parts

Anti-static bags are important tools to have at your disposal when servicing electronic components because they protect the sensitive electronic devices from stray static charges. These silver or pink bags are designed so that the static charges collect on the outside of the bags rather than on the electronic components.

You can obtain the bags from several sources. The most direct way to acquire anti-static bags is to go to an electronics supply store and purchase them in bulk. Most supply stores have several sizes available. Perhaps the easiest way to obtain them, however, is simply to hold on to the ones that come your way. That is, when you purchase any new component, it usually comes in an anti-static bag. After you have installed the component, keep the bag. It may take you a while to gather a collection of bags if you take this approach, but eventually you will have a fairly large assortment.

ESD Anti-static Mats

It is possible to damage a device by simply laying it on a bench top. For this reason, you should have an ESD mat in addition to an ESD strap. This mat drains excess charge away from any item coming in contact with it (see Figure 10.4). ESD mats are also sold as mouse/keyboard pads to prevent ESD charges from interfering with the operation of the computer. Many wrist straps can be connected to the mat, thus causing the technician and any equipment in contact with the mat to be at the same electrical potential and eliminating ESD. There are even ESD bootstraps and ESD floor mats, which are used to keep the technician's entire body at the same potential.

FIGURE 10.4   Proper use of an ESD anti-static mat

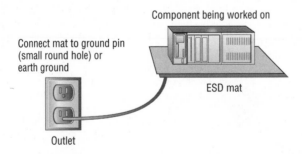

Other Protection Methods

Another preventative measure you can take is to maintain the relative humidity at around 50 percent. Be careful not to increase the humidity too far—to the point where moisture begins to condense on the equipment. Also, use anti-static spray, which is available commercially, to reduce static buildup on clothing and carpets.

If you don't have any anti-static spray, you can always use the "Downy solution." In a spray bottle, combine one part water with one part liquid fabric softener. Mist areas such as carpet and clothing that cause problems. If used regularly, it will keep static away and keep your office smelling nice too!

Vendors have methods of protecting components in transit from manufacture to installation. They press the pins of ICs into anti-static foam to keep all the pins at the same potential. In addition, circuit boards are shipped in anti-static bags, as discussed earlier. However, keep in mind that unlike anti-static mats, anti-static bags do not "drain" the charges away, and they should never be used in place of an anti-static mat.

Anti-static foam looks a lot like Styrofoam. However, there are huge differences between the two. While anti-static foam helps reduce the transfer of electricity, Styrofoam is a very able conductor. (Have you ever tried to get some of those small packing "peanuts" off of your hands?) Be careful to not mix the two up, lest you fry your components.

At the very least, you can be mindful of the dangers of ESD and take steps to reduce its effects. Beyond that, you should educate yourself about those effects so you know when ESD is becoming a major problem.

If an ESD strap or mat is not available, you can discharge excess static voltage by touching the metal case of the power supply. However, the power supply *must be plugged into a properly grounded outlet* for this technique to work as intended. Also, for this to work you need to maintain contact to continuously drain excess charge away. As you can see, it's easier to have an anti-static wrist strap.

Working in a Safe Environment

The Occupational Safety and Health Act states that every working American has the right to a safe and healthy work environment. To enforce the act, OSHA was formed. OSHA covers all private sector employees and post office workers. Public sector employees are covered by state programs, and federal employees are covered under a presidental executive order. In a nutshell, OSHA requires employees to "provide a workplace that is free of recognized dangers and hazards."

There are three overarching criteria to a safe work environment:

- The company and its employees have identified all significant hazards in the work setting.
- Preventative measures have been taken to address each significant hazard.
- The company and its employees understand how to respond to accidents or near-miss accidents if or when they occur.

The following sections explore specific responsibilities and creating a safe work environment plan.

Employer and Employee Responsibilities

Maintaining workplace safety is the responsiblity of employers as well as employees. Here are some of the important responsibilities of employers:

- Provide properly maintained tools and equipment.
- Provide a warning system, such as codes or labels, to warn employees of potential hazards or dangerous chemicals.
- Post the OSHA poster in a prominent location.
- Keep records of workplace injuries or illnesses.
- Continuously examine workplace conditions to ensure OSHA compliance.

It's also the responsibility of the employee to help maintain a safe work environment. Specifically, employees are charged with the following tasks:

- Read and understand OSHA posters.
- Follow all employer-implemented health and safety rules and safe work practices.
- Use all required protective gear and equipment.
- Report hazardous conditions to the employer.
- Report hazardous conditions that the employer does not correct to OSHA.

As you can see, both employers and employees need to work together to keep the workplace safe. It is illegal for an employee to be punished in any way for exercising their rights under the Occupational Safety and Health Act.

Safety Plans

It's recommended that your company create and follow a workplace safety plan. Having a safety plan can help avoid accidents that result in lost productivity, equipment damage, and employee injury or death.

A good safety plan should include the following elements:

- A written plan of the program, including who is responsible for implementing and managing the program
- Systematic perodic inspections to identify workplace hazards
- Procedures for eliminating hazards once identified

- Processes for investigating the cause of accidents, injuries, or illnesses

- A safety and health training program specific to the job duties performed

- A system for employees to communicate safety or health concerns, without fears of reprisal

- A system to ensure that employees comply with safety and health rules

- A system to maintain safety and health records, including steps taken to implement accident prevention initiatives

It might seem like a laundry list of items to consider, but a good safety program needs to be holistic in nature for it to be effective.

Many companies are also incorporating rules against drug or alcohol use in their safety and health plans. Specifically, employees are not allowed to come to work if under the influence of alcohol or illegal drugs. Employees who do come to work under the influence may be subject to disciplinary action up to and including termination of employment.

After your safety plan has been created, you need to ensure that all employees receive necessary training. Have each employee sign a form at the end of training to signify that they attended, and keep the forms in a central location (such as with or near the official safety policy). In addition to the training record, you should make available and keep records of the following:

- Safety improvement suggestion form

- Accident and near-accident reporting form

- Injury and illness log

- Safety inspection checklist

- Hazard removal form

- MSDSs

Safety rules and regulations will work only if they have the broad support of management from the top down. Everyone in the organization needs to buy into the plan, or it won't be a success. Make sure that everyone understands the importance of a safe work environment and make sure that the culture of the company supports safety in the workplace.

Handling Equipment

One of the ways IT employees get hurt is by moving equipment in an improper way. Changing the location of computers is a task often completed by IT personnel, and ensuring that you move things the right way can avoid injury.

Here are some safe lifting techniques to always keep in mind:

- Lift with your legs, not your back (bend at the knees when picking something up, not at the waist).

- Do not twist when lifting.

- Maintain the natural curves of the back and spine when lifting.

- Keep objects close to your body and at waist level.

- Push rather than pull if possible.

The muscles in the lower back aren't nearly as strong as those in the legs or other parts of the body. Whenever lifting, you want to reduce the strain on those lower back muscles as much as possible. If you want, use a back belt or brace to help you maintain the proper position while lifting.

Monitors can be heavy. (Thank goodness for flat screens!) When lifting and carrying a monitor, always keep the glass face toward your body. The front of the monitor is the heaviest part, and you want the heavy part closest to your body to reduce strain on your muscles.

If you believe the load is too much for you to carry, don't try to pick it up! Get assistance from another coworker. Another great idea is to use a cart. It will save you trips if you have multiple items to move, and it saves you the stress of carrying components.

When moving loads, always be aware of your surrounding environment. Before you move, scout out the path to see whether there are any trip hazards or other safety concerns such as spills, stairs, uneven floors (or ripped carpet), tight turns, or narrow doorways.

Following Disposal Procedures

After electronic devices reach the end of their useful life and it's time for them to fade away into the sunset, what do we do with them? With the proliferation of electronic devices over the last few decades, this has become an increasingly important question. Throwing them away puts them in landfills; is that a good or a bad thing? Other than throwing them in the trash, what are options for disposal? This section takes a look at three classifications of computer-related components and proper disposal procedures for each.

Batteries

The United States EPA estimates that there are over 350 million batteries purchased annually in the United States. One can only imagine what the worldwide figure is. Batteries contain several heavy metals and other toxic ingredients, including alkaline, mercury, lead acid, nickel cadmium, and nickel metal hydride.

Never burn a battery to destroy it. That will cause the battery to explode, which could result in serious injury.

When these batteries are thrown away and deposited into landfills, the heavy metals inside them will eventually find their way into the ground. From there, they can pollute water sources and eventually find their way into the supply of drinking water. In 1996, the United States passed the Battery Act to address two issues: to phase out the use of mercury in disposable batteries and to provide collection methods and recycling procedures for batteries.

There are several countries around the world with battery recycling programs. Information on battery recycling in various countries can be found at http://www.ibm.com/ibm/environment/products/batteryrecycle.shtml.

There are four types of batteries most commonly associated with computers and handheld electronic devices: alkaline, nickel cadmium (NiCd), nickel metal hydride (NiMH), lithium ion, and button cell.

Alkaline batteries   Alkaline batteries have been incredibly popular portable batteries for several decades now. Before 1984, one of the major ingredients in this type of battery was mercury, which is highly toxic to the environment. In 1984, battery companies began reduction of mercury levels, and in 1996 mercury was outlawed in alkaline batteries in the United States. Still, it's strongly recommended that you recycle these batteries at a recycling center. Although newer alkaline batteries contain less mercury than their predecessors, they are still made of metals and other toxins which contaminate the air and soil.

Nickel cadmium (NiCd)   Nickel cadmium is a popular format for rechargeable batteries. As their name indicates, they contain high levels of nickel and cadmium. Although nickel is only semi-toxic, cadmium is highly toxic. These types of batteries are categorized by the EPA as hazardous waste and should be recycled.

Nickel metal hydride (NiMH) and lithium ion   Laptop batteries are commonly made with NiMH and lithium ion. Unlike the previous types of batteries we have discussed, these are not considered hazardous waste, and there are no regulations on recycling them. However, these batteries do contain elements that can be recycled, so it's still a good idea to go that route.

Button cell   These batteries are named because they look like a button. They're commonly used in calculators and watches as well as portable computers. They often contain mercury and silver (and are environmental hazards due to the mercury), and need to be recycled.

You may have noticed a theme regarding disposal of batteries: recycling. Many people just throw batteries in the trash and don't think twice about it. However, there are several laws in the United States requiring the recycling of many types of batteries. Not only that, but recycling does indeed help keep the environment clean. For a list of recycling centers in your area, use your local yellow pages (under Recycling Centers) or do an Internet search.

If you're ever exposed to the electrolyte (the inside "juice") of the battery, immediately flush the exposed area with water. If exposed to the eye, wash the eye for 15 minutes and immediately contact a physician.

Display Devices

Computer monitors (CRT monitors, not LCD ones) are big and bulky, so what do you do when it's time to get rid of them? As we mentioned earlier in this chapter, monitors have capacitors in them that are capable of retaining a lethal electric charge after they've been unplugged. You wouldn't want anyone to accidentally set off the charge and die. But the thing we didn't mention earlier, which is important now, is that most CRT monitors contain high amounts of lead. Most monitors have several pounds of lead, in fact. Lead is very dangerous to humans and the environment, and must be dealt with carefully. Other harmful elements found in CRTs include arsenic, beryllium, cadmium, chromium, mercury, nickel, and zinc.

If you have a monitor to dispose of, contact a computer recycling firm. It's best to let professional recyclers handle the monitor for you.

Real World Scenario

How *Not* to Dispose of Your Monitors

This story comes from the technical support division of a now-defunct major computer manufacturer, who used a lot of computers at their own facility. At one time, they had as many as 500 technicians working the phones. So you can imagine that they burned out a lot of equipment.

Here's how dead monitors would be disposed of. An IT staff member would take the monitor out to the dumpster and bring along a sledgehammer. Setting the monitor on its back, he would take one good swing at the glass panel with the hammer to shatter the screen. (This was done, by policy, to ensure that no one would want to go out to the dumpster and try to salvage the dead monitor.) After glass went everywhere, he picked up the monitor and threw it in the dumpster.

One employee made an observation that it probably wasn't good for us to be spreading glass all over the parking lot by shattering monitors. That advice was taken, and the sledgehammer was done away with. Instead, an IT staff member would use a permanent black marker and draw all over the screen (again, so no one would want to try to salvage it), and again, it was thrown in the dumpster.

In our enlightened state today, we can see how this was not a good plan for disposing of broken monitors. In fact, many states today have laws prohibiting the disposal of computer monitors in trash bins. This is a good law, because with the amount of harmful elements in monitors, they're every bit the environmental hazard that batteries are.

Chemical Solvents and Cans

Nearly every chemical solvent you encounter will have a corresponding MSDS. On the MSDS you will find a section detailing the proper methods for disposing of that chemical. These chemicals were not designed to be released into nature, because they could cause significant harm to living organisms if they're ingested. If in doubt, contact a local hazardous materials handler to find out the best way to dispose of the chemical solvent.

Cans are generally made from metal or aluminum, neither of which is biodegradable. It's best to always recycle these materials. If the cans were used to hold a chemical solvent or otherwise hazardous material, contact a hazardous materials disposal center instead of a recycling center.

Summary

This chapter covered several aspects of safety and environmental issues. First, we looked at the importance of safety and environmental issues. We identified potential safety hazards and examined preventative actions. Then we talked about Material Safety Data Sheets (MSDSs) and their importance.

Next, we discussed the importance of using the right tool for the right job, and which tools to avoid using. That was followed by a section on handling accidents, including incident reporting.

Next, we outlined some methods to apply safe working environment policies and procedures. Included were prevention of electrostatic discharge (ESD), creating a safe work environment, and the proper handling of computer equipment.

Finally, we looked at proper disposal procedures for batteries, display devices, and chemical solvents and cans. These items need to be kept out of the environment because of the damage they can cause.

Exam Essentials

Know which computer components are particularly dangerous to technicians. The most dangerous are the power supply and the monitor. Both are capable of storing lethal charges of electricity, even when unplugged. You also need to be aware of parts that get incredibly hot, such as the processor, which can cause severe burns if touched.

Understand where to find safety information regarding chemicals. You can find this information on a Material Safety Data Sheet (MSDS). An MSDS might not have come with your purchase, but most suppliers will gladly supply one if requested.

Know which tool to use for which job. The majority of computer repair jobs can be handled with nothing more than a Phillips-head screwdriver. However, you might need cutters, extra light, or a mirror for some jobs. Never use magnetically tipped tools.

Understand methods to help prevent ESD. One of the biggest and most common dangers to electronic components is electrostatic discharge (ESD). There are several methods you can employ to help avoid ESD problems, such as grounding yourself; using an anti-static wrist strap, bag, or mat; and controlling the humidity levels.

Know proper disposal procedures for used computer parts, batteries, and chemical solvents. The specific disposal procedure depends on what you are trying to dispose of. However, the safe answer is to always recycle the component and not throw it in the trash bin.

Review Questions

1. Which of the following computer components can retain a lethal electrical charge even after the device is unplugged? (Choose all that apply.)

    A. Monitor

    B. Processor

    C. Power supply

    D. RAM

2. A computer is experiencing random reboots and phantom problems that disappear after reboot. What should you do?

    A. Tell the customer that it's normal for the computer to do that.

    B. Replace the motherboard.

    C. Boot clean.

    D. Replace the power supply.

    E. Open the cover, clean the inside of the computer, and reseat all cards and chips.

3. Which class of fire extinguisher is recommended for use in a wood and paper fire?

    A. A

    B. B

    C. C

    D. D

4. The electrical contacts on your video card are starting to become dirty. Which of the following should you use to clean those contacts?

    A. Cloth and water

    B. Isopropyl alcohol

    C. A pencil eraser

    D. Your fingers

5. Which of the following is used to properly discharge voltage from an unplugged computer monitor?

    A. Anti-static wrist strap

    B. Screwdriver

    C. High-voltage probe

    D. Power cord

6. Which of the following must contain information about a chemical solvent's emergency cleanup procedures?

   A. OSHA

   B. MSDS

   C. Product label

   D. CRT

7. Which of the following are usually contained on an MSDS? (Choose all that apply.)

   A. Boiling point

   B. Handling and storage instructions

   C. Personal protection instructions

   D. Firefighting measures

8. You are purchasing an inkjet printer cartridge for use in your home, which you know has an MSDS. How do you obtain the MSDS for this product?

   A. The store is required to give you one at the time of purchase.

   B. It's contained inside the packaging of the printer cartridge.

   C. You are not legally allowed to have an MSDS for this product.

   D. Visit the website of the printer cartridge manufacturer.

9. Which of the following are common types of screwdrivers? (Choose all that apply.)

   A. Flat-blade

   B. Phillips

   C. Torx

   D. Helix

10. What is the recommended use policy on magnetic-tipped screwdrivers inside computers?

    A. Do not use them.

    B. It's okay to use them, but keep them away from the processor.

    C. It's okay to use them, but keep them away from the RAM.

    D. It's okay to use them only if they're of the powered variety.

11. In the interest of a safe work environment, which of the following should you report? (Choose all that apply.)

    A. An accident

    B. A near-accident

    C. Dirt on the floor inside a building

    D. Water puddles in a hallway

12. What is the approximate minimum level of static charge for humans to feel a shock?

   A. 300 volts

   B. 3,000 volts

   C. 30,000 volts

   D. 300,000 volts

13. Which of the following measures can be implemented to reduce the risk of ESD? (Choose all that apply.)

   A. Anti-static wrist strap

   B. Anti-static bag

   C. Anti-static floor mat

   D. Anti-static hair net

14. Which of the following are OSHA requirements for a safe work environment that must be followed by employers? (Choose all that apply.)

   A. Attend yearly OSHA safe work environment seminars.

   B. Provide properly maintained tools and equipment.

   C. Keep records of accident reports.

   D. Display an OSHA poster in a prominent location.

15. Which of the following are OSHA requirements for a safe work environment that must be followed by employees? (Choose all that apply.)

   A. Immediately report all accidents to OSHA.

   B. Use all protective gear and equipment.

   C. Attend safety training.

   D. Follow all employer-implemented health and safety rules.

16. Which of the following are elements of a good workplace safety plan? (Choose all that apply.)

   A. Periodic workplace inspections

   B. A safety and health training program

   C. Retribution for employees who report violations

   D. An independent third-party auditor of the safety plan

17. When moving computer equipment, which of the following are good procedures to follow? (Choose all that apply.)

   A. Lift by bending over at the waist.

   B. Carry monitors with the glass face away from your body.

   C. Use a cart for heavy objects.

   D. Ensure that there are no safety hazards in your path.

18. You have four AA alkaline batteries that you just removed from a remote-control device. What is the recommended way to dispose of these batteries?

   A. Throw them in the trash.

   B. Incinerate them.

   C. Take them to a recycling center.

   D. Flush them in the sewer.

19. Which of the following types of batteries are *not* considered environmental hazards?

   A. Alkaline

   B. Nickel metal hydride (NiMH)

   C. Nickel cadmium (NiCd)

   D. Button cell

20. What is the proper way to dispose of a broken CRT monitor?

   A. Take it to a computer recycling center.

   B. Discharge the monitor with a high-volt probe and throw it away.

   C. Throw it away.

   D. None of the above.

Answers to Review Questions

1. A, C. Monitors and power supplies can retain significant electrical charges, even after they're unplugged. Don't open the back of a monitor or the power supply unless you are specifically trained to do so.

2. E. When a computer is experiencing random reboots and phantom problems that disappear after reboot, you should open the cover, clean everything (if it's dirty), and reseat all cards and chips. Some components could have gunk on them that carries an electrical charge, or could have experienced "chip creep," where they slowly work themselves out of their sockets.

3. A. Wood and paper fires can be put out by a class A fire extinguisher. If you have a combination Class ABC extinguisher, that will work fine.

4. B. To clean electrical contacts, use denatured isopropyl alcohol and a cotton swab. Water should never touch electrical components. A pencil eraser could leave traces of acids behind, and your fingers have oils on them that will damage the contacts.

5. C. A high-voltage probe is designed to release the electricity from high-voltage components, which are found in the back of CRT computer monitors.

6. B. The Material Safety Data Sheet (MSDS) contains information about chemical properties, including what to do if an accident occurs.

7. A, B, C, D. MSDSs contain a wealth of information on the product, including accident procedures and safety information. All of the above are included on an MSDS.

8. D. Companies are not legally required to provide MSDSs to consumers. However, most will if you ask. The best place to look is the manufacturer's website.

9. A, B, C. The three common types of screwdrivers are flat-blade, Phillips, and Torx. There is no helix screwdriver.

10. A. A good rule of thumb when it comes to magnetic-tipped screwdrivers is to avoid using them inside a computer case. Magnetic tools can damage data on disks which use a magnetic storage scheme.

11. A, B, D. Accidents and near-accidents should always be reported. Dirt isn't usually a safety issue, but water in a hallway could cause people to slip and fall.

12. B. Most people can feel an electric shock at about 3,000 volts. However, computer equipment can be damaged with as little as 100 volts.

13. A, B, C. Anti-static wrist straps, bags (for parts), and floor mats can all help reduce the risk of ESD. There are no anti-static hair nets.

14. B, C, D. Private sector employers are required by OSHA to maintain a safe work environment. This includes maintaining tools and equipment, keeping records of accidents, and displaying a safety information poster.

15. B, D. To maintain a safe work environment, all employees must follow certain protocols. These include using all protective gear and equipment, and following all health and safety rules. Accidents must be reported to the employer, not OSHA (unless action is not properly taken by the employer). There are no rules requiring safety training, although it is a good idea to have these sessions and for employees to attend them.

16. A, B. Good safety plans protect the interests of the workers and also help keep company costs down. Periodic workplace inspections and a training program are good components to implement. Employees cannot be punished in any way for reporting safety violations. Third-party auditing of safety programs is not necessary, but there are organizations that will do this for you.

17. C, D. You should always lift with your legs, not your back. This means bending at the knees and not the waist. Monitors should be carried with the glass face toward your body. Using carts for heavy objects is a good idea, as is ensuring that your path is free of safety hazards, such as trip hazards.

18. C. Alkaline batteries should always be recycled. Throwing them in the trash means they'll end up in a landfill where they can contaminate the environment. Burning batteries is always a bad idea, because they will explode.

19. A, B. Nickel metal hydride batteries are not considered environmental hazards. Alkaline batteries used to contain lead, which was an environmental hazard, but no longer do. All of the other battery types include harmful elements, such as mercury or lead. Even though they're not considered environmental hazards, it's still a good idea to recycle NiMH batteries.

20. A. Monitors should be recycled after the end of their useful life. They contain many harmful elements, including lead, that can cause environmental problems.

Chapter

11

Understanding Professionalism and Communication

THE FOLLOWING COMPTIA A+ ESSENTIALS EXAM OBJECTIVES ARE COVERED IN THIS CHAPTER:

✓ **8.1 Use good communication skills including listening and tact / discretion, when communicating with customers and colleagues**

- Use clear, concise and direct statements
- Allow the customer to complete statements – avoid interrupting
- Clarify customer statements – ask pertinent questions
- Avoid using jargon, abbreviations and acronyms
- Listen to customers

✓ **8.2 Use job-related professional behavior including notation of privacy, confidentiality and respect for the customer and customers' property**

- Behavior
  - Maintain a positive attitude and tone of voice
  - Avoid arguing with customers and / or becoming defensive
  - Do not minimize customers' problems
  - Avoid being judgmental and / or insulting or calling the customer names
  - Avoid distractions and / or interruptions when talking with customers
- Property
  - Telephone, laptop, desktop computer, printer, monitor, etc.

THE FOLLOWING COMPTIA A+ IT TECHNICIAN EXAM OBJECTIVES ARE COVERED IN THIS CHAPTER:

✓ **8.1 Use good communication skills including listening and tact / discretion, when communicating with customers and colleagues**

- Use clear, concise and direct statements
- Allow the customer to complete statements – avoid interrupting
- Clarify customer statements – ask pertinent questions
- Avoid using jargon, abbreviations and acronyms
- Listen to customers

✓ **8.2 Use job-related professional behavior including notation of privacy, confidentiality and respect for the customer and customers' property**

- Behavior
  - Maintain a positive attitude and tone of voice
  - Avoid arguing with customers and / or becoming defensive
  - Do not minimize customers' problems
  - Avoid being judgmental and / or insulting or calling the customer names
  - Avoid distractions and / or interruptions when talking with customers
- Property
  - Telephone, laptop, desktop computer, printer, monitor, etc.

THE FOLLOWING COMPTIA A+ REMOTE SUPPORT TECHNICIAN EXAM OBJECTIVES ARE COVERED IN THIS CHAPTER:

✓ **6.1 Use good communication skills, including listening and tact / discretion, when communicating with customers and colleagues**

- Use clear, concise and direct statements

- Allow the customer to complete statements – avoid interrupting
- Clarify customer statements – ask pertinent questions
- Avoid using jargon, abbreviations and acronyms
- Listen to customers

✓ **6.2 Use job-related professional behavior including notation of privacy, confidentiality and respect for the customer and customers' property**

- Behavior
  - Maintain a positive attitude and tone of voice
  - Avoid arguing with customers and / or becoming defensive
  - Do not minimize customers' problems
  - Avoid being judgmental and / or insulting or calling the customer names
  - Avoid distractions and / or interruptions when talking with customers
- Property
  - Telephone, laptop, desktop computer, printer, monitor, etc.

As a technician and a professional, it is important that you know how to interact with others. Those others may be customers, vendors, fellow employees, or managers. CompTIA recognizes the importance of this ability and has added it to the Essentials exam and two of the elective exams.

This chapter looks at the topic of professionalism and communication and discusses what you need to know for your exam study. Since the objectives are essentially the same between Essentials and the electives, this is the only chapter in this book that focuses on those topics. While many will argue that soft skills are really beyond the scope of an IT book, the level of coverage here is adequate for your exam preparation.

Using Good Communication Skills

Good communication includes listening to what the user or manager or developer is telling you and making certain that you understand completely what he is trying to say: Approximately half of all communication should be listening. Just because a user or customer does not understand the terminology or syntax or concepts that you use or understand does not mean he does not have a real problem that needs addressing. You must, therefore, be skilled not only at listening but also at translating.

Professional conduct encompasses politeness, guidance, punctuality, and accountability. Always treat the customer with the same respect and empathy you would expect if the situation were reversed. Likewise, guide the customer through the problem and the explanation. Tell him what has caused the problem he is currently experiencing and the best solution for preventing it from reoccurring in the future.

Customer satisfaction goes a long way toward generating repeat business. If you can *meet* the customer's expectations, you will almost assuredly hear from him again when another problem arises. However, if you can *exceed* the customer's expectations, you can almost guarantee that he will call you the next time a problem arises.

Customer satisfaction is important in all communication media—whether you are on-site, providing phone support, or communicating through e-mail or other correspondence. If you are on-site, follow these rules:

- When you arrive, immediately look for the person (user, manager, administrator, and so on) who is affected by the problem. Announce that you are there and assure that person that you will do all you can to remedy the problem.

- Listen intently to what your customer is saying. Make it obvious to her that you are listening and respecting what she is telling you. If there is a problem with understanding the

---

Real World Scenario

Communication Is Key

Marriages disintegrate when couples do not communicate effectively, or so many of the experts proclaim. Communication is ranked as one of the most important skills needed in order to make a marriage, or any similar partnership, work. The same can be said for business partnerships—it is important to make certain you are listening to your customers, whether they are truly customers in the traditional sense of the word or internal users that you support. The same can also be said of managers and vendors—you need to listen to their concerns and their information and then make sure you understand them before beginning a project.

Similarly, you need to make certain that the parties in question understand what you are saying to them. It isn't acceptable to resort to the "But I told you ..." excuse when customers or partners aren't pleased with the results. Making certain they understand what you are telling them is equally important as making certain you understand what they are telling you.

---

client, go to whatever lengths you need to in order to remedy the situation. Look for verbal and nonverbal cues that can help you isolate the problem.

- Share the customer's sense of urgency. What may seem like a small problem to you can appear as if the whole world were collapsing around your customer.

- Be honest and fair with the customer and try to establish a personal rapport. Explain what the problem is, what you believe is the cause of it, and what can be done in the future to prevent it from recurring.

- Handle complaints as professionally as possible. Accept responsibility for errors that may have occurred on your part, and never try to pass the blame elsewhere. Avoid arguing with a customer, as it serves no purpose; resolve her anger with as little conflict as possible. Remember: The goal is to keep her as a customer and not to win an argument.

- When you finish a job, notify the user that you have finished. Make every attempt to find the user and inform her of the resolution. If it is impossible to find her, leave a note explaining the resolution to find when she returns. You should also leave a means by which she can contact you should she have a question about the resolution or a related problem. In most cases, the number you should leave would be that of your business during working hours and that of your pager, where applicable, after hours. Notification should also be given to both managers—yours and the user's—that the job has been completed.

If you are providing phone support, keeps these guidelines in mind:

- Always answer the telephone in a professional manner, announcing the name of the company and yourself.

- Make a concentrated effort to ascertain the customer's technical level and communicate at that level, not above or below it.

- The most important skill you can have is the ability to listen. You have to rely on the customer to tell you the problem and describe it accurately. She cannot do that if you are second-guessing or jumping to conclusions before the whole story is told. Ask broad questions to begin, and then narrow them down to help isolate the problem. It is your job to help guide the description of the problem from the user. For example, you might ask:

  - Is the printer plugged in?

  - Is it online?

  - Are there any lights flashing on it?

- Complaints should be handled in the same manner as if you were on-site. Make your best effort to resolve the problem and not argue its points. Again, you want to keep the customer more than you want to accomplish any other goal.

- Close the incident only when the customer is satisfied that the solution you have given her is the correct one and the problem has gone away.

- End the telephone call in a courteous manner—thanking the customer for the opportunity to serve her is often the best way.

Talking to the user is an important first step in the troubleshooting process. Your first contact with a computer that has a problem is usually through the customer, either directly or by way of a work order that contains the user's complaint. Often, the complaint is something straightforward, such as "There's a disk stuck in the floppy drive." At other times, the problem is complex, and the customer does not mention everything that has been going wrong.

Real World Scenario

Communication Is Everywhere

Communication, and problems that can occur with it, are not isolated to the IT world. Almost every profession stresses the importance of good communication. As an example of this, Jamie Walters, founder and chief vision & strategy officer for Ivy Sea, Inc., and Sarah Fenson, Ivy Sea's guide to client services, wrote an article for Inc.com on steps to smooth conversations (http://www.inc.com/articles/2000/08/20000.html) that included this advice:

1. Don't take things personally. If some acts inappropriately toward you, just react in a calm manner. They are likely responding that way because of outside factors.

2. Admit when you don't know the answer to something. It's okay to defer to somebody else, or tell the user or customer that you'll have to look into their complaint and will get back with them as soon as possible.

3. It is better to validate one's feeling or respond to the information they have given you than reacting to them. For instance, if somebody complains that a help ticket has not been responded to in a timely manner, tell them you understand how they feel and will look into it versus reacting in a defensive manner.

4.   Don't let your personal opinions or feelings get in the way of what the real complaint is. Try to put yourself in the user's or customer's shoes.

5.   Be sympathetic. If you need a user to leave his or her laptop with you overnight, tell them you realize it's frustrating and apologize.

6.   Try to provide a solution that you both can benefit from. If, for instance, a user's machine is slow, explain to them that this might be a bigger issue than just his machine.

7.   Try and be as informative as possible when discussing a solution to their problem. Most people are uncomfortable with change, so explaining the benefits of a particular solution might help ease this discomfort.

8.   Try to keep a positive attitude and be optimistic.

9.   Don't be afraid to explain that you have an agenda as well, but explain to them that your ultimate goal is to make both you and the client happy. For instance, if you need replace a temperamental NIC, explain to the user that this will save you some time down the road if the NIC completely dies.

Elicit Problem Symptoms from Customers

The act of diagnosis starts with the art of customer relations. Go to the customer with an attitude of trust: Believe what the customer is saying. At the same time, retain an attitude of hidden skepticism, meaning *don't* believe that the customer has told you everything. This attitude of hidden skepticism is not the same as distrust, but just remember that what you hear isn't always the whole story, and customers may inadvertently forget to give some crucial detail.

WARNING   One of the best ways to become proficient in this is to put yourself in the shoes of the novice user. None of us are experts in every field, so think of an area where you are weak—auto repair, home repair, etc.—and imagine how you would want a professional in that area to discourse with you.

For example, a customer may complain that his CD-ROM drive doesn't work. What he fails to mention is that it has never worked and that he installed it himself. On examining the machine, you realize that he mounted it with screws that are too long and that these prevent the tray from ejecting properly.

Have the Customer Reproduce the Error

The most important part of this step is to have the customer show you what the problem is. The best method I've seen of doing this is to ask him, "Show me what 'not working' looks like." That way, you see the conditions and methods under which the problem occurs. The problem may be a simple matter of an improper method. The user may be doing an operation incorrectly or performing the operation in the wrong order. During this step, you have the opportunity to observe how the problem occurs, so pay attention.

Identify Recent Changes

The user can give you vital information. The most important question is, "What changed?" Problems don't usually come out of nowhere. Was a new piece of hardware or software added? Did the user drop some equipment? Was there a power outage or a storm? These are the types of questions you can ask a user in trying to find out what is different.

If nothing changed, at least outwardly, then what was going on at the time of failure? Can the problem be reproduced? Can the problem be worked around? The point here is to ask as many questions as you need to in order to pinpoint the source of the trouble.

Use the Collected Information

Once the problem or problems have been clearly identified, your next step is to isolate possible causes. If the problem cannot be clearly identified, then further tests will be necessary. A common technique for hardware and software problems alike is to strip the system down to bare-bones basics. In a hardware situation, this could mean removing all interface cards except those absolutely required for the system to operate. In a software situation, this may mean disabling elements within Device Manager.

Generally, then, you can gradually rebuild the system toward the point where the trouble started. When you reintroduce a component and the problem reappears, you know that component is the one causing the problem.

Using Appropriate Behavior

Critical to appropriate behavior is to treat the customer, or user, the way you want to be treated. Much has been made of the Golden Rule—treating others the way you would have them treat you. Six key elements to this, from a business perspective, are punctuality, accountability, flexibility, confidentiality, respect, and privacy. The following sections discuss these elements in detail.

Punctuality

Punctuality is important and should be a part of your planning process before you ever arrive at the site: If you tell the customer you will be there at 10:30 a.m., you need to make every attempt to be there at that time. If you arrive late, you have given her false hope that the problem will be solved by a set time. That false hope can lead to anger when you arrive late and appear not to be taking her problem seriously. Punctuality continues to be important throughout the service call and does not end with your arrival. If you need to leave to get parts and return, tell the customer when you will be back, and be there at that time. If, for some reason, you cannot return at the expected time, alert the customer and inform her of your new time.

In conjunction with time and punctuality, if a user asks how much longer the server will be down and you respond that it will up in five minutes, only to have it down for five more hours, you are creating resentment and possibly anger. When estimating downtime, always allow for more time than you think you will need just in case other problems occur. If you greatly underestimate the time, always inform the affected parties and give them a new time estimate. To use an analogy that will put it in perspective, if you take your car to get an oil change and the counter clerk tells you it will be "about 15 minutes," the last thing you want is to be still sitting there four hours later.

Exercise 11.1 tests the importance of punctuality.

EXERCISE 11.1

Understanding Punctuality

This is a simple exercise that you can modify and use as needed. Its purpose is to illustrate the importance of punctuality as it relates to situations with which you can associate.

1. Call someone important in your life—your spouse, a parent, an in-law, or a close friend— and tell him or her you have something very important you need to discuss. Give that person no other details, but ask him or her to meet you in exactly one hour at a location familiar to both of you.

2. Wait two hours before showing up.

3. Notice the person's reaction. How did that person feel about having to wait for you? Even though your lateness was not that great, what kind of an impact did it have on the person's mood and behavior?

This is an interaction with someone who matters in your life—imagine a customer who does not know you waiting for you when he perceives his system problem to be the most serious thing in his life at the moment. Punctuality can go a long way toward keeping dialog pleasant between any two parties.

Accountability

Accountability is a trait every technician should possess. When problems occur, you need to be accountable for them and not attempt to pass the buck to someone else. For example, you are called to a site to put a larger hard drive into a server. While performing this operation, you inadvertently scrape your feet across the carpeted floor, build up energy, and zap the memory in the server. Some technicians would pretend the electrostatic discharge (ESD) never happened, put the new hard drive in, and then act completely baffled by the fact that problems unrelated to the hard drive are occurring. An accountable technician would explain to the customer exactly what happened and suggest ways of proceeding from that point—addressing and solving the problem as quickly and efficiently as possible.

Flexibility

Flexibility is another equally important trait for a service technician. While it is important that you respond to service calls promptly and close them (solve them) as quickly as you can, you must also be flexible. If a customer cannot have you on-site until the afternoon, you must make your best effort to work them into your schedule around the time most convenient for them. Likewise, if you are called to a site to solve a problem, and the customer brings another problem to your attention while you are there, you should make every attempt to address that problem as well. Under no circumstances should you ever give a customer the cold shoulder or not respond to additional problems because they were not on an initial incident report.

 You should always follow the express guidelines of the company for which you work as they relate to flexibility, empowerment, and other issues.

Confidentiality

The goal of *confidentiality* is to prevent or minimize unauthorized access to files and folders and disclosure of data and information. In many instances, laws and regulations require confidentiality for specific information. For example, Social Security records, payroll and employee records, medical records, and corporate information are high-value assets. This information could create liability issues or embarrassment if it fell into the wrong hands. Over the last few years, there have been a number of cases in which bank account and credit card numbers were published on the Internet. The costs of these types of breaches of confidentiality far exceed the actual losses from the misuse of this information.

 Confidentiality entails ensuring that data expected to remain private is seen only by those who should see it. Confidentiality is implemented through authentication and access controls.

Just as confidentiality issues are addressed early in the design phase of a project, you—as a computer professional—are expected to uphold a high level of confidentiality. Should a user approach you with a sensitive issue—telling you his password, asking for assistance obtaining access to medical forms, and so on, it is your obligation as a part of your job to make certain that information passes no further.

Respect

Much of the discussion in this chapter is focused on respecting the customer as an individual. However, you must also respect the tangibles that are important to the customer. While you may look at a monitor they are using as an outdated piece of equipment that should be scrapped, the business owners may see it as a gift from their children when they first started their business.

Treat the customers' property as if it had value, and you will win their respect. Their property includes the system you are working on (laptop/desktop computer, monitor, peripherals, and the like) as well as other items associated with their business. Do not use their telephone to make personal calls or call other customers while you are at this site. Do not use their printers or other equipment, unless it is in a role associated with the problem you've been summoned to fix.

> The Customer Respect Group, http://www.customerrespect.com, measures the behavior of corporations and the respect they give to customers through their websites. Such items as privacy, responsiveness, attitude, simplicity, transparency, and business principles are combined to create a Customer Respect Index (CRI) ranking. The items they rank in the online world are just as important in the offline world and mirror those presented here.

Respecting the customer is not rocket science. All you need to do—for this exam and in the real world—is think of how you would want someone to treat you. Exercise 11.2 explores this topic further.

EXERCISE 11.2

Surprise Someone

This exercise, like Exercise 11.1, can be modified to fit your purpose or constraints. Its purpose is to illustrate the positive power of the unexpected:

1. Pick a random, toll-free number used for business solicitation and call it.

2. Chat with the operator for a few moments about the company's product or service, and then ask to speak to the supervisor.

3. When the supervisor comes on, tell her about the operator you have been speaking with and commend him for the job that he has done.

It is likely the operator became confused when you asked to speak to his supervisor; this almost always occurs only in a negative situation. How did the operator handle the request? Did it change the tone of the communication that was taking place? Did he fulfill your request even though he feared he could lose from it? How did the supervisor respond when she came to the phone—was she expecting negative comments? How did she accept the positive information you offered?

Ideally, this illustrated the importance of staying professional and keeping the channel of communication open even in a tough situation. You should be able to adapt this to the workplace when a customer asks to speak to your superior or has another request that is difficult for you to fulfill.

🌐 Real World Scenario

A Little Goes a Long Way

The following examples of respecting and disrespecting the customer come from my own experience:

My wife and I were in an unfamiliar part of Chicago without ready access to a vehicle when we started to get hungry. I am a meat-and-potatoes man and rarely take a chance on anything else. There were no restaurants of that type around, however, and we wound up in an Asian grill. Expecting not to like the buffet, we ordered a side of lettuce wraps and then two buffets and drinks. As it turned out, I liked the buffet a great deal and went back through the line many times. We also liked the drinks and got several of those. Everything was great, except the waiter forgot to bring the lettuce wraps. I dismissed it and made a mental note to inform the waiter when he brought the bill and have him deduct them from our tab. Instead, the manager brought the bill over when we were finished eating, and he had scribbled on it "no charge." When I asked him why, he apologized that no one brought the wraps and said he hoped we would come back another time. I was beside myself with disbelief and thanked him profusely, and since then I have told many people about the best place in Chicago I know of to eat.

In a very different situation, while driving home one night, a dashboard light came on reading "Low tire pressure." Upon inspection, I could hear the right-rear tire hissing. I drove to a tire store and explained the situation. I had used this same tire store over the past 14 years for tires, oil changes, exhaust, maintenance, and a number of other things on the vehicles I've owned. The manager came out and said they found a nail in the tire. They removed the nail, patched the tire, and charged me $13. I was delighted, expecting it to cost much more, and so I paid the bill and went on my way. The next morning, I woke up to find the right-rear tire completely flat. I canceled the morning's appointment, filled the tire with an air compressor, and drove back to the tire store. Shortly, the manager came out and told me that they found another nail in that tire; they were going to eat the $13 on this one, but it had better not happen again. I could not believe the insinuation—that I was driving about looking for nails to hit with that one tire just so I could spend my morning taking them for $13! Instead of offering the possibility that they had overlooked a nail the previous night, apologizing for the inconvenience, or anything of that sort, he shifted the responsibility to me. Needless to say, I have not been back since, and all of my repair business is now done elsewhere.

These two examples illustrate two different approaches to treating the customer. In the first example, the customer is well respected and treated better than expected. In the second example, the customer is disrespected and is treated as an inconvenience. Given the lifetime value of customers, it is always better to respect them—and retain them—than to offhandedly dismiss them.

One last area to consider that directly relates to this topic is that of ethics. Ethics is the application of morality to situations. While there are different schools of thought, one of the most popular areas of study is known as normative ethics, focusing on what is normal or practical (right versus wrong and so on). Regardless of religion, culture, and other influences, there are generally accepted beliefs that some things are wrong (stealing, murder, and the like) and some things are right (for example, the Golden Rule). You should always attempt to be ethical in everything you do because it reflects not only upon your character but also on the company for which you work.

Privacy

While there is some overlap between confidentiality and privacy, privacy is an area of computing that is becoming considerably more regulated. As a computing professional, you must stay current with applicable laws, because you're often one of the primary agents expected to ensure compliance.

In addition to the federal laws about computer crime, there are similar laws in most states. Check `http:/www.nsi.org/Library/Compsec/computerlaw/statelaws.html` for information on your state's regulations.

While the laws provide a minimal level of privacy, you should go out of your way to respect the privacy of your users beyond what the law establishes. If you discover information about a user that you should not be privy to, you should not share it with anyone, and you should alert the customers that their data is accessible and encourage them—if applicable—to remedy the situation.

Putting It All in Perspective

Whether you are dealing with customers in person or on the phone, there are five rules to which you should adhere. These were implied in the previous discussion, but you must understand them and remember them for the exam:

- Use clear, concise, and direct statements—customers want to know what is going on. They want to know that you understand the problem and can deal with it. Being honest and direct is almost always appreciated.

- Allow the customers to complete their statements and avoid interrupting them. Everyone has been in a situation where they have not been able to fully explain their problem without being interrupted or ignored. It is not enjoyable in a social setting, and it is intolerable in a business setting.

- Clarify customer statements and ask pertinent questions. The questions you ask should help guide you toward isolating the problem and identifying possible solutions. Don't be afraid to nod, ask questions, and repeat to the customer what you think they are saying to make sure you are understanding it correctly.

- Avoid using jargon, abbreviations, and acronyms. Every field has its own language, and outsiders feel lost when they start hearing it. Put yourself in the position of someone not in the field and explain what is going on by using words they can relate to.

- Listen to your customers. This is the most important rule of all—people like to know they are being heard, and, as simple an act as it is, this can make all the difference in making them feel at ease with your work.

When it comes to behavior, there are five rules that CompTIA expects you to adhere to. These were implied in the discussion of privacy, confidentiality, and respect, but specifically are:

- Maintain a positive attitude and tone of voice.

- Avoid arguing with customers and/or becoming defensive.

- Do not minimize customers' problems. While it may be a situation you see every day, it is a crisis to them.

- Avoid being judgmental and/or insulting or calling the customer names.

- Avoid distraction and/or interruptions when talking with customers.

Summary

In this chapter, you learned about the various issues related to professionalism and communication. These topics have been extracted from other domains in the previous iteration of the A+ exams and turned into a domain of their own.

You should treat your customers as you would want to be treated and let them know that you respect them and their business through your actions and behavior.

Exam Essentials

Use good communication skills. Listen to your customers. Let them tell you what they understand the problem to be, and then interpret the problem and see if you can get them to agree to what you are hearing them say. Treat your customers, whether they be end users or colleagues, with respect, and take their issues and problems seriously.

Use job-related professional behavior. The Golden Rule should govern your professional behavior. Five key elements to this, from a business perspective, are punctuality, accountability, flexibility, confidentiality, and privacy.

Review Questions

1. You are handling a service call in the field. When should you close this call?

    A. When you are handed the ticket

    B. When you arrive on location

    C. When you have solved the problem

    D. When the customer is satisfied

2. Roughly how much time spent communicating should be devoted to listening?

    A. 10 percent

    B. 25 percent

    C. 40 percent

    D. 50 percent

3. Which of the following are good ways to show you are listening to someone explaining a problem?

    A. Nodding

    B. Repeating what she is saying

    C. Asking questions

    D. All of the above

4. While troubleshooting a customer's LAN, you determine the server must be rebooted to restore the network to full functionality. What should you do?

    A. Broadcast a message to all users telling them the reboot is coming.

    B. Reboot as quickly as you can.

    C. Suggest the customer do the reboot while you are at lunch.

    D. Recommend the reboot be bypassed now and done by the customer after hours.

5. Upon arriving at a customer's site, you are told by the office manager that you are not welcome here. They are used to dealing with another technician—one who is currently unavailable—and want to deal only with him. What should you do?

    A. Push past her and continue toward the equipment you have been summoned to fix.

    B. Leave the site immediately.

    C. Tell the customer that the other technician isn't as qualified as you are.

    D. Call your manager and inform him of the situation.

6. While working on a user's system, you discover a sticky note attached to the bottom of the keyboard that has their username and password written on it. The user is not around, and you need to verify that the network connection is working. What should you do?

    A. Log in, verify access, and log out.

    B. Log in and stay logged in when you are finished.

    C. Page the user.

    D. Log in and change the user's password.

7. You promised a customer that you would be out to service his problem before the end of the day but have been tied up at another site. As it now becomes apparent that you will not be able to make it to his location, what should you do?

   A. Arrive first thing in the morning.

   B. Wait until after hours and then leave a message that you were there.

   C. Call the customer and inform him of the situation.

   D. Send off an e-mail letting him know you will be late.

8. A customer stresses to you how important her company's operations are and asks how she can get hold of you after hours if there is a problem. What should you provide her?

   A. Your home phone number.

   B. Your office phone number.

   C. Your pager number.

   D. It depends on company policy.

9. A customer is trying to explain a problem with his system to you. Unfortunately, he has such a thick accent that you are unable to understand what he is saying. What should you do?

   A. Just start working on the system and looking for obvious errors.

   B. Call your supervisor.

   C. Ask that another technician be sent in your place.

   D. Apologize and find another user or manager who can help you translate.

10. You have been trying to troubleshoot a user's system all day when it suddenly becomes clear that the data is irretrievably lost. Upon informing the customer of this, he becomes so angry that he shoves you against a wall. What should you do?

    A. Shove the user back, only a little harder than he shoved you.

    B. Shove the user back, only a little easier than he shoved you.

    C. Try to calm the user down, and leave the site if you cannot.

    D. Yell for everyone in the area to come quickly.

11. Which of the following would be the best way to show the customer you are listening to her description of a complicated problem?

    A. Take notes

    B. Smile

    C. Nod

    D. Wink

12. When providing phone support, a user suddenly asks for your name. What should you do?

    A. Hang up.

    B. Give your first name.

    C. Make a joke.

    D. Ask him why he wants to know.

13. While fixing a printer problem for a customer, you notice that a network switch is behaving erratically and is likely to fail soon. How should you respond?

    A. Focus only on the printer you were called out to fix.

    B. Inform the customer of the pending switch problem.

    C. Tell the customer he needs to fix the other problem now as well.

    D. Start working on the switch and add the charge to that for the printer.

14. A customer tells you that the last technician who was there spent three hours on the phone making personal calls. What should you do with this information?

    A. Nothing.

    B. Inform your manager.

    C. Talk to the technician personally.

    D. Ask the customer to prove it.

15. You arrive at the site of a failed server to find the vice president nervously pacing and worrying about lost data. What should you do?

    A. Offer a joke to lighten things up.

    B. Downplay the situation and tell him that customers lose data every day.

    C. Keep your head down and keep looking at manuals to let him know you are serious.

    D. Inform him that you've dealt with similar situations and will let him know what needs to be done as soon as possible.

16. You have been paged to solve a problem on a desktop computer. Upon arrival, the user is nowhere around. What should you do?

    A. Have the user paged.

    B. Sit and wait for the user.

    C. Use the phone to call your manager and check in on other jobs.

    D. Come back later.

17. Which of the following traits affecting IT support is also governed by law?

    A. Punctuality

    B. Accountability

    C. Privacy

    D. Respect

18. You're temporarily filling in on phone support when a caller tells you that they are sick and tired of being bounced from one hold queue to another. He wants his problem fixed, and he wants it fixed now. What should you do?

    A. Inform him up front that you are only filling in temporarily and won't be of much help.

    B. Transfer him to another technician who handles phone calls more often.

    C. Try to solve his problem without putting him on hold or transferring him elsewhere

    D. Suggest that he call back at another time when you are not there.

19. A user on the phone does not seem to be able to explain her problem to you without using profanity for every other word. That profanity is making you unable to understand their problem. What should you do?

   A. Ask the user to refrain from the offensive language.

   B. Overlook the profanity.

   C. Hang up.

   D. Show her that you know just as many expletives as she does.

20. At the end of the day, you finish a job only to find the user you were doing it for had to leave. What should you do?

   A. Notify your manager that the user has gone.

   B. Leave a note for the user detailing what was done and how to contact you.

   C. Notify the user's manager and your own that you have finished.

   D. All of the above.

Answers to Review Questions

1. D . Close the incident only when the customer is satisfied that the solution you have given is the correct one and the problem has gone away.

2. D. Roughly half the time spent communicating should be devoted to listening.

3. D. All of these actions can indicate to the speaker that you are listening to what she is saying.

4. A. You should be courteous to all workers and inform them that a reboot is needed and coming soon. You should not reboot without first informing them, and you should not leave it up to the customer to do in your absence since this is a part of your responsibility and a problem could occur in your absence.

5. D. You should never disrespect the customer or your fellow technician. The best response is to seek guidance from your manager and let him determine how to handle the situation.

6. C . You should page the user and let her know she needs to verify access. You also should tell her that you saw the sticky note and highly recommend that she change her password to a new value and not write it down. Logging in to the system using the information you found would be violating the privacy of that user and should not be done. Further, logging in with someone else's information makes you a potential scapegoat for any data that is corrupted or missing until the user changes the password.

7. C. While calling and sending e-mail are both solutions to this situation, calling the customer provides an immediate means of communication that you know will get there. Inform the customer of the situation and offer to be out the first opportunity you can—which will hopefully be first thing in the morning.

8. D. As a representative of your company, you must always follow company policy. Most likely there is a protocol for handling after-hours calls, and typically they are routed through a service that can document the call and make sure that someone responds even when the well-liked technician is on vacation and unavailable (a downfall of relying on home phone and pager numbers).

9. D. While there is no perfect solution to problems of this type, the best solution is to find someone else who can mediate and help you understand the problem.

10. C. Physical abuse violates respect and should be avoided at all costs. You should try to calm the user down. If you cannot do this, you should leave the site immediately and not return until it is safe to do so.

11. A. Taking notes will indicate that you are paying attention to the details and attempting to fully comprehend them.

12. B. Names are often used to establish rapport and put both parties in the conversation at ease. When answering the phone and providing support, you should give your name anyway. If a user asks it, offer him your first name and continue on with diagnosing and solving the problem.

13. B. Since the switch has not yet failed, and since it is not the problem you were called to work on, you should bring it to the attention of the customer and let him decide what to do next. Under no condition should you simply start working on it or demand that it be done—perhaps the customer is aware of the situation and has ordered a replacement that will arrive the next day.

14. B. The customer is expressing a concern that she was not shown respect by a technician from your company. You should apologize and make your manager aware of the situation or concern. Unless you are a supervisor, which is not implied in the question, you should not personally talk to the technician about the issue.

15. D. You should always act with confidence and in a way similar to how you would want to be treated if you were in the customer's situation. Ignoring, downplaying, or joking about the vice president's obvious concern are very poor choices.

16. A. The situation is serious enough that you were called. You should now have the user summoned and wait for her before proceeding. You don't have enough information to proceed and it is unreasonable to expect a user who has asked for assistance to stay at their desk until you arrive (unless a specific time has been arranged beforehand).

17. C. Privacy is governed by law at several levels.

18. C. The best solution is to meet the customer's needs and solve his problem. If that means you have to summon additional help or resources, you should do so.

19. A. While likely the profanity is linked to frustration, it hinders the communication and should be eliminated. There may be circumstances where it is necessary to overlook the profanity if your request is likely to make the already upset customer even angrier, as long as you can understand what is being said. The customer is not always right, but he is always our customer.

20. D. You should perform all of these operations to sign off on the job and leave the user with a sense that his problem has been taken care of.

Working with Personal Computer Components

THE FOLLOWING COMPTIA A+ IT TECHNICIAN EXAM OBJECTIVES ARE COVERED IN THIS CHAPTER:

✓ **1.1 Install, configure, optimize and upgrade personal computer components**

- Add, remove and configure personal computer components including selection and installation of appropriate components for example:
  - Storage devices
  - Motherboards
  - Power supplies
  - Processors / CPUs
  - Memory
  - Display devices
  - Input devices (e.g. basic, specialty and multimedia)
  - Adapter cards
  - Cooling systems

✓ **1.2 Identify tools, diagnostic procedures and troubleshooting techniques for personal computer components**

- Identify and apply basic diagnostic procedures and troubleshooting techniques
  - Isolate and identify the problem using visual and audible inspections of components and minimum configuration
- Recognize and isolate issues with peripherals, multimedia, specialty input devices, internal and external storage and CPUs

- Identify the steps used to troubleshoot components (e.g. check proper seating, installation, appropriate components, settings and current driver) for example:
  - Power supply
  - Processor / CPUs and motherboards
  - Memory
  - Adapter cards
  - Display and input devices
- Recognize names, purposes, characteristics and appropriate application of tools for example:
  - Multi-meter
  - Anti-static pad and wrist strap
  - Specialty hardware / tools
  - Loop back plugs
  - Cleaning products (e.g. vacuum, cleaning pads)
- ✓ **1.3 Perform preventative maintenance of personal computer components**
  - Identify and apply common preventative maintenance techniques for personal computer components for example:
    - Display devices (e.g. cleaning, ventilation)
    - Power devices (e.g. appropriate source such as power strip, surge protector, ventilation and cooling)
    - Input devices (e.g. covers)
    - Storage devices (e.g. software tools such as DEFRAG and cleaning of optics and tape heads)
    - Thermally sensitive devices such as motherboards, CPU, adapter cards memory (e.g. cleaning, air flow)

THE FOLLOWING COMPTIA A+ REMOTE SUPPORT TECHNICIAN EXAM OBJECTIVES ARE COVERED IN THIS CHAPTER:

- ✓ **1.1 Install, configure, optimize and upgrade personal computer components**
  - Add, remove and configure display devices, input devices and adapter cards including basic input and multimedia devices

✓ **1.2 Identify tools, diagnostic procedures and troubleshooting techniques for personal computer components**

- Identify and apply basic diagnostic procedures and troubleshooting techniques, for example:
  - Identify and analyze the problem/potential problem
  - Test related components and evaluate results
  - Identify additional steps to be taken if/when necessary
  - Document activities and outcomes
- Recognize and isolate issues with display, peripheral, multimedia, specialty input device and storage
- Apply steps in troubleshooting techniques to identify problems with components including display, input devices and adapter cards

✓ **1.3 Perform preventative maintenance on personal computer components**

- Identify and apply common preventative maintenance techniques for storage devices, for example:
  - Software tools (e.g., Disk Defragmenter, Check Disk)
  - Cleaning (e.g., optics, tape heads)

THE FOLLOWING DEPOT TECHNICIAN EXAM OBJECTIVES ARE COVERED IN THIS CHAPTER:

✓ **1.1 Install, configure, optimize and upgrade personal computer components**

- Add, remove and configure internal storage devices, motherboards, power supplies, processor/CPU's, memory and adapter cards, including:
  - Drive preparation
  - Jumper configuration
  - Storage device power and cabling
  - Selection and installation of appropriate motherboard
  - BIOS set-up and configuration
  - Selection and installation of appropriate CPU

- Selection and installation of appropriate memory
- Installation of adapter cards including hardware and software/drivers
- Add, remove and configure systems

✓ **1.2 Identify tools, diagnostic procedures and troubleshooting techniques for personal computer components**

- Identify and apply basic diagnostic procedures and troubleshooting techniques, for example:
  - Identify and isolate the problem using visual and audible inspection of components and minimum configuration
- Identify the steps used to troubleshoot components (e.g. check proper seating, installation, appropriate component, settings, current driver), for example:
  - Power supply
  - Processor/CPU's and motherboards
  - Memory
  - Adapter cards
- Recognize names, purposes, characteristics and appropriate application of tools, for example:
  - Multi-meter
  - Anti-static pad and wrist strap
  - Specialty hardware/tools
  - Loop back plugs
  - Cleaning products (e.g. vacuum, cleaning pads)

✓ **1.3 Perform preventative maintenance of personal computer components**

- Identify and apply common preventative maintenance techniques, for example:
  - Thermally sensitive devices (e.g. motherboards, CPU's, adapter cards, memory)
  - Cleaning
  - Air flow (e.g. slot covers, cable routing)
  - Adapter cards (e.g. driver/firmware updates)

You cannot become A+ certified without knowing personal computers inside and out. To that end, this chapter guides you through the installation, removal, and configuration of some of the most common devices found in modern computer systems. First, though, you are presented with tips on selecting components. Then you will dive right in to removal and installation of components. Finally, you are presented with troubleshooting techniques that you can use in case removing or installing components goes awry.

Removing, Installing, and Configuring Components

There are huge economies in choosing to upgrade the components of an existing computer. Think about it. You can spend hundreds, even thousands, of dollars on a nice new, shiny computer just to get that "gig" of *random access memory (RAM)* you wanted. Why not spend just a fraction of that and upgrade the RAM of the computer you have? Not enough horsepower for that new RAM upgrade? Replace the processor or the entire motherboard as well. You've still saved an appreciable sum. There is little need these days to perform a forklift upgrade on computers built within the last few years. Most of what you can identify as a shortcoming in your computer's characteristics can be remedied by a component upgrade.

This chapter details the upgrade process for various components. Bear in mind that an upgrade not only requires that you know how to install a component but by its very nature necessitates the removal of older hardware as well. Therefore, the process presented for each component in this chapter includes removal and installation, as well as any configuration for that component after the fact.

Selecting Components

Bus Types and Characteristics

When you're selecting upgrade devices, you may have a choice of bus types to which to connect the new device. It is important to understand the benefits of the various buses so you can choose wisely.

For example, you might have a choice of an ISA or PCI internal modem, or a COM port or USB external modem. Or you might need to choose between an AGP and a PCI video card.

For external ports, USB is better and faster than both COM (legacy serial) and LPT (legacy parallel), and is further advantageous because of its seamless Plug and Play integration and its hot-plugging ability.

For internal buses, AGP is the fastest and best, but it is only for video cards. PCI is the next most desirable. ISA is old technology and nearly obsolete, and you should avoid it whenever possible. One exception might be an internal modem. Because an internal modem operates at a maximum of only 56Kbps, it would be least affected by being relegated to the ISA bus. In contrast, a video card would suffer greatly on ISA.

Table 12.1 describes the speeds and characteristics of internal expansion buses.

TABLE 12.1   Comparison of ISA, PCI, and AGP Buses

Bus	Width	Speed	Uses
ISA	8-bit or 16-bit	8MHz	Avoid if possible, or use for slow devices like modems.
PCI	32-bit	33MHz to 66MHz	Mainly non-video internal expansion boards
PCIe	Serial	Bidirectional 250MB/s per lane	Current and next-generation video and non-video cards
AGP	64-bit	66MHz to 133MHz	Current and last-generation video cards

Memory Capacity and Characteristics

When you're selecting RAM for a memory upgrade, it is important to buy the right kind. On a modern system, you must match the RAM to the motherboard's needs in the following areas:

Physical Size   168-pin or 184-DIMMs or 184-pin RIMMs and more.

Type   SDRAM, Double Data Rate (DDR) SDRAM, or Rambus RAM.

Speed   PC100, PC133, and up, as well as the DDR-based speeds discussed in Chapter 1. Faster RAM than is required will work, but not slower.

Capacity   64MB, 128MB, 1GB, for example. The characteristics of the chips that make up memory modules lead directly to the overall capacity of the modules.

When you're shopping for RAM for a system, it's important to consult the motherboard manual to find out the type of memory you need and any special rules for installation. Without the manual, you must open the case and observe the memory slots or existing memory to determine what is needed. Some motherboards have complex charts showing the combinations and positions of the modules that they allow.

Motherboards may combine one or more RAM slots into a single logical bank. A bank must be filled completely, and all the RAM installed in that set of slots should or must be completely identical in every way. Check the motherboard documentation.

System/Firmware Limitations

One of the most common problems in upgrading to a larger hard disk is the BIOS's inability to support the larger disk size. In the original IDE specification, the size limit was 540MB. This limitation was upped to 8GB with the introduction of *Logical Block Addressing (LBA)* in 1996, which the BIOS must support. A BIOS update may be available for the motherboard to enable LBA if needed.

The 8GB limitation can be broken if the BIOS supports Enhanced BIOS Services for Disk Drives, a 1998 update. Again, a BIOS update for the motherboard may enable this support if it is lacking.

If no BIOS update is available, the choices are to replace the motherboard, to use the drive at the BIOS's maximum size it can recognize, or to install a utility program (usually provided with the hard disk) that extends the BIOS to recognize the new drive. Such utilities are very useful but can introduce some quirks in the system that cannot be easily undone, so their usage is not recommended except where no other alternative exists.

Power Supply Output Capacity

A power supply has a rated output capacity in watts, and when you fill a system with power-hungry devices, you must make sure that that maximum capacity is not exceeded. A simple Internet search can yield helpful yet generic tables to help you predict the power consumption of your components. Each manufacturer generally lists power requirements with their components and on the Web.

Selecting a CPU for a Motherboard

The CPU must be compatible with the motherboard in the following ways:

Physical Connectivity   The CPU must be in the right kind of package to fit into the motherboard.

Speed   The motherboard's chipset dictates its external data-bus speed; the CPU must be capable of operating at that external speed.

Instruction Set   The motherboard's chipset contains an instruction set for communicating with the CPU; the CPU must understand the commands in that set. For example, a motherboard designed for an AMD Athlon CPU cannot accept an Intel Pentium CPU, because the instruction set is different.

Voltage   The CPU requires a certain voltage of power to be supplied to it via the motherboard's interface. This can be anywhere from +5V for a very old CPU down to under +2V for a modern one. The wrong voltage can ruin the CPU.

Motherboards, CPUs, Memory, and Adapter Cards

While it's true that the motherboard is a relatively low-dollar component, you have to consider that the motherboard you choose to replace your existing board might require a different processor, memory, or both. Even your adapter cards might need to be replaced with newer versions, such as replacing ISA with PCI or PCI with PCI Express. Therein lies the rub. You could start out expecting to spend one amount and more than double your expenses before you are finished. A little homework goes a long way. Catalog your existing components before heading down to the computer store or going online to purchase replacements.

Removing the Motherboard, CPU, Memory, and Adapter Cards

Removing any component is frequently easier than installing the same part. It's generally as simple as disconnecting any cables and leads that attach to the existing board and removing or releasing any fastening hardware. The caveat is to be very cognizant of what you are removing; everything might need to be reinstalled in corresponding locations on the new motherboard. The issue that arises most often is that the case manufacturer might not mark their leads or their markings might be cryptic.

🌐 Real World Scenario

Power Isn't Always Power

A student of mine listened intently to the lecture that day concerning motherboard jumpers, connectors, and headers. When lab time came around, he was eager to get started installing the motherboard and connecting it to the rest of the system. At the first opportunity to power up the partially built computer, the student noticed that he had no power LED, but the power supply fan seemed to be running and there was an LED on the motherboard that illuminated. He raised his hand and called me over. Upon inspection of the lead coming from the power LED on the case, I noticed he had it plugged onto a pair of pins labeled PWR ON.

The difference between this location and the one labeled PWR LED is that the LED connection sends current through the green LED on the case whenever system power is on and the PWR ON connection supplies no such current. What it does do is allow an input from the physical power button on the front of the case to the motherboard that a compatible operating system can use to suspend and resume or completely power down, depending on how long the button is held. So, no LED illuminates by connecting in this location.

Where the student went wrong was that he not only zoned out when this was mentioned during lecture, but there was no corresponding lead from the case for the PWR ON connection, so he did not see a conflict when he plugged the LED lead into that position. No other lead appeared to belong there. The book that came with the motherboard explained the difference in pretty clear detail, but when you think you have it right, it's easy not to question yourself.

Question yourself, always.

It's advised that you document the removal of all external connections to your existing motherboard. In addition, try following each lead back to its source so that you can demystify similar abbreviations in your mind, reducing the amount of guesswork required when you attach them to the new motherboard.

In Exercise 12.1, you remove a motherboard, CPU, memory, and adapter cards.

EXERCISE 12.1

Removing the Motherboard, CPU, Memory, and Adapter Cards

To remove the motherboard, CPU, memory, and adapter cards from your computer, follow these steps:

1. With the power source removed from the system, ground yourself using an approved method, such as an antistatic wrist strap. Make sure the chassis of the computer has access to the same source of ground. This step protects you and the system from electrical hazards.

2. Remove the cover from the system, exposing the internal components. Your case might have a simple mechanical latch with a finger release mechanism, or it might have machine screws that need to be removed. Do not remove the screws that hold the power supply.

3. Detach each wiring lead and harness from the motherboard, cataloging each one as you go.

4. Remove any obstructions that might hinder motherboard removal, such as component cables attached to adapter cards.

5. Gather the appropriate antistatic packaging to plan ahead for all static-sensitive components that will be reused in the future. These include adapter cards, memory modules, and the CPU.

6. Remove all adapter cards from the motherboard, storing those to be reused in antistatic packaging. Different cases have different methods of attachment, from locking latches to machine screws.

7. If you will use the same processor, now is an excellent time to remove it from the mother- board, while the motherboard is protected from static discharge. Be sure to place it in anti- static packaging. Remove the CPU's fan and heat sink assembly from the CPU and from its power connection. Modern CPU sockets use a zero insertion force (ZIF) mechanism. Release the lever on the socket to loosen the clamps that hold the CPU pins.

8. If you will use the same memory in the new motherboard, remove it now. Dual inline memory modules (DIMMs), such as double data-rate (DDR) and synchronous dynamic random access memory (SDRAM), eject the same way. Pull the release tabs away from the module, but be careful to control the force with which the module ejects, because it can hit you or become damaged.

9. Remove or release all motherboard-to-chassis retaining hardware, which includes machine screws, barbed standoffs, and the like.

10. Maneuver the motherboard off of the chassis and out of the case. Depending on the combination of motherboard and case you have, this step can be as simple as lifting straight up and out. Sometimes a slight tilting of the motherboard is necessary to clear cages or other obstructions within the case.

Installing the Motherboard, CPU, Memory, and Adapter Cards

To say installation is the reverse of removal would be oversimplifying matters, because you need to be mindful of things that were not present during removal, even if you are reinstalling the same component. Furthermore, if you are building a system from scratch, there is no reverse to reference.

A new motherboard might locate connectivity for the same function in a different place from where the old motherboard did and call it something different. Installing the same motherboard can throw you a couple of curveballs as well. It's very much like traveling the same road in the other direction. The landmarks just appear to be different. The fact is your perspective when you install a component is different from when you remove the same component. Any documentation you already had or created for yourself will be quite useful, generally.

A word of caution: Take care to observe the path between the computer's front ventilation and the power supply. Anything installed between these two extremes alters the airflow circuit. Improper routing or sloppy placement of ribbon cables and other obstructions can defeat the manufacturer's engineering design and disrupt the smooth flow of air, resulting in components overheating and possible damage to them.

Along these same lines, be sure to use a blank bracket on the backplane for any adapter card you remove from the system. Failure to do so can result in the creation of dead pockets of air that might heat up to damaging levels. Additionally, unless you are in the most controlled of lab environments, never operate the system with all or part of the cover removed. In such a state, the cooling components are unable to generate the necessary pressure to draw air across the circuitry that needs it most at an effective rate.

In Exercise 12.2, you install a motherboard, CPU, memory, and adapter cards.

Installing the Motherboard, CPU, Memory, and Adapter Cards

To install the motherboard, CPU, memory, and adapter cards in your computer, follow these steps:

1. With the power source removed from the system, ground yourself and make sure the chassis of the computer has access to the same source of ground.

2. Remove the cover from the system, exposing the internal components.

3. If you are reusing a chassis from which a different motherboard has been removed, take care to ensure that any leftover mounting hardware, especially metallic hardware, is necessary for the new motherboard. Any unnecessary hardware, such as brass screw-hole standoffs, must be removed or short circuits can result on the underside of the motherboard. One of the best methods of comparing the chassis's mounting holes to those of the motherboard is to pick each of the holes in the chassis in turn and see if you can see it through a corresponding hole in the motherboard as you hold the motherboard close to the chassis exactly above the motherboard's correct placement. If you cannot see the chassis's hole through a corresponding hole in the motherboard, make sure you remove any mounting hardware that may have been left in that location, unless it is a flush plastic support, one that does not protrude through a motherboard hole. Additionally, you might be required to add mounting hardware. Motherboards are manufactured requiring a certain amount of support under delicate circuitry. If you leave crucial support mechanisms out, you could damage the motherboard and other components as they flex and fracture. See, this is not a reverse step of the removal process.

4. If you have the most common type of modern motherboard, it is an integrated motherboard. This means most of the components that used to be added to the system afterward on adapter cards, video, network, sound, for example, are built into the motherboard. The connectors for these components are on the back edge of the board and must mate properly with the bezel on the back of the case. Visually confirm that your motherboard's connectors all have an opening in the case. If not, perhaps you have a matching interchangeable bezel that you need to change out before mounting the motherboard.

5. Place the motherboard in position over the chassis so that any protruding mounting hardware pokes through the intended motherboard holes, paying attention to how the motherboard's connectors line up with the rear of the case.

6. Use the appropriate machine screws (there are two popular styles; one is thicker with wider or coarser threads) to secure the motherboard where screw-hole standoffs were placed in the chassis.

7. If you need to install the CPU, do so now. Make sure the lever on the socket is lifted before properly orienting and inserting the CPU, and don't force the CPU to seat. Check for bent pins on the CPU or improper orientation (look for pin 1 on the chip and socket) if it doesn't drop effortlessly into place. Drop the lever to secure the CPU. Use thermal grease and install the fan and heat-sink assembly.

8. If you need to install the memory, do so now. With DIMMs, make sure the release tabs are open before inserting the module. The tabs click and lock into place when the module is inserted completely. Take care to insert the module with firm, even pressure, using equal force near the ends of the module and in the orientation that matches the module's keying.

9. If you have any expansion cards to install, do so now. These adapter cards come in a variety of slot formats, making it necessary to match the card edge to the slot in the motherboard. If you do not have a slot in the motherboard that matches your card and you require its functionality, it will be necessary to acquire an expansion card with the appropriate edge format.

10. Using any documentation you might have, which can include the manufacturer's user guide, notes you took during removal, or silk-screened labels on the motherboard, find the proper location for each loose connection coming from the case and power supply and attach it, keeping in mind that not all connectors will be attached in all systems. It's more common to have one or more lose connectors than to have them all attached. Also reattach any obstructive cables or objects affected by motherboard removal.

Configuring the Motherboard, CPU, Memory, and Adapter Cards

Modern motherboards automatically configure themselves for the processor and memory installed, among other things. Older motherboards allowed or required you to set jumpers or configure the BIOS to indicate the type of processor installed, its frequency, its clock multiplier, or core and I/O voltage levels. Some also required you to manually configure the amount of RAM you installed, or the full amount might not be recognized. Methods of configuring these parameters vary with the motherboard, but the newer boards detect all of this and more automatically.

Even newer adapter cards, on the other hand, might require configuration. However, most can be recognized automatically by a Plug and Play operating system. In other words, the installation of device drivers is handled automatically. Consult the documentation provided with your adapter for additional configuration requirements or options. The more specialized the adapter, the more likely it will come with specialty configuration utilities.

Storage Devices

The removal and installation of storage devices, such as hard drives, floppy drives, CD/DVD drives, and tape drives, is pretty straightforward. There really isn't any deviation in the process of installing or exchanging the hardware. Fortunately, with today's operating systems, there is little to no configuration required for such devices. The *Plug and Play BIOS* and operating system work together to recognize such components. However, you still have to *partition* and *format* out-of-the-box hard drives before they will allow the installation of the operating system. Nevertheless, today's operating systems allow for a pain-free partition/format/install experience by handling the entire process if you let them.

Removing Storage Devices

Continuing the earlier discussion about removal usually being easier than installation, consider the fact that most people could destroy a house, perhaps not safely enough to ensure their well-being, but they don't have to know the intricacies of construction to start smashing away. Building a house, on the other hand, is an art of which very few people are capable. Similarly, many could figure out how to remove a storage device, as long as they can get into the case to begin with, but only a few could start from scratch and successfully install one without tutelage.

In Exercise 12.3, you remove an internal storage device.

This section details the removal of internal storage devices, and the section titled "Installing Storage Devices" details their installation. Be aware that external storage devices exist, but today's external storage devices are USB- and FireWire-attached, making them completely Plug and Play. Only the software preparation of external hard drives is a consideration, but the same procedure outlined for internal devices works for external devices as well.

EXERCISE 12.3

Removing an Internal Storage Device

To remove an internal storage device from your computer, follow these steps:

1. With the power source removed from the system, ground yourself and the computer to the same source of ground.

2. Remove the cover from the system, exposing the internal components.

3. Targeting the storage device you wish to remove, unplug all connections from the device. These include data and power connections as well as any other connections, such as audio connections to the sound card or motherboard. The beveled Molex power connectors can be difficult to remove, but they fit very tightly, so don't worry about how hard they seem to be to remove. There is no clip to release. Do, however, make sure to grip the connector, not the wires.

4. Gather the appropriate antistatic packaging to plan ahead for all static-sensitive components that will be reused in the future, including any adapter cards that the storage device plugs into.

5. Remove any obstructions that might hinder device removal, such as component cables attached to adapter cards or adapter cards themselves, storing those to be reused in antistatic packaging.

6. Remove related adapter cards from the motherboard, storing those to be reused in antistatic packaging.

EXERCISE 12.3 *(continued)*

7. Remove the machine screws holding the storage device to the chassis. These could be on the side of the device or on the bottom.

8. Some devices, especially hard drives because they have no front access from the case, pull out of the chassis toward the rear of the case, while others, such as CD/DVD and floppy drives, generally pull out from the front. A gentle nudge from the rear of the device starts it on its way out the front. Go ahead and remove the device from the case. If you discover other components that obstruct the storage device's removal, repeat step 5.

Installing Storage Devices

An obvious difference among storage devices is their form factor. This is the term used to describe the physical dimensions of a storage device. Common form-factor characteristics are these:

- 3.5 inches wide vs. 5.25 inches wide
- Half height vs. full height vs. 1 inch high and more
- Any of the laptop specialty form factors

You will need to figure out if you have an open bay in the chassis to accommodate the form factor of the storage device you want to install. Adapters exist that allow a device of small size to fit into a larger bay. For obvious reasons, the converse is not also true.

In Exercise 12.4, you install an internal storage device.

EXERCISE 12.4

Installing an Internal Storage Device

To install an internal storage device in your computer, follow these steps:

1. With the power source removed from the system, ground yourself and the computer to the same source of ground.

2. Remove the cover from the system, exposing the internal components.

3. Locate an available bay for your component, paying attention to your device's need for front access. If you do not see one, look around; some cases provide fastening points near the power supply or other open areas of the case. If you still do not see one, investigate the possibility of sacrificing a rarely or never used device to make room.

4. Remove any obstructions that might hinder device installation, such as component cables attached to adapter cards or adapter cards themselves, storing those to be reused in antistatic packaging.

5. Insert the storage device into the bay, keeping in mind that some insert from the rear of the bay and some from the front.

6. Line up the screw holes in the device with the holes in the bay. Note that many devices rarely insert as far as they can before lining up with the chassis's holes. So don't be surprised when pushing the device all the way into the bay results in misalignment. Other devices that require front access stop themselves flush with the front of the case, and still others require you to secure them while holding them flush.

7. Use at least two screws on one side of the device. This keeps the device from sliding in the bay, as well as from rotating, which happens when you use only one screw or one screw on each side. If the opposite side is accessible, go ahead and put at least one screw in the other side. Most devices allow for as many as four screws per side, but eight screws are not necessary in the vast majority of situations.

8. Connect the data cable from the device to the adapter card or motherboard header. Advanced technology attachment (ATA) devices, such as those that are designated as IDE drives, which include compatible hard drives and CD/DVD drives, use a 40-pin connector. Floppy drives and some tape backup drives that connect through the floppy subsystem use a 34-pin connector. They look the same except for the three rows of two pins that differentiate them. Note that if you use the master/slave and not the cable-select feature of IDE drives on the same chain, it does not matter which device connects to which connector on the cable. However, with floppy drives, drive A: must always be attached to the connector after the twist in the cable.

9. Attach a power connector from the power supply to the device, bearing in mind that there are two connector styles that are not very close in appearance. You should have no trouble telling them apart. Be sure to fully insert the connector. Watch out for the smaller connector. See "Do You Smell Something?" below.

🌐 **Real World Scenario**

Do You Smell Something?

In 1990, I started a PC sales and repair business. Those were the days when you could build a computer from scratch for relatively little expense and sell it with a great markup and still come in way under the prices of the name-brand systems.

One customer was especially price conscious. In those days, a floppy drive was not the afterthought that it is today, both in use and price. You needed a floppy drive and could actually save a bit of money if you were buying quite a few units, just by opting for a cheaper model. This customer was buying 45 computers. So, one of the corners that was cut to keep the invoice amount down was floppy drive quality. We went with a brand that I had never heard of but that my distributor listed as the cheapest. How bad could it be? How much of a difference could there have been between brands and models? I found out. The customer didn't.

The cheaper drive worked just like any other, from the perspective of the user, but the difference showed while we were building the systems. The manufacturer scrimped in the production of the power connector. Where most manufacturers create a casing to receive the power supply's connector with little chance of inserting the connector upside down, this manufacturer allowed the four pins of the connector to protrude in a nondescript manner without any keying or guidance for the power supply's connector.

Unlike the well-keyed, larger Molex power connectors used on hard drives and CD/DVD drives, the Berg connector used with floppy drives can be inserted upside down rather easily if there is no well-thought-out receptacle for it. An upside-down connector causes no problems when the power cable is attached to the system. It causes no problems when the system is turned on. It does, however, "fry" the floppy's circuit board the first time the drive is accessed, which is during the boot-up process, emitting the telltale aroma of burning plastic.

When one of my assistants flipped the connector on one of the floppy drives, it wasn't long before I realized someone learned a valuable lesson. The lesson was so clear you could smell it. Everyone smelled it. My assistant knew there was a right way and a wrong way to plug the connector, but it was just too easy. Out of 45 floppies, we were lucky to have lost only one. It could have been a lot worse.

Configuring Storage Devices

Aside from software configuration to partition and format a hard drive, there really is very little to be done post-installation with storage devices. The fact is, for non–hard-drive ATA devices, such as CD-ROM and DVD-ROM drives, the only setting is the jumper or jumpers that configure them as cable select, master, slave, or stand-alone, only one of which can be chosen per drive. For floppy drives, most BIOS configuration utilities allow the swapping of the A: and B: drives for booting purposes. Other than that, there's relatively nothing you can do to alter the way a floppy drive functions, although you might find that you have to specify the capacity of the disks your drive can handle. 1.44MB is often the default.

For a hard drive, after you install the hardware, the BIOS recognizes what you have installed and puts it to use. However, you must supply the operating system and make the drive bootable, if it is so desired. As mentioned earlier in this chapter, today's operating systems take care of all software setup tasks in a virtually unattended fashion. Nevertheless, it doesn't hurt for you to be aware of what is happening behind the scenes, especially when troubleshooting. It's essentially the same process as the one used on the very first hard drives used with IBM's PCs in the eighties.

The first step is to partition the drive. The FDISK command-line utility was and still can be used for this purpose. Partitioning a hard drive marks a contiguous stretch of the drive for the purpose of designating one or more drive letters. One physical drive can be made up of a single logical drive letter or many logical drives, each represented by a different letter. You can create one or more primary partitions and a single extended partition. Primary partitions can be made bootable and are represented by a single drive letter. Extended partitions are not bootable and can be further subdivided and represented by one or more drive letters.

The next step is to format the drive at the operating system level. The FORMAT commandline utility can be used for this task. This type of formatting is not to be confused with what is known as low-level formatting. IDE hard drives are low-level formatted by the manufacturer. Low-level formatting must be performed even before a drive can be partitioned. In low-level formatting, the drive controller and the drive meet for the very first time and learn to work together. Because IDE drives have their controllers integrated into the drive, lowlevel formatting is a factory process with these drives. Low-level formatting is not operating system dependent.

The formatting that is performed after partitioning lays down the logical data structures of the operating system within the boundaries of the logical drives created in the partitions. Structures such as the clusters or allocation units are created during the formatting. The root directory and the file table are created during this process. Only after formatting can a drive letter be accessed by the operating system. Only after formatting and transferring the necessary system files can a logical drive be used to boot the computer. In other words, form atting a hard drive creates the filesystem that the operating system uses to store and retrieve data. As a result, this is when you decide which filesystem to use. Examples are FAT, FAT32, and NTFS. Most operating systems offer the choice of one or two filesystems, not all of them.

Power Supplies

Sometimes power supplies fail. Sometimes you grow out of your power supply and require more wattage than it can provide. Often, it is just as cost effective to buy a whole new case with the power supply included rather than dealing with the power supply alone. However, when you consider the fact that you must move everything from the old case to the new one, replacing the power supply becomes an attractive proposition. Doing so is not a difficult task.

Regardless of which path you choose, you must make sure that the power connection of the power supply matches that of the motherboard to be used. A new power supply with the single 20-pin ATX power connector is not compatible with a motherboard that has only the older P8/P9 connectors, although there are adapters that allow interconnection. The very latest 24-pin PCI Express ATX power supply connection can also be adapted to a motherboard with the 20-pin ATX connector.

Exercise 12.5 details the process to remove an existing power supply. Use the reverse of this process to install the new power supply. Just keep in mind that you might need to procure the appropriate adapter if a power supply that matches your motherboard can no longer be found. There is no post-installation configuration for the power supply, so there is nothing to cover along those lines. Many power supply manufacturers have utilities on their websites that allow you to perform a presale configuration, so that you are assured of obtaining the most appropriate power supply for your power requirements.

EXERCISE 12.5

Removing a Power Supply

To remove a power supply from your computer, follow these steps:

1. With the power source removed from the system, ground yourself and the computer to the same source of ground.

2. Remove the cover from the system, exposing the internal components.

3. After locating the power supply, which can come in a variety of formats and appear on the left or right side of the case, follow all wiring harnesses from the power supply to their termini, disconnecting each one.

4. Remove any obstructions that appear as if they might hinder removal of the power supply.

5. Using the dimensions of the power supply, detectable from the inside of the case, note which machine screws on the outside of the case correspond to the power supply.

6. Remove the screws that you identified as those that hold the power supply in place. Be aware that the power supply is not light weight, so you must support it as you remove the final couple of screws.

7. Maneuver the power supply past any obstructions that did not have to be removed, and pull the power supply out of the case.

Display Devices

In the early days of the PC, when DOS was all you had, you could boot the system with no working monitor and make your way to a predefined location in the interface, just by watching drive activity and listening for audible cues. This ability continued into the early stages of Windows, because DOS was still in charge, so it was a simple feat to use the keyboard combinations to bypass the need for a mouse and the ability to see the cursor. If you were unlucky enough to choose a screen resolution or refresh rate that was unsupported by the hardware, you could key your way to the utility to change back to standard video settings. These days, booting up in normal mode, as Microsoft calls it, you're lucky if you get logged in without a monitor. On the bright side, you do have safe mode today, so working without a monitor is less likely to occur. VGA mode is also very helpful for correcting bad video settings. Whereas safe mode uses a Microsoft-generic VGA driver to boot the system. VGA mode uses the installed driver and resets a low resolution and refresh rate (640x480 with 8-bit color) that can then be reset.

The fact is, even as more and more display options are developed, dependency on them increases, not because there are more choices, but simply because modern software dictates it. Just in the basic class of monitors there exists a plethora of options, from the classic CRT to the LCD. Indeed, as television makes its way onto the computer monitor, it brings with it plasma and HDTV as well. Other less-popular options exist as well, including the antiquated use of a standard TV as a monitor, which isn't so bad, because the standard TV has improved quite a bit in recent years. Other display devices can be presentation related, such as the modern projector, or entertainment related, such as virtual-reality goggles.

Removing Display Devices

To remove any modern display device from a computer, simply follow its cables from the device to where they connect. Disconnect the cable or cables that are not power cables. Standard D-sub connectors found on most VGA monitors and their predecessors routinely have thumbscrews that might or might not be secured. If the connector does not pull right off of the computer's video adapter, unscrew the thumbscrews to release the connector.

Component video connectors use either a nonlocking RCA plug or a locking BNC connector. Simply pull the RCA plug from the receptacle. BNC connectors are spring-loaded and have a catch that locks them into place. Push the connector into the video adapter against the spring and twist counterclockwise past the catch. Releasing the pressure on the connector, pull the cable straight out from the adapter.

Installing Display Devices

If the cable isn't already plugged into the video adapter, it's a bit tougher to figure out where it goes. It takes more than just being able to trace a cable back to its connection point. It takes being able to recognize a video adapter's connector when you see it. Modern VGA technologies and the digital standards that came before them commonly use a D-sub connector that started out as a standard 9-pin interface in the days of digital monitors, such as monochrome, CGA, and EGA, the female connector on the adapter and the male on the cable. The gender pairing remained the same for VGA, but more pins were required, so the connector had to change. It appears to be roughly the same form factor as its predecessor, but upon closer inspection you realize it has three rows of pins, not two. In fact, it is a high-density 15-pin connector, known as a DE15. This connector is used only for computer video.

Installing a display device, whether it be a monitor, projector, or any of a host of other possibilities, is performed the same way for each type of connector. Find the female connector that matches the male on the end of the cable, and you find your connecting point. Simply remain mindful of any keying that might exist (RCA plugs have no keying), line up the connector, if necessary, and insert the device. If any thumbscrews exist, tighten them down, if desired. For a BNC connector, push straight in past the keying structure, which is also the catch that keeps the connector seated, turn the connector clockwise until it stops, and release.

There are other considerations you should keep in mind while installing a display device. Always pay attention to ergonomics. Make sure the placement of the device will not adversely affect the posture or comfort of the user. Do not place the device on an unstable surface. Many such devices are heavy enough to warrant consideration because of their weight alone. The display device can interfere with other electronic devices, as well as be interfered with by them and by magnetic fields. The device will need to be relatively close to the computer. While extension cables exist, they can be costly and might degrade the video quality, especially if they are not manufactured to exacting standards. Do your best to limit cable use to the original video cable for primary monitors and to a well-manufactured extension for presentation display devices, such as projectors, which often must be mounted away from the computer.

Configuring Display Devices

While there is not a great deal to consider in the realm of configuring a display device, because most of the configuration is performed on the adapter, not the monitor or similar device, these components are not completely without configuration. The following list contains the primary settings that you might be able to configure on a standard display device. Terms in parentheses are synonyms:

Brightness   The level of intensity by which the dot phosphors are made to glow.

Contrast   The ratio between the light intensity of true black and true white. Lower contrast reduces a screen's sharpness, while higher contrast increases it. See Exercise 12.6 for a quick and effective method of adjusting brightness and contrast.

Horizontal/Vertical (H/V) Position (Centering)   The left/right and up/down movement of the unaltered image within the viewable area of the screen. The ideal adjustment is for 100 percent of the software image (in pixels) to appear on the viewable screen (in dot phosphors). If this is not possible, once the image is centered, spacing might need to be adjusted.

> Think of the difference between the image and the viewable screen in reference to shooting a photograph. You can swivel the camera up and down or to the side and cut off part of your subject, but that doesn't mean the subject changed. Similarly, just because the image is partially off the screen doesn't mean that the video adapter has changed its feed to the monitor.

H/V Size (Spacing)   The number of dot phosphors it takes to display an image of a given number of pixels. Again, you can change how the image uses the viewable screen without changing what the video adapter sends to the monitor. Made too large, part of the centered image can disappear along all four edges of the viewable screen.

Pincushion   A type of distortion in which the edges of the display bend in a convex or concave manner. The adjustment attempts to return the image to a rectangular appearance and affects the vertical edges more than the horizontal ones. Overadjustment can lead to bulging edges.

Pin Balance   The balance of the convex or concave bends seen with the pincushion affect. Uneven pin balance can result in one side of the image being concave while the other side is convex, limiting the effectiveness of pincushion adjustment.

Trapezoidal (Keystone)   As in geometry, a trapezoidal image defines one that has two parallel sides, the horizontal sides, and two nonparallel sides, the vertical sides. This adjustment attempts to return the rectangular appearance of the image. If the top edge is narrower than the bottom edge, overadjustment can make the bottom edge narrower than the top edge.

Parallelogram (Key Balance)   The geometric state of both pairs of sides having parallel opposites but the vertical sides lean in the same direction. Contrast this with the trapezoidal effect in which the leaning sides lean in opposite directions. Therefore, neither the top nor bottom of the image is wider than the other; they simply slide in opposite directions from each other.

Tilt (Rotation)   The number of degrees from 0 that a potentially otherwise flawless image has rotated in the viewable screen, possibly clipping the corners of the image from view. Rotation can be thought of as to the left or to the right.

H/V Moiré   More of an incompatibility of patterns than a disturbance. Moiré is a distortion characterized by an effect that manifests itself as wavy lines and is often caused by interference between the image's pattern and that of the physical dot phosphors that make up the viewable screen. Adjustment attempts to reduce the interference, producing less of a perceived visual distortion. Images with less-patterned appearances might need no adjustment at all. These patterns tend to be unaffected by adjustment for more conflicting patterns, however.

Color Temperature   A term with a basis in physics that is used to describe the colors that are used to represent the signals coming from the video adapter. Common choices range from around 5000 Kelvin (K) to 9300K and higher. Adjusting the color temperature allows on-screen colors to more closely match printed colors. When screen whites have a printed red component, adjust the color temperature lower, so they appear redder on screen. When screen whites have a printed blue component, adjust the color temperature higher. When in doubt and when not attempting to match to printed output, choose 6500K, which is the color temperature most often used in the design of web graphics and electronics for video and photography, such as cameras and DVDs. The term *temperature* is used because of a specific relationship between the change in surface temperature of a black radiating body and the corresponding change in color of the surface.

H/V Linearity   The ability of a monitor to display geometric shapes anywhere on the screen without distortion.

H/V Convergence   The synchronization of the red, green, and blue components of the displayed image. You might need to adjust the convergence if you see ghosting of the primary colors around text and graphics, meaning that the red, green, or blue signals have wandered and stand out from the others.

Phase (Hue or Tint)   The emphasis of a particular portion of the color spectrum on the image, or the lack thereof. For a standard image, the phase adjustment should be centered for best results. Otherwise, one end of the phase adjustment adds a pinkish-purple overtone and the other end adds green.

Landing   Color irregularities in a corner of the viewable screen. With some monitors, you just have to live with that irritating discolored corner, but others give you controls to help reduce this distortion.

Degauss   Not really a configuration, but worth mentioning. CRT display devices use magnetic fields to guide or bend the cathode rays to the exact intended point on the viewable screen. External magnetic influences can magnetize the shadow mask, a perforated metal sheet that prevents stray electrons from exciting the wrong dot phosphors, causing discrepancies between where the ray is aimed and where it hits. Image distortion and "dirty" colors are common results. Degaussing, which most modern monitors and CRT-based televisions do each time they are turned on, reduces the magnetic influence on the shadow mask, improving the appearance of the image. A more thorough manual degaussing can be performed with the monitor on or off, but the built-in degauss feature requires that the monitor be on. Repeated power cycling to degauss is not recommended and can damage the component. You should wait 20 minutes or more between manual degaussing attempts.

EXERCISE 12.6

Adjusting Brightness and Contrast

Most of us can eyeball these settings and do a great job with it, but this exercise gives you a quick and easy way to reliably adjust these two important controls for optimal effect. To adjust brightness and contrast for your CRT monitor, follow these steps:

1. Boot up your computer and display your Windows Desktop. Make sure your monitor has been on for at least a half hour.

2. Start with the brightness adjustment. For this, you'll need a pure black image. One way to make sure the black covers the entire image area is to change your Desktop color to black. Choose Start ➢ Control Panel ➢ Display to open the Display Properties dialog.

3. On the Desktop tab, click the down-arrow beside the representation of the Desktop color in the Color field. Choose black from the color palette. Click OK.

4. Maximize the brightness control and then reduce it until the black of the image matches the black at the edge of the physical screen.

5. To adjust contrast, start with it at the maximum setting.

6. Open a screen with a plain-white background. A blank word processing document with default settings is a good choice. Notepad or Microsoft Word generally satisfies this step.

7. Reduce the contrast until the white area on your screen begins to look off-white or gray.

8. Gradually increase the contrast until the white area looks pure again. Generally, the final contrast setting is greater than 80 percent of maximum.

Input Devices

Of the large list of input devices on the market, the keyboard and the mouse are the two that almost every computing device today has installed. Many users with computers that have built-in pointing devices utilize an external mouse for the sheer convenience of it. Many laptop users employ docking stations with a semipermanent keyboard and mouse attached. Numerous personal digital assistant (PDA) users own an optional folding keyboard for when it's time to really get down to business. Most users who have never seen the inside of a computer are capable of finding where the keyboard and mouse plug into their system. Today, the color coding of these device connectors assists even the most novice of individuals in connecting these basic input devices.

For some users, however, the keyboard and mouse are just the tip of the iceberg. Depending on a user's primary application, she might find that a pen, touch-screen monitor, or digitizing tablet is the best input device for her needs, obviating the need for a mouse under most circumstances.

Still other users with very specific applications might require a secondary input device, such as a barcode reader or biometric scanner, in addition to their mouse. Input devices that do not require the user to use his hands in such an interactive manner are, for example, web cameras and other digital video and still cameras, microphones, and even page scanners. Page scanners are discussed in more detail in Chapters 7 and 15.

Technically, any device that is capable of externally altering the contents of the computer or a network to which it is connected could be considered an input device. Strictly speaking, however, this classification is more intuitive than that. For example, let's say you're playing a video game on your computer. You're tired of using cumbersome key sequences on your keyboard, an input device, to control your character. You try the mouse, another input device, but you don't have the precision in your movement that you need. You run down to the local computer store and procure a USB joystick, yet another input device. It's hard to question whether any of these three devices are input devices. It's obvious that they are.

Installing Standard Input Devices

There's little doubt we live in a USB world. Sure, FireWire is a readily available technology, but since USB 2.0 with speeds of 480Mbps came onto the market, it's hard to justify the coexistence of a similar technology with no outstanding advantages. USB is simply the motherboard manufacturer's choice. This industry support has led to a consumer market that accepts USB as the de facto standard.

The fact is it is conceivable that every input device you connect to your computer could be USB attached. Even though you have a mini-DIN keyboard and mouse connector, you can use a USB keyboard and mouse, in addition or instead. See the real-world scenario titled "How Many of Those Do You Need?" With USB, you are able to daisy-chain hubs in such a way as to add ports when you need them. While there is a technical limit of 127 USB devices connected to any USB controller, you would not be satisfied with the performance from that many devices. Still, the average user could never dream of adding enough USB devices to cause a problem.

Installing your input device is easy, regardless of the type of interface it has. All interfaces are keyed so that they will only connect the right way. The following list contains information on and tips for hooking up the most popular types of connectors:

DIN and Mini-DIN   These circular connectors are keyed to plug in only one way in the 360 degrees you have to choose from. Usually there are markings, such as an arrow pointing toward the end of the connector and embossed in the position corresponding to "up." The problem is that many systems have the motherboard in sideways, so which way is up? The good news is that you can place the connector on the interface and gently apply force as if to insert the connector as you turn the plug in one direction. Before you make a complete circle with the connector, you should feel it catch and insert farther. At that point, push the connector until it is fully seated. There is no locking mechanism, so you are finished.

USB and FireWire   These connectors are keyed to go in only one way. Markings on the USB Type A connector that plugs into a computer system tell you which way is up, but trial and error works well also. FireWire connectors are shaped in such a way that you would have little trouble matching the plug to the receptacle. In either case these plugs insert until they stop, and there is no locking mechanism for either one.

D-subminiature Connectors   Referred to as D-sub, these classic connectors were on the original IBM Personal Computer. The *D* refers to the shape of the connector, which is beveled on two of the four corners. Subminiature is an old label, because today these connectors are rather large by comparison. There are five broad classifications that relate to the shell size— DA, DB, DC, DD, and DE. Figure 12.1 shows the relative size of these connectors and the standard number of pins.

Note that these five classifications do not imply pin count without a numerical suffix. Unfortunately, all five classifications get referred to incorrectly as DB connectors. Most likely this is because the original PC had only the DB25 connectors, male and female, for the serial and parallel ports, respectively. The misconception was that *DB* referred to the overall D-sub style only, not the size. However, only those that measure about 1.5 inches by about a third of an inch are truly DB connectors.

If you have a computer today, it's almost guaranteed that it has at least one D-sub connector. The serial port is a 9-pin male DE, known as a DE9M. The printer port is a DB25F, *F* for female. The VGA video adapter interface is known as a DE15F, because it is the same size as the DE9 connector. The DE15 is often incorrectly referred to as a DB15-HD. The *HD* means high density, because 15 pins are squeezed in where only 9 used to be.

This effort to add to the name to imply density verifies the fact that many do not realize the size is in the name already, and there is no DB15 connector at all. The 15-pin game port, which looks the same as an old 15-pin network interface, is known as a DA15F. So calling a video interface a DE15F differentiates it from the game port connector just fine.

FIGURE 12.1   D-subminiature connectors

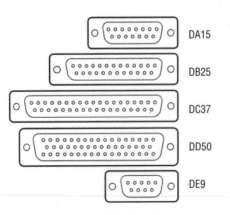

🌐 Real World Scenario

How Many of Those Do You Need?

When I decided to try out a Bluetooth keyboard and mouse on my home computer, the technology was still a bit new. As a result, the manufacturer might not have gotten everything quite right. What this meant to me was long frustrating sessions every time I rebooted my PC characterized by me trying to get the receiver to communicate with the keyboard and mouse. Finally, I broke down and added a PS/2-style mouse that I had lying around, so that I could at least click around on the utilities to attempt to bring the other input devices back to life. I'm a very patient person, it seems. Had I been less patient, I would have had two keyboards as well. Had I been even less patient, I would have had only one keyboard and one mouse—the "Bluetooth twins" would have been in pieces two floors below.

Anyway, one day I was pressing away on all the connect buttons—on the receiver, on the keyboard, on the mouse—exercising my usual level of self-control, thereby taking 10 times as long to achieve the same result. When it finally sunk in that these Bluetooth players were not going to be cooperating today, I reached under the desk to the top of my mini-tower case, where my backup wired mouse was. As I was tooling around with the backup mouse, my inquisitive youngest daughter, who had entered my home office unbeknownst to me, caught my peripheral vision as she leaned down to see what I was doing under the desk. Now looking me straight in the eye as I froze to figure out what she was up to, she asked earnestly, "How many of those do you need?"

The point is you really can have multiple input devices of the same type connected in various ways to the same computer. I could have added a USB mouse if I really wanted to blow my little girl's mind.

D-sub connectors are keyed by their shape and usually have a locking mechanism, such as thumbscrews or very small slotted screws. Push them straight onto the receptacle and tighten them down, if not tightening them might lead to accidental disconnection.

Configuring Input Devices

Configuration of an input device varies with the device type. There is no configuration for most keyboards beyond changing character maps for different languages or applications. The basic mouse gives you the ability to change its behavior through the Mouse applet in Control Panel.

In Exercise 12.7, we will show you how to adjust mouse behavior.

Specialty input devices might require additional configuration, from device driver installation to utility installation for configuration of features. Consult your input device's documentation or manufacturer's website for configuration specifics.

EXERCISE 12.7

Adjusting Mouse Behavior

If you obtain a mouse with special buttons and extra wheel functions, you get drivers and utilities that affect what you see in the Mouse applet in Control Panel. Regardless of the device you use, there are certain features all brands and styles of mouse have in common. To adjust some of the basic settings for your mouse, follow these steps:

1. Open Control Panel by the method of your choosing. For instance, Start ≻ Control Panel.

2. Find the icon labeled Mouse and double-click it.

3. Click on the tab labeled Pointer Options, an example of which is shown in the following screen shot.

4. In the Motion section, adjust the pointer speed slider depending on how far you want to have to move the physical mouse device compared to how far the pointer moves. Slower settings cause you to have to move a standard mouse farther on the physical surface or roll the ball of a trackball more than faster settings.

5. Also in the Motion section, check the Enhanced Pointer Precision box for better control when making small movements with the mouse. The mouse is able to stop more precisely on the screen when the interface detects the physical device slowing down or stopping.

6. In the Snap To section, check the box to cause the mouse pointer to jump to the default button in a dialog box whenever one pops up on the screen. In rare circumstances, this might not be the desired functionality, but in general this saves time over the course of a computing session.

7. In the Visibility section, check the Display Pointer Trails box to cause the on-screen mouse cursor to display residual cursors as you move away from a location in the screen. Certain monitors, such as some LCDs, have trouble displaying a mouse cursor that moves rapidly on a regular basis. This setting gives you more of a visual area for the cursor, making it harder to lose. The slider allows you to adjust exactly how large of an area the average moving cursor takes up on the screen.

8. The middle feature in the Visibility section, when enabled, hides the mouse cursor when you start typing. Many users position the I-bar mouse cursor where they intend to type and click to produce the blinking text cursor at that position. If the I-bar cursor remains, it obstructs the user's view of what she is typing. This setting prevents the frustration that ensues.

9. If you still seem to lose the mouse cursor, despite all other settings, the last feature in the Visibility section helps with that. Enabling the use of the Ctrl key to locate the cursor produces a reverse water-drop pattern with the cursor in the center, guiding your eyes to its location. To use it once it is enabled, press the Ctrl key and nothing else. When you release the Ctrl key, you see the animated beacon. The feature does not activate when you use the Ctrl key in sequence with other keys, so you do not have to worry about the signal becoming a hindrance.

Removing Input Devices

The removal of input devices is really quite simple and the reverse of their installation. For DIN, USB, and FireWire, simply grasp the connector firmly and pull straight out away from the receptacle. USB tends to be the easiest to remove because it offers very little resistance, only what is necessary to keep the connector from falling out on a regular basis. Each of the non-fastened connectors removes with very little effort.

D-sub connectors and other such fastening connectors remove quite easily as well. The difference is that you must ensure the connector is not fastened before attempting to disconnect it. Earlier connectors and today's do-it-yourself connectors are more likely to have small slotted screw heads that you need to use a screwdriver on, as opposed to the more convenient thumbscrew design of more modern connectors. While the thumbscrew can be tightened and loosened blindly, in most cases the slotted screw head almost forces you to move the system around so you can gain clearance to the screw to be tightened or loosened. Most people have trouble unless they can actually see the head of the screw because it's too easy for the screwdriver to slip if it is not straight.

Cooling Systems

Modern cooling systems that the technician might be faced with installing or exchanging range from the classic heat sink, which is fairly straightforward to install and remove, to the newer liquid-cooled systems that have multiple components and the danger of mixing water with electricity if you are not careful. Somewhere in the middle is today's ubiquitous active heat sink, which combines the classic passive heat sink with a powered fan to force airflow onto and away from the component being cooled. In addition, the technician needs to be comfortable adding and replacing secondary cooling components, such as chassis fans that more actively bring air into and out of the case through preengineered pathways.

Removing Cooling Systems

If you have a fan that fails, a good system alerts you to this fact and, when you are not around to be alerted, shuts the system down at a configurable threshold to prevent damage. Active and passive heat sinks often clip onto the socket they are designed for, using a spring-loaded approach to remain tightly interfaced to the surface of the component they cool. As a result, the technician must be aware that there can be multiple ways to orient the heat sink over the component and still secure the heat sink. Not all orientations always provide the same coverage for the component to be cooled. Poor coverage can result in component failure or damage.

For those heat sinks that have a metal band running through the middle of them with a clip on each end, the secret to releasing the clips secured to tabs on the socket or other location is to make sure you have the right tool for the job. Some implementations allow you to use your fingers to grip the larger end and push down to clear the tab, swing the clip away from the tab, and allow the clip's spring action to maneuver the clip up and away from the tab. At that point, the other end of the clip on the other side of the heat sink comes off when you lift up the heat sink from the component, angling it in the direction of the clip that's still attached.

In the case of harder-to-release clips with no finger holds, they are most often designed so that a small slotted screwdriver or, less often, a small Philips-head screwdriver can be inserted into the top portion of one end of the clip, offering you leverage to push down and pivot the clip away from the tab. You must take care to ensure that there is such a receptacle for one of these tools and that you use the right tool. Otherwise, slippage of the tool can result in a fatally wounded motherboard or other circuit board.

To remove chassis fans, you generally need to unscrew the fan from the chassis at two or more corners of the fan assembly. Better cases provide a snap-in carrier for these fans that you screw the fan into from the other side, making the simple removal of the carrier necessary in order to gain access to the screw heads. In the case of all actively powered cooling devices, you must remove the power connector from the motherboard or power-supply connector in order to remove it completely from the system. In general, you will find it easier to disconnect the power before demounting the unit.

The best liquid cooling systems provide a mechanism that acts somewhat like the multi-stage airlocks between hazardous and safe areas. What this means is that during the disconnection of the fluid lines, there is a valve mechanism that causes the fluid to retreat and be cut off from the end of the connecting interface, preventing even a single drip. Still, all power should be off and removed from the system before doing anything with fluid-filled conduits.

Many liquid cooling systems have sensors that allow them to shut the system down when they detect even a minute leak in the pathway for the liquid. Follow the manufacturer's specification for removal and installation of liquid cooling systems.

Installing Cooling Systems

Exercise 12.8 steps you through the process of installing a standard heat sink on a CPU. Such a component might be active, in that it has a powered fan on top of it, but the installation process is the same, with the exception of adding power to the situation. Heat sinks for other components install more easily in general.

EXERCISE 12.8

Installing a CPU Heat Sink

To install an active or passive heat sink on a CPU, follow these steps:

1. With the power source removed from the system, ground yourself and the computer to the same source of ground.

2. Remove the cover from the system, exposing the internal components.

3. If you are replacing an existing heat sink, follow the narrative in the "Removing Cooling Systems" section after removing any obstructions that might hinder removal and installation.

4. Position the heat sink over the CPU. If necessary, reorient the heat sink until the flat, smooth bottom of the heat sink fully covers the CPU's surface and the clips on the metal band running through the heat sink are in position over corresponding tabs in the socket. There are only four positions for the heat sink to square up with the CPU; two of these might appear to line up the clips with the tabs; only one of those two might also position the heat sink completely over the CPU. Pay attention to detail on this step. If, despite your best effort, you cannot seem to satisfy all of these criteria simultaneously, consider the possibility that you might have the wrong heat sink for the type of processor you have.

5. Put just a drop of thermal grease in the center of the surface of the CPU. The pressure from securing the heat sink will cause the grease to distribute thinly and evenly over the surface. There is no need to spread the grease around.

6. Using the orientation you discovered to be the best, hook the plainer clip on the end of the metal band running through the heat sink to its tab first. This clip does not have a finger or screwdriver hold on it, so it must be attached before the heat sink is in place.

7. Gently ease the mating surface of the heat sink onto the surface of the CPU, keeping your eye and possibly a finger on the attached clip, so that it does not spring free. The heat sink might have the tendency to spring back in the direction of the attached clip, so use your clip-support hand to hold the heat sink in place, once it is level with the surface of the CPU. The attached clip should be fine now.

EXERCISE 12.8 *(continued)*

8. Depending on the type of clip it is, use your fingers or a tool to maneuver the free clip of the metal band running through the heat sink onto its tab. Generally, you will need to guide the clip out and away from the socket as you apply downward pressure and then guide it back to catch it under the tab.

9. If you have an active heat sink, find the appropriate power connection and finalize the installation. Visually confirm the operation of an active heat sink before replacing the cover of the case. Because power connections vary, from onboard headers on the motherboard to harnesses coming from the power supply, you might require an adapter if your early-model motherboard does not have a header required by your active heat sink. Never operate an active heat sink without power. The CPU will quickly overheat.

Secondary fans can be installed at the front of the case, the rear of the case, or both. In any event, they generally come with a hole in each of the four corners, as well as four screws or other fastening devices. Modern case manufacturers machine the chassis to accept one or more secondary fans in the front and back each. At least two opposing fasteners should be used, but preferably all four. These devices are always powered because there is no heat sink associated with such fans. As a result, you must find the appropriate power connection or an adapter. They are of no use if they are not powered. The front fan should be mounted to draw air in through the front vents, while the rear fan should be mounted to blow air out through the rear of the case, as does the power supply's fan.

Liquid cooling systems require specialized installation. You should consult and follow the steps outlined in the manufacturer's documentation or website to install these components. One choice you might have to make is whether to mount the unit inside or outside the system unit. Some models don't give you a choice, but others fit nicely in the same space that a classic full-height 5.25-inch hard drive used to fit into. From there, all installation should follow the manufacturer's specification. However, one hurdle you might face is how much tubing to cut off during installation. Everyone likes a nice, neat installation. The temptation that arises is to slide the unit into the drive bay and cut the tubing to a length that reaches perfectly. Doing so, however, leads to disconnecting the tubing every time you need to slide the unit out for checking or refilling the water supply. Leave enough tubing so that you are able to slide the unit out enough to maintain it or even slide it out all the way.

Configuring Cooling Systems

There's no direct configuration of most cooling devices, but you might decide that you want to enter your system's BIOS management routine during startup to make your way to the environmental controls in order to adjust how your system responds to how well your cooling systems perform. While such utilities differ in how you access them and where the environmental controls are, if they exist at all, every BIOS management utility that has such a set of controls places them on a page together. The name of the page might not be intuitive, so you might need to look around the utility before you find it.

You'll know you've found the right page when you see temperature references, usually in both Celsius and Fahrenheit. Some entries simply tell you the current temperatures of key components, such as the temperature of the CPU and the ambient temperature of the inside of the case. Other entries tell you the revolutions per minute (RPM) of the fans that can be monitored inside the case, for example, the CPU's cooling fan speed. Still other entries allow you to configure the temperature and revolution thresholds that will generate audible alarms and eventually cause the system to shut itself down to prevent damage to sensitive components from excessive heat.

If the manufacturer of your specialty cooling system provides features that can be configured, they will provide documentation to guide you through the configuration process.

Using Tools and Diagnostic Procedures for Personal Computer Components

The various tools that you can use to discover the available resources on a PC can make installing new hardware a lot easier. Unfortunately, the tools are of little use unless you understand the information they present. In this section, we discuss the various resources that might be used by PC components and how those resources are used.

Memory address range, interrupt request lines, direct memory access channels, and input/output addresses are configurable aspects of the communication between the devices inside a PC. Memory addresses are numbers assigned to physical memory that allow software to access specific areas of memory. *Interrupt request (IRQ) lines* allow a device to signal the CPU to request its attention. *Input/output (I/O) addresses* are assigned to devices that allow the CPU to identify and signal the device. *Direct memory access (DMA) channels* allow a storage device or adapter card to send information directly into memory without passing through the CPU, which results in a faster data transfer rate.

At some point, every computer will require the installation of a new component, whether it's a new sound card, a memory upgrade, or the replacement of a failed device. As a technician, you will be required to perform this task time and time again. You should be well versed in determining the installation configuration and resources.

Whenever a new component is installed into a PC, its resources must be correctly configured or the device will not function correctly (those resources may be memory address range, IRQs, I/O addresses, and/or DMA channels). This is one of the most common problems when installing new circuit boards along with issues related to device drivers.

Many of the sub-objectives for the troubleshooting requirement of the specialist exams coincide in content with similar objectives for the Essentials exam. Read Chapter 2 before you read this section for greatest effect.

Understanding Computer Resources

In general, there are four main types of PC resources you might need to be aware of when installing a new component: interrupt request (IRQ) lines, memory addresses, direct memory access (DMA) channels, and I/O addresses.

Interrupt Request Lines

IRQs are appropriately named. Interrupts are used by peripherals to interrupt, or stop, the CPU and demand attention. When the CPU receives an interrupt alert, it stops whatever it is doing and handles the request. When simultaneous requests come in, special interrupt controller chips prioritize the competing requests, favoring lower interrupt numbers, making IRQ 0 the highest priority. See the sidebar titled "Why 15 Is Less than 3."

Each device is given its own interrupt to use when alerting the CPU. (There are exceptions; PCI devices can share with one another, for example, and USB devices all use a single interrupt.) AT-based PCs have 16 interrupts defined. Given the limited number of available interrupts, it is critical that you assign them wisely! Table 12.2 lists the standard use and other uses associated with each interrupt.

TABLE 12.2   AT Interrupts

Interrupt	Most Common Use	Other Common Uses
0	System timer	None
1	Keyboard	None
2	None; this interrupt is used to cascade to the upper eight interrupts (see sidebar following this table)	None
3	COM2	COM4
4	COM1	COM3
5	Sound adapter	LPT2
6	Floppy-disk controller	Tape controllers
7	LPT1	Any device
8	Real-time clock	None
9	None	Any device

TABLE 12.2   AT Interrupts *(continued)*

Interrupt	Most Common Use	Other Common Uses
10	None	Any device
11	None	Any device
12	PS/2-style mouse	Any device
13	Floating-point coprocessor	None
14	Primary IDE channel	SCSI controllers
15	Secondary IDE channel	SCSI controllers and network adapters

Most experienced field technicians have the standards (listed in the table) memorized. In studying for the exam, make sure you know all the default assignments, as well as the assignments for COM1–COM4 and LPT1–LPT2.

Why 15 Is Less than 3

Interrupt 2 is a special case. Earlier (XT-based) PCs had only eight interrupts because those computers used a single interrupt controller chip. The controller chip has a single output line that connects to the interrupt line of the processor. With the development of the AT, a second interrupt controller chip was added, providing eight more interrupts, but no mechanism was in place to treat the second controller's output separately. Rather than redesign the entire interrupt process, AT designers decided to use interrupt 2 as a gateway to *cascade* to the second chip and interrupts 8–15. The second controller chip's output connects to interrupt 2 of the first chip. Interrupt 2, often used for early VGA adapters, was replaced by interrupt 9. As a result, you should never configure your system so that both interrupt 2 and 9 are used.

The CPU has a single interrupt line for the entire I/O system. Interrupt controller chips (model 8250s) interface to this single line and arbitrate among the eight interrupt inputs, with lower interrupts having higher priority. Because the entire second controller chip replaces interrupt 2, its interrupts (8–15) replace IRQ2 in the hierarchy and are at a higher priority than interrupts 3–7. The result is that you cannot simply use the numerical value of the interrupts to determine priority. Although lower IRQ values have higher priority in general, IRQ 15 is at a higher priority than IRQs 3–7, making it appear "less than 3."

Memory Usage

The CPU is capable of differentiating between *system memory*, which is what you refer to when you say that your computer has 512MB or 1GB of RAM, and *I/O memory*, which is a resource allocated to an expansion card and other components external to the CPU. A single pin on the CPU, called the I/O_MEM line, allows the CPU to specify which group of memory it is referring to for read or write operations. In addition, the two blocks of memory can over-lap in value, due to the fact that the CPU refers to one or the other per operation, never both, eliminating the possibility of confusion.

Memory Addresses

Many components use blocks of system memory as part of their normal functioning, often finding their data elbow to elbow with application data and code. For example, network inter-face cards often buffer incoming data in a block of memory until it can be processed. Doing so prevents the card from being overloaded if a burst of data is received from the network.

When the device driver loads, it lets the CPU know which block of system memory should be set aside for the exclusive use of the component. This prevents other devices and software from overwriting the information stored there. Certain system components, such as the system board and the PCI bus, also need a memory address. Memory addresses are usually expressed in a hexadecimal range with eight digits, such as 00F0000–000FFFFF. When the CPU indi-cates MEM with the I/O_MEM line, it is referring to a memory address.

Direct Memory Access

Direct memory access (DMA) allows a device to bypass the CPU and place data directly into RAM. To accomplish this, the device must have a DMA channel devoted to its use.

All DMA transfers use a special area of memory set aside to receive data from the expansion card (or CPU, if the transfer is going the other direction) known as a *buffer*. The basic archi-tecture of the PC DMA buffers is limited in size and memory location.

No DMA channel can be used by more than one device. If you accidentally choose a DMA channel that another card is using, the usual symptom is that no DMA transfers occur and the device is unavailable.

Certain DMA channels are assigned to standard AT devices. DMA is no longer as pop-ular as it once was, because of advances in hardware technology, but it is still used by floppy drives and some keyboards and sound cards. The floppy-disk controller typically uses DMA channel 2. A modern system is not likely to run short on DMA channels because so few devices use them anymore.

I/O Addresses

I/O (input/output) addresses, also known as *port addresses*, are a specific area of memory that a component uses to communicate with the system. When the CPU indicates I/O with the I/O_MEM line, it is referring to an I/O address. Although I/O addresses sound quite a bit like mem-ory addresses, the major difference is that memory addresses are used to store information that will be used by the device itself. I/O addresses are used to store information that will be used by the system or to represent instructions for the device from the CPU. For instance, the I/O address range 01F0–01F7 for the primary IDE controller acts as a set of instructions allowing the CPU to control the activities of the IDE controller.

An I/O address is typically expressed using only the last four digits of the full address, such as 03E8, because the first four digits are always zeros. All I/O addresses fall within the first 640KB, starting at 0. Although the I/O addresses for a component are technically a range, such as 03E8–03EF for COM3, you more often refer to the *base I/O address*, just 03E8 in this case. The exam asks about a few I/O addresses; Table 12.3 lists a few of the hexadecimal addresses that you should know.

TABLE 12.3   I/O Addresses

Port	I/O Address
COM1	03F8–03FF
COM2	02F8–02FF
COM3	03E8–03EF
COM4	02E8–02EF
LPT1	0378–037F
LPT2	0278–027F
Primary IDE	01F0–01F7
Secondary IDE	0170–0177

Determining Available Resources

The best way to determine the PC's available resources is by using hardware-configuration-discovery utilities. These software programs talk to the PC's BIOS as well as the various pieces of hardware in the computer and display which IRQ, DMA, I/O addresses, and memory addresses are being used. Most operating systems include some way of determining this information, including Device Manager in Windows 2000/XP. Exercise 12.9 guides you through investigating your system resources.

EXERCISE 12.9

Displaying System Resources

To display the system resources currently in use, follow these steps:

1. Right-click My Computer and choose Properties to bring up the System Properties dialog.

2. Click the Hardware tab, and then click the Device Manager button.

3. To display a device's resources, open the category by clicking the plus sign next to it and double-clicking the device name. Then, look in the Resources tab for that device.

4. In order to see the specifics about how your system allocates a certain type of resource, click the View menu in Device Manager and select Resources By Type. Resources By Connection works as well, but some categories are less intuitive.

5. Notice that the four categories correspond to the four resources presented in this section—DMA, I/O address, IRQ, and memory address. Investigate each of the four categories by clicking on the plus sign in front of them. For example, expanding the Interrupt Request category shows you all components that have IRQs assigned to them in order of IRQ number.

EXERCISE 12.9 *(continued)*

You can also get this same information through the System Information utility. To run it, choose Start ➢ (All) Programs ➢ Accessories ➢ System Tools ➢ System Information. Click the plus sign next to Hardware Resources, and then click one of the categories in the left pane to see the information in the right pane.

Resource	Device	Status
IRQ 0	System timer	OK
IRQ 1	Standard 101/102-Key or Microsoft Natural PS/2 Keyboard	OK
IRQ 3	Intel(r) 82801BA/BAM USB Universal Host Controller - 2442	OK
IRQ 4	Communications Port (COM1)	OK
IRQ 6	Standard floppy disk controller	OK
IRQ 8	System CMOS/real time clock	OK
IRQ 9	Microsoft ACPI-Compliant System	OK
IRQ 9	Promise Technology Inc. Ultra IDE Controller	OK
IRQ 10	Creative SB Live! Value (WDM)	OK
IRQ 10	Intel(R) 82801BA/BAM SMBus Controller - 2443	OK
IRQ 11	NVIDIA GeForce2 GTS	OK
IRQ 11	3Com EtherLink XL 10/100 PCI For Complete PC Management ...	OK
IRQ 11	U.S. Robotics 56K Fax PCI	OK
IRQ 12	Microsoft PS/2 Mouse	OK
IRQ 13	Numeric data processor	OK
IRQ 14	Primary IDE Channel	OK
IRQ 15	Secondary IDE Channel	OK

System Summary
 Hardware Resources
  Conflicts/Sharing
  DMA
  Forced Hardware
  I/O
  IRQs
  Memory
 Components
 Software Environment
 Internet Settings
 Office 10 Applications

Find what:

Find   Close Find

☐ Search selected category only   ☐ Search category names only

---

Manually Specifying a Resource Assignment

In the Windows' Device Manager, you can manually specify the resources for a device to solve a problem with a *resource conflict*—that is, a situation in which two or more devices lay claim to the same resource. A resource conflict usually appears as a yellow exclamation point next to a device's name in Device Manager. Double-clicking the device opens its Properties box, and on the Resources tab you will find an explanation of the problem in the Conflicting Device list.

To change a device's resource assignments, clear the Use Automatic Settings check box and select a different configuration from the Settings Based On drop-down list. (See Figure 12.2.) If none of the alternate configurations resolves the conflict, you can double-click a specific resource on the Resource Type list and enter a manual setting for it.

Most modern computers use a power management and configuration method called ACPI (advanced configuration and power interface), which helps prevent resource conflicts but which also limits the amount of tinkering you can do with manual resource assignments. If you get a message that a particular resource cannot be changed, or if the Use Automatic Settings check box is unavailable, it is probably because of ACPI.

If the device is not Plug and Play compatible, it may have jumpers for hard-setting the resources assigned to it. If that's the case, Windows will not be able to change these assignments; it will use the assignments the device requires, based on its jumper settings.

FIGURE 12.2   Manually changing a resource assignment

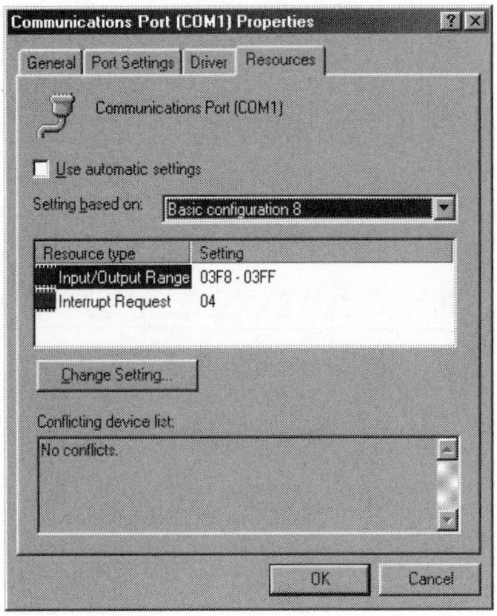

Diagnostic Resources

When you are stumped by a computer problem, where do you turn? Try manuals, the Web, and training.

User/Installation Manuals   Consult the manuals that came with the hardware and software.

Internet/Web Resources   Consult the websites of the companies that make the hardware and software. Updates and patches are often available for download, or the websites may offer knowledge bases of troubleshooting information and downloadable manuals as well as live forums for those with similar problems to discuss their issues.

Training Materials   If you have taken a class pertaining to the hardware or software, consult the materials you received for that class.

Diagnostic Tools and Utilities

A big part of being a successful technician is knowing what tools are appropriate to correct which problems. The following diagnostic tools and utilities are ones you should be comfortable with:

Task Manager   Lets you shut down nonresponsive applications selectively in all Windows versions. In Windows 2000/XP, it does much more, allowing you to see which processes and applications are using the most system resources. To display Task Manager, press Ctrl+Alt+Delete. Task Manager appears immediately in Windows 9*x*; in Windows 2000/XP, you must click the Task Manager button to display it after pressing Ctrl+Alt+Delete. Use Task Manager whenever the system seems bogged down by an unresponsive application.

Dr. Watson   This tool enables detailed logging of errors. Use it whenever you think an error is likely to occur (for example, when you're trying to reproduce an error).

Event Viewer   This tool enables you to see what's been going on behind the scenes in Windows NT/2000/XP. Use Event Viewer when you want to gather information about a system or hardware problem.

Device Manager   As already mentioned, Device Manager shows you what hardware is installed and lets you check its status. Use this when a device is not functioning and you are trying to figure out why.

WinMSD   Another name for System Information, the same utility you can select from the System Tools menu. (Running it at the Run command with `WINMSD` is an alternative.) WinMSD provides comprehensive information about the system's resource usage, hardware, and software environments. Use it when you need to gather information about the system.

Recovery CD   Some computers that come with Windows preinstalled do not come with a full version of Microsoft Windows; instead they come with a Recovery CD that can be used to return the PC to its original factory configuration. The important thing to know about these Recovery CDs is that they wipe out all user data and applications. Use one only when you cannot restore system functionality in any less-drastic way.

CHKDSK   One utility for checking the integrity of magnetic media that has been around since the dawn of the PC operating system, DOS that is, is `CHKDSK`. CHKDSK is run from a command prompt and scrubs the disk to varying degrees for surface-level and filesystem imperfections. The imperfections can even be corrected in many cases, if you request that they be. Table 12.4 lists the primary switches for CHKDSK and their descriptions. Switches can be specified in series and two of the switches imply the third switch without your explicitly specifying it.

TABLE 12.4   Common CHKDSK Software Switches

Switch	Description
/F	Attempts to fix any errors it finds.
/R	Searches for bad sectors and recovers readable information to good sectors elsewhere on the disk, if the bad sectors are not unreadable. The /F switch is automatically enabled with this switch so that errors found can be fixed.
/X	Forces the volume to dismount, if necessary, before CHKDSK runs. Any handles to the volume are invalidated and clients lose access to the server. The /F switch is automatically enabled with this switch so that errors found can be fixed.

Hardware Tools

In addition to the software tools included with the operating system, there are a number of hardware tools you should be familiar with as well. The exam objectives specifically mention familiarity with these tools:

Multi-meter   A multi-meter (also written as multimeter) combines a number of tools into one. While there can be slight deviations, they always include a voltmeter, ohmmeter, and ammeter (and are sometimes called VOMs, as an acronym for volt-ohmmeter).

Antistatic Pad and Wrist Strap   The need for an antistatic strap was discussed in the first objective of this chapter. A properly grounded strap can save you from suffering a nasty jolt. An antistatic pad works similarly and can not only protect you but also can protect sensitive equipment from static damage as well.

Another option is antistatic spray. Usually applied as a mist to carpets, chairs, and so on, this reduces the amount of static electricity present and can save computers and components.

Specialty Hardware/Tools   While specialty tools can include anything needed for a specific purpose, there are a few things you should always have: a parts grabber for picking up pieces that have fallen or are hard to hold on to, a chip extractor, and wire cutters/strippers/crimpers. These tools can be used to solve a number of problems.

Loop-Back Plugs   Also called wrap plugs, loop-back plugs take the signal going out and essentially echo it back. This allows you to test parallel and serial ports to make certain they are working correctly.

Cleaning Products   A good hand vacuum is a necessity. You need to be able to vacuum up dust, debris, and even toner on occasion. Because of this, you want a vacuum that is capable of collecting small particles and will not pass them through the bag and back in to the air. Spend the money on a good vacuum and you will be glad you did. Vacuums designed to be used safely inside the computer case are available, and only vacuums built for this purpose should be used.

An assortment of other cleaning supplies should also be available. This would include cleaning pads for monitors, contact cleaner, compressed air, tape-head and optical lens cleaners, and CD cleaning supplies.

Performing Preventative Maintenance for Personal Computer Components

If the best defense is a good offense, then preventative maintenance truly is the best defense. This section, although short, gets right to the point on maintaining some of the most common components.

Chapter 2 included a great deal of information on preventative maintenance products and procedures. Rather than repeating the information from objective 1.4 of the Essentials exam verbatim, it is expected that you read that information, and the content here builds upon that.

Display Devices   Keep them clean to prevent them from overheating, and make sure they have adequate ventilation. Depending upon the type and size of monitor, it may generate a considerable amount of heat. This heat needs to be vented away to keep the device working properly, and you must make sure the heat from the monitor does not go into other devices that are also heat sensitive.

Power Devices   In the days of old, it was common procedure to turn the power off on a computer and solve your problems with a reboot. Today, so many files on a system are open at any given time that doing so could cause irreparable harm to data. Just as you would no longer "pull the plug," you want to make sure this does not happen outside of your control. Therefore, you should consider adding surge protectors, power strips, UPSs, and other devices to the PC. Most UPSs now include software that can trigger the PC to safely shut down if the power stays off for a long enough time that the battery in the UPS begins to get low.

Input Devices   If you are working in an environment with a large amount of contaminants (a factory floor, for example), you should consider covering the input devices. Many supply houses carry disposable covers that can be placed over keyboards and other devices to keep out dirt, liquid, grime, and other impurities in these environments.

Storage Devices   Keep the hard drives defragmented as much as possible (use DEFRAG) to keep them working optimally. Monitor them for adequate storage space, and replace or add to them as needed.

Thermally Sensitive Devices   Motherboards, CPUs, adapter cards, and almost everything else in the PC will react negatively to high temperatures. Make sure there is adequate ventilation for your PCs and that you keep them clean to let the heat escape.

As with so many other topics on the exam, common sense should be your guide when answering questions about preventative maintenance and computer components.

Summary

In this chapter, you learned how to remove, install, and configure computer components. Specifically, you explored installing and exchanging motherboards, CPUs, memory, adapter cards, storage devices, power supplies, display devices, input devices, and cooling systems. You also learned about troubleshooting and preventative maintenance techniques that every specialized technician should know.

Exam Essentials

Know how to remove, install, and configure motherboards.   Know how to choose the correct motherboard for the chassis you have. Know how to choose the correct mounting hardware to avoid shorting out electrical components. Know the various connectors and headers associated with today's motherboards. Be aware that there are various formats of BIOS routines and methods to access them.

Know how to remove, install, and configure CPUs.   Know how to choose the right CPU for the motherboard you have. Know how to remove and install a CPU in a ZIF socket.

Know how to remove, install, and configure memory.   Know the difference between various memory form factors, especially SDRAM and DDR, so you know how to choose the correct memory for your motherboard. Be aware of the fastening mechanisms that modern memory modules employ, how they affect module installation, and how to release them during module removal.

Know how to remove, install, and configure adapter cards.   Be aware that adapter cards must match available expansion slots. Know how to remove and install them and how to secure them into the computer chassis.

Know how to remove, install, and configure storage devices.   Know the difference between the data and power connectors used on storage devices. Be aware of the master/slave relationship used with ATA devices and know the strategy for setting them. Know what it means to partition and format a hard drive. Be aware of the physical differences in storage-device form factors.

Know how to remove, install, and configure power supplies.   Know the difference between the modern motherboard power headers, and be aware of when an adapter might be required. Know the two most common device connectors coming from the power supply. Be familiar with how to fasten power supplies to the chassis, as well as how to unfasten them.

Know how to remove, install, and configure display devices.   Know the display device choices on the market today. Know the general configuration aspects of each type of device. Know the specific adjustments most commonly available.

Know how to remove, install, and configure input devices.   Be aware of what constitutes an input device. Know how to connect an input device to a computer and how to disconnect one. Familiarize yourself with common mouse configuration.

Know how to remove, install, and configure cooling systems.   Know that cooling systems range from passive heat sinks to liquid cooling systems. Know the specifics on removing and installing the more common devices and the general concept of dealing with the more complex devices.

Know the default IRQs for COM ports and common devices.   Know the default IRQs for COM ports and common devices such as modems, sound cards, disk drives, and so on.

Be familiar with Device Manager.   Device Manager can display information about the computer's memory, I/O ports, IRQs being used, and many other PC resources.

Understand how manual resource assignments are set.   Manual resource assignments for Plug and Play devices are set on the Resources tab of the device's Properties dialog box. For a non-PnP device, resource assignments are controlled by jumpers on the device itself.

Know the hardware tools mentioned.   Be able to name the hardware tools and their purpose, as discussed in this section.

Be aware of the need to keep systems well ventilated.   Heat can be a negative force to almost any PC component, and ventilation can help ensure there is not excessive heat buildup.

Review Questions

1. Which statement is true regarding upgrading a computer system?

   A. When upgrading RAM, you must also upgrade the CPU.

   B. When upgrading RAM, you must perform a forklift upgrade on the entire system.

   C. When upgrading RAM, it is possible that you can upgrade RAM only.

   D. RAM is the only upgrade you can perform on modern computer systems.

2. Which two of the following are today's best choices for video adapter technology?

   A. ISA

   B. PCI

   C. PCIe

   D. AGP

3. Which of the following is not a selection criterion for RAM?

   A. Physical size

   B. Solid state

   C. Speed

   D. Capacity

4. While installing a CPU, you apply gentle pressure to the surface of the CPU, but it will not seat. When you examine the pins of the CPU to see if they are straight, you find that a number of them are bent. Why are the bent pins not the original problem?

   A. The socket has a ZIF mechanism that must be released before inserting the CPU.

   B. The holes in the socket are large enough to accept pins bent up to 45 degrees from perpendicular.

   C. The bent metal protrusions around the edge of a chip are not pins. They are non-electronic tensioners to make sure the CPU maintains a tight connection.

   D. CPUs don't have pins. What you thought were pins were metallic designs in the likeness of the manufacturer's logo.

5. Which of the following statements regarding motherboard replacement is not true?

   A. As you remove any electronic components, including the motherboard and its adapters, you should place them in antistatic containers.

   B. Existing power supply connectors might not fit the new motherboard.

   C. Existing memory modules might not fit the new motherboard.

   D. When removing the motherboard, it is recommended that you not remove the expansion boards, so that you do not subject them to static.

6. Which statement concerning CPU and RAM configuration is most true?

    A. Modern motherboards have intelligent BIOS routines that automatically recognize and configure themselves for the CPU and RAM.

    B. The CPU and RAM modules have DIP switches on them that must be set the same as the DIP switch on the motherboard.

    C. The motherboard is preset from the factory to work with only one CPU and only one type of RAM module.

    D. You must use an external CPU/RAM programming station to pre-configure these components for your specific motherboard.

7. Which of the following statements is true, regarding working inside a computer system?

    A. You and the chassis should be grounded to the same ground, but power should not be supplied to the system.

    B. All internal components, except the power supply, are hot-swappable. Maintaining power to the system while working ensures interruption-free service for the customer.

    C. As long as the LEDs on the motherboard are lit, you are safe to work inside the chassis.

    D. Not since the original PC has the technician been able to work inside the computer system.

8. Which of the following is not a consideration when installing an internal storage device?

    A. You should match the form factor of the drive or adapt it to an available drive bay or slot.

    B. You should secure the drive with at least two screws on one side and preferably two on each side.

    C. Due to the high revolutions at which modern hard drives spin, you must secure external power source because the internal power supplies do not have the capacity.

    D. You need to be sure that the routing of the drive's ribbon cable, if applicable, does not obstruct the engineered flow of air across internal components.

9. Which of the following statements regarding floppy-drive installation is true?

    A. Like a hard drive, the floppy drive requires no external access.

    B. Like DVD-ROM drives, floppy drives have a 5.25-inch form factor and must be installed in the larger drive bays.

    C. Because it is antiquated technology, floppy-disk drives can no longer be purchased new.

    D. Although some drives might not clearly key the receptacle for the Berg power connector, you must insert the connector correctly or the drive can be damaged.

10. After manually formatting a hard drive and installing the operating system, you find that the computer does not function in the manner expected. Which of the following is a possible cause?

    A. You performed a high-level format, but neglected to perform a low-level format first.

    B. The operating system was distributed on two discs, but you only installed one.

    C. During formatting, you did not make the partition bootable.

    D. The operating system was larger than your hard drive and did not install completely.

11. What is the term for an operating-system independent operation that ties a hard drive to its controller card?

   A. High-level formatting

   B. Low-level formatting

   C. Partitioning

   D. Scrubbing

12. Which of the following is not a consideration when upgrading power supplies?

   A. You might find that you do not have a matching motherboard connector on your new power supply.

   B. You might find that your case has a nonremovable power supply.

   C. You might find that your power rating is not adequate on the new power supply.

   D. You might find that you do not have enough of the appropriate connectors coming from the power supply for the devices you have installed.

13. Which of the following is not a Microsoft boot mode?

   A. Normal mode

   B. Complete mode

   C. Safe mode

   D. VGA mode

14. Which of the following is not a configuration option for computer video?

   A. Pincushion

   B. Contrast

   C. Trapezoid

   D. Rhombus

15. Which of the following is not an example of a standard input device connector?

   A. 1/8-inch jack

   B. Mini-DIN

   C. D-subminiature

   D. USB

16. When installing a CPU fan and heat sink, which of the following is not a consideration to keep in mind?

   A. If a tool is needed, use only the tool for which the clip to be attached was designed.

   B. Orient the fan and heat sink to be square with the CPU and to match up with the tabs that receive the clips.

   C. Match the direction that the fan blows, up or down, to the model of CPU based on heat production.

   D. Determine if you have the appropriate power connector for the fan and obtain an adapter, if necessary.

17. Which system resource allows an expansion card, for instance, to signal the CPU that it requires some of the CPU's time?

   A. I/O memory

   B. DMA channels

   C. IRQ lines

   D. Memory addresses

18. Which of the following is considered a diagnostic utility in the Microsoft operating system?

   A. REGEDIT

   B. CACL

   C. CALC

   D. CHKDSK

19. Which one of the following statements is not accurate regarding preventive maintenance where heat is concerned?

   A. Make sure that outside air vents are not blocked or clogged.

   B. Use distilled water to rinse dust off of internal components regularly, but make sure to allow sufficient drying time or use a blow-dryer or compressed air for faster drying.

   C. Use a static-safe vacuum cleaner but do not touch the electronics to avoid dislodging minute items, such as jumpers and pluggable components.

   D. Regularly check the operating parameters of CPU and system fans.

20. What is the name of the utility that allows you to check hardware resources and alter them, if allowed?

   A. Device Manager

   B. Task Manager

   C. Program Manager

   D. Control Panel

Answers to Review Questions

1. C. Very often, computer systems prove to have an upgrade path for their RAM. Also, upgrading the RAM is the least expensive upgrade compared to the increase in performance that you can observe, up to a point.

2. C, D. ISA is an antiquated computer expansion bus. PCI is liable to be replaced by its high-performance cousin PCIe. AGP remains a popular video technology in today's market.

3. B. All RAM is solid state. The other three options are selection criteria.

4. A. You should never apply insertion pressure to a CPU. With ZIF sockets, you release the lever on the side of the socket, and the CPU should drop right in, sometimes with delicate urging but never with what could be considered pressure.

5. D. Removing the expansion boards from their slots is recommended, if not required. Any static that you discharge into the motherboard can affect the adapters while they're attached. The fact that a motherboard outside of the case is made more cumbersome with cards attached means that you are more likely to slip and discharge static with the motherboard in that state.

6. A. It's true. Sometimes you have to pat yourself on the back for being able to install the CPU and RAM, because kudos for configuring the motherboard for these components would be a bit of a stretch. The BIOS does this for you today. There are no DIP switches on these components, and there is no such thing as a CPU/RAM programming station. Manufacturers must remain more flexible than to produce motherboards for only one set of CPU and RAM modules.

7. A. You must make sure, for electrostatic-discharge reasons, that you are at the same electrical potential as the chassis and other components. The best way to do this is by using an antistatic wrist strap and ensuring it is clipped to the chassis and that the chassis is connected to ground. Alternatively, both you and the chassis can be connected in parallel to the same source of ground. Very few components on standard computer systems are hot-swappable, which is normally limited to certain drives and USB/PC Card applications. Servers are somewhat more resilient, but still not all components are hot-swappable. Motherboard LEDs light up when power is supplied to the board. This is an indication that you should not perform work inside the chassis. How many people would be out of a job if they could not work inside a computer system today?

8. C. Today's hard drives, regardless of their RPMs, have standard internal power connections. Each of the other options are valid concerns when installing an internal drive.

9. D. See the "Do You Smell Something" Real Word Scenario in this chapter. Inserting the Berg connector upside down will damage the drive the first time the motor is activated. Floppy drives require front access for floppy-disk insertion. Their form factor is only 3.5 inches, and you can still buy them new.

10. C. When manually performing a high-level format of a drive, you must make the partition bootable. Automatic operating-system installation takes care of this for you, making it easy to overlook. If a low-level format is required, you are not able to partition a drive and perform a high-level format without first performing the low-level format. You do not need to install each disc for your operating system separately. Operating systems prompt you for all required distribution media during installation and do not allow you to choose partial-media installations. If you do not have enough room on your hard drive to install an operating system, the installation routine will not perform the installation.

11. B. The question describes low-level formatting, which is performed by the manufacturer for ATA (IDE) drives but must be performed by the installer for SCSI drives. Partitioning and high-level formatting are based on the operating system being used, and scrubbing is an informal term used to describe the behavior of certain integrity-checking utilities.

12. B. Personal computers do not have permanently installed power supplies. Like other electrical and electronic components, power supplies can and do fail on a regular basis. Permanently mounting a power supply to a chassis would be a disservice to the consumer. You need to consider the cumulative power needs of your installed components and you might have to obtain adapters and splitters if you do not have enough or you have the wrong types of connectors coming from the power supply.

13. B. There is no such thing as complete mode. Without any adjustment to the boot process, you boot into normal mode. Safe mode and VGA mode are used during troubleshooting various problems that prevent successful booting in normal mode, including graphics issues.

14. D. Although a geometric shape like the trapezoid, rhombus is not a video configuration setting. The other three options are.

15. A. 1/8-inch jacks, or minijacks, are used for multimedia input devices, not standard input devices. Standard input devices include human interface devices, such as keyboards and mice. The other three options have and can be used for such devices.

16. C. The fan always blows downward to push the collected heat out through the fins of the heat sink. The other options are valid points to consider.

17. C. Interrupt request (IRQ) lines perform as stated in the question. The other three resources have nothing to do with this action.

18. D. Of the options listed, only CHKDSK is considered to be a diagnostic utility. The others either do not exist or are nondiagnostic in nature.

19. B. Please don't rinse your computer components. The other options are highly advisable to keep heat dissipation under control.

20. A. Only Device Manager allows you access to the resources being used by the various hardware components. Task Manager and Control Panel allow you to monitor and alter certain items, but not hardware resources the way Device Manager is designed to do.

Chapter

13

Working with Laptops and Portable Devices

THE FOLLOWING COMPTIA A+ IT TECHNICIAN EXAM OBJECTIVES ARE COVERED IN THIS CHAPTER:

✓ **2.1 Identify fundamental principles of using laptops and portable devices**

- Identify appropriate applications for laptop-specific communication connections such as Bluetooth, infrared, cellular WAN and Ethernet

- Identify appropriate laptop-specific power and electrical input devices and determine how amperage and voltage can affect performance

- Identify the major components of the LCD including inverter, screen and video card

✓ **2.2 Install, configure, optimize and upgrade laptops and portable devices**

- Removal of laptop-specific hardware such as peripherals, hot-swappable and non-hot-swappable devices

- Describe how video sharing affects memory upgrades

✓ **2.3 Use tools, diagnostic procedures and troubleshooting techniques for laptops and portable devices**

- Use procedures and techniques to diagnose power conditions, video, keyboard, pointer and wireless card issues for example:

  - Verify AC power (e.g. LEDs, swap AC adapter)
  - Verify DC power
  - Remove unneeded peripherals
  - Plug in external monitor
  - Toggle Fn keys
  - Check LCD cutoff switch

- Verify backlight functionality and pixilation
- Stylus issues (e.g. digitizer problems)
- Unique laptop keypad issues
- Antenna wires

THE FOLLOWING COMPTIA A+ DEPOT TECHNICIAN EXAM OBJECTIVES ARE COVERED IN THIS CHAPTER:

✓ **2.1 Identify the fundamental principles of using laptops and portable devices**

- Identify appropriate applications for laptop-specific communication connections, for example:
  - Bluetooth
  - Infrared devices
  - Cellular WAN
  - Ethernet
- Identify appropriate laptop-specific power and electrical input devices, for example:
  - Output performance requirements for amperage and voltage
- Identify the major components of the LCD (e.g. inverter, screen, video card)

✓ **2.2 Install, configure, optimize and upgrade laptops and portable devices**

- Demonstrate the safe removal of laptop-specific hardware including peripherals, hot-swappable and non hot-swappable devices
- Identify the affect of video sharing on memory upgrades

✓ **2.3 Identify tools, diagnostic procedures and troubleshooting techniques for laptops and portable devices.**

- Use procedures and techniques to diagnose power conditions, video issues, keyboard and pointer issues and wireless card issues, for example:
  - Verify AC power (e.g. LED's, swap AC adapter)

- Verify DC power
- Remove unneeded peripherals
- Plug in external monitor
- Toggle Fn keys
- Check LCD cutoff switch
- Verify backlight functionality and pixilation
- Stylus issues (e.g. digitizer problems)
- Unique laptop keypad issues
- Antenna wires

Even though prices on laptops have dropped dramatically over the last several years, laptop computers clearly aren't going to out-muscle their similarly priced desktop counterparts. But what laptops do provide is flexibility—the flexibility to work wirelessly from anywhere and the flexibility to change peripherals in the blink of an eye.

Laptops also pose a different set of challenges to the technician than desktops because of technology differences between the platforms. Although wireless networking is becoming more commonplace with desktops, it's a fundamental technology of mobile computing. Similarly, liquid crystal display (LCD) screens are springing up on desktops everywhere but are again squarely at the center of the laptop world. As you move forward in the computer industry, it's important to have a good grasp of the different technologies, especially now that mobile computers make up over half of new computer sales each year.

This chapter takes a look at applications of wireless networking, laptop power requirements, LCD technologies, removing laptop hardware, video sharing, and troubleshooting. Each of these themes is particularly relevant in the mobile computing world.

Using Laptops and Portable Devices

Perhaps a sports analogy is appropriate here. (After all, you can't get through an entire computer book without at least one sports analogy, right?) If you can't outmuscle your opponent, you need to be quicker or more adaptable than your opponent to have an advantage—especially if you're the smaller player. That's exactly what laptops do. They're not bigger or stronger or faster, but they provide the quickness and flexibility that desktops can't provide because of their stationary nature.

The biggest advantage that laptops offer is mobility. But in being mobile, you still need to be able to attach to a network and its resources to be productive in today's computing environment. This is why wireless networking is a fundamental component of mobile computing.

Sticking to the mobility theme, laptops have different power requirements than their desktop brethren. Power adapters are mobile, and nearly all laptops have built-in or removable batteries to work when there's no wall socket available. Consequently, laptops have slightly different power requirements than desktops.

Finally, LCD technology is paramount to the rise of laptop popularity. While it's likely that LCD would have been successful without laptops, it's difficult to imagine laptops being as widely used if it weren't for this compact display technology. If you're going to be trouble-shooting laptops, you need to know how this technology works and what to look at if and when display troubles pop up.

Identifying Applications for Laptop-Specific Communication Connections

There are four common wireless communication methods available to mobile devices, from cell phones and PDAs to laptop computers. They are Bluetooth, infrared, cellular, and Ethernet. Each has its distinct performance characteristics, thus each has its own appropriate use for applications.

Bluetooth

In 1998, a consortium of companies formed the *Bluetooth Special Interest Group (SIG)*, and formally adopted the name *Bluetooth* for its technology. The name comes from a 10th-century Danish king named Harald Blatand, known as Harold Bluetooth in English. (One can only imagine how he got that name.) King Blatand had successfully unified warring factions in the areas of Norway, Sweden, and Denmark. The makers of Bluetooth were trying to unite disparate technology industries, namely computing, mobile communications, and the auto industry.

Current membership in the Bluetooth SIG includes Microsoft, Intel, Apple, IBM, Toshiba, and several cellular phone manufacturers. The technical specification IEEE 802.15.1 describes a *Wireless Personal Area Network (WPAN)* based on Bluetooth version 1.1.

The first Bluetooth device on the market was an Ericsson headset and cell phone adapter, which arrived on the scene in 2000. By 2002, there were over 500 Bluetooth certified products, and as of 2005 over 5 million Bluetooth chipsets shipped each week. The current Bluetooth specification is Version 2.0+ Enhanced Data Rate.

Bluetooth Networks

According to the Bluetooth SIG, "Bluetooth wireless technology is a short-range communications technology intended to replace the cables connecting portable and/or fixed devices while maintaining high levels of security." Bluetooth also operates at low power and low cost and can handle simultaneous voice and data transmissions.

One of the unusual features of Bluetooth networks is their temporary nature. With other popular wireless standards, you need a central communication point, such as a hub or router. Bluetooth networks are formed on an ad hoc basis, meaning that whenever two Bluetooth devices get close enough to each other, they can communicate directly with each other. This dynamically created network is called a *piconet*. A Bluetooth-enabled device can communicate with up to seven other devices in one piconet.

Within the piconet, one device is the master and the other seven devices are slaves. Technically, communication can occur only between the master and a slave. While this might sound like a problem, the role of master rotates quickly among the devices in a round-robin fashion. In this way, all devices in a piconet can communicate with each other directly. Current Bluetooth specifications allow for connecting two or more piconets together in a *scatternet*. In a scatternet, one or more devices would serve as a bridge between the piconets. Those devices are not currently on the market, but they should be by 2007.

Bluetooth Technical Specifications

There are two different supported versions of Bluetooth. Version 1.2 was adopted in November 2003, and it supports data transmissions of up to 1 megabit per second (Mbps). Version 2.0+ EDR, adopted in November 2004, can support data rates up to 3Mbps. Both standards transmit in the 2.4–2.485GHz range.

> The 2.4GHz range is unlicensed, meaning that any wireless technology can use it. Indeed, many cell phone technologies as well as wireless networking technologies do use it. To avoid interference, Bluetooth can "signal hop" at different frequencies to avoid conflicts with devices using other technologies in the area.

Bluetooth is a short-range technology. There are three different device classes, and each one is detailed in Table 13.1.

TABLE 13.1   Bluetooth Classes

Class	Range	Use	Power
1	100 meters (300 feet)	Industrial usage	100 milliwatts
2	10 meters (30 feet)	Mobile devices	2.5 milliwatts
3	1 meter (3 feet)	Rarely used	1 milliwatt

Class 2 is the most common Bluetooth class, and it operates at 2.5 milliwatts (mW) of power.

For security, Bluetooth uses the *Secure and Fast Encryption Routine (SAFER+)* encryption routine, a 128-bit algorithm developed in 1998. There have been questions surrounding how secure Bluetooth really is, and the best advice is to not leave powered-on devices unattended.

Bluetooth Devices

As mentioned earlier, the first device was a wireless headset for a cell phone, and Bluetooth continues to excel in this field, considering its low power consumption and ample bandwidth for voice communications.

Bluetooth-enabled computer peripherals include keyboards and mice, printers, digital cameras, and MP3 players. The technology is also prevalent in PDAs and handheld computers as well as in several cars, including those made by BMW and Toyota (and Lexus).

Cards for laptops come in serial, USB, and PCMCIA Type II varieties. Figure 13.1 shows a USB model by Linksys.

FIGURE 13.1 Bluetooth USB adapter

Figure 13.2 shows a card made for printers—quite handy to have if you're on the road with a mobile printer!

FIGURE 13.2 USB print server

All in all, Bluetooth is a solid technology that should be around for a while. It doesn't have the range of cellular or the capacity of WiFi (discussed later in this chapter), but it fills a nice niche, uses low power, and has developed a critical mass of devices that support it.

Infrared

Infrared waves have been around since the beginning of time. Infrared waves are longer than light waves but shorter than microwaves. The most common use of infrared technology is the television remote control, although infrared is also used in night-vision goggles and medical and scientific imaging.

In 1994, the *Infrared Data Association (IrDA)* was formed as a technical consortium to support "interoperable, low-cost infrared data interconnection standards that support a walk-up, point-to-point user model." The key terms here are "walk-up" and "point-to-point," meaning that you need to be at very close range to use infrared, and it's designed for one-to-one communication. Infrared requires line of sight, and generally speaking the two devices need to be pointed at each other to work. If you point your remote away from the television, how well does it work?

More information on the IrDA standard can be found at the organization's website: http://www.irda.org.

Most laptops have a built-in infrared port, which is a small, dark square of plastic, usually black or dark maroon. For easy access, infrared ports are located on the front or sides of devices that have them. Figure 13.3 shows an example of an infrared port.

FIGURE 13.3   Infrared port

Infrared Networks

An infrared network is a point-to-point network between two devices. There is no master or slave or hub-type device required. Simply point one infrared-enabled device at another and transmit.

Infrared Technical Specifications

Current IrDA specifications allow transmission of data up to 16Mbps, and IrDA claims that 100Mbps and 500Mbps standards are on the horizon. Because it does not use radio waves, there are no concerns of interference or signal conflicts. Atmospheric conditions can play a role in disrupting infrared waves, but considering that the maximum functional range of an IrDA device is about one meter, weather is not likely to cause you any problems.

Security is not an issue with infrared. Consider the fact that the maximum range is about one meter with an angle of about 30 degrees, and the signal does not go through walls. If someone is going to intercept an infrared signal, you will know that the person is there and trying to intercept the signal. The data is directional, and you choose when and where to send it.

Infrared Devices

Infrared mice were all the rage a few years ago and are still popular today. Also readily available are infrared keyboards and printers. Perhaps some of the most useful infrared devices are keyboards for PDAs. They're smaller than standard laptop keyboards (but not by much), and they generally fold up to a convenient travel size. Speaking of PDAs, many of them are infrared-enabled, as are many cellular phones. Finally, don't forget the almighty remote control. Although not necessarily computer related, it's hard to imagine society without that ubiquitous device of convenience.

Cellular (Cellular WAN)

The cellular phone, once a clunky brick-like status symbol of the well-to-do, is now pervasive in our society. It seems that everyone from kindergarteners to 80-year-old grandmothers has a cell. The industry has revolutionized the way we communicate and, some say, contributed to the furthering of an attention deficit disorder–like, instant-gratification-hungry society.

Regardless of your feelings about cell phones, whether you text-message like a maniac or long for the good old days when you could escape your phone, because it had a functional radius as long as your cord, you need to understand the basics of cell technology. It's primarily been developing in the realm of small handheld communications devices (phones, and now the BlackBerry), but technologies converge, and that's definitely what's happening between cell phones and computers.

Cellular Networks

Cellular networks are very complex behind the scenes, but unless you are working at a major cell provider, learning a ton of information won't give you a lot of practical help. What you do need to know is that cell communications require the use of a central access point, generally a cell tower, which is connected to a main hub. Cellular networks are very large mesh networks with extensive range. The term *cell* refers to a cellular phone network.

Cellular Technical Specifications

There are two major cell standards in the United States. The *Global System for Mobile Communications (GSM)* is the most popular, boasting over 1.5 billion users in 210 countries. The other standard is *Code Division Multiple Access (CDMA)*, which was developed by Qualcomm and is available only in the United States. GSM and CDMA are not compatible with each other.

GSM uses a variety of bands to transmit. The most popular are 900MHz and 1800MHz, but 400, 450, and 850MHz are also used. Because of this, one phone cannot work at full capacity on all the GSM networks in the world. GSM splits up its channels by time division, in a process called Time Division Multiple Access (TDMA).

The maximum rate for GSM is about 270 kilobits per second (Kbps). While this is incredibly low based on current networking standards, it's ample for voice communications. The maximum functional distance of GSM is about 22 miles (35 kilometers). For security, GSM uses the A5/1 and A5/2 stream ciphers.

A newer enhancement to GSM is called General Packet Radio Service (GPRS). It's designed to provide data transmissions over a GSM network at up to 171Kbps.

CDMA is considered a superior technology to GSM because it doesn't break up its channels by time but rather by a code inserted into the communicated message. This allows for multiple transmissions to occur at the same time without interference. CDMA was first used by the English in World War II, and today it is used in Global Positioning Systems (GPSs) as well.

Current CDMA-based technologies support download rates of over 3Mbps, with upload speeds of nearly 2Mbps. Not only does CDMA have better transmission speeds than GSM, but it works in ranges up to 100 kilometers.

Newer takeoffs of the CDMA technology include Wideband Code Division Multiple Access (W-CDMA), CDMA2000, and Evolution Data Optimized (EVDO).

Cellular Devices

Cellular communication is still much further developed in the phone industry than the computer industry. Cell phones and BlackBerries are the most common cellular-equipped devices you'll find. However, cellular modems are widely available for laptops, most of them with a PC Card interface.

Ethernet

Ethernet is the most common networking standard used today in the world, and it likely will be for the foreseeable future. It's not the most efficient method ever devised—after all, the technology is predicated upon the idea that packet collisions happen, and when they do, oops, we'll just resend the message. It works pretty well, though, except in extremely large networks, and is relatively cheap to implement.

For the fundamentals of Ethernet networking, see Chapter 8. In this chapter, I'll keep the focus on wireless networking, which is really a core strength of mobile technology.

Ethernet Networks

Ethernet networks are often set up as *spoke-and-wheel* networks. If you think about the construction of a wheel, at the center is a hub, and the spokes radiate from the hub to support the outside of the wheel. At the center of most Ethernet networks is a connectivity hub (a hub, switch, or router), and connected to it in some way are the computers on the network. One hub can be, and often is, connected to other hubs to extend the network.

Although we focus mainly on a spoke and wheel setup, Ethernet networks can also be configured as a linear bus, where the computers are physically connected in a serial line fashion. This was more common in the past, when 10Base2 and 10Base5 coaxial cabling was more popular than 10BaseT. If your network is configured as a bus rather than a star (spoke and wheel), you don't need a hub.

Wireless networking hubs often have wired connections, too, either for a computer that isn't wireless enabled or for uplinking to another hub. Figure 13.4 shows a Linksys wireless router.

FIGURE 13.4   Wireless router

You can't see the wired ports on the router shown in Figure 13.4, as they're located on the back of the device.

Another common type of central hub you will see is called a *Wireless Access Point (WAP)*. They look nearly identical to wireless routers and provide central connectivity like wireless routers, but they don't have nearly as many features. The main one most people worry about is Internet connection sharing.

Think of a router as a bridge between your computer and the outside world, say the Internet. When you sign up for high-speed access to the Internet, your *Internet Service Provider* (ISP) generally assigns you one IP address, and if you want more, you need to pay for more. When you set up your router, the external "side" of it gets that IP address. On the internal "side," the router assigns all computers on your network different IP addresses and handles all the translation for you in a process called *Network Address Translation* (NAT). The end result is that your ISP gives you (and charges you for) only one IP address, yet you can have as many computers on your internal network as your router can handle, and each of them has Internet access. It doesn't make your ISP happy, but it's great for end users.

For more information on TCP/IP and IP addressing, see Chapter 8.

Now back to the WAP: It can't do NAT. Therefore, there is no Internet connection sharing, unless you have software that can handle the connection for you, such as Microsoft's Internet Connection Sharing (ICS). But if you are only networking internally, a WAP is a fine connectivity device and is usually a bit cheaper than a wireless router.

Ethernet Technical Specifications

The most common wireless networking connection is called *WiFi*, short for wireless fidelity. Specifically, WiFi is a collection of IEEE 802.11x standards.

🌐 Real World Scenario

I'll Just Use My Neighbor's Wireless Connection

There's no doubt that wireless networking has become popular in mainstream America. People from all walks of life are discovering the joys of wire-free Internet access. Consequently, many homes now have wireless routers.

To continue the great news, wireless routers have become easier to set up than they were in the past, and most people can configure one with no more than a little assistance from the manual. However, setting a router up and setting a router up properly are two different things.

The part that most people forget is to secure their wireless network. For example, you can set your router to only accept connections from certain network cards or computer names. (By the way, if you have a wireless router and haven't restricted access to it yet, now is a good time to review the manual to find out how.)

If someone hasn't up the security on his router, anyone with a wireless card and within signal range (usually a few hundred yards) can access it. A phenomenon that's become popular in recent years is called *wardriving*: getting in your car with your laptop and driving around neighborhoods looking for wireless connections that you can hack.

You might be tempted to save the money on a wireless router and just access your neighbor's network, without her knowing. Don't do it. In July 2005, a UK man was convicted of using wireless without permission. He received 12 months of probation, was fined the equivalent of $872, and had his laptop confiscated. Several cases like this are pending in U.S. courts as well.

The most common standard for the last several years has been *802.11b*, which provides wireless speeds up to 11Mbps. Newer still is *802.11g*, which is backward compatible with 802.11b and provides data transmission of up to 54Mbps. Both 802.11b and 802.11g operate in the 2.4GHz band, and they use compatible encoding schemes.

Another standard you will occasionally run into is 802.11a. This standard operates at a different frequency (the 5GHz band), uses a different encoding scheme than 802.11b and 802.11g, and is not compatible with either of them.

Ethernet Devices

Most laptops today come with an internal 802.11 adapter. Often the laptop will claim to be 802.11b/g compatible, meaning it can handle either type of network. If your laptop doesn't have a network card, you can purchase USB or PC Card network adapters from any electronics store.

Other than network cards, all you really need is a central connectivity device. The most popular today are wireless routers, but you can also find wireless switches and access points. Finally, printing can be wireless as well. Many wireless routers will have a USB connection on them for a printer, or you can purchase a wireless print server, which will hook to your printer and interface with your wireless router as well.

Identifying Laptop-Specific Power Requirements

Laptops can get power from two sources. The first is an internal battery, and the second is an external source, such as a wall outlet. You have two different choices in external sources: AC power from a wall outlet or DC power from other outlets such as in cars or on airplanes.

Regardless of your external power source, you need to make sure the power adapter you are using will provide the right level of power to your laptop. The two numbers you need to pay particular attention to are those for amps and volts.

It would be nice to be able to give you specifics on exactly what your laptop requires for amps and volts, but it's not that easy. Seemingly, each laptop has a different power requirement. For example, a quick Internet search shows that a certain Dell laptop requires 20 volts and 5.5 amps, one model of IBM laptop needs 16 volts and 4 amps, and one Compaq laptop requires 22 volts and 2.7 amps.

So how do you know what you need? The first place to check is the bottom of your laptop. It should have a sticker on it that tells you the required power output. Figure 13.5 shows the sticker on the bottom of a Dell Latitude C640, which shows a need for 20 volts and 3.5 amps.

FIGURE 13.5 Laptop power requirement

The general rule to follow is this: Don't use a power adapter that provides anything other than exactly what your laptop requires. At best, your laptop won't work. At worst, you'll fry your system. If you're not sure, and your laptop doesn't have a sticker on the bottom, there are a few sources of information that might be able to help. You can look in the manual or check the manufacturer's website. If neither of those help, there are third-party websites, such as http://www.atbatt.com/computer-power-supply.asp, that can help you track down what you need.

Understanding LCD Technology

As discussed in Chapter 3, LCD technology is one of the core reasons why laptop computers have had a rapid rise in popularity. Before LCD technology, displays were big and bulky and hardly mobile. Because LCD is a totally different technology than cathode-ray tube (CRT), some different components are required. This section looks at some of the components that make LCD work.

Video Card

The video card in a laptop or desktop with an LCD monitor does the same thing a video card supporting a CRT monitor would do. It's responsible for generating and managing the image sent to the screen. The big difference is that most LCD monitors are digital, meaning you need a video card that puts out a digital image. Obviously, laptop manufacturers put video cards in laptops that are compatible with the display, but with desktops it can get a bit confusing. Figure 13.6 shows an ABIT video card, with a digital video interface (DVI) port on the left and an analog (VGA) port on the right. The port in the middle is an S-video/composite video port.

FIGURE 13.6   Video card

On the market, you can find digital-to-analog video converters, if you need to plug in an older analog monitor to a digital video card.

Backlight

LCD displays do not produce light, so to generate brightness, many LCD displays have a *backlight*. A backlight is a small fluorescent lamp placed behind, above, or to the side of an LCD display. The light from the lamp is diffused across the screen, producing brightness. The typical laptop display uses a *cold cathode fluorescent lamp (CCFL)* as its backlight. They're generally about eight inches long and slimmer than a pencil. Best of all, they generate little heat, which is always good thing to avoid with laptops.

Inverter

The only problem with fluorescent lighting, and LCD backlights in particular, is that they require fairly high-voltage, high-frequency energy. Another component is needed to provide the right kind of energy, and that's the *inverter*.

The inverter is a small circuit board installed behind the LCD panel that takes AC power and converts (inverts) it for the backlight. If you are having problems with flickering screens or dimness, it's more likely that the inverter is the problem and not the backlight itself.

There are two things to keep in mind if you are going to replace an inverter. One, they store and convert energy, so they have the potential to discharge that energy. To an inexperienced technician, they can be dangerous. Two, make sure that the replacement inverter was made to work with the LCD backlight you have. If they weren't made for each other, you might have problems with a dim screen or poor display quality.

LCD Screen

The screen on an LCD monitor does what you might expect—it produces the image that you see. There are two broad categories of LCD screens: active matrix and passive matrix.

For more information on active- and passive-matrix screens, see Chapter 3.

Removing Devices and Video Sharing

Because of the compact nature of laptop computers, space is at a premium. Consequently, most laptops have few extra bells and whistles installed internally. Most peripherals and expansion hardware, with the exception of PC Card devices, are plugged in through a port such as a USB port and reside outside the laptop case.

Space is also at a premium with what is built in, such as the motherboard, processor, and memory. You normally can't upgrade the processor, for example, because it's soldered onto the motherboard as opposed to being in a removable socket.

While you can upgrade the memory on laptops, you need to be aware of how your laptop allocates memory. Instead of having completely separate video memory, many laptops use system memory for applications as well as video, and you need to be cognizant of this if you plan on performing a video upgrade.

This section looks at removing hardware devices from laptops, as well as the effect of video sharing on memory upgrades.

Removing Laptop-Specific Hardware

In the grand scheme of things, there are two types of peripherals: internal and external. We've already discussed that laptops weren't exactly made for internal expandability. So when it comes to opportunities to remove internal hardware, you'll find them few and far between. The most likely thing you will do is add or remove memory. To do that, you usually need to remove a screw or two holding a plate on the bottom of the laptop to reveal the memory compartment. Always check with the laptop's manual and your warranty information before attempting these types of procedures.

External hardware is much easier to remove from the computer. Just unplug it, right? Well, it's not always quite that simple. If you have USB-type devices plugged in, removing them *is* as easy as disconnecting them, but other peripherals require more work.

Devices that can be removed when the computer is powered on are called hot-swappable devices. If you need to turn the computer off first, then the device is not hot-swappable. There are several different hot-swappable peripherals, including mice, keyboards, some hard drives, network cards, printers, and others. Good examples of non-hot-swappable devices include motherboards and internal IDE hard drives. Odds are if it's internal to your computer case, then it's not hot-swappable. Always be sure to check your hardware documentation to see if the device is safe to plug in or disconnect with the system powered on.

 WARNING   Although most of the time you can just remove a USB device, make sure it's not in use when you remove it.

In Exercise 13.1, we will show you the recommended method to remove a device.

EXERCISE 13.1

Removing a Device from Your Laptop

To remove a device from your laptop, follow these steps:

1. You need to stop the device first (this is even good policy for USB devices), using the icon in the system tray that looks like a card with a green arrow over it.

EXERCISE 13.1 *(continued)*

2. Click on the Safely Remove Hardware icon, and you will get a screen similar to the one shown here.

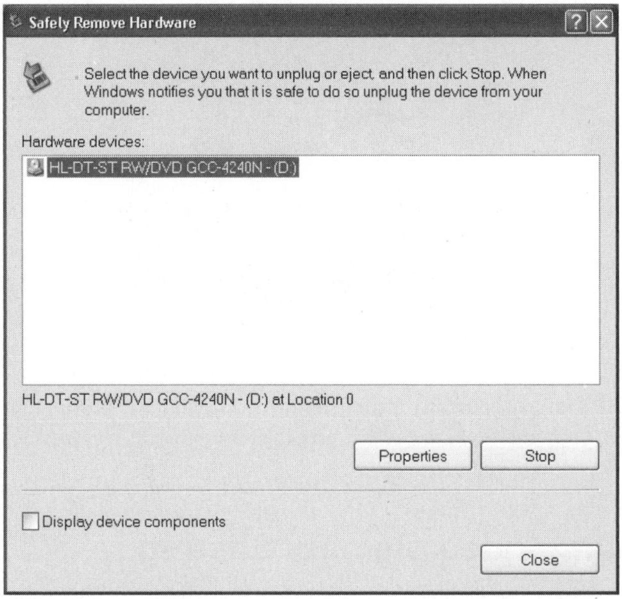

3. Highlight the device you want to remove, and click Stop. Windows will then notify you it's safe to remove the device. If it's a cabled device, just detach it. If it's PCMCIA, then you can press the Eject button next to the slot in which the card is located. Other types of hardware in some laptops require you to release a latch. The following photo shows a modular front-load bay, and the right side has a CD-ROM in it.

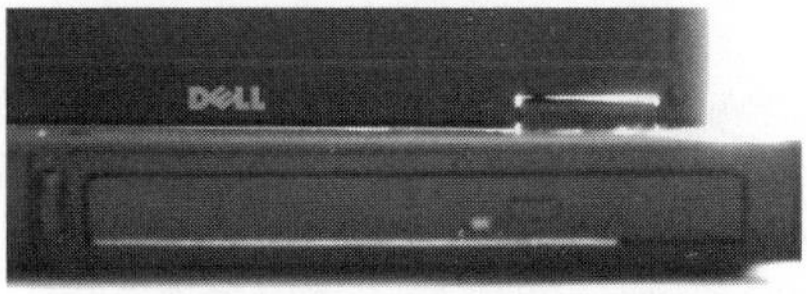

EXERCISE 13.1 *(continued)*

4. Turn the computer over, and you can see the release latch. Slide it to the side, and pull on the grip on the underside of the CD-ROM. Out it comes.

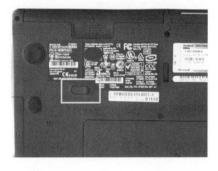

Adding a device to a laptop generally means that the computer will automatically recognize and enable the device for you, unless there's no compatible driver available. In cases like these, Windows will tell you that it detected new hardware and ask you to provide an appropriate driver.

Understanding Video Memory Sharing

Most laptop motherboards have the video card built into them. Just as with everything else inside the laptop case, there's simply no room for expansion cards inside most machines.

If your video card is built into your motherboard, odds are that it doesn't have its own memory but shares system memory with the processor. Note that there is nothing wrong with this type of setup; in fact, it often brings the cost of the laptop down. It's just that instead of having 512MB of RAM and 64MB of video RAM (for example), you would only have 512MB total. So if your video card were using 64MB, the system would only be left with 448MB.

How much of a difference does all of this make? Well, it depends on what you're doing with your laptop. If you're using it for the Internet and light work, probably not much difference. If you're working with more video-intensive applications, using a computer with shared memory might slow you down some. This usually brings up two questions. One, what's the optimal balance? Two, where do I change this?

To answer question one, again, it depends on what you are doing. If you perform more video-intensive operations (or if you're gaming), then you might want to set aside more memory for the video card. If you're not as concerned with rapid pixilation, then less is fine. Which brings us to the second question, which is where do you set it? Shared memory is configured in the system BIOS. Each BIOS is different, so be sure to consult your owner's manual if you have any questions. Keep in mind that some BIOSs will only allow you set aside a certain amount of memory—say, 128MB—for video memory.

How does this affect your computer when you upgrade the memory? First, keep in mind that some of your memory will be taken by the video card, so you might want to upgrade to more than you originally planned for. Also, after upgrading the memory, you will need to go into the BIOS and reconfigure how much you want allocated to the video card.

⊕ Real World Scenario

But My BIOS Won't Let Me Configure My Video Memory!

As the price of memory has dropped, and the size of components has gotten smaller and smaller, more laptop manufacturers are including video cards with their own memory in the system. If this is the case, then the BIOS might still display the video memory, but it won't let you change it. If this is your situation, the only way to increase video memory is to upgrade your video card.

In Exercise 13.2, we will show you how to remove and install video memory.

EXERCISE 13.2

Removing and Installing Video Memory

To remove and install the memory package, perform the following steps:

1. With the laptop turned off, locate the latches that secure the memory access panel. Remove the cover.

2. Gently slide the memory package out of its slot. Some laptops have clips or locks that hold the memory package in place. Release them first before removing the memory package.

3. Inspect the memory package and the slot.

4. Replace the memory package and ensure that it locks back into place.

5. Replace the access panel.

To install a PCMCIA memory card:

6. Locate the PCMCIA Type I slot and insert the memory card.

When handling memory packages, it is a good idea to also remove the battery and hard drive to prevent any corruption of data or damage from electrostatic discharge (ESD) to the drive connectors.

Troubleshooting Laptops

Troubleshooting is both an art and a science. There's a lot of intuition or gut feel that can go into it, but ultimately your success also depends on taking a methodological approach. Nothing can replace experience when it comes to troubleshooting. After all, if you've seen and fixed a problem before, odds are you have a pretty good idea of what will fix it this time. That doesn't mean that an inexperienced person has to struggle as a troubleshooter, though. It just means that the inexperienced troubleshooter needs to stick to a more methodical plan to get things fixed.

This section starts with an overview of troubleshooting steps. There's not a single book in the world that can tell you how to troubleshoot every situation, but if you follow some principles and guidelines, you'll get to the bottom of almost every problem. After reviewing the general guidelines, we'll move into diagnosing specific laptop problems.

Identifying Specific Safety Issues

The safety of the technician and the computer must be considered when a laptop computer is being repaired or updated.

A laptop is designed to take more shock than a PC; however; you still need to take care not to drop or shock any of the components as you remove them from the laptop.

Before you remove the hard drive, it is a good idea to back up any of the information stored on it if possible. Never remove the hard drive while the system is powered on or in hibernate mode.

Although you can safely remove a PCMCIA card while the system is on, doing so can cause an unexpected error to your programs or the operating system. Many operating systems have an icon representing the device in the Taskbar. By clicking on the device's icon (or by using the Safely Remove Hardware icon in the system tray), you can access an option to disable the device/slot before removing it. The same is true for undocking the laptop from a docking station.

A docking station is a common addition for many laptops. The docking station allows the laptop to extend its functionality by providing additional external connectors and a power source. When the laptop is in a docked state, the docking station takes on the function of providing power. In addition, it will normally have connectors for a monitor, keyboard, mouse, network, and USB. Each manufacturer may have additional options as well.

Diagnosing Laptop Problems

Before getting into specific laptop-type issues, remember that good troubleshooting means acting in a methodical manner. You need to find out if the device or software ever worked or what happened before the problem occurred. What changes were made (if any) to try to isolate the problem? Then test one fix at a time.

There are four typical areas where laptops could have different problems than their desktop counterparts: power, video, input, and wireless networking.

Power Concerns

Is it plugged in? Everyone hates getting asked that question if their computer doesn't work. But it's the critical first question to ask. After all, if it's not plugged in, who knows if it will work or not? You can't assume that the battery is working (or is attached) like it's supposed to. Always check power and connections first!

Most laptop power adapters have a light on them indicating they're plugged in. If there's no light, check to make sure the outlet is working, or switch outlets. Also, most laptops have a power-ready indicator light when plugged into a wall outlet as well. Check to see if it's lit. If the outlet is fine, try another power adapter. They do fail on occasion.

If you're working on a DC adapter, the same thing applies. Check for lights, try changing plugs if possible (many newer cars have secondary power sources, such as ones in the console between the seats), or try another adapter if you have one.

Another thing to remember when troubleshooting power problems is to remove all external peripherals. Strip it down to the base computer, so there isn't a short or other power drain coming from an external device.

In Exercise 13.3, we will show you how to remove and install a laptop battery.

EXERCISE 13.3

Removing and Installing Laptop Batteries

To remove and install the battery assembly, perform the following steps:

1. With the laptop turned off, locate the latches that secure the battery assembly. Release the latches.

2. Slide the battery assembly out of its slot.

3. Inspect the battery and the slot.

4. Replace the battery and ensure the latches lock it back into place.

Identifying Video Issues

Video problems are usually caused by the video card (built into the motherboard on most laptops) or the display unit. Of course, make sure the computer is on before diagnosing it as a video problem!

Here are a few things to try:

- Plug in an external monitor that you know works. On most laptops, you need to press the function (Fn) key and another key (often F8) to direct the video output to an external monitor.

- Check the LCD cutoff switch. Remember the function+F8 idea? Try toggling it a few times, waiting a few seconds between each press of the toggle key to let the display power up. Most laptops have three display states: LCD only, external only, and both.

- Raise or lower the brightness level. This is usually done with a function key combination as well, such as function+F5 or function+F6. Check your keyboard for function keys that look like the Sun.

- If you have a handheld computer, try turning the backlight feature on or off. For specifics on how to do this, check your manual.

If the display is not working, you can order a new one from the laptop manufacturer. If the computer won't output a display to an external monitor as well, you likely need a new motherboard.

Identifying LCD Issues

There are a couple of specific problems that you might encounter with LCD screens that are outside of the scope of normal video troubleshooting. This is just a feature of LCD technology.

The most common "problem" with LCD screens is a dim screen, one that you can never seem to make brighter. This is generally caused by one of two things: a failing inverter or a failing backlight. Unfortunately, the only real way to test it for sure is to replace a part, unless you have an inverter power tester handy. Many repair shops will be able to test your inverter and see if it's the cause of the problem.

Speaking of backlight issues, there are four things that can cause backlight problems. They are (in order of likelihood) the inverter, the backlight lamp, the video card, and the backlight circuitry on the motherboard.

If your screen is flickering, or there's no display but your monitor is getting power, then odds are, once again, that it's the inverter. When you replace an inverter, make sure it's designed to work with the LCD backlight in your system. Having a mismatched inverter could cause video display problems, such as a dim or flickering screen.

In Exercise 13.4, we will show you how to clean an LCD display.

EXERCISE 13.4

Cleaning an LCD Display

To clean an LCD display, perform the following steps:

1. Open the laptop to reveal the screen. With the laptop powered off, it is easier to see fingerprints and dirt on the screen.

2. Using a lint-free cloth moistened with water, gently wipe away any fingerprints, smudges, and dirt.

WARNING   Although most laptop screens can be cleaned with glass cleaner, some screens have a capacitive coating that can be damaged by the glass cleaner. Never spray any liquid directly onto the screen. Droplets from the liquid may cause electrical shorts in the system. Do not apply excessive pressure while cleaning the LCD panel. It is very easy to crack the screen if too much pressure is applied.

Identifying Input Problems

Laptop keyboards aren't as easy to switch out as desktop keyboards. You can, however, very easily attach an external keyboard to your laptop if the keys on your laptop don't appear to work. If you have the wrong type of connector, most electronics stores will have USB-to-PS/2 or PS/2-to-USB converters.

Another unique problem to laptop keyboards is the function key. (It can be your friend or your enemy.) If the function key is "stuck" on, the only keys that will work are those with functions on them. Try toggling it, just as you would a Caps Lock key.

A lot of laptops now have touchpads. While they're usually thought of as very handy (I love mine), some people find that they're annoying. If you are using the Touchpoint, for example, your palm might rest on the touchpad, causing erratic mouse behavior. You can turn the touchpad off through the Mouse applet in Control Panel or through the system BIOS. Keeping in mind that you can turn it off on purpose, remember that it can be turned off "accidentally" as well. Check to make sure it's enabled. Some laptops allow you to disable or change the sensitivity of the Touchpoint as well

On handhelds or other touch-screen devices, the screen input can occasionally fail. This represents a problem with the digitizer and generally means you need a repair or a replacement.

An issue seen more often on palmtop computers rather than full size laptops is a problem with the stylus input area. This is the area in which you write; your handwriting is (theoretically) recognized by the system and digitized. If this area isn't working properly, try resetting the device. If it still doesn't work, then the digitizer could need replacement.

Identifying Networking Troubles

Nearly all modern laptops are equipped with wireless networking built into the computer. In many cases, the wireless antenna is run into the LCD panel. This allows the antenna to stand up higher and pick up a better signal.

If your LCD panel was just replaced, and your wireless network isn't working like it should, it could be that your wireless card antenna wasn't reconnected properly.

If your wireless isn't working, check to make sure that the LEDs on your network card are functioning. If there are no lights, it could indicate a problem with the card itself or, on some cards, that there is no connection or signal. First, make sure that the wireless card is enabled through Windows. Using Windows XP, you generally do this by right-clicking on My Network Places, selecting Properties, right-clicking the wireless network connection, and selecting Properties in order to look at the network card properties. However, some network cards have their own proprietary configuration software. While looking at the wireless network connection properties, you can also click the Wireless Networks tab to see if you're getting a signal and the strength of that signal.

If you have a USB network adapter, try unplugging it and plugging it back in. Make sure that Windows recognizes the card properly.

When wireless fails but the network card appears to be working, plug it in. Most laptops with wireless cards also have wired RJ-45 network ports. Plug the card in and see if you get lights, and see if the network works.

Summary

In this chapter, you learned about the various laptop issues that are on the A+ 220-602 and 220-604 exams. We discussed differences between laptops and desktops, including the various components that make up a laptop and how they differ in appearance and function from those on a desktop.

You also learned how to configure power management in laptops, as well as remove laptop-specific hardware. Finally, we explored troubleshooting procedures and preventative maintenance techniques. Keep in mind that each brand of laptop is different. For a lot of these issues, it is important to refer to the service manual for specific proper procedures.

Exam Essentials

Know what situations best utilize Bluetooth technology. Bluetooth is designed to run in a Wireless Personal Area Network. It works best if you have a small physical range of communications but need to have easy connectivity to several devices. Bluetooth can connect your phone to your car and several computer peripherals (keyboards, mice, printers, and so on) to your laptop.

Understand infrared technology strengths and weaknesses. Infrared is quick, easy to configure (that is, no configuration is required, other than ensuring your port is enabled), and highly secure. However, it is limited to line-of-sight, point-to-point communications, at a range of about one meter.

Know what advantages cellular communications have over other wireless options. The single biggest advantage cellular has is range. While other technologies are limited to a few hundred meters at best, cellular can span several kilometers without a problem. If you need range, cellular is the way to go.

Know when to use wireless Ethernet. Wireless Ethernet is basically an extension of your wired network. Transmission rates are pretty good (54Mbps for 802.11g), and properly encrypting transmissions allows for reasonably tight security. If you want a wireless network to connect several computers, wireless Ethernet is by far the best choice available.

Know the components of an LCD screen and what they do.   The backlight provides brightness, because by themselves LCDs do not generate light. The inverter provides power to the backlight. The video card generates images and sends them to the screen, and the screen provides the physical display.

Understand how video memory sharing affects your laptop.   In order to save space, many laptops forgo specialized video memory and just tap into system memory instead. Of course, this reduces the amount of system memory available and also limits the amount of video memory you can logically use. In a nutshell, it slows your computer down a bit, but it's also usually a lot cheaper than having separate video memory.

Know how to remove laptop-specific hardware.   For most devices, you should use the Safely Remove Hardware icon in the Taskbar to stop the device and then physically remove it.

Understand laptop-specific troubleshooting issues.   Laptops have unique issues when it comes to power (AC and DC adapters), external peripherals, inputs (such as the touchpad and Fn key), video output, and wireless networking.

Review Questions

1. Which two of the following are standards for cellular communications?

    A. GSM

    B. SIG

    C. CDMA

    D. CCFL

2. Which of the following standards would you want to use if you need high-bandwidth network communications?

    A. Bluetooth

    B. Ethernet

    C. Cellular

    D. Infrared

3. If you want to set up a wireless network and have multiple computers share one Internet connection, which of the following connectivity devices should you use (provided you don't have any Internet connection–sharing software)?

    A. Wireless access point

    B. Wireless hub

    C. Wireless switch

    D. Wireless router

4. Your laptop has shared video memory. You want to increase the amount of memory available to the video card from 32MB to 64MB. Where do you do this?

    A. The video applet in Control Panel

    B. Moving a jumper on the video card

    C. The system BIOS

    D. You can't reallocate shared memory.

5. You lost your laptop AC power adapter and need to purchase another one. How can you tell what power output it needs to provide? (Choose all that apply.)

    A. It doesn't matter, because all laptops have the same power requirements.

    B. Look for a sticker on the bottom of the laptop.

    C. Consult the owner's manual.

    D. Look at the manufacturer's website.

6. Which of the following technologies' networks is called a piconet?

   A. Bluetooth

   B. Ethernet

   C. Cellular

   D. Infrared

7. Which of the following communication methods is point-to-point, limited to a distance of about one meter?

   A. Bluetooth

   B. Wireless Ethernet

   C. Cellular

   D. Infrared

8. The _____ provides power to the backlight of most LCD monitors.

   A. LCD backlight power adapter

   B. Inverter

   C. Video card

   D. LCD backlight motherboard circuitry

9. A flickering LCD screen is most likely caused by what?

   A. A failing inverter

   B. A faulty LCD backlight

   C. The video board circuitry

   D. A crack in the LCD display

10. Which of the following standards supports communications up to 54Mbps?

   A. 802.11*x*

   B. 802.11b

   C. 802.11g

   D. Bluetooth

11. A piconet is limited to how many devices?

   A. Six

   B. Seven

   C. Eight

   D. Unlimited

12. Which of the following communication technologies has the longest range?

    A. Bluetooth

    B. Wireless Ethernet

    C. Cellular

    D. Infrared

13. Which of the following communication technologies is designed for use with peripheral devices such as keyboards, mice, and wireless headsets?

    A. Bluetooth

    B. Ethernet

    C. Cellular

    D. Infrared

14. Which one of the following types of PCMCIA cards is 10.5 millimeters thick?

    A. Type I

    B. Type II

    C. Type III

    D. Type IV

15. What is the easiest way to brighten your laptop screen if you are working around a strong light source?

    A. Use the function key along with the appropriate key to brighten the screen.

    B. Replace the LCD backlight with a more powerful backlight.

    C. Adjust the brightness settings in the Video applet of Control Panel.

    D. Use the thumbwheels on the front of the monitor to adjust the brightness.

16. Which of the following best describes the function of SAFER+?

    A. It protects the computer against hacker attacks.

    B. It encrypts Bluetooth communications.

    C. It password-protects the system BIOS.

    D. It produces an audit log of failed system services.

17. You have inserted a flash memory drive into the USB port on your laptop and copied files to it. Now you want to remove the device. What is the recommended way to remove the device?

    A. Use the Safely Remove Hardware icon in the system tray to stop the device, and then unplug it.

    B. Use the Add/Remove Hardware applet in Control Panel to stop the device, and then unplug it.

    C. Unplug the device from the USB port.

    D. Turn off the laptop, and then unplug it.

18. Your department has several different models of laptops. You need to find a power adapter for one of them, and all of the extra power adapters are thrown into a drawer. The sticker on the bottom of the laptop indicates output requirements of 16 volts and 4 amps. Which of the following power supplies can you use? (Choose all that apply.)

    A. AC power adapter, 16V 4A

    B. DC power adapter, 16V 4A

    C. AC power adapter, 18V 5A

    D. DC power adapter, 18V 5A

19. The touchpad on one of your client's laptop computers is not working. Where can you check to ensure that the device is enabled? (Choose all that apply.)

    A. The Safely Remove Hardware icon in the system tray

    B. The Add/Remove Hardware applet in Control Panel

    C. The Mouse applet in Control Panel

    D. The system BIOS

20. Which of the following is the encryption method used by infrared devices to secure transmissions?

    A. SAFER+

    B. Shared-key encryption

    C. Public-key encryption

    D. None of the above

Answers to Review Questions

1. A, C. The Global System for Mobile Communications (GSM) and Code Division Multiple Access (CDMA) are cellular standards. A SIG is a Special Interest Group, and cold cathode fluorescent lamp (CCFL) is a backlight on a laptop.

2. B. Ethernet is the best of the four wireless communication methods for networking, and it has the highest bandwidth of all four options.

3. D. A wireless router will allow you to set up multiple computers to share one Internet connection. The other options will allow you to connect multiple computers in a wireless network, but none of them provide Network Address Translation (NAT).

4. C. To reallocate shared memory, enter the system BIOS.

5. B, C, D. As convenient as it would be for all laptops to have the same power requirements, it's not the case. You can look for power requirements on the bottom of the laptop, in the manual, or on the manufacturer's website.

6. A. Bluetooth networks are called piconets. Ethernet networks are typically called networks or nets. Cellular networks are cells. Infrared doesn't really make networks, as it's a point-to-point communication method.

7. D. Infrared communications are point-to-point only and are limited to about one meter. Bluetooth can work up to 100 meters, depending on the version. Wireless Ethernet network signals can travel for several hundred meters, and cellular communications can span several kilometers.

8. B. The inverter is responsible for powering the LCD backlight. There is no LCD backlight power adapter, by name. The video card is responsible for the video signal.

9. A. If the screen is flickering, the most likely culprit is the inverter, which supplies power to the LCD backlight. If the backlight were to fail, you would likely have no video, and the same goes for the video board itself. If the LCD display is cracked, you'll be lucky to get an image at all.

10. C. The 802.11g standard supports speeds up to 54Mbps. 802.11x refers to the family of 802.11 standards, and 802.11b supports only up to 11Mbps. Bluetooth is limited to 3Mbps.

11. C. A piconet (Bluetooth network) can have eight devices on it. One device can communicate with seven other devices on the same network.

12. C. Infrared communications are point-to-point only and are limited to about one meter. Bluetooth can work up to 100 meters, depending on the version. Wireless Ethernet network signals can travel for several hundred meters, and cellular communications can span several kilometers.

13. A. Bluetooth was made to work as a Wireless Personal Area Network (WPAN). As such, it's perfect for computer peripherals such as keyboards, mice, and wireless headsets.

14. C. Type III PCMCIA cards are 10.5 millimeters thick. Type I cards are 3.3mm thick, and Type II cards are 5mm thick. Currently, there are no Type IV PCMCIA cards.

15. A. On laptops, you control the brightness of the screen with the function (Fn) key along with the appropriate key to brighten the screen (it usually has a Sun-like icon on it).

16. B. The Secure and Fast Encryption Routine (SAFER+) is the encryption method used by Bluetooth devices.

17. A. With USB devices, you can typically just unplug them. However, the recommended way to remove any device is to first stop it with the Safely Remove Hardware icon in the system tray and then unplug the device. With a flash drive, this is a good idea because the system may still be accessing the device, and improper removal can result in the loss of data.

18. A, B. Whenever using a power adapter for a laptop, ensure that it produces exactly the power that the laptop needs. Laptops can use either AC or DC power adapters.

19. C, D. The touchpad can be enabled or disabled through the Mouse applet in Control Panel or through the system BIOS.

20. D. Infrared devices do not encrypt data transmissions. Infrared devices are limited to about one meter and must be pointed directly at the device intended to receive the message. Therefore, encryption is not considered a major concern for these devices.

Installing, Configuring, Optimizing, and Upgrading Operating Systems

---

THE FOLLOWING COMPTIA A+ IT TECHNICIAN EXAM OBJECTIVES ARE COVERED IN THIS CHAPTER:

✓ **3.1 Identify the fundamental principles of operating systems**

- Use command-line functions and utilities to manage operating systems, including proper syntax and switches, for example:
  - CMD
  - HELP
  - DIR
  - ATTRIB
  - EDIT
  - COPY
  - XCOPY
  - FORMAT
  - IPCONFIG
  - PING
  - MD/CD/RD
- Identify concepts and procedures for creating, viewing, and managing disks, directories, and files on operating systems
  - Disks (for example, active, primary, extended, and logical partitions and file systems including FAT32 and NTFS)
  - Directory structures (for example, create folders, navigate directory structures)

- Files (for example, creation, attributes, permissions)
- Locate and use operating system utilities and available switches, for example:
  - Disk management tools (for example, DEFRAG, NTBACKUP, CHKDSK, FORMAT)
  - System management tools
    - Device and Task Manager
    - MSCONFIG
    - REGEDIT
    - REGEDT32
    - CMD
    - Event Viewer
    - System Restore
    - Remote Desktop
- File management tools (for example, Windows Explorer, ATTRIB)

✓ **3.2 Install, configure, optimize, and upgrade operating systems**

- Identify procedures and utilities used to optimize operating systems, for example:
  - Virtual memory
  - Hard drives (for example, disk defragmentation)
  - Temporary files
  - Services
  - Startup
  - Application

✓ **3.3 Identify tools, diagnostic procedures, and troubleshooting techniques for operating systems**

- Demonstrate the ability to recover operating systems (for example, boot methods, Recovery Console, ASR, ERD)
  - Windows-specific printing problems (for example, print spool stalled, incorrect/incompatible driver for print)
  - Auto-restart errors

- Blue-screen error
- System lockup
- Device drivers failure (input/output devices)
- Application install, start, or load failure
- Recognize and resolve common error messages and codes, for example:
  - Boot (for example, invalid boot disk, inaccessible boot drive, missing NTLDR)
  - Startup (for example, device/service failed to start, device/program in Registry not found)
  - Event Viewer
  - Registry
  - Windows reporting
- Use diagnostic utilities and tools to resolve operational problems, for example:
  - Bootable media
  - Startup modes (for example, safe mode, safe mode with command prompt or networking, step-by-step/single-step mode)
  - Documentation resources (for example, user/installation manuals, Internet/web-based training materials)
  - Task and Device Manager
  - Event Viewer
  - MSCONFIG
  - Recovery CD / recovery partition
  - Remote Desktop Connection and Assistance
  - System File Checker (SFC)

✓ **3.4 Perform preventative maintenance for operating systems**

- Demonstrate the ability to perform preventative maintenance on operating systems including software and Windows updates (for example, service packs), scheduled backups/restore, restore points

THE FOLLOWING COMPTIA A+ REMOTE SUPPORT TECHNICIAN EXAM OBJECTIVES ARE COVERED IN THIS CHAPTER:

✓ **2.1 Identify the fundamental principles of using operating systems**

- Use command-line functions and utilities to manage Windows 2000, XP Professional, and XP Home, including proper syntax and switches, for example:
  - CMD
  - HELP
  - DIR
  - ATTRIB
  - EDIT
  - COPY
  - XCOPY
  - FORMAT
  - IPCONFIG
  - PING
  - MD/CD/RD
- Identify concepts and procedures for creating, viewing, and managing disks, directories, and files in Windows 2000, XP Professional, and XP Home, for example:
  - Disks (for example, active, primary, extended, and logical partitions)
  - File systems (for example, FAT32, NTFS)
  - Directory structures (for example, create folders, navigate directory structures)
  - Files (for example, creation, extensions, attributes, permissions)
- Locate and use Windows 2000, XP Professional, and XP Home utilities and available switches
  - Disk management tools (for example, DEFRAG, NTBACKUP, CHKDSK, FORMAT)
  - System management tools

- Device and Task Manager
- MSCONFIG
- REGEDIT
- REGEDIT32
- CMD
- Event Viewer
- System Restore
- Remote Desktop
- File management tools (for example, Windows Explorer, ATTRIB)

✓ **2.2 Install, configure, optimize, and upgrade operating systems**

- Identify procedures and utilities used to optimize the performance of Windows 2000, XP Professional, and XP Home, for example:
  - Virtual memory
  - Hard drives (for example, disk defragmentation)
  - Temporary files
  - Services
  - Startup
  - Applications

✓ **2.3 Identify tools, diagnostic procedures, and troubleshooting techniques for operating systems**

- Recognize and resolve common operational problems, for example:
  - Windows-specific printing problems (for example, print spool stalled, incorrect/incompatible driver for print)
  - Auto-restart errors
  - Blue-screen error
  - System lockup
  - Device drivers failure (input/output devices)
  - Application install, start, or load failure

- Recognize and resolve common error messages and codes, for example:
  - Boot (for example, invalid boot disk, inaccessible boot device, missing NTLDR)
  - Startup (for example, device/service has failed to start, device/program references in Registry not found)
  - Event Viewer
  - Registry
  - Windows
- Use diagnostic utilities and tools to resolve operational problems, for example:
  - Bootable media
  - Startup modes (for example, safe mode, safe mode with command prompt or networking, step-by-step/single-step mode)
  - Documentation resources (for example, user/installation manuals, Internet/web-based training materials)
  - Task and Device Manager
  - Event Viewer
  - MSCONFIG
  - Recovery CD / recovery partition
  - Remote Desktop Connection and Assistance
  - System File Checker (SFC)

✓ **2.4 Perform preventative maintenance for operating systems**

- Perform preventative maintenance on Windows 2000, XP Professional, and XP Home including software and Windows updates (for example, service packs)

Without software to run on them, computer components are nothing more than expensive paperweights. The most important piece of software your computer has is the operating system.

In the simplest of contexts, the operating system is a translator between you and the hardware in your computer. Just leaving it at that level, though, means you miss out on so many of the intricate details that make operating systems so complex and interesting.

Although complexity and interesting features can be fun, they can also be problematic. The more moving parts something has, the more likely it is that one of those parts will fail and need repair.

This chapter covers several aspects of the Windows 2000 and Windows XP operating systems. We'll start off with a discussion of how to run an operating system, including from a command prompt, and move into managing Windows and using Windows utilities. We'll also look at optimizing Windows, resolving specific error messages, and performing preventative maintenance.

Using Operating Systems

One of the niceties of the Windows operating system is its flexibility. There are often several ways to accomplish one system management task. For example, you can manage your files and directories in Windows Explorer, but if you are a cagey DOS-era veteran, you can still do the same thing from the command line. In this section, you will look at various ways that you can perform system management tasks in Windows. This includes using the command line (even if you're not a cagey DOS-era veteran) as well as using graphical tools. We'll cover the following topics:

- Using command-line utilities

- Managing disks, files, and directories

- Using Windows utilities

Although we'll focus specifically on the Windows 2000 and Windows XP operating systems, many of these utilities (especially the command-line functions) are universal throughout the Windows family.

Using the Command Prompt

Even though we've made quantum leaps in technology over the last 20 to 30 years, the Windows operating system's ancestor, the Microsoft Disk Operating System (MS-DOS), still plays a role in Windows today.

MS-DOS was never meant to be extremely friendly. Its roots are in CP/M, which, in turn, has its roots in Unix. Both of these older OSs are command line–based, and so is MS-DOS. In other words, they all use long strings of commands typed in at the computer keyboard to perform operations. Some people prefer this type of interaction with the computer, including many folks with technical backgrounds. Although Windows has left the full command-line interface behind, it still contains a bit of DOS, and you get to it through the command prompt.

There are several command-line utilities that can be useful in managing a Windows-based computer. One important thing to point out, though, is that the DOS interface really has gone the way of the dinosaur. Although you probably can't tell from looking at it (see Figure 14.1), the Windows command prompt is actually a 16- or 32-bit Windows program that is intentionally *designed* to have the look and feel of a DOS command line. Because it is, despite its appearance, a Windows program, the command prompt provides all the stability and configurability you expect from Windows.

Running a Utility or Program from the Command Prompt

Windows includes several command-line utilities you can use to configure and maintain your system. Among these is the IPCONFIG utility, which allows you to check on the TCP/IP settings of the machine. (TCP/IP is the protocol that allows networked computers to use the Internet, and as such is something you will probably see a lot of. It's discussed in detail in Chapter 8.)

You can access a command prompt by running either the 16-bit COMMAND.COM or the 32-bit CMD.EXE.

There are few actual text-based applications in newer versions of Windows. However, for a taste of the old days, check out the EDIT program (see Figure 14.2), which is still provided free of charge with even the newest versions of Windows. EDIT is often used to modify batch files and text configuration files. Exercise 14.1 gives you some exposure to the EDIT program.

EXERCISE 14.1

Using the *EDIT* Program

In this exercise, you get to use one of the most rudimentary text-editing programs, EDIT. (Thank goodness for the word-processing programs of our day!)

1. Open a command prompt. The quickest way to do this is to click Start ➢ Run, type **CMD** (or **COMMAND**) in the Open field, and click OK.

2. Type **EDIT** and press Enter.

3. The EDIT utility opens. In the text area, type **hello**.

4. To save the file, press Alt+F. This brings up the File menu. Press A.

5. In the Save As window, type **HELLO.TXT** and click OK.

6. To exit from EDIT, press Alt+F and press X for Exit.

FIGURE 14.1   The Windows command prompt

FIGURE 14.2   The EDIT program

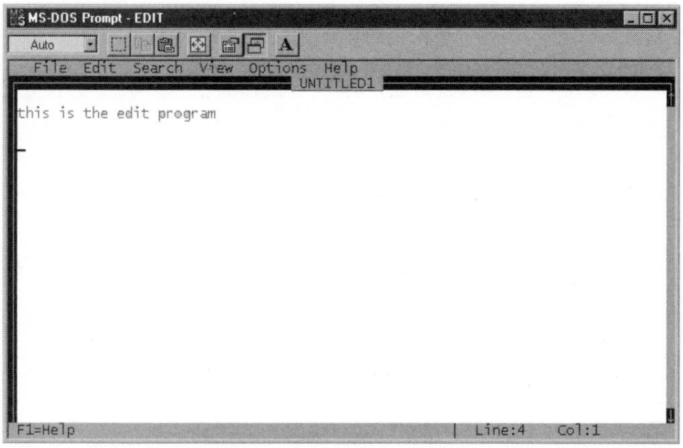

Issuing Text Commands

In general, older versions of Windows, such as Windows 98, use more *text-based commands* than newer versions, such as Windows 2000/XP. Look for standard commands in the \Windows\ System32 directory. Some commands are not listed in this directory (such as dir, CD, and CLS), but are internal to the operating system. These commands are executed by COMMAND.COM. Table 14.1 lists some of the available Windows text commands in Windows 2000 and Windows XP.

TABLE 14.1   Windows Text Commands

Command	Purpose
ATTRIB	Allows the user to set or remove file attributes.
CD	Changes your current folder to another folder (same as CHDIR).

TABLE 14.1 Windows Text Commands *(continued)*

Command	Purpose
CHKDSK	Examines the machine's hard drives.
CLS	Clears the screen.
CONVERT	Converts a FAT file system to an NTFS file system.
COPY	Copies a file into another directory.
DEFRAG	Defragments (reorganizes) the files on your machine's hard drives, which can result in better performance.
DEL	Deletes a file from the folder.
DIR	Displays the contents of the current folder.
DISKCOPY	Duplicates floppy disks.
DISKPART	Manages partitions on the computer's hard drives.
ECHO	Repeats typed text back to the screen. Can be used to send text to a file or device by using redirection.
EDIT	Allows you to edit text files.
FIND	Searches for a text string in one file or several files.
FORMAT	Prepares a drive for use.
HELP	Displays the list of commands you can execute.
IPCONFIG	Displays the computer's IP configuration.
MD	Creates a new folder (same as MKDIR).
MEM	Provides information about how much memory is available to the system.
MOVE	Moves files from one folder to another.
PING	Establishes a connection to the specified host.
REN	Renames a file (can also use RENAME).

TABLE 14.1   Windows Text Commands *(continued)*

Command	Purpose
RD	Deletes a directory (same as RMDIR).
SET	Sets, displays, and removes DOS environment variables.
SETVER	Sets the version and reports the version numbers of DOS utilities.
TYPE	Displays the contents of text files.
VER	Checks the current version of the OS.
XCOPY	Duplicates files and subdirectories. An extension of the COPY command.

To issue a command from the command prompt, you need to know the structure the command uses, generally referred to as its *syntax*. You should also be familiar with the command's available switches. *Switches* enable you to further configure the command's actions. Exercise 14.2 shows you how to learn about a command's syntax and available switches and then run that command. The command in the exercise is ATTRIB, which is used to allow a user to set one of four attributes on a file: Read-Only, Archive, System, or Hidden.

To identify the options or switches for a DOS command, you can use the built-in Help system. Type the command followed by a forward slash and a question mark (/?). Doing so displays all the options for that command and how to use them properly, as shown in Figure 14.3.

FIGURE 14.3   Options available for ATTRIB.EXE

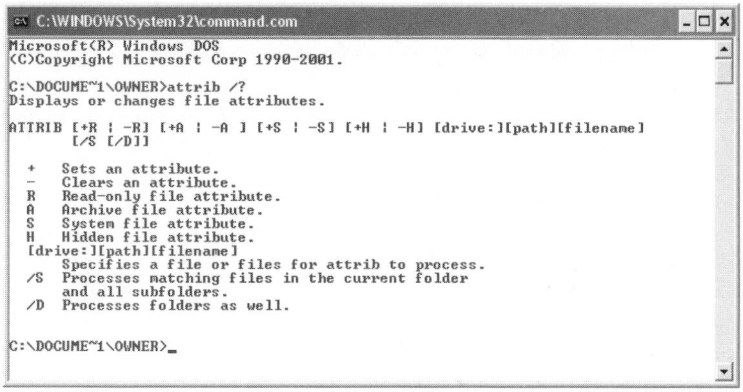

```
C:\WINDOWS\System32\command.com                                    _ □ x
Microsoft(R) Windows DOS
(C)Copyright Microsoft Corp 1990-2001.

C:\DOCUME~1\OWNER>attrib /?
Displays or changes file attributes.

ATTRIB [+R ¦ -R] [+A ¦ -A ] [+S ¦ -S] [+H ¦ -H] [drive:][path][filename]
       [/S [/D]]

  +    Sets an attribute.
  -    Clears an attribute.
  R    Read-only file attribute.
  A    Archive file attribute.
  S    System file attribute.
  H    Hidden file attribute.
  [drive:][path][filename]
       Specifies a file or files for attrib to process.
  /S   Processes matching files in the current folder
       and all subfolders.
  /D   Processes folders as well.


C:\DOCUME~1\OWNER>_
```

EXERCISE 14.2

Changing a File Attribute on Windows XP

You can change file attributes from within Windows, but also from a command prompt. In this exercise you learn how to change attributes from the command prompt.

1. Open a command prompt. To do this, click Start ≻ Run, type **CMD** in the Open field, and click OK.

2. In the command prompt window, type **CD /D C:** and press Enter.

3. Type **DIR** and press Enter. A list of all the files in the root of C: is shown.

4. Type **ATTRIB /?** and press Enter. Examine the available options.

5. Type **ATTRIB AUTOEXEC.BAT** and press Enter. The current attributes of the file are displayed.

6. Type **ATTRIB +R AUTOEXEC.BAT** and press Enter.

7. Repeat step 5 to view the changed attribute, and then repeat step 6 with the **–R** switch to return the file to its original attributes.

8. Type **EXIT** to close the command-prompt window.

You can use commands you've already typed at the command prompt again without having to type the same or a similar command over and over. To do so, press the up arrow on the keyboard. This steps backward one at a time through the commands you've entered, and can make working with command-prompt commands much quicker. When you've found the command you're looking for, you can either press Enter to execute it again or use the left and right arrow keys to navigate through the command to make minor modifications, such as specifying a different switch.

In the next few sections, we'll look at how to use some of the more popular commands and their associated switches.

Unless otherwise specified, switches can be entered in lowercase or uppercase, and have the same effect.

ATTRIB

As mentioned earlier in this chapter, the ATTRIB command is used to set file attributes, such as Read-Only or Hidden. Table 14.2 lists the switches available with ATTRIB.

TABLE 14.2   *ATTRIB* Switches

Switch	Purpose
+	Sets an attribute
–	Clears an attribute
R	Read-Only file attribute
A	Archive attribute
S	System attribute
H	Hidden attribute
/S	Makes the change on all matching files in the current folder (directory) and any subfolders
/D	Makes the change to the folder (directory) as well

An easy mnemonic device to remember the commonly used ATTRIB switches is the word *RASH*, for Read-Only, Archive, System, and Hidden.

For an exercise on using ATTRIB, please refer back to Exercise 14.2. But here's the proper syntax for using ATTRIB:

`ATTRIB [switch] [drive:][path][filename][/S [/D]`

If the file you are setting the attribute on is in the directory you're in, you don't need to specify a drive or path, just the filename, as in the following:

`ATTRIB +R BOOT.INI`

This will make the BOOT.INI file read-only, but it will work only if your current directory is the directory containing the file (usually the root of C:), or in a directory that is listed in the system's search path (the PATH environment variable).

CD/MD/RD

The CD, MD, and RD commands are used to change (or display), make, and remove directories, respectively. They're shorthand versions of the CHDIR, MKDIR, and RMDIR commands. Table 14.3 lists their usage and switches.

TABLE 14.3   *CD/MD/RD* Usage and Switches

Command	Purpose
CD *[path]*	Changes to the specified directory.
CD /D *[drive:][path]*	Changes to the specified directory on the drive.
CD ..	Changes to the directory that is up one level.
CD\	Changes to the root directory of the drive.
MD *[drive:][path]*	Makes a directory in the specified path. If you don't specify a path, the directory will be created in your current directory.
RD *[drive:][path]*	Removes (deletes) specified directory.
RD /S *[drive:][path]*	Removes all directories and files in the specified directory, including the specified directory itself.
RD /Q *[drive:][path]*	Quiet mode. It won't ask whether you're sure you want to delete the specified directory when you use /S.

Now that you've looked at the available switches, let's use them in Exercise 14.3.

EXERCISE 14.3

Command-Line Directory Management

For technicians who have been around for years, managing directories from a command line is second nature. It's important to be able to get around and manage directories in a command prompt, so in this exercise you'll learn how to do this.

1. Open a command prompt. To do this, click Start ➢ Run, type **CMD** in the Open field, and click OK.

2. Change to the root of your C: drive by typing **CD /D C:** and pressing Enter. (Note: If you are already in C:, all you have to type is **CD** and press Enter.)

3. Create a directory called C14 by typing **MD C14** and pressing Enter.

4. Change to the C14 directory by typing **CD C14** and pressing Enter.

5. Create several layers of subdirectories at once. Type **MD A1\B2\C3\D4** and press Enter.

EXERCISE 14.3 *(continued)*

Notice that these commands created each of the directories you specified. You now have a directory structure that looks like this: C:\C14\A1\B2\C3\D4.

6. Change back to your root directory by typing **CD**.

7. Attempt to delete the C14 directory by typing **RD C14** and pressing Enter.

Windows won't let you delete the directory, because the directory is not empty. This is a safety measure. Now let's really delete it.

8. Delete the C14 directory and all subdirectories by typing **RD /S C14** and pressing Enter. It will ask whether you're sure. If you are, type **y** and press Enter.

Note that if you had used the /Q option in addition to /S, your system wouldn't have asked whether you were sure; it would have just deleted the directories.

COPY

The COPY command does what it says: It makes a copy of a file in a second location. (To copy a file and remove it from its original location, use the MOVE command.) Here's the syntax for COPY:

COPY [filename] [destination]

It's pretty straightforward. There are several for COPY, but in practice they are rarely used. The two most used ones are /V, which verifies that the files are written correctly after the copy, and /Y, which suppresses the prompt asking whether you're sure you want to overwrite files if they exist in the destination directory.

The COPY command cannot be used to copy directories. Use XCOPY for that function.

One useful tip is to use wildcards. For example, in DOS (or at the command prompt), the asterisk (*) is a wildcard that means *everything*. So you could type **COPY *.EXE** to copy all files that have an .EXE extension, or you could type **COPY *.*** to copy all files in your current directory.

DIR

The DIR command is short for *directory* and gives you a listing of everything in your current directory. Its usefulness is readily apparent, as it's always good to know where your files are located. There are several switches available for DIR. Table 14.4 captures some of the most commonly used ones.

TABLE 14.4 Common *DIR* Switches

Switch	Purpose
/A	Displays files with specified attributes.
/O	Lists the files in a sorted order. Options for sorting are N for name, E for extension, G for directories first, S by size, and D by date.
/P	Pauses after a full screen is displayed.
/Q	Displays the owner of the files and directories.
/S	Shows all files in that directory, and any subdirectories of that directory.
/W	Displays the files and directories in wide format.

If you're in the DOS world, the two most common commands you are ever going to use are CD and DIR. You need to get around and see what's there. Exercise 14.4 gives you some practice with the DIR command.

EXERCISE 14.4

Seeing What's Out There with *DIR*

The DIR command is one of the fundamental command-line utilities that every technician needs to know how to use. You'll get some practice with it in this exercise.

1. Open a command prompt. To do this, click Start ➢ Run, type **CMD** in the Open field, and click OK.

2. Obtain a directory listing by typing **DIR** and pressing Enter.

3. Switch to the root directory by typing **CD** and pressing Enter.

4. Look at the files in named order by typing **DIR /ON** and pressing Enter.

5. Check out what's on your hard drive! Type **DIR /S** and press Enter.

You'll probably have time to read the rest of this chapter before the listing stops. You can manually stop it by holding down your Ctrl key and pressing Break.

6. Let's make it so you can actually read what's in which directories. Type **DIR /S /P** and press Enter.

This command displays one page and asks you to press any key to continue. After doing that gets tiring, you might want to press Ctrl+Break and then any key.

If you have too much displayed on your screen, you can use the CLS command to clear your screen.

FORMAT

The FORMAT command is used to wipe data off of disks and prepare them for new use. Before a disk can be formatted, it must have partitions created on it. (Partitioning was done in the DOS days with the FDISK command, but that command does not exist in Windows 2000 and Windows XP.) The syntax for FORMAT is as follows:

FORMAT *[volume]* *[switches]*

The *volume* parameter describes the drive letter (for example, D:), mount point, or volume name. Table 14.5 lists some common format switches.

TABLE 14.5   *FORMAT* Switches

Switch	Purpose
/FS:*[filesystem]*	Specifies the type of file system to use (FAT, FAT32, or NTFS)
/V:*[label]*	Specifies the new volume label
/Q	Executes a quick format

There are other options as well to specify allocation sizes, the number of sectors per track, and the number of tracks per disk size. However, it's not recommended you use these unless you have a very specific need. The defaults are really just fine.

So, if you wanted to format your D: as NTFS, with a name of HDD2, you could type the following:

FORMAT D: /FS:NTFS /V:HDD2

Before you format anything, be sure you have it backed up or are prepared to lose whatever is on that drive!

HELP

The HELP command does what it says: It gives you help. Actually, if you just type **HELP** and press Enter, your computer gives you a list of system commands you can type. To be useful, type the name of a command you want to know about after typing HELP. For example, type **HELP RD** and press Enter, and you will get information about the RD command.

As a reminder, you can also get the same help information by typing **/?** after the command, as you did in Exercise 14.2 earlier in this chapter.

> The /? switch is slightly faster and provides more information than the HELP command. The HELP command only provides information for system commands (it does not include network commands). For example, if we type **help ipconfig** at a command prompt, we get no useful information (except to try /?); however, typing **ipconfig /?** provides the help file for the ipconfig command.

IPCONFIG

In a world where it seems every computer is connected to a network, you'll do a lot of network connection troubleshooting. The IPCONFIG command is one of the first ones you should use when troubleshooting why someone can't get on the network. In fact, it's often the first one I do use. The IPCONFIG command checks your computer's IP configuration. Figure 14.4 shows a sample output.

Table 14.6 lists useful switches for IPCONFIG.

TABLE 14.6   *IPCONFIG* Switches

Switch	Purpose
/ALL	Shows full configuration information
/RELEASE	Releases the IP address, if you are getting addresses from a Dynamic Host Configuration Protocol (DHCP) server
/RENEW	Obtains a new IP address from a DHCP server
/FLUSHDNS	Flushes the domain name server (DNS) name resolver cache

FIGURE 14.4   IPCONFIG display

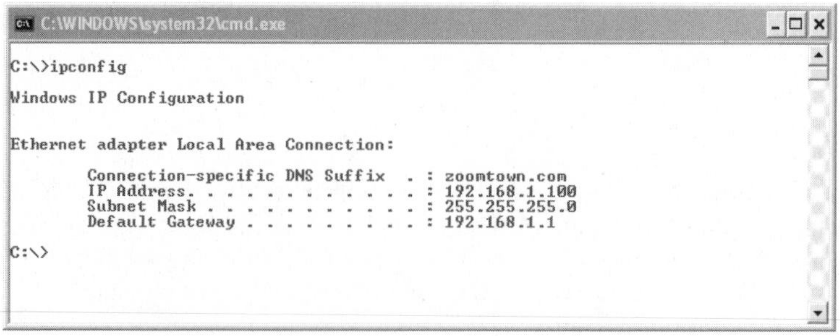

```
C:\>ipconfig

Windows IP Configuration

Ethernet adapter Local Area Connection:

        Connection-specific DNS Suffix  . : zoomtown.com
        IP Address. . . . . . . . . . . : 192.168.1.100
        Subnet Mask . . . . . . . . . . : 255.255.255.0
        Default Gateway . . . . . . . . : 192.168.1.1

C:\>
```

Running IPCONFIG can tell you a lot. For example, if the network cable is disconnected, it will tell you. Also, if your IP address is 0.0.0.0, you're not going to connect to any network resources.

If you get an IP address from a DHCP server but are having connectivity problems, a common troubleshooting method is to release the IP address with IPCONFIG /RELEASE, and get a new one with IPCONFIG /RENEW.

> More often than not, when you release and renew an IP address, you'll get the same one you had before. This in itself isn't a problem. The idea is that you basically "reset" your network card to try to get it working again.

> For a full discussion of network troubleshooting, including IP addresses, please see Chapter 8.

PING

Another useful connectivity troubleshooting tool is PING, which stands for *packet Internet groper*. The PING command sends out four 32-byte packets to a destination and waits for a reply. Figure 14.5 shows a PING command.

FIGURE 14.5   Pinging www.yahoo.com

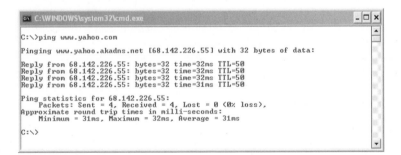

If you cannot make a connection to the remote host, you will get back the following:

```
Request timed out.
Request timed out.
Request timed out.
Request timed out.
```

Keep in mind that some Internet sites block pings as a precautionary security measure, so make sure to use a site that you know accepts them, if you're using PING as a troubleshooting tool. Generally, you don't use any switches with PING. Just type in **PING *IPaddress*** or **PING *hostname*** and see if it works. However, switches are available to persistently ping (until we press Ctrl-C to stop ping), change the packet size, change the number of packets sent, and various other things.

Along with IPCONFIG and PING, another handy connectivity troubleshooting command is TRACERT, or trace route. It traces the route between your computer and the destination computer, and can help determine where the breakdown is if you're having connectivity problems.

XCOPY

If you are comfortable with the COPY command, learning XCOPY shouldn't pose too many problems. It's basically an extension of COPY with one notable exception—it's designed to copy directories as well as files. The syntax is as follows:

XCOPY [source] [destination][switches]

There are 26 XCOPY switches; some of the more commonly used ones are listed in Table 14.7.

TABLE 14.7 *XCOPY* Switches

Switch	Purpose
/A	Copies only files that have the Archive attribute set, and does not clear the attribute. (Useful for making a quick backup of files, while not disrupting a normal backup routine.)
/E	Copies directories and subdirectories, including empty directories.
/F	Displays full source and destination filenames when copying.
/G	Allows copying of encrypted files to a destination that does not support encryption.
/H	Copies hidden and system files as well.
/K	Copies attributes. (By default, XCOPY resets the Read-Only attribute.)
/O	Copies file ownership and ACL information (NTFS permissions).
/R	Overwrites Read-Only files.
/S	Copies directories and subdirectories, but not empty directories.
/U	Copies only files that already exist in the destination.
/V	Verifies each new file.

Perhaps the most important switch is /O. If you use XCOPY to copy files from one location to another, the file system creates a new version of the file in the new location, without changing the old file. In NTFS, when a new file is created, it inherits permissions from its new parent directory. This could cause problems if you copy files. (Users who didn't have access to the file before might have access now.) If you want to retain the original permissions, use XCOPY /O.

Managing Disks, Directories, and Files

It's easy to get in the mind-set of calling most pieces of hardware in a computer the "most critical" piece in the system. After all, if the motherboard dies, your computer is useless. Same goes for the processor and RAM. Want to see what your computer is telling you? It's important that your video card works. But when it really comes down to it, the hard drive is the piece that most people can't afford to lose, because it contains the thing that's the hardest to get back: data. You can replace a motherboard, processor, RAM, or video card and still have your data intact. But if your hard drive crashes, you better hope you made a recent backup. (And everyone makes regular backups, right?)

In this section, we'll look at some specifics in managing disks in your computer. Some of this information will be similar to what was covered in Chapter 4, but knowing how to manage disks, directories, and files is a critical skill for any computer technician.

Preparing Hard Disks to Store Files

Before files can be stored on a hard disk, that hard disk must be properly prepared. The first step in this process is called *partitioning*, and the second step is *formatting*.

A *partition* is a logical division on a hard drive. If you put a partition down the middle of a room, it would divide the room in two. In computer terms, think of the partition as the area of space available that is provided by that barrier. Hard drives can have more than one partition.

Formatting prepares the partition with a file system and gets the partition ready to store files. Here's an analogy for you: Take a blank piece of printer paper. That's your unpartitioned and unformatted hard drive. You're going to make that piece of paper suitable to store information, with each piece of information being in its own area. Now draw a big box (or rectangle if you prefer, I'm not picky) on the paper. That's your partition—the area you cordoned off for files. To format your box, you need to draw horizontal and vertical lines through the box to make a grid. Now you have lots of little boxes that are ready to hold information. That's essentially how your hard drive is laid out after you partition and format.

You'll see partitions designated as active, primary, extended, and/or logical. Here's a review of each type:

- The partition that the operating system boots from must be designated as *active*. Only one partition on a disk may be marked active.

- The first partition created on a hard disk is usually a primary partition. *Primary* partitions cannot be further subdivided. In Windows 2000/XP, each hard disk can have up to four primary partitions. (Older operating systems such as DOS would recognize only one primary partition on a disk, hence the name primary.)

- *Extended* partitions can be logically subdivided into multiple drives. Each physical hard disk can contain only one extended partition.

- A *logical* partition is any partition that has a drive letter associated with it.

> If you are using dynamic disks, logical partitions can span multiple hard drives or multiple primary or extended partitions.

Under Windows 2000/XP, each hard disk can be divided into a maximum of four partitions—either four primary partitions, or three primary and one extended partition. If you have one partition on your hard drive and install Windows XP on it (C:), then C: will be active, primary, and logical.

You have several choices to consider when formatting your hard drives' partitions. The two most common ones in Windows 2000/XP are FAT32 and NTFS:

FAT32   FAT32 support is included in Windows 98/Me/2000/XP and is an extension of the FAT file system. It's more efficient than FAT (it uses smaller clusters) and can support partitions of up to 2TB (2048GB). FAT32 still isn't as efficient in storage as NTFS, and it does not support file system security.

> Older versions of Windows (Windows 3.*x* and Windows 95 original release) as well as all versions of DOS cannot read FAT32 partitions.

New Technology File System (NTFS)   NTFS is a much more advanced file system in almost every way than all versions of FAT. It includes features such as individual file security and compression, RAID support, as well as support for extremely large file and partition sizes and disk transaction monitoring. It is the file system of choice for higher-performance computing.

> Unless you are dual-booting with an older operating system that can't read NTFS (such as Windows 98), there is really no reason to use anything besides NTFS on your hard drives.

Understanding and Navigating Directory Structures

With over several thousand files in a default installation, it is necessary to have a structure that allows you to find things. Windows provides this by allowing you to create directories, also known as folders, in which to organize files.

Here's another analogy for you. You have a filing cabinet. That's your hard drive. Although it would be possible for you to put all of your papers (files) directly into the cabinet, it wouldn't be easy to find them later. Instead, you put them into folders (directories) that are placed in other folders (directories) inside the cabinet. The order among the possible chaos makes it much easier to locate items you want, provided, of course, that you named everything in a way that makes sense to you.

To navigate through directory structures, you can use the CD command from a command prompt (along with DIR to see what's there). Or you can use the graphical Windows Explorer. The ability to use drag-and-drop techniques and other graphical tools to manage directories and files makes Windows Explorer a utility that you need to be very familiar with. It's shown in Figure 14.6.

Some of the tasks you can accomplish by using Explorer include viewing files and directories, opening programs or data files, creating directories and files, copying or moving files or directories to other locations, deleting or renaming files or directories, searching for a particular file or type of file, changing file attributes, or formatting new disks (such as floppy disks). You can access many of these functions by right-clicking a file or folder and selecting the appropriate option, such as Copy or Delete, from the context menu.

Using Windows Explorer is simple. Some common actions in Explorer include the following:

Expanding a Folder   You can double-click a folder in the left pane to expand the folder (show its subfolders in the left pane) and display the contents of the folder in the right pane. Clicking the plus sign (+) to the left of a folder expands the folder without changing the display in the right pane.

Collapsing a Folder   Clicking the minus sign (–) next to a folder unexpands/collapses it.

Selecting a File   If you click a file in the right pane, Windows highlights the file by marking it with a darker color.

Selecting Multiple Files   The Ctrl and Shift keys allow you to select multiple files at once. Holding down Ctrl while clicking individual files selects each new file while leaving the currently selected file(s) selected as well. Holding down Shift while selecting two files selects both of them and all files in between.

FIGURE 14.6   The Windows Explorer program

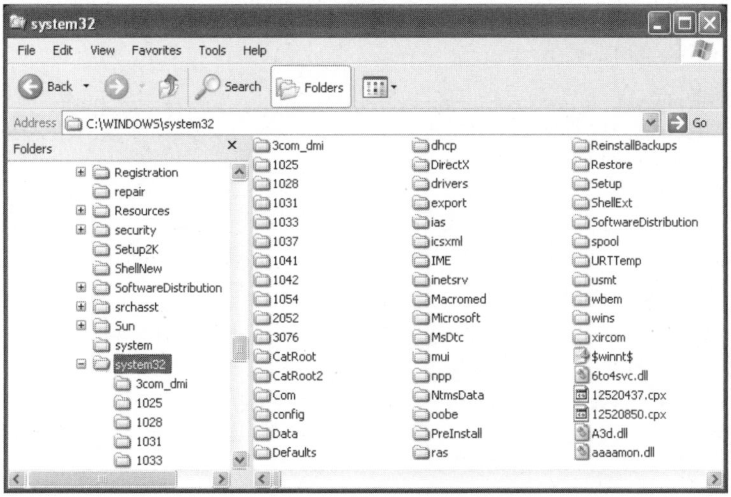

Opening a File   Double-clicking a file in the right pane opens the program if the file is an application; if it is a data file, it will open by using the application that has been associated with the data file's file extension.

Changing the View Type   Windows 2000 has five view types: Large Icons, Small Icons, List, Details, and Thumbnail. In Windows XP, the Tiles view was added. In XP, you can still choose to view objects with icons, but you can no longer choose between large and small icons. You can move between these views by clicking the View menu and selecting the view you prefer.

Finding Specific Files   This option is accessed by using the Search button. You can search for files based on their name, file size, file type, and other attributes.

Creating New Objects   To create a new file, folder, or other object, navigate to the location where you want to create the object and then right-click in the right pane (without selecting a file or directory). In the menu that appears, select New and then choose the object you want to create. Exercise 14.5 walks you through another way to complete this process.

EXERCISE 14.5

Creating a New Folder

Earlier you created and managed folders from a command prompt. In this exercise, you will create a new folder from within Windows.

1. Open up Windows Explorer. One shortcut to do this is to hold down the Windows key and then press E.

2. In the left-hand Folders pane, click once on your C:. That should display the contents of C: in the right-hand pane. (If you don't have the Folders pane on the left side, click View ➢ Explorer Bar ➢ Folders.)

3. Click File ➢ New ➢ Folder. In the right-hand pane, a new folder appears with the high-lighted name New Folder.

4. Type in the name of your new folder and press Enter.

Deleting Objects   Select the object and press the Del key on the keyboard, or right-click the object and select Delete from the menu that appears.

Managing File Attributes

File attributes determine what specific users can do to files or directories. For example, if a file or directory is flagged with the Read-Only attribute, users can read the file or directory but not make changes to it or delete it. Attributes include Read-Only, Hidden, System, and Archive, as well as Compression, Indexing, and Encryption. Not all attributes are available with all versions of Windows.

You can view and change file attributes either with the ATTRIB command-prompt command or through the properties of a file or directory. (From a command prompt, you can only manage Read-only, Archive, System, and Hidden. Windows allows you to manage advanced attributes as well.) To access the properties of a file or directory in the Windows GUI, right-click the file or directory and select Properties. Figure 14.7 shows the Properties dialog box of a file in Windows XP. In Windows XP, you can view and configure the Read-Only and Hidden file attributes on the General tab. To view and configure additional attributes, click Advanced.

System files are usually flagged with the Hidden attribute, meaning they don't appear when a user displays a directory listing. You should not change this attribute on a system file unless absolutely necessary. System files are required for the OS to function. If they are visible, users might delete them (perhaps thinking they can clear some disk space by deleting files they don't recognize). Needless to say, that would be a bad thing!

File System Advanced Attributes

Windows 2000 and XP can use NTFS, which gives you options that are not available on earlier file systems such as FAT or FAT32. Some of these options are implemented through the use of the Advanced Attributes dialog box. To reach these options in Windows 2000/XP, right-click the folder or file you wish to modify and select Properties from the menu. On the main Properties page of the folder or file, click the Advanced button in the lower-right corner.

WARNING   In the Advanced Attributes dialog box you can set archiving, indexing, compression, and encryption.

FIGURE 14.7   The General tab of a Windows XP file's properties

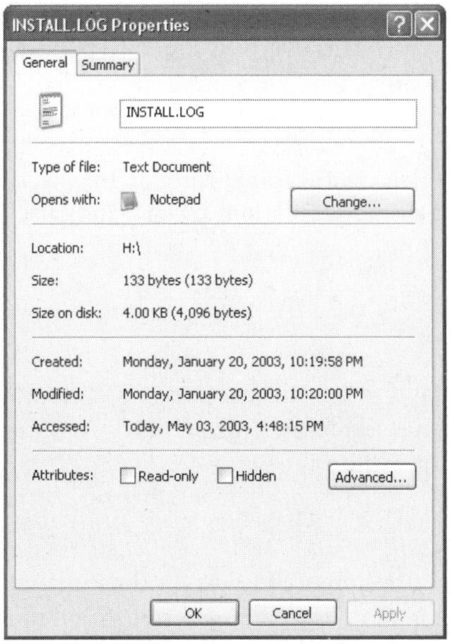

File Permissions

Windows 2000 and XP also support the use of file permissions, because these OSs use the NTFS file system, which includes file-level security (rather than just shared-folder permissions, as is the case with Windows 9x/Me). Permissions serve the purpose of controlling who has access, and which type of access, to particular files or objects. Several permissions are available, such as Read, Write, Execute, Delete, Change Permissions, Take Ownership, Full Control, and so on. The list is quite extensive. For a complete list, consult the Windows Help files. These permissions are called special permissions.

 The significance of file-level security in XP/2000 is that earlier OSs (e.g., 9x) only allowed permissions to be set for an entire drive or folder. The distinction between share-level security or user-level security has to do with how access is determined: share-level control lets you specify a password for each shared resource, whereas user-level control lets you specify who has access to each resource through user accounts.

Assigning special permissions individually could be a tedious task. To make it easier for administrators to assign multiple permissions at once, Windows incorporates standard permissions. Standard permissions are collections of special permissions. The most common ones are as follows:

- Full Control
- Modify
- Read & Execute
- Read
- Write

Each of these standard permissions automatically assigns multiple special permissions at once. To see which special permissions are assigned by the different standard permissions, type **File Permissions (List)** into the Help system's index keyword area.

 You can assign permissions to individual users or to groups. However, when you have multiple users it's best to assign permissions by using groups.

Using Windows Utilities

Microsoft provides various utilities with Windows to manage common operations. One such tool is one you're already familiar with: Windows Explorer. This section covers some useful tools that can help you manage disks and the operating system.

Disk Management Tools

Preserving information on hard drives has never been more important than it is today. Not only do you want to keep your own information, you have the legal obligation to manage company records if you work for a publicly held firm. Here are some disk management utilities to be familiar with.

CHKDSK

You can use the Windows CHKDSK utility to create and display status reports for the hard disk. CHKDSK can also correct file system problems (such as cross-linked files) and scan for and attempt to repair disk errors. You can manually start CHKDSK by right-clicking the problem disk and selecting Properties. This will bring up the Properties dialog box for that disk, which shows the current status of the selected disk drive.

By clicking the Tools tab at the top of the dialog box, and then clicking the Check Now button in the Error-checking section, you can start CHKDSK. Exercise 14.6 walks you through starting CHKDSK in Windows XP.

EXERCISE 14.6

Running *CHKDSK* in Windows XP

1. In this exercise, you will check your hard disk for errors.

2. Open Windows Explorer by holding down the Windows key and pressing E.

3. Right-click C: and choose Properties.

4. Click the Tools tab and then click the Check Now button.

5. Choose your options: You can automatically fix file system errors and/or scan for and attempt recovery of bad sectors.

6. After you have selected your options, click Start.

DEFRAG.EXE

Defragmenting a disk involves analyzing the disk and then consolidating fragmented files and folders so they occupy a contiguous space, thus increasing performance during file retrieval. Although you can easily run a defrag through Windows, you can also do it through the command-line command DEFRAG.

We'll cover the steps to run DEFRAG later in this chapter, in the "Optimizing Operating Systems" section.

NTBACKUP.EXE

If you want to back up your system, you can run the NTBACKUP.EXE utility located in the \Windows\System32 directory. You can also run it by clicking Start ➤ All Programs ➤ Accessories ➤ System Tools ➤ Backup. No matter how many times it's said, few people seem to listen: If your data is important, back up your files often.

System Management Tools

Keeping the complicated Windows 2000 and Windows XP operating systems up and running can seem like a daunting task. There are so many different modules and applications—it can get overwhelming at times. The good news is, Microsoft is aware of this, and ever since the Windows NT days has made significant advancements in making system management easier. The following sections describe some of the more commonly used system management utilities found in Windows 2000 and Windows XP.

Computer Management

Windows 2000/XP includes a new piece of software to manage computer settings: the Computer Management Console. Because Windows 2000 is more advanced as a platform, the Computer Management Console can manage more than just the installed hardware devices. In addition to a Device Manager that functions almost identically to the one in Windows 9x, the Computer Management Console can also manage all the services running on that computer. It contains an Event Viewer to show any system errors and events, as well as methods to configure the software components of all the computer's hardware. Figure 14.8 shows an example of the Computer Management Console running on Windows XP.

To access the Computer Management Console in Windows 2000, choose Start ➤ Settings ➤ Control Panel ➤ Administrative Tools ➤ Computer Management. In Windows XP, you can access Control Panel through the Start button directly. In both operating systems, you can also access Computer Management by right-clicking the My Computer icon and choosing Manage.

FIGURE 14.8   Windows XP Computer Management Console

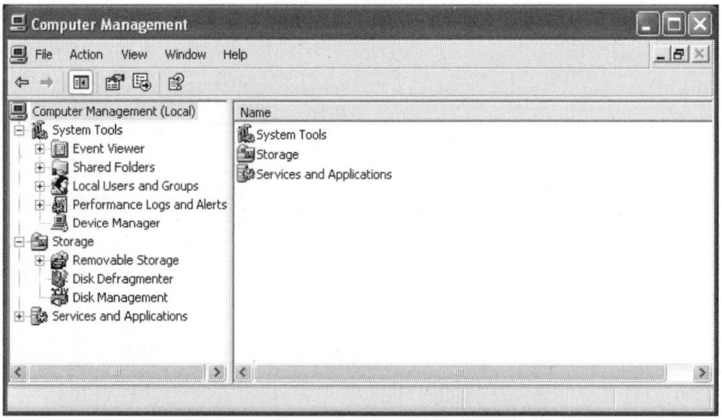

After you are in Computer Management, you will see all of the tools available. This is one power-packed interface, which includes the following system tools:

Device Manager   Lets you manage hardware devices.

Event Viewer   Allows you to view application error logs, security audit records, and system errors.

Shared Folders   Allows you to manage all of your computer's shared folders.

Local Users and Groups   Allows you to create and manage user and group accounts.

Performance Logs and Alerts   Shows you how your system hardware is performing, and alerts you if system performance goes under a threshold you set.

Computer Management also has the Storage area, which lets you manage removable media, defragment your hard drives, or manage partitions through the Disk Management utility. Finally, you can manage system services and applications through Computer Management as well. Exercise 14.7 walks you through stopping and restarting the print spooler service.

EXERCISE 14.7

Stopping and Restarting a Service

One problem you will run into on occasion is a misbehaving service. For example, say you are sending print jobs to a printer, but nothing is printing. The printer is turned on, plugged in, online, and everything appears to be in working order, but nothing prints. One solution is to stop and restart the print spooler, which is done through Computer Management. In this exercise you will stop and restart the print spooler.

1. Open Computer Management by right-clicking the My Computer icon and selecting Manage.

2. In the left pane, expand Services And Applications, and select Services.

3. In the right pane, scroll down to Print Spooler and click on it.

EXERCISE 14.7 *(continued)*

4. Stop the print spooler either by right-clicking it and choosing Stop, or by clicking the Stop button (the black square) above the services list.

5. Restart the service by either right-clicking it and choosing Start, or by clicking the Start button (the black arrow to the left of the square) above the services list.

Device Manager

From Windows *9x* forward, Microsoft has provided the Device Manager, a tool that analyzes hardware-related problems. The Device Manager displays all of the devices installed in a computer (as shown in Figure 14.9). If a device is malfunctioning, a yellow circle with an exclamation point inside it is displayed. If the device is disabled, it will have a red X through it, as shown in Figure 14.10.

With this utility, you can view the devices installed in a system and any of those devices that are failing, and also double-click a device to view and set its properties (as shown in Figure 14.11). On the General tab, you will see the status of the device (whether it's working). The other tabs are used to configure the individual devices, add or update drivers, and verify the version of drivers installed.

FIGURE 14.9   The Windows XP Device Manager

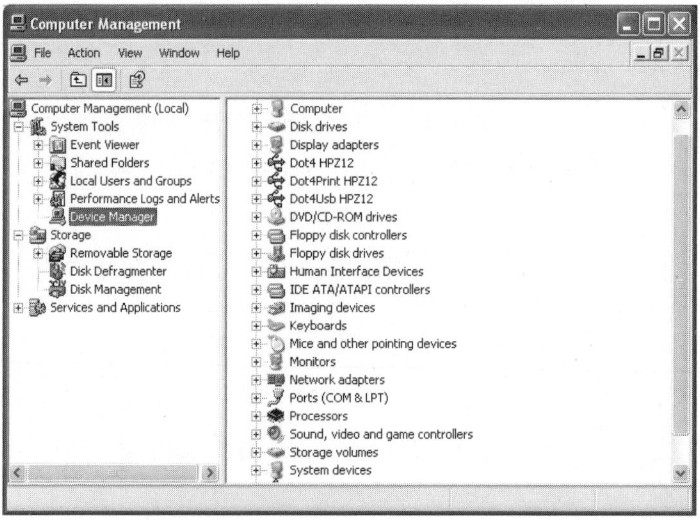

FIGURE 14.10   Disabled device in Device Manager

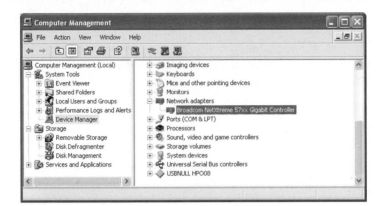

FIGURE 14.11   Properties of a network card

In Windows 2000 and XP, you can access the Device Manager in one of three ways:

- Right-click the My Computer icon, choose Manage (which takes you to Computer Management), and then select Device Manager in the left pane.

- Right-click the My Computer icon, choose Properties, and then click the Hardware tab. On the Hardware tab, click the Device Manager button.

- Open Control Panel and double-click the System applet. In the System Properties dialog box, click the Hardware tab. On the Hardware tab, click the Device Manager button.

If you're having problems with a hardware device, Device Manager is a good place to check to ensure it's enabled and being recognized by Windows. Device Manager is also a key resource to help you upgrade device drivers.

> If you right-click on a hardware device and choose Properties, it opens the device's Properties window. On the General tab, there's a Troubleshoot button. Clicking this button will start the hardware troubleshooter, which can help you resolve problems.

Task Manager

Another tool you can use to check on and control your Windows 2000/XP environment is the Task Manager. Anytime you run a program, it displays as a button on the Taskbar. Sometimes, however, you run into problems with running tasks. For example, a task (program) may hang. You'll know this has happened because you won't be able to use any of the program's functions—the program will be unresponsive. To deal with this situation, as well as for other reasons, you can use the Task Manager (see Figure 14.12).

To access the Task Manager, press Ctrl+Alt+Del. In Windows 2000, you then have to click Task Manager on the Windows Security screen. In Windows XP, whether the Security screen displays depends on whether you're using the Windows XP Welcome screen (you can change this setting on the Screen Saver tab of the computer's Display Properties). By default, in Windows XP, the Windows Security screen does not display if you press Ctrl+Alt+Del; instead, Task Manager opens right away.

FIGURE 14.12 The Task Manager in Windows XP

To get to the Task Manager directly in any of the Windows versions that include it, you can press Ctrl+Shift+Esc.

In Windows 2000, the Task Manager has three tabs: Applications, Processes, and Performance. In Windows XP, the Task Manager can include two additional tabs: Networking and Users. The Networking tab is only shown if your system has a network card installed. The Users tab is displayed only if the computer you are working on has Fast User Switching enabled, and is a member of a workgroup or is a standalone computer. The Users tab is unavailable on computers that are members of a network domain. Let's look at these tabs in more detail:

Applications   The Applications tab lets you see which tasks are open on the machine. You also see the status of each task, which can be either Running or Not Responding. If a task/ application has stopped responding (that is, it's hung), you can select the task in the list and click End Task. Doing so closes the program, and you can try to open it again. Often, although certainly not always, if an application hangs you have to reboot the computer to prevent the same thing from happening again shortly after you restart the application. You can also use the Applications tab to switch to a different task or create new tasks.

Processes   The Processes tab lets you see the names of all the processes running on the machine. You also see the user account that's running the process, as well as how much CPU and RAM resources that each process is using. To end a process, select the process in the list and click End Process.

Performance   The Performance tab contains a variety of information, including overall CPU usage percentage, a graphical display of CPU usage history, page-file usage in MB, and a graphical display of page-file usage. This tab also provides you with additional memory-related information such as physical and kernel memory usage, as well as the total number of handles, threads, and processes. Total, limit, and peak commit-charge information also displays. Some of the items are beyond the scope of this book, but it's good to know that you can use the Performance tab to keep track of system performance. Note that the number of processes, CPU usage percentage, and commit charge always display at the bottom of the Task Manager window, regardless of which tab you have currently selected.

Networking (Windows XP Only)   The Networking tab provides you with a graphical display of the performance of your network connection. It also tells you the network adapter name, link speed, and state. If you have more than one network adapter installed in the machine, you can select the appropriate adapter to see graphical usage data for that adapter.

Users (Windows XP Only)   The Users tab provides you with information about the users connected to the local machine. You'll see the username, ID, status, client name, and session type. You can right-click on any connected user to perform a variety of functions, including sending the user a message, disconnecting the user, logging off the user, and initiating a remote-control session to the user's machine.

MSCONFIG (Windows XP Only)

A new utility was introduced with Windows 98: MSCONFIG.EXE (aka the System Configuration Utility). (Even though it was introduced with Windows 98, Windows 2000 does not include it. Windows XP does.) It allows a user to manage their computer system's configuration. MSCONFIG.EXE allows a user to boot Windows in diagnostic mode, in which they can select which drivers to load interactively. If you suspect a certain driver is causing problems during boot, you can use MSCONFIG.EXE to prevent that driver from loading. Additionally, each of the major configuration files (CONFIG.SYS, AUTOEXEC.BAT, WIN .INI, SYSTEM.INI) and the programs loaded at startup can be reconfigured and reordered by using a graphical interface.

REGEDIT and REGEDT32

The most flexible (and possibly the most dangerous) utility in Windows is the Registry Editor, also known by its executable names REGEDIT.EXE and REGEDT32.EXE. The Registry stores all Windows configuration information. If you edit the Registry, you are directly changing the configuration of Windows. The Registry Editor is used to manually change settings that are usually changed by other means (such as through Setup programs and other Windows utilities).

 In Windows 2000, REGEDIT and REGEDT32 open different programs. REGEDIT has more robust search options, and REGEDT32 can be made read-only. In Windows XP, both commands open the same program, which is the Windows 2000 REGEDIT.

   In addition to changing Windows settings, you can use REGEDIT to back up and restore the Registry. To back up the Registry, choose the Export Registry File command under the Registry menu (or File ➤ Export in later versions). This command allows you to save the Registry file to backup media. You can restore it later by choosing the Import Registry File command under the Registry menu.

CMD

If you ever need to type in a command (for example, you want to view your environment variables the old-fashioned way or you want to test network connectivity), use the Start button. From Start, choose Run, type **CMD**, and press Enter. That will open a command prompt where you can enter your commands.

Event Viewer

Windows 2000/XP employs comprehensive error and informational logging routines. Every program and process theoretically could have its own logging utility, but Microsoft has come up with a rather slick utility, Event Viewer, which, through log files, tracks all events on a particular Windows 2000/XP computer. Normally, though, you must be an administrator or a member of the Administrators group to have access to Event Viewer.

To start Event Viewer, log in as an administrator (or equivalent) and choose Start ➢ Programs ➢ Administrative Tools ➢ Event Viewer. From here, you can view the System, Application, and Security log files: .

- The System log file displays alerts that pertain to the general operation of Windows.
- The Application log file logs application errors.
- The Security log file logs security events such as login successes and failures.

These log files can give a general indication of a Windows computer's health.

One situation that does occur with the Event Viewer is that the Event Viewer log files get full. Although this isn't really a problem, it can make viewing log files confusing because there are many entries. Even though each event is time- and date-stamped, you should clear the Event Viewer every so often. To do this, open the Event Viewer and choose Clear All Events from the Log menu. Doing so erases all events in the current log file, allowing you to see new events more easily when they occur.

System Restore

Windows XP contains a new feature called System Restore. It's designed to provide automatic backups of your system configuration, which can be restored in the event that a system change causes problems.

System Restore does *not* back up files and folders, just system configuration.

System Restore works by creating restore points, or copies of your system configuration. There are three ways restore points are created:

- Windows creates them automatically by default.
- You can manually create them by using System Restore.
- During the installation of some programs, a restore point is automatically created before the installation.

Restore points are useful for when Windows fails to boot but the computer appears to be fine otherwise, or if Windows doesn't seem to be acting right and you think it was because of a recent configuration change.

To open System Restore, click Start ➢ All Programs ➢ Accessories ➢ System Tools ➢ System Restore. This opens a screen like the one in Figure 14.13.

Notice in Figure 14.13 that you have two options. The first is to restore your computer to an earlier time (if you feel Windows is misbehaving), and the second is to manually create a restore point.

If you need to use a restore point and Windows won't boot, you can reboot into Safe Mode. After Safe Mode loads, you will have the option to work in Safe Mode or use System Restore. Choose System Restore and you'll be presented with restore points (if any) you can use.

One other option in Figure 14.13 is a link on the left side, which takes you to System Restore settings. You can also get to the same place by opening the System control panel (right-clicking the My Computer icon and choosing Properties) and selecting the System Restore tab, as shown in Figure 14.14.

FIGURE 14.13   System Restore

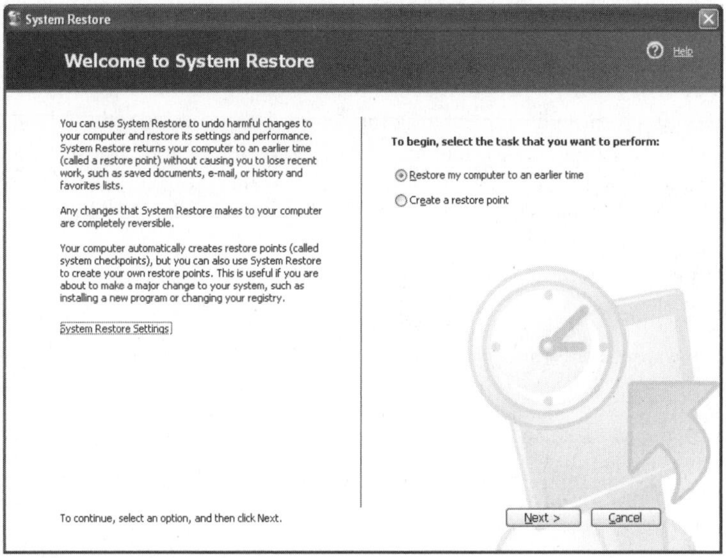

FIGURE 14.14   System Restore options

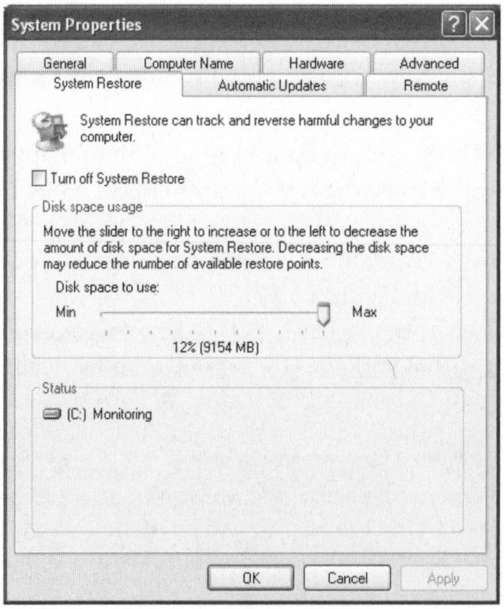

First, notice that you can turn off System Restore. Don't, unless you really don't care if your computer crashes and you can't recover it without a reinstallation. The other option is to select how much disk space is available for System Restore. The less disk space you make available, the fewer restore points you will be able to have. If you have multiple hard drives, you can allocate a different amount of space per hard drive.

Creating a restore point manually is also done through the System Restore utility. Exercise 14.8 walks you through this process.

EXERCISE 14.8

Creating a Restore Point

Windows XP will automatically create restore points for you. If you're going to make system changes, though, you might want to create one manually. This exercise shows you how to do that.

1. Open System Restore by clicking Start ➤ All Programs ➤ Accessories ➤ System Tools ➤ System Restore.

2. Choose Create A Restore Point, and click Next.

3. Provide a restore point description. Click Create.

4. Within a minute, you will be presented with a confirmation screen with the time, date, and name of your restore point.

Now that you have created a restore point, it's time to look at how to perform a system restoration. To restore your system to a previous state, choose the Restore My Computer To An Earlier Time radio button, as in Figure 14.13. Click Next. On the next screen, you will be shown a calendar and available restore points, as shown in Figure 14.15.

On days when restore points were created, the calendar date will be bolded. You can choose any restore point you want, and click Next. The next screen confirms the restore point you have chosen, as in Figure 14.16.

Note that at the bottom of the screen, it tells you to click Next and the system will be restored to the point you selected. And as the screen tells you, restoring the system restores only the configuration and does not cause you to lose recently saved files or documents.

Remote Desktop Connection and Assistance

Windows contains two remote connectivity applications, called Remote Desktop connection and Remote Assistance. The following sections describe each in more detail.

Remote Desktop Connection

The *Remote Desktop* feature of Windows would probably be more accurately named remote control. Remote Desktop allows you to connect to another computer and take control over that computer as if you were sitting in front of it. This utility can allow you to connect to your work computer from home, for example, and it can also work as a great troubleshooting tool. On the flip side, it can also be a huge security risk.

Remote Desktop classifies computers into two categories: home computer and remote computer. The *home computer* is the one that you are sitting at. For it to use Remote Desktop, it needs to have *Remote Desktop Connection* installed (which it is by default in Windows XP). The *remote computer* is the one you are connecting to. It needs to have Remote Desktop installed, which is separate from Remote Desktop Connection.

Windows XP Home does not have Remote Desktop, only Remote Desktop Connection. Therefore, Windows XP Home computers can be only home computers, not remote computers.

When using Remote Desktop, keystrokes and mouse movements are transmitted from the home computer to the remote computer. Programs that you open on the remote computer (from the home computer) run normally on the remote computer. You (from the home computer) can see the Desktop of the remote computer, just as if you were sitting there. Finally, sound can be passed from the remote computer to the home computer. This is enabled by default, but it consumes a lot of bandwidth so you might not want to use it.

You can connect to more than one remote computer at a time, but if you do, the connections will likely be very slow because this application is bandwidth-intensive.

FIGURE 14.15   Available restore points

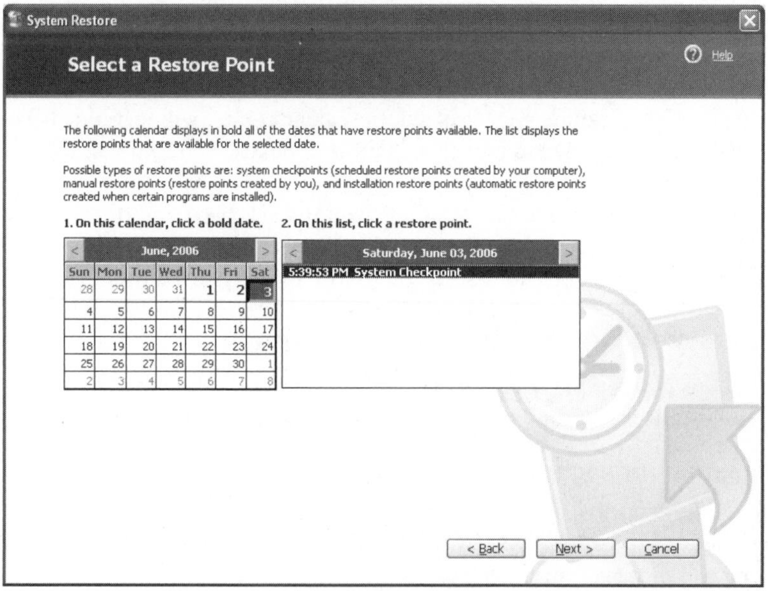

FIGURE 14.16   Confirming restore point selection

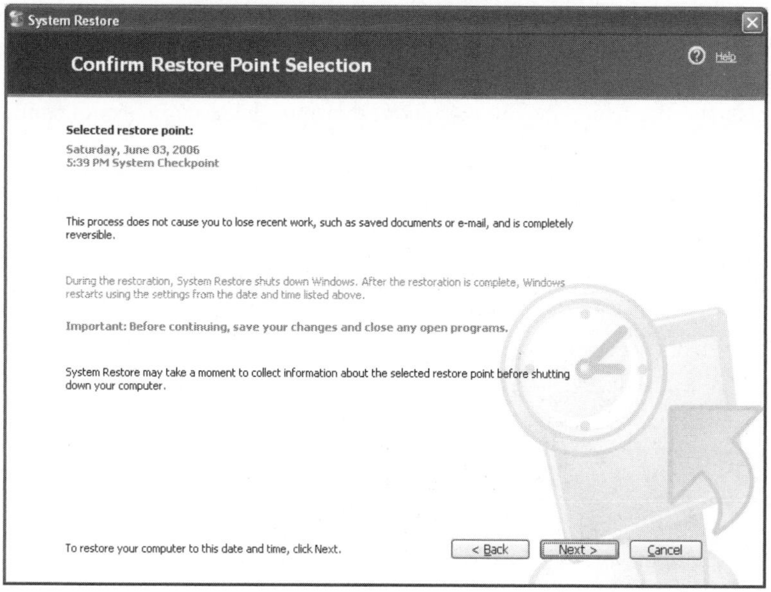

FIGURE 14.17   System Properties Remote tab

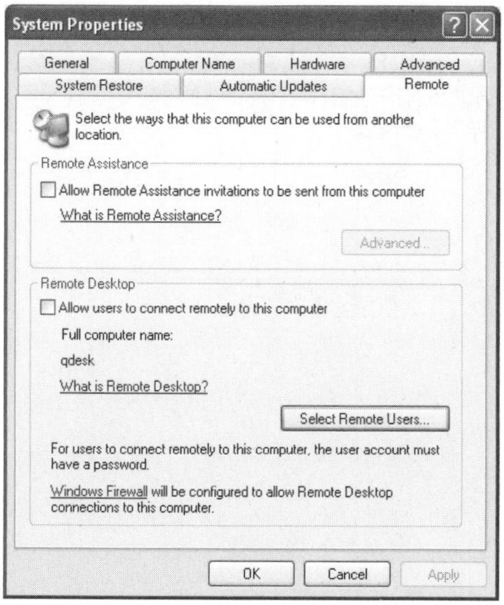

By default, users are not allowed to remotely connect to your computer. To change this, you need to open System Properties (right-click My Computer and select Properties) and click the Remote tab, as shown in Figure 14.17.

Check the Allow Users To Connect Remotely To This Computer check box to enable access. Then to choose which users can connect remotely, click the Select Remote Users button. For users to be able to access your computer, they must have a user account and password on your computer.

To configure Remote Desktop Connection options, open Remote Desktop Connection by clicking Start ➢ All Programs ➢ Accessories ➢ Communications ➢ Remote Desktop Connection. This opens a window like the one in Figure 14.18.

This is the window you would use to connect to another computer. By clicking the Options button, you can configure desired settings. Looking at Figure 14.19, you can see that there are five tabs of configuration options.

FIGURE 14.18   Remote Desktop Connection

FIGURE 14.19   Remote Desktop Connection options

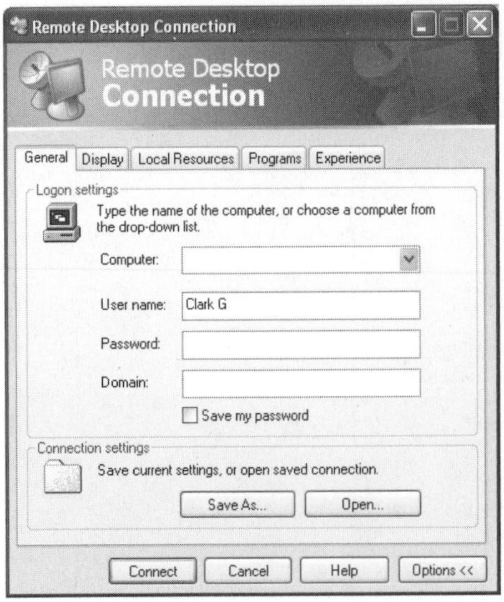

On the bottom of the General tab, you'll notice that you can save these settings into different profiles. This might be handy if you connect to different computers.

The Display tab lets you set the size of your Remote Desktop window, up to full screen. It also allows you to configure the depth of color used, much like when you configure your own Desktop.

The Local Resources tab (shown in Figure 14.20) lets you configure sound (good to leave off unless absolutely necessary), keyboard settings, and connectivity to local devices.

On the Programs tab, you can choose to start applications when the remote connection is made.

Finally, the Experience tab lets you choose your connection speed as well as a few graphical options (such as allowing themes or the Desktop background) designed to help optimize your connection.

Remote Assistance

Have you ever tried explaining a computer problem you're having to someone else, and it just isn't sinking in? Or how about being on the other end, and having a user trying in vain to explain a problem to you but they just don't have the right words to get their point across?

The Remote Assistance feature of Windows allows you to access someone else's computer in an effort to repair it.

Looking back at Figure 14.17, you will see a check box marked Allow Remote Assistance invitations to be sent from this computer. By checking that box, you can send an invitation to a person on another computer to connect to yours, with the intention of letting them fix a problem. By clicking on the Advanced button, you can choose whether or not to allow remote users to be able to take control over your machine. If you want them to fix the problem, then let them take control. Otherwise, you can just give them a guided tour once they're connected.

FIGURE 14.20   Local Resources Tab

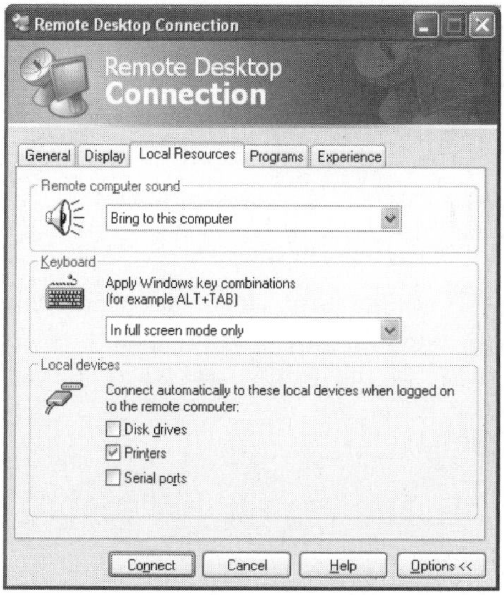

For Remote Assistance to work, you must be running either Windows Messenger or a MAPI-compliant e-mail system such as Outlook or Outlook Express.

Once you have enabled Remote Assistance on the Remote tab of your system properties, you can send an invitation to others to connect to your computer. Here's how:

1. Click on Start ➢ Help and Support.

2. Click on the link that says Invite A Friend To Connect To Your Computer With Remote Assistance. That will take you to another Help and Support menu.

3. Click on Invite someone to help you.

4. If you use Windows Messenger (or MSN messenger), highlight the person on your contacts list and click Invite This Person. If you do not use Messenger, type their e-mail address in the Type An E-mail Address Box, And Click Invite This Person.

Upon receiving the invitation, the user will be given the opportunity to accept. After they accept, you will be notified that they have accepted, and the session is started.

To end a Remote Assistance session, click the Disconnect or Close buttons in the Remote Assistance window.

Differences between Remote Desktop and Remote Assistance

Both remote programs use the same base technology, but there are differences. Remote Desktop was designed to give you remote access to a Windows session running on your computer, even if you're not there. For example, you can be at home and log in to your work computer to access files or applications.

Remote Assistance allows a friend or a technician to use an Internet connection to access your computer to provide help. By default, the friend sees your Desktop and communicates with you through a messenger window. If you choose, you can allow that friend to have control over your computer.

Optimizing Operating Systems

For the most part, Windows runs pretty well. Over the years, a lot of the operational bugs have been ironed out, and Windows 2000 and Windows XP are pretty adaptable. However, you can still perform several tasks to make your system run better. Areas where you can optimize Windows performance include the following:

- Managing virtual memory
- Defragmenting disks
- Controlling temporary files
- Managing services, the startup environment, and applications

In this section, you will learn how to optimize Windows performance.

Managing Virtual Memory

As we discussed in Chapter 5, Windows is a resource hog. Because of heavy resource needs, virtual memory technology was developed. *Virtual memory* is the general term for a type of computer technology that uses hard disk space as a kind of backup memory.

Windows uses a swap file to provide virtual memory to the system. The *swap file* is hard drive space where idle pieces of programs are placed, while active parts of programs are kept in or swapped into main memory. The programs running in Windows believe that their information is still in RAM, but Windows has moved it into near-line storage on the hard drive. When the application needs the information again, the data is swapped back into RAM so it can be used by the processor.

 For full details on managing virtual memory, see Chapter 5.

Although both Windows 2000 and Windows XP configure virtual memory on their own, there are ways you can help your system. First, keep in mind that the recommended minimum page-file size is 1.5 times the amount of RAM in your computer. Second, realize that simply increasing the size of your page file might not help system performance. Increase its size only if you have been instructed to do so, or if you're testing for optimal performance.

 If you reduce the minimum or maximum size of the page file, you will have to reboot your computer. However, in Windows 2000/XP, increases don't require a restart.

 If you need to delete a paging file, set both the minimum and maximum sizes to zero in Windows 2000. In Windows XP, choose the No Paging File radio button.

One of the best ways to increase virtual memory performance is to create page files on multiple physical disks. This is because Windows has the ability to read and/or write from multiple disks at the same time. If you create a page file that spans disks, Windows essentially treats it as one volume, and can then perform multiple simultaneous reads/writes on it. This should increase your system performance.

 Do *not* create multiple page files on one physical disk (for example, if it has multiple partitions). Each physical disk has only one set of read/write heads, and having multiple page files on one disk will cause performance issues.

Exercise 14.9 walks you through setting up virtual memory on multiple physical disks.

EXERCISE 14.9

Optimizing Virtual Memory

In this exercise, you will see how to optimize virtual memory. This exercise will work only if you have multiple partitions that can contain a page file.

1. Open System Properties by right-clicking My Computer and choosing Properties.

2. Go to the Advanced tab, and click the Settings button in the Performance section.

3. Click the Advanced tab (again) and click the Change button in the Virtual Memory section. You will get a dialog box similar to the following.

4. Highlight the drive you want to create the second page file on (F:, in this example), click the Custom Size radio button, and enter an initial size and maximum size.

5. Click Set. Click OK.

6. You will need to reboot your system for the changes to take effect.

In Windows XP, you can choose to have Windows dynamically manage the size of your paging file by choosing the System Managed Size radio button. If you have a RAID array in your computer, setting up virtual memory on that array can also speed up your system.

Defragmenting Disks

When Windows is installed on a new disk, all the full clusters are contiguous. That is, they are located one after another rotationally on the disk. However, as files and programs are installed and deleted, the blocks of disk space get less and less contiguous. This can hinder Windows' performance, because it has to constantly go looking for more sections of different files. You've probably seen a symptom of a fragmented disk: the hard-drive light flickers madly, and the system seems slow as a snail when switching programs, starting a new program, or opening a file. This symptom is known as *disk thrashing*.

To solve this problem, Microsoft includes a utility with Windows for reorganizing, or *defragmenting*, the hard disk. With earlier versions of Windows, this was a separate utility you ran to defragment your disk; in later versions, it is integrated into the operating system.

Defragmenting in Windows 2000 Professional

To begin defragmenting, close all programs and then double-click the My Computer icon. Right-click on the hard disk you want to defragment and choose Properties to bring up the Local Disk Properties dialog box. Click the Tools tab and then click the Defragment Now button to start the defragmentation program.

You can also start the program by choosing Start ➢ Programs ➢ Accessories ➢ System Tools ➢ Disk Defragmenter.

After you have started the Disk Defragmenter, you can do one of two things: analyze a disk to see whether it needs defragmentation (by clicking the Analyze button) or go ahead with the defragmentation (by clicking the Defragment button). If you click the Defragment button to begin the defragmentation, Disk Defragmenter will analyze the disk to get a map of where files are stored, and then rearrange them into contiguous disk space. This process will take some time, and it may be best to start it in the evening before you go to bed.

Defragmenting in Windows XP Professional

As in other operations that modify key parts of the Windows installation or hardware (especially disk drives), you must be logged in as an administrator in order to perform a defragmentation on Windows XP. However, the process for starting the Disk Defragmenter is exactly the same as in previous versions of Windows. To open the Disk Defragmenter, go to Properties in My Computer on any drive you want to defragment, click the Tools tab, and then click Defragment Now. As with Windows 2000, click Defragment to begin the process.

Managing Temporary Files

A *temporary file (temp file)* is just that—temporary. It is designed to store information for a short period of time and then be deleted. Almost every program of any size today uses temp files. There is one problem, however: Often, the temp files become more permanent. Eventually, they begin taking up considerable disk space.

One thing you can do to improve system performance is to delete any temporary files that exist on your system. Temp files can be found in a variety of locations, including the following:

```
C:\Temp
C:\Tmp
C:\Windows\Temp
C:\Windows\Tmp
```

The way to know for sure where they're located is to determine what values the TEMP and TMP environment variables are set to. An *environment variable* is a setting that stays permanent throughout a Windows or DOS session. It is set by an entry in an .INI file, the Registry, or one of the MS-DOS configuration files (CONFIG.SYS or AUTOEXEC.BAT).

To find out where the temporary files are stored in your machine, start a command-line session (choose Start ➢ Run and type in either **CMD** or **COMMAND**). At the command prompt, type **SET**. This command returns all the environment variables for your system. Look for TEMP= or TMP= (or both). These variables point to directories on your hard disk; in these locations, you will find the temporary files.

In Windows XP, you can find where your temp files are going by opening the System control panel, clicking the Advanced tab, and then the Environment Variables button. The temp location will be shown in the User Variables box at the top as well as the System Variables at the bottom.

After you have found the temporary files, use Windows Explorer to delete them. You may need to reboot, and then try to delete the temp files. Otherwise, some of them may be in use, and you won't be able to delete them.

Managing Services, Startup, and Applications

Windows runs a lot of programs behind the scenes, and we often forget that they're there. But everything that runs takes system resources, and Windows can run a lot of things that might not be necessary for your system to run as you want it to. This section looks at those behind-the-scenes services, configuring startup, and managing applications.

Windows Services

To configure Windows services, open Administrative Tools in Control Panel, and choose Services (or, right-click My Computer, choose Manage, and then Services under Services and Applications). You'll see a window similar to the one in Figure 14.21.

FIGURE 14.21 Windows services

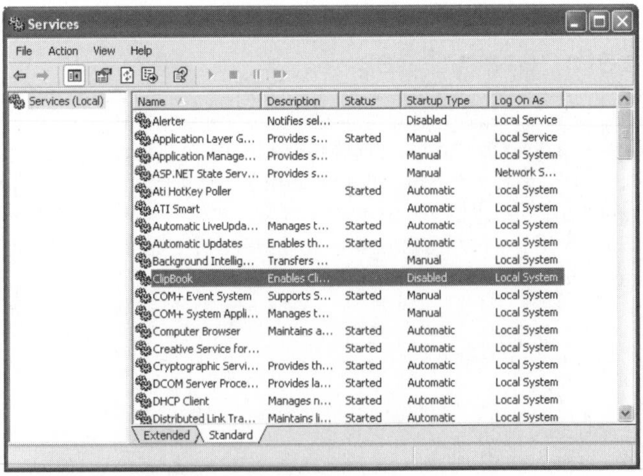

The services are listed in alphabetical order by default. You can also see which services are started, and if they start automatically when Windows boots or if they need to be started manually. If you're not sure what the service does, double-clicking it will give you more details. For example, Figure 14.22 gives you more description about what the DHCP client service does.

If a service is running but it's not needed, you can stop it in this applet. Also, the various tabs of the service's properties allow you to configure how it operates.

The General tab gives you a description of the service, lets you configure its startup options, and start, stop, or pause the service. Under the Logon tab, you can set the account the computer will use to run the service. Unless you have a very specific need, there's no need to change this. Recovery lets you specify actions to take if the service fails, and the Dependencies tab lets you see what services are dependent on this service, as well as what services this one is dependent on. If this service has dependents, disabling it will affect those dependents as well.

Windows Startup

You can configure several aspects of the Windows startup environment. Grouping these aspects into two buckets, you get how the system behaves and what applications are automatically started.

To configure how your system behaves at startup, open System Properties, choose the Advanced tab, and click the Settings button under the Startup And Recovery section. You'll see a dialog box like Figure 14.23.

Here, you can choose the default operating system (the Edit button manually opens the BOOT.INI file), set system failure options, and set debugging information variables.

FIGURE 14.22   DHCP client service properties

FIGURE 14.23 Startup And Recovery options

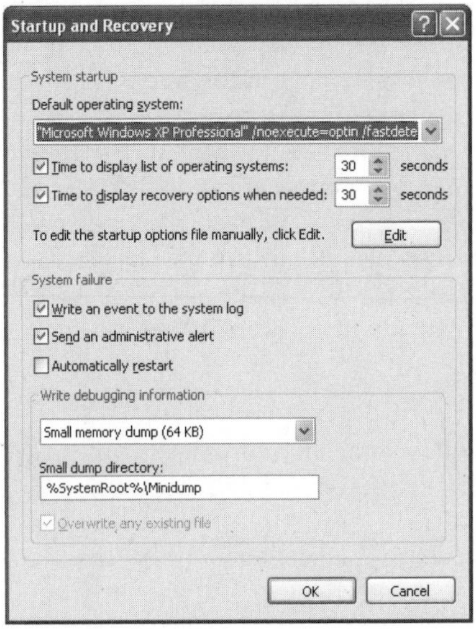

If you click your Start button and navigate to the `Startup` folder (under All Programs in Windows XP, and Programs in Windows 2000), you might or might not see applications there. If applications are there, those apps will run when Windows starts. If you want an application to start every time Windows loads, place it in this folder.

Managing Applications

Other than placing applications in the `Startup` folder to run automatically, you can configure the amount of system resources available. To access these options, open System Properties, click the Advanced tab, and click the Settings button under Performance. Go to the Advanced tab (just as when you configure virtual memory), and you'll get a dialog box like that in Figure 14.24.

Here you can set options for both processor scheduling and memory usage for programs. The default in both cases is to adjust performance to best suit programs.

Troubleshooting Windows

It is impossible for one person to know the solutions to all possible problems a computer can have. There's just too much technology out there, and frankly too many problems out there, to memorize all of the solutions. The key axioms of troubleshooting, then, can be summarized in a few short points. One, use a regimented process (and document your work!). Two, know where to find the answers to problems you don't immediately know how to solve.

FIGURE 14.24   Performance options

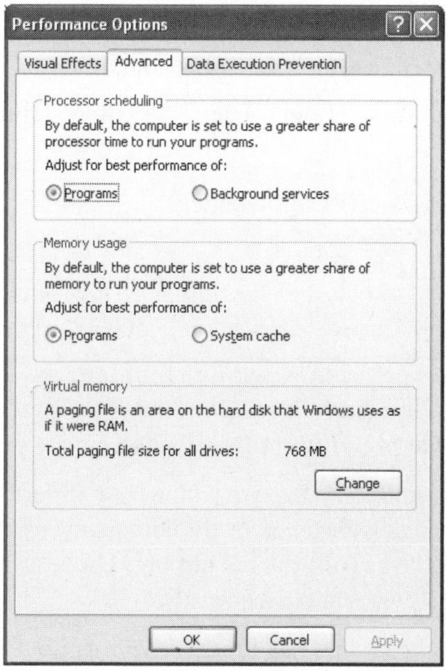

This section will give you more background to help you build your troubleshooting repertoire by showing you how to perform the following tasks:

- Recover Windows

- Recognize and resolve common operational problems and error codes

- Use Windows diagnostic utilities

Recovering Windows

Recovering Windows can take many forms, from resolving boot problems, which are usually relatively simple, to performing system recoveries by using tools such as the Recovery Console, Automated System Recovery (ASR), and the Emergency Repair Disk (ERD).

For example, to be able to fix boot issues, you need to know how the boot process runs normally. That way, if Windows isn't booting properly, you know where to start your troubleshooting. To that end, let's review the Windows 2000/XP boot process and the critical files involved.

The Windows 2000/XP Boot Process

To protect Windows system files from accidental deletion, and to get them out of the way of the average user, they are hidden from the user by default. Because of this, many of the files we are about to talk about will not be visible to you. To make them visible, you need to change the display properties of Windows Explorer. Follow these steps:

1. Open Windows Explorer.
2. Choose Tools ➢ Folder Options. The Folder Options dialog box opens.
3. Select the View tab, and scroll until you find the Hidden Files And Folders option.
4. Select Show Hidden Files And Folders.
5. Deselect Hide Protected Operating System Files (Recommended).
6. Uncheck Hide File Extensions For Known File Types.
7. Click OK. You will now be able to see the Windows system files discussed in the following sections. For security reasons, you should set these attributes back after you've read this chapter.

Windows 2000 and XP use different startup procedures and different startup files than older versions of Windows. Windows 2000/XP are both based on Windows NT and as such use the same key boot files as Windows NT. Here's the Windows 2000/XP boot process:

System self-checks and enumerates hardware resources.   Each machine has a different startup routine, called the POST (power-on self-test), which is executed by the commands written to the motherboard of the computer. Newer Plug and Play (PnP) boards not only check memory and processors, they also poll the systems for other devices and peripherals.

MBR loads and finds the boot sector.   After the system has finished with its housekeeping, the Master Boot Record (MBR) is located on the first hard drive and loaded into memory. The MBR finds the bootable partition and searches it for the boot sector of that partition.

MBR determines the file system and loads NTLDR.   Information in the boot sector allows the system to locate the system partition and to find and load into memory the NTLDR file located there.

NTLDR switches the system from real mode to protected mode and enables paging.   Protected mode enables the system to address all of the available physical memory. It's also referred to as *32-bit flat mode*. At this point, the file system is also started.

NTLDR processes BOOT.INI.   BOOT.INI is a text file that resides in the root directory. It specifies what OSs are installed on the computer. During this step of the boot process, you may be presented with a list of the installed OSs (depending on how your startup options are configured and whether you have multiple OSs installed). If you're presented with the list, you can choose an OS; or, if you don't take any action, the default selection is chosen automatically. If you have multiple OSs installed and you choose a DOS-based OS from the list (such as Windows 9x), NTLDR turns over the boot processes BOOTSECT.DOS and terminates. The MBR code contained in BOOTSECT.DOS is run and IO.SYS is loaded, starting the DOS-based OS's boot process. We will, however, continue with the 2000/XP boot process.

NTLDR loads and runs NTDETECT.COM.   NTDETECT.COM checks the system for installed devices and device configurations and initializes the devices it finds. It passes the information to NTLDR, which collects this information and passes it to NTOSKRNL.EXE after that file is loaded.

NTLDR loads NTOSKRNL.EXE and HAL.DLL.   NTOSKRNL.EXE holds the OS kernel, and also what's known as the executive subsystems. *Executive subsystems* are software components that parse Registry control set configuration information and start services and drivers. HAL.DLL enables communication between the OS and the installed hardware.

NTLDR loads the HKEY_LOCAL_MACHINE\SYSTEM Registry hive and loads device drivers.   The drivers that load at this time serve as boot drivers, using an initial value called a *start value*.

NTLDR transfers control to NTOSKRNL.EXE.   NTOSKRNL.EXE initializes loaded drivers and completes the boot process.

WINLOGON loads.   At this point, you are presented with the Logon screen. After you enter a username and password, you're taken to the Windows Desktop.

Advanced Startup Options

If Windows doesn't load properly, you can also make additional selections for advanced startup options. In Windows 2000/XP, you access the options by pressing the F8 key when you're presented with the list of OSs installed on the computer or when you see the Starting Windows display during Windows boot-up. If you don't have the system configured to display the list of OSs (for example, if you have only one OS installed), press F8 when a message on the screen tells you that you can do so.

Here are the advanced startup options available in Windows 2000 and Windows XP:

Safe Mode   Starts Windows 2000/XP by using only basic files and drivers (mouse, except serial mice; monitor; keyboard; mass storage; base video; default system services; and no network connections). Once in safe mode, you can restore files that are missing or fix a configuration error.

Safe Mode With Networking   Same as safe mode, but tries to load networking components as well.

Safe Mode With Command Prompt   Similar to safe mode, but doesn't load the Windows GUI. Presents the user with a Windows 2000/XP command-line interface.

Enable Boot Logging   *Boot logging* logs all boot information to a file called NTBTLOG.TXT. This file can be found in the \Winnt directory. You can then check the log for assistance in diagnosing system startup problems.

Enable VGA Mode   Starts Windows 2000/XP by using the current video driver but at a 640 X 480 resolution, and loads the rest of the system as normal. If you happen to set your resolution to something your monitor can't handle, this allows you to get into the system to fix the problem.

Last Known Good Configuration   Useful if you have changed a configuration setting in the Registry, which then causes the system to have serious problems, and you're not able to log in. Use *Last Known Good Configuration* to restore the system to a prior, functional state, which will allow you to log in again. It will not save you from a corrupt file or a deleted file error.

Directory Services Restore Mode   Used only with domain controllers. If chosen, boots into a mode that doesn't load directory services. This enables you to restore directory services, such as Active Directory, to the machine. (You can't restore directory services if directory services are running.)

Debugging Mode   A sort of advanced boot logging. It requires that another machine be hooked up to the computer through a serial port. The debug information is then passed to that machine during the boot process. This option is rarely used and should not be bothered with in most cases. If it comes to this, reinstalling is far faster!

Boot Normally (Start Windows Normally)   Continues the boot normally.

Reboot (Windows XP Only)   As the name implies, reboots the computer (warm boot).

Return To OS Choices Menu (Windows XP Only)   Self-explanatory; returns you to the choice of installed OSs.

Using Boot Disks, Emergency Repair Disks, and Automated System Recovery

If you find yourself in a situation where the system won't boot up anymore, or where you are experiencing some other type of critical error, you might need to use boot disks. In Windows 2000 we use an Emergency Repair Disk, and in Windows XP we use Automated System Recovery (ASR).

> To use boot disks, an ERD, or ASR, you must have first created the appropriate disks. Chapter 5 walks you through the procedures on how to create these disks.

Windows 2000 Boot Disks and ERD

To recover from a Windows 2000 emergency, you need four OS boot disks (or a Windows 2000 bootable CD), as well as an *Emergency Repair Disk (ERD)*. If Windows won't boot, you need to boot to either the boot disks or the Windows 2000 CD. This will start the Windows 2000 Setup program. At an early point in the Setup program, you'll be asked whether you want to install or repair Windows 2000. Choose Repair. Windows 2000 Setup will continue and at a later point ask you for the ERD.

> Emergency Repair Disks are computer-specific. Using an ERD created on one computer to fix another computer generally does not work.

Automated System Recovery in Windows XP

Windows XP introduces *Automated System Recovery (ASR)* as a replacement for the ERD. ASR creates a backup of your system partition and then creates a recovery disk. Using these two components, you can recover from a system crash and restore the system back to a functional state.

To use ASR to recover from a system failure, run Setup from the Windows XP CD. During the text portion of the Setup program, you'll see a message to *Press F2 to run the Automated System Recovery Process*; do so, and you'll be prompted to insert the ASR disk. The system then guides you through the rest of the process.

To obtain setup boot disks for Windows XP, you have to go to Microsoft's download website at `http://www.microsoft.com/downloads` and download them. These disks can be used to install XP if you can't boot from CD-ROM. You'll need six floppy disks during the download; they should be formatted and blank.

Using the Recovery Console

If Windows is not booting properly and safe mode and other startup options don't work, you might want to try the Recovery Console. The Recovery Console is a command-line utility you can use to format drives, read data from and write data to local hard drives, stop and start services, and perform several other administrative tasks.

You can run the Recovery Console directly from the Windows installation CD, or you can install it on your hard drive and run it as one of the advanced boot options.

Here's how to install the Recovery Console:

1. Put the Windows installation CD in the CD-ROM drive.

2. Click Start and then Run.

3. In the Run box, type **D:\i386\winnt32.exe /cmdcons** (where D:\ is your CD-ROM drive letter).

4. Follow the instructions on screen.

In order to run the Recovery Console, you must be an administrator or have administrative privileges. Once you are logged in, the Recovery Console will allow you to perform activities such as changing directories or viewing files, as well as administrative duties such as trying to repair the boot sector of the hard drive. The Recovery Console is a command-line interface; much like in a Windows command prompt, you can type **help** at the Recovery Console prompt to get a list of available commands. Table 14.8 lists the available Recovery Console commands and a brief description of their functions.

TABLE 14.8   Recovery Console commands

Command	Function
ATTRIB	Changes the attributes of a file or folder.
BATCH	Runs the commands specified in a text file so that you can perform many tasks in one step.
CD or CHDIR	Changes directories.
CHKDSK	Runs the hard-disk checker.
CLS	Clears the screen of previous output.

TABLE 14.8   Recovery Console commands *(continued)*

Command	Function
COPY	Copies files from removable media to the system folders. (Note: With the Console, you cannot use wildcards!)
DEL or DELETE	Deletes files.
DIR	Lists the contents of a directory.
DISABLE	Disables a specified service or driver.
DISKPART	Creates or deletes disk partitions.
ENABLE	Enables a specified service or driver.
EXTRACT	Extracts compressed installation files (ones with .CAB extensions) to the system partition. This command only works if you run the Console from the installation CD.
FIXBOOT	Writes a new boot sector on the system partition.
FIXMBR	Writes a new master boot record for the partition boot sector.
FORMAT	Formats the selected disk.
HELP	Displays a list of available Recovery Console commands.
LISTSVC	Lists all services and drivers running in Windows.
LOGON	Logs on to Windows.
MAP	Displays the drive letter mappings currently recognized. Can be helpful to use before DISKPART.
MD or MKDIR	Creates a directory.
MORE or TYPE	Displays the contents of a specified file.
RD or RMDIR	Deletes a directory.
REN or RENAME	Renames a file.
SYSTEMROOT	Makes the current directory the system root of the drive you are logged in to.

While the Console can do many things, it's important to note the things that the Console *can't* do. Most notably, it can't be used to back up files. Files can be copied from media to the local hard drive (specifically, to the system partition), but not the other way around. In addition, although you can change to partitions other than the system partition, you can't read files on them. So the Console is handy, but it's not a save-all; don't think of it as a duplicate of the command prompt.

 The key functions of the Recovery Console are to be able to repair your system partition or make minor tweaks to Windows to get the operating system functional.

Recognizing and Resolving Common Operational Problems and Error Messages

Earlier I said that it was impossible to know all possible fixes. Although this is true, there are issues that are more common than others. Having a good grasp on how to begin fixing these common issues can greatly speed up your troubleshooting processes.

Fixing Boot Errors

If the files that are needed to boot the operating system aren't present and accounted for, you will get an error message at boot. But not all files are needed for every boot situation. For example, if you don't use a SCSI boot drive, you don't need the `NTBOOTDD.SYS` file.

Let's take a brief look at some common Windows 2000/XP boot errors, what might be causing them, and how to solve them:

Invalid Boot Disk   You get the *Invalid boot disk* error when the BIOS finds a partition that could be bootable but is missing the essential system files. You can correct this problem by reinstalling the OS.

Operating System Not Found   This error means exactly what it says. Essentially, the system BIOS could not find an OS, or even a valid boot partition, on any of the boot devices (floppy, hard disk, or CD-ROM). You will get this error on a brand-new computer that you have just built, until you install the OS. Other causes are a corrupted boot sector or boot files.

There are a couple of solutions to the Invalid Boot Disk and Operating System Not Found problems. First, if the file or files are missing, copy them from the original setup diskettes or CD-ROM, or copy them from a backup (assuming you have one). The same holds true if you have a corrupt file, except you must delete the corrupt files first, and then replace them with new copies.

Inaccessible Boot Device   If, on bootup, you receive an error that states *STOP: 0x0000007B inaccessible boot device*, you may have one of several problems. The most common is that Windows could not load the driver for the disk controller on the boot device. This could be because it is the wrong driver or because the disk controller is conflicting with some other hardware in the system.

This issue could also be caused by a unique installation procedure. If you are trying to run Windows 2000/XP Setup from a SCSI CD-ROM, Setup will not allow you to install a third-party SCSI driver when you boot from the SCSI CD-ROM. You will have to try using the boot disks to install 2000/XP.

Missing *NTLDR* or Missing or Corrupt *NTOSKRNL.EXE* As you've learned, NTLDR is relied on heavily during the boot process. If it is missing or corrupted, Windows NT will not be able to boot, and you'll get an error similar to *Can't find NTLDR*.

On the other hand, if you get an error such as *NTOSKRNL.EXE missing or corrupt* on bootup, it may be an error in the BOOT.INI file. This is a common occurrence if you have improperly used the multi(0)disk(0)rdisk(0)partition(1)\WINDOWS="Microsoft Windows XP Professional" syntax for partition entries or had the partition table modified in a multidisk setup. If these entries are correct, the NTOSKRNL.EXE file may be corrupt or missing. Boot to a startup disk and replace the file from the setup disks or CD-ROM.

Solving Auto-Restart and Startup Errors

Sometimes you will have a computer that won't get past the Windows splash screen (the screen that tells you Windows is loading, but it's not yet to the screen that lets you log in). The splash screen will load, and the computer will sit there for a bit and then reboot itself. This process repeats itself over and over.

This can mean that there is a corrupt driver or an error in the Registry. If you can get the system to boot into the advanced options, you can try to resolve the problem by using an ERD or ASR.

Other causes of auto-restart errors could be an overheating computer, power supply problems, bad RAM, and viruses.

You will also sometimes see the system booting into Windows, but it will give you an error message such as *The xxxx device/service has failed to start* or *A device/program referenced in the Registry cannot be found.*

Generally speaking, these errors are not fatal, but they are annoying. If it's a device that's not starting, check Device Manager to see whether there are problems with the device driver. If so, uninstall and reinstall the device. If problems persist, it might be a defective device. If you have just updated the driver in Windows XP and problems started, you can use a feature called driver rollback to uninstall the driver and restore a previous version. Exercise 14.10 walks you through this process.

For failing services, check the Services applet in the Administrative Tools in Control Panel (or in Computer Management). Some services are dependent on other services, so having one fail to start could cause a chain reaction. If the service failed, you can try starting the service manually and ensuring that the service and its upstream services are scheduled to start automatically.

EXERCISE 14.10

Rolling back a device driver

Maybe you wanted new features or you were having compatibility issues, so you installed a new device driver. For whatever reason, your system seems to be worse off than it was before. One way to help solve this new problem is to roll back the device driver with the device driver rollback feature in Windows XP. Here's how:

1. Open Device Manager.

2. Navigate to the device you're having problems with.

3. Right-click on the device and select Properties.

4. Go to the Driver tab, and click the Roll Back Driver button.

5. The system will ask you, *Are you sure you would like to roll back to the previous driver?* Click Yes.

The previous driver will be restored!

Errors involving the Registry are generally cause for concern. The most common cause of a computer telling you that a Registry reference can't be found is that someone tried to uninstall a program or device but did so improperly. You can try to remove the device through Device Manager, or remove the program through Add/Remove Programs. If that doesn't help, you can always edit the Registry manually, searching for entries that match the device or program causing the error.

Resolving Printing Problems

Another major category of problems you might be asked to troubleshoot are those problems that occur during printing. If a printer is not printing at all, always check the cables first and reseat them. If they appear okay and the printer is online but still will not print, then you will want to look in the direction of the printer driver.

One common source of printer-driver errors is corruption of the driver. If a printer doesn't work, you can delete the printer from the printer settings (Printers and Faxes) window and reinstall it. If this method fails, the problem may be that related printer files were not replaced. Delete all printers from the computer and reinstall them. If this second method fails, the printer driver is not compatible with Windows or with the printer, and you will need to obtain an updated driver.

A quick way to test the printer functionality is to use the Print Test Page option. This option is presented to you as the last step when setting up a new printer in Windows. Always select this option when you're setting up a new printer so you can test its functionality. To print a test page for a printer that's already set up, look for the option on the Properties menu for the particular printer.

After the test page is sent to the printer, the computer will ask whether it printed correctly. The first few times, you'll probably want to answer no and use the troubleshooting wizard that appears; but after you have troubleshot a few printer problems, you may prefer to answer yes and bypass the wizard.

 For steps on how to stop and restart the print spooler, see Exercise 14.7.

Resolving Device, Application, and Other Failures

Some common Windows problems don't fall into any category other than "common Windows problems." They include the following:

General Protection Faults (GPFs)   A *general protection fault (GPF)* happens in Windows when a program accesses memory that another program is using or when a program accesses a memory address that doesn't exist. Generally, GPFs are the result of sloppy programming. To fix this type of problem, a simple reboot will usually clear memory. If GPFs keep occurring, check to see which software is causing the error. Then find out whether the manufacturer of the software has a patch to prevent it from GPFing.

Illegal Operation   Occasionally, a program will quit, apparently for no reason, and present you with a window that says *This program has performed an illegal operation and will be shut down. If the problem persists, contact the program vendor.* An *illegal operation error* usually means that a program was forced to quit because it did something Windows didn't like. Windows then displays this error window. The name of the program that quit appears at the top of the window, along with three buttons: OK, Cancel, and Details. The OK and Cancel buttons do the same thing: dismiss the window. The Details button opens the window a little further and shows the details of the error, including which module experienced the problem, the memory location being accessed at the time, and the registers and flags of the processor at the time of the error.

System Lockup   It is obvious when a system lockup occurs. The system simply stops responding to commands and stops processing completely. System lockups can occur when a computer is asked to process too many instructions at once with too little memory. Usually, the cure for a system lockup is to reboot. If the lockups are persistent, it may be a hardware-related problem instead of a software problem.

Dr. Watson   Windows 2000 and Windows XP include a special utility known as Dr. Watson. This utility intercepts all error conditions and displays a slew of information that can be used to troubleshoot the problem. The information is typically more useful to programmers than it is to technicians.

Failure to Start GUI   Occasionally, the Windows GUI won't appear. The system will hang just before the GUI appears. Or sometimes the *Blue Screen of Death (BSOD)*—not a technical term, by the way—appears. The BSOD is another way of describing the blue-screen error condition that occurs when Windows 2000/XP fails to boot properly or quits unexpectedly. Because it is at this stage that the device drivers for the various pieces of hardware are installed, if your Windows GUI fails to start properly, more than likely the problem is related to a misconfigured driver or misconfigured hardware. Try booting Windows in safe mode to bypass this problem.

Option (Sound Card, Modem, SCSI Card, or Input Device) Will Not Function   When you are using Windows, you are constantly interacting with pieces of hardware. Each piece of hardware has a Windows driver that must be loaded in order for Windows to be able to use it. Additionally, the hardware must be installed and functioning properly. If the device driver is not installed properly or the hardware is misconfigured, the device won't function properly.

Cannot Log On to the Network (Option—NIC Not Functioning)   If your computer is hooked up to a network (and more and more computers today are), you need to know when your computer is not functioning on the network properly and what to do about it. In most cases, the problem can be attributed to either a malfunctioning network interface card (NIC) or improperly installed network software. The biggest indicator in Windows that some component of the network software is nonfunctional is that you can't log on to the network or access any network service. To fix this problem, you must first fix the underlying hardware problem (if one exists), and then properly install or configure the network software.

Networking software is covered in Chapter 8.

Applications Don't Install   We've all experienced this frustration. You are trying to install the coolest new program, and, for whatever reason, it just won't install properly. It may give you one of the previously mentioned errors or a cryptic installation error. If a software program won't install and it gives you any of the errors we've mentioned (such as a GPF or illegal operation), use the solutions for those errors first. If the error that occurs during installation is unique to the application being installed, check the application manufacturer's website for an explanation or update. These errors generally occur when you're trying to install over an application that already exists, or when you're trying to replace a file that already exists but that another application is using. When you're installing an application, it is extremely important that you first quit all running programs so the installer can replace any files it needs to.

Application Will Not Start   After you have an application successfully installed, you may run across a problem getting it to start properly. This problem can come from any number of sources, including an improper installation, a software conflict, or system instability. If your application was installed incorrectly, the files required to properly run the program may not be present, and the program can't function without them. If a shared file that's used by other programs is installed, it could be a different version than should be installed that causes conflicts with other already-installed programs. Finally, if one program GPFs, it can cause memory problems that can destabilize the system and cause other programs to crash. The solution to these problems is to reinstall the offending application, first making sure that all programs are closed.

Invalid Working Directory   Some Windows programs are extremely processor intensive. These programs require an area on the hard disk to store their temporary files while they work. This area is commonly known as a *working directory*, and its location is usually specified during that program's installation. However, if that directory changes after installation and the program still thinks its working directory is in the same location, the program will issue an error that says something such as *Invalid working directory*. The solution is to reinstall the program with the correct parameters for the working directory.

Always Reboot First...

Troubleshooting software problems can be tricky. There are so many files that could be causing the problem, and it's often hard to know where to start. If you are having a software problem, such as specific error messages, or worse yet the Blue Screen of Death, the first step should always be the same: Save your work (if you can) and reboot.

To reboot, turn the computer completely off. Wait 10 seconds (it gives the hard disk time to stop spinning, which is important), and power the system back on.

Performing a hard reboot does two things. One, it clears the memory, which could have caused the problem. Two, it should clear out temporary files, which are a common culprit as well. After you reboot, try the application again.

If the error doesn't come back, and you can't make it happen again, it's not a problem. If it comes back, you have something to fix. This "solution" frustrates a lot of end users, but it's the absolutely critical first step to solving software (including operating system) problems.

To avoid *Invalid working directory* errors, many programs use the Windows Temp directory as their working directory. You will see this error only if the programmer chose to use a working directory that could be set by the user.

Remember that there are two universal solutions to Windows problems: rebooting, and obtaining an update from the software manufacturer.

Using Windows Diagnostic Utilities

Microsoft provides several tools with Windows to help troubleshoot problems. These resources are the best to use if you have no other troubleshooting tools available, or they can also be used as a starting point for troubleshooting a computer. Here are the diagnostic utilities you can expect to see on the A+ technician exams:

- Bootable media
- Startup modes
- Documentation resources
- Task Manager
- Device Manager
- Event Viewer
- MSCONFIG
- Recovery CD / recovery partition
- Remote Desktop Connection and Assistance
- System File Checker (SFC)

Several of these resources are covered in this section. Startup modes are discussed in the "Advanced Startup Modes" section earlier in this chapter. Task Manager, Device Manager, Event Viewer, and MSCONFIG are talked about in the "System Management Tools" section earlier in this chapter. Remote Desktop Connection and Assistance is covered in the "Remote Desktop Connection and Assistance" section earlier in this chapter.

Bootable Media

In the old days of computer troubleshooting, one of the items that every technician needed to carry was a bootable floppy disk. When CD-ROMs became common, you made sure that your floppy had the CD-ROM drivers on it too, because operating systems (and their installation files) were being offered on that media as well.

Today it seems fewer and fewer computers even have floppy disk drives. And most, if not all, of today's computer BIOSs are capable of booting from the CD-ROM or DVD drives.

The moral of the story is, even though technology has changed, the fundamental reason we carried and still need to carry bootable media has not. If the operating system won't start but the computer appears to POST just fine, you need to somehow find a way to figure out exactly what's wrong. Booting to a command line or to an installation program gets you a step closer to solving the problem.

I would still recommend carrying a bootable floppy disk, just because you never know when you'll need it. It's also a good idea to carry bootable CD-ROMs of popular operating systems, such as Windows 98, Me, 2000, and XP.

Documentation Resources

Whenever troubleshooting, always consider the use of the following resources.

User/Installation Manuals

Technicians are the most guilty of not using this readily available resource when troubleshooting a system. In fact, most often, a technician will rely on their own experience and try to install a new component without reading the manual. Then, when the installation doesn't work, the technician might go back and look at the manual after spending time looking for the solution to a problem that might have been avoided in the first place.

Typically, in addition to the steps needed to install software or a device, a manual includes a section on the most common problems and the solutions to those problems. This area of the manual would be especially useful for the technician we just described.

Internet/Web Resources

Possibly the most useful resource to the technician is the Internet. As mentioned throughout this book, a manufacturer's website is the best place to get the most current drivers, fixes, and technical information. Often you can search a hardware or software vendor's website for a problem you might be having with that hardware or software, and find the fix for it. In addition, Microsoft's website contains a wide variety of known problems and issues with Windows and its interaction with other software. Sometimes an issue that can't be solved at the software vendor's website can be solved by viewing the Microsoft support website, because Microsoft has a larger staff and has been able to document a larger variety of problems. If you can't find an answer at the manufacturer's or Microsoft's website, you might try entering your problem into one of the many search engines, such as Yahoo (`http://www.yahoo.com`) or Google (`http://www.google.com`).

There are websites dedicated to communities of technical individuals (such as yourself) that can be a great source of information. Chances are, if you're having a computer or technical problem, someone else, somewhere in the world, has the solution—and the Internet can bring you together. You can post your problem to any number of website bulletin boards and newsgroups and receive a response, possibly within minutes.

Training Materials

The final resource is one that most people overlook. Individuals do not acquire knowledge magically—they either learn it by themselves with self-study materials or are taught by an experienced instructor. In either case, books and other training materials (such as the one you are reading right now) are excellent sources of information. Although training materials don't often contain patches or updates, they can and do teach concepts that you can apply to help you with troubleshooting. After all, if you had not read this book, you might not have gotten the information you needed to pass the A+ exam.

Now ask yourself: Did I learn anything? Will the information I learned be able to help me troubleshoot a computer problem?

Recovery CD / Recovery Partition

Many times a computer will have more problems than can be fixed easily, or the fix may result in only a temporary solution. Usually such a case calls for a complete formatting and reinstallation of the OS and applications, and restoration of data. However, many new computers today don't come with a true OS CD-ROM. Instead, they come with one or more recovery CDs.

A *recovery CD* is a CD-ROM that comes with a particular model and brand of computer. The CD-ROM contains an image of the entire Windows installation, along with applications, utilities, and drivers specifically for that computer. In the case of a serious system failure, you can insert this CD-ROM into the CD-ROM drive of your computer, boot to it, and completely restore the system back to the way it was when you bought it.

These CDs are also known as *restoration CDs*.

However, these CDs will *erase the hard drive first*! Therefore, any data and settings that you've created will be gone, including data files, e-mail configuration settings, Internet favorites, and so on. The computer will be *exactly* as it was out of the box.

If you ever need to use a recovery CD-ROM, *back up your data* before booting to the CD. Most recovery CDs don't give you the option of backing up before the restoration. You *will* lose all your data when you use one of these CDs for a recovery.

A *recovery partition* is basically the same as a recovery CD. The difference is that instead of being portable, it's a partition on a hard drive. There are numerous third-party utilities on the market that can help you create recovery partitions, such as Norton's Ghost.

To use a recovery partition, you would boot the problematic computer by using a boot disk (or CD). Depending on how you have it configured, the recovery process starts automatically or you enter a simple command to begin the process. Just as with a recovery CD, all information previously on the computer will be removed.

System File Checker (SFC)

The System File Checker (SFC) is a command line–based utility that checks and verifies the versions of system files on your computer. If system files are corrupt, the SFC will replace the corrupt files with correct versions.

The syntax for the System File Checker is as follows:

SFC *[switch]*

Table 14.9 lists the switches available for SFC.

T A B L E 1 4 . 9   *SFC* Switches

Switch	Purpose
/CACHESIZE=*X*	Sets the Windows File Protection cache size, in megabytes
/PURGECACHE	Purges the Windows File Protection cache and scans all protected system files immediately
/REVERT	Reverts SFC to its default operation
/SCANNOW	Immediately scans all protected system files

TABLE 14.9 *SFC* Switches *(continued)*

Switch	Purpose
/SCANONCE	Scans all protected system files once
/SCANBOOT	Scans all protected system files every time the computer is rebooted

To run the SFC, you must be logged in as an administrator or have administrative privileges. If the System File Checker discovers a corrupt system file, it will automatically overwrite the file by using a copy held in the *%systemroot%*\system32\dllcache directory. If you believe that the dllcache directory is corrupt, you can use SFC /SCANNOW, SFC /SCANONCE, or SFC /SCANBOOT, or SFC /PURGECACHE to repair its contents.

Performing Preventative Maintenance

In this section you'll take a look at some preventative steps you can take to help keep Windows 2000 and Windows XP running smoothly. They include the following:

- Updating Windows regularly
- Scheduling backups
- Creating restore points

Updating Windows

Windows 2000 and Windows XP include *Windows Update*, a feature designed to keep Windows current by automatically downloading and installing updates such as patches and security fixes.

By default, Windows Update will run automatically when any Administrator user is logged in. However, if you want to run it manually, you can do so by clicking Start ➤ All Programs ➤ Windows Update in Windows XP, or by clicking Start Windows Update (Windows XP), or by clicking Start ➤ Windows Update in Windows 2000. You can also go to http://windowsupdate.microsoft.com to start the process.

 Often, updates to Windows are called *service packs*.

Here is an overview of how Windows Update works:

1. Windows Update starts (either by itself or manually).
2. Windows Update goes online to check what updates are available. It compares the update list to the updates that have already been applied to the computer or have been refused by the Administrator.

3. If updates are available, they are downloaded automatically in the background.

4. After the updates are downloaded, Windows Update notifies you that the download is complete and asks whether you want to install them.

If you choose not to install the updates right away, Windows will do so for you when you shut off the computer. Instead of shutting off right away, Windows Update will install the updates first and then perform a proper shutdown.

By default, Windows Update is enabled. But at times you might want to configure it. Exercise 14.11 shows you how to configure Windows Update in Windows XP.

EXERCISE 14.11

Configuring Windows Update in Windows XP

Windows Update should be enabled by default. However, you can change this option if you prefer. This exercise shows you how to do that.

1. Open the System Properties dialog box (right-click My Computer and choose Properties, or double-click the System icon in Control Panel).

2. Click the Automatic Updates tab.

3. Choose the option that best suits your needs. You have four choices:

   Automatically download recommended updates for my computer and install them

   Download updates for me, but let me choose when to install them

   Notify me but don't automatically download or install them

   Turn off Automatic Updates

It's not a problem if you want to choose to have control over which updates get installed and when. However, it really is in your best interest to have Windows Update enabled to ensure that you have the most current patches available.

Scheduling Backups

This is one of the areas that most users, and even most companies, fail to manage properly. At the same time, it's one of the most important. Backups serve several key purposes, such as protecting against hard drive failure, protecting against accidental deletion, protecting against malicious deletion or attacks, and making an archive of important files for later use. Any time you make major changes to your system, including installing new software, you should perform a *backup* of important files before making the changes.

Both Windows 2000 and Windows XP allow you to schedule backups, which is a great feature that not all versions of Windows have had.

Now that you know you can schedule backups to make your life easy—and of course you want to make backups because it's the right thing to do—the question becomes: How often do you need to back up your files?

The answer really depends on what the computer does and what you do on the computer. How often does your data change? Every day? Every week or every month? How important are your files? Can you afford to lose them? How much time or money will it cost to replace lost files? Can they be replaced? By answering these questions, you can get an idea of how often you want to run scheduled backups. As a rule of thumb, the more important it is, and the more often it changes, the more often you want to back up. If you don't care about losing the data, there's no need for backups—but most of us do care about losing our stuff.

Exercise 14.12 walks you through scheduling a backup in Windows XP.

EXERCISE 14.12

Scheduling Backups in Windows XP

Backups are critical, and not enough people make them. This exercise shows you how to do it, so now you have no excuses not to!

1. Open Windows Backup by choosing Start ➢ All Programs ➢ Accessories ➢ System Tools ➢ Backup. This opens up the Backup Or Restore Wizard. The wizard will walk you through all of the options you can use, or you can click the Advanced Mode link to set up things manually.

2. On the Backup Or Restore Wizard screen, click Next to continue.

3. Choose Back Up Files And Settings and click Next.

4. Choose what you want to back up (as shown in the following graphic), and click Next.

5. Confirm the backup type and destination, and give the backup file a name (it will have a .BKF extension). For the destination, you can click the Browse button to select the right location, which might be a floppy drive, CD or DVD burner, or a network drive. Click Next.

6. At the Completing the Backup Or Restore Wizard confirmation page, review the settings. If you're happy with them, click Finish to begin the backup. Clicking on Advanced will give you more options; continue with step 7.

7. Specify the type of backup. If you're not sure, choose Normal. Click Next.

8. Choose your backup options: Verify data, hardware compression, and disable volume shadow copy. It's a good idea to verify data, but it does take extra time. Click Next.

9. Choose to replace the current backup file (if one exists) or append the data to the end of the backup. Click Next.

10. Here is where you can schedule the backup. Choose Later, and then click the Set Schedule button. (If you didn't want to schedule, but just back up files now, click Now.)

EXERCISE 14.12 *(continued)*

11. In the Schedule Job dialog box, choose how often and at what time you would like to run backups, and click OK. Click Next.

12. You will be prompted for a username and password to run the backup. This is because only certain user accounts (such as the Administrator) have the ability to run backups. When the process starts, Windows will log itself in as the user account you specify to perform the backup. Click Next.

13. Review the information on the confirmation page and click Finish.

One key point to remember is that for the backups to run properly as scheduled, the computer needs to be on when the scheduled backup is supposed to take place.

Backup Lessons

People don't back up data enough, plain and simple. Scheduling regular backups is a good protective measure, but just because you are backing up your data doesn't mean you're completely saved if something goes wrong.

Several years ago, one of my former students related a story to me about a server crash at his company. A server had mysteriously died over the weekend, and the technicians were greeted with the problem first thing Monday morning. Not to worry, they thought, because they made regular backups.

After several attempts to restore the backup tape, a second, more serious problem was readily apparent. The backup didn't work. They couldn't read data from the tape, and it was the only backup tape they had. It wasn't going to be a very good Monday. Ultimately, they ended up losing a lot of data from the server, because their backup didn't work.

How do you prevent tragedies like this from happening? Test your backups. After you make a backup, ensure that you can read from it. If you've just backed up a small amount of data, restore it to an alternate location and make sure you can read it. If you are backing up entire computers, a good idea is to run a test restore on a separate computer. No matter your method, test your backups, especially when it's the first one you've made after setting up backups or have made backup configuration changes. It isn't necessary to fully test each single backup after that, but it is a good idea to spot-check backups on occasion.

Here are two more ideas that will help too. One, rotate backup tapes (or CDs). Alternate tapes every other backup period, or use a separate tape for each day of the week. This lessens the risk of having a bad tape bring you down. Two, store your backups off-site. If your backup is sitting on top of the server, and you have a fire that destroys the building, then your backup didn't do you any good. There are data archiving firms that will, for a small fee, come and pick up your backup tapes and store them in their secure location.

Be religious about backing up your data, and in the event of a failure, you'll be back up and running in short order.

Creating Restore Points

As noted earlier in this chapter, Windows XP has a feature called System Restore, which lets you create and use restore points to "roll back" a system's configuration to a previous state.

Windows XP is configured to create restore points automatically, but you can also create them manually if you so choose. Detailed instructions on creating restore points are given earlier in this chapter in the "System Restore" section, as well as in Exercise 14.8.

Summary

In this chapter, you learned about several aspects of using, optimizing, and troubleshooting Windows. We started with an overview of several command-line utilities you can use in Windows, including proper syntax and switches. Then we showed you how to manage disks, directories, and files, as well as several useful Windows-based utilities.

Next, we discussed ways to optimize Windows, including virtual memory, hard drives, temporary files, services, startup, and applications.

We reviewed the Windows boot process, as well as how to recover Windows from a boot failure. From there, we presented several common Windows problems and solutions. Finally, we looked at preventative maintenance tasks to help keep Windows running smoothly.

Exam Essentials

Understand what each of the following command-line utilities does: CMD, HELP, DIR, ATTRIB, EDIT, COPY, XCOPY, FORMAT, MD, CD, and RD. Many utilities that come with Windows help you navigate through or manage files and directories from a command prompt. The CMD command opens a command line, where you can type the rest of the commands. If you're not sure which utility to use, HELP will give you information. The MD, CD, and RD commands make, change, and delete (remove) directories, respectively, and the DIR command shows you what's inside the directory. To set file attributes, use ATTRIB; to modify file contents, use EDIT. The FORMAT command formats hard drives, and both COPY and XCOPY are used to copy files.

Know what the IPCONFIG and PING utilities are for.   Both IPCONFIG and PING are network troubleshooting commands. You can use IPCONFIG to view your computer's IP configuration, and PING to test connectivity between two network hosts.

Know how to create, format, and manage partitions in Windows 2000 and Windows XP.   The Disk Management utility is used to create, format, and manage partitions in Windows 2000 and Windows XP.

Know how and when to use Windows 2000 and Windows XP utilities.   Utilities that you need to be familiar with include Device Manager, Task Manager, MSCONFIG, ATTRIB, REGEDIT and REGEDT32, Event Viewer, System Restore, Remote Desktop, and Windows Explorer.

Understand ways in which you can optimize Windows performance.   Some common areas for optimization include virtual memory, hard drives (disk defragmentation), temporary files, services, startup, and applications.

Know how to fix common Windows problems.   You need to be familiar with how to fix printing problems, boot and auto-restart errors, system lockups, driver failures, application failures, and Registry problems.

Understand how to perform preventative maintenance in Windows.   The maintenance you should do includes the following: Perform regular backups, apply current patches and service packs (generally through Windows Update), and create restore points.

Review Questions

1. You just clicked Start ➤ Run. Which of the following can you type to open a command prompt? (Choose all that apply.)

   A. RUN

   B. CMD

   C. COMMAND

   D. OPEN

2. Which of the following command-line utilities is primarily used to modify text files?

   A. EDIT

   B. EDT

   C. NOTEPAD

   D. WORDPAD

3. Which of the following types of partitions is the one the operating system must boot from?

   A. Primary

   B. Logical

   C. Extended

   D. Active

4. Which of the following types of partitions is defined by it being assigned a drive letter?

   A. Primary

   B. Active

   C. Extended

   D. Logical

5. Which of the following are valid hard drive file systems available in Windows 2000? (Choose all that apply.)

   A. FAT32

   B. NTFS

   C. CDFS

   D. NFS

6. You are in Device Manager and want to temporarily disable your network card while you make configuration changes. What's the best way to temporarily disable the card?

   A. Highlight the network card and hit the Del key on your keyboard.

   B. Highlight the network card, right-click, and click Uninstall.

   C. Highlight the network card, right-click, and click Disable.

   D. Device Manager does not allow you to disable hardware.

7. Which of the following are methods to open Task Manager? (Choose all that apply.)

   A. Right-click My Computer and select Tasks.

   B. Press Ctrl+Alt+Del.

   C. Press Ctrl+Shift+Esc.

   D. Press the Windows key and Esc.

8. In Windows 2000, which utility contains Event Viewer, Disk Defragmenter, and Services?

   A. Task Manager

   B. System Manager

   C. Computer Management

   D. Device Manager

9. Which of the following utilities creates backups of the system configuration called restore points?

   A. Registry Backup

   B. Backup

   C. System Restore

   D. Configuration Manager

10. Which of the following operating systems by default contain the software to act as a home computer using Remote Desktop? (Choose all that apply.)

    A. Windows XP Home

    B. Windows XP Professional

    C. Windows 98

    D. Windows Me

11. Your printer appears to be hung and is not printing jobs sent to it. You have checked the printer and it is online and has paper. You have powered the printer off and back on to no avail. Which troubleshooting step should you try next?

    A. Delete and reinstall the printer.

    B. Unplug the printer from the wall outlet, and plug it back in.

    C. Stop and restart the print spooler.

    D. Map the printer to LPT2.

12. You have just installed Windows XP and want to optimize the virtual memory. What is the minimum recommended page-file size in Windows XP?

    A. As big as the amount of RAM in your computer.

    B. One and a half times the amount of RAM in your computer.

    C. Two and a half times the amount of RAM in your computer.

    D. There is no minimum recommended page-file size in Windows XP.

13. Which of the following files is responsible for switching the system from real to protected memory mode during the boot process?

    A. NTOSKRNL

    B. BOOT.INI

    C. NTDETECT.COM

    D. NTLDR

14. Your Windows 2000 computer will not boot into Windows. You believe that the problem is the video resolution you just set isn't supported by your monitor. Which of the following options should you try at boot to troubleshoot the problem?

    A. Safe Mode

    B. Safe Mode With Networking

    C. Last Known Good Configuration

    D. VGA Mode

15. Which of the following operating systems uses an Emergency Repair Disk (ERD) to restore its configuration in the event of a system failure?

    A. Windows 2000

    B. Windows XP Home

    C. Windows XP Professional

    D. None of the above

16. You believe that your system files are corrupted in Windows XP. You run System File Checker. What do you do to make System File Checker automatically repair your system files if repair is needed?

    A. Run SFC /AUTOREPAIR

    B. Run SFC /REPAIR

    C. Run SFC /REVERT

    D. Run SFC /SCANNOW

17. You are at a command prompt, and your current directory is C:\Windows\Temp\Files\Old. Which command will get you to the root of D:?

    A. CD..

    B. CD\

    C. CD /D D:\

    D. D:

18. Which of the following commands can you use to convert a FAT partition to an NTFS partition?

   A. CONVERT

   B. CONVPART

   C. CONV

   D. You cannot convert a FAT partition to NTFS.

19. You are at a command prompt. Which utility can you use to see whether you have a network connection to another computer?

   A. IPCONFIG

   B. CONNECT

   C. PING

   D. IP

20. You are at a command prompt. You want to make a file called WORK.DOC a read-only file. Which command do you use to accomplish this?

   A. ATTRIB +R WORK.DOC

   B. ATTRIB +RO WORK.DOC

   C. ATTRIB WORK.DOC

   D. READONLY WORK.DOC

Answers to Review Questions

1. B, C. To open a command prompt, you can use CMD or COMMAND.

2. A. The EDIT command is a holdover from the DOS days, and is used to edit text-based files. Notepad and Wordpad are both Windows-based utilities, and EDT does not exist.

3. D. The operating system boots from the active partition. Often this is also a primary partition and the first partition created on a hard drive.

4. D. A logical partition is any partition that has a drive letter. It can be primary, active, or extended. However, a logical partition can also span multiple hard disks or multiple primary or extended partitions.

5. A, B. The FAT32 and NTFS file systems are available for hard drives in Windows. CDFS is a file system, but it's restricted to compact discs. NFS is also a file system, but it's not available in Windows.

6. C. The best way to disable a device is to right-click on it and click Disable. Deleting or uninstalling the card will make it not work, but the card will be automatically reinstalled via Plug and Play when Windows is rebooted.

7. B, C. Task Manager can be opened by pressing Ctrl+Alt+Del or by pressing Ctrl+Shift+Esc.

8. C. In both Windows 2000 and Windows XP, the Computer Management utility contains Event Viewer, Disk Defragmenter, and Services.

9. C. The System Restore application creates restore points, which are backups of system configuration.

10. A, B. Windows XP Home and XP Professional both have the necessary software (Remote Desktop) to act as home computers. However, Windows XP Home cannot act as a remote computer.

11. C. If you are sending jobs to the printer but no printing is occurring, you should stop and restart the print spooler service. This is done through the Services applet in Administrative Tools in Control Panel, or Services in Computer Management.

12. B. The minimum recommended page-file size is 1.5 times the amount of physical memory in your computer.

13. D. The NTLDR file is responsible for switching from real to protected mode during the Windows 2000/XP boot process.

14. D. VGA mode will load your video driver, but only at 640 × 480 resolution. Your monitor should be able to handle that. If you had just installed a new video driver, then the other options might be of more use.

15. A. The Windows 2000 operating system uses ERDs to back up the Registry, which contains system configuration items.

16. D. The SFC command will run System File Checker. The /SCANNOW option will scan files, and SFC automatically repairs files it detects as corrupt.

17. D. To change drives at the command prompt, simply type in the drive letter and a colon, and press Enter. However, if you were previously at a specific directory in D: (say, D:\TEMP), then typing D: and pressing Enter would take you to D:\TEMP.

18. A. The CONVERT command is used to convert FAT partitions to NTFS. You cannot convert NTFS to FAT, however.

19. C. The PING command tests to see whether you can reach a remote host on the network.

20. A. The ATTRIB command is used to set file attributes. To add attributes, use the plus sign (+). To remove attributes, use the minus sign (−). The Read-Only attribute is designated by R.

Chapter 15

Installing, Configuring, Optimizing, and Upgrading Printers and Scanners

THE FOLLOWING COMPTIA A+ IT TECHNICIAN EXAM OBJECTIVES ARE COVERED IN THIS CHAPTER:

✓ **4.1 Identify the fundamental principles of using printers and scanners**

- Describe processes used by printers and scanners including laser, ink dispersion, thermal, solid ink and impact printers and scanners

✓ **4.2 Install, configure, optimize and upgrade printers and scanners**

- Install and configure printers / scanners
    - Power and connect the device using local or network port
    - Install and update device driver and calibrate the device
    - Configure options and default settings
    - Install and configure print drivers (e.g. PCL™, Postscript™, GDI)
    - Validate compatibility with operating system and applications
    - Educate user about basic functionality
- Install and configure printer upgrades including memory and firmware
- Optimize scanner performance including resolution, file format and default settings

✓ **4.3 Identify tools and diagnostic procedures to troubleshooting printers and scanners**

  ▪ Gather information about printer / scanner problems

  ▪ Review and analyze collected data

  ▪ Isolate and resolve identified printer / scanner problem including defining the cause, applying the fix and verifying functionality

  ▪ Identify appropriate tools used for troubleshooting and repairing printer / scanner problems

    ▪ Multi-meter

    ▪ Screwdrivers

    ▪ Cleaning solutions

    ▪ Extension magnet

    ▪ Test patterns

✓ **4.4 Perform preventative maintenance of printers and scanners**

  ▪ Perform scheduled maintenance according to vendor guidelines (e.g. install maintenance kits, reset page counts)

  ▪ Ensure a suitable environment

  ▪ Use recommended supplies

THE FOLLOWING COMPTIA A+ REMOTE SUPPORT TECHNICIAN EXAM OBJECTIVES ARE COVERED IN THIS CHAPTER:

✓ **3.1 Identify the fundamental principles of using printers and scanners**

  ▪ Describe processes used by printers and scanners including laser, ink dispersion, impact, solid ink and thermal printers.

✓ **3.2 Install, configure, optimize and upgrade printers and scanners**

  ▪ Install and configure printers and scanners

    ▪ Power and connect the device using network or local port

    ▪ Install/update the device driver and calibrate the device

- Configure options and default settings
- Install and configure print drivers (e.g. PCL™, Postscript™ and GDI)
- Validate compatibility with OS and applications
- Educate user about basic functionality
- Optimize scanner performance for example: resolution, file format and default settings

✓ **3.3 Identify tools, diagnostic procedures and troubleshooting techniques for printers and scanners**

- Gather information required to troubleshoot printer/ scanner problems
- Troubleshoot a print failure (e.g. lack of paper, clear queue, restart print spooler, recycle power on printer, inspect for jams, check for visual indicators)

THE FOLLOWING COMPTIA A+ DEPOT TECHNICIAN EXAM OBJECTIVES ARE COVERED IN THIS CHAPTER:

✓ **3.1 Identify the fundamental principles of using printers and scanners**

- Describe the processes used by printers and scanners including laser, inkjet, thermal, solid ink, and impact printers

✓ **3.2 Install, configure, optimize and upgrade printers and scanners**

- Identify the steps used in the installation and configuration processes for printers and scanners, for example:
  - Power and connect the device using network or local port
  - Install and update the device driver
  - Calibrate the device
  - Configure options and default settings
  - Print test page
- Install and configure printer/scanner upgrades including memory and firmware

✓ **3.3 Identify tools, diagnostic methods and troubleshooting procedures for printers and scanners**

- Gather data about printer/scanner problem
- Review and analyze data collected about printer/scanner problems
- Implement solutions to solve identified printer/scanner problems
- Identify appropriate tools used for troubleshooting and repairing printer/scanner problems
  - Multi-meter
  - Screw drivers
  - Cleaning solutions
  - Extension magnet
  - Test patterns

✓ **3.4 Perform preventative maintenance of printer and scanner problems**

- Perform scheduled maintenance according to vendor guidelines (e.g. install maintenance kits, reset page counts)
- Ensure a suitable environment
- Use recommended supplies

There's definitely been a movement in modern society to avoid the use of paper when possible. Many office environments are proud to call themselves "paper-free" environments. No matter the level of your "paper-freeness," odds are you still need to print things off, whether it's in the office or at home. Electronic records are great to keep, but many situations still call for an old-fashioned hard copy.

Printers are computer peripherals that specialize in putting ink to paper. There are several different ways that this can be accomplished, but the end result is all pretty much the same.

In a sense, scanners are the exact opposite of printers. While printers put ink to paper, transforming an electronic file into a paper one, scanners transform a paper file into an electronic one. (In fact, how many times has someone sent you a hard copy of something, only for you to need to scan it into your computer?) Scanners are devices that make an electronic copy of the hard-copy paper or picture you have. Scanners are very handy devices. Their usefulness runs a gamut from scanning necessary legal documents to scanning pictures of the family to send to relatives.

In this chapter, we look at different ways printers physically work, as well as how to make them play nice with your computer. After we cover those basics, we'll look at ways to optimize printing, upgrade printers, fix printers when things don't work right, and help prevent things from going wrong in the first place. In addition, we'll look at scanners throughout this chapter as well. There aren't as many user-fixable moving parts on scanners as there are on printers, but some of the high points we'll cover include optimizing scanner performance and troubleshooting scanner problems.

By design this chapter focuses mainly on printers and not on scanners. There are two reasons for this. First, there are far more printer questions than scanner questions on the A+ exams. Second, printers are far more "technician-friendly." There are a lot more things you can do to clean and fix printers than you can scanners. Still, we'll cover scanner-specific material where it's appropriate.

Understanding Printer and Scanner Processes

You can find several different types of printers and scanners on the market today. As with all other computer components, there have been significant advancements in printer technology over the years. Most of the time when faced with the decision of purchasing a printer, you're going to be weighing performance versus cost. Some of the higher-quality technologies, such as color laser printing, are rather expensive for the home user. Other technologies are less expensive but might not provide the same level of quality.

In this section, you will learn about five different types of printer technologies and how they function. Specifically, we'll look at the following:

- Impact printers

- Ink-dispersion printers (such as inkjet and bubble-jet)

- Laser printers

- Other printers (such as solid ink and thermal)

 The following sections cover the processes used by each of these printing technologies. For a detailed discussion of all components involved with each printer technology, please see Chapter 7.

Impact Printers

Impact printers are so named because in order to transfer ink to paper, the printhead actually makes impact with the paper. This printing technology is one of the oldest around, and it usually provides a fairly low level of print quality.

A good way to think of an impact printer is to imagine it as a typewriter attached to your computer (that is, if you can remember what a typewriter is). Like typewriters, most impact printers have an ink ribbon that goes between the paper and the printhead. The printhead strikes the ink ribbon and presses it against the paper, which transfers the ink from the ribbon to the paper.

The two major types of impact printers are daisy wheel and dot matrix.

Daisy-Wheel Printers

Daisy-wheel printers contain a wheel (called the *daisy wheel* because it looks like a daisy) with raised letters and symbols on each "petal" (see Figure 15.1). When the printer needs to print a character, it sends a signal to the printhead, which is the mechanism that contains the wheel. The printhead rotates the daisy wheel until the required character is in place. An electromechanical hammer (called a *solenoid*) then strikes the back of the petal containing the character. The character pushes up against an inked ribbon that strikes the paper, making the impression of the requested character.

Daisy-wheel printers were one of the first types of impact printer developed. Their speed is rated by the number of *characters per second (cps)* they can print. The early printers could print only between two and four characters per second. Aside from their poor speed, the main disadvantage to this type of printer is that it makes a lot of noise when printing—so much, in fact, that special enclosures were developed to contain the noise.

The daisy-wheel printer has a few advantages, of course. First, because it is an impact printer, you can print on multipart forms (like carbonless receipts), assuming they can be fed into the printer properly. Second, it is relatively inexpensive compared to the price of a laser printer of the same vintage. Finally, the print quality is comparable to that of a typewriter because it uses a very similar technology. This typewriter level of quality was given a name: *letter quality (LQ)*.

Dot-Matrix Printers

The other common type of impact printer is the *dot-matrix printer*. These printers work in a manner similar to daisy-wheel printers, but instead of a spinning, character-imprinted wheel, the printhead contains a row of pins (short, sturdy stalks of hard wire). These pins are triggered in patterns that form letters and numbers as the printhead moves across the paper (see Figure 15.2).

FIGURE 15.1   A daisy-wheel printer mechanism

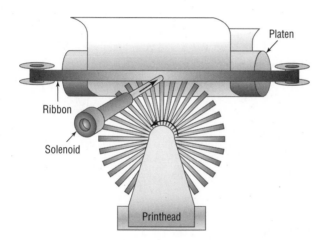

FIGURE 15.2   Formation of images in a dot-matrix printer

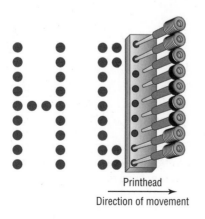

The pins in the printhead are wrapped with coils of wire to create a solenoid and are held in the rest position by a combination of a small magnet and a spring. To trigger a particular pin, the printer controller sends a signal to the printhead, which energizes the wires around the appropriate print wire. This turns the print wire into an electromagnet, which repels the print pin, forcing it against the ink ribbon and making a dot on the paper. The arrangement of the dots in columns and rows creates the letters and numbers you see on the page. Figure 15.2 shows this process.

The main disadvantage of dot-matrix printers is their image quality, which can be quite poor compared to the quality produced with a daisy wheel. Dot-matrix printers use patterns of dots to make letters and images, and the early dot-matrix printers used only nine pins to make those patterns. The output quality of such printers is referred to as *draft quality*—good mainly for providing your initial text to a correspondent or reviser. Each letter looked fuzzy because the dots were spaced as far as they could be and still be perceived as a letter or image. As more pins were crammed into the printhead (17-pin and 24-pin models were eventually developed), the quality increased because the dots were closer together. Dot-matrix technology ultimately improved to the point that a letter printed on a dot-matrix printer was *almost* indistinguishable from typewriter output. This level of quality is known as *near letter quality (NLQ)*.

Dot-matrix printers are noisy, but the print wires and printhead are covered by a plastic dust cover, making them quieter than daisy-wheel printers. They also use a more efficient printing technology, so the print speed is faster (typically in the range of 36 to 72cps). Finally, because dot-matrix printers are also impact printers, they can use multipart forms. Because of these advantages, dot-matrix printers quickly made daisy-wheel printers obsolete.

Neither type of impact printer used ink cartridges like we're familiar with in today's printers. As we mentioned, the ink was contained in a ribbon that was pressed up against the paper. As each character was struck, the ribbon would advance slightly so that the new character had a fresh supply of ink. As you would imagine, these ink ribbons would eventually run out of life and need to be replaced.

Ink-Dispersion Printers

With impact printers, the printhead must impact the ink ribbon, which comes in contact with the paper to create an image. In an ink-dispersion printer, the printhead comes very close to the paper and squirts out its ink (disperses it) in a specific pattern to create the image.

Ink-dispersion printers are the most popular type of printer on the market today, but you probably don't recognize them by this moniker. If someone mentioned the terms *inkjet* or *bubble-jet* printers though, you'd probably recognize them.

Both inkjet and bubble-jet printers spray ink on the page, but inkjet printers use a reservoir of ink, a pump, and an ink nozzle to accomplish this. They are messy, noisy, and inefficient. Bubble-jet printers work much more efficiently and are much cheaper. In a *bubble-jet printer,* bubbles of ink are sprayed onto a page and form patterns that resemble the items being printed.

The printing process for inkjet and bubble-jet printers is identical. For the sake of brevity, we'll refer to the process only from the more current bubble-jet technology.

So, you want to get something from your computer screen onto a piece of paper? Here's how the bubble-jet printing process works:

1. You click the Print button (or similar button), which initiates the printing process.

2. The software you are printing from sends the data to be printed to the printer driver you have selected.

The functionality of printer drivers is discussed in detail in Chapter 7.

3. The printer driver uses a page-description language to convert the data being printed into the proper format that the printer can understand. The driver also ensures that the printer is ready to print.

4. The printer driver sends the information to the printer via whatever connection method is being used (parallel, USB, network, and so on).

5. The printer stores the received data in its onboard *print buffer* memory. A print buffer is a small amount of memory (typically 512KB to 16MB) used to store print jobs as they are received from the printing computer. This buffer allows several jobs to be printed at once and helps printing to be completed quickly.

6. If the printer has not printed in a while, the printer's control circuits activate a cleaning cycle. A *cleaning cycle* is a set of steps the bubble-jet printer goes through in order to purge the printheads of any dried ink. It uses a special suction cup and sucking action to pull ink through the printhead, dislodging any dried ink or clearing stuck passageways.

7. Once the printer is ready to print, the control circuitry activates the paper-feed motor. This causes a sheet of paper to be fed into the printer until the paper activates the paper-feed sensor, which stops the feed until the printhead is in the right position and the leading edge of the paper is under the printhead. If the paper doesn't reach the paper-feed sensor in a specified amount of time after the stepper motor has been activated, the Out of Paper light is turned on and a message is sent to the computer.

8. Once the paper is positioned properly, the printhead stepper motor uses the printhead belt and carriage to move the printhead across the page, little by little. The motor is moved one small step, and the printhead sprays the dots of ink on the paper in the pattern dictated by the control circuitry. Typically, this is either a pattern of black dots or a pattern of *cyan, magenta, yellow, and black (CMYK)* inks that are mixed to make colors. Then the stepper motor moves the printhead another small step; the process repeats all the way across the page. This process is so quick, however, that the entire motion of starts and stops across the page looks like one smooth motion.

9. At the end of a pass across the page, the paper-feed stepper motor advances the page a small amount. Then the printhead repeats step 8. Depending on the model, the printhead either returns to the beginning of the line and prints again in the same direction only, or it moves backward across the page so that printing occurs in both directions. This process continues until the page is finished.

10. Once the page is finished, the feed-stepper motor is actuated and ejects the page from the printer into the output tray. If more pages need to print, printing the next page begins again at step 7.

11. Once printing is complete and the final page has been ejected from the printer, the print-head is *parked* (locked into rest position) and the print process is finished.

This sounds like a complex process, and in reality it is. But even though it's complex, it's a lot faster than impact printers. Some of the faster bubble-jet printers approach speeds of 20 pages per minute when printing text.

Laser Printers

In the office environment, laser printers are the most common type of printer found. Of the common printer types, laser printers provide the best speed and print quality. The reason more people don't have them at home is because historically they've been quite a bit more expensive than their bubble-jet counterparts. Although this isn't always the case anymore, laser printers still have the stigma of being cost-prohibitive for home use.

There are two major categories of laser printers: those that use the electrophotographic (EP) print process and those that use the light-emitting diode (LED) print process. Each works in basically the same way, with slight differences.

Electrophotographic (EP) Print Process

The *EP print process* is the process by which an EP laser printer forms images on paper. It consists of six major steps, each with a specific goal. Although many different manufacturers call these steps different things or place them in a different order, the basic process is still the same. Here are the steps in the order you will see them on the exam:

1. Cleaning
2. Charging
3. Writing
4. Developing
5. Transferring
6. Fusing

The details of these steps were discussed in depth in Chapter 7. You will want to review them thoroughly before taking your A+ elective examination.

LED Laser Printer Print Process

The other major category of laser printer is the light-emitting diode (LED) page printer. This technology is primarily developed and used by Okidata and Panasonic. Because the A+ exam does not currently cover LED page printers, we will discuss only the differences between them and laser printers.

The LED page printer uses the same process as a laser printer, with one major exception: It uses a row of small light-emitting diodes held very close to the photosensitive drum to expose it. Each LED is about the same size as the diameter of the laser beam used in laser printers. These printers are basically the same as EP process printers, except that in the writing step, they use LEDs instead of a laser. This makes these printers much cheaper and smaller than their EP cousins, but their resolution is worse and they're also messier.

Other Printers

The vast majority of the printers on the market are laser and ink-dispersion printers. Impact printers used to enjoy significant popularity, but their slow speed and relatively low quality doomed them from the start.

Some other types of printers you might run across include solid-ink printers, thermal printers, and dye-sublimation printers.

 These printers were discussed in Chapter 7. Please refer to that chapter for more information.

Solid-Ink Printers

Solid-ink printers are a lot like bubble-jet printers, except that the ink comes in a waxy solid form instead of a liquid. One key difference is that many solid-ink printers will print an entire line at a time, making them faster than bubble jets. Still others will print an entire page in a single pass. Proponents of solid-ink printers point to this feature as a mark of superiority over color dispersion and color laser printers. With one pass, there is no chance of misalignment of colors on a page.

Because many solid-ink printers will print an entire page in one pass, printing in color is not slower than printing in black and white. In addition, since the printer does not use a fuser (unlike laser printers), they are great for printing transparencies, which tend to melt in laser printer fusers.

Thermal Printers

Based on their name, you might guess that these types of printers use heat to print, and you would be correct. Many older fax machines use this technology, but it's less common today.

Thermal printers use a special waxy paper that typically comes on a roll. When the paper comes in contact with heat it changes color, usually to black or dark brown. Some thermal printers can print in two colors. The second color is usually red, and is created by applying less heat to the paper than is required to produce black images.

The key components of a thermal printer are the thermal head, platen, spring, and controller boards. The thermal head generates the heat and prints on the paper. It can either be the width of the paper or movable, much like an inkjet printhead. The platen is a rubber roller that feeds the paper. A spring applies pressure to the back of the thermal head, causing it to contact the paper, and the controller board is the brains of the outfit.

As the paper passes between the platen and the thermal head, an electrical current heats the head in the desired print pattern. The spring engages and presses the thermal head to the paper, which causes a chemical reaction in the paper and "prints" the image.

The advantages of thermal printers are that they're fast and quiet, and the only consumable is paper.

Dye-Sublimation Printers

Dye-sublimation printers use sheets of solid ink that *sublimate*, or go from the solid phase directly to gas. During printing, a printhead passes over these sheets (one each of cyan, magenta, yellow, and gray for tonal change) inside the printer. As it passes over the page, spots on the printhead heat up, causing the ink under those spots to sublimate into gas. This gas then passes through the paper being printed, where the ink turns back into a solid, embedded into the paper. The printhead in most printers makes four passes, one for each color.

These types of printers tend to be slow, but they do a great job of printing photo images.

Scanner Processes

There are two types of scanners that have been popular computer peripherals: handheld scanners and flatbed scanners. In terms of the scanning technology, both use similar processes. However, due to the difficulty of obtaining quality images from handheld scanners, flatbed scanners are the far more popular option today.

Flatbed (or desktop) scanners have a glass plane, also called the scanner window. Images are placed on this pane. Under the pane, a movable scanner head and a light source handle the dirty work. The scanner head is called a charged-couple device, and the light source is typically a cold cathode fluorescent or xenon light.

After the image is placed face-down on the glass, the scanner head and light source move across the image, reading it as a series of light and dark spots. Images are only visible to the charged-couple device based on the light that they reflect, hence the need for the light source. Color scanners typically have three charge-coupled devices, one each for red, green, and blue.

Some scanners have automatic feed mechanisms, eliminating the need to manually feed or change each page. In these types of scanners, the scanning head is usually stationary, and the image passes over it at a constant speed. These types of scanners often look a lot like large, office-style laser printers. In fact, many office-style multifunction devices can scan and print using one input area.

Installing, Configuring, Optimizing, and Upgrading Printers and Scanners

By themselves, printers and scanners make pretty good paperweights, other than the fact that they're usually rather bulky. As peripherals, these devices don't achieve their full potential alone; they must be connected to a computer for that. Once the device is installed, there are several things you can configure to enhance and optimize the peripheral's performance. If it's still not performing the way you would like, perhaps it's time to think of an upgrade, such as a memory upgrade for a printer.

As an A+ technician, you need to know the procedures required to install, configure, optimize, and upgrade printers and scanners. This section covers those procedures.

Printer and Scanner Installation Procedures

Although every device is different, there are certain accepted methods used for installing any device. Printers and scanners are just two sides of the same coin. Both devices use similar hookups, but one is an input device, and the other is an output device. The following procedure works for installing both kinds of devices:

1. Attach the device using a local or network port and connect the power.

2. Install and update the device driver and calibrate the device.

3. Configure options and default settings.

4. Print/scan a test page.

5. Verify compatibility with the operating system and applications.

6. Educate users about basic functionality.

Before installing any device, read your device's installation instructions. There are exceptions to every rule.

Step 1: Attach the Device Using a Local or Network Port and Connect the Power

When installing a printer or scanner, you must first take the device out of its packaging and set it up on a flat, stable surface. Then connect the device to either the host computer with its power off (if it is a stand-alone device) or to the network (if it is a network device). However, USB devices usually require that you install the software first and then connect the device.

Once you have connected the device, connect power to it using whatever supplied power adapter comes with it. Some devices have their own built-in power supply and just need an A/C power cord connecting the device to the wall outlet, while others rely on an external transformer and power supply. Finally, turn on the device.

Some USB scanners are very low power and run off the power supplied by the USB cable.

Step 2: Install and Update the Device Driver and Calibrate the Device

Once you have connected and powered up the device, boot up the computer and wait for Windows to recognize the device. It will pop up a screen similar to the one shown in Figure 15.3. This wizard will allow you to configure the driver for the printer or scanner (depending on the device). You can insert the driver CD-ROM that comes with the device, and the wizard will guide you through the device driver installation. If Windows fails to recognize the device, you can use the Add Hardware Wizard to troubleshoot the installation and to install the device drivers.

FIGURE 15.3   The Windows Add Hardware Wizard

Once the driver is installed, the device will function. But some devices, such as inkjet printers and scanners, require that you calibrate the device. *Calibration* is the process by which a device is brought within functional specifications. For example, inkjet printers need their printheads aligned so they print evenly and don't print funny-looking letters and unevenly spaced lines. The process is part of the installation of all inkjet printers.

Each manufacturer's process is different, but a typical alignment/calibration works like this:

1. During software installation, the installation wizard asks you if you would like to calibrate now, to which you respond Yes or OK.

2. The printer prints out a sheet with multiple sets of numbered lines. Each set of lines represents an alignment instance.

3. The software will ask you which set(s) looks the best. Enter the number and click OK or Continue.

4. Some alignment routines end at this point. Others will reprint the alignment page and see if the alignment "took." If not, you can reenter the number of which one looks the best.

5. Click Finish to end the alignment routine.

Understanding and Installing PCL, PostScript, and GDI Drivers

For your printer to work properly, you need to install the right driver for the device. In addition, you need to make sure you're talking to the device in the language that it speaks.

There are several printer communication languages in existence, but the three most common ones are Printer Command Language (PCL), PostScript, and Graphics Device Interface (GDI).

PCL was developed by Hewlett-Packard in 1984 and originally intended for use with inkjet printers. Since then, its role has been expanded to virtually every printer type, and it's a de facto industry standard.

PostScript (PS) is a page description language which allows computers to communicate with printers. One of the early advantages of PS was that it allowed any font to be scaled to any size and printed properly. This might not sound like an earth-shattering feature, but at the time it was revolutionary for home and business printers. (Previously, these types of features were only found on high-end image plotters.)

GDI is actually a Windows component and is not specific to printers. Instead, it's a series of components that govern how graphics images are presented to both monitors and printers. GDI printers work by using computer processing power instead of their own. The printed image is rendered to a bitmap on the computer, and then sent to the printer. This means that the printer hardware doesn't need to be as powerful, which results in a less expensive printer. Generally speaking, the least expensive laser printers on the market are GDI printers.

When you install your printer driver, you will often have to make the choice between PCL and PS or PCL, PS, and GDI drivers. Figure 15.4 shows the Add Printer Wizard to illustrate an example of this.

You're installing a LaserJet 8150. Do you select PS or PCL? It depends on if your printer is set for PS or PCL mode. This can be configured through your printer's menu system. If you have a PS driver and your printer is set for PCL, it will only print garbage. If you're not sure how to do this, check your printer's manual.

FIGURE 15.4   PS and PCL print drivers

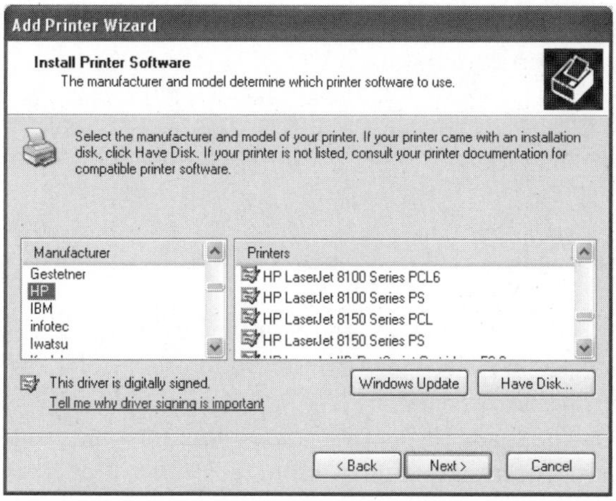

Many newer printers can handle both PS and PCL (and GDI), and will automatically translate for you. Therefore, it's less likely that you'll install the "wrong" print driver than it was several years ago.

Calibrating Scanners

Scanners may need to be color calibrated with the monitor so that what scans in is accurate to what's on screen. Many include a test pattern that can be scanned in, and the color on the screen can be corrected for variations in color. This pattern is commonly known as an *IT8 scanner target.*

When working with print media, it is especially important to calibrate all your hardware, including your monitor, scanner, printer, and digital camera, to ensure color matching.

Step 3: Configure Options and Default Settings

Once you have installed the software and calibrated the device, you can configure any options for either the scanner or printer. Scanners may require setting options such as configuring sheet feeders within the driver software. These settings and how to change them can be found in your hardware's manual.

Most of the time, scanner properties and options are configured from within the scanner software that came with the device. Common configuration options include the resolution at which you want to scan, the use of color or grayscale, and the compression method to use after the document has been scanned.

Where you configure specific printer properties depends a lot on the printer itself. Figure 15.5 shows the Printers and Faxes window in Windows XP. On the left-hand side under Printer Tasks, you can see that there's an option to select printing preferences and another option to set printer properties (in addition, both options can be executed by right-clicking on the printer and choosing Printing Preferences or Properties, respectively).

If you don't see these options under Printer Tasks, highlight the printer first.

Various configuration features can be set from each menu option. The Printing Preferences window of this printer is shown in Figure 15.6.

Under Printing Preferences (for this printer) you can select the quality of the print job, layout (portrait vs. landscape), paper size, two-sided printing, and use of color. By contrast, Figure 15.7 shows the printer Properties screen.

Here the options are different. The printer Properties is less about how the printer does its job and more about how people can access the printer. From the printer Properties, you can share the printer, set up the port that it's on, and configure when the printer will be available throughout the day (and to which specific users). Figure 15.8 shows the important Advanced tab of the printer Properties.

FIGURE 15.5   Printers and Faxes

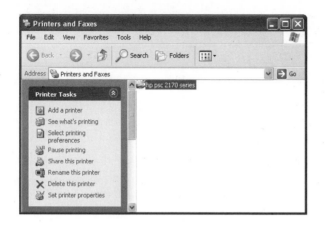

FIGURE 15.6   Printing Preferences

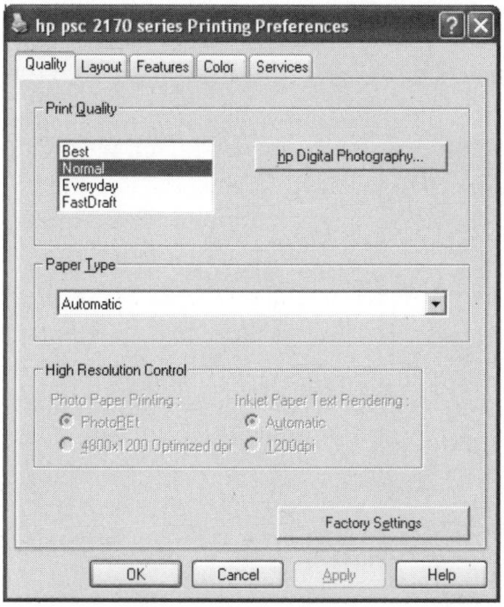

On this tab, you can configure the printer to be available only during certain hours of the day. This might be useful if you're trying to curtail after-hours printing of non-work-related documents, for example. You can also configure the spool settings. It's recommended to always spool the jobs instead of printing directly to the printer. However, if the printer is printing garbage, you can try printing directly to it to see if the spooler is causing the problem.

Regarding the check boxes at the bottom, you will want to always print spooled documents first, as it speeds up the printing process. If you need to maintain an electronic copy of all printed files, check the Keep Printed Documents check box. Keep in mind that this will eat up a lot of hard disk space.

FIGURE 15.7 Printer Properties

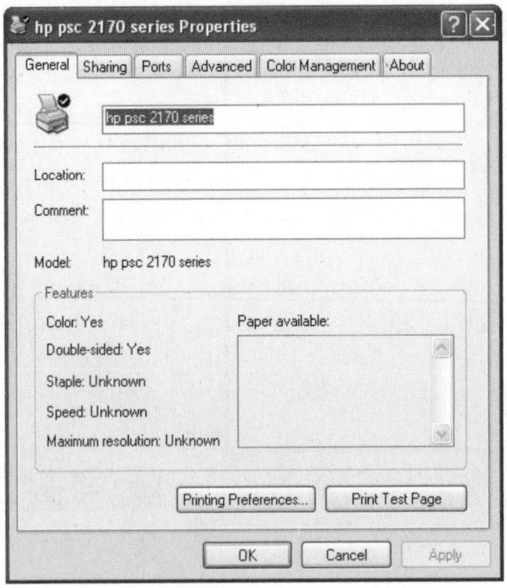

FIGURE 15.8 Printer Properties Advanced tab

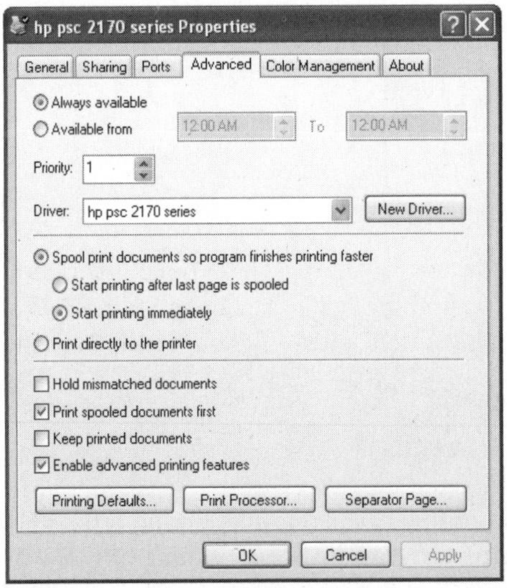

Finally, the Printing Defaults button takes you to the Printing Preferences (see Figure 15.6), Print Processor lets you select alternate methods of processing print jobs (not usually needed), and Separator Page lets you specify a file to use as a separator page (a document that prints out at the beginning of each separate print job, usually with the user's name on it), which can be useful if you have several (or several dozen) users sharing one printer.

Step 4: Print/Scan a Test Page

Once you have done all of these steps, you are finished and can print a test page to test the output of the printer. Windows has a built-in function for doing just that. To print a test page, right-click on the printer you installed from within the Printer control panel and click Properties. On the General tab of the printer Properties (as shown back in Figure 15.7), there will be a Print Test Page button. Click that button, and Windows will send a test page to the printer. If the page prints, your printer is working. If not, check all of your connections, and then read ahead in the troubleshooting section, "Using Printer and Scanner Troubleshooting Tools and Techniques."

For scanners, run the scanning software that came with the scanner. Place a single page on the scanner. Press the Scan button on the scanner (or in the software) to initiate a test scan. If the scan comes through on the screen, then you know everything was set up correctly.

In Exercise 15.1 we'll step through the process of installing a USB printer.

EXERCISE 15.1

Installing a USB Printer

In this exercise, you will install a USB printer. You will need the following:

- A USB printer

- A USB printer cable

- The software driver CD or disk that came with the printer

- A computer with a free USB port and a CD-ROM drive

1. Turn on the computer.

2. Plug in the printer and turn it on.

3. Insert the printer driver CD into the computer's CD-ROM drive. The driver CD's auto-run should automatically start the installation program. If not, click on Start ➢ Run and type in **D:\setup** or **D:\install** (if your CD-ROM drive letter is different than *D* substitute that letter for *D*).

4. Follow the prompts in the installation program to install the driver.

5. Once the software has been installed, plug one end of the USB cable into the printer and the other end into the free USB port. Some installation programs will prompt you for this step.

6. Windows will automatically detect the new printer, install the driver, and configure it. Windows will display a balloon in the lower-right-hand corner of the screen saying, *Your hardware is now installed and is ready to use.*

7. Print a test page to see if the printer can communicate and print properly.

Step 5: Validate Compatibility with Operating System and Applications

Once your printer or scanner is installed and you have tried out a test page, everything else should work well, right? That's usually true, but it's good practice to verify compatibility with applications before you consider the device fully installed.

With printers, this process is rather straightforward. Open the application you wonder about and print something. For example, open up Microsoft Word, type in some gibberish (or open a real document if you want), and print it out. If you are running non-Microsoft applications (such as a computer-aided drafting program or accounting software) and have questions about their compatibility with the printer, try printing from those programs as well.

It's also usually pretty easy to test a scanner's compatibility. The main reason is that most scanners come with their own proprietary software to scan in images. Once the image is scanned in and saved as a file (usually a picture format such as .JPG, .GIF, or .BMP), then opening the file in other programs is not an issue. The only concern is if you are trying to use a scanning application that did not come with the scanner itself. This can be a tricky process (compatibility is a big issue) to configure. It's recommended that you check your scanner (or software) manual for advice on getting this working properly.

Step 6: Educate Users about Basic Functionality

Most users today know how to print, but not everyone knows how to install the right printer or print efficiently. This can be a significant issue in work environments.

Say that your workplace has 10 different printers, and you just installed number 11. First, your company should use a naming process to identify the printers in a way that makes sense. Calling a printer HPLJ4 on a network does little to help users understand where that printer is in the building. After installing the printer, offer installation assistance to those who might want to use the device. Show users how to install the printer in Windows (or if printer installation is automated, let them know they have a new printer and where it is). Also let the users know the various options available on that printer. Can it print double-sided? If so, you can save a lot of paper. Show users how to configure that. Is it a color printer? Do users really need color for rough drafts of documents or presentations? Show users how to print in black-and-white on a color printer to save the expensive color ink or toner cartridges.

Not as many people are familiar with scanners. Offer education to the users who will be using it. Show them how to scan an image, as well as give them some basics about the software use, such as how to modify images and compress them so the saved image files aren't positively huge.

Installing Printer Upgrades

The printer market encompasses a dizzying array of products. You can find portable printers, photo printers, cheap black-and-white printers for under $30, high-end color laser printers for over $5,000, and everything in between. Most of the cheaper printers do not have upgrade options, but higher-end printers will have upgrade options including the memory and firmware.

Real World Scenario

Which Printer Did That Go To?

I used to work at a satellite office for a company whose headquarters were in Houston. Because of recent printer problems, we just had a new network printer installed, and it had a different network name than the previous printer.

At the end of the month, one of our accountants printed off her monthly reconciliation report, which typically ran about 400 pages. Puzzled when it didn't come out on the printer, she printed it again. And again. And again. After the fourth time (and a few hours later), she decided to ask someone in IT what the problem was.

It turns out that she had mapped (installed) the new network printer but had gotten a few letters wrong in the printer name. Instead of being at our office, all of her print jobs were sent to a printer in the Houston office. And of course, there were people in Houston trying to print similar reports and who just kept refilling the printer with paper because they didn't want to cut someone else's report off in the middle.

While this wasn't a catastrophic failure, it was annoying. She had unintentionally wasted three reams of paper, the associated toner, and hours of printer life. It wasn't a malicious act and she was a literate computer user, but it's illustrative of the need to educate and help users with installing and configuring devices. Had the printer been mapped correctly the first time, the waste could have been avoided.

Installing Printer Memory

When purchasing a memory upgrade for your printer, you need to make sure of two things. First, buy only memory that is compatible with your printer model. Most printers today use a standard computer DIMM, but check your manual or the manufacturer's website to be sure. If you're not sure, purchasing the memory through the manufacturer's website (or an authorized reseller) is a good way to go. Second, be sure that your printer is capable of a memory upgrade. It's possible that the amount of memory in your printer is the maximum that it can handle.

Once you have obtained the memory, it's time to perform surgery. The specific steps required to install the memory will depend on your printer. Check with the manual or the manufacturer's website for instructions tailored to your model.

Exercise 15.2 walks you through the general steps for installing memory into a laser printer.

Upgrading Printer Firmware

As with upgrading memory, methods to upgrade a printer's firmware depend on the model of printer you have. Most of the time, upgrading a printer's firmware is a matter of downloading and/or installing a free file from the manufacturer's website. Printer firmware upgrades are generally done from the print server. Firmware files can easily be several megabytes in size, so they might take a bit to download.

EXERCISE 15.2

Installing Memory into a Laser Printer

Providing additional memory to your printer can speed up the printing process, especially in heavily utilized environments. While the specific steps for your printer might be slightly different, follow these general steps for installing printer memory:

1. Turn off the printer.

2. Disconnect all cables from the printer (power and interface cables).

3. Find the area in which you need to install the memory.

4. On most HP LaserJet printers, this is in the back, on a piece of hardware called the formatter board. The formatter board is held in by tabs near the top and bottom of the board. Remove the formatter board from the printer. Other brands have different configurations. For example, on many Xerox laser printers you remove a panel on the top of the unit (underneath the paper output tray) to get to the memory.

5. If your printer requires you to remove a component (such as the formatter board) to upgrade the memory, place that component on a grounded surface such as an antistatic work mat. Otherwise, proceed to step 6.

6. If you are replacing an existing memory module, remove the old module, being careful not to break off the latches at the end of the module that hold it in.

7. Insert the new memory module, making sure that any alignment notches on the memory module are lined up with the device before inserting the memory module.

8. Replace the removable component (if necessary).

9. Reconnect the power and interface cables.

10. Power on the printer.

11. Follow the printer manual's instructions on running a self-test to ensure that the memory is recognized.

Some printers require that you manually enable the added memory. Here are the steps to do that in Windows 2000/XP:

1. Open the Printers and Faxes window.

2. Right-click on the printer and choose Properties.

3. On the Device Settings tab, click the Printer Memory button in the Installable Options section.

4. Select the amount of memory that is now installed.

5. Click OK.

Upgrading firmware is usually done for one of two reasons. One, if you are having compatibility issues, a firmware upgrade might solve them. Two, firmware upgrades can offer newer features not available on previous versions.

Optimizing Scanner Performance

Scanners pretty much either work or they don't, and there's not a lot of "fixing" that can be done from the field technician vantage point. However, there are a lot of options that you can configure to optimize the scanning process. In this section, we'll look at some of those options.

 Here we focus on what you can (or should be able to) change. The exact "how" will depend on your scanner software. The software shown in this chapter is intended to serve as an example.

Scanner Resolution and Output Size

One of the most common questions or concerns regarding scanning is the output file size. For a full 8.5″ × 11″ scanned picture, the output file can easily exceed 1GB in size. You can change this by modifying the scanned resolution of the image. Look at Figure 15.9 as an example.

FIGURE 15.9   Scanner software window

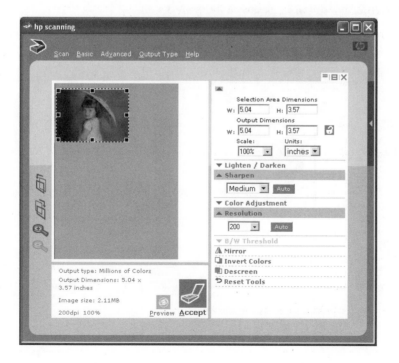

If you look near the bottom of Figure 15.9, you'll see that the output file for this scan is 2.11MB, but the picture is only at 200 dots per inch (dpi). On the right-hand size of this screen, notice that there is a Resolution section where you can change this. Lowering the resolution to 75dpi (the lowest available in this particular software) drops the output file to under 300KB. Increasing the resolution to 300dpi more than doubles the file size, to 4.75MB, and when you bump the resolution all the way to the maximum of 9600dpi, the output file is a whopping 4.86GB. All of this is for a 3.5-inch by 5-inch picture.

So what is the right resolution to scan at? Well, that depends on what you're planning on doing with the scanned image. For most uses, 200–300dpi will work just fine. If you're scanning text documents, you can even go lower. If the picture will be blown up to a large size or it's for a high-end graphical presentation, then a higher resolution might be in order. Just keep in mind that higher resolutions and larger outputs mean very large files. (For example, the picture in Figure 15.9 blown up to 30 inches by 21 inches at 9600dpi would produce an output file of 175GB—it's hardly likely that you will want to or be able to store a file that big.)

File Formats

After a scanner scans a picture in, you can save it in a variety of file formats. The format you choose often depends on the anticipated use of the file. For example, your brochure printer might require that files be in .JPG or .TIF format.

As with changing resolution, the specific way to change file types depends on the scanner software. In the case of the HP scanner software we are using, we have to click the Accept button at the bottom to scan the image (see Figure 15.9), and then the software sends the image to the Photo & Imaging software, as shown in Figure 15.10.

FIGURE 15.10   HP Photo & Imaging

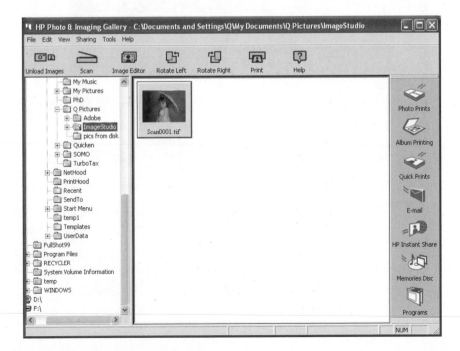

By default, this scanner software saves files in a .TIF format. For us to change the format, we have to highlight the image, click on Image Editor, and then choose Save As. At that point, we can change the file format. Some scanning programs will let you choose the file format when the picture is scanned. Others, like the one we have, let you change the file format in the bundled photo-editing software.

Default Scanner Settings

Each scanner's software has different options, but they all have the same basic functionality for the most part. In Figure 15.11, you can see that this particular software's options are configured to the right.

FIGURE 15.11 Scanner configuration options

Table 15.1 lists some of the standard configuration options and descriptions of each.

TABLE 15.1 Scanner Configuration Options

Option	Description
Resize	This can make the picture larger or smaller. You can choose to have the picture proportions locked or not. Changing picture proportions can result in distorted pictures.
Lighten/Darken	Some scanned items are too light, or "washed out," while others are too dark for you to see details. This option lets you adjust light settings.

TABLE 15.1 Scanner Configuration Options *(continued)*

Option	Description
Sharpen	If a picture looks fuzzy, you can help clear it up with this setting.
Color Adjustment	This can either cause colors to stand out more or make the palette more of a monotone. If you are scanning in black-and-white, this option will not be available.
Resolution	This controls how many dots per inch (dpi) the scanned image will contain. Higher resolution means better quality but larger files.
Black/White Threshold	For scanning black-and-white items, this can help adjust the contrast between the black and white portions of the image.
Mirror	Flips the image on the y-axis. Most scanning programs also let you rotate the image 90 degrees each way.
Invert Colors	Produces the image in negative color.
Descreen	Causes the scanner to scan the image again.
Reset Tools	Sets the scanner software back to the defaults.

Using Printer and Scanner Troubleshooting Tools and Techniques

Printers are some of the more mechanically complex devices used in computing. They contain many moving parts, and the more moving parts you have, the more likely you are to encounter a problem. Add to that the sheer number of different printers on the market, and you have plenty of opportunity to work on your troubleshooting skills.

Scanners are different beasts entirely. They don't have any moving parts that most technicians can fix, other than the lid. Sure, you can crack open a scanner to try to fix the lamp or scanner apparatus inside, but that's not a good idea unless you've been specifically trained on how to do that.

Regardless of whether you're troubleshooting a laser printer or a scanner, there are some general steps to keep in mind:

1. Gather data about the printer/scanner problem.

2. Review and analyze the collected data.

3. Isolate and resolve the identified printer/scanner problem.

4. Apply the fix and verify functionality.

Good troubleshooting is always done in a methodical fashion. Haphazard troubleshooting rarely works and is difficult if not impossible to replicate.

The details of these troubleshooting steps were discussed in Chapter 7. However, in addition to being familiar with these steps, every A+ technician should also have a set of tools to work with when troubleshooting printers and scanners, and we will look at these in the following sections.

Multi-meter

Multi-meters are used for testing electrical issues. For example, problems with the power supply output can be detected with a multi-meter. Multi-meters can also be used to perform resistance tests. When testing fuses, a good fuse will have a resistance of zero ohms.

If you are using a multi-meter on a circuit of unknown voltage, set the multi-meter to its highest setting in order to avoid damage to the tool.

Multi-meters can be useful if you turn on your printer and it doesn't respond normally. That could indicate a power problem.

A laser printer's DC power supply provides three different DC voltages to printer components. This can all be checked at a power interface labeled J210, which is a 20-pin female interface. Pin 1 will be in the lower-left corner, and the pins along the bottom will all be odd numbers, increasing from left to right.

Using the multi-meter, you should find the following voltages:

- Pin 1 +5v
- Pin 5 −5v
- Pin 9 +24v

If none of the voltages are reading properly, then you probably need to replace the fuse in the DC power supply. If one or more (but not all) of the voltages aren't reading properly, then the first thing to do is remove all optional hardware in the printer (including memory) and testing again. If the readings are still bad, it's likely you need to replace the DC power supply.

Screwdrivers

Screwdrivers are easily the most important tool every PC technician carrys with him. There are three major categories of screwdrivers: flat-blade (or flathead), Phillips, and Torx. In addition, there are devices that look like screwdrivers, except they have a hex-shaped indented head on them. They're called hex drivers and belong in the screwdriver family.

Straight-slot screws have one slot on their head. They work just fine as far as screws go, but screwdrivers slip easily out of the slot. Phillips screws, on the other hand, have two slots at right angles to each other, forming a cross or an X pattern. Screwdrivers stay in these slots much easier. The final type is Torx, which was used primarily by Compaq in the mid- to late-1990s and is still used by some manufacturers today. Torx screws have a six-sided, star-shaped hole in the head of the screw. Of course, regular Phillips screwdrivers won't work in Torx screws—you need a Torx driver.

Whenver picking a screwdriver, always keep in mind that you want to match the size of the screwdriver head to the size of the screw. Using a screwdriver that's too small will cause it to spin inside the head of the screw, stripping the screw and making it useless. And if the screwdriver is too large, you won't be able to get the head in far enough to generate any torque to loosen the screw. Of course, if the screwdriver is way too big, it won't even fit inside the screw head at all. Common sizes for Phillips-head screws are 000, 00, 0, 1, 2, and 3. When dealing with Torx screws, the two most common sizes are T-10 and T-15.

Cleaning Solutions

With all of the ink or toner they use, printers get dirty. While most of the time we don't notice problems, if printers get too dirty or if the printheads get dirty, we'll notice print problems. No one wants this to happen.

Most printers have a self-cleaning utility that is activated through a menu option or by pressing a combination of buttons on the printer itself. It's recommended that you run the cleaning sequence every time you replace the toner or ink cartridges. If you experience print-quality problems, such as lines in the output, run the cleaning routine.

Sometimes the self-cleaning routines aren't enough to clear up the problem. If you are having print-quality issues, you might want to consider purchasing a cleaning kit, which frequently comes with a cleaning solution.

Cleaning kits are often designed for one specific type of printer and should be used only on that type of printer. For example, don't apply an inkjet cleaning solution to a laser printer.

Each cleaning kit comes with its own instructions for use. Exercise 15.3 walks you through the steps of using an inkjet cleaning solution.

EXERCISE 15.3

Using an Inkjet Cleaning Solution

Inkjet (and bubble-jet) printers are very common today. If you are experiencing print-quality issues and the self-cleaning routine isn't doing the trick, you might need to purchase a cleaning solution and apply it. Here's how. (Note: The steps for your printer might differ slightly; please consult your manual for specific instructions.)

1. Power on the printer, and open the top cover to expose the area containing the print cartridges.

2. Initiate a self-cleaning cycle. When the printer head moves from its resting place, pull the AC power plug. This lets you freely move the printheads without damaging them.

3. Locate the sponge pads on which to apply the cleaning solution. They'll be in the area where the printheads normally park. Use a cotton swab or paper towel to gently soak up any excess ink in the pads.

4. Using the supplied syringe, apply the cleaning solution to the sponge pads, until they are saturated.

5. Plug the printer back into the wall outlet, and turn it on. The printheads will park themselves.

6. Turn the printer back off. Let the solution sit for at least three hours.

7. Power the printer back on, and run three printer cleaning cycles. Print a nozzle check pattern (or a test page) after each cleaning cycle to monitor the cleaning progress.

That should take care of it! If not, again, refer to your printer's manual for more instructions.

Extension Magnets

An extension magnet looks like a pen and fits nicely into pockets or PC toolkits. It's made so that it can extend, often providing you with an additional two feet of reach. Because of its small size, it can fit into tight areas with no problem.

As its name implies, an extension magnet has a magnetic tip, meaning that it can pick up small, magnetized objects that may have fallen into an area you can't reach. Other extension devices come with lights or lights and a mirror, so you can see into otherwise inaccessible areas for troubleshooting.

Test Patterns

Most printers will print a test page, which contains both colors and patterns, based on your printer's capabilities. Although the exact style of pattern may vary, the idea is the same for all printers. You're checking to ensure that the printer can do what it's capable of. Many test patterns will measure gradients and resolution as well as letter qualities at various font sizes. Color printers will also print color sections, whereas black-and-white printers will often produce patterns in grayscale.

If you are experiencing print-quality issues, running a test pattern is a good way to check to see what's wrong with the printer.

    To test a scanner, print off a test pattern from your printer and then scan it in.

Performing Preventative Maintenance

Considering the amount of work they do, printers last a pretty long time. Some printers can handle over 100,000 pages per month, yet they're usually pretty reliable devices. These next sections on preventative maintenance focus on things you can do to help keep the printer running smoothly. After all, going to get your print job from the printer and discovering that the printer's in the shop is a very frustrating experience!

Performing Scheduled Maintenance

When shopping for a printer, one of the characteristics you should look for is the printer's capacity. This is often quoted in monthly volume. If the printer will be serving in a high-load capacity, you need to be able to account for that. Regardless of the printer's capacity, every printer needs periodic maintenance. Printers that can handle a lot of traffic just typically need it less frequently. Check the printer specifications to see how often scheduled maintenance is suggested. Never, ever fall behind on performing scheduled maintenance on a printer.

Many laser printers have LCD displays that provide useful information, such as error messages or notices that you need to replace a toner cartridge. The LCD display will also tell you when the printer needs scheduled maintenance. How does it know? Printers keep track of the number of pages they print, and when the page limit is reached, they display a message, usually something to the simple effect of *Perform user maintenance*. The printer will still print, but you should perform the maintenance.

Being the astute technician that you are, you clean the printer with the recommended cleaning kit or install the maintenance kit you purchased from the manufacturer. Now, how do you get the maintenance message to go away? You want to reset the page count, and it will be a menu option. For example, on many HP laser printers, you press the Menu button until you get to the Configuration Menu. Once there, you press the Item key until the display shows *Service Message = ON*. Then press the plus key (+) to change the message to *Service Message = OFF*. Bring the printer back online, and you're ready to go.

Ensuring a Suitable Environment

Printers won't complain if the weather outside is too hot or too cold, but they are susceptible to environmental issues. Here are some things to watch out for in your printer's environment:

Heat   Laser printers can generate a lot of heat. Because of this, ensure that your laser printer is in a well-ventilated area. Resist the temptation to put the laser printer in the little cubbyhole in your desk, as overheating will reduce the shelf life of your printer.

Light   The laser printer's toner cartridge contains a photosensitive drum. Exposing that drum to light will ruin the drum. While the drum is encased in plastic, it's best to avoid exposing the printer or toner cartridges to extreme light sources. Under no circumstance should you open the toner cartridge, unless you're ready to get rid of it as well as clean up a big mess.

Ozone   Laser printers that use corona wires (and many of them do) produce ozone as a by-product of the printing process. In offices, ozone can cause respiratory problems in small con-centrations, and it can be seriously dangerous to people in large amounts. Ozone is also a very effective oxidizer and can cause damage to printer components.

Fortunately, laser printers don't produce large amounts of ozone, and most laser printers have an ozone filter. Ozone is another reason to ensure that your printer area has good ventilation. Also, replace the ozone filter periodically; check your printer's manual for recommendations on when to do this.

Ammonia   Ammonia isn't produced by the printer, but it is contained in many cleaning products. Ammonia can greatly reduce the printer's ability to neutralize ozone and can cause permanent damage to toner cartridges. It's best to avoid using ammonia-based cleaners near laser printers.

Using Recommended Supplies

To properly maintain a printer, you need to replace consumables such as toner or ink cartridges, assemblies, filters, and rollers on occasion. It can be tempting to cut costs by saving money on these supplies, but it's rarely a good idea in the long run.

Whenever purchasing supplies for your printer, always get supplies from the manufacturer or from an authorized reseller. This way, you'll be sure that the parts are of high quality. Using unauthorized parts can damage your printer and possibly void your warranty.

When it comes to printer paper, you have more flexibility. However, if your printer calls for a certain type of paper, it's best to use that paper. Not doing so can cause damage to the feed mechanism or can cause waste if the printer does not feed properly.

The area in which this is the biggest concern is ink and toner cartridges. Many businesses have sprung up around recycling your toner or ink cartridges for you, refilling them, and then selling them back to you at a discount to new cartridges. Don't buy them. While some busi-nesses that perform this "service" are more legitimate than others, using recycled parts is more dangerous to your hardware than using new parts. The reason for this is that refilled cartridges are more likely to break or leak than new parts, and this leakage could cause extensive damage to the inside of your printer. And again, using secondhand parts can void your warranty, so you're left with a broken printer that you have to pay for. Avoid problems like this by buying new parts. It's best to recycle your old parts—just don't buy recycled parts.

Summary

In this chapter, you learned about printers and scanners. First, we talked about the processes used by various types of printers, including impact, ink-dispersion, laser, solid-ink, thermal, and dye-sublimation printers.

After reviewing how each type works, we covered installing printers and scanners. Proper steps include connecting the device, installing the driver, configuring options, validating application and operating system compatibility, and educating users on how to use the device. Next, we looked at how to install upgrades in printers as well as optimizing scanner performance.

From there we moved on to troubleshooting and covered the tools that are useful to the troubleshooting process.

Finally, we looked at performing preventative maintenance. Items discussed include performing scheduled maintenance, making sure the environment is suitable for the printer, and using recommended supplies.

Exam Essentials

Know the six steps in the laser printing print sequence.   The six steps are cleaning, conditioning, writing, developing, transferring, and fusing.

Understand how impact printers work.   Impact printers (such as dot-matrix printers) work by using a printhead that strikes an ink ribbon, which in turn strikes the paper producing an image.

Know how ink-dispersion printers work.   Ink-dispersion printers work by squirting ink (or in the case of bubble-jets, small bubbles of ink) from the printhead onto the paper.

Know how to install printers and scanners.   There are six steps to installing printers and scanners. One, attach the device to the computer and to the power source. Two, install the device driver. Three, configure options and settings. Four, test the device to ensure it works. Five, validate the device's compatibility with crucial applications. Six, don't forget to educate your users on proper usage!

Understand how to upgrade printer memory and firmware.   Printer memory is upgraded by installing an additional or replacement memory chip. To do this, you must remove a panel from the printer. The specific steps depend on your printer model. Firmware is upgraded by downloading a file from the manufacturer's website and installing it.

Know what scanner options you can optimize.   When scanning images, you can modify several options including size of picture (both physically and the amount of disk space it will take), resolution, colors, and file format.

Know what environmental hazards to watch out for around printers.   Heat, excessive light, ozone, and ammonia are all bad things for printers to be around.

Review Questions

1. Your laser printer has recently starting printing vertical black lines on documents it prints. What is the most likely cause of the problem?

   A. The print driver is faulty.

   B. The fuser is not heating properly.

   C. There is toner on the transfer corona wire.

   D. There is a scratch on the EP drum.

2. In which step of the laser printer printing process does a uniform −600VDC charge get applied to the EP drum?

   A. Conditioning

   B. Charging

   C. Developing

   D. Transferring

3. Which of the following most accurately describes how to obtain a firmware upgrade for your laser printer?

   A. Download the firmware upgrade for free from the manufacturer's website.

   B. Pay to download the firmware upgrade from the manufacturer's website.

   C. Have a certified laser printer technician come to your site and install a new firmware chip.

   D. Contact the manufacturer of the printer, and they will send you the firmware upgrade on a floppy disk.

4. You support an old dot-matrix printer at work. When the printer prints, the text is always goes from darker to lighter as it moves across the page. What is the most likely cause of the problem?

   A. The print ribbon is old and needs to be replaced.

   B. The print ribbon is not advancing properly.

   C. The printhead needs to be replaced.

   D. The wrong print driver is installed.

5. What type of printers can use ink that comes in a wax form? (Choose all that apply.)

   A. Bubble-jet

   B. Thermal

   C. Solid-ink

   D. Dye-sublimation

6. You believe your laser printer has a power issue. Using a multi-meter, what reading should you get from pin 9?

   A. +5V

   B. −5V

   C. +24V

   D. −24V

7.   Your laser printer has recently starting printing vertical white lines on documents it prints. What is the most likely cause of the problem?

   A. The print driver is faulty.

   B. The fuser is not heating properly.

   C. There is toner on the transfer corona wire.

   D. There is a scratch on the EP drum.

8.   In which step of the laser printing process is a laser used to reduce the charge to −100VDC on areas of the photosensitive drum?

   A. Charging

   B. Writing

   C. Developing

   D. Cleaning

9.   Which of the following are possible causes of paper jams in a laser printer? (Choose all that apply.)

   A. Worn pickup rollers

   B. Worn exit rollers

   C. Worn corona wire

   D. Paper that is too moist

10.   What type of printer uses ink that goes from solid to gaseous form?

   A. Bubble-jet

   B. Thermal

   C. Solid-ink

   D. Dye-sublimation

11.   You have an inkjet printer. Recently, papers are being printed with excessive amounts of ink, and the ink is smearing. What is the most likely cause of the problem?

   A. A faulty ink cartridge

   B. A corrupt print driver

   C. A faulty fuser

   D. Too much humidity in the air

12.   Which step in the laser printer printing process occurs immediately after the writing phase?

   A. Charging

   B. Fusing

   C. Transferring

   D. Developing

13. A user calls to complain about the scanner. When she turns it on, the scanner makes grinding noises for about 15 seconds and then stops. The scanned images appear normal. What should you do?

    A. Tell the user that the noises are normal and not to worry about it.

    B. Replace the stepper motor.

    C. Run the scanner calibration test to realign the scanner head.

    D. Open the scanner's case and oil the scanner motor.

14. You support an old dot-matrix printer at work. When the printer prints, there is always a blank horizontal line in the middle of each line of output. What is the most likely cause of the problem?

    A. The print ribbon is old and needs to be replaced.

    B. The print ribbon is not advancing properly.

    C. The printhead needs to be replaced.

    D. The wrong print driver is installed.

15. When you print documents on your laser printer, you see residue from previous images on the output. What two things are the most likely causes of this problem? (Choose two.)

    A. A faulty transfer corona wire

    B. An overheating printer

    C. A bad erasure lamp

    D. A broken cleaning blade

16. Which of the following elements can damage your laser printer? (Choose all that apply.)

    A. Heat

    B. Light

    C. Ozone

    D. Ammonia

17. You have scanned in a photograph for a company brochure. It appears fuzzy in the scanning software. Which of the settings should you look to adjust?

    A. Color adjustment

    B. Lightness/darkness

    C. Descreen

    D. Sharpen

18. After printing documents, the toner smears on the output pages whenever you touch it. Otherwise, things appear to be working properly. What is the most likely cause of the problem?

    A. The print driver is faulty.

    B. The fuser is not heating properly.

    C. There is toner on the transfer corona wire.

    D. There is a scratch on the EP drum.

19. You believe your laser printer has a power issue. Using a multi-meter, what reading should you get from pin 5?

   A. +5V

   B. –5V

   C. +24V

   D. –24V

20. Which component of the laser printer is responsible for making the image permanent on the paper?

   A. Fuser

   B. Exit roller

   C. Transfer corona wire

   D. Presser

Answers to Review Questions

1. D. Vertical black lines are caused by a scratch or a groove in the EP drum. If the fuser was not heating properly, toner would not bond to the paper and you would have smearing. Toner on the transfer corona wire would most likely cause white streaks, not black streaks. Faulty print drivers will cause garbage to print or there will be no printing at all.

2. B. During the charging phase, the charging corona applies a uniform –600VDC charge to the photosensitive drum. The drum is then ready for the image to be written on it.

3. A. Firmware upgrades for laser printers are downloaded for free from the manufacturer's website. A technician does not need to install a new chip, as firmware is upgraded via software. The majority of firmware upgrades are too big to fit on a floppy disk.

4. B. If a dot-matrix printer outputs dark to light across a page, that means that the printer ribbon is not advancing properly; the gear likely needs to be replaced. If the output were consistently faded, then you would replace the ribbon.

5. B, C. A solid-ink printer uses ink that comes in a solid, wax form. Thermal printers use either heat only or heat along with a ribbon that contains a wax-based ink. Bubble-jet and dye-sublimation printers use liquid ink.

6. C. Pin 9 on a laser printer should read +24V. Pin 1 is +5V, and pin 5 is –5V.

7. C. White streaks on printouts are most likely caused by toner on the transfer corona wire. Vertical black lines are caused by a scratch or a groove in the EP drum. If the fuser was not heating properly, toner would not bond to the paper and you would have smearing. Faulty print drivers will cause garbage to print or there will be no printing at all.

8. B. During the writing process, a laser shines on the photosensitive drum and reduces the charge from –600VDC to –100DVC. The areas where the charge is reduced will form the image.

9. A, B, D. Worn pickup or exit rollers can definitely cause paper jams, as they fail to feed paper through the system properly. Paper that is too moist can also cause paper jams.

10. D. Dye-sublimation printers use sheets of solid ink that immediately convert to gaseous form and then adhere to the paper.

11. A. If an ink cartridge is faulty or develops a hole, it can release excessive amounts of ink, which will lead to smearing.

12. D. Developing happens after writing. The correct order is cleaning, charging, writing, developing, transferring, and fusing.

13. A. When turning a scanner on or beginning to scan a document, some noises are normal. There is probably nothing to worry about.

14. C. If there is a consistent blank space, it likely means that a pin is not firing properly, and the printhead needs to be replaced.

15. C, D. Seeing images from previous print jobs is a phenomenon called ghosting. It's most likely due to a bad erasure lamp or a broken cleaning blade.

16. A, B, C, D. Heat, light, ozone, and ammonia can all damage laser printers.

17. D. If the image is fuzzy, you will likely want to sharpen it. It's possible that the fuzziness could be due to low scanner resolution as well.

18. B. If the fuser does not heat properly, toner will not bond to the paper and you will have smearing. White streaks on printouts are most likely caused by toner on the transfer corona wire. Vertical black lines are caused by a scratch or a groove in the EP drum. Faulty print drivers will cause garbage to print or there will be no printing at all.

19. B. Pin 5 on a laser printer should read −5V. Pin 1 is +5V, and pin 9 is +24V.

20. A. The fuser is responsible for fusing the image to the paper and making the image permanent.

Installing, Configuring, Optimizing, and Upgrading Network Systems

---

THE FOLLOWING COMPTIA A+ IT TECHNICIAN EXAM OBJECTIVES ARE COVERED IN THIS CHAPTER:

✓ **5.1 Identify the fundamental principles or networks**

- Identify names, purposes, and characteristics of basic network protocols and terminologies, for example:
  - ISP
  - TCP/IP (for example, gateway, subnet mask, DNS, WINS, static and automatic address assignment)
  - IPX/SPX (NWLink)
  - NetBEUI/NetBIOS
  - SMTP
  - IMAP
  - HTML
  - HTTP
  - HTTPS
  - SSL
  - Telnet
  - FTP
  - DNS
- Identify names, purposes, and characteristics of technologies for establishing connectivity, for example:
  - Dial-up networking

- Broadband (for example, DSL, cable, satellite)
- ISDN networking
- Wireless (all 802.11)
- LAN/WAN
- Infrared
- Bluetooth
- Cellular
- VoIP

✓ **5.2 Install, configure, optimize, and upgrade networks**

- Install and configure browsers
  - Enable/disable script support
  - Configure proxy and security settings
- Establish network connectivity
  - Install and configure network cards
  - Obtain a connection
  - Configure client options (for example, Microsoft, Novell) and network options (for example, domain, workgroup, tree)
  - Configure network options
- Demonstrate the ability to share network resources
  - Models
  - Configure permissions
  - Capacities/limitations for sharing for each operating system

✓ **5.3 Use tools and diagnostic procedures to troubleshoot network problems**

- Identify names, purposes, and characteristics of tools, for example:
  - Command-line tools (for example, IPCONFIG.EXE, PING.EXE, TRACERT.EXE, NSLOOKUP.EXE)
  - Cable-testing device
- Diagnose and troubleshoot basic network issues, for example:
  - Driver/network interface

- Protocol configuration
  - TCP/IP (for example, gateway, subnet mask, DNS, WINS, static and automatic address assignment)
  - IPX/SPX (NWLink)
- Permissions
- Firewall configuration
- Electrical interference

✓ **5.4 Perform preventative maintenance of networks including securing and protecting network cabling**

THE FOLLOWING COMPTIA A+ REMOTE SUPPORT TECHNICIAN EXAM OBJECTIVES ARE COVERED IN THIS CHAPTER:

✓ **4.1 Identify the fundamental principles of networks**

- Identify names, purposes, and characteristics of the basic network protocols and terminologies, for example:
  - ISP
  - TCP/IP (for example, gateway, subnet mask, DNS, WINS, static and automatic address assignment)
  - IPX/SPX (NWLink)
  - NetBEUI/NtBIOS
  - SMTP
  - IMAP
  - HTML
  - HTTP
  - HTTPS
  - SSL
  - Telnet
  - FTP
  - DNS
- Identify names, purposes, and characteristics of technologies for establishing connectivity, for example:
  - Dial-up networking

- Broadband (for example, DSL, cable, satellite)
- ISDN networking
- Wireless
- LAN/WAN

✓ **4.2 Install, configure, optimize, and upgrade networks**

- Establish network connectivity and share network resources

✓ **4.3 Identify tools, diagnostic procedures, and troubleshooting techniques for networks**

- Identify the names, purposes, and characteristics of command-line tools, for example:
  - `IPCONFIG.EXE`
  - `PING.EXE`
  - `TRACERT.EXE`
  - `NSLOOKUP.EXE`
- Diagnose and troubleshoot basic network issues, for example:
  - Driver/network interface
  - Protocol configuration
    - TCP/IP (for example, gateway, subnet mask, DNS, WINS, static and automatic address assignment)
    - IPX/SPX (NWLink)
  - Permissions
  - Firewall configuration
  - Electrical interference

As a technician, you will find the world is one where everything is now connected. Rare is the PC that does not communicate with a network or the Internet, and rarer still is the user who does not expect this as a seamless part of their computing experience. You must know far more than just how PCs operate, you must know how they communicate. This chapter focuses on the technologies that make this communication possible.

It is highly recommended that you read Chapter 8, "Understanding Networking Fundamentals," as you study for your technician exam, in addition to this chapter. You are expected to have the essentials down before preparing for the elective.

Understanding Networking

One of the newest buzz phrases going about is "online oxygen." It means that users feel as if they have to be connected—able to check messages, reach the Web, and so on—at all times. If they cannot do that, they feel as if they are missing out of touch, or missing something as precious as the oxygen needed to sustain life.

As a technician, it often falls upon you to provide the oxygen that users need. You must make sure their computers can connect, they can get their e-mail, and downtime is something that resides only in history books. To be able to make that a reality, you must understand as much as you can about networking and the topics discussed in this section.

There is a great amount of overlap between this chapter and Chapter 8. Don't let that lull you, however, into a false sense of security. Every attempt has been made to avoid repetition, so you should read what is here fresh and make sure you understand it for the elective exam you are preparing for.

Identifying Network Protocols and Technologies

Understanding the various network protocols and technologies, and what purpose they serve, is an important aspect of any technician's job. In the following sections, you will look at a number of network protocols you should be familiar with.

DNS

Domain Name System (DNS) is the network service used in TCP/IP networks to translate hostnames to IP addresses. The first attempts at this used static files called hosts files. When the systems grew too large for the hosts files to be feasible, DNS was created to handle it and runs as a service on port 53.

Real World Scenario

A Need to Be Unique ...

One of the main issues with hosts files is that they are read in sequential order. As soon as a match is found, the search stops and results are used. If any duplicate entries exist within the file, only the first entry would be found and the other one ignored.

In the days when these files were more widely used, they caused a problem if you did not keep track of hostnames very carefully. For example, suppose the tenth line in the file read:

```
110.2.3.4   jupiter machine
```

Then both "jupiter" and "machine" would be translated to 110.2.3.4. If the fifth line in the file read:

```
110.5.6.7 saturn – next to jupiter
```

Then four hostnames would map to 110.5.6.7: "saturn," "next," "to," and "jupiter." Since this line appears first in the file, then anyone attempting to go to jupiter would be sent to this machine instead.

As simple a problem as it is (requiring the use of a pound sign for comments), it could take some time to figure out what is causing the problem and correct it.

While DNS is a database, the easiest way to think of it is as a hierarchical tree with a set number of top-level domains, and then entries beneath each of those. Table 16.1 contains a list of popular top-level domains.

TABLE 16.1   Common Domains

Domain	Meaning
.biz	Business
.com	Commercial
.edu	Educational

TABLE 16.1   Common Domains *(continued)*

Domain	Meaning
.info	Information
.mil	Military
.gov	Government
.net	Network—ISP
.org	Original/organization
.xx	Two-character country identifier, such as .ca for Canada

You do not have to use DNS for name resolution; it is simply the most practical and accepted way to do so. On a small network with a few hosts, it is still possible to use static HOSTS files (/etc/hosts on Linux) or %systemroot%/System32/Drivers/Etc/hosts in the Microsoft world (where you can also opt to use WINS which is discussed later in this chapter).

In hosts files, each line is limited to 255 characters, but there can be an unlimited number of lines within the file. The file is read sequentially until a match is found, and then the search stops and the found entry is used. Each line represents its own entry. The first column of each line is the IP address of the host. The second column—and all subsequent columns—are text names associated with that IP address (the hostnames). White space and a delimiter—either a space or a tab—must be used to separate the columns. Whichever delimiter is used must be used to separate subsequent columns as well. A pound sign (#) can be used to turn any line into a comment line that is ignored during processing.

DNS Zones

With the enormous number of hosts and sites on the Internet, it is not possible for a single server to hold all the address resolutions needed, regardless of the capabilities of the database. Instead of a single server, DNS resolution for the Internet is performed by multiple servers, each responsible for a zone.

By using multiple servers for multiple zones, the load and the administrative burden of managing the database is diffused. Administrators manage only the DNS database records stored in their zones, which can be any portion of the domain name space. For each zone, there is a primary server (responsible for all updates), and one or more secondary servers. Any changes made to the zone file must be made on the primary server because the zone file on the secondary server(s) is a read-only copy. Zones are copied from the primary to the secondary name servers through replication (also known as zone transfer).

In addition to primary and secondary, there are also servers known as caching-only servers. A caching-only DNS server doesn't have zone files, and its only function is to make DNS queries, return the results, and cache the results. Whereas primary and secondary servers always store files locally, a caching-only server has no stored DNS information when the server first starts. The caching-only server builds this information over time as it caches results of queries made after the server starts.

DNS Records

Each DNS zone file contains records that consist of a number of entries. The entries are also known as resource records and can vary ever so slightly in format. The following sections examine the most common record types.

SOA RECORD

Every database file starts with an SOA (Start of Authority) record. This record identifies the zone and contains several other parameters, including the following:

Source Host   The name of the primary server (with the read/write copy of the file)

Contact E-mail   E-mail address for the administrator of the file

Serial Number   The incrementing version number of the database

Refresh Time   The delay in seconds that secondary servers wait before checking for changes to the database file.

Retry Time   The time in seconds that a secondary server waits before another attempt if replication fails

Expiration Time   The number of seconds on secondary servers before the old zone information is deleted

Time to Live (TTL)   The number of seconds that a caching-only server can cache resource records from this database file before discarding them and performing another query

NS RECORD

The Name Server record simply specifies the other name servers for the domain, or maps a domain name to that of the primary server for the zone.

A RECORD

The Address record holds the IP address of the name.

CNAME RECORD

The Canonical Name record is an alias field allowing you to specify more than one name for each TCP/IP address.

MX RECORD

The Mail Exchange record specifies the name of the host that processes mail for this domain.

HINFO RECORD

The Host record is the record that actually specifies the TCP/IP address for a specified host. All hosts that have static TCP/IP addresses should have an entry in this database.

PTR RECORD

Pointer records are used for reverse-lookup entries. They specify the IP address in reverse order and the corresponding hostname.

FTP

File Transfer Protocol (FTP) is both a TCP/IP protocol and software that permits the transferring of files between computer systems. Because FTP has been implemented on numerous types of computer systems, files can be transferred between disparate computer systems (for example, a personal computer and a mainframe).

FTP is the most widely used file-transfer mechanism in use. First defined in RFC 959, FTP runs on ports 20 and 21.

> **NOTE** FTP requires user interaction to work; a user must initiate a download/upload in order for the operation to take place. A derivative of FTP is Trivial File Transfer Protocol — TFTP — which works in the absence of user interaction. Instead of using TCP, TFTP uses UDP and port 69. It is commonly used to provide startup configurations to devices lacking an operating system.

HTML

Hypertext Markup Language (HTML) is a set of codes used to format text and graphics that will be displayed in a browser. The codes define how data will be displayed.

HTTP

Hypertext Transfer Protocol (HTTP) is the protocol used for communication between a web server and a web browser. By default, it uses port 80.

HTTPS

Hypertext Transfer Protocol (Secure) is a combination of HTTP with Secure Sockets Layer (SSL) to make for a secure connection. It uses port 443 by default, and the beginning of the site address becomes `https://`.

IMAP

Internet Message Access Protocol (IMAP) is a protocol with a store-and-forward capability. It can also allow messages to be stored on an e-mail server instead of downloaded to the client. The current version of the protocol is 4 (IMAP4), and the counterpart to it is POP3 (Post Office Protocolv3). IMAP uses port 143, while POP uses port 110.

IPX/SPX

Internetwork Packet Exchange / Sequenced Packet Exchange (IPX/SPX) is a connectionless, routable network protocol based on the Xerox XNS architecture. It's the default protocol for versions of NetWare before NetWare 5. IPX operates primarily at the Network layer of the OSI model and is responsible for addressing and routing packets to workstations or servers on other networks. SPX operates at the Transport layer only. The Microsoft transport protocol that is compatible with IPX/SPX is NWLink.

ISP

An Internet service provider (ISP) is a company that provides direct access to the Internet for home and business computer users.

NetBEUI/NetBIOS

NetBIOS is the Network Basic Input/Output System. In its most generic form, it is the API (application programming interface) that Microsoft originally used to allow Windows to utilize networking. The NetBIOS Extended User Interface (NetBEUI) expanded on this, and is used to transport NetBIOS across a local area network (LAN).

 An API is a set of routines, protocols, and tools for building software applications.

NetBEUI advantages are that it is easily configured, has low overhead, and is configured for (and therefore fast and efficient on) LANs. Disadvantages are that it is not routable and does not handle large networks well.

SMTP

Simple Mail Transfer Protocol (SMTP) is a protocol for sending e-mail between SMTP servers. Clients typically use either IMAP or POP to access the e-mail. By default, SMTP uses port 25.

SSL

Secure Sockets Layer (SSL) is a protocol that secures messages by operating between the Application layer (the HTTP protocol) and the Transport layer.

TCP/IP

Transmission Control Protocol / Internet Protocol (TCP/IP) is a suite of networking protocols and applications. It is elaborated on in Chapter 8, and you should reread that material—particularly the discussion on addressing—when studying for the elective exam.

Telnet

Telnet is a protocol that functions at the Application layer of the OSI model, providing terminal-emulation capabilities. Telnet uses the connection-oriented services of the TCP/IP protocol for communications at port 23. With Telnet, the command to initiate the session is TELNET itself, or TELNET followed by an IP address or hostname to connect to a specific remote host.

The remote host system must be running a Telnet daemon or service, and after a connection is established, you must log on to the server by using a valid username and password (plain text) as if you were sitting at the server. If you connect to a remote host by using the Connect/Remote system option, you may be prompted for the information required for a Telnet session.

WINS

Windows Internet Name Service (WINS) provides a centralized method of name management that is both flexible and dynamic. A WINS server automatically collects entries whenever a client is configured with that WINS server's address. By default, non-WINS clients cannot directly communicate with a WINS server to resolve a name, but resolution can be done by installing a *WINS proxy agent* that works by using broadcasts. The proxy agent forwards broadcasts for name resolution to the WINS server if the values are not locally cached, and gets the resolution. The proxy does not send the resolution back to the requester, but instead waits for it to request it again, at which time it finds the entry in cache and responds back. The proxy agent must be located on the same subnet as non-WINS clients so the proxy agent receives the broadcast for name resolution (broadcasts don't go through routers).

 WINS is an alternative to DNS and the Microsoft equivalent to a hosts file is LMHosts in a WINS system.

Any Windows-based WINS client can be a WINS proxy agent, but it cannot be a WINS server. After you configure a WINS client to be a proxy agent, you must reboot the machine for this change to take effect. No other configuration is needed for this proxy agent. This WINS client remains a proxy agent until you turn off the proxy agent parameter and reboot the computer.

Identifying Network Connectivity Technologies

As a technician, there are a number of network connectivity technologies that you should be familiar with. Many of these were discussed in Chapter 8, and it is highly recommended that you skim that chapter once again when studying for this exam.

Bluetooth

Bluetooth is a wireless standard that uses radio waves in the 2.4 to 2.485 GHz range. Class 2 is limited to about 35 feet in range. While it does not require a clear line of sight, having a clear line of sight greatly enhances the device. Therefore, it is commonly used for connecting mice, keyboards, scanners, printers, and so on to PCs. Class 1 has a range of approximately 100 meters (328 feet). The most common uses of Bluetooth technology are currently related to cell phones (especially hands-free headsets).

Broadband (DSL, Cable, Satellite)

There are essentially three methods of broadband access (using a single medium for several channels) that CompTIA looks at. Digital Subscriber Line (DSL) employs high-speed connections from telephone-switching stations. Cable uses a cable modem and the cable line from providers who used to carry only television signals. Satellite replaces the terrestrial cable with signals through the air. The opposite of broadband is baseband, which allows only one signal at a time to be transmitted.

> ### 🌐 Real World Scenario
>
> #### Sometimes, the Choices Are Limited …
>
> Before you decide which broadband connection sounds the most appealing to you, you should also factor in something very important: what is available in your area. DSL is available at different rates of connectivity based upon distance from a central station. If you live far enough from a central station, or near a central station that has not been updated lately (such as in the middle of rural America), DSL may not be an option.
>
> Similarly, not all cable providers are willing to take the steps necessary to run a connection in all situations. I once had a small business within a section of an old industrial building. The cable provider said the office where the modem was desired was too far from their nearest pole and there was nothing that could be done about it. We offered to pay the expense to have an additional pole placed closer to the location, but they would not discuss it further.
>
> Make certain you know the available options—not just the technological options—before you spend too much time determining what is best for you.

Cellular

Cellular networking is a means of communication utilizing geographic regions known as *cells*. The cells divide the area and handle communications within them by assigning each connection or conversation a separate frequency.

Dial-up Networking

One of the first ways of communicating with ISPs and remote networks was through dial-up connections. Although this is still possible, dial-up is not used much anymore due to limitations on modem speed. Dial-up modems operate over the Plain Old Telephone System (POTS) and cannot compare to speeds possible with DSL and cable modems. According to a recent study, dial-up Internet connections dropped from 74 percent of all U.S. residential Internet connections in 2000 to 60 percent in 2003, and 36 percent in 2006.

Infrared

Infrared networking requires a line of sight and is useful for small areas (a few feet), but is not used much beyond that. Many printers have infrared (IrDA) capabilities, as do mice and other wireless peripherals.

ISDN

Integrated Services Digital Network (ISDN) is a WAN technology that performs link management and signaling by virtue of packet switching. The original idea behind ISDN was to let existing phone lines carry digital communications by using multiplexing to support multiple channels.

LAN/WAN

A local area network (LAN) is a network that is geographically confined within a small space. That small space can be only a single room, a floor, or a building, for example. By being confined, it has tighter security and can normally offer higher speeds. A wide area network (WAN) is a collection of two or more LANs, typically connected by routers. The geographic limitation is removed, but WAN speeds are traditionally less than LAN speeds.

VoIP

Voice over IP (VoIP) is also known as IP telephony or and Internet telephony. It is simply the routing of voice traffic over the Internet. (Although the routing could be across any smaller IP-based network, generally it is over the Internet.)

Wireless

Wireless networking is defined by the 802.11 body of standards and was discussed earlier in Chapter 8. It is also highly recommended that you reread the section on wireless security in Chapter 9, "Understanding Network Security Fundamentals."

Working with Additional Network Components

As an IT Technician or Depot Technician, you will find that hardware is only one part of the equation that you must master in order to optimize connectivity. In addition to the physical side, you must also know how to configure application and operating system components in order to meet the needs of the user and abide by the rules (security, usage, etc.) of the organization you work for. This section looks beyond the pure hardware issues and introduces some of the software elements of connectivity.

Contrary to what the "Install, configure, optimize, and upgrade networks" objective may make you first think of, this objective expects basic knowledge of browsers, with an emphasis on Internet Explorer as well as network connectivity and network resources. Each of these items is discussed in detail in this section.

Working with Browsers

A browser is any application allowing you to interact with software or code. Web browsers provide an interface for web pages by showing the text, figures, hyperlinks, and other information coded in HTML.

> There are many types of browsers, and although CompTIA uses only the word *browser* in the objective, what they really mean is a *web browser*.

A handful of web browsers are available, and most are freely distributed. Two of the most popular are Microsoft Internet Explorer and Mozilla Firefox. Almost every operating system from Windows to Linux ships with a web browser of some type installed, or packaged, with it. If you do not want to use that browser, you can download another and install it according to the instructions supplied by the vendor.

> Netscape, Safari, and Opera are also popular browsers at the time of this writing.

You can configure such things as script support, proxy settings, and other variables directly within the browser. Within Internet Explorer, for example, choose Internet Options from the Tools menu, and then choose the Security tab. From here, you can pick a default level of security, or customize your own for each of four security zones (Internet, Local Intranet, Trusted Sites, and Restricted Sites), or customize each zone by clicking the Custom Level command button. This opens a myriad of choices, as shown in Figure 16.1.

> In Internet Explorer, you can click on Tools, then Manage Add-ons to enable/disable add-ons.

FIGURE 16.1 Configure custom security choices in Internet Explorer

Choosing the Connections tab, you can configure dial-up and VPN (Virtual Private Network) settings, as well as click on LAN Settings to configure proxy settings.

In Mozilla Firefox, choose Preferences from the Edit menu, then Advanced, and you can configure similar security information, as shown in Figure 16.2. This will differ based upon version. On some versions, configuration screens are in the Tools ➢ Options menu. The General icon ➢ Connection Settings button is where you can configure proxy settings. The Advanced icon ➢ Security tab allows setting allows selection of security protocols and certificate configuration.

FIGURE 16.2   One way to configure custom choices in Mozilla Firefox

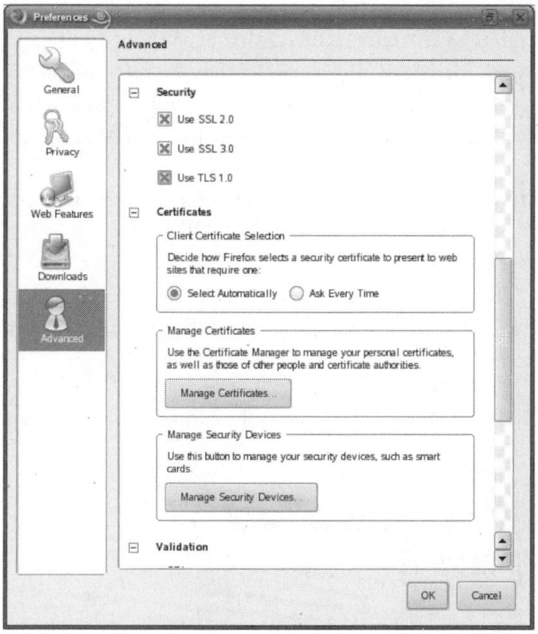

From the General tab in Firefox 1.5.0.4, you can choose Connection Settings and configure proxy values.

Establishing Network Connectivity

For network connectivity to occur, there must be a network card and a language shared between the hosts. The network card can be a wired card requiring LAN cabling, or it can be a wireless card. The language can be the TCP/IP protocol (the most popular), IPX/SPX, or any of a number of other possibilities.

The traditional NIC card is installed in a machine in the same way any adapter card would be:

1. Disconnect all power and other cords from the PC.

2. Take appropriate antistatic precautions (ESD mat and/or wrist strap) and remove the cover.

3. Remove a blank from the PC case and insert the NIC into an expansion slot. Secure it with the screw or clip previously used to hold the blank.

4. Reinstall the case, and reconnect all cords including power.

To configure a Windows XP client on a new network, choose My Network Places (depending on the desktop used, it may be on the desktop or accessible from the Start menu) and then choose Set Up A Home Or Small Office Network (or Set Up A Wireless Network For A Home Or Small Office, if appropriate) beneath Network Tasks. This will start the Network Setup Wizard, shown in Figure 16.3, (or the Wireless Network Setup Wizard) and walk you through the configuration of the client.

After initially configuring the network, you can always go to Network Tasks (in My Network Places) and choose Add A Network Place when needed. This will start the Add Network Place Wizard and allow you to configure Internet connections as well as create shortcuts to websites, FTP sites, and other network locations. If you click View Network Connections and then right-click on a LAN or high-speed connection and choose Properties, you can install, uninstall, and change the properties for any available client, service, or protocol, as shown in Figure 16.4.

The Advanced tab allows you to configure Windows Firewall and Internet Connection Sharing parameters.

Different Linux vendors include the same functionality but use different tools. With SUSE Linux, for example, you can start YaST (Yet Another Setup Tool), and then choose the options between either Network Devices or Network Services to configure the same parameters. Figure 16.5 shows the settings for the network card in SUSE Linux.

FIGURE 16.3   The Network Setup Wizard walks you through the process of adding an XP client to a network.

FIGURE 16.4   Configure the client, service, and protocol settings in XP.

FIGURE 16.5   Configure network card parameters in SUSE Linux.

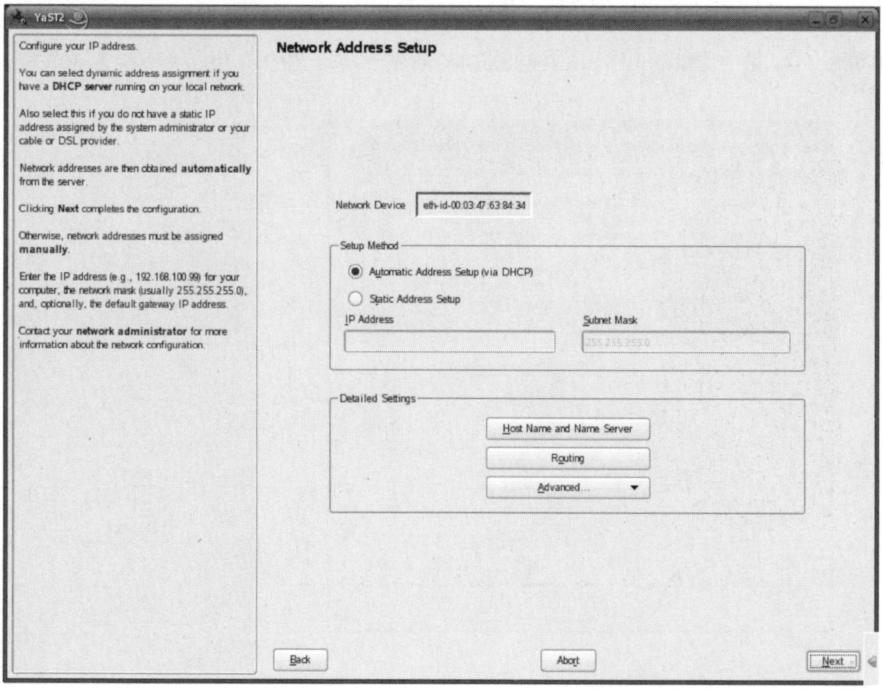

Sharing Network Resources

The real reason for having a network is to be able to share resources, whether those resources are printers, files, or something altogether different. Within each operating system, sharing is almost as simple as configuring network access.

While there are a number of hybrids that can be created, there are essentially two models for networking. The first is server-based (also known as client/server or domain model). In this model, one machine (the server) is given responsibility for maintaining the network in terms of resource sharing and permission management. The other model is a peer-to-peer network (also called a workgroup). In this model, there is no server and a group of clients share resources (files, printers, etc.) between each other. This model is easier to set up, but the security is not nearly as stringent. Sometimes, you are limited to which model you can use by the operating system: Windows XP Home Edition, for example, cannot join a domain.

With the Microsoft Windows operating systems, those in a workgroup that are to share must have the File And Printer Sharing For Microsoft Networks client installed (it need not be installed for those who are only going to access). You can then choose to share printers by right-clicking on them in Printers and Faxes (Printers in Windows 2000), click Sharing, and choosing Share This Printer (Shared As in Windows 2000), as shown in Figure 16.6.

Similarly, to share folders, right-click on them and choose Properties, and then click Sharing tab (you can also just choose Sharing And Security from the pop-up menu). This will offer the choices shown in Figure 16.7.

When a folder is shared, a hand will appear beneath the folder and others will be able to access it.

FIGURE 16.6   Configure printer sharing in Windows XP.

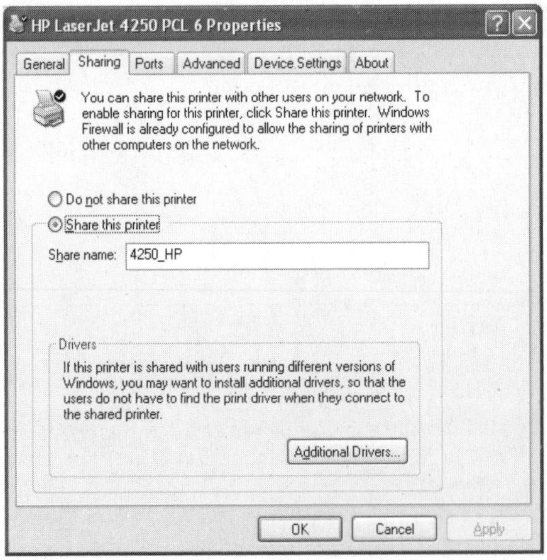

FIGURE 16.7   Configure folder sharing in Windows XP.

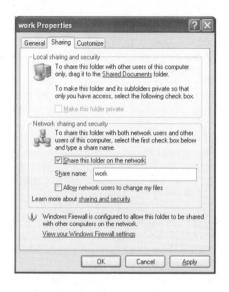

Files behave differently than folders. Files only provide a Security tab (accessed through the file properties) where NTFS permissions may be set.

Share permissions apply only when a user is accessing a file or folder through the network. Local permissions and attributes are used to protect the file when the user is local. Using the NTFS file system, files and folders can use NTFS permissions to protect local files and folders.

If you are not using a workgroup configuration, then files to be shared are typically placed on the server. Rights associated with the operating system where the files are stored (on the server or local machine) can be used to differentiate users. Table 16.2, for example, lists NTFS permissions.

TABLE 16.2   NTFS Permissions

NTFS Permission	Meaning
Full Control	Gives the user all the other choices and the ability to Change Permission. The user also can take ownership of the directory or any of its contents. Full Control is also the only permission that allows deleting subfolders and files.
Modify	Combines the Read & Execute permission with the Write permission and further allows the user to delete everything in the folder, including the folder itself.

TABLE 16.2   NTFS Permissions *(continued)*

NTFS Permission	Meaning
Read & Execute	Combines the permissions of Read with those of List Folder Contents (which applies only to folders) and adds the ability to run executables. Read & Execute applied to folders allows moving through folders to reach other files and folders (even if the users don't have permission for those folders). When applied to files, Read & Execute runs applications and allows all actions permitted by the Read permission.
List Folder Contents	The List Folder Contents permission (known simply as List in previous versions) allows the user to view the contents of a directory and to navigate to its subdirectories. It does not grant the user access to the files in these directories unless that is specified in file permissions. This permission applies only to folders.
Read	Allows the user to navigate the entire directory structure, view the contents of the directory, view the contents of any files in the directory (when applied to a folder), and see ownership and attributes.
Write	Allows creating new files and subfolders within a folder, overwriting a file, changing file or folder attributes, and viewing ownership and permissions

With Linux, you can choose to copy files/directories to the `Public` folder (`public_html`) to make them available across the network, and you can share printers in much the same way as with Windows. One key protocol/suite that should be installed on Linux is Samba in order to allow Linux and Windows hosts to communicate with each other. After this is installed, the Linux hosts can generally communicate on a Windows-based network as easily as any other client.

Permissions in Linux are divided into Read, Write, and Execute and are set separately for the owner of the resource, the group the owner belongs to, and everyone else (others). Figure 16.8 shows the permissions for a file in the public folder.

FIGURE 16.8   Configure permissions for shared files in Linux.

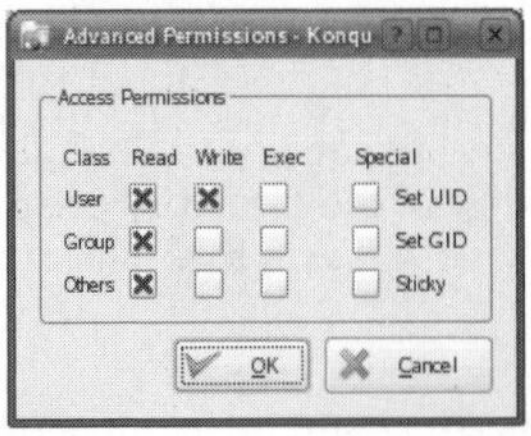

Using Network Tools and Diagnostics

You should have a good knowledge of diagnostic procedures and the ability to recognize the right tool to use for a particular situation. In addition to knowing the purpose of each of the utilities discussed here, you should be able to recognize the output that they provide and be able to identify the tool used just by looking at that output.

In this section, we will look at common tools, followed by a list of some of the symptoms of common problems you are likely to encounter during your days as a technician.

Network Tools to Use

The following list of utilities, some of which were also discussed in Chapter 8, "Understanding Network Fundamentals," are tools you should be familiar with as an technician.

CompTIA also expects you to be familiar with cable-testing devices. This is a broad category of any type of device that can isolate a break or problem with a cable or termination.

IPCONFIG.EXE

With Windows-based operating systems, you can determine the network settings on the client's network interface cards as well as any that a DHCP server has leased to your computer, by typing the following command at a command prompt:

```
IPCONFIG /ALL
```

IPCONFIG /ALL also gives you full details on the duration of your current lease. You can verify whether a DHCP client has connectivity to a DHCP server by releasing the client's IP address and then attempting to lease an IP address. You can conduct this test by typing the following sequence of commands from the DHCP client at a command prompt:

```
IPCONFIG /RELEASE
IPCONFIG /RENEW
```

This is one of the first tools to use when experiencing problems accessing resources, as it will show you whether an address has been issued to the machine. If the address displayed falls within the 169.254.*x*.*x* category, then the client was unable to reach the DHCP server and has defaulted to automatic Private IP addressing, which will prevent the card from communicating outside of its subnet, if not altogether.

In the Linux world, a utility similar to IPCONFIG is IFCONFIG.

In Exercise 16.1, you will renew an IP address on a Windows XP system within the graphical interface. In Exercise 16.2, you will perform this same operation from the command line.

EXERCISE 16.1

Renew an IP Address on a Windows XP System

This exercise assumes the use of Windows XP and dynamic IP assignments from a DHCP server:

1. From the Start menu, choose Control Panel and then click the Network Connections icon. A list of the LAN or high-speed Internet connections presently known appears.

2. Right-click on your connection and choose Status. The first tab that appears is General and it shows such things as whether you are connected, the speed of the connection, and how long the connection has been there.

3. Click the Support tab. From here, you can see whether the address is static or assigned by DHCP, the present address, subnet mask, and default gateway values.

4. Click the Details button. This expands the information by also showing you the physical (MAC) address and lease information, among other things. Note the date and time of the Lease Obtained values. Click Close.

5. Back at the Support tab, click the Repair button. This will attempt to establish or renew the connection. If the network (DHCP) is functioning properly, a notification that it finished will appear in a short time. Click the Details button again. The Lease Obtained values should reflect the current date and time.

This interface in Windows XP provides a convenient way to interact with the network components. The next exercise shows how to perform a similar action, only using the command line to do so.

EXERCISE 16.2

Renew an IP Address from the Command Line

This exercise assumes the use of Windows XP and dynamic IP assignments from a DHCP server:

1. Open a command prompt (Start ➢ Run ➢ **CMD**).

2. Type **IPCONFIG** and view the abbreviated list of information.

3. Type **IPCONFIG /ALL** to see the full list. Notice the date and time on the lease for the IP address.

4. Type **IPCONFIG /RENEW** followed by **IPCONFIG /ALL**. The date and time on the lease for the IP address should be the current date and time.

5. Close the command-prompt window by typing **EXIT**.

NSLOOKUP.EXE

NSLOOKUP is a command-line utility that enables you to verify entries on a DNS server. You can use NSLOOKUP in two modes: interactive and noninteractive. In interactive mode, you start a session with the DNS server, in which you can make several requests. In noninteractive mode, you specify a command that makes a single query of the DNS server. If you want to make another query, you must type another noninteractive command.

One of the key issues regarding the use of TCP/IP is the ability to resolve a hostname to an IP address—an action usually performed by a DNS server.

PING.EXE

The PING command is one of the most useful commands in the TCP/IP protocol. It sends a series of packets to another system, which in turn sends back a response. This utility can be extremely useful for troubleshooting problems with remote hosts.

The PING command indicates whether the host can be reached and how long it took for the host to send a return packet. Across wide area network links, the time value will be much larger than across healthy LAN links.

TRACERT.EXE

TRACERT is a command-line utility that enables you to verify the route to a remote host. Execute the command TRACERT *hostname*, where *hostname* is the computer name or IP address of the computer whose route you want to trace. TRACERT returns the different IP addresses the packet was routed through to reach the final destination. The results also include the number of hops needed to reach the destination. If you execute the TRACERT command without any options, you see a help file that describes all the TRACERT switches.

The TRACERT utility determines the intermediary steps involved in communicating with another IP host. It provides a road map of all the routing an IP packet takes to get from host A to host B.

Timing information from TRACERT can be useful for detecting a malfunctioning or overloaded router.

Troubleshooting Network Issues

Having looked at the tools available to use for finding problems, there are a number of common network problems that you should be aware of. This section introduces those problems and their symptoms, and should be helpful in your role as a technician.

Identifying DNS Problems

Problems with DNS not properly working or being incorrectly configured often manifest themselves in a host being unable to communicate by using hostnames or Fully Qualified Domain Names (FQDNs), but still able to communicate if IP addresses are used.

A FQDN includes the hostname and domain name. A DNS entry has record information. A zone is a database within DNS, and an alias is another name by which a host is known.

Identifying Driver Problems

Hardware devices use drivers to communicate. With the release of new sets of files, you can change drivers, fix related problems, or add functionality that is currently lacking. Problems with drivers can usually be identified by an inability to perform functions that should be allowed.

In a network, symptoms generally occur with device drivers for the network interface card (NIC). Problems with the NIC are manifested by an inability to connect to the network, My Network Places not showing other computers on the network, error messages while installing NIC drivers, a yellow exclamation point next to the name of the NIC in Device Manager, or no link light appearing. Updating or reinstalling drivers for the NIC can often resolve these problems. If this solution does not work, you should try another NIC.

Identifying Electrical Interference Problems

Electrical interference will degrade the network performance. This can be identified by a slow network and/or excessive network errors. Be sure to run cables around (not over) fluorescent light ballasts, and other items that can cause EMI, such as motors and transformers found in fans, heaters, microwaves, and air conditioners.

Identifying Firewall Configuration Problems

Problems with firewalls can prevent access to data. After firewalls are enabled, they tend to limit access to resources by default, and you must configure them to let through the traffic that you want to pass.

Identifying Gateway Problems

A gateway allows traffic out of the network. If the gateway is not configured properly, the hosts will have no difficulty communicating on the network, but will be unable to communicate beyond the LAN.

 A gateway is any upper-layer device that can work between different applications, such as e-mail, and send data between dissimilar networks.

Identifying IPX/SPX (NWLink) Problems

IPX/SPX uses frames. Problems with IPX/SPX typically involve not selecting the correct frame type. It is important that all hosts using IPX/SPX agree on the frame type. With Windows XP, you can choose Auto Detect or one of the other four choices (802.2, 802.3, Ethernet II, and SNAP).

Identifying Network Interface Problems

If there are problems with the network card, you usually will not be able to communicate at all. Check the card for a status light and verify that it is on. Blinking typically indicates link activity, and a solid light can indicate that all is working well. A light that is off can indicate that there is no activity, and the card should be replaced.

This can also indicate a network cable problem or a problem with the device at the other end of the cable. Check the possibility of each of these before replacing the card.

Identifying Permission Problems

Issues with permissions prevent users from accessing resources. Make sure that the users or groups have the appropriate permissions to be able to use the resource as intended.

Identifying Static and Automatic Address Assignment Problems

If DHCP is used to issue automatic addresses, you must make sure that the host can be reached and has enough addresses within its scope to be able to service all clients. If you are using static addresses, one of the most common problems is issuing the same address to two clients, which causes both to be unable to communicate. Every host on the network must have a unique IP address.

Identifying Subnet Mask Problems

Problems with subnet masks (incorrect values) prevent the client from being able to communicate with other hosts on the network. A common mistake is leaving the default value and forgetting to set this to a value that your network is using.

Identifying WINS Problems

Windows Internet Name Service provides name resolution for Microsoft networks. If your network uses WINS for name resolution, your computer needs to be configured with the IP address of a WINS server. (The IP address of a secondary WINS server can also be specified.) Although hostnames (and thus DNS) are understood on *all* operating systems running TCP/IP, NetBIOS names (and thus WINS) are understood only in the world of Microsoft operating systems. Eventually, WINS will be completely phased out in favor of DNS.

Performing Preventative Network Maintenance

Various types of cabling can be used in setting up a network. Each has its own benefits and susceptibilities, and all were examined in Chapter 8. You should know that regardless of the type of cabling you employ, you should go to lengths to make certain you protect it the best you can.

Protecting the cabling entails running it in such a way at to prevent it from being damaged (or degraded) by its environment and making sure it is not accessible to those wishing to harm your network. It is fairly easy to tap into a 10Base-T cable without being detected, but much harder to do so with fiber cabling. Likewise, it can be easy to tap into a wireless network, and you will want to make it as difficult as possible for those you do not want on the network to do so.

Aside from the cabling, you can secure the network by using firewalls, strong authentication, and a great deal of common sense when establishing the rules of the network.

> CompTIA offers an entire certification on network security. It is the Security+ exam, and the *CompTIA Security+ Study Guide, Third Edition* (Sybex, 2006) can help you prepare for it.

Summary

In this chapter, you learned about the various issues related to networking that appear on the CompTIA A+ electives. We looked at networking protocols and technologies and discussed various common problems and solutions. You also learned of networking tools and problem areas and how to identify and address them.

Each of the protocols discussed were those that you are likely to encounter as a technician, and you should know why each exists and when it is used. The networking discussion also included a look at preventative maintenance and some basic networking issues.

Exam Essentials

Know the definitions for various networking protocols.   You should be familiar with all the protocols and technologies listed in this chapter and be able to differentiate between them.

Know the connectivity options.   Be able to discriminate between various connectivity options based on definitions given. A knowledge of the choices available today is required.

Know that different browsers exist.   The most popular web browsers are Internet Explorer (IE) and Mozilla Firefox, but you can download any of a number of others and choose to use them as well.

Know how to establish network connectivity.   To connect a client to a network, you need a network card and a language (protocol) shared between the client and other hosts.

Know how to share resources.   Printers and files are the most commonly shared network resources. You can share them easily by using wizards or other tools.

Know which utilities can be used for troubleshooting.   The objectives include four utilities that work in the Windows world, and you should know each of them. The four utilities discussed are: IPCONFIG.EXE, PING.EXE, TRACERT.EXE, and NSLOOKUP.EXE.

Know common symptoms of network problems.   Review the list potential network problems given in this chapter and make sure you know common issues and problems and how they manifest themselves.

Know the importance of protecting your network.   You can protect your data by securing and protecting the cabling and the network to keep those who should not be accessing it from doing so.

Review Questions

1. Which of the following is a company that provides direct access to the Internet for home and business computer users?

   A. ASP

   B. ISP

   C. DNS

   D. DNP

2. Two of the most popular web browsers are Internet Explorer and _____.

   A. Mozilla Firefox

   B. Microsoft Access

   C. Microsoft Browser

   D. Novell Web

3. What is the hardware connectivity device you should use to transfer e-mail between dissimilar networks?

   A. Gateway

   B. Bridge

   C. Router

   D. Hub

4. Which character can be used at the beginning of a line in a hosts file to make the line a comment?

   A. @

   B. #

   C. !

   D. (

5. What is the maximum number of entries that can be in a hosts file?

   A. 255

   B. 1024

   C. 12,000

   D. Unlimited

6. Which domain should be used for an institution of higher learning in Oklahoma?

   A. .ok

   B. .gov

   C. .edu

   D. .sa

7. Within a DNS record, the entry type used to hold an alias would be which of the following?

   A. SOA

   B. HINFO

   C. A

   D. CNAME

8. Which DNS record type is used for reverse lookup?

   A. CNAME

   B. NS

   C. PTR

   D. REV

9. What is the name of the entity (which includes the host and domain names) that is used to signify an address that DNS can use for name resolution?

   A. FDDI

   B. DDOS

   C. CNAME

   D. FQDN

10. What is a DNS server that has no record file of its own known as?

   A. Primary

   B. Secondary

   C. Caching-only

   D. Authoritative

11. On which port does FTP run by default?

   A. 21

   B. 25

   C. 63

   D. 89

12. By default, on which port does Telnet run?

   A. 110

   B. 80

   C. 57

   D. 23

13. Which service, by default, runs on port 69?

   A. FTP

   B. TFTP

   C. DNS

   D. WINS

14. Which troubleshooting tool can be used at the command line to see the IP configuration data given by a DHCP server to a Windows XP workstation?

   A. IFCONFIG

   B. IPCONFIG

   C. WINIPCFG

   D. HIJACK

15. Which service is used to transfer e-mail between e-mail servers?

   A. DNS

   B. FTP

   C. SMTP

   D. IMAP

16. Which of the following protocols can be used by a client to access e-mail on a server?

   A. DNS

   B. FTP

   C. SMTP

   D. IMAP

17. Which tool can be used to test connectivity and see the path taken to reach another host?

   A. PING

   B. IPCONFIG

   C. TRACERT

   D. NSLOOKUP

18. Which of the following is a command-line utility that enables you to verify entries on a DNS server?

   A. PING

   B. IPCONFIG

   C. TRACERT

   D. NSLOOKUP

19. When SSL and HTTP are used together, what does the beginning of a site address become?

   A. https://

   B. ssl://

   C. asp://

   D. tcp://

20. What port does HTTPS use by default?

   A. 443

   B. 119

   C. 81

   D. 80

Answers to Review Questions

1. B. An Internet Service Provider (ISP) is a company that provides direct access to the Internet for home and business computer users.

2. A. Two of the most popular web browsers are Internet Explorer and Mozilla Firefox.

3. A. A gateway is an upper-layer device that can work between applications, such as different e-mail protocols, and send between dissimilar networks.

4. B. The pound sign (#) signifies the line as a comment line to ignore when processing.

5. D. There can be an unlimited number of entries in a hosts file, and each entry is limited to 255 characters.

6. C. Institutes of learning use the .edu domain.

7. D. CNAME is the Canonical Name record used to hold aliases for the host. SOA is the Start of Authority record, which holds the time to live and related information. HINFO records hold the TCP/IP address information, as do A records.

8. C. The PTR record holds the pointer information and is used for reverse-lookup entries. NS is the Name Server record and maps to the primary server for the zone. There are no record types of REV or VER; they are invalid entries.

9. D. A fully qualified domain name (FQDN) includes the host and domain names. A DNS entry has record information. A zone is a database within DNS, and an alias is another name by which a host is known.

10. C. A caching-only server holds the results of queries it has performed but does not have a zone file of its own.

11. A. By default, FTP runs on port 21. Port 20 is also used by this protocol, but was not one of the answer choices.

12. D. By default, Telnet runs on port 23.

13. B. By default, TFTP runs on port 69.

14. B. The IPCONFIG utility can be used at the command line with Windows XP to see the networking configuration values.

15. C. The Simple Mail Transfer Protocol (SMTP) service is used to transfer e-mail between e-mail servers.

16. D. Internet Mail Access Protocol (IMAP) is used by clients to access mail on the server.

17. C. The TRACERT (trace route) utility can be used to test connectivity and see the path taken to reach another host.

18. D. NSLOOKUP is a command-line utility that enables you to verify entries on a DNS server.

19. A. When SSL and HTTP are used together, the beginning of the site address becomes `https://`.

20. A. By default, HTTPS uses port 443.

Installing, Configuring, Upgrading, and Optimizing Security Systems

THE FOLLOWING COMPTIA A+ IT TECHNICIAN EXAM OBJECTIVES ARE COVERED IN THIS CHAPTER:

✓ **6.1 Identify the fundamentals and principles of security**

- Identify the purposes and characteristics of access control, for example:
  - Access to operating system (for example, accounts such as user, admin, and guest; groups; permission actions, types, and levels), components, restricted spaces
- Identify the purposes and characteristics of auditing and event logging

✓ **6.2 Install, configure, upgrade, and optimize security**

- Install and configure software, wireless and data security, for example:
  - Authentication technologies
  - Software firewalls
  - Auditing and event logging (enable/disable only)
  - Wireless client configuration
  - Unused wireless connections
  - Data access (for example, permissions, basic local security policy)
  - File systems (converting from FAT32 to NTFS only)

✓ **6.3 Identify tools, diagnostic procedures, and troubleshooting techniques for security**

- Diagnose and troubleshoot software and data security issues, for example:
  - Software firewall issues
  - Wireless client configuration issues
  - Data access issues (for example, permissions, security policies)
  - Encryption and encryption technology issues

✓ **6.4 Perform preventative maintenance for security**

- Recognize social engineering and address social engineering situations

---

THE FOLLOWING COMPTIA A+ REMOTE SUPPORT TECHNICIAN EXAM OBJECTIVES ARE COVERED IN THIS CHAPTER:

✓ **5.1 Identify the fundamental principles of security**

- Identify the names, purposes, and characteristics of access control and permissions
  - Accounts including user, admin, and guest
  - Groups
  - Permission levels, types (for example, file systems and shared) and actions (for example, Read, Write, Change, and Execute)

✓ **5.2 Install, configure, optimize, and upgrade security**

- Install and configure hardware, software, wireless and data security, for example:
  - Smart card readers
  - Key fobs
  - Biometric devices
  - Authentication technologies
  - Software firewalls
  - Auditing and event logging (enable/disable only)

- Wireless client configuration
- Unused wireless connections
- Data access (for example, permissions, security policies)
- Encryption and encryption technologies

✓ **5.3 Identify tools, diagnostic procedures, and troubleshooting techniques for security issues**

- Diagnose and troubleshoot software and data security issues, for example:
  - Software firewall issues
  - Wireless client configuration issues
  - Data access issues (for example, permissions, security policies)
  - Encryption and encryption technology issues

✓ **5.4 Perform preventative maintenance for security**

- Recognize social engineering and address social engineering situations

---

THE FOLLOWING COMPTIA A+ DEPOT TECHNICIAN EXAM OBJECTIVES ARE COVERED IN THIS CHAPTER:

✓ **4.1 Identify the names, purposes, and characteristics of physical security devices and processes**

- Control access to PCs, servers, laptops, and restricted spaces
  - Hardware
  - Operating systems

✓ **4.2 Install hardware security**

- Smart card readers
- Key fobs
- Biometric devices

In this chapter, we will look at we will look at security from a more detailed viewpoint than was done in Chapter 9. Not only is the topic important enough that CompTIA added it to the Essentials exam with the latest version, but they also added it to every elective exam as well. So ubiquitous is the topic, you cannot escape it in the real world or the exam world.

It is highly recommended that you read Chapter 9 as you study for your elective exam, in addition to this chapter.

Understanding Security Baselines

One of the first steps in developing a secure environment is to develop a baseline of the minimum security needs of your organization. A *security baseline* defines the level of security that will be implemented and maintained. You can choose to set a low baseline by implementing next to no security, or a high baseline that doesn't allow users to make any changes at all to the network or their systems. In practicality, most implementations fall between the two extremes; you must determine what is best for your organization.

Microsoft provides a tool for establishing a security baseline and for subsequent evaluations of security on Windows 2000 and higher OSs with the Microsoft Security Baseline Analyzer.

The baseline provides the input needed to design, implement, and support a secure network. Developing the baseline includes gathering data on the specific security implementation of the systems with which you'll be working.

One of the newest standards for security is *Common Criteria (CC)*. This document is a joint effort between Canada, France, Germany, the Netherlands, the United Kingdom, and the United States. The standard outlines a comprehensive set of evaluation criteria, broken down into seven *Evaluation Assurance Levels (EALs)*. EAL 1 to EAL 7 are discussed here:

EAL 1 EAL 1 is primarily used when the user wants assurance that the system will operate correctly, but threats to security aren't viewed as serious.

EAL 2 EAL 2 requires product developers to use good design practices. Security isn't considered a high priority in EAL 2 certification.

EAL 3 EAL 3 requires conscientious development efforts to provide moderate levels of security.

EAL 4   EAL 4 requires positive security engineering based on good commercial development practices. It is anticipated that EAL 4 will be the common benchmark for commercial systems.

EAL 5   EAL 5 is intended to ensure that security engineering has been implemented in a product from the early design phases. It's intended for high levels of security assurance. The EAL documentation indicates that special design considerations will mostly likely be required to achieve this level of certification.

EAL 6   EAL 6 provides high levels of assurance of specialized security engineering. This certification indicates high levels of protection against significant risks. These systems will be highly secure from penetration attackers.

EAL 7   EAL 7 is intended for extremely high levels of security. The certification requires extensive testing, measurement, and complete independent testing of every component.

EAL certification has replaced the Trusted Computer Systems Evaluation Criteria (TCSEC) system for certification. The recommended level of certification for commercial systems is EAL 4.

Currently, only a few operating systems have been approved at the EAL 4 level, and even though one may be, that doesn't mean that your own individual implementation of it is functioning at that level. If your implementation doesn't use the available security measures, you're operating below that level. The network is only as strong as its weakest component. If users can install software, delete files, and change configuration, then these actions can be done within software programs such as viruses and malware as well.

Windows XP (SP2), Windows Server 2003 (SP1) Standard, Enterprise, and Datacenter editions, Red Hat Enterprise Linux Version 4 update 1AS and 1WS, Windows 2000 Professional, Server, and Advanced Server (SP3) have all achieved EAL 4.

Hardening a System

Hardening is the process of reducing or eliminating weaknesses, securing services, and attempting to make your environment immune to attacks. Typically, when you install operating systems, applications, and network products, the defaults from the manufacturer are to make the product as simple to use as possible and to allow it to work with your existing environment as effortlessly as possible. That isn't always the best scenario when it comes to security.

You want to make certain that your systems, and the data within them, are kept as secure as possible. The security prevents others from changing the data, destroying it, or inadvertently harming it.

In addition to hardening a system, you can also harden components of it. Application hardening, for example, involves making an application more difficult for non-authorized individuals to access, exploit, and so on.

Hardening the OS and NOS

Any network is only as strong as its weakest component. Sometimes, the most obvious components are overlooked, and it's your job as a security administrator to make certain that doesn't happen. You must make certain that the operating systems running on the workstations and on the network servers are as secure as they can be.

Hardening an operating system (OS) or network operating system (NOS) refers to the process of making the environment more secure from attacks and intruders. This section discusses hardening an OS and the methods of keeping it hardened as new threats emerge. This section will also discuss some of the vulnerabilities of the more popular operating systems and what can be done to harden those OSs.

Hardening Microsoft Windows 2000

Windows 2000 entered the market at the millennium. It includes workstation and several server versions. The market has embraced these products, and they offer reasonable security when updated. Windows 2000 provides a Windows Update icon on the Start menu; this icon allows you to connect to the Microsoft website and automatically download and install updates. A large number of security updates are available for Windows 2000—make sure they're applied.

> In the Windows environment, the Services Manager or applet is one of the primary methods (along with policies) used to disable a service.

The server and workstation products operate in a similar manner to Windows NT 4. These products run into the most security-related problems when they're bundled with products that Microsoft has included with them. Some of the more attack-prone products include IIS, FTP, and other common web technologies. Make sure these products are disabled if they aren't needed, and keep them up-to-date with the most recent security and service packs.

Many security updates have been issued for Windows 2000. The Microsoft TechNet and Security websites provide tools, white papers, and materials to help secure Windows 2000 systems.

> You can find the Microsoft TechNet website at http://technet.microsoft.com/default.aspx. The Microsoft security website is at http://www.microsoft.com/security/.

Windows 2000 includes extensive system logging, reporting, and monitoring tools. These tools help make the job of monitoring security fairly easy. In addition, Windows 2000 provides a great deal of flexibility in managing groups of users, security attributes, and access control to the environment.

The Event Viewer is the major tool for reviewing logs in Windows 2000. Figure 17.1 shows an example Event Viewer. Several types of events can be logged by using Event Viewer, and administrators can configure the level of events that are logged.

FIGURE 17.1   Event Viewer log of a Windows 2000 system

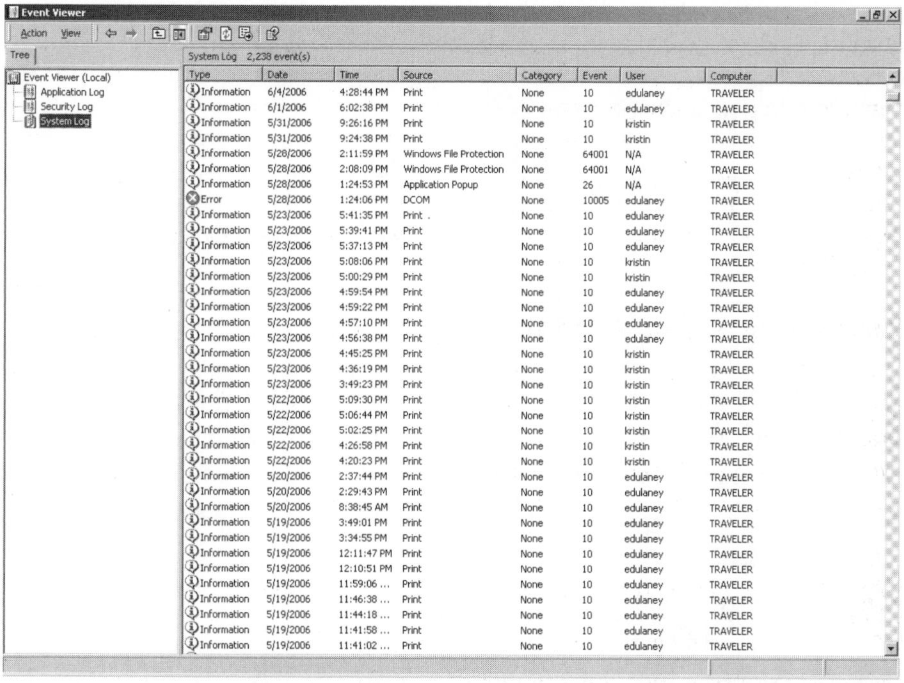

Another important security tool is Performance Monitor. As an administrator of a Windows 2000 network, you must know how to use Performance Monitor. This tool can be a lifesaver when you're troubleshooting problems and looking for resource-related issues.

Windows 2000 servers can run a technology called *Active Directory (AD)*, which lets you control security configuration options of Windows 2000 systems in a network. Unfortunately, the full power of AD doesn't work unless all the systems in the network are running Windows 2000 or higher.

Hardening Microsoft Windows XP

Windows XP functions as a replacement for both the Windows 9x family and Windows 2000 Professional. There are multiple versions of Windows XP, including the Home, Media Center, and Professional editions.

Windows XP Home Edition was intended specifically to replace Windows 9x clients and could be installed either as an upgrade from Windows 9x or as a fresh installation on new systems. Media Center adds entertainment options (such as a remote control for TV), while Windows XP Professional is designed for the corporate environment. Windows XP Professional has the ability to take advantage of the security possible from Windows 200x servers running Active Directory.

With Microsoft's increased emphasis on security, it's reasonable to expect that the company will be working hard to make this product secure. At the time of this writing, the second service pack for XP is available. The service packs fix minor security openings within the operating system, but nothing substantial has been reported as a weakness with XP.

Hardening Windows Server 2003

The update for Microsoft's Windows 2000 Server line of products is Windows Server 2003, which is available in four varieties:

- Web edition
- Standard edition
- Enterprise edition
- Datacenter edition

   This product introduced the following features to the Microsoft server line:

- Internet connection firewall (now called the Windows Firewall)
- Secure authentication (locally and remotely)
- Wireless connections as secure as they can be in today's environments
- Software restriction policies
- Secure Web Server (IIS 6)
- Encryption and cryptography enhancements
- Improved security in VPN connections
- PKI and X.509 certificate support

   In short, the goal was to make a product that is both secure and flexible.

Hardening Unix/Linux

The Unix environment and its derivatives are some of the most-installed server products in the history of the computer industry. Over a dozen versions of Unix are available; the most popular is a free derivative called *Linux*.

   Unix was created in the 1970s. The product designers took an open-systems approach, meaning that the entire source code for the operating system was readily available for most versions. This open-source philosophy has allowed tens of thousands of programmers, computer scientists, and systems developers to tinker with and improve the product.

   Linux and Unix, when properly configured, provide a high level of security. The major challenge with the Unix environment is configuring it properly.

   Unix includes the capacity to handle and run almost every protocol, service, and capability designed. You should turn off most of the services when they aren't needed by running a script during system startup. The script will configure the protocols, and it will determine which services are started.

   All Unix security is handled at the file level. Files and directories need to be established properly in order to ensure correct access permissions. The file structure is hierarchical by nature, and when a file folder access level is set, all subordinate file folders usually inherit this access. This inheritance of security is established by the system administrator or by a user who knows how to adjust directory permissions.

Keeping patches and updates current is essential in the Unix environment. You can accomplish this by regularly visiting the developer's website for the version/flavor you're using and downloading the latest fixes.

Linux also provides a great deal of activity logging. These logs are essential in establishing patterns of intrusion.

An additional method of securing Linux systems is accomplished by adding *TCP wrappers*, which are low-level logging packages designed for Unix systems. Wrappers provide additional detailed logging on activity by using a specific protocol. Each protocol or port must have a wrapper installed for it. The wrappers then record activities and deny access to the service or server.

As an administrator of a Unix or Linux network, you're confronted with many configuration files and variables that you must work with in order to keep all hosts communicating properly.

Hardening Novell NetWare

Novell was one of the first companies to introduce a NOS for desktop computers, called NetWare. Early versions of NetWare provided the ability to connect PCs into primitive but effective LANs. The most recent version of NetWare, version 6.5, includes file sharing, print sharing, support for most clients, and fairly tight security.

NetWare functions as a server product. The server has its own NOS. The NetWare software also includes client applications for a number of types of systems, including Macintoshes and PCs. You can extend the server services by adding NetWare Loadable Modules (NLMs) to the server. These modules allow executable code to be patched or inserted into the OS.

NetWare version 6.*x* is primarily susceptible to denial of service (DoS) attacks, as opposed to exploitation and other attacks. NetWare security is accomplished through a combination of access controls, user rights, security rights, and authentication.

 The heart of NetWare security is the NetWare Directory Services (NDS) or eDirectory (for newer Novell implementations). NDS and eDirectory maintain information about rights, access, and usage on a NetWare-based network.

A number of additional capabilities make NetWare a product worth evaluating in implementation. These include e-commerce products, document retrieval, and enhanced network printing.

 Prior to version 5, NetWare defaulted to the proprietary IPX/SPX protocol for networking. All newer versions of NetWare default to TCP/IP.

Hardening Apple Macintosh

Macintosh systems seem to be most the most vulnerable to physical access attacks targeted through the console. The network implementations are as secure as any of the other systems discussed in this chapter.

Macintosh security breaks down in its access control and authentication systems. Macs use a simple 32-bit password encryption scheme that is relatively easy to crack. The password file is located in the Preference folder; if this file is shared or is part of a network share, it may be vulnerable to decryption.

Macintosh systems also have several proprietary network protocols that aren't intended for routing. Recently, Macintosh systems have implemented TCP/IP networking as an integral part of the operating system.

Hardening File Systems

Several file systems are involved in the operating systems we've discussed, and they have a high level of interoperability between them—from a network perspective, that is. Through the years, the different vendors have implemented their own sets of file standards. Some of the more common file systems include the following:

Microsoft FAT   Microsoft's earliest file system was referred to as File Allocation Table (FAT). FAT is designed for relatively small disk drives. It was upgraded first to FAT16 and finally to FAT32. FAT32 allows large disk systems to be used on Windows systems. FAT allows only two types of protection: share-level and user-level access privileges. If a user has Write or Change access to a drive or directory, they have access to any file in that directory. FAT is very insecure in an Internet environment. Share-level permissions apply when the file is accessed through sharing (over the network): they do not factor in if the user is local. User-level permissions apply to the file based upon the user who is accessing it and allow/restrict their actions accordingly.

Microsoft NTFS   The New Technology File System (NTFS) was introduced with Windows NT to address security problems. Before Windows NT was released, it had become apparent to Microsoft that a new file system was needed to handle growing disk sizes, security concerns, and the need for more stability. NTFS was created to address those issues.

Although FAT was relatively stable if the systems that were controlling it kept running, it didn't do so well when the power went out or the system crashed unexpectedly. One of the benefits of NTFS was a transaction tracking system, which made it possible for Windows NT to back out of any disk operations that were in progress when Windows NT crashed or lost power.

With NTFS, files, directories, and volumes can each have their own security. NTFS security is flexible and built-in. Not only does NTFS track security in Access Control Lists (ACLs), which can hold permissions for local users and groups, but each entry in the ACL can specify what type of access is given—such as Read, Change, or Full Control. This allows a great deal of flexibility in setting up a network. In addition, special file-encryption programs were developed to encrypt data while it was stored on the hard disk.

Full control, Change, and Read are permissions available in FAT32. NTFS offers six permissions (Full Control, Modify, Read and Execute, List Folder Contents, Read, and Write) that are preconfigured from a list of 14 granular permissions (Advanced Permissions).

Microsoft strongly recommends that all network shares be established using NTFS. Several current operating systems from Microsoft support both FAT32 and NTFS. It is possible to convert from FAT32 to NTFS without losing data, but you cannot do the operation in reverse (you would need to reformat the drive and install the data again from a backup tape).

Novell Storage Services   Novell, like Microsoft, implemented a proprietary file structure called NetWare File System. This system allows complete control of every file resource on a NetWare server. The NetWare File System was upgraded to Novell Storage Services (NSS) in version 6. NSS provides higher performance and larger file storage capacities than the Net-Ware File System. NSS, like its predecessor, uses the NDS or eDirectory to provide authentication for all access.

Unix File System   The Unix file system is a completely hierarchical file system. Each file, subdirectory, and file system has complete granularity of access control. The three primary attributes in a Unix file or directory are Read, Write, or Execute. The ability to individually create these capabilities, as well as to establish inheritance to subdirectories, gives Unix the highest level of security available for commercial systems. The major difficulty with Unix is that establishing these access-control hierarchies can be time-consuming when the system is initially configured. Figure 17.2 illustrates this hierarchical file structure. Most current operating systems have embraced this method of file organization.

Unix Network File System   Network File System (NFS) is a Unix protocol that allows systems to mount file systems from remote locations. This ability allows a client system to view the server or remote desktop storage as a part of the local client. NFS, while functional, is difficult to secure. The discussion of this process is beyond the scope of this book; the major issue lies in Unix's inherent trust of authentication processes. NFS was originally implemented by Sun Microsystems, and it has become a standard protocol in Unix environments.

Apple File Sharing   Apple File Sharing (AFS) was intended to provide simple networking for Apple Macintosh systems. This system used a proprietary network protocol called *AppleTalk*. An AppleTalk network isn't routed through the Internet and isn't considered secure. AFS allows the file owner to establish password and access privileges. This process is similar to the Unix file system. OS X, the newest version of the Macintosh operating system, has more fully implemented a file system that is based on the Unix model. In general, Apple networking is considered as secure as the other implementations discussed in this section. The major weakness of the operating system involves physical control of the systems.

Each of these file system implementations requires careful consideration when you're implementing them in a network. You must evaluate their individual capabilities, limitations, and vulnerabilities when you're choosing which protocols or systems to implement.

FIGURE 17.2 Hierarchical file structure used in Unix and other operating systems

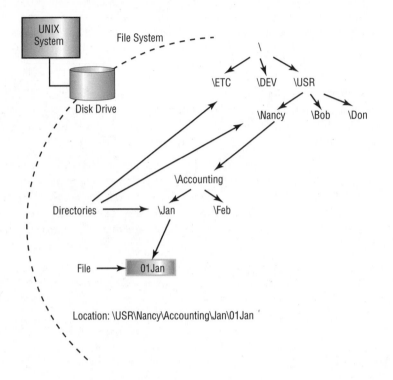

Most OS providers support multiple protocols and methods. Turn off any protocols that aren't needed, because each protocol or file system running on a workstation or server increases your vulnerability and exposure to attack, data loss, or DoS attacks.

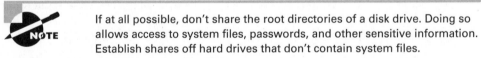

> If at all possible, don't share the root directories of a disk drive. Doing so allows access to system files, passwords, and other sensitive information. Establish shares off hard drives that don't contain system files.

Make sure you periodically review the manufacturers' support websites and other support resources that are available to apply current updates and security patches to your systems. Doing this on a regular basis will lower your exposure to security risks.

Working with Access Control Lists

Access Control Lists (ACLs) enable devices in your network to ignore requests from specified users or systems, or to grant them certain network capabilities. You may find that a certain IP address is constantly scanning your network, and thus you can block this IP address from your network. If you block it at the router, the IP address will automatically be rejected any time it attempts to utilize your network.

ACLs allow a stronger set of access controls to be established in your network. The basic process of ACL control allows the administrator to design and adapt the network to deal with specific security threats.

Working with Group Policies

One of the most wide-sweeping administrative features that Windows 200*x* offers over its predecessors and other operating systems is that of *Group Policy*. A part of IntelliMirror, the Group Policy feature enables administrators to control desktop settings, utilize scripts, perform Internet Explorer maintenance, roll out software, redirect folders, and so forth. All of these features can be an administrator's dream in supporting LAN users.

To use an analogy: When you connect a television set to the subscription cable coming through the living room wall, you get all the channels to which you subscribe. If you pay an extra $50 per month (depending on where you live), you can get close to 100 channels, including a handful of premium channels.

When you turn on the television, you are free to watch any of the channels—regardless of whether the content is questionable or racy. And when you are gone, your children are free to do the same. Enter the V-chip. Before leaving your children alone with the television, you simply enable the V-chip. The V-chip enables you (the "administrator") to restrict access to the stations that air questionable or racy programming.

How is this example analogous to an operating system? On Windows 2000 Professional, for example, users can do just about anything they want to do. They can delete programs and never be able to run them again; they can send huge graphics files to a tiny printer that can print only one page every 30 minutes; they can delete the Registry and never be able to use the system again; and so forth. Enter Group Policy.

Group Policy places restrictions on what a user/computer is allowed to do. It takes away liberties that were otherwise there; as such, they are never implemented for the benefit of the user (restrictions do not equal benefits), but are always there to simplify administration for the administrator.

From an administrator's standpoint, if you take away the ability to add new software, you don't have to worry about supporting nontested applications. If you remove the ability to delete installed printers (accidentally, of course), you don't have to waste an hour reinstalling the printer. In other words, by reducing what the users can do, you are reducing what you must support and reducing the overall administrative cost of supporting the network/computer/user.

Before going any further, it is important to differentiate between roaming users and mobile users, because the two are often confused. As the name indicates, *roaming users* are simply users who roam throughout the LAN. One example is a secretary within a secretarial pool. On Monday, she may be working in Accounting, on Tuesday in Human Resources, and for the remainder of the week in Marketing. Within each department, she has a different computer but is still on the same LAN. Given this, by simply placing her profile on the network and configuring her as a roaming user, she will have the same desktop and access to all resources regardless of where she works that day. Not only that, but the same Group Policy will apply (and be routinely refreshed) to prevent her from permanently deleting software that has been assigned, changing her desktop, and so forth.

An example of a *mobile user*, on the other hand, is a salesperson who is in the field calling on customers. In his possession is a $6,000 laptop capable of doing everything shy of changing the oil of the company car. Whenever the salesperson has a problem with the computer, he calls from 3,000 miles away and begins the conversation with, "It did it again." You not only have no idea to whom you are talking, you have no idea to what the *it* refers.

In short, roaming users use different computers within the same LAN, whereas mobile users use the same workstation but do not connect to the LAN. Because you cannot force mobile users to connect to a server on your LAN each time they boot (and when they do, it is over slow connections), you are less able to enforce administrative restrictions—such as Group Policies. That having been said, however, you should never think it impossible to apply administrative restrictions on mobile users.

System Policies are the predecessors of Group Policies (used in Windows 9*x*) and restrict what they can govern to Registry settings only, whereas Group Policies exceed that functionality.

In the absence of a regular connection to the LAN (and, therefore, to Active Directory), there are automatically a number of Group Policy restrictions that you cannot enforce or utilize (a cruel fact you must accept). Therefore, it is always in the best interest of the administrators to have the systems connect to the network (and require them to do so), whenever possible. The following is a list of some of the restrictions that cannot be enforced without such a connection:

Roaming Profiles   By placing a user's profile on the server, that user is able to have the same desktop regardless of which computer they use on a given day.

Assigning and Publishing Software   The Software Installation snap-in enables you to centrally manage software. You can publish software to users and assign software to computers.

Redirecting Folders   The Folder Redirection extension enables you to reroute special Windows 2000 folders—including My Documents, Application Data, Desktop, and the Start menu—from the user profile location to elsewhere on the network.

Installing the Operating System Remotely   The Remote Installation Services (RIS) extension enables you to control the Remote Operating System Installation component, as displayed to the client computers.

Aside from these, you can place all the other settings directly on the mobile computer—making them local policies. Local policies can apply to the following:

Administrative Templates   The administrative templates consist mostly of the Registry restrictions that existed in System Policies. They enable you to manage the Registry settings that control the desktop, including applications and operating system components.

Scripts   Scripts enable you to automate user logon and logoff.

Security Settings   The Security Settings extension enables you to define security options (local, domain, and network) for users within the scope of a Group Policy object, including Account Policy, encryption, and so forth.

Creating the Local Policy

You can create a local policy on a computer by using the Group Policy Editor. You can start the Group Policy Editor in one of the following two ways:

- From the Start button, choose Run and then enter **gpedit.msc**.

  or

- From the Start button, choose Run and then enter **MMC**. Within the MMC console, choose Console ➢ Open, and then select GPEDIT.MSC from the System32 directory.

When opened, a local policy has two primary divisions: Computer Configuration and User Configuration. The settings that you configure beneath Computer Configuration apply to the computer, regardless of who is using it. Conversely, the settings that you configure beneath User Configuration apply only if the specified user is logged on. Each of the primary divisions can be useful with a mobile workforce. Note that the Computer Configuration settings are applied whenever the computer is on, whereas the User Configuration settings are applied only when the user logs on.

The following options are available under the Computer Configuration setting:

Software Settings   These settings typically are empty on a new system.

Administrative Templates   These settings are those that administrators commonly want to apply.

Windows Settings   The Windows Settings further divide into the following:

Scripts   Scripts are divided into Startup and Shutdown, both of which enable you to configure items (for example, .EXE, .CMD, and .BAT files) to run when a computer starts and stops. Although your implementation may differ, for the most part, little here is pertinent to the mobile user.

Security Settings   Security Settings are divided into Account Policies, Local Policies, Public Key Policies, and IP Security Policies on the local machine.

The following sections examine Account Policies and Local Policies choices.

Account Policies

The Account Policies setting further divides into Password Policy and Account Lockout Policy. The following seven choices are available under Password Policy:

Enforce Password History   This allows you to require unique passwords for a certain number of iterations. The default number is 0, but it can go as high as 24.

Maximum Password Age   The default is 42 days, but values range from 0 to 999.

Minimum Password Age   The default is 0 days, but values range to 999.

Minimum Password Length   The default is 0 characters (meaning no passwords are required), but a number up to 14 can be specified.

Passwords Must Meet Complexity Requirements Of The Installed Password Filter   The default is disabled.

Store Password Using Reversible Encryption For All Users In The Domain   The default is disabled.

User Must Logon To Change The Password   The default is disabled, thus allowing a user with an expired password to specify a new password during the logon process.

Because the likelihood of laptops being stolen always exists, it is strongly encouraged that you make use of good password policies for this audience. An example policy is as follows:

- Enforce password history: 8 passwords remembered

- Maximum password age: 42 days

- Minimum password age: 3 days

- Minimum password length: 6 to 8 characters

Leave the other three settings disabled.

The Account Lockout Policy setting divides into the following three values:

Account Lockout Counter   This is the number of invalid attempts it takes before lockout occurs. The default is 0 (meaning the feature is turned off). Invalid attempt numbers range from 1 to 999. A number greater than 0 changes the values on the following two options to 30 minutes; otherwise, they are Not Defined.

Account Lockout Duration   This is a number of minutes ranging from 1 to 99999. A value of 0 is also allowed here and signifies that the account never unlocks itself—administrator interaction is always required.

Reset Account Lockout Counter After   This is a number of minutes, ranging from 1 to 99999.

When you are working with a mobile workforce, you must weigh the choice of a user calling you in the middle of the night when she has forgotten her password against keeping the system from being entered if the wrong user picks up the laptop. A good recommendation is to employ lockout after five attempts for a period of time between 30 and 60 minutes.

Local Policies

The Local Policies section divides into three subsections: Audit Policy, User Rights Assignment, and Security Options. The Audit Policy section contains nine settings, the default value for each being No Auditing. Valid options are Success and/or Failure. The Audit Account Logon Events entry is the one entry you should consider turning on for mobile users to see how often they are logging in and out of their machines.

When auditing on an event is turned on, the entries are logged in the Security log file.

The User Rights Assignment subsection of Local Policies is where the meat of the old System Policies comes into play. User Rights Assignment has 34 options, most of which are self-explanatory. Also shown in the list that follows are the defaults for who can perform these actions, with Not Defined indicating that no one is specified for this operation.

The list of rights and default permissions include the following:

- Access This Computer From The Network: Everyone, Administrators, Power Users

- Act As Part Of The Operating System: [blank]

- Add Workstations To Domain: [blank]
- Backup Files And Directories: Administrators, Backup Operators
- Bypass Traverse Checking: Everyone
- Change The System Time: Administrators, Power Users
- Create A Pagefile: Administrators
- Create A Token Object: [blank]
- Create Permanent Shared Objects: [blank]
- Debug Programs: Administrators
- Deny Access To This Computer From The Network: [blank]
- Deny Logon As A Batch Job: [blank]
- Deny Logon As A Service: [blank]
- Deny Logon Locally: [blank]
- Enable Computer And User Accounts To Be Trusted For Delegation: [blank]
- Force Shutdown From A Remote System: Administrators, Power Users
- Generate Security Audits: [blank]
- Increase Quotas: Administrators
- Increase Scheduling Priority: Administrators, Power Users
- Load And Unload Device Drivers: Administrators
- Lock Pages In Memory: [blank]
- Log On As A Batch Job: Administrator
- Log On As A Service: [blank]
- Log On Locally: Everyone, Administrators, Users, Guests, Power Users, Backup Operators
- Manage Auditing And Security Log: Administrators
- Modify Firmware Environment Values: Administrators
- Profile Single Process: Administrators, Power Users
- Profile System Performance: Administrators
- Remove Computer From Docking Station: [blank]
- Replace A Process Level Token: [blank]
- Restore Files And Directories: Administrators, Backup Operators
- Shut Down The System: Everyone, Administrators, Users, Power Users, Backup Operators
- Synchronize Directory Service Data: [blank]
- Take Ownership Of Files Or Other Objects: Administrators

This is the default list. You can add additional groups and users to the list, but you cannot remove them. (This functionality is not needed.) If you want to "remove" users or groups from the list, simply uncheck the box granting them access. If your mobile users need to be able to install, delete, and modify their environment, make them a member of the Power Users group.

The Security Options section includes 38 options, which, for the most part, are Registry keys. The default on each is Not Defined, with the two definitions that can be assigned being Enabled and Disabled, or a physical number (as with the number of previous logons to cache).

The ability to backup a system, and recover/restore it is extremely important. Exercise 17.1 discusses recovering a Windows XP system.

EXERCISE 17.1

Recovering a Windows XP System

This exercise assumes the use of Windows XP and asks you to rate your knowledge of the tools available within it:

1. Assume you created a backup set with ASR, as done in Exercise 9.1. Do you know how to restore it and why you would need to?

2. If the GUI were inaccessible, do you know enough about the command-line NTBACKUP.EXE options to be able to restore a backup?

3. Are you familiar with the Safe Mode boot options? What is the difference between the options, and why would you choose one over another?

4. Is Recovery Console installed on your server(s)? If not, do you know how to do so and why you would use it?

Virtually every network operating system offers tools of this sort, although their names differ. If you aren't running Windows XP, make certain you know the equivalent tools in the operating system you're running. You must know how to recover a system and not just how to back it up in order to be an effective administrator.

Exercise 17.2 walks you through the process of creating a backup in a different operating system—SuSE Linux.

EXERCISE 17.2

Create a Backup with SuSE Linux

This exercise assumes the use of SuSE Linux Enterprise Server 9. To create a backup:

1. Log in as root and start YaST.

2. Choose System and System Backup.

3. Click Profile Management and choose Add; then enter a name for the new profile, such as fullsystemback.

4. Click OK.

5. Enter a backup name (using an absolute path), and make certain the archive type is set to a tar variety. Then click Next.

6. At the File Selection window, leave the default options and click Next.

7. Leave the Search Constraints as they are and click OK.

At the main YaST System Backup dialog box, click Start Backup. After several minutes of reading packages, the backup will begin.

Auditing and Logging

Most systems generate *security logs* and *audit files* of activity on the system. These files do absolutely no good if they aren't periodically reviewed for unusual events. Many web servers provide message auditing, as do logon, system, and application servers.

The amount of information these files contain can be overwhelming. You should establish a procedure to review them on a regular basis. A rule of thumb is to never start auditing by trying to record everything, because the sheer volume of the entries will make the data unusable. Approach auditing from the opposite perspective and begin auditing only a few key things, and then expand the audits as you find you need more data.

These files may also be susceptible to access or modification attacks. The files often contain critical systems information including resource sharing, security status, and so on. An attacker may be able to use this information to gather more detailed data about your network.

In an access attack, these files can be deleted, modified, and scrambled to prevent system administrators from knowing what happened in the system. A logic bomb could, for example, delete these files when it completes. Administrators might know that something happened, but they would get no clues or assistance from the log and audit files.

You should consider periodically inspecting systems to see what software is installed and whether passwords are posted on sticky notes on monitors or keyboards. A good way to do this without attracting attention is to clean all the monitor faces. While you're cleaning the monitors, you can also verify that physical security is being upheld. If you notice a password on a sticky note, you can "accidentally" forget to put it back. You should also notify that user that this is an unsafe practice and not to continue it.

Under all conditions, you should always work within the guidelines established by your company.

You should also consider obtaining a vulnerability scanner and running it across your network. A *vulnerability scanner* is a software application that checks your network for any known security holes; it's better to run one on your own network before someone outside the organization runs it against you. One of the best-known vulnerability scanners is SAINT— Security Administrator's Integrated Network Tool.

Updating Your Operating System

Operating system manufacturers typically provide product updates. For example, Microsoft provides a series of regular updates for Windows 2000 (a proprietary system) and other applications. However, in the case of open-source systems (such as Linux), the updates may come from a newsgroup, the manufacturer of the version you're using, or a user community.

In both cases, public and private, updates help keep operating systems up to the most current revision level. Researching updates is important; when possible, so is getting feedback from other users before you install an update. In a number of cases, a service pack or update has rendered a system unusable. Make sure your system is backed up before you install updates.

 Make sure you test updates on test systems before you implement them on production systems.

Three types of updates are discussed here: hotfixes, service packs, and patches.

Hotfixes

Hotfixes are used to make repairs to a system during normal operation, even though they might require a reboot. A hotfix may entail moving data from a bad spot on the disk and remapping the data to a new sector. Doing so prevents data loss and loss of service. This type of repair may also involve reallocating a block of memory if, for example, a memory problem occurred. This allows the system to continue normal operations until a permanent repair can be made. Microsoft refers to a bug fix as a *hotfix*. This involves the replacement of files with an updated version.

Service Packs

A *service pack* is a comprehensive set of fixes consolidated into a single product. A service pack may be used to address a large number of bugs or to introduce new capabilities in an OS. When installed, a service pack usually contains a number of file replacements.

Make sure you check related websites to verify that the service pack works properly. Sometimes a manufacturer will release a service pack before it has been thoroughly tested. An untested service pack can cause extreme instability in an operating system or, even worse, render it inoperable.

Patches

A *patch* is a temporary or quick fix to a program. Patches may be used to temporarily bypass a set of instructions that have malfunctioned. Several OS manufacturers issue patches that can be applied either manually or by using a disk file to fix a program.

When you're working with customer support on a technical problem with an OS or applications product, customer service may have you go into the code and make alterations to the binary files that run on your system. Double-check each change to prevent catastrophic failures due to improperly entered code.

When more data is known about the problem, a service pack or hotfix may be issued to fix the problem on a larger scale. Patching is becoming less common, because most OS manufacturers would rather release a new version of the code than patch it.

Revisiting Social Engineering

Social engineering attacks can develop very subtly. They're also hard to detect. Let's look at some classic social engineering attacks:

- Someone enters your building wearing a white lab jacket with a logo on it. He also has a toolbox. He approaches the receptionist and identifies himself as a copier repairman from a major local copier company. He indicates that he's here to do preventative service on your copier. In most cases, the receptionist will let him pass and tell him where the copier is. Once the "technician" is out of sight, the receptionist probably won't give him a second thought. Your organization has just been the victim of a social engineering attack. The attacker has now penetrated your first and possibly even your second layer of security. In many offices, including security-oriented offices, this individual would have access to the entire organization and would be able to pass freely anywhere he wanted. This attack didn't take any particular talent or skill other than the ability to look like a copier repairman. Impersonation can go a long way in allowing access to a building or network.

- The next example is a true situation; it happened at a high-security government installation. Access to the facility required passing through a series of manned checkpoints. Professionally trained and competent security personnel manned these checkpoints. An employee decided to play a joke on the security department: He took an old employee badge, cut his picture out of it, and pasted in a picture of Mickey Mouse. He was able to gain access to the facility for two weeks before he was caught.

Social engineering attacks like these are easy to accomplish in most organizations. Even if your organization uses biometric devices, magnetic card strips, or other electronic measures, social engineering attacks are still relatively simple. A favorite method of gaining entry to electronically locked systems is to follow someone through the door they just unlocked, a process known as *tailgating*. Many people don't think twice about this event—it happens all the time.

Famed hacker Kevin Mitnick coauthored a book called *The Art of Deception: Controlling the Human Element of Security* in which 14 of the 16 chapters are devoted to social engineering scenarios that have been played out. If nothing else, the fact that one of the most notorious hackers known—who could write on any security subject he wants—chose to write a book on social engineering, should emphasize the importance of the topic to you.

As an administrator, one of your responsibilities is to educate users to not fall prey to social engineering attacks. They should know the security procedures that are in place and follow them to a tee. You should also have a high level of confidence that the correct procedures are in place, and one of the best ways to obtain that confidence is to check your users on occasion.

Preventing social engineering attacks requires more than just providing training about how to detect and prevent them. It also involves making sure that people stay alert. One form of social engineering is known as *shoulder surfing*, which is nothing more than watching someone when they enter their username/password/sensitive data.

Social engineering is easy to do, even with all of today's technology at our disposal. Education is the one key that can help.

Don't overlook the most common personal motivator of all: greed. It may surprise you, but people can be bribed to give away information. If someone gives out the keys, you won't necessarily know it has occurred. Those keys can be literal—as in the keys to the back door—or figurative—the keys to decrypt messages.

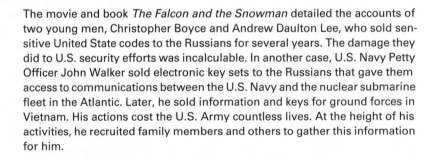

The movie and book *The Falcon and the Snowman* detailed the accounts of two young men, Christopher Boyce and Andrew Daulton Lee, who sold sensitive United State codes to the Russians for several years. The damage they did to U.S. security efforts was incalculable. In another case, U.S. Navy Petty Officer John Walker sold electronic key sets to the Russians that gave them access to communications between the U.S. Navy and the nuclear submarine fleet in the Atlantic. Later, he sold information and keys for ground forces in Vietnam. His actions cost the U.S. Army countless lives. At the height of his activities, he recruited family members and others to gather this information for him.

It is often comforting to think that we cannot be bought. We look to our morals and standards and think that we are above being bribed. The truth of the matter, though, is that almost everyone has a price. Your price may be so high that for all practical purposes you don't have a price that anyone in the market would pay, but can the same be said for the other administrators in your company?

Social engineering can have a hugely damaging effect on a security system, as the previous note illustrates.

Recognizing Common Attacks

Most attacks are designed to exploit potential weaknesses. Those weaknesses can be in the implementation of programs or in the protocols used in networks. Many types of attacks require a high level of sophistication and are rare. You need to know about them so that you can identify what has happened in your network.

In this section, we'll look at these attacks more closely.

Back Door Attacks

The term *back door attack* can have two meanings. The original term *back door* referred to troubleshooting and developer hooks into systems. During the development of a complicated operating system or application, programmers add back doors or maintenance hooks. These back doors allow them to examine operations inside the code while the code is running. The back doors are stripped out of the code when it's moved to production. When a software manufacturer discovers a hook that hasn't been removed, it releases a maintenance upgrade or patch to close the back door. These patches are common when a new product is initially released.

The second type of back door refers to gaining access to a network and inserting a program or utility that creates an entrance for an attacker. The program may allow a certain user ID to log on without a password or to gain administrative privileges.

Such an attack is usually used as either an access or modification attack. A number of tools exist to create back door attacks on systems. One of the more popular tools is Back Orifice, which has been updated to work with Windows Server 2003 as well as earlier versions. Another popular back door program is NetBus. Fortunately, most conventional antivirus software will detect and block these types of attacks.

 Back Orifice and NetBus are remote administration tools used by attackers to take control of Windows-based systems. These packages are typically installed by using a Trojan horse program. Back Orifice and NetBus allow a remote user to take full control of systems that have these applications installed. Back Orifice and NetBus run on all of the current Windows operating systems.

Spoofing Attacks

A *spoofing attack* is an attempt by someone or something to masquerade as someone else. This type of attack is usually considered an access attack. A common spoofing attack that was popular for many years on early Unix and other time-sharing systems involved a programmer writing a fake logon program. This program would prompt the user for a user ID and password. No matter what the user typed, the program would indicate an invalid logon attempt and then transfer control to the real logon program. The spoofing program would write the logon and password into a disk file, which was retrieved later.

The most popular spoofing attacks today are IP spoofing and DNS spoofing. With *IP spoofing*, the goal is to make the data look as if it came from a trusted host when it didn't (thus spoofing the IP address of the sending host). With *DNS spoofing*, the DNS server is given information about a name server that it thinks is legitimate when it isn't. This can send users to a website other than the one they wanted to go to, reroute mail, or do any other type of redirection wherein data from a DNS server is used to determine a destination.

 Always think of spoofing as fooling. Attackers are trying to fool the user, system, and/or host into believing that they're something they aren't. Since the word *spoof* can describe any false information at any level, spoofing can occur at any level of a network.

The important point to remember is that a spoofing attack tricks something or someone into thinking something legitimate is occurring.

Man-in-the-Middle Attacks

Man-in-the-middle attacks tend to be fairly sophisticated. This type of attack is also an access attack, but it can be used as the starting point for a modification attack. The method used in these attacks clandestinely places a piece of software between a server and the user that neither the server administrators nor the user are aware of. This software intercepts data and then sends the information to the server as if nothing were wrong. The server responds back to the software, thinking it's communicating with the legitimate client. The attacking software continues sending information on to the server, and so forth.

If communication between the server and user continues, what's the harm of the software? The answer lies in whatever else the software is doing. The man-in-the-middle software may be recording information for someone to view later or altering it, or in some other way compromising the security of your system and session.

A man-in-the-middle attack is an active attack. Something is actively intercepting the data and may or may not be altering it. If it's altering the data, the altered data masquerades as legitimate data traveling between the two hosts.

In recent years, the threat of man-in-the-middle attacks on wireless networks has increased. Because it's no longer necessary to connect to the wire, a malicious rogue can be outside the building intercepting packets, altering them, and sending them on. A common solution to this problem is to enforce Wired Equivalent Privacy (WEP) or WPA (Wi-Fi Protected Access) across the wireless network.

Replay Attacks

Replay attacks are becoming quite common. These attacks occur when information is captured over a network. Replay attacks are used for access or modification attacks. In a distributed environment, logon and password information is sent between the client and the authentication system. The attacker can capture this information and replay it again later. This can also occur with security certificates from systems such as Kerberos: The attacker resubmits the certificate, hoping to be validated by the authentication system and circumvent any time sensitivity.

If this attack is successful, the attacker will have all the rights and privileges from the original certificate. This is the primary reason that most certificates contain a unique session identifier and a time stamp: If the certificate has expired, it will be rejected, and an entry should be made in a security log to notify system administrators.

Password-Guessing Attacks

Password-guessing attacks occur when an account is attacked repeatedly. This is accomplished by sending possible passwords to the account in a systematic manner. These attacks are initially carried out to gain passwords for an access or modification attack. There are two types of password-guessing attacks:

Brute Force Attack   A *brute force attack* is an attempt to guess passwords until a successful guess occurs. This type of attack usually occurs over a long period. To make passwords more difficult to guess, they should be much longer than two or three characters (six should be the bare minimum), be complex, and have password lockout policies.

Dictionary Attack   A *dictionary attack* uses a dictionary of common words to attempt to find the user's password. Dictionary attacks can be automated, and several tools exist in the public domain to execute them.

Some systems will identify whether an account ID is valid and whether the password is wrong. Giving the attacker a clue as to a valid account name isn't a good practice. If you can enable your authentication to either accept a valid ID/password group or require the entire logon process again, you should.

Denial of Service (DoS) and Distributed DoS (DDoS) Attacks

Denial of service (DoS) attacks prevent access to resources by users authorized to use those resources. An attacker may attempt to bring down an e-commerce website to prevent or deny usage by legitimate customers. DoS attacks are common on the Internet, where they have hit large companies such as Amazon.com, Microsoft, and AT&T. These attacks are often widely publicized in the media. Most simple DoS attacks occur from a single system, and a specific server or organization is the target.

There isn't a single type of DoS attack, but a variety of similar methods that have the same purpose. It's easiest to think of a DoS attack by imagining that your servers are so busy responding to false requests that they don't have time to service legitimate requests. Not only can the servers be physically busy, but the same result can occur if the attack consumes all the available bandwidth.

🌐 Real World Scenario

Responding to an Attack...

As a security administrator, you know all about the different types of attacks that can occur, and you're familiar with the value assigned to the data on your system. Now imagine that the log files indicate that an intruder entered your system for a lengthy period last week while you were away on vacation.

The first thing you should do is make a list of questions you should begin asking to deal with the situation, using your network as a frame of reference. Some of the questions you should be thinking of include the following:

1. How can you show that a break-in really occurred?

2. How can you determine the extent of what was done during the entry?

3. How can you prevent further entry?

4. Whom should you inform in your organization?

5. What should you do next?

The most important question on the list, though, is whom you should inform in your organization. It's important to know the escalation procedures without hesitation and be able to act quickly.

Several types of attacks can occur in this category. These attacks can deny access to information, applications, systems, or communications. In a DoS attack on an application, the attack may bring down a website while the communications and systems continue to operate. A DoS attack on a system crashes the operating system (a simple reboot may restore the server to normal operation). A DoS attack against a network is designed to fill the communications channel and prevent authorized users access. A common DoS attack involves opening as many TCP sessions as possible; this type of attack is called a TCP SYN flood DoS attack.

Two of the most common types of DoS attacks are the ping of death and the buffer overflow attack. The *ping of death* crashes a system by sending *Internet Control Message Protocol* (ICMP) packets (think echoes) that are larger than the system can handle. *Buffer overflow attacks*, as the name indicates, attempt to put more data (usually long input strings) into the buffer than it can hold. Code Red, Slapper, and Slammer are all attacks that took advantage of buffer overflows, and sPing is an example of a ping of death.

A *distributed denial of service (DDoS)* attack is similar to a DoS attack. This type of attack amplifies the concepts of a DoS by using multiple computer systems to conduct the attack against a single organization. These attacks exploit the inherent weaknesses of dedicated networks such as DSL and cable. These permanently attached systems usually have little, if any, protection. An attacker can load an attack program onto dozens or even hundreds of computer systems that use DSL or cable modems. The attack program lies dormant on these computers until they get an attack signal from a master computer. This signal triggers these systems, which launch an attack simultaneously on the target network or system.

The master controller may be another unsuspecting user. The systems taking direction from the master control computer are referred to as *zombies*. These systems merely carry out the instruction they've been given by the master computer.

Remember that the difference between a DoS attack and a DDoS attack is that the latter uses multiple computers—all focused on one target.

The nasty part of this type of attack is that the machines used to carry out the attack belong to normal computer users. The attack gives no special warning to those users. When the attack is complete, the attack program may remove itself from the system or infect the unsuspecting user's computer with a virus that destroys the hard drive, thereby wiping out the evidence.

Can You Prevent Denial Attacks?

In general, there is little you can do to fully prevent DoS or DDoS attacks. Your best method of dealing with these types of attacks involves countermeasures and prevention. Many operating systems are particularly susceptible to these types of attacks. Fortunately, most operating system manufacturers have implemented updates to minimize their effects. Make sure your operating system and the applications you use are up-to-date.

TCP Attacks

TCP operates by using synchronized connections. The synchronization is vulnerable to attack; this is probably the most common attack used today. As you may recall, the synchronization, or handshake, process initiates a TCP connection. This handshake is particularly vulnerable to a DoS attack referred to as a *TCP SYN flood attack*. The protocol is also susceptible to access and modification attacks, which are briefly explained in the following sections.

TCP SYN or TCP ACK Flood Attack

The *TCP SYN flood*, also referred to as the *TCP ACK attack,* is very common. The purpose of this attack is to deny service. The attack begins as a normal TCP connection: The client and server exchange information in TCP packets.

In this attack, the client continually sends and receives the ACK packets but doesn't open the session. The server holds these sessions open, awaiting the final packet in the sequence. This causes the server to fill up the available sessions and denies other clients the ability to access the resources.

This attack is virtually unstoppable in most environments without working with upstream providers. Many newer routers can track and attempt to prevent this attack by setting limits on the length of an initial session to force sessions that don't complete to close-out. This type of attack can also be undetectable. An attacker can use an invalid IP address, and TCP won't care, because TCP will respond to any valid request presented from the IP layer.

TCP Sequence Number Attack

TCP sequence number attacks occur when an attacker takes control of one end of a TCP session. This attack is successful when the attacker kicks the attacked end off the network for the duration of the session. Each time a TCP message is sent, either the client or the server generates a sequence number. In a TCP sequence number attack, the attacker intercepts and then responds with a *sequence number* similar to the one used in the original session. This attack can either disrupt or hijack a valid session. If a valid sequence number is guessed, the attacker can place himself between the client and server.

In this case, the attacker effectively hijacks the session and gains access to the session privileges of the victim's system. The victim's system may get an error message indicating that it has been disconnected, or it may reestablish a new session. In this case, the attacker gains the connection and access to the data from the legitimate system. The attacker then has access to the privileges established by the session when it was created.

This weakness is again inherent in the TCP protocol, and little can be done to prevent it. Your major defense against this type of attack is knowing that it's occurring. Such an attack is also frequently a precursor to a targeted attack on a server or network.

TCP/IP Hijacking

TCP/IP hijacking, also called *active sniffing*, involves the attacker gaining access to a host in the network and logically disconnecting it from the network. The attacker then inserts another machine with the same IP address. This happens quickly and gives the attacker access to the session and to all the information on the original system. The server won't know that this has occurred and will respond as if the client were trusted.

TCP/IP hijacking presents the greatest danger to a network because the hijacker will probably acquire privileges and access to all the information on the server. As with a sequence number attack, there is little you can do to counter the threat. Fortunately, these attacks require fairly sophisticated software and are harder to engineer than a DoS attack, such as a TCP SYN attack.

UDP Attacks

A *UDP attack* attacks either a maintenance protocol or a UDP service in order to overload services and initiate a DoS situation. UDP attacks can also exploit UDP protocols.

One of the most popular UDP attacks is the ping of death discussed earlier in the section, "Denial of Service (DoS) and Distributed DoS (DDoS) Attacks."

UDP packets aren't connection oriented and don't require the synchronization process described in the previous section. UDP packets, however, are susceptible to interception, and UDP can be attacked. UDP, like TCP, doesn't check the validity of IP addresses. The nature of this layer is to trust the layer below it, the IP layer.

The most common UDP attacks use *UDP flooding*. UDP flooding overloads services, networks, and servers. Large streams of UDP packets are focused at a target, causing the UDP services on that host to shut down. UDP floods also overload the network bandwidth and cause a DoS situation to occur.

ICMP Attacks

ICMP attacks occur by triggering a response from the ICMP protocol when it responds to a seemingly legitimate maintenance request. From earlier discussions, you'll recall that ICMP is often associated with echoing.

ICMP supports maintenance and reporting in a TCP/IP network. It's part of the IP level of the protocol suite. Several tools, including ping, use the ICMP protocol. Until fairly recently, ICMP was regarded as a benign protocol that was incapable of much damage. However, it has now joined the ranks of common methods used in DoS attacks. Two primary methods use ICMP to disrupt systems: smurf attacks and ICMP tunneling.

Smurf Attacks

Smurf attacks are becoming common and can create havoc in a network. A smurf attack uses IP spoofing and broadcasting to send a ping to a group of hosts in a network. When a host is pinged, it sends back ICMP message traffic information indicating status to the originator. If a broadcast is sent to a network, all of the hosts will answer back to the ping. The result is an overload of the network and the target system.

The attacker sends a broadcast message with a legal IP address. In this case, the attacking system sends a ping request to the broadcast address of the network. This request is sent to all the machines in a large network. The reply is then sent to the machine identified with the ICMP request (the spoof is complete). The result is a DoS attack that consumes the network bandwidth of the replying system, while the victim system deals with the flood of ICMP traffic it receives.

Smurf attacks are very popular. The primary method of eliminating them involves prohibiting ICMP traffic through a router. If the router blocks ICMP traffic, smurf attacks from an external attacker aren't possible.

ICMP Tunneling

ICMP messages can contain data about timing and routes. A packet can be used to hold information that is different from the intended information. This allows an ICMP packet to be used as a communications channel between two systems. The channel can be used to send a Trojan horse or other malicious packet.

The countermeasure for ICMP attacks is to deny ICMP traffic through your network. You can disable ICMP traffic in most routers, and you should consider doing so in your network.

General Rules for the Exam

There are a number of general rules to adhere to, regardless of which operating systems are employed on your servers and clients. Most of these are common sense. There are various

New Attacks on the Way

The attacks described in this section aren't comprehensive. New methods are being developed as you read this book. Your first challenge in these situations is to recognize that you're fighting the battle on two fronts.

The first front involves the inherently open nature of TCP/IP and its protocol suite. TCP/IP is a robust and rich environment. This richness allows many opportunities to exploit the vulnerabilities of the protocol suite. The second front of this battle involves the implementation of TCP/IP by various vendors. A weak TCP/IP implementation will be susceptible to all forms of attacks, and there is little you'll be able to do about it except to complain to the software manufacturer. Fortunately, most of the credible manufacturers are now taking these complaints seriously and doing what they can to close the holes they have created in your systems. Keep your updates current, because this is where most of the corrections for security problems are implemented.

ways to look at these rules, but one way is to make sure that you understand each of them and would be able to justify them should you see a test question on them. Some of these topics were discussed in Chapter 9, others were discussed here, many were in both chapters, and some is new to here so read this list very carefully:

- Limit access to the operating system to only those who need it. As silly as it may sound, every user should be a user who has to access the system. This means that every user has a unique username and password and it is shared with no one else. You do not allow users to use guest accounts or admin accounts (whether your operating system calls them administrator (Windows), root (Unix), supervisor (NetWare), and so forth). The default Systems Administrator (SA) account on Microsoft's SQL Server is often targeted by hackers because it's well documented and known to them.

- Not only do you require users to have unique access, but you limit that access to only what they need access to. In other words, you start out assuming that they need access to nothing, and then back slowly off of that. It is always better to have a user who has too little permission, and you have to tweak their settings a bit, than to have one who has too much and "accidentally" deletes important files.

- Encourage users to use passwords that are difficult to guess. A long password composed of both uppercase and lowercase letters, numbers, and symbols is the most resistant to being broken.

- Trying to manage individual users becomes more of a nightmare as the size of the systems increases. For that reason, management should be done—as much as possible—by groups. Users with similar traits, job duties, and so forth are added to groups, and the groups are assigned the permissions that the users need. If a user needs access to more than what a specific group offers, you make them a member of multiple groups—you do not try to tweak their settings individually.

- All administrative tools, utilities, and so forth should be safely guarded behind secure rights and permissions. You should regularly check to see who has used such tools (see auditing later in this list) and make sure they are not being used by users who should not be able to do so.

- Control permissions to resources as granularly as possible. Know the ones that exist in your environment and how to use them effectively.

- Know the authentication possibilities for the operating systems you use and know what each allows. In addition to those that come standard with the operating system, you can also employ add-on devices such as biometric scanners to increase the security of the authentication process.

- Understand that firewalls can be software or hardware based, and are usually some combination of the two. Software-only firewalls are usually limited to home use and provide the first line of defense preventing outside users from gaining access to the home computer.

- Block as much coming in to your network as possible. This includes traffic (turn off protocols/services that you do not need) and data (do not allow in e-mail with attachments containing .SCR, .PIF, and other red-flag files).

- Event logging is used to record events and provide a trail that can be followed to determine what was done. Auditing involves looking at the logs and finding problems.

- Wireless clients can be configured to access the network in the same way as wired clients, but wireless security is a touchy issue. There are protocols that can be used to add security, but it is still difficult to secure a wireless network in the same way that you can secure a wired one. Unused wireless connections are the same as leaving a security door open.

- Data access can be limited in a number of ways. Permissions to the data and basic local security policies are two universal ways that should be used regardless of the operating system you are employing.

- The file system you are using can determine what permissions you have available to assign to resources. NTFS offers a great deal of granularity in terms of permissions, whereas FAT32 offers very few choices. You can convert from FAT32 to NTFS, without data loss, by using the convert utility.

- To increase the level of authentication, you can employ biometrics, key fobs, and smart cards. Smart card readers may be contact based (you have to insert the card) or contactless (the card is read when it is in proximity to the reader). Key fobs are used to provide access to a resource, and may incorporate a randomly generated number that you can enter for authentication. Biometric devices identify the user by some physical aspect (such as a thumbprint).

- Typically, software-only firewalls are suitable only for home use. They protect the computer they are running on, but require resources of that computer (which could slow down the computer and other applications sharing the computer).

- Wireless networks need to be carefully configured to allow access to the legitimate clients and only the legitimate network clients.

- Data access and encryption can work together. Hopefully, you are able to limit the access to only those eyes that need to see the data, but encrypting it helps to keep it secure if it does fall into the wrong hands.

Summary

In this chapter, we covered the key elements that an information technology specialist should be familiar with as related to security. Security is a set of processes and products. In order for a security program to be effective, all of its parts must work and be coordinated by the organization.

Typically, your network will run many protocols and services. These protocols allow connections to other networks and products. However, they also create potential vulnerabilities that must be understood. You must work to find ways to minimize the vulnerabilities. Many protocols and services offered by modern operating systems are highly vulnerable to attack. New methods of attacking these systems are developed every day.

Exam Essentials

Know the purpose and characteristics of access control.   The purpose of access control is to limit who can access what resources on a system. The characteristics are dependent on the type of implementation utilized. You should always harden your systems to make them as secure as possible.

Know the purpose and characteristics of auditing and logging.   Log files are created to hold entries about the operations that take place on the system. Auditing entails selecting which security events are logged and viewing those log files. There is often a fair amount of granularity in choosing what you want to allow into a log and what you do not; the danger in recording too much information is that it can overwhelm you when you then examine it.

Know the concepts of data security.   You should know that it is imperative to keep the system up-to-date and to install all relevant upgrades as they become available. You should also understand the importance of using a secure file system.

Diagnose and troubleshoot software and data security issues.   It is important to know the reason why policies exist and the types of possibilities they offer to an administrator. What were once called System Policies have now become Group Policies in the Microsoft world, and they can allow you to lock down workstations and prevent users from making changes that you do not want to them to be able to make.

Know how social engineering works.   Social engineering is the process by which intruders gain access to your facilities, your network, and even to your employees by exploiting the generally trusting nature of people.

Review Questions

1. Which of the following terms refers to the prevention of unauthorized disclosure of keys?

    A. Authentication

    B. Integrity

    C. Access control

    D. Nonrepudiation

2. Which of the following is a hacker's favorite target account on any network operating system?

    A. Ordinary user account

    B. Default administrator account

    C. Temporary user account

    D. Print operators

3. You're in the process of securing the IT infrastructure by using authentication methods. The methods you intend to implement include cameras, smart cards, biometric devices, and security personnel to protect access to locked rooms that contain network equipment and servers. This type of security is an example of which of the following? (Choose all that apply.)

    A. Access control

    B. Physical barriers

    C. Biometrics

    D. Softening

4. Which file extension should *not* be allowed with an e-mail attachment?

    A. .DOC

    B. .SCR

    C. .TXT

    D. .XLS

5. An application running on a network operating system (NOS) with a directory service can use NOS authentication or NOS authentication combined with application internal authentication. Removing the option to use the internal authentication would normally be considered a security improvement. What is this security measure called?

    A. Operating system hardening

    B. Application hardening

    C. Device hardening

    D. Network operating system hardening

6. Which account do attackers most often target on Unix network operating systems?

    A. Root

    B. Administrator

    C. Supervisor

    D. SA

7. Which account do attackers often target on a database application?

    A. Root

    B. Administrator/Systems

    C. Supervisor

    D. Database local account

8. Complex passwords are recommended for security. Which of the following passwords would be the most resistant to brute force, dictionary, and guessing attacks?

    A. Gigabitx

    B. Gigabit

    C. 1W3s&7yZ1

    D. 7891

9. Your company is creating a security policy that includes plans to distribute information and educate employees about who is authorized to discuss information related to information systems and data, what they can discuss, and when and how it's appropriate. What type of attack should the policy be effective against?

    A. Mathematical attack

    B. DDoS attack

    C. Worm attack

    D. Social engineering attack

10. Which file extension should *not* be allowed with an e-mail attachment?

    A. .DOC

    B. .PIF

    C. .TXT

    D. .XLS

11. Which type of attack denies authorized users access to network resources?

    A. DoS

    B. Worm

    C. Logic bomb

    D. Social engineering

12. As the security administrator for your organization, you must be aware of all types of attacks that can occur and plan for them. Which type of attack uses more than one computer to attack the victim?

    A. DoS

    B. DDoS

    C. Worm

    D. UDP attack

13. A server in your network has a program running on it that bypasses authentication. Which type of attack has occurred?

    A. DoS

    B. DDoS

    C. Back door

    D. Social engineering

14. An administrator at a sister company calls to report a new threat that is making the rounds. According to him, the latest danger is an attack that attempts to intervene in a communications session by inserting a computer between the two systems that are communicating. Which of the following types of attacks does this constitute?

    A. Man-in-the-middle attack

    B. Back door attack

    C. Worm

    D. TCP/IP hijacking

15. You've discovered that an expired certificate is being used repeatedly to gain logon privileges. Which type of attack is this most likely to be?

    A. Man-in-the-middle attack

    B. Back door attack

    C. Replay attack

    D. TCP/IP hijacking

16. A junior administrator comes to you in a panic. After looking at the log files, he has become convinced that an attacker is attempting to use an IP address to replace another system in the network to gain access. Which type of attack is this?

    A. Man-in-the-middle attack

    B. Back door attack

    C. Worm

    D. TCP/IP hijacking

17. A server on your network will no longer accept connections using the TCP protocol. The server indicates that it has exceeded its session limit. Which type of attack is probably occurring?

    A. TCP ACK attack

    B. Smurf attack

    C. Virus attack

    D. TCP/IP hijacking

18. A smurf attack attempts to use a broadcast ping on a network; the return address of the ping may be a valid system in your network. Which protocol does a smurf attack use to conduct the attack?

    A. TCP

    B. IP

    C. UDP

    D. ICMP

19. Your system log files report an ongoing attempt to gain access to a single account. This attempt has been unsuccessful to this point. What type of attack are you most likely experiencing?

    A. Password-guessing attack

    B. Back door attack

    C. Worm attack

    D. TCP/IP hijacking

20. A user reports that she is receiving an error indicating that her TCP/IP address is already in use when she turns on her computer. A static IP address has been assigned to this user's computer, and you're certain this address was not inadvertently assigned to another computer. Which type of attack is most likely underway?

    A. Man-in-the-middle attack

    B. Back door attack

    C. Worm

    D. TCP/IP hijacking

Answers to Review Questions

1. C. *Access control* refers to the process of ensuring that sensitive keys aren't divulged to unauthorized personnel.

2. B. The default administrator account is a favorite target of hackers on any network operating system.

3. A, B, C. Some of the technologies used for physical access are equally applicable to computer access. When these are combined, you achieve the highest levels of security.

4. B. The .SCR extension is used for screen savers. Screen savers, as executables, actually have the ability to do nasty things, such as lock the screen, and can wreak havoc.

5. B. The described security measure is called application hardening.

6. A. The root account is a target on Unix networks because this account exists in every implementation and is well known to hackers.

7. D. The database local account is known to exist in almost every database application and is thus a target for hackers.

8. C. A long password composed of both uppercase and lowercase letters, numbers, and symbols is the most resistant to being broken.

9. D. During a social engineering attack, an attacker might pretend to be a company technician, call an employee, and ask her to reveal her username and password. Knowing what to say and what not to say will go a long way toward preventing this type of attack from being successful.

10. B. The .PIF extension is used for Program Information Files—a type of file that allows legacy executable programs to run.

11. A. Although the end result of any of these attacks may result in denying authorized users access to network resources, a DoS attack is specifically intended to prevent access to network resources by overwhelming or flooding a service or network.

12. B. A DDoS attack uses multiple computer systems to attack a server or host in the network.

13. C. In a back door attack, a program or service is placed on a server to bypass normal security procedures.

14. D.

15. C. A replay attack attempts to replay the results of a previously successful session to gain access.

16. D. TCP/IP hijacking is an attempt to steal a valid IP address and use it to gain authorization or information from a network.

17. A. A TCP ACK attack creates multiple incomplete sessions. Eventually, the TCP protocol hits a limit and refuses additional connections.

18. D. A smurf attack attempts to use a broadcast ping (ICMP) on a network. The return address of the ping may be a valid system in your network. This system will be flooded with responses in a large network.

19. A. A password-guessing attack occurs when a user account is repeatedly attacked using a variety of different passwords.

20. D. One of the symptoms of a TCP/IP hijacking attack may be the unavailability of a TCP/IP address when the system is started.

Glossary

802.11b   A wireless standard that provides wireless speeds up to 11Mbps.

802.11g   A wireless standard that is backward compatible with 802.11b, and provides data transmission of up to 54Mbps.

802.3   An IEEE standard that defines a bus topology network that uses a 50-ohm coaxial baseband cable and carries transmissions at 10Mbps. This standard groups data bits into frames and uses the Carrier Sense Multiple Access with Collision Detection (CSMA/CD) cable access method to put data on the cable.

A (Address) record   DNS record that holds the IP address of the name.

AC adapter   The adapter for AC current that connects to the wall outlet.

Accelerated Graphics Port (AGP)   A bus developed to meet the need for increased graphics performance.

access point (AP)   The device that allows wireless devices to talk to each other and the network. It provides the functions of network access as well as security monitoring.

accessory bay   Also called media bays, these external bays allow you to plug your full-sized devices into them and take your laptop with you (e.g., a full-size hard drive that connects to an external USB or FireWire port).

accountability   Being held accountable for an item or entity.

active hub   A type of hub that uses electronics to amplify and clean up the signal before it is broadcast to the other ports.

active partition   The partition from which an operating system boots.

adapter card   A daughter card that extends the capabilities of the motherboard.

Advanced Configuration and Power Interface (ACPI)   A standard that defines common interfaces for hardware recognition and configuration, and more importantly, power management.

answer file   In an unattended installation, this file contains all of the correct parameters (time zone, regional settings, administrator user name, and so on), needed for installation.

AppleTalk   A proprietary network protocol for Macintosh computers.

aspect ratio   Gives a proportion of how wide the screen is versus how tall it is (specifically, it's the image width divided by image height). Basically, it's another way of looking at resolution.

AT system connector   The power-supply connector pair for the AT motherboard often marked P8 and P9 that was used in the original IBM PC but is now associated by name with the PC/AT.

Attached Resource Computer Network (ARCNet)   A network technology that uses a physical star, logical ring and token passing access method. It is typically wired with coaxial cable. It was developed in 1977 for IBM mainframe networks.

attended installation   An installation where a user is required to provide answers to options during the installation process.

ATX motherboard   A smaller successor to the AT motherboard that uses space more wisely and places related components closer together.

ATX system connector   The single, larger power-supply connector that powers the ATX motherboard.

authentication   A process that proves that a user or system is actually who they say they are.

Automated System Recovery (ASR)   ASR first creates a backup of your system partition and then creates a recovery disk. Using these two components, you can recover from a system crash and restore the system to a functional state.

autorun   When a compact disc automatically begins its program when it's inserted into the computer.

baby AT   A form factor that denotes AT compatibility but in a smaller size.

backside bus   A set of signal pathways between the CPU and Level 2 cache memory.

backup   A copy of files stored in a location other than where they originally came from.

backlight   A small fluorescent lamp placed behind, above, or to the side of an LCD display.

bandwidth   In communications, the difference between the highest and the lowest frequencies available for transmission in any given range. In networking, the transmission capacity of a computer or a communications channel stated in megabits or megabytes per second; the higher the number, the faster the data transmission takes place.

Basic Rate Interface (BRI)   An ISDN line with two B channels: one for a voice call and one for data transmissions.

basis weight   A measurement of the "heaviness" of paper. The number is the weight, in pounds, of 500 17″× 22″ sheets of that type of paper.

Bearer, or B, channel   The ISDN channel that carries 64Kbps of data.

Berg connectors   The official name for the smaller peripheral power-supply connectors that most often attach to floppy disk drives.

bidirectional   A satellite connection wherein the satellite is used for both uploads and downloads.

biometric devices   Devices that use physical characteristics to identify the user.

blue screen of death (BSOD)   The blue-screen error condition that occurs when Windows 2000/XP fails to boot properly or quits unexpectedly.

Bluetooth   A popular standard for wireless communication.

Bluetooth Special Interest Group (SIG)   The consortium of companies that developed the Bluetooth technology.

BNC   A type of connector used to attach stations to a Thinnet network.

bonding   Combining two bearer channels into one 128Kbps data connection to maximize throughput.

boot logging   Logs all boot information to a file called NTBTLOG.TXT. You can then check the log for assistance in diagnosing system startup problems.

boot ROM   A piece of hardware (often built into a network card) that is capable of downloading a small file that contains enough information to boot the computer and attach it to the network.

bridge   A type of connectivity device that operates in the Data Link layer of the OSI model. It is used to join similar topologies (Ethernet to Ethernet, Token Ring to Token Ring) and to divide traffic on network segments. This device passes information destined for one particular workstation to that segment, but it does not pass broadcast traffic.

broadband   The general designation for higher-speed Internet connections.

broadcast   To send a signal to all entities that can listen to it. In networking, it refers to sending a signal to all entities connected to that network.

brouter   In networking, a device that combines the attributes of a bridge and a router. A brouter can route one or more specific protocols, such as TCP/IP, and bridge all others.

bubble-jet printer   A type of sprayed-ink printer. It uses an electric signal that energizes a heating element, causing ink to vaporize and be pushed out of the pinhole and onto the paper.

cable   A conductive metallic or optical fiber sheathed assembly used to transmit data between electronic devices.

cable access methods   Methods by which stations on a network get permission to transmit their data.

cable Internet   Internet access across a common cable television service.

calibration   The process by which a device such as a printer or a scanner is brought within functional specifications.

caliper   The thickness measurement of a given sheet of paper, which can affect a printer's feed mechanism.

carriage belt   The printer belt placed around two small wheels or pulleys and attached to the printhead carriage. The carriage belt is driven by the carriage motor and moves the printhead back and forth across the page during printing.

carriage motor   A stepper motor used to move the printhead back and forth on a dot-matrix printer.

carriage stepper motor   The printer motor that makes the printhead carriage move.

case   The external container for the system.

case frame   The metal reinforcing structure inside the laptop that provides rigidity and strength and that most components mount to.

cell   A cellular phone network.

central processing unit (CPU)   The microprocessor chip that gives a computer its fundamental characteristics.

centralized processing   A network processing scheme in which all "intelligence" is found in one computer and all other computers send requests to the central computer to be processed. Mainframe networks use centralized processing.

certificates   A common form of authentication.

Challenge Handshake Authentication Protocol (CHAP)   An authentication protocol that challenges a system to verify identity.

characters per second (cps)   A rating of how fast dot-matrix printers can produce output.

charge coupled device (CCD) array   A matrix of photosensitive capacitors arranged so that one capacitor charges its neighbor, resulting in a representative sample for a row of capacitors. CCD arrays are used as photoreceptors in scanners and digital photographic equipment.

charging corona   The wire or roller that is used to put a uniform charge on the EP drum inside a toner cartridge.

charging step   The step in EP printing at which a special wire in the toner cartridge gets a high voltage from the HVPS. It uses this high voltage to apply a strong, uniform negative charge (around −600VDC) to the surface of the photosensitive drum.

chipset   A small group of larger chips that takes the place of a large number of earlier chips to perform a similar function.

clamshell design   A popular design for laptops.

cleaning cycle   A set of steps the bubble-jet printer goes through in order to purge the printheads of any dried ink.

cleaning step   The step in the EP print process at which excess toner is scraped from the EP drum with a rubber blade.

client computer   A computer that requests resources from a network.

client software   Software that allows a device to request resources from a network.

CMOS battery   The battery that maintains without external power the contents of the special memory chip that holds the alterations made to the BIOS settings.

CNAME (Canonical Name) record   DNS record that is an alias field allowing you to specify more than one name for each TCP/IP address

coaxial cable   A medium for connecting computer components that contains a center conductor, made of copper, surrounded by a plastic jacket, with a braided shield over the jacket.

Code Division Multiple Access (CDMA)   A cellular standard of Qualcomm. It allows for multiple transmissions to occur at the same time without interference.

collision   When two or more stations transmit onto a shared medium simultaneously, invalidating the data sent from each station.

collision light   The LED on a network device that indicates the detection of a collision.

communication network riser (CNR)   Sixty-pin slots found on some Intel motherboards that are a replacement for AMR slots. Using CNR slots, a motherboard manufacturer can implement a motherboard with certain integrated features and leave room for future expansion.

compact disc-recordable (CD-R) and compact disc-rewritable (CD-RW) drives   Compact disc drives with the capability to "burn" contents to specially manufactured discs.

compact installation   Also known as a minimal installation, it installs only the files necessary to run Windows.

compression   A feature in Windows 2000 and XP that gives you the option of compressing existing files in a particular folder. If the feature is turned on, Windows 2000 and XP automatically compress the subfolders and files. If not, only new files created in the directory are compressed.

computer name   The name by which a computer will be known if it participates on a network.

confidentiality   Keeping data secret.

connectivity device   Any device that facilitates connections between network devices. Some examples include hubs, routers, switches, and gateways.

contact image sensor (CIS)   A technology capable of replacing CCDs in scanning devices. Unlike CCD-based scanning, CIS-based imaging places the array of sensors in close proximity to the object being scanned, not using mirrors.

contention   Competition between two or more devices for the same bandwidth.

contrast ratio   The measure of the ratio between the lightest color and the darkest color the screen is capable of producing.

corona roller   A type of transfer corona assembly that uses a charged roller to apply charge to the paper.

corona wire   A type of transfer corona assembly. Also, the wire in that assembly that is charged by the high-voltage supply. It is narrow in diameter and located in a special notch under the EP print cartridge.

custom installation   An installation method where the user gets to choose which components are installed.

cyan, magenta, yellow, and black (CMYK)   The four colors typically used by color printers to create images. Depending on the printer model, there will be up to four separate cartridges. Other printers will combine cyan, magenta, and yellow into one cartridge.

D-subminiature connectors   Known as D-sub connectors, a series of D-shaped connector shells with a variety of pin counts and used to connect external peripherals to the computer system.

daisy-wheel printer   An impact printer that uses a plastic or metal print mechanism with a different character on the end of each spoke of the wheel. As the print mechanism rotates to the correct letter, a small hammer strikes the character against the ribbon, transferring the image onto the paper.

Data Over Cable Service Internet Specification (DOCSIS)   The standard used by most cable systems for transmitting Internet traffic to a subscriber via television cable.

daughterboard   Any circuit board connected to the motherboard.

DC adapter   The adapter which provides DC current to the laptop.

de facto   Latin translation for "by fact." Any standard that is a standard because everyone is using it.

de jure   Latin translation for "by law." Any standard that is a standard because a standards body decided it should be so.

dedicated server   The server that is assigned to perform a specific application or service.

defragmenting   Reorganizing files on a hard disk so they are in consecutive order.

delay   An impedance to the flow of a signal that causes the moment of transmission by the source to be earlier than the moment of receipt by the destination.

Delta channel   The signaling channel of an ISDN circuit also referred to as the D channel. Contrast with Bearer channel or B channel.

Denial of Service (DoS) attacks   Attacks that prevent access to resources by users authorized to use those resources.

developing roller   The roller inside a toner cartridge that presents a uniform line of toner to help apply the toner to the image written on the EP drum.

developing step   The step in the EP print process at which the image written on the EP drum by the laser is developed—that is, it has toner stuck to it.

device driver   A software file that allows an operating system to communicate with a hardware device. Also called a driver.

dialer   A special program for dial-up networking that initiates the connection with the ISP, takes the phone off hook, dials the ISP's access number, and establishes the connection.

dial-up   An Internet connection wherein the computer connecting to the Internet uses a modem to connect to the ISP over a standard telephone line.

Digital Subscriber Line (DSL)   A broadband Internet access technology that uses the existing phone line from your home to the phone company to carry digital signals at higher speeds.

digitally signed driver   A driver that has been digitally "signed" by Microsoft with a special value that only Windows can read. This signature tells the Windows installer that the driver being installed has been tested for security and stability on the chosen Windows platform and that the driver is from a reputable source.

DIMM   See *Dual Inline Memory Module.*

direct-solder method   A method of connecting a peripheral port by directly soldering individual ports to the motherboard. This method is used mostly in integrated motherboards in non-clone machines.

disk cache   A small amount of memory that is used to hold data that is frequently accessed from the hard disk.

diskette   One of variously sized magnetic-coated Mylar disks packaged in a square protective cover.

distributed processing   A computer system in which processing is performed by several separate computers linked by a communications network. The term often refers to any computer system supported by a network, but more properly refers to a system in which each computer is chosen to handle a specific workload and the network supports the system as a whole.

DIX Ethernet   The original name for the Ethernet network technology. Named after the original developer companies: Digital, Intel, and Xerox.

docking port   A port used to connect the laptop to a special laptop.

docking station   An extension of the motherboard of a laptop.

dot-matrix printer   An impact printer that has a printhead containing a row of pins (short, sturdy stalks of hard wire) that are used to strike the ink ribbon to create an image.

dot phosphor   The phosphorescent chemical dots that coat the back of a CRT monitor's screen. Electron beams excite these dots and cause them to glow.

dot pitch   The average measurement between two dot phosphors on a CRT screen. The smaller the dot pitch, the better the picture quality.

drive interfaces   The connectors and related technology used to attach drives and similar devices to adapters or the motherboard. Examples include ATA, SCSI, and ESDI.

driver   A software file that allows an operating system to communicate with a hardware device. Also called a device driver.

DSL endpoint   The device used to access DSL, commonly referred to mistakenly as a DSL modem.

dual-boot configuration   A computer that has more than one operating system installed. During boot, the user can choose which operating system to start.

Dual Inline Memory Modules (DIMMs)   Memory sticks that install in slots on motherboards and specialty devices to act as primary memory in service of the CPU. DIMMs are so named for the fact that the pins on each side of the module are independent of one another. Contrast with Single Inline Memory Modules (SIMMs).

dye-sublimation printer   A printer that uses heat to diffuse solid dyes onto the printing surface as a gas that resolidifies without ever going through a liquid state.

electron gun   The device that shoot a beam of electrons at the back of a CRT screen to illuminate the dot phosphors, thus producing an image on the front of the screen.

electromagnetic interference (EMI)   Any electromagnetic radiation released by an electronic device that disrupts the operation or performance of any other device.

electronic stepper motor   A special electric motor in a printer that can accurately move in very small increments. It powers all of the paper transport rollers as well as the fuser rollers.

emergency repair disk (ERD)   A disk that contains backup copies of portions of your Registry. It can be used to recover the system in the event of an operating system failure.

enhanced capabilities port (ECP)   A printer or parallel port setting that allows bidirectional communications and can be used with newer inkjet and laser printers, scanners, and other peripheral devices. Along with EPP, ECP is one of the two IEEE 1284 standards.

enhanced parallel port (EPP)   A high-speed bidirectional parallel port specification for nonprinter devices. Along with ECP, EPP is one of the two IEEE 1284 standards.

envelope feeder   A special device for feeding envelopes into a printer.

environment variable   A setting that stays permanent throughout a Windows or DOS session.

Ethernet   A network technology based on the IEEE 802.3 CSMA/CD standard. The original Ethernet implementation specified 10MBps, baseband signaling, coaxial cable, and CSMA/CD media access.

Ethernet port   A LAN interface that follows the Ethernet standard. Ethernet ports can be the most popular eight-pin modular connector, referred to as an RJ-45, or it can be a fiber or coaxial interface. The Ethernet port is found on the NIC in a computer system.

expansion card   A daughter card that expands the capabilities of a motherboard. Also known as an adapter card.

expansion slots   Slots on a motherboard to receive expansion cards. Expansion cards and slots must be of the same type, PCI, PCIe, or AGP, for example.

Extended Graphics Array (XGA)   Introduced in 1990 by IBM, this is often thought of as a synonym for the 1024×768.

fax modem   An adapter that fits into a PC expansion slot and provides many of the capabilities of a full-sized fax machine, but at a fraction of the cost.

feed roller   The rubber roller in a laser printer that feeds the paper into the printer.

feeder   A device that feeds paper or other media into a printer.

File Allocation Table (FAT) 16   An acronym for the file on this filesystem used to keep track of where files are. Many OSs have built their filesystem on the design of FAT, but without its limitations. A FAT filesystem uses the *8.3 naming convention* (eight letters for the name, a period, and then a three-letter file identifier). This later became known as *FAT16* (to differentiate it from FAT32) because it used a 16-bit binary number to hold cluster-numbering information. Because of that number, the largest FAT disk partition that could be created was approximately 2GB.

file locking   A feature of many network operating systems that "locks" a file to prevent more than one person from updating the file at the same time.

file permissions   These serve the purpose of controlling who has access and what type of access to what files or objects they have.

Files and Settings Transfer Wizard   A Windows XP utility that transfers files and individual application settings from an old computer to a new one.

finger mouse   A type of pointing device.

finisher   A device on a printer that performs such final functions as folding, stapling, hole punching, sorting, or collating the documents being printed.

FireWire   A trade name for IEEE 1394, FireWire is a competing standard of USB.

firmware   Software encoded on hardware. The BIOS routine and its chip is an example of firmware.

flatbed scanner   An optical device that can be used to digitize a whole page or a large image.

floppy disk   See *diskette*.

floppy drive   The hardware device that reads and writes to a floppy disk.

floppy drive interfaces   The drive interface for the floppy subsystem, which consists of 34 pins and is not compatible with the various hard drive interfaces.

floppy drive power connectors   See *Berg connectors*.

font   The typestyle used for printing a document. The font can be loaded onto the hard drive of the computer or the onboard memory of the printer.

format   To prepare a volume to receive files and folders by defining the file structure

formatting   The process of preparing the partition to store data in a particular fashion.

frame   The Data Link layer product that includes a portion of the original user data, upper-layer headers, and the Data Link header and trailer.

frontside bus   A set of signal pathways between the CPU and main memory.

full AT   The original AT form factor, which was followed by the baby AT form factor.

full-duplex communication   Communications where both entities can send and receive simultaneously.

full installation   An installation method that installs every component, even those that may not be required or used frequently.

fuser   A device on an EP printer that uses two rollers to heat the toner particles and melt them to the paper. The fuser is made up of a halogen heating lamp, a Teflon-coated aluminum fusing roller, and a rubberized pressure roller. The lamp heats the aluminum roller. As the paper passes between the two rollers, the rubber roller presses the paper against the heated roller. This causes the toner to melt and become a permanent image on the paper.

fusing step   The step in the EP printing process during which the toner image on the paper is fused to the paper using heat and pressure. The heat melts the toner, and the pressure helps fuse the image permanently to the paper.

game port   A DA15F interface designed for joysticks and other game controllers.

gateway   In networking, a shared connection between a local area network and a larger system, such as a mainframe computer or a large packet-switching network. Usually slower than a bridge or router, a gateway typically has its own processor and memory and can perform protocol conversions. Protocol conversion allows a gateway to connect two dissimilar networks; data is converted and reformatted before it is forwarded to the new network.

general protection fault (GPF)   A general protection fault (GPF) happens in Windows when a program accesses memory that another program is using or when a program accesses a memory address that doesn't exist.

glass plate   The surface of a scanner bed on which you place the original to be scanned.

global states   The various states that a computer is capable of working in.

Global System for Mobile Communications (GSM)   The most popular cellular standard. It uses a variety of bands to transmit. The most popular are 900 MHz and 1800 MHz, but 400, 450, and 850 MHz are also used.

graphics mode   As opposed to text mode, graphics mode displays shapes and images not based on text characters.

half-duplex communication   Communications that occur when only one entity can transmit or receive at any one instant.

handheld PC (HPC)   Shrunken laptops that run an operating system known as Windows Mobile.

handheld scanner   A type of scanner that is small enough to be held in your hand. Used to digitize a relatively small image or artwork, it consists of the controller, CCD, and light source contained in a small enclosure with wheels on it.

hard disk interfaces   Examples of drive interfaces.

hardening   The process of reducing or eliminating weaknesses, securing services, and attempting to make your environment immune to attacks.

Hardware Compatibility List (HCL)   A list of all the hardware that works with Windows and which versions of Windows it works with.

header   Information attached to the beginning of a network data frame.

heat spreaders   Metal covers for memory modules that act as heat sinks.

hermaphroditic data connector   A connector that is both male and female.

hibernation   A state that laptops are capable of entering in.

high-voltage probe   A tool with a very large needle, a gauge that indicates volts, and a wire with an alligator clip used to discharge electricity from electronic devices.

HINFO (Host Info) record   DNS record that actually specifies the TCP/IP address for a specified host.

home computer   In Remote Desktop, the home computer is the one you are sitting at, and the computer that makes the connection to the remote computer.

hostname   Computer name on a network.

hub   A connectivity device used to link several computers together into a physical star topology. A hub repeats any signal that comes in on one port and copies it to the other ports.

I/O memory   Standard memory locations attributed to devices connected through expansion buses and accessed by the I/O signal of the I/O_MEM line from the processor to the memory controller

IBM data connector (IDC)   A unique, hermaphroditic connector commonly used with IBM's Token Ring technology and Type 1 or 2 STP cable.

illegal operation error   An illegal operation error usually means that a program was forced to quit because it did something Windows didn't like.

image   An exact replica of an installed computer, used to install an operating system on other computers.

impact printers   Any printer that forms an image on paper by forcing a character image against an inked ribbon. Dot-matrix, daisy-wheel, and line printers are all impact printers, whereas laser printers are not.

Industry Standard Architecture (ISA) expansion slot   An old, nearly obsolete type of expansion slot in a motherboard.

Infrared Data Association (IrDA) standard   A personal area network (PAN) standard for the exchange of data over short distances using infrared light.

infrared port   A serial port that uses line-of-sight to attach to another infrared port for the exchange of data using IrDA.

infrared transmissions   Wireless transmission between devices that use radiation in the infrared range of the electromagnetic spectrum.

ink cartridge   A reservoir of ink and a printhead, in a removable package.

inoculating   Making the computer resistant to computer viruses.

Integrated Services Digital Network (ISDN)   A worldwide digital communications network emerging from existing telephone services, intended to replace all current systems with a completely digital transmission system. Computers and other devices connect to ISDN via simple, standardized interfaces, and when complete, ISDN systems will be capable of transmitting voice, video, music, and data.

integrated system board   A motherboard with components built in, reducing the need for a large number of expansion cards.

interface   The port or connection through which a device attaches to an external component, such as a printer's parallel or USB port for connection to a computer, as well as the software that enables the port to communicate with the external component, such as a Windows XP driver for an HP LaserJet.

interface circuitry   Circuitry that converts the signals from the interface into the datastream that the printer or other device uses.

interface software   The operating system-specific driver that enable communication between the computer and a peripheral.

interlaced   A video standard that scans alternate lines on the monitor with each pass, effectively halving the nominal refresh rate. Contrast with progressive.

Internet Control Message Protocol (ICMP)   An element of the TCP/IP protocol suite that transmits error messages and network statistics.

Internet Protocol (IP)   The underlying communications protocol on which the Internet is based. IP allows a data packet to travel across many networks before reaching its final destination.

Internet service providers (ISP)   A company that provides Internet access and e-mail addresses for users. Generally, ISPs are local or regional companies.

internetwork   Any TCP/IP network that spans router interfaces. Anything from a small office with two subnets to the Internet itself can be described as an internetwork.

Internetwork Packet Exchange/Sequenced Packet Exchange (IPX/SPX)   The default communication protocol for versions of the Novell NetWare operating system before NetWare 5. IPX and SPX correspond loosely to IP and TCP, respectively, in the TCP/IP protocol suite.

inverse multiplexing   See *bonding*.

inverter   A a small circuit board installed behind the LCD panel that takes AC power and converts (inverts) it for the backlight.

IPX network address   An eight-digit hexadecimal number used by IPX addresses for the network portion. This number can be assigned randomly by the installation program or manually by the network administrator.

ISDN terminal adapter   The device that connects a computer to an ISDN line.

IT8 scanner target   A test pattern that can be scanned in, and then the color on the screen can be corrected for variations in color.

joystick port   See *game port*.

Kerberos   An authentication protocol designed by MIT that allows for a single sign-on to a distributed network.

keyboard/mouse port   The port that the keyboard or mouse connects to.

laser printer   A generic name for a printer that uses the electrophotographic (EP) print process.

Last Known Good Configuration   An advanced boot option that lets you restore the system to a prior, functional state, which will allow you to log in again.

letter quality (LQ)   A category of dot-matrix printer that can print characters that look very close to the quality a laser printer might produce.

liquid cooling   The use of a circulating liquid, such as water, to dissipate heat.

local area networks (LAN)   A group of computers and associated peripherals connected by a communications channel, capable of sharing files and other resources among several users.

logical topology   The topology that defines how the data flows in a network.

MAC address   The unique physical address for each NIC.

main motor   A printer stepper motor that is used to advance the paper.

maintenance station   Provides a zero position for the an ink- or bubble-jet printhead and keeps the print nozzles clear between print jobs.

master computer   In sysprep, the master computer is the one that is used to make an image.

Material Safety Data Sheet (MSDS)   A document that contains safety information about a given product. Information provided includes safe handling procedures, what to do in case of an accident, and disposal information.

mesh topology A type of logical topology in which each device on a network is connected to every other device on the network. This topology uses routers to search multiple paths and determine the best path.

MicroDIMM A 45.5mm × 30mm memory module that is over 50 percent smaller than a SoDIMM. MicroDIMMs were designed for ultralight and portable subnotebook computers and have 144 or 172 pins.

minimal installation Also known as a compact installation, it installs only the files necessary to run Windows.

Mini PCI An adaptation of the Peripheral Component Interconnect (PCI) standard used in desktop computers designed primarily for laptops.

mopiers A laser printer that includes copier-like functions (coalition, stapling, and so on), so each "copy" is essentially an original.

modem A concatenation of modulator/demodulator. Modems allow the transmission of a digital bit stream over an analog medium, such as a standard phone line.

Molex connector The larger peripheral power connector used on such devices as hard drives and CD/DVD drives.

monochrome Using a single color to display text and graphics on a screen with a contrasting background.

motherboard The main system board of a computer. Daughterboards interface with the motherboard to expand its capabilities.

multifunction printers A peripheral that is essentially a printer, copier, scanner, and fax machine all in one.

multiplexer A network device that combines multiple data streams into a single stream for transmission. Multiplexers can also break out the original data streams from a single, multiplexed stream.

multipurpose server A server that has more than one use. For example, a multipurpose server can be both a file server and a print server.

multistation access unit (MAU) The central device in a Token Ring network that provides both the physical and logical connections to the stations.

MX (Mail Exchange) record DNS record that specifies the name of the host that processes mail for this domain.

native resolution The resolution that a display will natively run in.

near letter quality (NLQ) A category of dot-matrix printer that can come close to the quality of a laser printer, but still is lacking somewhat in print quality.

NetBEUI (NetBIOS Extended User Interface)   A network device driver for the transport layer supplied with Microsoft's LAN Manager.

NetBIOS   In networking, a layer of software, originally developed in 1984 by IBM and Sytek, that links a network operating system with specific network hardware. NetBIOS provides an application program interface (API) with a consistent set of commands for requesting lower-level network services to transmit information from node to node.

NetBIOS Extended User Interface   See *NetBEUI (NetBIOS Extended User Interface)*.

network   A group of computers and associated peripherals connected by a communications channel capable of sharing files and other resources between several users. A network can range from a peer-to-peer network (which connects a small number of users in an office or department) to a local area network (which connects many users over permanently installed cables and dial-up lines) or to a wide area network (which connects users on several different networks spread over a wide geographic area).

network interface card (NIC)   In networking, the PC expansion board that plugs into a personal computer or server and works with the network operating system to control the flow of information over the network. The network interface card is connected to the network cabling (twisted-pair, coaxial, or fiber optic cable), which in turn connects all the network interface cards in the network.

network install   An installation method where the installation is performed over a network as opposed to from a device (such as a CD-ROM) attached to the computer.

nondedicated server   A computer that can be both a server and a workstation. In practice, by performing the functions of both server and workstation, this type of server does neither function very well. Nondedicated servers are typically used in peer-to-peer networks.

nonintegrated system board   A motherboard that does not have peripheral interfaces, other than keyboard and mouse, permanently attached. These features must come from expansion cards.

Northbridge   A portion of a motherboard's overall chipset that is responsible for communications with integrated video and between the processor and memory.

null modem serial cable   A serial cable that crosses signal lines so that a modem is not necessary to connect two computers directly.

NS (Name Server) record   DNS record that specifies the other name servers for the domain, or maps a domain name to that of the primary server for the zone.

NWLINK   The Microsoft version of the IPX/SPX protocol.

Occupational Safety and Health Administration (OSHA)   A United States federal agency in charge of administering the Occupational Safety and Health Act. OSHA is responsible for ensuring that employees have a safe work environment.

open access point   A wireless access point that employs no encryption or authentication, allowing any device that receives the signal potential access to the connected network.

Open Systems Interconnection (OSI)   See *OSI (Open Systems Interconnection) model.*

original   In scanning, the object being scanned.

packet   A group of bits ready for transmission over a network. It includes a header, data, and a trailer.

page-description language   Describes the whole page being printed. The controller in the printer interprets these commands and turns them into laser pulses or firing print wires.

paper-feed mechanism   The portion of the printer that picks up paper from the paper drawer and feeds it into the printer.

paper feeder   See *feeder.*

paper pickup roller   A D-shaped roller that rotates against the paper and pushes one sheet into a printer.

paper tray   The tray that holds paper until it is fed into a printer.

paper pickup roller   A D-shaped roller that rotates against the paper and pushes one sheet into a printer.

parallel interface   See *parallel port.*

parallel port   A peripheral port that is used most often for printer connection and that transfers data in parallel instead of one bit at a time.

parked   When the print head is in the locked, resting position.

partition   A logical grouping of data organized to fall under a single drive letter for primary partitions and multiple drives for extended partitions

partitioning   The process of assigning part or all of a hard drive for use by the computer.

passive hub   A type of hub that electrically connects all network ports together. This type of hub is not powered.

Password Authentication Protocol (PAP)   An authentication protocol that offers no true security, but it's one of the simplest forms of authentication. The username and password values are both sent to the server as clear text and checked for a match.

PC card   What was formerly known as PCMCIA. See *Personal Computer Memory Card International Association (PCMCIA).*

PCI Express (PCIe)   A more advanced expansion-bus standard to compete with AGP that is backward compatible with PCI.

Peripheral Component Interconnect (PCI)   Today's most popular expansion-bus standard.

peripheral interface   Any port that allows external devices to connect to the computer system.

personal computer (PC)   Any of a class of computer systems that allows a single user to perform day-to-day personal and business functions, such as word processing and networking. Also IBM's original product name for such a computer system.

Personal Computer Memory Card International Association (PCMCIA)   A standard way of expanding portable computers.

phase-change cooling   A component cooling method that uses the effect from a liquid's change of state to a gas to cool the inside of a PC.

photosites   The individual cells within a CCD array.

physical topology   A description that identifies how the cables on a network are physically arranged.

pickup rollers   See *paper pickup roller*.

pickup stepper motor   The motor that turns the pickup roller in a printer.

piconet   A Bluetooth network. A Bluetooth-enabled device can communicate with up to seven other devices in one piconet.

pins   The minute projections that terminate signal lines and, for example, appear on a male connector at the end of a cable.

pixels   Short for picture elements, pixels are the individual dots that the software projecting the image is capable of controlling. Viewable screen sizes, such as 1024×768, refer to the number of pixels in a matrix. Contrast with dot phosphors.

planar board   A synonym for motherboard that generally has no processor but instead has a modular interface for a processor card.

plenum-rated   When referring to coaxial covering, a designation that means the coating does not produce toxic gas when burned (as PVC does) and is rated for use in air plenums that carry breathable air.

Plug and Play BIOS   A BIOS that communicates with Plug and Play components to adapt to their existence without the installation of device drivers

Plug and Play (PnP)   A standard set of specifications that was developed by Intel to enable a computer to detect a new device automatically and install the appropriate driver.

port   See *interface*.

portable installation   A Windows installation method that installs components needed for portable system installations on laptops. It includes such features as power management and LCD display software.

POTS line   A Plain Old Telephone Service line, the original analog technology for phone lines still in use today for standard phone service.

power circuits   The set of conductive pathways that converts 110V or 220V house current into the voltages a bubble-jet printer uses (usually 12V and 5V) and distributes those voltages to the other printer circuits and devices that need it.

power supply   The component that converts AC wall voltages to DC voltages that other computer components require. Rated in watts, the power supply must be able to handle the demand placed on it by these components.

primary partition   The first partition created in an operating system.

Primary Rate Interface (PRI)   An ISDN interface known as 23B+D, which means it has 23 B channels and one D channel.

print buffer   A small amount of memory located on the printer used to hold print jobs.

print consumables   Products a printer uses in the print process that must be replaced occasionally. Examples include toner, ink, ribbons, and paper.

print media   Another name for the media being printed on. Examples include paper, transparencies, and labels.

printer control circuits   Runs a printer's stepper motors, loads paper, and so on. Monitors the health of the printer and reports that information back to the computer.

printer controller assembly   A large circuit board in a laser printer that converts signals from the computer into signals for the various parts in a printer.

printer-resident fonts   Fonts that are stored locally in the printer's onboard memory to speed up printing.

printer ribbon   A fabric strip that is impregnated with ink and wrapped around two spools encased in a cartridge. This cartridge is used in dot-matrix printers to provide the ink for the print process.

printhead   The part of a printer that creates the printed image. In a dot-matrix printer, the printhead contains the small pins that strike the ribbon to create the image, and in an ink-jet printer, the printhead contains the jets used to create the ink droplets as well as the ink reservoirs. A laser printer creates images using an electrophotographic method similar to that found in photocopiers and does not have a printhead.

printhead alignment   The process by which the printhead is calibrated for use. A special utility that comes with the printer software is used to do this.

printhead carriage   The component of a bubble-jet printer that moves back and forth during printing. It contains the physical as well as electronic connections for the printhead and (in some cases) the ink reservoir.

product activation   The process of registering your Windows product with Microsoft to ensure you have a licensed copy.

product key   A unique key that you enter into Windows during installation to signal that you have a licensed copy of the software.

propagation delay   In satellite Internet, the delay caused by the length of time required to transmit data and receive a response via satellite.

proprietary design   A nonstandard design that serves the marketing interests of the manufacturer, as opposed to the general interests of the consumer.

protocol   In networking and communications, the specification that defines the procedures to follow when transmitting and receiving data. Protocols define the format, timing, sequence, and error-checking systems used.

PTR (Pointer) record   DNS record used for reverse lookup entries.

Public Switched Telephone Network (PSTN)   The network that carries standard, non-packetized voice and data traffic from subscribers. Traffic can originate from POTS, ISDN, and DSL lines but does not include DSL's data-band traffic.

PS/2 port   A mini-DIN connector that is used to connect keyboards and mice, so named for the IBM Personal System/2, where it was originally seen.

rag stock   Paper made from cotton.

random access memory (RAM)   Memory, usually in chip form, that can be read from or written to in any order

resource   Anything on a network that clients might want to access or use.

rasterizing   The process of converting signals from the computer into signals for the various assemblies in a laser printer.

recovery CD   A CD-ROM that comes with a particular model and brand of computer and usually contains an image of the entire Windows installation, along with applications, utilities, and drivers specifically for that computer. Also called a restoration CD.

recovery partition   A section of hard drive space, usually on a server, that contains an exact image of a computer's files and configuration.

refresh rate   The number of times per second, measured in hertz (Hz), that an electron gun retraces the image on a screen. Higher refresh rates produce better images to the human eye. Lower refresh rates can cause headaches and poor-quality images.

registered jack (RJ)   A series of modular jacks usually modified by a numerical identifier, such as RJ-11, which identifies the characteristics of that particular registered jack.

remote computer   In Remote Desktop, the remote computer is the one that you are not sitting at; it's the one you make a connection to while sitting at the home computer.

Remote Desktop   A feature of Windows that allows you to connect to another computer and take control over that computer as if you were sitting in front of it. Also the name of the software that lets your computer be a remote computer in a remote desktop connection.

Remote Desktop Connection   The software that lets a computer act as a home computer in the Remote Desktop application.

resolution   The number of dots in a square inch used to represent the image to be scanned or printed. Resolution is measured based on a grid of dots in the horizontal and vertical planes. For example, a resolution of 600×600 dpi indicates the device uses 360,000 dots to represent each square inch of the image.

restoration CD   A CD-ROM that comes with a particular model and brand of computer and that usually contains an image of the entire Windows installation, along with applications, utilities, and drivers specifically for that computer. Also called a recovery CD.

restore point   A copy of your system configuration at a given point in time.

ribbon cartridge   The container that holds the printer ribbon.

RIMM   The module used to carry Rambus DRAM.

RIMM slot   The motherboard slot designed to receive a RIMM.

riser card   A card that has no functional circuitry of its own but that provides connecting points for other cards parallel to the motherboard.

router   In networking, an intelligent connecting device that can send packets to the correct local area network segment to take them to their destination. Routers link LAN segments at the Network layer of the International Standards Organization's Open Systems Interconnect (ISO/OSI) model for computer-to-computer communications.

RS-232 cables   See *serial cables*.

satellite Internet   A type of Internet connection that uses a satellite dish to receive data from a satellite and a relay station that is connected to the Internet.

safe mode   Starts Windows 2000/XP using only basic files and drivers, such as mouse (except serial mice), monitor, keyboard, mass storage, base video, and default system services.

scanner   An optical device used to digitize images such as line art or photographs, so that they can be merged with text by a page-layout or desktop publishing program or incorporated into a CAD drawing.

scatternet   A network of two or more piconets.

secondary partition   Any partition not designated the primary partition in an operating system.

security tokens   Similar to certificates, they contain the rights and access privileges of the token bearer as part of the token.

security baseline   Defines the level of security that will be implemented and maintained.

separator pads   Rubber patches that help keep the paper in place so that only one sheet goes into a printer.

serial cables   Cables used for serial communications. See *serial communications*.

serial communications   The transmission of information from computer to computer or from computer to a peripheral, one bit at a time. Serial communications can be synchronous and controlled by a clock or asynchronous and coordinated by start and stop bits embedded in the data stream..

serial ports   Interfaces that connect peripheral components using a serial communications stream. Also a specific term for the ANSI/EIA/TIA-232 ports (formerly RS-232) on a PC.

service packs   Major patches or upgrades to the Windows operating system are released in groups known as service packs.

Service Set Identifier (SSI)   The unique name of a wireless network that differentiates it from other wireless networks that are also in range of a wireless client.

sheet-fed scanner   A scanner that feeds each original sheet across the imaging mechanism from an input hopper. Contrast with flat-bed scanner.

signal channel   See *Delta channel*.

Single Inline Memory Modules (SIMMs)   Memory modules that have mated pins in the same position on each side of the module, each pair performing the same function so that the module's pin count considers each pair to be only one pin. Contrast to DIMMs, where each pin in the pair performs a potentially separate function.

single-purpose server   A server that is dedicated to one purpose (for example, a file server or a printer server).

site license   A software license that is valid for all installations at a single site.

Small Outline DIMM (SoDIMM)   A smaller form-factor memory module that is used in smaller systems, such as laptops. Only MicroDIMMs are currently smaller.

smart card   A type of badge or card that gives you access to resources including buildings, parking lots, and computers.

SOA (Start of Authority) record   DNS record that identifies the zone and contains several other parameters.

solenoid   In daisy-wheel printers, the small electromechanical hammer that strikes the back of the petal containing the character.

solid-ink printers   A printer that uses ink is in a waxy solid form, rather than in liquid form. This allows the ink to stay fresh and eliminates problems like spillage.

Southbridge   A portion of a motherboard's overall chipset that is responsible for control of non-AGP video and other I/O communications, such as serial, parallel, and USB ports.

special permissions   Permissions in Windows operating systems, including Read, Write, Execute, Delete, Change Permissions, Take Ownership, and Full Control.

spoofing   An attempt by someone or something to masquerade as someone else.

stabilizer bar   A small metal bar on a printer that holds the printer carriage as it crosses the page.

standard peripheral power connector   See *Molex connector*.

standard permissions   Collection of special permissions, including Full Control, Modify, Read & Execute, Read, and Write. Each of these standard permissions automatically assigns multiple special permissions at once.

standard serial cable   A serial cable that is used to connect the serial port of a computer to that of a modem. The signal lines run straight through a standard cable. Contrast to null modem serial cable.

standby   A mode that laptops can operate in.

static-charge eliminator strip   The device in EP process printers that drains the static charge from the paper after the toner has been transferred to the paper.

stepper motor   A very precise motor that can move in very small increments. Often used in printers.

straight tip (ST)   One of the most common fiber-optic connectors similar in style to the BNC connector used in 10Base2 Ethernet.

sublimate   To go from a solid state to a gaseous state without passing through a liquid state.

subnet mask   A required part of any TCP/IP configuration, used to define which addresses are local and which are on remote networks.

Super Video Graphics Array (SVGA) port   A DE15F interface that has the capability of accepting a wide variety of signals using various screen resolutions.

swap file   Also called the page file, the swap file is the virtual memory in Windows.

switch   A Layer 2 device similar to a hub in its port count but more advanced with the ability to filter traffic based on the destination MAC address of each frame.

syntax   The specific structure required by a text-based command to work properly.

sysprep   A utility used to make an image of a computer for installation on other computers.

system board   See *motherboard*.

system memory   The primary computer memory that holds instructions and data for currently executing software

System Tray   Located on the Windows Taskbar, contains a clock by default, but other Windows utilities (for example, screensavers or virus-protection utilities) may put their icons here when running to indicate that they are running and to provide the user with a quick way to access their features.

tailgating Following someone through the door they just unlocked.

TCP/IP (Transmission Control Protocol/Internet Protocol) A set of computer-to-computer communications protocols that encompasses media access, packet transport, session communications, file transfer, e-mail, and terminal emulation. TCP/IP is supported by a very large number of hardware and software vendors and is available on many different computers from PCs to mainframes.

temporary file (temp file) A file designed to store information for a short period of time and then be deleted.

Temporary Internet Files A directory on your hard drive where Internet Explorer copies any images or HTML files from websites you visit frequently. Used to speed up Internet access.

text-based commands Commands that are executed from the command prompt, such as DIR, CD, or FORMAT.

text mode As opposed to graphics mode, text mode displays only alphanumeric characters on the screen, not graphical images.

thermal printer A nonimpact printer that uses a thermal printhead and specially treated paper to create an image.

thrashing When you have an extremely slow system and a disk that is constantly being accessed.

throttling Not allowing to operate at full capacity.

token passing A media-access method that gives every NIC equal access to the cable. The token is a special packet of data that is passed from computer to computer. Any computer that wants to transmit has to wait until it has the token, at which point it can add its own data to the token and send it on.

Token Ring network A local area network with a ring structure that uses token passing to regulate traffic on the network and avoid collisions. On a Token Ring network, the controlling computer generates a token that controls the right to transmit. This token is continuously passed from one node to the next around the network. When a node has information to transmit, it captures the token, sets its status to busy, and adds the message and the destination address. All other nodes continuously read the token to determine if they are the recipient of a message; if they are, they collect the token, extract the message, and return the token to the sender. The sender then removes the message and sets the token status to free, indicating that it can be used by the next node in sequence.

toner A black carbon substance mixed with polyester resins and iron oxide particles. During the EP printing process, toner is first attracted to areas that have been exposed to the laser in laser printers and is later deposited and melted onto the print medium.

topology A way of laying out a network. Can describe either the logical or physical layout.

transfer corona assembly The part of an EP process printer that is responsible for transferring the developed image from the EP drum to the paper.

transferring step   The step in the EP print process when the developed toner image on the EP drum is transferred to the print medium using the transfer corona

Transmission Control Protocol (TCP)   See *TCP/IP (Transmission Control Protocol/Internet Protocol)*.

typical installation   Installs the most commonly used components of the software, but not all of the components.

unattended installation   An installation method that does not require human intervention once started, and is frequently used when installing over the network. Unattended installations use answer files to supply the necessary parameters to Windows Setup.

unidirectional   A form of satellite Internet wherein the satellite is used for only one part of the connection: downloading from the Internet.

universal data connector (UDC)   Another name for an IBM data connector.

Universal Serial Bus (USB)   One of the latest standards for external peripheral connectivity to the computer system. USB competes with FireWire.

User Datagram Protocol (UDP)   Part of the TCP/IP suite that performs a similar function to TCP, with less overhead and more speed but with lower reliability.

virtual memory   A general term for a type of computer technology where hard disk space is used to supplement a computer's physical memory.

virus   A small, deviously genius program that replicates itself to other computers, generally causing those computers to behave abnormally.

Voice over IP   The technology that encapsulates voice traffic into IP packets and transmits it across a TCP/IP network.

vulnerability scanner   A software application that checks your network for any known security holes.

watt   The unit of measure for power. Used to rate power supplies and the related requirements of the various powered components.

WiFi   Short for wireless fidelity, it is a collection of IEEE 802.11x standards.

wide area networks (WAN)   A network that expands LANs to include networks outside of the local environment and also to distribute resources across distances.

window   A rectangular area created on the screen when an application is opened within Windows.

Windows Catalog   A list of all the hardware that works with Windows and which versions of Windows it works with. The new name for the Hardware Compatibility List.

Windows Update   A feature designed to keep Windows current by automatically downloading updates such as patches and security fixes and installing these fixes automatically.

wireless access point (WAP)   A central hub that looks nearly identical to wireless routers, and provide central connectivity like wireless routers, but doesn't have nearly as many features. The main one most people are concerned with is Internet connection sharing.

wireless Internet   An Internet access technology that uses radio frequency signals to communicate between ISP and user. It allows the user to roam about a particular area while remaining connected to the Internet.

wireless card   An adapter card that gives its host the ability to join a wireless LAN.

working directory   An area on the hard disk where programs store their temporary files while they work.

workstation   1) In networking, any personal computer (other than the file server) attached to the network. 2) A high-performance computer optimized for graphics applications such as computer-aided design, computer-aided engineering, and scientific applications.

writing step   The step in the EP print process during which the items being printed are written to the EP drum. In this step, the laser is flashed on and off as it scans across the surface of the drum. The area on which the laser shines is discharged to almost ground (–100V).

Index

Note to the Reader: Throughout this index **boldfaced** page numbers indicate primary discussions of a topic. *Italicized* page numbers indicate illustrations.

C

G

P

Wiley Publishing, Inc.
End-User License Agreement

The Absolute Best CompTIA A+ Book/CD Package on the Market!

Get Ready for CompTIA new A+ Exams with the most comprehensive and challenging sample tests anywhere!

The Sybex Test Engine features:

- All the review questions, as covered in each chapter of the book.

- Challenging questions representative of those you'll find on the real exam.

- A total of 8 full length bonus exams available only on the CD: two each for the Essentials, IT Technician, Remote Support Technician, and Depot Technician.

- An Assessment Test to narrow your focus to certain objective groups.

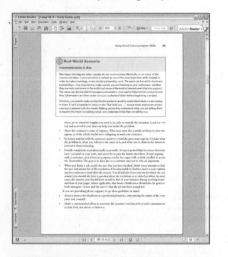

Search through the complete book in PDF!

- Access the entire *CompTIA A+ Complete Study Guide*, complete with figures and tables, in electronic format.

- Search the *CompTIA A+ Complete Study Guide* chapters to find information on any topic in seconds.

Use the Electronic Flashcards for PCs or Palm devices to jog your memory and prep last-minute for the exam!

- Reinforce your understanding of key concepts with these hardcore flashcard-style questions.

- Download the Flashcards to your Palm device and go on the road. Now you can study for the CompTIA A+ Exams any time, anywhere.

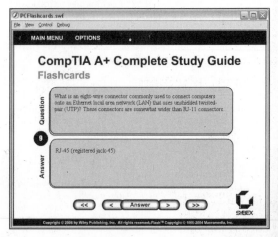